SECOND EDITION

# Compensation Decision Making

### Frederick S. Hills
Late of *Virginia Polytechnic Institute and State University*

### Thomas J. Bergmann
*University of Wisconsin–Eau Claire*

### Vida G. Scarpello
*Georgia State University*

**The Dryden Press**
Harcourt Brace College Publishers

Fort Worth   Philadelphia   San Diego   New York   Orlando   Austin   San Antonio
Toronto   Montreal   London   Sydney   Tokyo

Acquisitions Editor: Ruth Rominger
Developmental Editor: Traci Keller
Project Editor: Sheila M. Spahn
Art Director: Bill Brammer
Production Manager: Eddie Dawson
Literary Permissions Editor: Shirley Webster
Publisher: Elizabeth Widdicombe
Director of Editing, Design, & Production: Diane Southworth

Copy Editor: Donna Regen
Indexer: Michael Ferreira
Electronic Publishing Coordinator: Cathy Spitzenberger
Electronic Publishing Supervisor: Mike Beaupré
Text type: 10/12 Janson Text

Requests for permission to make copies of any part of the work should be mailed to: Permissions Department, Harcourt Brace & Company, 8th Floor, Orlando, FL 32887.

*Address for Editorial Correspondence*
The Dryden Press, 301 Commerce Street, Suite 3700, Fort Worth, TX 76102

*Address for Orders*
The Dryden Press, 6277 Sea Harbor Drive, Orlando, FL 32887
1-800-782-4479, or 1-800-433-0001 (in Florida)

ISBN: 0-03-033058-0

Library of Congress Catalog Number: 93-80337

Printed in the United States of America
3 4 5 6 7 8 9 0 1 2    0 1 6    9 8 7 6 5 4 3 2 1

The Dryden Press
Harcourt Brace College Publishers

*In memory of Frederick S. Hills*

# The Dryden Press Series in Management

# The Harcourt Brace College Outline Series

Pentico
**Management Science**

Pierson
**Introduction to Business Information
Systems**

Sigband
**Business Communication**

Compensation decision making is a critical organization activity. Organizations are vitally interested in attracting and retaining employees and in motivating them to high levels of performance. Indeed, organizational survival requires that they do so. One needs only to observe the U.S. economy to realize that while some organizations have a difficult time attracting, retaining, and motivating people, others do not. As a result, some organizations achieve unprecedented productivity growth, but others watch their productivity slip to the point where they can no longer compete, and many fail altogether.

Organizations must compete for a strong work force while simultaneously surviving within a range of other constraints. Growth in product competition (both domestic and imported) and legal pressures, has organizations today more constrained than ever in making compensation decisions. Recent events show these two constraints at work in the United States. The auto industry emerged from its most severe recession ever by updating technology and controlling labor costs. The textile industry is in trouble because of the influx of less costly foreign products. The electric razor industry, with one exception, has become entirely a foreign industry because of high labor costs. The computer industry is experiencing significant restructuring, with Burroughs and like organizations no longer acting as major players and IBM experiencing downsizing.

In the case of legal constraints, organizations are routinely taken to court for violating nondiscrimination and other wage-related laws. In the early 1990s with the passage of such legislation as the Americans with Disabilities Act, the Family and Medical Leave Act, various tax reforms, and the pending health care legislation it is increasingly more difficult to design an effective and efficient compensation program. As a result of this new legislation, compensation decision makers will face a new round of governmental agency and court rulings that will determine if implementation programs are within the law. Organizations are faced with an incredible tension between their need for the best labor and the constraints placed on them by their own ability to pay and by the legal system. This book is about the dynamic tension between these and other competing forces.

The compensation field has been depicted variously as a group of theories, a set of administrative practices, or a set of techniques. These pages are an effort to make sense out of these conflicting depictions by relating theory to practice and presenting techniques to aid in developing sound compensation practice.

The ultimate goal of the text is to make compensation decision makers out of its readers. No book can provide all the answers nor can it provide a fail-safe formula. What it can provide are the knowledge and techniques that lead to answers. All compensation decisions are made under a set of decision-making constraints. This book analyzes those constraints. A thorough understanding of them will assist the reader, since a careful consideration and judicious weighing of all the constraints should result in more rational compensation decisions.

Stated another way, the reader will make compensation decisions for some organization in the future. These decisions will determine whether the company achieves its goals or fails. The decisions have an impact upon the company achieving high productivity or slowly slipping into oblivion. To aid in preparing for compensation decisions, these pages were written to provide readers with the skills to make wise decisions in a complex and ever-changing environment.

## Organization of the Text

*Compensation Decision Making* is divided into six parts. Each part covers a critical block of material. The parts are divided into chapters and are documented with references for further reading. Each chapter also has highlighted key terms, and most chapters have discussion questions and exercises to use as learning aids.

Parts One and Two set the parameters in which compensation decisions are made. In Part One, Chapter 1 provides an overall introduction to the compensation field. The focus in Chapter 2 is the economics of compensation: that is, why organizations that hire workers face an ability-to-pay constraint. Chapter 3 discusses theoretical frameworks that are useful in understanding human behavior as it applies to compensation, such as why people work and what motivates people. The implications of theories of economics and human behavior are also discussed in each chapter. The three chapters in Part Two examine institutional constraints that influence compensation decision making and compensation strategy. Chapter 4 examines the institutional constraints of internal labor markets and labor unions. Chapter 5 then examines the major federal legislation that affects compensation decision making. Chapter 6 focuses on strategy planning as it relates to compensation decision making.

In Part Three, each of the two chapters deals with one or more administrative activities that are important in designing a good pay system. Chapter 7 covers job analysis and job descriptions. Studying jobs and documenting the results of these studies are critical for all compensation work. How jobs are studied, uses of the data, and techniques for studying jobs are all discussed in this chapter. Chapter 8 focuses on establishing internal equity among jobs within the organization. A step by step procedure for implementing either the ranking, job classification, factor comparison, or point method of job evaluation is presented. In addition, a number of single factor methods and the position analysis questionnaire techniques are discussed. The chapter ends with a discussion of job grades and the relative "goodness" of job evaluation methods. Because Part Three emphasizes skill building, there are cases and exercises to use in mastering job analysis and job evaluation.

Part Four contains three chapters. Chapter 9 completes the design of a basic wage or salary system. It examines the topic of conducting wage and salary surveys. It focuses on the organization's wage payments in light of what other organizations are doing. Chapter 10 discusses how organizations use wage surveys and it integrates them with job evaluation data. Chapter 11 deals with the important subject of performance assessment in a merit pay context.

In Part Five, Chapters 12 and 13 discuss individual performance pay. Chapter 12 focuses on several types of individual and group incentive plans used by organizations. Chapter 13 takes up the subject of employee benefits. The chapter examines the types of benefits that are provided and trends for future benefits

Part Six completes the discussion of the design of the compensation system. Chapter 14 covers the important topic of compensation control and administration. Once a comprehensive compensation program is designed and installed, it must be administered on a day-to-day basis, and control must be maintained in the system. The chapter presents numerous techniques that help to determine if the goals of the compensation system are actually being achieved in practice. Chapter 15 focuses on special compensation situations involving executives, international operations, boards of directors, paying for knowledge and sales personnel.

## New to This Edition

The second edition has two new chapters. Chapter 6, dealing with strategic planning as it relates to compensation decision making, is new. The purpose of this chapter is to discuss how compensation decision making must be integrated into the broader context of the competitive and changing environment within which a firm operates. In addition, compensation strategies and practices may have to vary at the business unit level because different business units within an organization may be operating in significantly different product environments. Chapter 15, on special compensation situations, is also new. The topics of executive and sales compensation have received more development in this edition and discussions of international compensation, board of directors compensation, two-tier plans, and knowledge-based compensation have been added.

In addition to the new chapters, the chapters on labor markets, labor unions, and performance assessments have had significant amounts of new material added. The legal chapter has been reorganized and expanded. A number of new cases and exercises have been incorporated to give the reader practice in application of the material presented.

## Acknowledgments

We would like first to thank the Industrial Relations Department of the University of Minnesota for providing us with the educational background in compensation and developing within us a love of the area. The interdisciplinary nature of the program provides us with the appropriate framework in which to study compensation issues. Second, we want to acknowledge the undergraduate and graduate students that we have had in our compensation classes who have stimulated our thought processes, making this edition possible.

As anyone who has attempted to write a book knows, criticism is easily bestowed but not always useful. Constructive criticism, therefore, is especially valued. A host of colleagues improved various manuscripts of both the first and second editions with their constructive criticism. We would like to thank Chris Berger, Purdue University; Richard R. Camp, Eastern Michigan University; Ruth Curran, California State University–Northridge; Kermit R. Davis, Jr., Auburn University; James W. Hathaway, Appalachian State University;

Sandra Jennings, Miami University of Ohio; Timothy J. Keaveny, Marquette University; Linda A. Krefting, Texas Tech University; Robert M. Madigan, Virginia Polytechnic Institute and State University; Luis R. Gomez-Mejia, University of Florida; Michael K. Mount, University of Iowa; Paul M. Muchinsky, Iowa State University; Robert V. Nally, Villanova University; Craig J. Russell, Rutgers University; and Michael N. Wolfe, University of Houston–Clear Lake. We owe these colleagues a special thanks for the extra effort they put into reviewing the manuscript.

To those of you who may attempt to write a book, allow us to recommend The Dryden Press to you. A competent staff of many, including Ruth Rominger, Sheila M. Spahn, Eddie Dawson, Traci Keller, Bill Brammer, Shirley Webster, Mike Beaupré, Cathy Spitzenberger, and Matt Ball, were just wonderful. They cajoled, encouraged, and always pleasantly nudged the project towards completion.

We want to pay special tribute to Marilyn A. Bergmann who spent many long hours editing the second edition of this text. Without her help editing and reorganizing the material, the second edition would not have become a reality. In addition, we would like to thank Debra Mosey and Kari Becker for their library assistance.

Finally, we must recognize all those practitioners and academicians who write, teach, and work in compensation. Whether named or unnamed in these pages, your collage of contributions, we hope, is accurately presented here.

This book is a collection of empirical facts, general beliefs, and our own biases. Errors of fact are our responsibility. Our interpretation of general beliefs is, hopefully, accurate and our own biases tolerable.

The untimely death of our friend and colleague, Fred Hills, before the completion of this second edition, leaves us thankful for the fine work he did on this text but saddened that he could not witness its arrival in print.

Frederick S. Hills, Late
School of Business
Virginia Polytechnic Institute and State University
Blacksburg, Virginia

Thomas J. Bergmann
School of Business
University of Wisconsin–Eau Claire
Eau-Claire, Wisconsin

Vida G. Scarpello
School of Business
Georgia State University
Atlanta, Georgia

**Preface** *vii*

**PART ONE**

**Introduction and Theoretical Foundations**

**2**

## Chapter 3

**PART FOUR**

Pay Structure
Decisions
260

# Chapter 9

## Chapter 10

# Chapter 11

**PART FIVE**

**Individual
Equity
386**

# Chapter 12

# Chapter 13

# Chapter 14

# Chapter 15

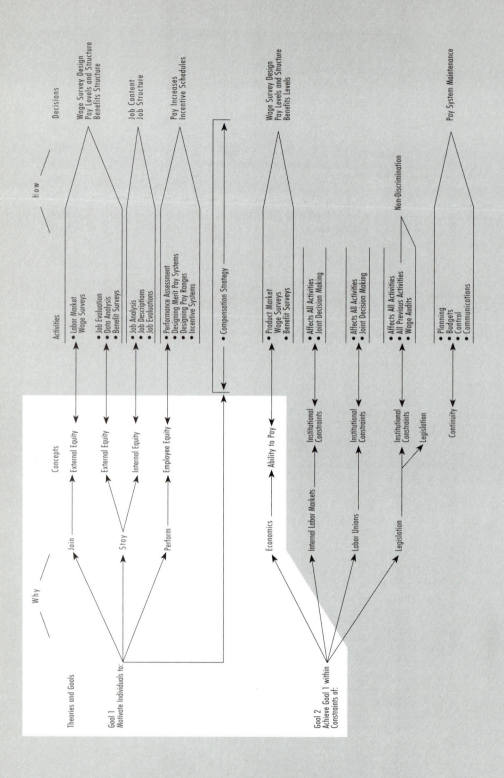

# I

# Introduction and Theoretical Foundations

CHAPTER

# 1

# Introduction to Compensation

# Learning Objectives

To become aware of the complexity of compensation as an area of study.

To understand how compensation-related issues affect individuals, organizations, and society at large.

To define the term *compensation* and to identify the components of compensation.

To introduce the viewpoint of this textbook.

To identify and discuss the goals of an organization's compensation system.

To recognize that compensation goals are determined within economic, legal, and institutional constraints.

To understand how compensation theory relates to compensation practice.

# The Impact of Compensation Issues

Compensation is probably one of the most controversial topics in corporate America today. It has an impact on individual members of society, on organizations (public, private, and nonprofit), and on society as a whole. To understand the vital importance of this topic to those groups, it is useful to look at some specific compensation issues and see how they impact the parties involved.

## Individual Concerns

**Wages as Income**    Individuals usually receive income from two sources, earnings and investments. Relatively few people realize most of their income from investments. The largest portion of most people's income results from what economists call earnings and what this text calls wages.[1] Wages are defined herein as income received for labor services.[2]

Wages affect people's lives in pervasive and intimate ways. People's wages influence whether they drive a Dodge Shadow or a Mercedes-Benz or whether they own a luxurious home or rent a small apartment. Wages help define socioeconomic status and influence friendships, neighborhood choice, clothing choice, eating behaviors, and so on. In general, the level of compensation individuals receive is significant in determining their social status and that of their family, their self-esteem, and their ability to provide for their current needs and long-term security.

**Wage Comparisons**   Why is a Madison, Wisconsin, engineer with an income of $65,000 better off financially than a New York City engineer with an income of $70,000? Why do maintenance workers at the local industrial plant make more than mechanics at the local gas station? Why is a bachelor's degree in engineering worth one and one-half to three times in wages what a bachelor's degree in education is worth? Why does one person get a 3 percent raise when another gets a 6 percent raise?

Why does a marketing manager in the electronics industry generally get paid twice what a marketing manager in textiles gets paid for virtually identical work? Why does a first-year teacher in one school system make $16,000 when a first-year teacher in another school system makes $20,000?

**Wage Fairness**   Most of these questions relate to the issue of fairness. Are these differences in compensation fair? What are the bases for the differences? Do supply and demand dictate which individuals work, where they work, and how much they earn? Is the assessment of employees' performances objectively determined or is it based on bias and favoritism? How does such assessment relate to compensation? One of the objectives of this book is to answer the kinds of questions raised above, about why individuals are paid certain wages.

A specific fairness issue that is of concern to the individual is wage compression. *Wage compression* refers to the narrowing of the wage differential between jobs of different relative value. Employees usually have a perception of what is an appropriate wage differential between positions, and when that gap narrows, they question the fairness of the total compensation program. This narrowing can be caused by the job market increasing the pay associated with a position faster than the overall percentage increase granted within the organization. To remain competitive with the external job market, the organization must provide greater pay increases for that position than the pay increases given comparable jobs within the organization. Compression problems also arise if minimum wage law increases the pay of minimum pay jobs in the organization by, say, 12 percent but the organization's overall wage increase is limited to 5 percent; then the minimum wage jobs' increase will be significantly higher than non-minimum wage jobs' increase and, again, the differential will narrow. This book attempts to offer suggestions for dealing with fairness issues such as the compression issue.

## *Organizational Considerations*

Organizations must constantly deal with compensation issues. Their decisions in this regard will ultimately help determine the success—or failure—of their enterprise.

**Labor Costs**   Labor costs represent a substantial proportion of total costs to the average company, whether it is in the public, private, or nonprofit sectors of the economy.[3]

Labor costs as a proportion of total costs vary tremendously from industry to industry and even from employer to employer, as depicted in Exhibit 1.1.

| EXHIBIT 1.1 | PAYROLL AS A PERCENTAGE OF VALUE OF INVENTORY SHIPMENTS |

| | Payroll (million $) | Value of Industry Shipments (million $) | Percentage |
|---|---|---|---|
| Food and kindred products | 32,108.4 | 364,403.7 | 8.8 |
| Textile mill products | 11,836.7 | 67,321.5 | 17.6 |
| Apparel and other textile products | 14,047.5 | 63,398.6 | 22.2 |
| Lumber and wood products | 13,359.6 | 74,328.4 | 18.0 |
| Furniture and fixtures | 9,737.7 | 41,152.3 | 23.7 |
| Paper and allied products | 18,396.9 | 131,366.3 | 14.0 |
| Printing and publishing | 36,643.8 | 149,911.8 | 24.4 |
| Chemicals and allied products | 28,475.1 | 278,084.9 | 10.2 |
| Petroleum and coal products | 4,181.5 | 143,702.1 | 2.9 |
| Rubber and miscellaneous plastic | 19,660.2 | 98,416.8 | 20.0 |
| Leather and leather products | 1,860.8 | 9,852.1 | 18.9 |
| Stone, clay, and glass products | 12,955.8 | 63,555.9 | 20.4 |
| Primary metal industries | 22,155.5 | 152,967.5 | 14.5 |
| Fabricated metal products | 37,224.0 | 162,181.1 | 23.0 |
| Industrial machinery and equipment | 56,247.3 | 253,642.1 | 22.2 |
| Electronic and other electric equipment | 42,156.6 | 192,617.7 | 21.9 |
| Transportation equipment | 62,378.3 | 365,980.7 | 17.0 |
| Instruments and related products | 30,633.5 | 118,486.1 | 25.9 |

Constructed from information in *Annual Survey of Manufacturers* (1991), (Washington, DC: U.S. Department of Commerce, Bureau of the Census).

Some organizations are relatively more labor intensive (labor cost as a percentage of total costs) than others. These organizations tend to pay lower wages for the same type of worker than less labor-intensive employers pay. The fact that labor costs on average represent a substantial cost relative to total costs for employers, however, means that one way to manage business costs effectively is to manage labor costs effectively.

Because organizations must increasingly compete in a global marketplace, not only the cost of domestic but also foreign competitors must be considered. The average wage rate in the United States ($13.90) in 1988 was fourth highest in the world, trailing only West Germany, Switzerland, and Sweden. Many American organizations are moving or considering moving all or parts of their organizations to other countries such as Mexico ($1.57) or Brazil ($1.49) to more effectively compete in world markets.[4]

**Legal Constraints**   While numerous variables and constraints are involved when organizations consider compensation issues, legal constraints are certainly among the most powerful influences. Organizations must assure themselves and their employees that they are in compliance with legislative and administrative legal constraints so that they behave in a socially responsible way and avoid legal penalties.[5] For example, the Equal Pay Act of 1963 is a piece of federal legislation that prohibits discrimination in wage payments on the basis of sex. The average differential between what men receive and what women receive has ranged between 65 and 70 percent, depending on the source referenced. Regardless of the exact percentage difference, there is always a part of the difference that cannot be explained by such variables as experience, occupation choice, and industry. The remaining difference is probably a result of discrimination (or some other unmeasured variable) in such practices as designing the pay structure in an organization, weighing what organizations value, or assessing performance in the allotment of pay increases.

If the organization violates any of the laws relating to discrimination in the workplace, it is subject to prosecution (causing more costs). If a violation is found, the organization may be faced with redressing it. This could involve back pay with interest (more costs) plus attorney's fees for the plaintiff (more costs).[6] For example, age discrimination is legally prohibited. IDS Financial Services settled an age discrimination lawsuit with 32 former IDS managers for $35 million. The lawsuit, originally filed in January 1989, claimed IDS began discriminating against managers older than 40 years in 1984. Besides the financial settlement, IDS agreed to monitor treatment of managers older than 40 years.[7]

## Societal Concerns

As far back as the Middle Ages, when plagues were sweeping Europe, the Church and State became concerned over the increases in wages for occupations experiencing labor shortages. To ensure that relative wages of occupational groups remained constant, the Church and State evolved a Just Wage Doctrine. This doctrine held that each occupational group should receive its just wage. *Justice* was defined as the relative wage of the occupation before the plague.[8]

A current issue of social concern and one of today's hottest topics is the issue of executive compensation. Executive compensation is not only being discussed in academic and professional journals but in newspapers across the country. This issue is controversial enough to catch the ear and eye of Congress. Radical actions have been suggested, such as putting a cap on executive pay or not permitting companies to deduct executive compensation in excess of $1 million as a business expense. The issue of fairness of wage distribution for executives (or for any employees) must include not only the amount allocated (distributive justice) to each person or position but also the process (procedural justice) by which the dollars are allocated. A significant section of this text deals with equity theory (distributive and procedural justice), which is at the heart of this matter.

The public outcry of excessive payments to executives and the perceived short-term perspective of executive decisions has resulted in organizations placing less emphasis on base pay (salary paid to perform a job) for executives and more emphasis on incentive-based pay (compensation which depends on the long-term performance of the organization).[9]

From very early times to the dawn of the twenty-first century then, societies have historically been concerned with the wages of their members. This concern is one of the reasons for the myriad of legislation encountered by compensation decision makers in our democratic society.

**Income Maintenance**    In a democracy, legislation is the logical response to a societal concern. Early in this century, there was concern over workers becoming injured on the job and not receiving adequate compensation for the injury. An outcome of that concern was workers' compensation laws.[10] In the 1930s, there was concern about the financial ability of workers to live in retirement. The Social Security Act of 1935 was passed in part to provide a supplemental retirement income.

**Labor Law Reform**    In the 1930s, society also decided there was a need to protect employees' rights to organize, join a union, and bargain collectively with management. One of the issues that workers have a right to negotiate under the provisions of the Wagner Act of 1935 is the wage rate. But society's concern about a just wage, a wage that would keep workers out of poverty, went even farther. In response to this concern, the Fair Labor Standards Act (FLSA) of 1938, among other provisions, established the first minimum wage. The changes in the minimum wage since 1938 are reflected in Exhibit 1.2. Recently, a short term training wage which is below minimum wage was legalized. The training wage, which took effect April 1, 1991, is $3.61 per hour.

**Civil Rights**    Significant civil rights activity started in the United States in the 1960s and is continuing today. That movement, supported by societal interest groups such as the National Association for the Advancement of Colored People (NAACP), the Black Caucus, the National Organization of Women (NOW), and others, fought hard for change. In an attempt to eradicate unjustified male/female wage differentials, Congress passed the Equal Pay Act of 1963.[11] With the Civil Rights Act of 1964, Congress moved to prohibit discrimination in the terms and conditions of employment on the basis of race, color, creed, sex, and national origin.[12] In recent years, new legislation has been passed that attempts to protect further the civil rights of employees. For example, in the late 1980s, federal legislation to prohibit the use of polygraph tests in most employment decisions was passed. In the 1990s, two major pieces of federal legislation were passed that have significant impact on human resources practices. The first is the Americans with Disabilities Act of 1990 which requires employers to distinguish between essential and nonessential job requirements and to try to make "reasonable accommodations" for all jobs within the organizations. This will likely lead to increased emphasis on job analysis and work design. The second major law is the Civil Rights Act of 1991. The key elements in this law

| EXHIBIT 1.2 | CHANGES IN MINIMUM WAGE |
| --- | --- |

| Month/Year | Minimum Wage |
| --- | --- |
| Oct. 1938 | .25 |
| Oct. 1939 | .30 |
| Oct. 1945 | .40 |
| Jan. 1950 | .75 |
| Mar. 1956 | 1.00 |
| Sept. 1961 | 1.15 |
| Sept. 1963 | 1.25 |
| Feb. 1967 | 1.40 |
| Feb. 1968 | 1.60 |
| May 1974 | 2.00 |
| Jan. 1975 | 2.10 |
| Jan. 1976 | 2.30 |
| Jan. 1978 | 2.65 |
| Jan. 1979 | 2.90 |
| Jan. 1980 | 3.10 |
| Jan. 1981 | 3.35 |
| April 1990 | 3.80 |
| April 1991 | 4.25 |

SOURCE: U.S. Department of Labor, Employment Standards Administrator, *Minimum Wage and Maximum Hours Standards under the Fair Labor Standards Act* (1991), annual, and unpublished data.

re-emphasize the concept of "business necessity" (qualifications that must exist to perform the job) rather than "business justification" (job-related qualifications) and increase the financial cost of illegal discrimination for employers.

Legislation influencing pay decision making is discussed in detail in Chapter 5.

## Compensation Defined

Compensation consists of four distinct components:

> Compensation = Wage or salary + Employee benefits + Nonrecurring financial rewards + Nonpecuniary rewards

The following sections will discuss each of these components in turn.

## Wage or Salary

The first component of compensation is wage or salary. Some legal distinctions between wage and salary are discussed in a later chapter, but for now, the two are treated the same. Wage or salary can be defined in two ways. First, it can be expressed as the rate of pay per unit of time. Thus, it can be expressed as dollars per hour or dollars per month or year. Wage or salary can also be expressed as the rate of pay per unit of output. For example, under piece rate systems an employee is paid so many dollars or cents for each unit produced. Piece rate systems are discussed in more detail in Chapter 12. The concept of wage or salary refers to the gross wage or salary and should not be confused with take-home pay, net pay, or earnings (after deductions for taxes, insurance, etc.).

## Employee Benefits

Employee benefits are defined herein as the indirect and recurring monetary rewards that an employee receives from employment. Examples of employee benefits are company contributions to retirement and insurance plans, as well as company-paid vacation days and personal days off. Employee benefits, sometimes called fringe benefits, are an important part of compensation decision making. They are treated separately from wage or salary partly because they tend to influence different worker behaviors than do wage or salary. It is also useful to think of direct economic rewards (wage or salary) as opposed to indirect rewards (employee benefits).

Employee benefits today represent about 28 percent of total compensation when both large and small employers are surveyed. The percentage is significantly larger when only larger firms are studied (range: 30 to 40 percent).[13] There are many controversial issues surrounding employee benefits. Health care is probably one of the country's most significant current problems. The increasing costs of health care have resulted in both labor and management suggesting that significant changes must be made if reasonable health care is to be provided to all members of society within the limited resources available. Some of the areas of consideration that are discussed in future chapters are levels of employee contributions, size of deductibles, managed health care, health maintenance organizations, preferred providers, mandated minimum benefits, and a national health care system. These are just a few of the considerations when examining the health care issue. It is essential that organizations be proactive in forging a workable solution to health care within the limited resources the nation has to deal with this problem.

A second benefits issue that is very important to many employees is the availability and cost of child, elder, and sick care.[14] The cost of dependent care (child, spouse, parent) can run up to 75 percent of an employee's yearly income. Also, finding providers that can match the work schedule of working parents is often difficult. It is especially difficult for a single parent who may be required to work long hours or travel to make career progress. How an organization deals with this issue may have a significant impact on the availability of high-quality employees in the future.

A third benefits issue that will receive greater attention in the next decade is the degree to which benefits should be taxed. It seems certain that benefits such as health care will be taxed in some form in the future, but what other benefits will be added to the taxable list as the budget deficit continues to plague the nation? Key questions will be how this changes the value of an employee's total compensation package and what impact it has on an organization's ability to attract and retain employees. Will some organizations with a greater ability to pay increase their employees' wages to compensate for the additional tax burden or will most refrain from this strategy and thus reduce the potential impact on those organizations that are unable to do such?

The next decade will definitely be a time of change for employee benefits packages, and compensation managers will need to keep in touch with the changing needs of their employees and design and administer a program that will maximize the return to the employees while minimizing the cost to the employer.

## Nonrecurring Financial Rewards

Nonrecurring financial rewards are defined as those monetary rewards that a person can earn through employment but that do not occur automatically. Examples of these rewards include special commissions such as those in sales promotions and prizes won in special absenteeism or tardiness control programs. Increasingly important as a nonrecurring financial reward is the practice of profit sharing (paid only when the employer has a profitable year). Such incentives may be dependent on any number of performance measures, such as return on assets (earnings divided by assets), earnings per share (earnings divided by total shares outstanding), labor cost/total cost ratio, or market share. In each of these, the reward is not automatic with passage of time but occurs only when the established measure of performance is achieved. At the executive level, many of the traditional incentive programs have come under increasing criticism for focusing executive behaviors to emphasize the short-term measures (for example, earnings per share) instead of long-term performance measures (for example, market share). Newer approaches to executive compensation are discussed in Chapter 15, which addresses some of the more compelling criticisms of past executive compensation programs. Employee incentive plans at the nonexecutive level are now focusing more on group incentives and gainsharing plans (employees share in cost reduction). It is estimated that these plans will increase in popularity as more organizations focus on developing internal work teams.

## Nonpecuniary Rewards

The three components of compensation just defined (wage or salary, employee benefits, and nonrecurring financial rewards) comprise what many people call the monetary or economic components of a compensation program. Another component to compensation is the nonpecuniary reward. Nonpecuniary rewards are defined in this text as the noneconomic rewards associated with employment. Examples are one's colleagues, company reputation, a sense of accomplishment in one's job, and a sense of power from one's work. In the fiercely competitive environment facing all organizations today, it is essential that organizations take every advantage of nonpecuniary rewards. Organizations during the past few decades have stepped up their efforts to use nonfinancial rewards, including increased participation and autonomy, as a means of influencing employee behaviors. The recent interest in team building and self-managed teams is an illustration of this new approach to managing and a way to provide employees nonpecuniary rewards. Chapter 3 examines nonpecuniary rewards. The text focuses primarily, however, on the monetary components of pay and on making decisions about wages and salaries, employee benefits, and nonrecurring economic rewards.

## Perspective of the Text

The purpose of this textbook is to approach the compensation field from the organizational decision-making perspective. Each of the chapters is designed to provide the reader with what information will be needed to make compensation decisions, the issues that surround each decision, the constraints that the decision maker faces, and a general procedure for approaching the decision. Specific answers often cannot be provided, but the reader, after completing the text, should have acquired essential knowledge and developed a critical thinking approach that can be used to address compensation issues effectively.

An example of the kind of issues that might face a compensation decision maker may be in order. A typical fast-food restaurant pays the minimum wage to its employees. The fast-food restaurant may wish to pay a higher average wage, but because of product market competition, it may not have adequate profit margins to pay a premium unless definite increases in productivity are realized. A wage and salary survey of other types of work that the fast-food restaurant's employees could perform determines that these employees could make more money if they worked at other organizations. This finding establishes the restaurant is a low-wage employer. On top of that, the benefits these employees receive are also low. What steps did the fast-food organization go through to arrive at its decision to offer low wages and low benefits (that is, low economic compensation) relative to other organizations in the area? Why did the fast-food restaurant decide to be a low-compensation organization—what forces or variables caused or encouraged the organization to be a low-compensation organization?

Given their position as a low-wage employer, should the company hire students or attempt to employ only older employees? If it decides to hire students, does it hire workers younger than 16 years and cope with state and federal child labor laws that limit the number of hours worked and when those hours can be worked? If it hires adult workers, does it need to provide special benefits such as child care or very flexible work hours? Is the retention rate currently acceptable? Are any wage adjustments financially feasible? Should the managers be paid a straight salary or should a part of their compensation be in some form of incentive? If an incentive is to be used, what percentage of total compensation should the incentive be? Could incentives be used for nonmanagerial employees? These are just a few of the compensation decisions that must be made for the fast-food restaurant. Each of these decisions could have a significant effect on the restaurant's ability to attract, retain, and motivate employees while remaining competitive within the product market.

# Goals of the Compensation System

Before an organization can act on compensation decisions, it must decide what goals to accomplish. There are, in essence, two goals of every compensation system. The first is to influence individuals who participate in the labor force to make personal decisions about employment that are congruent with the organization's needs. The second goal is for the compensation system to operate effectively within a range of constraints. Exhibit 1.3 shows these goals.

## *Influencing Employment Behavior*

The first goal of all compensation systems is to influence individuals who participate in the labor force to make personal decisions that are congruent with the organization's needs. There are at least three areas of employment covered by this goal: (1) motivate people to join the organization, (2) motivate people to stay with the organization, and (3) motivate people in the organization to perform at above-minimum levels.

**Motivating Individuals to Join the Organization**   Motivating people to join the organization is a critical objective of the compensation system. Every organization uses people in the process of producing its unique goods or services.

---

**EXHIBIT 1.3**   GOALS OF COMPENSATION

---

**First Goal of Compensation:**  To elicit desired behaviors from employees.

1. Motivate people to join the organization
2. Motivate people to stay with the organization
3. Motivate people in the organization to perform at high levels

**Second Goal of Compensation:**  To achieve the first goal within a set of constraints.

1. The organization's ability to pay
2. Legislation
3. Labor unions
4. Internal labor market
5. External labor market

---

Whether manufacturing tires, fixing teeth, managing a monetary fund, training college graduates, or franchising restaurants is the organization's business, labor is an absolutely essential factor in the production process. Organizations must create this labor force by motivating appropriate individuals to join the organization.

*Compensation versus Other Motivators*   It should be apparent that many factors other than economic compensation influence individuals to join a particular organization. For example, an individual may decide to work at organization X because she or he identifies with the product, or a person may decide to join organization Y because it is the only organization within easy commuting distance. Regardless of these forces, compensation is the main area in which the organization can influence individual decisions regarding employment. Benefits have been found to influence the attractiveness of a potential employer in the eyes of applicants.[15]

Probably the most critical compensation decisions that organizations must make are those identifying the **wage level.** Wage level is defined as the average wage paid to all workers in the organization or in a given job or occupation. The wage level is important in attracting labor. If one organization pays more than another, the high-wage employer will attract more and possibly better-qualified individuals who wish to work than the low-wage employer will, all other factors being equal. Wage level is used in a relative sense—that is, workers would value $10 per hour over $8 per hour because of the greater purchasing power of the $10 per hour. The reasons for being concerned about relative wage levels are developed in Chapter 3, in which the subject of motivating workers to join from a theoretical perspective is explored. Chapter 10 covers the administrative aspects of pay structure.

**Motivating Employees to Stay with the Organization**   Motivating individuals to join the organization does little good if the organization cannot retain them. Like motivating people to join, motivating individuals to stay with an organization is also influenced by a complex set of variables. The intrinsic rewards from the job itself (nonpecuniary rewards) partly influence the employee's decision to stay. The attitudes and leadership style of an employee's supervisor can also influence the decision to remain with the organization. Many variables beyond the economic compensation system influence this decision. Regardless of these influences over the individual's decision to stay, organizations can use the compensation system to influence staying in at least three ways.

*External Compensation Equity*   First, the organization must continue to provide its employees with a feeling that they are treated equitably in an external sense, referred to herein as **external equity.** By external equity, we mean that if an employee is hired at a pay rate that is relatively equal to other organizations' pay rates, then this feeling of equity to other organizations must be maintained by continually ensuring that the wage level remains comparable with pay in other organizations. Labor market and product market wage and benefits surveys are used to determine the going rate. These concepts are discussed in depth in Chapter 9. External equity is defined in Exhibit 1.4.

| EXHIBIT 1.4 | DEFINITIONS OF EXTERNAL AND INTERNAL EQUITY |
|---|---|

**External equity:** External equity occurs when the organization's pay rates are at least equal to market rates.

**Internal equity:** Internal equity occurs when people feel that performance or job differences result in corresponding differences in pay rates.

*Internal Compensation Equity*   Not all jobs are readily assessed in terms of external equity. Once individuals work for an organization for a while, they may lose track of their market worth. They move into jobs that are not readily comparable across organizations, and they simply lose track of pay rates in the marketplace. This phenomenon is attributed to the operation of the internal labor market (normal progression an individual follows while moving up within a firm), which results in employees becoming isolated from the external labor market. Once an employee reaches this point, external equity probably becomes less relevant than the second influence, the perception of **internal equity** defined in Exhibit 1.4. That is, it is more important to ensure that individuals believe they are treated equitably with respect to others within the organization. This concern over internal equity is investigated theoretically in Chapter 3 and administratively in Chapter 8, in which the process of establishing the **wage structure** is explored. For the time being, wage structure within the firm is defined as the system of relative wage rates among jobs within the firm.

*High Cost of Departure*   A third way that employers can influence the individual's decision to stay with the organization is to increase the costs associated with leaving. While there are probably other reasons for providing employee benefits, one principal reason is to motivate employees to stay. For example, many benefits grow as a function of length of service (amount of vacation time or size of the monthly retirement stipend), so that to change employers involves costs to the employee that the average person may not be willing to incur. An example of a progressive vacation schedule (giving more time off with longer seniority) can be seen in Exhibit 1.5. A 1987 study indicates that employees perceive benefits as positively influencing their decision to remain with their current employer.[16]

Organizations must make compensation decisions that will motivate people to stay with the organization. These decisions focus on internal and external wage levels, internal wage structures, and the types and amounts of benefits to provide.

**Motivating Individuals to Perform**   Most organizations would like to motivate employees to perform beyond minimally acceptable levels. Organizations do many things other than use wage payments to elicit high performance. For example, there is an extensive body of leadership literature that suggests that leaders and their behavior can influence the level of performance that workers exhibit.[17]

| EXHIBIT 1.5 | EXAMPLE OF A COMPANY'S VACATION POLICY |
| --- | --- |

### Vacations

Policy

Newman Co. provides vacation with pay to all eligible employees.

Comment

Full-time employees will be provided with paid vacation in each calendar year within the following guidelines:

1. Full-time employees receive 10 days of paid vacation each calendar year. Each employee on the staff on January 1 accrues vacation time as of that date. This does not apply to part-time or temporary employees. Full-time employees receive 15 days of accrued vacation time on January 1 following the year in which they complete 10 years of employment with Newman Co.

2. New employees—During the first calendar year of employment, those employed after January 1 will receive vacation time based on the month of employment as follows:

Number of Vacation Days

January ....................................10 days
February................................ 9 days
March ..................................... 7 days
April, May, June.................... 5 days
July through December ........ 0 days

Accrued vacation time will not be credited to you until the end of your probationary period.

3. All officers are entitled to 15 days of vacation.

4. Part-time and temporary employees are not eligible for paid vacations.

5. Vacations must be taken in the year earned. Unused, accrued vacation time cannot be carried over beyond December 31.

6. No vacation pay will be granted if the employee was dismissed for cause (misconduct or willful violation of policies) or failed to give at least 2 weeks notice of resignation.

7. The department supervisor is responsible for notifying the Payroll Department in writing of employees' vacation days actually taken.

---

Other literature suggests that the way jobs are designed may influence performance levels.[18] Although there may be multiple variables, interacting in complex ways, that have an impact on individuals' motivation to perform, it should be clear that compensation is also one of the ways in which organizations influence performance. According to one study, employees perceived that benefits did impact the amount of effort they exerted on the job.[19] A merit pay policy is one way organizations attempt to use money to motivate high performance. One organization's merit pay policy is presented in Exhibit 1.6.

A main objective of compensation systems is to motivate performance. Before compensation managers can make decisions about the compensation system's design that will motivate performance, several earlier steps are necessary. It is important first to understand what motivates people and then to understand how to carry out the process of motivation. Finally, compensation system decision makers must be able to design components of the compensation system that put that understanding into practice and tie all rewards to the organization's overall goals. Recognizing the stimuli that motivate people to perform and understanding the process of motivation are covered in Chapters 3, 11, 12, and 15.

## Constraints of the Compensation System

The first goal of the organization's compensation system is to motivate employees to behave in ways that are congruent with the organization's needs. That goal includes motivating individuals to join the organization, to stay with the organization, and to perform well for the organization. The second main goal of an organization's compensation system (summarized in Exhibit 1.3) is to accomplish the first goal within certain constraints. The five principal constraints faced by the organization are its ability to pay, legal constraints, collective bargaining, the internal labor market, and the external labor market.

**Ability to Pay**  Statements such as "I want to pay all my employees as little as possible to maximize profits" and "I want to keep all my employees in poverty" are often attributed to the early capitalists of the industrial revolution. Since the advent of the public corporation in the twentieth century, it is unlikely that managers would make such statements. It is true, however, that managers do want to hire people as cheaply as possible.

---

**EXHIBIT 1.6**    **EXAMPLE OF A MERIT PAY POLICY**

---

**Salaries**

---

Policy

    Employees are paid twice a month, on the 15th and the last day of the month, by automatic deposits to their checking accounts. When these dates fall on weekends or holidays, employees will be paid on the preceding business day.

Comment

1. Your employee rating is based on merit, and you are considered for a salary increase after the first year of employment and every anniversary date thereafter.

2. Salary increases are not automatic, nor are they based on length of service. Salary adjustments are based on a thorough review of your performance and noted improvement in performance or continued excellent performance of your actual job requirements.

3. Salaries are confidential, and you are expected to respect and maintain this confidentiality.

If you were to ask a typical contemporary manager what type of wages an employee in the firm should make, you might get an answer such as "A fair wage, a living wage that allows, if not a luxurious life-style, at least a tolerably civil life-style." Yet, that same manager might actually pay minimum wages for almost all jobs. What dictates that an organization whose managers might like to pay more will not? The **ability to pay** is the determining factor, and it varies considerably from organization to organization and industry to industry. The competitive nature of most product markets today results in shrinking profit margins, which restrict the discretion of the organization in the compensation area. It is extremely difficult to compete with a foreign operation that has an average wage significantly below what must be paid domestic workers. For example, in 1988, workers in Mexico received an average hourly compensation of $1.57 and those in Taiwan received $2.71 compared with U.S. workers whose average was $13.90.[20] Regardless of the intentions of management, the product market may determine the maximum compensation that the organization can pay even if the organization makes maximum use of technology and creativity. Chapter 2 discusses product markets and labor markets and their effect on the organization's ability to pay.

The productivity of labor and the *elasticity* (degree to which change in price of a product results in change in demand) of the organization's product demand are two critical variables that dictate an employer's ability to pay. Chapter 2 discusses these concepts and why ability to pay is such a main constraint to many organizations. However, these considerations are theoretical and do not readily translate into practice. The practical approach to ability-to-pay constraints is discussed briefly in Chapter 2 and in considerable detail in Chapters 4, 8, and 10.

**Legal Constraints**    Legal issues in compensation are so pervasive as to consume much of the time of compensation managers. For example, the board of directors of the XYZ company recently suggested that the company investigate the possibility of having a private pension plan. The company's compensation director, Al Ladd, must decide several things: How large a plan should XYZ have, how should the employee and the company contributions be calculated, and what kind of legal liability does the company have? Al remembers from graduate school that the Employee Retirement Income Security Act of 1974 and other tax laws have provisions regulating vesting, funding, portability, and fiduciary standards. He starts to ask his benefits manager to investigate this. Al's secretary interrupts to inform him that a local attorney is in the waiting room about an employee complaint regarding pay. The attorney serves papers on XYZ on behalf of Rosie Laughlin and 246 other women who are charging XYZ with sex-related pay discrimination under Title VII of the Civil Rights Act of 1964 and the Equal Pay Act of 1963. Although the Equal Employment Opportunity Commission just investigated that issue 6 weeks ago and found no probable cause for a suit, they did give Laughlin a **letter of right to sue.** Al is also aware that the Civil Rights Act of 1991 has increased the potential monetary liability of XYZ, should the court find against it. Concurrently with these problems, Al must contend with minimum wage legislation, complex issues over when the company must pay overtime (FLSA of 1938), and provisions of the Davis Bacon Act that will affect the wages XYZ must pay workers on a government contract in Alaska.

Where does it all end? The simplistic answer to the question is that it ends when a compensation manager knows and understands the myriad of legislation and administrative law that constrains the compensation behavior of the organization. These particular constraints are enormously complex, and an entire text could be devoted to them; the goal in this book is to give the reader a comprehensive exposure to these constraints, with further exposure left to outside readings or an advanced course on compensation. Chapter 5 deals with these complex legal constraints.

**Collective Bargaining**   A famous labor leader once reputedly said when asked what the union wanted, "We want more—more money, more days off with pay, more benefits—more, more, more!" The world has changed since that early labor leader's statement of union goals. Although unions may still want more, there is a systematic trend that started in the 1970s and 1980s and is gaining momentum in the 1990s for labor to be willing to negotiate for less (that is, pay and benefit cuts.[21]) Sagging U.S. industry, many plant closings, buy-outs, takeovers (sometimes by foreign owners), and competition from foreign firms with cheap labor costs have changed the position and the goals of many unions. Regardless, anyone wanting to be familiar with compensation practices must appreciate the constraint imposed by labor unions. In one sense, the labor union as an entity could be considered part of the legal constraint because the requirement of management to bargain over compensation is mandated by law. However, labor unions have a distinct life apart from the law. As a result, once management is required by law to bargain with the union, the union's presence provides a new dynamic to compensation decision making. Chapter 4 focuses on this dynamic and briefly examines the legal foundations for labor unions, examines what unions bargain for, and attempts to answer the question, "What impact does the union have on the compensation system?" It examines the role of labor organizations in the compensation decision-making process and labor's influence on the level and structure of wages and benefit packages for its members and for nonunion employees.

**Internal Labor Market**   An internal labor market can be thought of as all the jobs within an organization and the relationship among these jobs. In organizations in which an internal labor market is present, there are usually entry level jobs and then other jobs into which employees can move only after being in entry level positions. Movement to these higher level jobs is controlled by organizational rules and procedures. Internal labor markets have extremely important implications for the design of compensation systems. Chapter 4 discusses internal labor markets, how they arise, what purposes they serve, and how they influence the compensation of employees.

**External Labor Market**   All employers must bid for labor in the marketplace. Under the reasonable assumption that individuals would rather work for more money than for less money, employers are obligated to try to pay competitive wages. The going rate in the labor market is an additional constraint that employers must try to meet. The going rate is really an array of rates paid by other employers in a given labor market area. Generally, there are sound economic reasons (including ability to pay and willingness to pay) for this array. From the standpoint of trying to motivate individuals to join and stay with them, organizations in theory would want to pay at least the market rate. In reality, this is often not done. The reasons are strongly linked to the economics of the organization—although employers might want to pay at market, they may be unable to do so.[22] This inherent tension between the external labor market constraint and the ability-to-pay constraint is a main theme of this text.

## Roles of Theory and Practice

It is the perspective of this text that sound theory helps to understand practice. A theory can be envisioned as a conceptual framework that links two or more variables together. For example, a person might suggest a theory that the amount of pay one gets is determined solely by power. This theory says that Pay = $f$ (power). That is, "pay is a function of power." A theory is verified by testing it in the physical world. The theorist needs to find some people who vary in terms of the amount of power they have and ascertain if the more powerful get more money and if the less powerful get less money.

Suppose very little association is found between what people make as a wage and the power they have. Now, the theorist is in a position to refine this theory along several paths. Another variable can be added. For example, Pay = $f$(power and the market value of the job). That is, pay is determined by the power the individual has and the market value of the job. The theorist can go to the physical world and empirically test the theory again. If the theory is still inadequate, more and more variables can be added until a theory that accurately captures reality results.

This process is the way in which theory evolves. Exhibit 1.7 depicts this process graphically. Even Einstein continually tested his theories about light, energy, and mass until he was able to refine a generalized theory of relativity. In much the same way, theories of wages have evolved. The theory of wages is less elegant and refined than a general theory of relativity. In fact, it would be appropriate to say that there are many theories explaining how organizational decisions about compensation are shaped. The purpose of using theory in this text is to describe general behavioral tendencies and to show why compensation departments function the way they do.

Theory and practice go hand in hand. Because theory is shaped by what occurs in the physical world, one could even argue that theory is simply an abstraction of reality and that the only reason theory exists is because it provides a rationale for practice. This text uses theory to help the reader understand the practices that go on in organizations. Theory can aid in understanding the relationships between what otherwise seem like disjointed pieces of administrative practice. The theory presented here is meant to be a useful crutch for organizing facts.

Because of the multidimensionality of compensation, compensation practices are developed from an array of disciplines. In other words, compensation practices are based on theories and concepts from the disciplines of economics,

| EXHIBIT 1.7 | RELATIONSHIP BETWEEN THE CONCEPTUAL AND PHYSICAL WORLD AND THE DEVLEOPMENT OF THEORY |
|---|---|

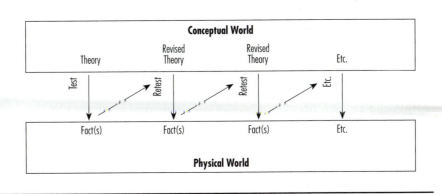

psychology, sociology, philosophy, and finance/accounting. For example, in assessing performance, psychological theories such as reinforcement theory and equity theory provide the bases on which many of the practices are built. Economic theory is a primary means of determining the ability of the organization to pay. Philosophy is essential in the notion of fairness underlying employees' satisfaction or dissatisfaction with the compensation package and its administration. The sociologic concept of social status has an effect on the value employees give to the hierarchical position of jobs within the organization and on what they perceive as rewards. Finance and accounting concepts are the main criteria used in determining the final design of fringe benefits and incentive programs. The above are just a few illustrations of how different disciplines are used in determining compensation policies and practices.

The precise specifications of different theoretic frameworks presented in Chapters 2 and 3 should not be taken literally. For example, among advanced students and scholars, there is often debate over the precise specifications of a model (or theory). To the extent that alternate specifications cause different results—different behavioral conclusions or outcomes—then the alternate specifications are important. However, if alternate specifications of a model or theory result in the same behavioral conclusions, the distinctions make little difference for the purposes in this text. The theories presented are taken to be generally valid or explanatory of individual or market behavior. They are meant to serve as pedagogical devices with which to organize and understand the compensation world.

Every theoretic framework has behind it a set of assumptions. When it is found that the theory does not predict behavior, it is usually because the cases being used to disprove the theory violate one or more assumptions that are necessary for the theory to work. In that situation, it would be more appropriate to suggest that the theory was misapplied than to say the theory is not valid.

# Summary

This introductory chapter on compensation decision making was designed to do three things. First, it introduces the parties who have an interest in compensation decision making: individuals, organizations, and society at large. The questions asked by individuals about compensation payments are also asked by organizations and society at large, although from slightly different perspectives.

Second, the chapter defines compensation, describes the components of compensation, and identifies the two basic goals of compensation systems. The first goal is to elicit desired behaviors from potential employees and current employees; the second goal is to accomplish the first goal within the constraints of ability to pay, the legal environment, the institutional process of collective bargaining, and the internal and external labor markets.

Finally, this chapter presents the framework of the text and discusses how theory and practice are intimately related to each other. The study of theory helps in understanding why certain compensation decisions are made, and the study of common practices helps us understand how certain compensation decisions are made.

# Discussion Questions

1. "Theory is good for theoreticians, but it is irrelevant for the average person." Discuss.

2. Discuss the two organizational compensation goals presented. What other goals for compensation might have been included? Why do you think those goals were excluded?

3. Discuss the forces that might cause an employer such as McDonald's Hamburgers to be a low-wage employer.

4. Define the following terms:

   *External equity*

   *Internal equity*

   *Wage level*

   *Wage structure*

   *Ability to pay*

   *Wage compression*

5. Define the term *compensation.*

6. Why are organizations concerned with compensation as a managerial tool? For example, what should a compensation program accomplish?

7. Identify some of the ways in which society has influenced compensation decision making—for example, what are some of the constraints that compensation decision makers must deal with?

8. Why has the issue of compensation practices become such a hot topic?

## References

[1] In fact, the top 5 percent of income recipients in the United States receive more than two thirds of all dividend payments and nearly half of all property income. Lloyd G. Reynolds, *Labor Economics and Labor Relations*, 6th ed. (Englewood Cliffs, NJ: Prentice–Hall, 1974), 308.

[2] H. G. Heneman, Jr. and D. Yoder, *Labor Economics*, 2d ed. (Cincinnati, OH: South-western, 1965).

[3] U.S. Chamber of Commerce, *Annual Employee Benefits Survey* (Washington, DC, 1982).

[4] T. Karier, "Trade Deficits and Labor Unions: Myths and Realities," in *Unions and Economic Competitiveness*, eds. L. Mischel and P. B. Voos (Armonk, NY: M. E. Shape, 1992), 15–37.

[5] G. A. Steiner and John F. Steiner, *Business, Government, and Society*, 4th ed. (New York: Random House, 1985), 525.

[6] M. Zall. "What to Expect from the Civil Rights Act," *Personnel Journal* 71 (March, 1992), 46–50.

[7] "IDS Settles Age Discrimination Suit with Managers," *National Underwriters* 96 (September 21, 1992), 11.

[8] *Corning Glass Works v. Brennan*, 417 U.S. 188, 9 FEP 919 (1974).

[9] G. Colvin, "How to Pay the CEO Right," *Fortune* 125 (April 6, 1992), 60–70.

[10] The first workers' compensation law was passed in Maryland in 1902. W. L. French, *The Personnel Management Process*, 5th ed. (Boston: Houghton Mifflin, 1982).

[11] Equal Pay Act of 1963, enacted as section 6(d) of the Fair Labor Standards Act, 29 U.S.C., section 206(d), 1976.

[12] Civil Rights Act of 1964, 42 U.S.C., section 2000e, 1964.

[13] _____ "Employee Benefits 1990," U.S. Chamber of Commerce (Washngton, DC: U.S. Chamber of Commerce, 1991).

[14] J. Zampetti, "Building ABC's for an On Site Child Care Center," *Management Review* 80 (March 1991), 54–55+.

[15] T. J. Bergmann and M. A. Bergmann, "Empirical Analysis of the Role of Fringe Benefits in a Company's Compensation System," *Personnel* 64 (1987), 59–64.

[16] *Ibid.*

[17] G. Yukl and D. D. Van Fleet, "Theory and Research on Leadership in Organization" in *Handbook of Industrial and Organizational Psychology*, 2d ed., vol. 3, eds. M. D. Dunnette and L. M. Hough (Palo Alto, CA: Consulting Psychologist Press, 1992), 147–198.

[18] R. J. Hackman and G. R. Oldham, *Working Redesign* (Reading, MA: Addison-Wesley, 1980); R. A. Guzzo, R. D. Jettle, and R. A. Katzell, "The Effects of Psychological Based Intervention Programs and Workers Productivity," *Personnel Psychology* 38 (1985), 275–291.

[19] T. J. Bergmann and M. A. Bergmann, "Empirical Analysis of the Role of Fringe Benefits in a Company's Compensation System," *Personnel* 64 (1987), 59–64.

[20] T. Karier, "Trade Deficits and Labor Unions: Myths and Realities," in *Unions and Economic Competitiveness*, eds. L. Mischel and P. B. Voos (Armonk, NY: M. E. Shape, 1992).

[21] J. J. Lacombe, III, and J. R. Conley, "Major Agreements in 1984 Provide Record Low Wage Increases," *Monthly Labor Review*, U.S. Department of Labor, Bureau of Labor Statistics, vol. 108 (4) (April 1985), 39–45.

[22] L. Nay, "The Determinants of Concession Bargaining in the Airline Industry," *Industrial and Labor Relations Review* 44 (January 1991), 307–323.

# 2

# Theoretic Framework I: Economic Constraints

## Learning Objectives

**To learn that organizations have an ability-to-pay constraint.**

**To learn that the demand for labor is a derived demand; that is, it is derived from the demand for the good or service that the employer produces.**

**To learn that marginal revenue productivity (MRP) theory is the theoretic base for understanding the organization's ability-to-pay constraint.**

**To learn through simple examples how MRP theory translates into ability to pay wages.**

**To learn the consequences associated with an organization that is a high-wage or low-wage employer.**

**To learn that the concept of ability to pay is directly related to the concept of the wage level.**

**To learn about other wage theories and how they are relevant today.**

## Introduction

The basic issue of this chapter is to lay out the concept of ability to pay. Organizations differ in their ability to pay. To illustrate this difference, this chapter discusses the concepts of demand for labor as a derived demand, marginal revenue productivity theory, and labor supplies. It includes a section on the significance of ability to pay in compensation practice; specifically, firms conduct product market wage and salary surveys to estimate their ability to pay. The chapter concludes with a brief discussion of several historical wage theories and their current application.

Every labor market area has both a high-wage employer and a low-wage employer, with many employers who pay a range of rates between the extremes. Restaurants and gas stations are relatively low-wage employers. However, oil firms and computer companies may be relatively high-wage employers. In the simplest case, one might not expect large wage differences among employers within a labor market area. Organizations in a given labor area might be expected to pay the same rate to influence workers to join and stay with them (the first main goal of the compensation system). Yet, there are large wage differences within a given labor market area. One classic study found that for truck drivers in the Boston labor area, the highest paying firms paid 96 percent more than the lowest paying firms, even though the truck drivers were unionized.[1]

By developing the concept of ability to pay, this chapter develops the theoretic framework to explain why these wage differentials exist. It is primarily the relative ability to pay wages among employers that causes wage differences. This chapter also deals with the consequences for a firm if its economic situation forces it to be a low-wage payer or permits it to be a relatively high-wage payer.

## Wage Differentials—A Technical Meaning

Wage differentials are often attributed to differences in the skill mix of employees used by different organizations or industries in producing a good or service.[2] In this context, a computer company, on average, will pay higher wages than a restaurant because the computer company usually uses more highly skilled workers.

Wage differentials between geographic areas also exist.[3] Geographic wage differentials are often attributed to the difference in the skill mix and supply of labor offered in various regions of the United States. Variation in the composition of industry among geographic regions is also a partial explanation for geographic wage differentials.

Adam Smith[4] identifies five reasons for wage differentials among workers within a given geographic area. First, different kinds of work vary in terms of their agreeableness. Some work is simply cleaner, more enjoyable, or more honorable than others. Bank work involves working in a prestigious and pleasant environment which may explain why the banking industry pays relatively low wages. An organization that can provide more agreeable work may be able to pay lower wages than other organizations for the same quality of employee (nonpecuniary rewards). Second, wages for work vary as a function of the expense of learning the business. Some labor is paid more, presumably because training time is longer and workers must receive a higher wage for their training investment. Third, constancy of employment affects wages. Employment that is stable presumably can be lower-paying than unstable employment, because unstable employment requires higher wages to offset less time at work. Fourth, wages vary with the level of trust that must be placed in the worker: A physician's pay is relatively higher than a groundskeeper's pay because of the level of trust people must have in the physician's work. Fifth, wages vary as a function of the likelihood of success in the employment. If chances of success are low (for example, professional athletics), wages should be correspondingly higher for the athlete who does succeed or who shows great potential to succeed.

The above notions of wage differentials are not the main focus of this chapter. When high- and low-wage employers are referred to, it means that within a given labor area, holding constant the job under consideration, some organizations pay more than others for the same type of work. If an employee in one organization is paid less than an employee doing the same work in another organization, it is because different organizations have different abilities to pay.

It is also true that just because an organization has a high ability to pay does not necessarily mean that it pays high wages. For example, a millionaire and an average wage earner have different abilities to pay someone to remove snow from their driveways, but both may pay the same. Other forces than ability to pay influence whether the millionaire pays more than the average wage earner.

# Marginal Productivity Theory

## Marginal Productivity Assumptions

Marginal productivity theory proposes a relationship between employment, wages, and productivity. It provides a useful way of looking at labor costs and how they must be examined to remain competitive in today's global marketplace.[5] The theory is based on a series of ten assumptions. First, employers attempt to maximize profit. It is probably true that employers would like to maximize profits; however, this desire is often constrained by the environment in which they operate. Such factors as the degree of product market competition or government regulation prohibit the organization from absolute profit maximization. Second, employers use the most efficient combination of factors of production. In reality, union–management contracts and customs often limit the ability of employers to substitute technology for labor. Third, the law of diminishing proportions holds between different factors of production. That is, the marginal revenue product will at some point decrease as additional units of labor are added to a fixed work site. This assumes that employers hire workers one at a time and can measure the marginal physical output of each additional worker. But, employers often hire employees in groups and thus do not hire sequentially and do not have the ability to measure the marginal output of each additional worker hired. Fourth, because all workers are equal (homogeneous), the wage paid each unit of labor is where marginal cost equals marginal revenue. Fifth, employees have perfect knowledge of the labor market. This means that if an employer attempts to pay below where marginal cost equals marginal revenue, employees will leave that employer and switch to an employer who pays at the appropriate level. It is obvious that employees do not have perfect knowledge of the labor market, but, if an employer does get too far out of line (substandard wages), the quality of labor that can be attracted does decrease. Sixth, the market is a purely competitive market and there are many buyers and sellers of labor, so that neither labor nor employer can fix the price of labor. While this may be true in some areas, it is not a universally true statement. Seventh, capital and labor are fully employed. The unemployment figures during the past decades have shown less than full employment of labor. Even the concept of full employment generates a high level of debate among economists; they question what level of unemployment causes an economy to drop out of being classified as fully employed. Eighth, all laborers are homogeneous. Clearly, a typical employer does not hire homogeneous workers; rather the employer hires computer programmers, lathe operators, data entry clerks, and others who receive great differences in wage rates. Ninth, all goods and services at a set price are sold, so there is no build up of finished products waiting to be sold. Warehouses worldwide verify that this is not the case. Tenth, the attractiveness of a job is measured by its hourly rate. In fact, the attractiveness of a job is much broader than money wages and includes such factors as fringe benefits, geographic location, and intrinsic value of the job itself. Obviously, these ten assumptions represent the theoretic realm; each requires modification and variation in the real world as the comment after each assumption indicates. Nevertheless, Marginal Productivity Theory has proven itself to be very useful in understanding labor cost.

### Labor Demand as a Derived Demand

Labor services, in and of themselves, have no value. Labor is valued only by an employing organization to the extent that the labor is combined with other factors of production (for example, land, plant, capital) to produce a good or service. Ford Motor Company and Ace Hardware want workers only because they are part of the resource mix needed to make cars or to sell hardware. Therefore, the demand for labor is a derived demand—that is, it is derived from the demand for the goods or services of the employing organization.[6] When the demand for Ford cars is down, workers are laid off; new workers are hired by Apple Computers when demand for home computers grows.

### Intuitive Example of Labor's Value

The value of labor is determined, in part, by how it is applied to other factors of production, as shown in the following example. Suppose an employer is in the business of digging ditches and can sell all the linear feet of ditch that can be dug at $1 per foot. The employer has a total of five shovels (a fixed production facility); no other tools or equipment are used, and the shovels are paid for (no capital costs). All laborers hired are interchangeable. What happens to productivity (feet of ditch dug) and revenues as the employer hires each worker?

If a typical laborer can dig 30 feet of ditch in a day, the productivity of the first laborer hired will be 30 feet of ditch. Similarly, the second through the fifth worker hired each add 30 feet of ditch per day. Regardless of whether the employer uses one, two, three, four, or five workers per day, the average productivity is 30 feet of ditch, even though total productivity goes up 30 times the number of workers employed. Total productivity is 30 feet in the case of one worker, 60 feet in the case of two workers, and so forth, up to 150 feet for five workers. The relationship between labor's productivity and number of workers hired in this example is summarized in Exhibit 2.1.

What happens to marginal productivity as workers one through five are added? Marginal productivity can be defined as the increment in productivity resulting from the addition of one more worker. As the employer adds the first worker, marginal productivity goes from zero (with no workers) to 30 (when the first worker is added). When the second worker is added, marginal productivity is 30 and is equal to average productivity. That is, the second worker increased total output to 60 feet of ditch, but the second worker is no more productive than the first worker. For workers one through five, then, marginal productivity is 30 feet of ditch, and average productivity is 30 feet of ditch. Each worker is using one more shovel and adding the same amount to the total productive capacity of the ditch digging company.

| EXHIBIT 2.1 | LABOR'S PRODUCTIVITY AND THE IMPACT ON LABOR'S DEMAND PRICE | | | | | |
|---|---|---|---|---|---|---|

| No. of Workers | Total Product (ft of ditch) | Average Product[a] | Marginal Product[b] | Price | Average Revenue Product[c] | Marginal Revenue Product[d] |
|---|---|---|---|---|---|---|
| 1 | 30 | 30 | 30 | $1 | $30 | $30 |
| 2 | 60 | 30 | 30 | 1 | 30 | 30 |
| 3 | 90 | 30 | 30 | 1 | 30 | 30 |
| 4 | 120 | 30 | 30 | 1 | 30 | 30 |
| 5 | 150 | 30 | 30 | 1 | 30 | 30 |
| 6 | 210 | 35 | 60 | 1 | 35 | 60 |
| 7 | 280 | 40 | 70 | 1 | 40 | 70 |
| 8 | 320 | 40 | 40 | 1 | 40 | 40 |
| 9 | 333 | 37 | 13 | 1 | 37 | 13 |
| 10 | 280 | 28 | -53 | 1 | 28 | -53 |

[a]Average productivity = total productivity divided by the number of workers.
[b]Marginal productivity = the increment in total productivity realized by moving from $N$ to $N + 1$ workers.
[c]Average revenue product = average productivity multiplied by the unit price of the product.
[d]Marginal revenue product = marginal productivity multiplied by the unit price of the product.

The company now adds a sixth worker to the work crew. This worker sharpens the shovel blades while the other five workers rest, gets water for them (and thereby shortens their breaks), and spells them periodically. With the addition of the sixth worker, total productivity goes from 150 feet of ditch (with five workers) to 210 feet of ditch. The marginal productivity of the sixth worker is 60 feet of ditch, and the average productivity of the six workers is now 35 feet of ditch. The employer is realizing an economy scale; that is, workers are becoming more productive because they are more efficiently using the fixed factor of production (the five shovels).

Now the seventh worker is added to the work crew. This worker sharpens shovels even more often, spells the other workers more frequently, and drives the stakes to show where the ditch is to be dug. Workers who are digging no longer have to stop digging to plan the route of the ditch. This work crew can now dig 280 feet of ditch per day. The marginal productivity of the seventh worker is 70 feet of ditch and average productivity is 40 feet of ditch per day. Labor is becoming more productive as it is applied to the fixed factor of production (shovels).

An eighth worker is now added to the work crew. This worker also spells other workers periodically and moves large stones out of the way of the planned ditch. Total productivity now goes to 320 feet of ditch. Marginal productivity is now 40 feet of ditch, and average productivity is 40 feet of ditch. Average productivity did not go up because marginal productivity of the eighth worker was exactly equal to the average productivity of the first seven workers. In other words, the eighth worker did not increase marginal productivity (although total productivity increased).

The ninth worker is added now. This ninth worker also helps remove obstacles from the path of the ditch and spells other workers on breaks. With this ninth worker, productivity is 333 feet of ditch. Marginal productivity of this ninth worker is 13 feet of ditch, and average productivity is 37 feet of ditch per worker. Average productivity fell, even though total productivity increased slightly, because marginal productivity is falling.

The tenth worker now is added to the work crew. This tenth worker is always underfoot bumping into the other nine workers and generally disrupting their work. Now, total productivity is 280 feet of ditch. This tenth worker has a negative marginal productivity of 53 feet of ditch, and average productivity is 28 feet of ditch.

This intuitive example demonstrates two important aspects of labor's productivity. The first is what economists call the law of diminishing marginal proportions.[7] This law states that as a variable factor of production (labor in the example) is added to a fixed factor of production (shovels in the example), the resulting additions to output initially increase because of economies of scale but will eventually decrease (third assumption).

The second point is that the employer's ability to pay will vary with labor's productivity. Average productivity can be translated to average revenue productivity because it is assumed that the ditch digging company can sell each foot of ditch dug for $1. When average physical productivity is multiplied by revenue, average revenue productivity for the work crew is $30 per day in the case of five workers, $35 per day in the case of six workers, and so on, to $28 per day for ten workers. Depending on labor's productivity at different combinations of employment, the firm's ability to pay varies. These relationships are depicted in column six of Exhibit 2.1. With a five-person crew of workers, the firm could pay up to $30 per day per worker; with a crew of seven, the firm could pay up to $40 per day per worker; and with a crew of ten, the firm could pay up to $28 per day per worker.

The ditch digging example is deficient in several respects. First, it is extremely simplistic in that there are usually several costs of production, and firms do wish to make a profit. Second, the concept of ability to pay is much richer than portrayed here. The example suggests that ability to pay varies within a fixed production technology. Although this is true, it fails to make the important point that ability to pay varies across technologies. Third, any change in selling price of the product or service will significantly affect the number of workers that can be hired, all other factors held constant. Fourth, the example does not adequately develop the concept of an employer's demand for labor. The demand for labor is important in understanding why firms are concerned about the wages they pay their employees. This concept is developed in the next section.

## *Employer's Demand for Labor*

To illustrate the employer's demand for labor, assume a small hamburger stand sells miniburgers and fries for $1 per serving. Each of these servings is called a meal. The owner of this stand figures out the amount of labor to hire by running an experiment in which one worker at a time is hired and the marginal physical product of each is determined. It is assumed that all workers are homogeneous, and the owner can sell all the meals produced at $1 each.

Using the same analysis as in the ditch digging example, the owner hires one worker and records the total productivity, the average productivity (AP), the marginal productivity (MP), the average revenue productivity (ARP), and the marginal revenue productivity (MRP) of that worker. The employer then adds more workers at the rate of one worker to each hourly shift to see how these five variables change. The results appear in Exhibit 2.2, which shows that total productivity varies from zero output with no workers to 225 meals with 10 workers.

Based on these productivity figures, it can be seen that going from one to two workers will increase ARP from $10 to $15 and MRP from $10 to $20. Each additional worker, for workers one through five, results in an increase in both ARP and MRP. However, when worker six is employed, ARP remains unchanged but MRP decreases! With the addition of workers eight through ten, both ARP and MRP decrease. These changes in ARP and MRP are due to changes in labor's productivity as a result of the law of diminishing marginal proportions as demonstrated in the ditch digging example. The ARP and MRP data from Exhibit 2.2 can be plotted on a graph, as shown in Exhibit 2.3.

What are the profit levels of this hamburger stand at different levels of employment given a total hourly wage rate of $10, $20, $30, $40, and $50 per hour, respectively? The hamburger stand is most profitable at combinations of wages and employment along the portion of the MRP schedule from the point where MRP = ARP and to the right. All levels of employment to the left of this point are less profitable, and the employer is not maximizing profits (that is, it pays to hire more workers). The firm's demand schedule for labor is equal to the MRP schedule for labor, and the relevant portion of this schedule is from where ARP = MRP to the right.

An employer can pay varying amounts for labor, depending on where the employer is on the demand schedule. This ability to pay wages of varying amounts is because labor has a given productivity level at different levels of employment as it is applied to the physical plant. However, employers do not normally set wages unilaterally. That is, employers also set wages based on what they must pay to attract and retain labor, which is, in turn, partly determined by the labor supply, which is discussed next.

| EXHIBIT 2.2 | MARGINAL REVENUE PRODUCTIVITY ANALYSIS (PER-HOUR BASIS) |
| --- | --- |

| Units of Labor | Total Productivity | Average Physical Product | Marginal Physical Product | Price per Unit | Average Revenue Product | Marginal Revenue Product |
| --- | --- | --- | --- | --- | --- | --- |
| 0 | 0 | 0 | 0 | $1 | $ 0 | $ 0 |
| 1 | 10 | 10 | 10 | 1 | 10 | 10 |
| 2 | 30 | 15 | 20 | 1 | 15 | 20 |
| 3 | 60 | 20 | 30 | 1 | 20 | 30 |
| 4 | 100 | 25 | 40 | 1 | 25 | 40 |
| 5 | 150 | 30 | 50 | 1 | 30 | 50 |
| 6 | 180 | 30 | 30 | 1 | 30 | 30 |
| 7 | 210 | 30 | 30 | 1 | 30 | 30 |
| 8 | 220 | 27.5 | 10 | 1 | 27.5 | 10 |
| 9 | 225 | 25 | 5 | 1 | 25 | 5 |
| 10 | 225 | 22.5 | 0 | 1 | 22.5 | 0 |

| EXHIBIT 2.3 | AVERAGE AND MARGINAL REVENUE PRODUCTIVITY CURVES |
|---|---|

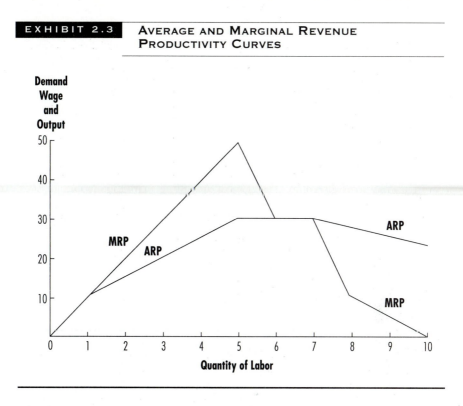

## Labor Supply in the Marketplace

An example of a theoretic labor supply schedule is depicted in Exhibit 2.4. In theory, this labor supply schedule could be constructed by asking potential employees in the labor market how many of them are willing to work at different wage rates—How many would be willing to work for $4 per hour, how many would be willing to work for $5 per hour, and so forth. In general, the higher the wage offered in the marketplace, the larger the quantity of labor willing to work. The owner in the hamburger stand example is faced with a supply schedule of labor in the marketplace and must pay (under assumptions of competition for labor) a rate that will attract sufficient labor to make the meals.

The wage that is offered is dependent on the joint function of the labor supply's acceptable wage and other employers' demands for labor. That is, if all the labor in the market that is willing to work for $5 per hour is already employed, the employer will not be able to hire labor at $5 per hour. In most cases, however, it is reasonable to assume that an adequate labor supply is available and that the supply of labor is highly elastic with respect to price. The hamburger stand owner can obtain all the labor desired at the going market rate. The labor supply schedule for the hamburger stand resembles the one that appears in Exhibit 2.5. The employer here can obtain all the labor desired at a given wage.[8]

The labor demand schedule in Exhibit 2.4 and the labor supply schedule in Exhibit 2.5 can now be combined into the graph in Exhibit 2.6.

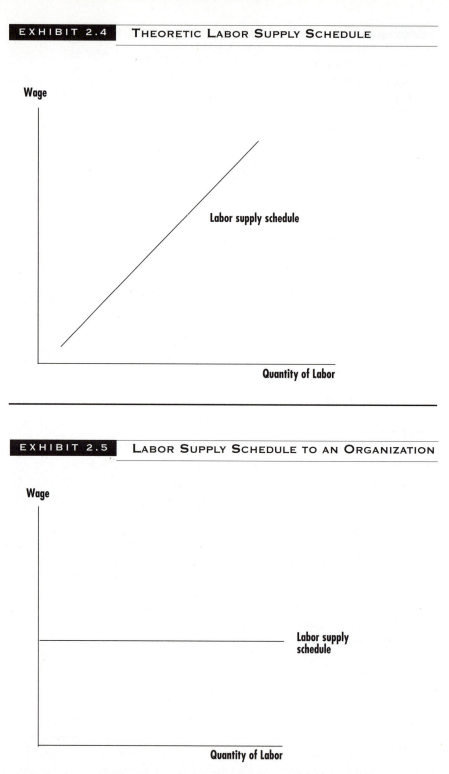

**EXHIBIT 2.4    THEORETIC LABOR SUPPLY SCHEDULE**

Wage

Labor supply schedule

Quantity of Labor

**EXHIBIT 2.5    LABOR SUPPLY SCHEDULE TO AN ORGANIZATION**

Wage

Labor supply
schedule

Quantity of Labor

Using Exhibit 2.6, it is now possible to determine what the wage will be and what employment will be. The wage rate will be the equilibrium rate at $W$, and employment will be at the equilibrium level $Q$.

According to the graph in Exhibit 2.6, an employer has little control over wages paid. That is, wage rates presumably are a joint function of labor productivity and the labor supply's willingness to work at different wage levels. Although this is partially true, it is erroneous to conclude that management has no control over wage rates. It should also be recognized that marginal revenue productivity theory as developed to this point is a theory of employment—given the productivity of labor (the demand schedule for labor) and the price of labor, the organization decides how many units of labor to employ.

To better understand the role of MRP theory's impact on ability to pay wages, it is useful to conduct a slightly different kind of analysis, which is done in the next section.

## Marginal Revenue Productivity Theory and Ability to Pay

Why is an organization constrained by it ability to pay? One of the factors that is critical in an employer's ability to pay is the productivity of labor units.[9] An

---

**EXHIBIT 2.6**    **INTERACTION OF LABOR SUPPLY AND DEMAND**

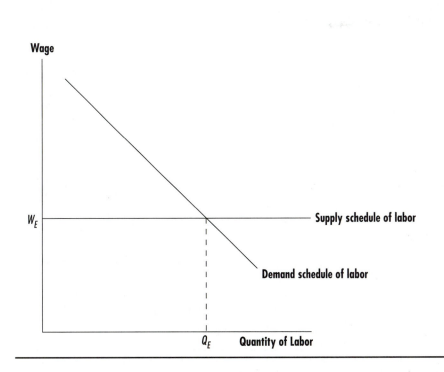

organization that makes and sells a product must sell it for a price that allows the organization to cover the costs of production and make a profit. The more productive each unit of labor employed by the organization, the more valuable that labor unit is to the employer (the cheaper each unit of labor is, per unit of product). The following example, using two hamburger stands, illustrates why. In this example, employer A has a relatively efficient labor force, and employer B has a relatively inefficient labor force.

Assume that both employers A and B are determining what hourly wage rate they could offer workers. Each employer has a targeted level of output of 220 meals per hour. These meals sell for $1 each, and for convenience let's assume that the employer can sell all units produced in the hour. The amount targeted output and the revenue associated with that output can be depicted in a graph, as shown in Exhibit 2.7.

### Average and Total Revenue

In Exhibit 2.7, the line designated as price is the $1 per meal that the employer can charge for the product. The amount of the product to be produced is 220 meals, and the area under the curve is the total revenue to be realized: $1 \times 220$ meals $=$ $220. This line also represents average revenue per unit of product.

**EXHIBIT 2.7**    **ANALYSIS OF AVERAGE NET REVENUE PRODUCT**

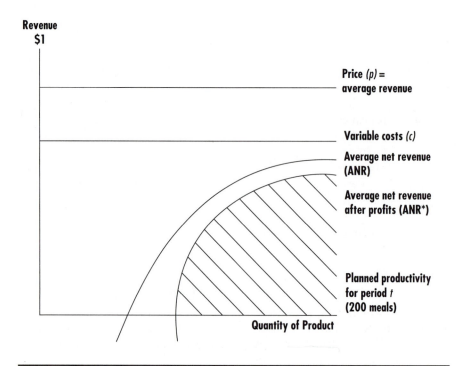

## Variable Costs

Every employer who manufactures a product must be concerned about variable costs.[10] Variable costs are the direct costs that go into the manufacture of the finished good. Examples of variable costs for a meal are the cost of the hamburger, pickles, buns, potatoes, and so forth. These costs are variable with respect to the level of production (the number of units produced) but are fixed with respect to each unit produced. For example, the same amount of hamburger goes into each meal.

It is possible to represent these variable costs on the graph in Exhibit 2.7. The area between price $(p)$ and the line $c$ represents these variable costs. In the example, assume variable costs represent $ .40 per unit. Total variable costs for 220 meals (output) is $88.

## Fixed Costs

Every employer also has fixed costs. Fixed costs are items such as rent on the building, capital expenditures on equipment, and utilities.[11] This type of cost is fixed for a given planning cycle but is variable with respect to output. For example, whether an employer produces zero units of output during an hour or 220 units per hour, fixed costs remain the same. However, fixed costs per unit of output decrease as output increases in that hour.

Assume fixed costs in the example are constant at $30 per hour. These fixed costs can be represented on the graph in Exhibit 2.7 as the area between the curve $c$ and the average net revenue (ANR) curve. The area remaining under the curve is the ANR after both variable and fixed costs have been deducted from total revenues.

## Profits

All employers in the private sector desire a profit from their endeavors. It is reasonable to assume that employers would like to have a constancy of profits from their operations. An employer will express a desired level of profits with respect to a planning period (quarterly, semiannually, or annually). In the example, each employer would like to make $18 per hour profit from the hamburger stand.

The difference between the ANR and ANR* curves represents profit—that is, the difference between ANR and ANR after profits (ANR*) is profits. Like fixed costs, profits are variable with respect to units produced: If a fixed profit level is desired within the planning period, the more units produced, the smaller must be the contribution of each unit toward profitability.

## Labor's Share

The remaining area under the ANR* curve would be thought of as the pool of money from which to pay for labor's services. That is, after taking into consideration product price, output, fixed and variable costs, and profit, the employer is able to pay labor from this remaining pool of resources. In the example, the remaining pool to pay labor is $84.

# Labor's Productivity and Ability to Pay

To determine a firm's ability to pay, the resources available to pay labor must be converted into an ANR product for labor.[12] Conceptually, the ANR* is divided by the amount of labor that it took to produce ANR*.

To continue with the example, the two hamburger stands are across the street from each other, and both can sell 220 meals per hour. Despite the identical cost structures depicted in Exhibit 2.6, their labor is not equally productive. Employer A has very modern grills, french friers, and so on, and uses only 5 workers to produce 220 meals in an hour. Employer B requires 10 workers to produce the 220 meals because of old and obsolete production processes.

Based on this analysis, employer A can afford to pay up to $16.80 per hour for each worker on average, whereas employer B can afford to pay up to $8.40 per hour on average for its workers.

## *A Caution on Labor's Productivity*

It would be easy to infer that labor's productivity varies with different abilities among workers (workers are not homogeneous) and differences in motivation levels among workers. Although workers do differ in these important dimensions, the differences in productivity among workers in different firms are due overwhelmingly to the technologic and other organizational differences among firms.

Productivity differences among employers account for large differences in ability to pay both within and across industries. For example, within an industry such as construction, a firm that digs ditches with bulldozers will have a higher ability to pay relative to a firm that digs ditches by pick and shovel because of labor's higher productivity per unit of time when working with a bulldozer. Similarly, firms that computerize their accounting procedures are realizing greater efficiency than firms that continue to handle all accounting procedures with traditional manual systems.

## *Wage Level versus Wage Structure Concepts*

Will an employer always pay more if the firm has a higher ability to pay than another firm does? A relatively high ability to pay may cause an employer to pay a higher wage rate than another employer would. However, it does not mean that this will always happen.

To use the hamburger stand example, although employer A has a higher ability to pay than employer B, employer A may not pay more. In fact, employer A may choose to take the excess over actual labor costs for profit.

If employer A chose to pay a higher average wage than employer B, how that money would be allocated among different types of workers would be a major issue for the firm's compensation decision makers. The ability-to-pay constraint on employers influences the wage level for the firm. To be more specific, some possible decisions on the part of employers A and B can be considered. First, both owners could decide that all employees should make the same wage. If the owner works for an hour, she or he could be considered one of the employees for wage purposes. Second, the employers might decide to pay as little as they have to (minimum wages) and pocket the difference as their "managerial wage." In this case, employer A would make a higher managerial wage than employer B. Still another decision might be for employer A to pay $1 per hour premium to its employees and still make more profit than employer B. These decision-making strategies and their influence on wages of workers and employers are summarized in Exhibit 2.8.

Ability to pay constrains the average wage that an employer can afford to pay. It does not specify how an employer will actually decide to distribute that average wage among different types of employees. That issue is the question of wage structure determination and is dealt with more deeply in future chapters.

## Ability to Pay and Industry Characteristics

The previous section discussed the importance of labor productivity as it influences the amount of money available to pay labor. It is not likely that management actually calculates all the variables that go into establishing the wage fund (it is unlikely that organizations even think in terms of a wage fund). If organizations do not calculate the relative productivity of labor, how do they estimate their relative ability to pay? The most direct method is to conduct product market surveys of wages or salaries and benefits.[13]

| EXHIBIT 2.8 | STRATEGIES FOR DISTRIBUTING THE AVERAGE WAGE AND THE EFFECT ON WAGES FOR DIFFERENT EMPLOYEES |
|---|---|

|  | Employer A | Employer B |
|---|---|---|
| Pool of money for wages | $84.00 per hour | $84.00 per hour |
| Number of employees (owner is one of workers) | 5 per hour | 10 per hour |

**Strategy A:** Distribute wages equally to all employees, including owner who works for that hour.

|  | Employer A | Employer B |
|---|---|---|
| Wage rate (employees) | $16.80 per hour | $8.40 per hour |
| Wage rate (owner) | $16.80 per hour | $8.40 per hour |

**Strategy B:** Pay minimum wage ($4.25/hr) to all nonowner employees, and owner take balance.

|  | Employer A | Employer B |
|---|---|---|
| Wage rate (employees) | $4.25 per hour | $4.25 per hour |
| Wage rate (owner) | $67.00 per hour | $45.75 per hour |

**Strategy C:** Same as strategy B, but employer A pays a $1 premium to all nonowner employees.

|  | Employer A | Employer B |
|---|---|---|
| Wage rate (employees) | $5.25 per hour | $4.25 per hour |
| Wage rate (owner) | $63.00 per hour | $45.75 per hour |

Labor productivity is largely determined by the application of technology to units of labor. The application of technology may be highly standardized within an industry. For example, within the brewing industry there is great homogeneity of technology among Budweiser, Coors, and Miller. The same is true for the U.S. auto industry, the fast-food industry, dentistry, and so forth. Failure to keep up to date technologically can mean eventual death of a company because technologically superior firms are in a position to receive larger productivity returns from labor.[14] This increased efficiency can result in lower per-unit labor costs that allow the firm to be more competitive in the product market. The more efficient firm may then be able to sell its products more cheaply than less-efficient firms, thereby driving the less-efficient firms out of business.

Given the high degree of technologic homogeneity within an industry, it is relatively easy for an employer to estimate its ability to pay. An employer determines what other competing organizations in the product market are paying and then behaves in a similar manner.[15] The employer cannot know for sure that the wage level paid will result in optimal operations. All the employer knows is that by behaving like competing employers, at least the organization should be able to be competitive and profitable. The employer tries to assure that comparisons are made with other relevant organizations, meaning those with which this organization competes in the product market, organizations with similar technology, organizations of similar size (roughly equal economies of scale), and so forth.[16] The employer can then infer that if the organization does not behave much differently in its wage payments relative to its competitors, it can survive and be profitable. The marginal productivity theory is crucial to understanding the importance of labor productivity as it has an effect on a firm's ability to pay. Organizations seldom actually go through the calculations of determining demand schedules for labor or their ANR*. Instead, they rely on a commonly accepted administrative practice known as product market surveys of wages or salaries and benefits. These surveys allow the organization to estimate its relative ability to pay, thus ensuring that they do not violate this crucial constraint (upper limit to wages).

## Importance of Product Market Surveys

Up to this point, homogeneity of technology within product markets has been assumed. However, the concern over ability to pay is not constant for all firms within an industry or for firms among industries. Does the Budweiser plant in Williamsburg, Virginia, pay much attention to what the A-1 brewery in Arizona pays? Would the Leinenkugel brewery in Chippewa Falls, Wisconsin, pay the same wages as the Miller brewery in Milwaukee, Wisconsin? The answers reside with the importance of the ability-to-pay constraint for any given industry and firm.

Five factors affect the importance of the ability-to-pay constraint:

1. Elasticity of the demand for the product

2. Elasticity of demand for the brand

3. Proportion of labor costs to total costs

4. Substitutability of other factors of production

5. Supply curves of productive services other than labor

## *Elasticity of Demand for the Product*

The demand for labor is a derived demand in the sense that labor services are demanded only after there is a demand for a good or service in the product market. The elasticity of the demand for labor is also determined in large part by the elasticity of demand for the product. Elasticity of demand for a product is defined as the ratio of the proportionate change in the demand for a product to the proportionate change in the price of the product in moving between any two points on the product demand schedule. Conceptually, there are three alternate elasticities that can occur: (1) A 1 percent unit change in price can result in a greater than 1 percent change in demand; (2) a 1 percent change in price can result in a 1 percent change in demand; or (3) a 1 percent change in price can result in less than a 1 percent change in demand. In the first case, product demand is said to be elastic with respect to price; in the third case, product demand is relatively inelastic with respect to price. The second case is referred to as unit elasticity.[17] Exhibit 2.9 illustrates these three cases.

In general, the more elastic product demand in an industry is with respect to price, the more concerned employers will be about not behaving differently from each other. This will be even more important as firms move toward a global product market. The wages paid by foreign firms operating in other countries have become a relevant concern for U.S. firms attempting to be competitive in a global market. For example, in one industry, product demand is highly elastic with respect to price, and in another, product demand is inelastic with respect to price. In the first case, assume that elasticity is equal to 2 (a 1 percent price increase results in a 2 percent decrease in demand). In the second case, product demand elasticity is .01 (a 1 percent increase in price will result in a .01 percent decrease in demand). Assume firms in both industries are faced with wage increases that will result in price increases of 2 percent. Firms in the first industry will be hurt more in terms of decreases in the demand for their products (4 percent versus .02 percent decreases in demand, respectively). Firms in the first industry will be much more concerned about not allowing any increases in costs, including wages, that would result in product price increases.[18] Firms in the first industry would want to pay wages that are highly consistent with their product market competitors (to ensure similar cost structures for labor) and to resist wage increases.

At the lower end of the restaurant industry, for example (hamburger houses, short-order establishments), product demand is quite elastic with respect to price, and if all these businesses in an area raised wages by 50 percent and meal prices by 25 percent, customers would find other food sources (for example, ground beef at the grocery store and cook at home; go to a fast-food outlet).

| EXHIBIT 2.9 | CONCEPTUAL PORTRAYAL OF THREE ELASTICITY CONDITIONS IN DEMAND FOR THE PRODUCT |
|---|---|

### Elastic Product Demand

The percentage change in price is less
than the percentage change in demand.

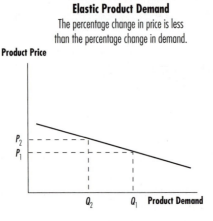

### Unit Elasticity

The percentage change in price equals
the percentage change in demand.

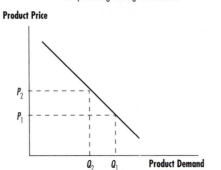

### Inelastic Product Demand

The percentage change in price is greater
than the percentage change in demand.

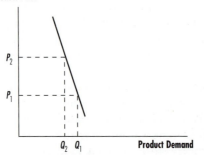

The elasticity of product demand may be related to product life cycle. If the product is in its early stages and there are few (if any) alternatives, a consumer may be willing to purchase it even if the price increases substantially. Whereas, if the product market is mature and there are many competitors and alternative products, the consumer may substitute an alternative product or switch brands as is discussed next.

### Elasticity of Demand for the Brand

Elasticity of demand for a brand also operates within an industry. In general, the more elastic brand demand is with respect to price, the more concerned an organization will be about not behaving differently in its wage payments relative to its competitors. For example, two firms in the same industry face highly elastic brand demand and currently charge the same price for their product—elasticity is 2.5. If firm A raises wages relative to B so that firm A's final product is now priced 10 percent higher than firm B's, firm A would face a decrease in demand of 25 percent. If brand elasticity is only .20 and firm A raises wages so that its product price goes up by 10 percent, there will be only a 2 percent decrease in brand demand.

In the first case, firm A would be very concerned that its wage payments not significantly vary from firm B. The more elastic the demand for the brand, the greater the concern firms in that industry will have that their wage rates (and therefore their wage level) not vary from their competitors. In the restaurant business, for example, a firm cannot afford to have its hamburgers sell for a very different price than its competitors' (brand demand is highly elastic with respect to price).

### Capital/Labor Ratio

The third main consideration in conducting a product market survey is the proportion of total costs represented by labor costs.[19] Both product demand and brand demand elasticities influence this variable. For example, two firms manufacture and sell beer. Firm A's case of beer costs $9 to manufacture, as does firm B's. Firm A's labor costs are only 10 percent of the costs of the case of beer, whereas firm B's are 80 percent. Firm A is more capital intensive than firm B, so its labor costs are small relative to capital costs. The union requests a 10 percent increase in wages from both firms, and both agree to the wage increase. What is the impact of this wage increase on the two firms, and what impact will it have on the cost of beer at the grocery store?

Firm A's costs will increase by $.09 per case: $9 × 10 percent (labor cost) × 10 percent (wage increase) = $.09. Firm B's costs will increase by $.72: $9 × 80 percent (labor cost) × 10 percent (wage increase) = $.72. For both firms to still recoup their other costs of overhead, malt, hops, profits, and so on, they will have to pass the increased labor costs on to the consumer. Firm A's new cost for beer will be $9.09, and firm B's will be $9.72. Under the assumption that the brand demand for beer is elastic with respect to the price, the wage increases would have a particularly harsh impact on the demand for firm B's beer. The above example is summarized in Exhibit 2.10.

| EXHIBIT 2.10 | IMPACT OF THE CAPITAL/LABOR RATIO ON PRODUCT PRICE WHEN WAGES CHANGE | |
|---|---|---|

|  | Firm A | Firm B |
|---|---|---|
| Total cost of product | $9.00 | $9.00 |
| Labor cost per unit of product (dollars) | $ .90 | $7.20 |
| Labor cost per unit of product (percentage) | 10% | 80% |
| *If wages go up by 10% in both firms* | | |
| New wage costs | $ .09 | $7.92 |
| New total costs | $9.09 | $9.72 |

Firm B will be unwilling to pay wages equal to firm A's in the first place, because unless there is an initial direct trade-off between capital and labor productivity, firm B cannot be as profitable as firm A at the same wage level. More importantly, firm B would be extremely concerned that its wage costs not rise as fast as firm A's because of the negative impact of wage increases on demand for its beer. Firm B would be very concerned about what its competitors are paying in wages (for example, firm A) and also that firm B would be a low-wage employer relative to firm A, even though they are both in the brewing industry.

### Substitutability of Other Factors of Production

The importance of product market surveys also rests on a fourth factor, the substitutability of other factors of production for labor. In some industries, technology is very standardized and rigid; whereas, in others, there is considerable flexibility in substituting other factors of production for labor.[20]

In cases in which it is difficult to substitute for labor, employers will be very concerned that their wage levels do not exceed their competitors' because of the negative impact on sales. However, if other factors of production can be substituted for labor, technologic changes can be made if wages become too high, actually reducing the total wage bill. In this case, employers are less likely to be as concerned about following the wage pattern of others in the industry.

### Supply Curves of Other Factors of Production

Finally, the supply curves of other factors of production will influence an employer's concern over wage rates. For example, a firm increases wages relatively more than its competitors. Because of this wage increase and the resulting increase in the price of the product, product demand falls. The firm's demand for other resources in the production process also falls. This drop in demand for these other resources results in a decrease in the price of these other resources, which, in turn, offsets the relatively large increase in labor costs. In this case, the employer is in a position to apply these savings against the wage increase, and it is not as crucial to follow the wage patterns of other firms in the industry.[21]

Although most employers do pay very close attention to the wages paid by other firms in their industry, several factors affect the degree of concern over following the competition. The most critical of these is the elasticity of demand for the product. Second is the elasticity of demand for the brand. Third, employers whose labor costs represent a large proportion of total costs are very concerned about what the product market competition is doing with regard to wage payments. Fourth, the substitutability of other factors of production for labor, and fifth, the supply curves of other resources also affect the importance of observing wage patterns in the industry.

## Wage Level Concept

*Wage level* applies to the notion of an average wage, whereas wage rate refers to the actual amount of money paid for a specific job. A firm surveys a subset of jobs in doing a wage survey. The firm looks at the subset of wage rates paid to these jobs. Knowing the numbers of people working in each of these jobs would allow an employer to estimate the wage level for the surveyed organization.

For the estimated wage level obtained in wage surveys to be meaningful in relation to the wage level in the surveying firm, the technologies of all the organizations have to be highly similar. The discussion of levels and rates in this chapter holds true only where technology is standardized. The purpose of product market surveys is to make these inferences, whereas the purpose of labor market surveys is to satisfy equity considerations.

# Consequences of Different Wage Levels

Employers conduct wage and benefit surveys in the relevant labor market area so that they can assess the going wage rates for particular types of labor. The theoretic rationale for this is to pay a wage level for jobs that is competitive and ensures that the firm can attract and retain labor.

To achieve external equity, employers attempt to pay a wage that will be perceived as equitable to present and potential employees. However, employers do attempt to adhere to wage levels within their industry. Because of the ability-to-pay constraint, the organization will be reluctant to pay much different wages than its product market competitors.

These two forces may yield different results.[22] The product market wage levels may be considerably lower or higher than the labor market wage levels. There are negative consequences for a firm that is at the low end of the wage distribution in a labor market and benefits for the firm at the high end.

## Low-Wage Employer

A low-wage employer is very likely to be at the low end of a hiring queue. Within every labor market, it is appropriate to think of organizations being ranked into a queue. The criterion for the queue is the relative desirability of employment with the firm as perceived by the work force. High-wage employers are at the top of the queue and are preferred by the labor force. Low-wage employers are the least preferred and, as might be expected, usually have the most difficult time attracting labor. Being on the low end of the hiring queue also means that the organization probably gets less productive workers in the work force because the better workers are accepted into the high-wage firms. As jobs open up at high-wage firms, workers will leave low-wage firms and move up the queue. A low-wage employer thus finds it difficult to retain labor because individuals move up the queue. Low-wage employers are left with hiring the poorest-qualified workers and can expect higher turnover.[23]

Faced with the ability-to-pay constraint, a low-wage employer may wish to do a careful analysis of the costs of recruiting, selection, training, turnover, and so on. It may be possible to reduce some of these costs substantially by offering a hiring wage that is more competitive. Thus, wage costs may be offset by savings in other human resource areas. The employer also should look at all labor costs, not just the direct costs associated with wages and benefits.

### High-Wage Employer

Many benefits accrue to a high-wage employer, many of them the obverse of the difficulties faced by the low-wage employer. First, the high-wage employer takes a position at the top of the hiring queue. As a consequence, the firm has a substantially larger and more qualified labor pool from which to make selection decisions. Second, the quality of labor hired ought to be higher because of the better pool of candidates. Third, because wages are relatively high, the employer ought to have less of a problem with external equity and turnover. It is much preferred to be a high-wage employer than a low-wage employer, although as discussed earlier, the choice is not really the employer's; it is dictated by that firm's ability-to pay constraint, which is influenced by the productivity of the employer's labor and characteristics of the product market.

Why wouldn't a firm just pay the labor market rate in a labor area if it is less than its product market constraint? Such a wage strategy would be highly profitable: The difference between the product market wage and the labor market wage would be pure profit. However, the employer is not likely to put the total difference between product market and labor market wages into profits because of the benefits accruing to a high-wage employer. It may be more sensible to take a middle-of-the-road course and maintain a higher place in the hiring queue and also be marginally more profitable.[24]

## Other Wage Theories

As this chapter has indicated up to this point, wage determination is not a simple operation. Since the beginning of the concept of wages, theories have been put forth to explain how wages are or should be determined. The following theories are wage theories that have historical significance. Each of the theories had a following at the time developed, but none of them adequately explain wage level determination. Each theory is briefly discussed, and an example of how each theory has either directly or indirectly had an effect on compensation practices and policies is illustrated.[25] It must be pointed out that there is no single economic wage theory that completely explains wage determination but that many theories are operating simultaneously to shape wage determination.

## Just Wage Theory

The just wage theory was developed during the Middle Ages and was an extension of the just price theory. As people became free labor instead of slaves or serfs, a mechanism had to be developed to determine the wages to be paid to this human resource. The wage under this system would be set at a rate such that laborers could maintain themselves at their current economic level. The church and governmental bodies would monitor pay practices to ensure that employers were providing fair pay and that employees were not taking advantage of a temporary shortage and unfairly increasing their wage. In current wage-setting practices, the call by unions and others that management's offer is unfair is related to the concept expressed in the just wage theory. In addition, as U.S. corporations attempt to compete with foreign competitors and adjust wages accordingly, the cry of an unjust wage is again common. The concept of a just wage also enters in with regard to public outcry at the wages of some CEOs.

## Subsistence Theory

Subsistence theory essentially states that over a long period of time the wage level paid to labor will not rise above the amount necessary to sustain labor. This theory was developed by Malthus and Ricardo (early nineteenth century) and was a result of observing population increasing at a faster rate than the food supply. Subsistence theory proposes that when wages are above the subsistence level (because of labor shortages) people will have more children, which increases the population and thus the supply of labor. When this new supply of labor enters the labor force, the increased supply of labor causes wages to decrease and eventually fall below the subsistence level. When the wage level is below subsistence level, people delay having additional children and more people die of disease and starvation, which reduces the surplus supply of labor, which in turn leads to increases in the wage level. This theory is not valid because data have proved that as family income increases, family size does not correspondingly increase. Also, major gains have been made in food production, and many nations have a surplus of food. The minimum wage policy of the United States is somewhat based on the notion of subsistence in that increases in minimum wage are usually based on the belief that the existing level is not adequate to support the employee economically. Some underdeveloped countries do operate close to a subsistence wage level and are direct competitors (in the global market) with domestic producers. This competitive advantage may result in the domestic manufacturer going out of business or moving operations abroad.

## Wage Fund Theory

The wage fund theory was proposed by John Stuart Mills (late nineteenth century) and states that the wage level is a function of the number of employees required to deliver a set level of goods or services and the total dollars set aside to pay labor for their work. The wage fund is fixed in the short run, and if the number of workers required to complete the project increases, the wage level of each unit of labor has to decrease. Likewise, if labor becomes more productive, the funds have to be distributed over a smaller number of workers and the wage level of each increases. The fund is established for the operating period based on the resources accumulated during the past operating period. It is obvious that, in reality, a fixed fund is not established before the operating year to pay workers but that workers over the year are paid out of operating revenues. Supplementary unemployment funds are examples of a modified wage fund theory. The amount and the number of months an unemployed worker can draw from the fund depends on the size of the fund and the number of other unemployed workers also drawing from the fund. The fund is not fixed but is increasing as those who are still employed continue to result in dollars being contributed by the employer to the fund. Governmental budgets operate similarly to a wage fund theory. A set amount is allocated to payroll for a fiscal period, and if negotiated wages exceed the dollars allocated, employment levels will have to be reduced to compensate for the difference.

## Investment Theory

Gitelman proposed a wage theory (mid-twentieth century) that emphasizes the input side of the employment exchange. Employees' productivity, and thus their value, is a function of the personal attributes of the individuals and the technology the organization provides. The workers' attributes are their values, beliefs, and abilities, which are manifested through the workers' decision to invest in education, training, and experience. The specific value of an individual employee is the amount of investment that the employee makes in himself or herself as a human resource. The organization makes the assumption that there is a relationship between investment in human capital and individual productivity. The increased skills of the employee increase the geographic labor market for that individual and thus his or her corresponding value. The investment concept is related to wage setting practices of many firms through the job evaluation system in which one job is paid more than another because of the skills or education required to perform the job task. Two individuals with the same education may be paid differently because of differences in productivity, ability of the company to pay, cost of living, and other factors, but income data have shown a positive relationship between education and employee income for the U.S. economy as a whole.

## National Income Theory

The national income theory is not a wage theory but an employment theory. It was proposed by John Maynard Keynes (early twentieth century) in response to the inability of price system to regulate employment as proposed by the classical economist. He proposed that at some level of spending all the goods and services provided by the economy would be consumed and that full employment would be reached. Spending was in the form of either consumer (for example, food), investment (for example, plant equipment), or government (for example, education, health defense) spending. To have full employment, government must regulate the spending level of the three components of spending by monetary and fiscal policy. If the economy is operating at less than full employment, government can spur spending directly by such things as increasing government programs or indirectly by lowering interest rates, providing investment tax credits, or cutting taxes. The government in the early 1990s, to spur the economy out of recession, used monetary policy (reduced the discount rate to a 27-year low) to increase personal and business spending. The national income theory is a macro theory that looks only at general wage levels and does not explain wage differentials or wage structures, nor does it consider specific labor costs. Even though this is not a wage theory, it does illustrate the need for business executives to become more active in the political arena so that special interest groups do not pressure government to exercise the inappropriate monetary or fiscal policy. If the economy becomes overstimulated, it will result in too many dollars chasing too few goods, causing higher inflation. The higher inflation brings increasing demand for higher wages, which may add to the problem and may result in U.S. firms becoming less competitive in the global marketplace.

## Job Competition Theory

The job competition theory (mid-twentieth century) states that workers compete against each other for jobs based on the relative time it takes to be trained, rather than on the wage each will accept.[26] When workers enter the job market they come with different degrees of ability (for example, formal education, experience) and must be trained to perform the specific task effectively and efficiently for the organization. During times when labor is in short supply, the organization must hire workers with less ability. Those lower quality workers will require more training time to learn the job adequately, but they will earn the same wages. Two workers with identical backgrounds (for example, education) may earn different wages because the on-the-job training each receives is different.

## Bargaining Power Theory

The bargaining power theory essentially states that there is an upper limit and a lower limit to wages and that the wage will fall between these two limits because of the bargaining power of the parties to the employment exchange. The upper limit is that wage level beyond which the employer will refuse to hire and will either close the plant or move it to another location. The upper limit is determined by the physical productivity of labor, degree of product market competition (domestic and foreign), and the ability of management to substitute capital for labor. The lower limit is the wage level workers will refuse to accept for employment. The lower limit is determined by the subsistence level, government regulations (for example, Fair Labor Standards Act, Davis Bacon Act), and workers' knowledge of what other employers are paying. The actual wage is a function of the bargaining power of the parties in the employment exchange. The power coefficient is determined by the prosperity of the general economic cycle, size and the quality of labor in the labor market, political and social attitudes at the time, and the strategies that each party will be willing to execute to obtain its demands. For example, if the economy is booming, shortages of qualified labor are occurring, organizations are recording record-high profits, and labor is willing to withhold its services, then the power coefficient favors the worker and the relative wage will move closer to the upper limit than if the reverse is true.

## Summary

This chapter focuses on the economic constraints faced by an organization in making compensation decisions. The firm's ability to pay is the main economic constraint. A firm's ability to pay is influenced by labor's productivity and characteristics of the product market. Ability to pay accounts for why some employers are relatively high-wage employers within a labor market area and why other employers are relatively low-wage employers within that same labor area. High-wage employers generally have a larger and better qualified pool of applicants and can anticipate lower turnover. Low-wage employers can anticipate higher turnover and greater difficulty in attracting labor. Also, historical wage theories are presented, along with some current applications of those theories.

## Discussion Questions

1. A basketball team signs 6-foot, 6-foot 3-inch, 6-foot 10-inch, 7-foot 3-inch, 6-foot 5-inch, 6-foot 1-inch, and 5-foot 4-inch players in that order. Graph the average height and marginal height of the team as each new player is added. How is this like marginal revenue productivity analysis?

2. Major State University and Community State College are located within 20 minutes of each other in Ideal State, USA. Both employ professors, yet MSU pays, on average, 40 percent more than CSU for professors. Why?

3. Discuss the concept of the product market. How does a product market differ from a labor market? Compare and contrast these two markets—how are they alike and how are they different?

4. Major oil refining companies pay about twice as much as trucking companies for their computer programmers. Why?

## Minicase: The Automobile Industry Recession

During the 1970s, the U.S. automobile industry faced a severe depression in demand for cars. Although Americans continued to buy cars, they generally shied away from U.S.-built cars and bought imported cars. The depression in demand was so severe that Chrysler Corporation was forced into bankruptcy.

In the early 1980s, U.S. automakers took several steps to reverse this trend. First, they sought wage concessions from their employees. Second, they began to build smaller cars that more favorably met consumer preferences. Third, they modernized production plants by introducing robotics. By the mid-1980s, the U.S. auto industry looked like it was on its way to profitability.

Since then, the auto industry has had varying levels of success. Between 1989 and 1991, General Motors, Ford, and Chrysler have announced a reduction in force totaling 147,165 employees and massive plant closings. In addition, stock performance has been poor and record losses have been posted.

Using the auto industry, trace through all of the forces that threw the industry into its initial depression. Identify how each of these forces influenced the demand for cars and what each did to the demand for labor. Also, trace through what the auto industry recovery temporarily did to the industry's demand for labor. Finally, examine the current situation in the auto industry. Relate this case to as many concepts as you can from this chapter.

## References

[1] J. T. Dunlop, "Suggestions toward a Reformulation of Wage Theory," in *Compensation and Reward Perspectives*, ed. T. A. Mahoney (Homewood, IL: Irwin, 1979), 105–113.

[2] M. W. Reder, "The Occupational Wage Structure," in *Perspectives on Wage Determination: A Book of Readings*, ed. C. R. McConnell (New York: McGraw–Hill, 1970), 199–206.

[3] H. M. Douty, "Regional Wage Differentials; Forces and Counterforces," in *Perspectives on Wage Determination: A Book of Readings*, ed. C. R. McConnell (New York: McGraw–Hill, 1970), 207–217.

[4] A. Smith, "Wages in the Different Employments of Labour," in *Perspectives on Wage Determination: A Book of Readings*, ed. C. R. McDonnell (New York: McGraw–Hill, 1970), 187–190.

[5] For a more thorough analysis, see H. G. Heneman and D. Yoder, *Labor Economics* (Cincinnati, OH: Southwestern Publishing, 1965), 587–612.

[6] L. G. Reynolds, *Labor Economics and Labor Relations*, 6th ed. (Englewood Cliffs, NJ: Prentice-Hall, 1974), 87–111.

[7] *Ibid.*, 90

[8] T. A. Mahoney, ed., *Compensation and Reward Perspectives* (Homewood, IL: Irwin, 1979), 58.

[9] *Ibid.*, 97.

[10] A. E. Gruenwald and E. Esser Nemmers, *Basic Managerial Finance* (Philadelphia: Holt, Rinehart & Winston, 1970), 70.

[11] *Ibid.*, 97.

[12] Mahoney, *Compensation and Reward Perspectives*, 120.

[13] *Ibid.*, 123.

[14] G. E. Crystal, "The Re-Emerging Role of Industry Pay Differences," *Compensation Review* 3d quarter (1983), 29–32.

[15] *Ibid.*

[16] Dunlop, "Suggestions toward a Reformulation of Wage Theory," 107; Mahoney, *Compensation and Reward Perspectives*, 121.

[17] Reynolds, *Labor Economics and Labor Relations*, 93.

[18] Mahoney, *Compensation and Reward Perspectives*, 122.

[19] Reynolds, *Labor Economics and Labor Relations*, 93.

[20] *Ibid.*

[21] *Ibid.*

[22] Crystal, "The Re-Emerging Role of Industry Pay Differences," 29–32.

[23] J. F. Burton, Jr., and J. E. Parker, "Interindustry Variations in Voluntary Labor Mobility," *Industrial and Labor Relations Review* 22 (1969), 199–216.

[24] M. Bronfenbrenner, "Potential Monopsony Power in Labor Markets," *Industrial and Labor Relations Review* 9 (1956), 577–588.

[25] For a more detailed explanation of the following theories, please refer to Heneman and Yoder, *Labor Economics*, 569–638.

[26] L. C. Thurow, *Generating Inequality* (New York, NY: Basic Books, 1975).

# 3

# Theoretic Framework II: Worker Behaviors

## Learning Objectives

**To develop an understanding of equity, need, expectancy, and reinforcement theories of human behavior and their relationship to compensation decision making.**

**To learn how organizations attempt to achieve external pay equity (labor market wage surveys).**

**To learn how organizations attempt to achieve internal pay equity (job evaluation).**

**To understand how reinforcers and the schedules used to administer them can influence human behavior.**

**To learn how an employee may decide to be a high or low performer.**

## Introduction

The previous chapter focused on how economic theory could be used to understand wage-setting practices. In this chapter, the focus is on providing several conceptual frameworks for analyzing and discussing human behavior specifically as it relates to compensation. The goal of the chapter is to provide the reader with some insights into understanding why people behave the way that they do—why people choose to work at all, why people feel properly or improperly treated, and why people choose or choose not to expend high levels of effort at work. The frameworks used here are not the only ones that might be used but were selected because of their use for understanding the behavior of people.

## Sociologic Value of Occupations

There are strong beliefs about the appropriate criteria for determining the pay level of different occupations and jobs and the criteria for determining pay increases. The hierarchical position that a person occupies within an organization is generally a strong determinant for what is perceived as a fair pay level for the job and helps determine the social status of the person occupying that position. Likewise, the individual contribution that the person makes within the position is considered a criteria for fair wage increase.

Hierarchy is one of the most universal characteristics of modern organizations and is a primary determinant of a person's social and economic position in society. Employees occupying higher levels within organizations earn a higher base pay and have a wider array of incentives available to them. Until the passage of the Tax Reform Act of 1986, employees at higher hierarchical positions were often provided an array of nontaxable additional fringe benefits. The nondiscriminatory provision of the act made any benefit that discriminated in favor of "highly paid" employees a nonqualified benefit, thus eliminating the tax benefits and, indirectly, many of the additional benefits themselves.

The wage differential between occupations and jobs should be based on organizational contributions (for example, necessary qualifications, value of output) and the perceived value of these different contributions. Empirical evidence supports a relationship between hierarchical level and pay.[1] Mahoney[2] found that pay differential between different levels of management should be about 30 percent and that hierarchical position within the organization was a significant determinant of value and status within organizations. The wage structure represents the value that the organization places on different work activities, reflects the internal labor market, and identifies the career paths available within the organization.[3] The differentiation between wages within an organization is done to provide internal equity (relative compensation) and is normally carried out through job evaluation. The perception by employees that the job structure and the corresponding wage structure is internally fair is essential in making the organization attractive to potential and existing employees. The process of determining the relative value of jobs within an organization is called job evaluation and will be thoroughly discussed in Chapter 8.

A fundamental belief of American culture is that individual contributions should be rewarded. This traditionally has been operationalized by basing pay increases to individuals within a position on either seniority or performance. In recent years, there has been a movement to measure performance contributions more from the perspective of a team contribution and less from the perspective of a single individual contribution. Performance has been measured by employee evaluation programs that identify a set of specific behavioral or outcome criteria to which individual or team contributions are compared. Viewing managers and other employees as agents of the stockholders, the pay system should be developed to reward employees for increasing the short- and long-term wealth of the shareholders. The topic of performance assessment is covered in detail in Chapter 11. This chapter will focus on the many psychological and social-psychological theories (for example, equity theory, need theory, expectancy theory, reinforcement theory) that form the bases for the role of compensation in affecting human behavior.

## Equity Theory

Adams' equity theory is the process used by employees to determine if the employment relationship is fair and equitable. For an employee, the determination of the fairness of the employment relationship is critical in influencing the decision to join and remain with the firm and the amount of effort exerted on the job. The employee's determination of fairness is based on the comparison of the value and cost of that individual's employment relationship to the value and cost of another party's.[4] This social comparison is more relevant when made to another individual (relevant other) rather than to an absolute standard (ideal other). The comparison examines the fairness of wage level of a position and the wage increases granted from year to year. The employee compares the wage level of the position with other positions within the organization and outside the organization to determine if the treatment is fair. Likewise, the employee examines the wage increases granted from year to year to determine if the increases are being allocated fairly within the organization and how they compare with other firms in the market. In both cases, the most relevant comparisons are those made within the organization.[5] For an employment relationship to continue over time, it must be perceived as fair by both the employer and the employee. If either party believes the relationship is unjust, that party is motivated to engage in behavior to correct the injustice. There are two forms of justice—distributive justice and procedural justice. Distributive justice focuses on the fairness of the outcomes, whereas procedural justice focuses on the methods used to arrive at those outcomes.

## *Distributive Justice*

According to the equation, each party in an employment relationship receives a set of outcomes (or inducements) and offers a set of inputs (or contributions) as identified in Exhibit 3.1. Thus each has a ratio of outcomes to inputs. The focal person $f$ asks if this exchange is equitable—am I equitably treated?

Assessments of fairness are not made in a vacuum. To assess whether the relationship is fair, the focal person must look to some referent or relevant other $o$. The focal person $f$ observes the ratio of the other's outcomes to inputs to determine if distributive-justice exists.

Three consequences are possible when the ratio of the focal person $f$ is compared with the ratio of the other $o$. First, the focal person may find that the two ratios are about equal and that a state of equity exists. In this situation, the focal person believes that things are satisfactory. Second, the focal person might find that the other's ratio is greater than that of the focal person. This is a condition of inequity, and the focal person will feel under-rewarded relative to the other. Third, the focal person's ratio may be seen by the focal person as greater than the other's ratio. This inequitable condition would be a condition of over-reward relative to the other. The unpleasant psychological state that may occur in the second or third situation is called *cognitive dissonance*.[6]

---

**EXHIBIT 3.1**    OUTCOMES/INPUT RATIOS IN EQUITY COMPARISONS

$$\left( \frac{\text{Outcomes}}{\text{Inputs}} \right)_f \quad \gtrless \quad \left( \frac{\text{Outcomes}}{\text{Inputs}} \right)_o$$

## *Procedural Justice*

Procedural justice deals with the perceived fairness of the methods used to allocate the outcomes. The theory was first developed by Thibaut and Walker in 1975 and then further refined by Leventhal in 1980 and Bies and Moag in 1986.[7] Process control and decision control are two important elements to procedural justice. Process control refers to the amount of participation employees are permitted in resolving disputes in which they are involved; whereas, decision control is the amount of effect they have on the actual outcomes.[8] Individuals evaluate the amount of control or input they have on the following seven elements to determine the fairness of decisions: (1) selection of the decision maker, (2) determination of the ground rules, (3) method for gathering the information, (4) decision-making procedure, (5) appeal procedure decisions, (6) process to ensure the decision maker is correctly using his or her power, and (7) appeal procedure to review the decision-making process.[9] Also, four interpersonal communication criteria have been identified as criteria in evaluating the fairness of decision making. The four elements are truthfulness, respect, propriety of questions, and justification.[10]

## *Research on Equity Theory*

Considerable research has been conducted on equity theory, particularly in the context of wage and salary payments. One subset of this research concerns the reactions of an individual for whom a state of inequity exists.

In theory, there are at least six actions that a person experiencing under-reward can take: (1) increase outcomes (for example, by asking for a pay raise); (2) decrease the inputs (for example, by not working as hard); (3) select a different referent person; (4) abandon the present outcome and input ratio; (5) rationalize any differences in outcomes and inputs; or (6) change the referent's outcomes or inputs.[11]

When a state of over-reward exists, theoretically there are at least six actions a person might take: (1) increase inputs; (2) decrease outcomes; (3) change the referent person; (4) vacate the field (abandon the present outcome and input ratio for a new one); (5) rationalize the differences in outcomes and inputs; or (6) change the referent's outcomes or inputs.

Research generally shows that people do react to inequity in all these ways. For example, one study suggests that if people believe they are overpaid, they increase their inputs.[12] This is accomplished by producing more if outcomes are expressed as an hourly rate or by improving quality if outcomes are expressed as a piece rate.[13] In studies conducted of under-rewarded employees, the results indicate the individuals try to restore equity. This is accomplished by coming to work late, taking long lunch breaks, or using all possible sick leave. Besides reducing inputs, employees can attempt to increase outcomes. Examples include asking for more pay or benefits, a promotion, or better working conditions. If all attempts to restore equity fail, employees may leave their position to remove the inequity. This research suggests that referents can be internal (for example, coworkers), external (for example, neighbors), or personal (themselves). If individuals choose someone other than themselves, most research has shown that they prefer to select a referent who has abilities and opinions similar to their own.[14] One study found that employees compare themselves to multiple people, not just one other person, in making this comparison.[15] Other components that may have an effect on referent selection are gender, race, age, tenure, level of professionalism, and position.[16]

Several studies have found that individuals in a variety of situations who have process control (that is, participation in decision making) perceive the process as being fairer than those who lack such input.[17] Two studies have found a relationship between interpersonal communication and procedural justice.[18] One study also found a significant positive relationship between procedural and distributive justice.[19] More research needs to be conducted to obtain a better understanding of these processes, but it is clear that the research to date lends credence to the general validity of the equity model.

## *Implications for Compensation*

Equity theory is especially useful to the compensation decision maker in understanding why individuals decide to join the organization and why they decide to stay with the organization. The first goal of a compensation system is to elicit desired behaviors from individuals, including motivating people to join and stay with the organization. Equity theory is useful in understanding how individuals are likely to assess the employment relationship (either offered or present) to make the decision to join and stay. Specifically, they must first believe that a potential employment relationship with the organization is equitable and, then, once they are members of the organization, they must perceive that the employment contract remains equitable. These are minimum requirements to attract and retain people, yet they are fundamental in that if the organization is unable to attract and retain people, all other human resource activities are meaningless.[20] Three important activities commonly practiced by organizations are directly related to attracting and retaining employees: labor market surveys of wages and benefits, job evaluation, and performance assessment. All three are essentially concerned with ensuring that the organization's compensation system is perceived as equitable.

**External Equity and Labor Market Surveys**     In the case of labor market surveys of wages and benefits, the concern is with external equity considerations that presumably influence the decision to join the organization. That is, unless the organization's pay and benefit rates are seen as equitable relative to other firms in the labor market, the organization may have a difficult time attracting labor.[21] It may also have a difficult time retaining labor, in some cases, if its wages and benefits are not perceived to be satisfying an external equity standard.[22]

In conducting labor market surveys, the organization asks: Given a certain job with required inputs, what do other firms pay for this job? That is, are the outcomes to the organization's employees (wages and salary) relative to the employee inputs (job requirements) going to be perceived as equitable? Exhibit 3.2 shows, in equation form, a job in one company that requires a college education and pays $20,000 per year. The organization doing a survey is asking what a job that requires an equivalent college education should be paid so that the organization's wage rate is equitable.

**Internal Equity and Job Evaluation**    Organizations are also concerned that wage rates among jobs within the organization are perceived as equitable, often referred to as internal equity. Internal equity is traditionally achieved through job evaluation. Job evaluation can be defined as the process of establishing the relative worth of jobs within the organization. (The details of conducting job evaluations are the subject of Chapter 8.) One goal of job evaluation is to achieve internal equity to influence individuals to stay with the organization. Employee involvement in the job evaluation process can contribute significantly to the acceptance of the final job structure throughout the organization. Again, in equity theory terms, when the firm does job evaluation, it is trying to answer the question: Given that jobs have different requirements (skill, effort, and so forth), what would be equitable pay rates for these jobs? That is, what should the outcomes (pay) be for this job given the required inputs (skill)?[23] Exhibit 3.3 shows one example of this question in equation form.

**Employee Equity and Performance Assessment**    The concept of procedural justice is very critical to the level of acceptance of the organization's performance assessment process. Employees perceive that performance assessment is fairer when they have input into the evaluation procedure.[24] Employees' perception of the fairness of the procedure, the raters, and the outcomes is increased when they are permitted input into the information being used in the assessment.[25] There is a positive relationship between employees' perception of procedural justice and employees' satisfaction with pay raises.[26] Two studies have found a significant relationship between interpersonal communication and procedural justice.[27] The above findings are very important to performance assessment because acceptance or nonacceptance of the outcomes of performance assessment will have an impact on employee behavior. In fact, a recent study found a positive relationship between employees' perception of pay equity and product quality.[28] With the increased emphasis on quality by U.S. business, this finding is very important.

---

**EXHIBIT 3.2**    **LABOR MARKET COMPARISONS AND PAY EQUITY**

$$\left( \frac{\text{Labor Market Other}}{\text{Outcomes} = \$20,000} \middle/ \frac{}{\text{Inputs} = \text{College education}} \right) = \left( \frac{\text{Employees}}{?} \middle/ \frac{}{\text{Inputs} = \text{College education}} \right)$$

**EXHIBIT 3.3**    JOB-TO-JOB COMPARISONS FOR INTERNAL
                   EQUITY DETERMINATION

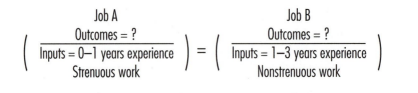

$$\left( \frac{\text{Job A}}{\underset{\text{Strenuous work}}{\text{Inputs} = 0\text{–}1 \text{ years experience}}}\ \frac{\text{Outcomes} = ?}{} \right) = \left( \frac{\text{Job B}}{\underset{\text{Nonstrenuous work}}{\text{Inputs} = 1\text{–}3 \text{ years experience}}}\ \frac{\text{Outcomes} = ?}{} \right)$$

The concepts of social comparison, cognitive dissonance, referent other, and distributive and procedural justice have a great deal to contribute to the design and administration of an effective compensation system. These theories are critical to understanding human behavior, and a working knowledge of them is necessary for all compensation managers. The above concepts are only part of the behavioral theories that significantly affect compensation design and administration. The following section provides additional theories and concepts that also must be mastered if the compensation manager is to design and administer an effective system.

## Need Theories of Motivation

Probably the most basic question that can be asked about people is why do they engage in specific behaviors. Why do they work, play golf, go to church, eat, sleep, and so on? The answer is that people have basic human needs that must be satisfied. What needs do people have and how do these needs affect behavior? The first part of this question is answered here, and the second is answered later in the chapter.[29]

Content theories of motivation, theories that describe what motivates people, share the common feature of identifying the different needs that people have.[30] Although different theorists have identified different needs, all of them are attempting to identify what motivates people to behave in particular ways. For example, a person might belong to a bowling team because of the need to affiliate with others. Or a person might work at a job because of the need to provide food, clothing, and shelter. In this section, several content theories of motivation are reviewed.

### Maslow's Hierarchy of Needs Theory

One of the more popular ways to look at human needs uses a hierarchy of needs, first articulated by Abraham Maslow. According to Maslow's theory, all individuals have a common set of needs that are satisfied in a hierarchical fashion, shown in Exhibit 3.4.[31]

**EXHIBIT 3.4**　　MASLOW'S HIERARCHY OF NEEDS

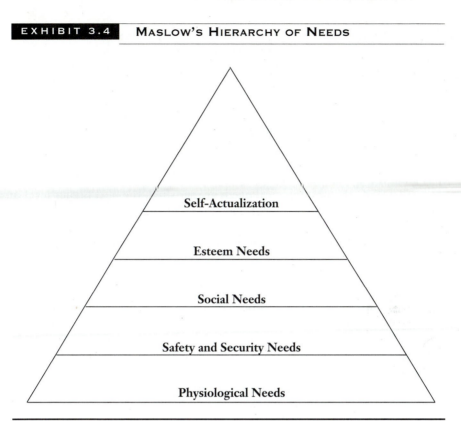

*Physiological needs:* The most basic human needs according to Maslow are "physiological," including the need for clothing, food, and shelter. Satisfaction of these needs is essential to the maintenance of the human organism.

*Safety and security needs:* Once physiological needs are satisfied, individuals will then be able to satisfy safety and security needs. These needs are not as straightforward as the physiological needs. Basically, individuals need to be free from bodily harm or injury and to be safe and secure in their environment.

*Social needs:* According to Maslow, all individuals need social interaction. The theory holds that people are gregarious and do not function well without social support structures around them. The particular ways in which people try to meet social needs can range from being part of a family unit to having "buddies" at the office, but most normal people will be motivated to find and maintain social relationships.

*Esteem needs:* Maslow also suggests that all people have a need for esteem. This means that people need a high opinion of themselves and also want others to have a high opinion of them. Some writers even talk about a "love" need that people have—that is, people need to be loved and respected by others.

*Self-actualization:* Finally, Maslow argues that people are driven to self-actualize. Although the concept of self-actualization may be somewhat vague, Maslow suggests that people need to become all that they can be. People have a need for accomplishment, to feel that they are using their abilities to the fullest.

Maslow argues that these needs are arranged in a prepotent order: Lower-order needs in the hierarchy must be satisfied before people can satisfy higher-order needs. For example, a person who has been unable to satisfy physiological needs will not be very concerned about meeting social needs. However, once the physiological needs are satisfied, the next higher level of needs (safety and security) will become important as an activator of behavior.

Maslow's view is only one way to look at the structure of human needs. Other researchers and writers view human needs differently.

### Alderfer's Need Theory

A second content theory of motivation is proposed by Clayton Alderfer.[32] Alderfer speaks of three common needs that all people have:

*Existence needs:* The desire for material things (such as, clothes, money, and food).

*Relatedness needs:* The desire for sharing feelings and thoughts with other people.

*Growth needs:* The desire to use ability and to pursue interests to the utmost.[33]

### Herzberg's Two-Factor Need Theory

Frederick Herzberg approaches the motivation question from a slightly different direction than other writers.[34] He asks the question: What things in a work environment do people find satisfying and dissatisfying? Based on his work with accountants and engineers, he identifies two sets of items that he calls motivational (or intrinsic) factors and hygiene (or extrinsic) factors. Examples of these factors are summarized in Exhibit 3.5 and are discussed below.

Intrinsic factors

*Achievement:* Completing an important task successfully.

*Recognition:* Being singled out for praise.

*Responsibility:* Having control and authority over one's work.

*Advancement:* Moving ahead through promotion.

*Work itself:* Accomplishing challenging tasks.

| EXHIBIT 3.5 | HERZBERG'S TWO-FACTOR THEORY |
| --- | --- |

| Hygienic Factors | Motivation Factors |
| --- | --- |
| Salary | Achievement |
| Supervision | Recognition |
| Interpersonal relations | Responsibility |
| Company policy | Advancement |
| Working conditions | The work itself |
| Job security | |

Extrinsic factors

*Salary:* Money one receives for doing a job.

*Technical supervision:* Competency of supervisors.

*Interpersonal relations:* Quality of supervision.

*Company policy and administration:* Fair, equitable policies and their applications.

*Working conditions:* Physical surroundings

*Job security:* Confidence in one's future with the firm.

**How Factors Motivate**  Herzberg maintains that intrinsic and extrinsic factors work in different ways on people. He suggests that satisfaction with work is a two-dimensional construct and that intrinsic factors contribute to a person being motivated while extrinsic factors do not. More specifically, if intrinsic factors (recognition, achievement, and so on) are present in a job, the worker will be motivated. If the intrinsic factors are not present, the worker will not be motivated. Similarly, if the intrinsic factors are present, the person will be satisfied with the job, but if they are not present, a person will not be. That is, job satisfaction will be neither positive nor negative; it will be zero.[35]

According to Herzberg, the presence of extrinsic factors in the job ensures that a person is not dissatisfied with the job. Conversely, if extrinsic factors are not present in the job, the worker will be dissatisfied with the job. In no case, however, will extrinsic factors have an impact on motivating people to perform.[36]

**Money in Herzberg's Theory**  The role of money in Herzberg's two-factor theory has been a source of debate. Specifically, if money is a hygiene factor, then how can it motivate? There are two partial answers. First, the fact that money is a hygiene factor is consistent with the way money is dealt with in this text. Most issues faced by compensation managers relate to using money to ensure fair or equitable treatment. In this sense, money (or lack of it) can only dissatisfy; it has marginal value as a true motivator. Second, money can be a motivator if it is highly valued by the employee. Even Herzberg recognizes that money can be a motivator; he specifically notes that money has symbolic value and can be a surrogate for recognition and achievement. Thus, although money may have limited value as a motivator, the proper implementation of an economic reward system can motivate performance.[37]

### Research on Need Theories

The theories proposed by Maslow, Alderfer, and Herzberg are intuitively appealing, but the amount of empirical support they have received is weak. Also, the studies that do support the theories present serious methodologic problems that raise questions about the findings.[38] In a review of the literature, Wahba and Bridwell are not able to support the five levels of need structure of Maslow or the three-level structures of Alderfer. In a review of the literature regarding need strength and prepotency, little support can be found.[39] The research on Herzberg's two-factor theory is inconclusive. Some studies support the model whereas others can find no support. Herzberg's theory receives criticism based on the method used to collect the data and the original sample he used. Even though empirical evidence is weak, need theories have strong employee appeal and thus warrant a thorough discussion. Also, the concepts of needs and value placed on need satisfaction are used in other behavioral theories, such as expectancy theory.

## Expectancy Theory

Expectancy theory is a process model of motivation which answers the question: How do individuals become motivated? That is, what steps do they go through in deciding to engage in particular behavior? Influencing individuals to join and stay are two critical parts of the overall goal of influencing workers to behave in ways desired by the organization. Having people in jobs within the organization, however, is not enough. The organization also would like to influence employees to work at higher than minimally acceptable performance levels. In short, the organization would like to motivate high levels of performance. This section develops the instrumentality and expectancy theory as a conceptual framework for the activities that motivate high performance.

### Expectancy Model

The concept of instrumentality and expectancy is usually attributed to Victor Vroom.[40] The theory is useful in understanding the process by which people are motivated to action.

Instrumentality and expectancy theory holds that effort or motivation toward a behavior is dependent on five variables: expectancies $(E)$, instrumentalities $(I)$, valences $(V)$, first-level outcomes, and second-level outcomes.[41] These five variables are combined in the following way:

$$\text{Effort (motivation)} = E * \sum VI$$

where $E$ = the expectation that a given behavior will result in a first-level outcome (for example, greater performance);

$I$ = the instrumentality, or degree of belief, that a first-level outcome will result in a second-level outcome;

$V$ = the valence, or value, that the individual places on the second-level outcome;

First-level outcome = some immediate result associated with a behavior;

Second-level outcome = a secondary result of the first-level outcome.

The easiest way to understand the theory is with an example. Why does Adair decide that she will expend only enough energy to be an adequate employee? Her fictional decision is presented in Exhibits 3.6 and 3.7.

Adair is deciding which of two behaviors she is going to engage in. Choice A is to put in 80 hours per week on her job, and choice B is to put in 40 hours per week on her job. She first asks herself what first-level outcomes are associated with working 80 hours per week. She ascertains that there are two likely outcomes: She could be a superior performer, or she could be an average performer. Adair now asks what first-level outcomes are associated with working 40 hours per week. She determines that working only 40 hours per week, she still can be an average performer but cannot be a superior performer.

The next step for Adair is to decide on the probability (expectancy) of a first-level outcome occurring given her behavior. Suppose that in her mind the

---

**EXHIBIT 3.6**  **EXAMPLE OF INSTRUMENTALITY EXPECTANCY THEORY**

|   | Choice | $E$ | First-Level Outcome | $I$ | Second-Level Outcome | $V$ |
|---|--------|-----|---------------------|-----|----------------------|-----|
| **A.** | Work 80 hours per week | .90 | Superior performance | .50 | Promotion | +3 |
|   |   |   |   | .50 | Supervisor recognition | +2 |
|   |   |   |   | 1.00 | Peer recognition | -3 |
|   |   |   |   | .60 | Pay raise | +2 |
|   |   | .10 | Average performance | .70 | Promotion | +3 |
|   |   |   |   | .50 | Supervisor recognition | +2 |
|   |   |   |   | 1.00 | Peer recognition | +3 |
|   |   |   |   | .50 | Pay raise | +2 |
| **B.** | Work 40 hours per week | 1.00 | Average performance | .70 | Promotion | +3 |
|   |   |   |   | .50 | Supervisor recognition | +2 |
|   |   |   |   | 1.00 | Peer recognition | +3 |
|   |   |   |   | .50 | Pay raise | +2 |

probability or expectancy $E$ of her being a superior performer is 0.90 if she works 80 hours per week and that the expectancy of her being an average performer, working 80 hours per week, is 0.10. She also asks what the expectancy is that she can be an average performer working 40 hours per week. Suppose that in her mind she is so confident of her abilities and the job is so unchallenging to her that she decides that she can be an average performer with a 40-hour commitment to her job ($E = 1.0$).

What second-level outcomes are associated with each of Adair's first-level outcomes? Assume that the same four outcomes are associated with each second-level outcome: (1) a promotion, (2) recognition from the supervisor, (3) recognition from peers, and (4) a pay raise.

Adair must now assess the likelihood of each second-level outcome occurring given the first-level outcome. That is, she must determine how instrumental $(I)$ the first-level outcome is for each second-level outcome. She assumes that the degree of association between first- and second-level outcomes (instrumentalities) corresponds to the instrumentalities column in Exhibit 3.6. She also values each of the second-level outcomes in the amounts indicated in the valences column in Exhibit 3.6.

Given this set of $E$s, $V$s, $I$s, and first- and second-level outcomes for Adair, applying the arithmetic of the expectancy model will show that she will elect to expend low effort. Her effort score for choice A is 1.34 units, and her effort score for choice B is 7.10 units. The calculations for determining her effort score for each choice are provided in Exhibit 3.7.

There may be several questions about this example. Why did Adair assign a negative value to the peer recognition outcome when high performance was the first-level outcome but assign a positive value to it when average performance was the first-level outcome? If the peer response under a high-performance condition is negative (she will be viewed as making her peers look bad), she may value it negatively. Alternately, the peer response under the average performance condition is probably positive (she will be viewed as "one of the gang"), and she may value that positively.

A second question is, Why is there a greater likelihood of a promotion resulting from average performance than high performance? The answer might be that Adair is afraid that if she is too good her supervisor might try to keep her in the department. She might also think that promotions go to people with the most seniority with little regard to variation in performance.

A third question is, Do people really act this way—that is, do people actually compute all these values? People probably do not sit down and figure out a decision tree like this. However, everyone goes through this process subconsciously when they make choices. Behavior is influenced by what individuals perceive as the relationships between that behavior, the first- and second-level outcomes, and the value attached to those outcomes.

### Research and Implications on Expectancy Theory

Expectancy theory has been thoroughly researched during the past three decades. In general, support for the theory has been encouraging. The predictive

| EXHIBIT 3.7 | CALCULATIONS FOR DETERMINING BEHAVIORAL CHOICE |
|---|---|

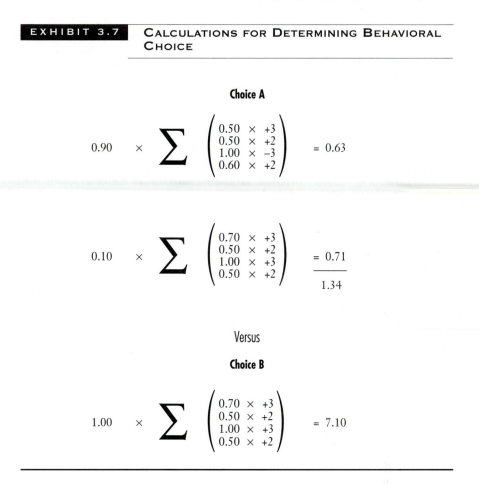

**Choice A**

$$0.90 \quad \times \quad \sum \begin{pmatrix} 0.50 \times +3 \\ 0.50 \times +2 \\ 1.00 \times -3 \\ 0.60 \times +2 \end{pmatrix} = 0.63$$

$$0.10 \quad \times \quad \sum \begin{pmatrix} 0.70 \times +3 \\ 0.50 \times +2 \\ 1.00 \times +3 \\ 0.50 \times +2 \end{pmatrix} = \frac{0.71}{1.34}$$

Versus

**Choice B**

$$1.00 \quad \times \quad \sum \begin{pmatrix} 0.70 \times +3 \\ 0.50 \times +2 \\ 1.00 \times +3 \\ 0.50 \times +2 \end{pmatrix} = 7.10$$

power has been stronger for job choice than it has been for job effort.[42] The model has been refined over the years, but the basic concepts of the original model have remained in all revisions and extensions. The vast bulk of the research during the past decade has focused on methodologic problems and specific propositions associated with the theory.[43]

Expectancy is the probability that increased effort will yield increased job performance. The organization and the immediate supervisor may have a significant impact on the employee's perception and ability to perform the job at a higher level. Research has shown an employee's treatment in the first few weeks on the job can significantly influence that employee's ability to perform the task and desire to remain with the organization.[44]

The value attached to second-level outcomes may be influenced by several factors. First, the values attached to second-level outcomes are in large part determined by how much each contributes to satisfying the needs that people bring to the work place. For example, because Adair has a strong need to achieve, she will value a promotion more than someone with a low need to achieve. Two studies found that, when using expectancy theory, the outcome list should be generated by the participants and that list should contain only 10 to 15 outcomes.[45] This supports the practice of organizations using flexible benefits to satisfy a variety of employee needs. Second, not only can one second-level outcome satisfy more than one need, but different second-level outcomes may contribute to satisfying any one need. Third, instrumentalities and second-level outcomes may be controllable by the organization. For example, Adair's perceptions about the relationship between performance level and a promotion were probably learned by observing what happens where she works. If management wants its employees to believe that promotion results from high performance, it must act that way.[46] This concept is developed with the design of a pay-for-performance system in Chapter 11.

Research has revealed an interesting characteristic of the expectancy theory: Although positive and negative consequences influence an individual's level of motivation, the two outcomes may be processed differently.[47] It has been proposed that the magnitude of the outcome is important if it is positive, but for negative outcomes, the magnitude of the outcome is not considered.[48] In general, the theory identifies the importance of managers taking a proactive approach to identifying which outcomes are most valued for each employee and designing a flexible compensation program that can address as many needs as possible.

Compensation decision makers have considerable control over shaping employee perceptions or reinforcing employee behaviors. They can influence employee beliefs about the instrumentalities and outcomes associated with performance. For example, if promotions are given only for high levels of performance, employees learn that high performance and not something else results in promotion. If pay raises go only to those who are high performers, employees learn that performance results in more money. All this suggests that valid performance assessment systems and pay-for-performance systems are an absolute necessity for employees to believe in merit pay systems and be motivated by money.[49]

Monetary outcomes are one of the main ways in which an organization can influence behavior. Money appeals to all the needs that people have.[50]

Once again, two organizational goals of the compensation system include influencing employees' decisions to join and stay and influencing their decision to perform at high levels. There are several ways a firm can influence the decisions that people make in the context of these goals. First, the absolute level of hiring wages can influence people to join the organization. For example, if a firm offers a wage rate of $10 per hour for a given type of work and everyone else is offering $8 per hour, job applicants are likely to choose the higher-paying firm, all other things being equal. Second, money can influence the decision to stay. If wages in the firm fall below the going rate, people may start leaving the firm. Money in the form of employee benefits may also influence the decision to stay. A senior employee who is entitled to 6 weeks of paid vacation may be reluctant to leave for a better paying job if it means losing the vacation time. Third, organizations can use money to influence the decision to perform, as shown in the Adair example.

A series of conditions must exist before money will motivate high levels of performance. Those conditions are (1) the person must believe that by expending the effort, he or she is capable of high performance ($E$ is close to 1.0);

(2) the person must have needs that money will satisfy; and (3) the person must believe that high performance will result in money.

# Reinforcement Theory

The concept of reinforcement theory is based primarily on the work of B.F. Skinner. Three essential elements of reinforcement theory are relevant for this chapter. *Stimulus* is something in the environment that energizes the individual to react in a certain way. *Response* is the individual's reaction (for example, performance or lack of it) to the stimulus being present. *Reinforcement* is the consequences to the individual for the selection of a specific response. The basic model for reinforcement theory is stimulus–response–reinforcement, which is illustrated in Exhibit 3.8. The individual learns over time which responses are appropriate based on the consequences of prior response selection. The individual will select those responses that lead either directly or indirectly to desired goals.[51] To change behavior, the consequences associated with the behaviors must be changed, and thus one must be in control of those consequences and know the level of importance of each to the individual whose behavior is trying to be shaped.[52] A reinforcer can be primary or secondary. A primary reinforcer is satisfying or dissatisfying because of innate properties and not because of past experience (for example, food, water). Secondary reinforcers have their value because of past experience (for example, money, praise). The compensation manager is mostly concerned with developing a reward system in which secondary reinforcers can be manipulated to motivate employee behavior within the work environment.

## *Types of Reinforcement*

Four types of reinforcement are of primary concern to compensation managers in the design of a compensation system: positive reinforcement, negative reinforcement, extinction, and punishment. *Positive reinforcement* is the application of a reinforcer to increase the probability that the desired behavior will be repeated in similar situations in the future. *Negative reinforcement* is the removal of aversive stimulus when the employee establishes or returns to a desired behavior. For example, Rebecca has traditionally arrived at work on time. She has always contributed to the team output, and her supervisor and coworkers have always been nice to her. Now, suppose that during one week Rebecca is late for work several times, and she is nagged by her coworkers and supervisor. She makes a renewed effort to get to work on time, and the nagging ceases. This is negative

---

**EXHIBIT 3.8**　　**REINFORCEMENT MODEL**

Stimulus ——— Response ——— Reinforcement

---

reinforcement. *Extinction* is the removal of a previous positive reinforcer to eliminate an undesirable behavior. For example, Karen, a salesperson, receives a financial bonus for several months because she surpasses a set number for new accounts opened during each month. The past month, however, she did not reach the minimum number, and thus the bonus was not awarded. *Punishment* is the application of the reinforcer to decrease the probability that the undesired behavior will be repeated. For example, John, an employee who is late for work, has his pay reduced for the inappropriate behavior.

## Schedule of Reinforcement

Schedule of reinforcement is used when each behavior is not individually reinforced but rather some of the behaviors or groupings of behaviors are reinforced. The schedule selected deals with the method by which the reinforcers are applied within the business situation. The four schedules of reinforcement are fixed interval, fixed ratio, variable interval, and variable ratio. *Fixed interval* is the application of the reinforcer on a fixed time schedule. For example, an executive is paid $1800 salary every two weeks. Whether the executive works 80 or 100 hours in that time period, the amount of pay remains the same. *Fixed ratio* is the application of the reinforcer based on a fixed number of behavioral responses. For example, a seamstress is paid for each garment produced. The paycheck is different based on the number of finished garments produced in the period covered by the paycheck. *Variable interval* is the application of the reinforcer based on variable time intervals. For example, a supervisor has determined that each of his/her employees should receive praise two times per week. The supervisor provides overt praise but not at the same times each week. *Variable ratio* is the application of the reinforcer based on a variable number of behavioral responses. For example, an owner of a small company takes the work team out to dinner after some major accomplishment or if the team has just performed well throughout a very busy and successful work period. The above schedules are used when each response is not reinforced but rather a selected number of responses are reinforced. *Continuous reinforcement* is when the reinforcer is applied after each behavior. For example, an independent contractor purchases items for a set amount and resells them to customers; compensation occurs with each resale and is based on the spread between the selling price and cost times the amount sold.

## Research and Implications on Reinforcement Theory

Although reinforcement theory was originally developed by a psychologist examining noncognitive animal behavior, it has extensive application for understanding human behavior. Research shows that reinforcers such as financial incentive plans, behavioral analysis, praise and criticism, and self-management programs are successful in reinforcing desired behavior.[53] Within an organization, effective performance by employees must be positively reinforced, poor performance must not be reinforced, and in some situations punishment may be effective in influencing human behavior.[54] Studies of financial incentive plans find the effectiveness of such plans ranges from small to significant.[55] In one recent review of the literature, the authors conclude that salary plans are effective in maintaining satisfactory performance levels (to avoid termination) but do not influence behavior above that, commission pay is effective in initiating higher levels of performance but cannot sustain the behaviors and usually does not raise performance to the full potential of the employee, and contests are effective in creating a meaningful increase in performances during the contests themselves but do not have a sustaining effect on the performance of the employee. Possible causes for the wide variation in studies of incentive systems include the challenge of both measuring performance equitably and providing adequate payment amount and the presence of contemporary social values that hinder the effectiveness of incentive plans.[56] There is a contention that extrinsic rewards may actually reduce intrinsic motivation of the worker on the job; however, there is no empirical evidence from the workplace to support this belief.[57] Work can be designed that provides both intrinsic motivation and extrinsic rewards.[58]

Self-management is a form of nonfinancial reward. The reinforcer works by providing training to individuals in self-observation and then having them compare their behaviors with the goals that they have set. Based on self-observation, individuals will administer reinforcers or punishers to help achieve and/or sustain their established goals.[59] One benefit of self-management is that individuals believe they have control over their own behavior.[60]

There is little doubt that employees consciously or unconsciously have their behaviors reinforced through outcomes provided by the organization. For example, money has been viewed as a secondary reinforcer in the sense that money can purchase things to satisfy basic needs.[61] Thus managers have available to them a wide array of financial and nonfinancial reinforcers to shape the behaviors of employees.

## Employment Exchange Contract

Every individual who participates in the labor force also participates in what has been called the *employment exchange contract* or the *inducements and contributions contract*.[62] These terms mean that every individual agrees, at least implicitly, to engage in activities desired by the employer (or to make contributions and offer inducements), and the employer agrees to provide certain outcomes for the individual (or offers inducements and makes contributions).

### Psychological Contract

The employment exchange contract is a psychological contract, not an actual legal contract. Although some employees do have legally binding contracts with their organizations, the employment exchange contract is considered an informal, unspoken agreement between the employee and the organization.

### Both Parties Profit

Both parties to the employment exchange contract see themselves as better off than they were before they made the contract. From the organization's viewpoint, the contributions made by the organization must be less than the inducements made by the individual. Similarly, from the individual's view, the contributions made by the individual must be less than the inducements made by the organization. How is it possible for these two views to be true at the same time? Because the contract exists only in the minds of the employee and the organization, each party has the opportunity to consider different factors as inducements and contributions. What one party sees as an inducement may not be considered relevant in the exchange by the other party.[63] In this manner, both parties see the exchange as profitable. The list of inducements and contributions in Exhibit 3.9 reflects the possible differences between the parties in making their assessments of each other.

Compensation decision makers must be aware that all behavior is activated by the drive to satisfy one or more needs. Before an individual will work at a job, the individual must psychologically agree to the employment exchange contract.[64] The following example illustrates the contract between both parties.

Al Ladd has to decide whether to work for ABC Corporation. Al considers the contributions he must make (show up at 8 A.M. each day, offer his skills as a compensation expert, make judgmental decisions using his 20 years of experience, and so on). He also considers the inducements offered by ABC Corporation in return (the work is near his home, the salary is acceptable, the

---

**EXHIBIT 3.9    EMPLOYMENT EXCHANGE CONTRACT**

---

**Employee's perception**[a:]

| | |
|---|---|
| Inducements = | Money wage |
| | Benefits |
| | Company prestige |
| | Company location |
| | Challenging work |
| Contributions = | Perform engineering tasks |
| | Work from 8:00 to 5:00 each workday |

**Employer's perception**[b:]

| | |
|---|---|
| Inducements = | Perform engineering work |
| | Work from 8:00 to 5:00 each workday |
| | Candidate has degree from prestigious engineering school |
| | Candidate has managerial potential |
| | Candidate was honor student |
| Contributions = | Money Wage |
| | Benefits |
| | Company prestige |

---

[a]Employee sees inducements from employer as greater than employee contributions.
[b]Employer sees inducements from employee as greater than employer contributions.

office overlooks Lake Michigan, and so on). If Al believes that he will profit from the exchange, he will decide to accept the job if it is offered. ABC Corporation goes through the same process. It looks at the contributions it will give Al (good pay, a high level of responsibility, and so on) and looks at the inducements Al is offering (20 years of experience, good verbal and writing skills, and so on). ABC Corporation may then decide that if Al is interested in the job, they will make an employment offer. In short, the two parties have arrived at an acceptable exchange.

## Summary

This chapter establishes a theoretic framework for understanding human behavior. The compensation decision maker must understand how people behave so that the reward system will positively influence their behavior. The chapter starts out by taking a brief look at the sociologic value of occupations and the corresponding hierarchy that develops within organizations.

The point is made that the hierarchical position of a job in an organization provides the job holder not only higher status within the firm and in society but also higher wages. Also, traditionally, Americans believe that individual rewards should be heavily influenced by individual performance. That belief is being slightly modified lately such that team rewards are becoming more prevalent in business.

This chapter discusses equity theory, need theory, expectancy theory, and reinforcement theory as they pertain to compensating employees within an organization. A brief review of the relevant literature is provided for each of these theories.

It is critical for employees to feel equitably treated in their wage and benefit payments. The just treatment includes both distributive and procedural justice. At least two forms of equity should be considered: external and internal equity. Employers are concerned about external equity because they want to influence people to join and stay with the organization. External equity is accomplished by conducting labor and product market wage and benefit surveys when feasible. Employers are concerned about internal equity because of the compensation goals of influencing workers to stay with the organization. Concerns about internal equity cause employers to engage in the administrative practice of job evaluation.

Expectancy and reinforcement theory provide understanding of the process of motivating higher levels of performance. If organizations want high levels of performance, they must design the compensation system to accomplish that goal. Administratively, organizations must have a valid merit pay system or incentive system that requires, among other things, an effective performance appraisal process. This process aids in establishing employee equity.

In conclusion, this chapter presents the concept of the employment contract which implicitly exists between employee and employer. This is a psychological contract in which both parties believe the inducements for them outweigh the contributions by them.

## Discussion Questions

1. Discuss the concepts of internal and external pay equity.

2. What is the distinction between distributive and procedural justice?

3. Think about the things that have happened to you at work (even if it has been a part-time job). How do those things relate to the needs that you may have? Relate these needs back to some of the terminology used by the different need theorists.

4. Think about a time when you felt unfairly treated. What seemed to be unfair about that situation to you? Can you identify the comparison standard—the relevant other?

5. Most of you have had to think about spending two hours at your favorite sport or studying for that examination the next day. Which decision did you make and why? Can you recast that decision using instrumentality and expectancy theory terminology?

6. Identify a list of contributions you intend to make to your employer, and also list the inducements that you expect your employer to make to get you to work.

7. What is the role of reinforcement theory in influencing a salesperson's behavior?

*References*

[1] J. E. Rosenbaum, "Hierarchical and Individual Effects on Earnings," *Industrial Relations* 19 (Winter 1980), 1–14; B. G. Malkiel and J. A. Malkiel, "Male–Female Differentials in Professional Employment," *American Economic Review* 63 (September 1973), 693–705.
[2] T. A. Mahoney, "Organizational Hierarchy and Position Worth," *Academy of Management Journal* (1979), 726–737.
[3] T. A. Mahoney, *Compensation and Reward Perspectives* (Homewood, IL: Irwin, 1979), 168–169.
[4] J. S. Adams, "Inequity in Social Exchange," in *Advances in Experimental Social Psychology*, ed. L. Berkowitz (New York: Academic Press, 1965), 267–299.
[5] Mahoney, *Compensation and Reward Perspectives*, 169.
[6] L. A. Festinger, *A Theory of Cognitive Dissonance* (Evanston, IL: Row, Peterson, 1957).
[7] J. Thibaut and L. Walker, *Procedural Justice: A Psychological Analysis* (Hillsdale, NJ: Lawrence Erlbaum, 1975); G. S. Leventhal, "What Should Be Done with Equity Theory?" in *Social Exchange: Advances in Theory and Research*, eds. K. J. Gergen, M. S. Greenberg, and R. H. Willis (New York: Plenum, 1980), 27–55; R. J. Bies and J. S. Moag, "Interactional Justice: Communication Criteria of Fairness" in *Research on Negotiation in Organizations*, vol. 1, eds. R. J. Lewicki, B. H. Sheppard, and B. H. Bazerman (Greenwich, CT: JAI Press, 1986), 43–55.

[8] Thibaut and Walker, *Procedural Justice: A Psychological Analysis.*

[9] Leventhal, "What Should Be Done with Equity Theory?"

[10] Bies and Moag, "Interactional Justice: Communication Criteria of Fairness."

[11] J. S. Adams, "Toward an Understanding of Inequity," *Journal of Abnormal and Social Psychology* 67 (1963): 442–435; Paul Goodman and Abraham Friedman, "An Examination of Adams' Theory of Inequity," *Administrative Science Quarterly* (September 1971), 271–277.

[12] Adams, "Inequity in Social Exchange."

[13] For reviews of equity theory findings, see R. D. Prichard, "Equity Theory: A Review and Critique," *Organizational Behavior and Human Performance* (May 1969), 176–211.

[14] For a review of alternative references, see F. S. Hills, "The Relevant Other in Pay Comparisons," *Industrial Relations* 19, (Fall 1980), 346–351; G. R. Oldham, C. T. Kulik, M. L. Ambrose, L. P. Stepina, and J. F. Brand, "Relations Between Job Facet Comparison and Employee Reactions," *Organizational Behavior and Human Performance* 38 (1986), 28–47.

[15] P. S. Goodman, "An Examination of Referents Used in the Evaluation of Pay," *Organizational Behavior and Human Performance* 12 (1974), 170–195.

[16] C. T. Kulik and M. L. Ambrose, "Personal and Situational Determinants of Referent Choice," *Academy of Management Review* 17 (1992), 212–237.

[17] E. A. Lind and T. Tyler, *The Social Psychology of Procedural Justice* (New York: Plenum, 1988); R. J. Bies and D. L. Shapiro, "Voice and Justification: Their Influence on Procedural Fairness Judgements," *Academy of Management Journal* 31 (1988), 676–685; J. Alderfer, "An Empirical Test of a New Theory of Human Needs," Organizational Behavior and Human Performance 4 (1969), 142–175.

[34] B. Herzberg and B. Snyderman, *The Motivation to Work*, 2d ed. (New York: Wiley, 1959).

[35] R. Steer and R. Mowday, "The Motivational Properties of Tasks," *Academy of Management Review* (October 1977), 645–658.

[36] F. Herzberg, "One More Time: How Do You Motivate Employees?" *Harvard Business Review* (January/February 1968), 56–57.

[37] S. R. Maddi, *Personality Theories*, 3d ed. (Homewood, IL: The Dorsey Press, 1976), 19–174.

[38] R. Kanfer, "Motivation Theory and Industrial and Organizational Psychology," in *Handbook of Industrial and Organizational Psychology*, 2d ed., vol. 1, eds. M. D. Dunnette and L. M. Hough (Palo Alto, CA: Consulting Psychologist Press, 1990), 75–170.

[39] *Ibid.*

[40] V. H. Vroom, *Work and Motivation* (New York: Wiley, 1964).

[41] J. R. Hackman and L. W. Porter, "Expectancy Theory Prediction of Work Effectiveness," *Organizational Behavior and Human Performance* 12 (1968), 417–426; H. G. Heneman III and D. P. Schab, "Evaluation of Research on Expectancy Theory Predictions of Employee Performance," *Psychological Bulletin* 79 (July 1972), 1–9; R. D. Pritchard and M. S. Sanders, "The Influence of Valence, Instrumentality, Expectancy on Effort and Performance," *Journal of Applied Psychology* 57 (1973), 55–60; L. Reinharth and M. A. Wahba, "Expectancy Theory as Predictor of Work Motivation, Effort Expenditure, and Job Performance," *Academy of Management Journal* 18 (September 1975), 520–537; E. E. Lawler, III, and J. L. Suttle, "Expectancy Theory and Job Behavior," *Organizational Behavior and Human Performance* 71 (1973), 482–503; T. Matsui et al., "Validity of Expectancy Theory as a Within Person Behavioral Choice Model for Sales Activities," *Journal of Applied*

*Psychology* (December 1977), 764–767; J. E. Mathieu, "The Influence of Positive and Negative Outcomes on Force Model Expectancy Predictions: Mixed Results From Two Samples," *Human Relations* 40 (1987), 817–832.

[42] R. Kanfer, "Motivation Theory and Industrial and Organizational Psychology."

[43] *Ibid.*

[44] D. T. Hall, *Careers in Organizations* (Pacific Palisades, CA: Goodyear, 1976); W. H. Mobely, *Employee Turnover: Causes, Consequences, and Control* (Reading, MA: Addison–Wesley, 1982).

[45] D. F. Parker and L. Dyers, "Expectancy Theory as a Within-Person Behavioral Choice Model: An Empirical Test of Some Conceptual and Methodological Refinements," *Organizational Behavior and Human Performance* 17 (1976), 97–117; D. P. Schwab, J. D. Olian–Gottlieb, and H. G. Heneman, "Between Subject Expectancy Theory Research: A Statistical Review of Studies Predicting Effort and Performance," *Psychological Bulletin* 86 (1979), 139–147.

[46] T. Mitchell, "Expectancy Models of Job Satisfaction; Occupational Preference and Effort," *Psychological Bulletin* 81 (1974), 1053–1056.

[47] Mathieu, "The Influence of Positive and Negative Outcomes on Force Model Expectancy Prediction: Mixed Results from Two Samples," *Human Relations* 40, 817–832; F. R. Leon, "The Role of Positive and Negative Outcomes in the Causation of Motivational Forces," *Journal of Applied Psychology* 66 (1981), 45–53.

[48] Leon, "The Role of Positive and Negative Outcomes in the Causation of Motivational Forces."

[49] R. L. Opsahl and M. D. Dunnette, "The Role of Financial Compensation in Industrial Motivation," *Psychological Bulletin* 66, (1966), 94–118.

[50] *Ibid.*

[51] B. F. Skinner, *Contingency Reinforcement: A Theoretical Analysis* (New York: Appleton–Century Crofts, 1969).

[52] *Ibid.*

[53] R. A. Katzell and D. E. Thompson, "Work Motivation: Theory and Practice," *American Psychologist* 45 (1990), 144–153.

[54] R. D. Arvey and J. M. Ivancevich, "Punishment in Organizations: A Review, Propositions, and Research Suggestions," *Academy of Management Review* 5 (1980), 123–132.

[55] R. A. Guzzo, R. D. Jette, and R. A. Katzell, "The Effects of Psychologically Based Intervention Programs on Workers Productivity: A Meta-analysis," *Personnel Psychology* 38 (1985), 275–291.

[56] E. E. Lawler III, "Pay For Performance: A Motivational Analysis," in *Incentives. Cooperation and Risk Sharing*, ed. H. Nalbantian (Totowa, NJ: Rowman and Littlefield, 1987).

[57] E. L. Deci, "The Effects of Contingent and Non-Contingent Rewards and Controls in Intrinsic Motivation," *Organizational Behavior and Human Performance* 8 (1972), 217–229.

[58] J. L. Farr, "Task Characteristics, Reward Contingency, and Intrinsic Motivation," *Organizational Behavior and Human Performance* 16 (1976), 292–307.

[59] P. Karoly and F. H. Kanfer, *Self-Management and Behavior Change: From Theory to Practice* (New York: Pergamen Press, 1982).

[60] C. A. Frayne and G. P. Latham, "Application of Social Learning Theory to Employee Self-Management of Attendance," *Journal of Applied Psychology* 72 (1987), 387–392.

[61] Opsahl and Dunnette, "The Role of Financial Compensation in Industrial Motivation."

[62] The inducements and contributions contract concept is more fully developed by J. G. March and H. A. Simon in Chapter 4, "Motivational Constraints: The Decision to Participate," *Organizations* (New York: Wiley, 1958), 83–111.

[63] J. Kotter, "The Psychological Contract: Managing the Joining Up Process," *California Management Review* 15 (Spring 1973), 91–99.

[64] D. Yankelovich, "New Psychological Contracts at Work: Employee Incentives," *Personnel Psychology* 24 (1971), 501–518; D. Berlew and D. T. Hall, "The Socialization of Managers: Effect of Expectations on Performance," *Administrative Science Quarterly* (September 1966), 207–223.

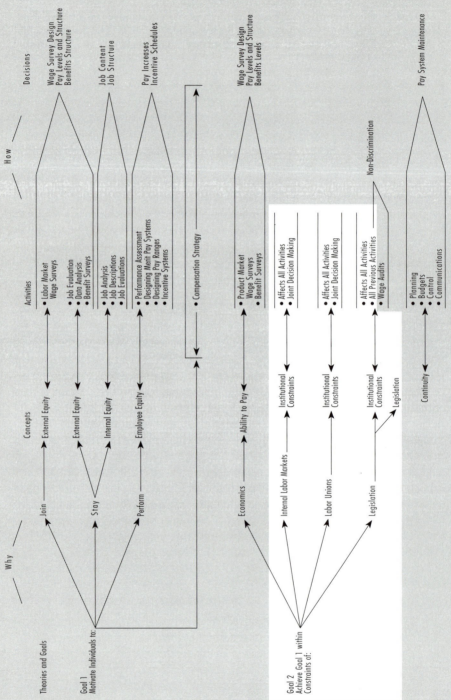

# II

# *Institutional Constraints in Compensation*

# 4

# Institutional Constraints: Labor Markets and Labor Unions

## Learning Objectives

**To learn about the internal labor market concept.**

**To learn how internal labor markets influence compensation decision making.**

**To learn the causes of interindustry wage structure.**

**To understand how unions bargain and the issues that the unions bargain over.**

**To learn how labor unions have an effect on compensation decisions.**

**To learn that unions also bargain over nonwage and nonbenefit issues that have an indirect impact on labor costs.**

## Introduction

This chapter explores two of the more important constraints faced by compensation decision makers: labor markets and labor unions. The notion of an internal labor market as a constraint is important because, as an institution, the internal labor market (internal relationship of all positions within an organization) shapes both individual and organizational perceptions of social relationships. These perceptions of social relationships translate into an institutional force that also shapes compensation decision making. Interindustry wage structures often exist over extended periods of time and thus limit the organization's discretion in setting wages. Labor unions are an important institutional constraint because, as the representatives of employees, they are involved in joint labor–management decision making over compensation issues.

The concept of the internal labor market and its significance is developed first. Interindustry wage structure is defined, and the causes for such wage structure differentials are briefly discussed. The subject of labor unions is examined along with a discussion of their impact on the terms and conditions of employment in general and on wages and benefits in particular.

This chapter addresses a number of pertinent questions: Why are entry-level jobs often the dirtiest and hardest, yet also the lowest paid? What is a job hierarchy, and how is it related to the organization's pay system? Why do job hierarchies arise in the first place? Why does one industry consistently pay more than a different industry? What do unions bargain for? How do they bargain, and do they affect the wage level of bargaining unit nonunion employees? Do unions affect the wage structure?

## Internal Labor Markets

The internal labor market of a firm is comprised of all those employees who work for the organization. However, the term *internal labor market* is used with more precision in this text. Conceptually, an internal labor market consists of all the positions within an organization and the relationship of these positions to each other as well as the relationship of these positions to the external environment of the organization.[1] Exhibit 4.1 depicts the internal labor market for an office clerical work force of a company.

Individuals enter into the internal labor market from the external labor market through what is often called a port of entry.[2] The port of entry is the job or jobs for which new employees are hired. In Exhibit 4.1, new employees are hired into job 1, job I, or job A. These are the lowest jobs in each of three progression lines. Progression lines denote job hierarchy within a firm. One example of a line of progression would be the three jobs of data clerk, computer programmer, and computer department supervisor. Higher-level jobs in each of the progression lines are generally filled by movement from the lower-level jobs. This movement is controlled by a set of administrative rules. Typically, these rules base movement on some combination of merit and seniority. The exact combination is usually highly organization-specific. Rules also may vary within an organization (that is, they may be different for production jobs and marketing jobs within the same company).[3]

Job A, job 1, and job I represent several positions. A *job* can be defined as a collection of tasks that can be performed by one person. A *position* is defined as a collection of tasks assigned to one person. A job is the generic grouping of tasks and duties, whereas a position is the actual assignment of those tasks or duties to a specific individual. A company may have one job of data entry clerk (one collectively of tasks), yet have 20 positions in that job (20 people who work as data entry clerks).

The broken lines with arrows in Exhibit 4.1 depict the points at which employees can transfer from one progression line to another. Transfers are possible from job D to job ¢. Transfers are also possible from job A to job I. Job 3, however, is a dead-end job: Once an employee rises to job 3, there is nowhere to go.

## Organizations and Internal Labor Markets

Most organizations have one or more internal labor markets.[4] Typically, there are internal labor markets for production jobs (maybe even separate progression lines for skilled and unskilled jobs), marketing jobs, finance jobs, and so forth. There may or may not be points of transfer from one set of jobs to another—such as transfer from unskilled to skilled jobs and transfer from human resource jobs to general management.

A common misconception is that internal labor markets are perfectly closed. Exhibit 4.1 depicts an internal labor market in which hiring occurs only at the bottom jobs in a progression line. Although this is often true, sometimes higher-level jobs are filled directly from outside of the firm. There is a degree of openness in the internal labor market.[5] In other words, some internal labor markets are relatively closed (they hire only into bottom jobs), whereas others are relatively open (they hire into all jobs). A host of factors affects the extent to which an internal labor market is closed. For example, to keep a perfectly closed internal labor market, the company has to train people for advancement, plan for future human resource needs, hire people in the lower jobs who are capable of being trained, and so forth. For simplicity, the following sections assume a relatively closed internal labor market.

## Implications of the Internal Labor Market for Compensation

The existence and use of the internal labor market has a series of implications for compensation decision makers.[6] First, because people enter the organization and, in many cases, spend years moving into higher-level jobs, it is often argued that people become isolated from the external labor market.[7] One of the benefits of this isolation effect for the organization is the latitude its compensation decision makers gain in setting wage rates for higher-level jobs. Because the employees who are isolated within higher-level jobs have a difficult time assessing external pay rates, the organization is in a position to exercise discretion in pay rates.

Second, many jobs are organization-specific. Every organization combines tasks and duties into unique jobs. An administrative secretarial job in one company may be quite different from an administrative secretarial job in another company. When employees in different companies do dissimilar work, it becomes difficult for them to assess what constitutes fair pay for their job by looking to workers outside their own company. This makes it more critical on the part of the compensation decision makers to have pay rates perceived as equitable among jobs within the internal labor market than to have pay equity across companies. As is noted later in the chapter, there is evidence of long-term interindustry wage structure in which similar jobs are paid different wages across different industries.

Third, employee mobility is reduced. If employees leave a high-level job in their present company, they may have to start over at the bottom or near the bottom of the progression line with another company.[8] They are likely to realize that such a move will involve a cut in pay, a loss of seniority, a loss of vacation,

---

**EXHIBIT 4.1**    HYPOTHETICAL LABOR MARKET FOR OFFICE/CLERICAL EMPLOYEES

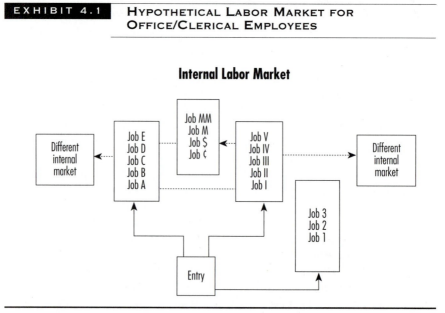

SOURCE: Reprinted by permission of the publisher from "Internal Labor Markets and Indirect Pay Discrimination," by F. S. Hills and Thomas J. Bergmann, *Compensation Review*, Fourth Quarter, 1982, p. 46. 1982 AMACOM periodicals Division, American Management Association, New York. All rights reserved.

and changes or reductions in other benefits. With these negative outcomes, the probability that they will leave is likely to decrease. In one sense, such employees are immobile or locked into the organization. The implication for the compensation decision maker is that perceptions of equity in pay (and other terms and conditions of employment) are extremely important. Given that there are many long-time employees in an organization who stand to lose a lot by leaving, it is to the organization's advantage to see that they believe they are equitably treated. Because present employees in higher jobs are somewhat immobile, relative equity among wage rates for jobs within the firm (internal equity) is probably more important than equity of wages between firms (external equity).

Finally, given that an organization tends to hire into port-of-entry jobs, it is particularly important that these jobs pay wage rates that are competitive in the external labor market. After all, the people hired into these jobs will be the employees moving through the lines of progression. Entry jobs are often considered key jobs and are subject to analysis of competitive wage rates when product and labor market surveys are undertaken by the compensation decision makers.

### Pressures to Maintain Internal Labor Markets

Why are internal labor markets maintained—why don't they eventually disappear so that all jobs are subject to purely competitive wage pricing? There are benefits to both employers and employees with internal labor markets.[9] From the organization's standpoint, an internal labor market provides a number of advantages: (l) It provides cheap training, because lower-level employees can learn informally about higher jobs;[10] (2) it reduces the risk of hiring unknown people who might fail in more responsible jobs; (3) it allows for systematic planning of human resource replacement;[11] and (4) it allows for socialization of employees into the organization's culture.

Employees also benefit in several ways: (1) They have a career in the company if they can demonstrate competence;[12] (2) they probably will be buffeted from layoffs the longer they are employed, as most organizations use a last-in, first-out layoff system; and (3) as they move up the job ladder, they will earn more money.

Internal labor markets also have disadvantages for both employees and employers. From the employees' standpoint, probably one of the greatest disadvantages is that their jobs often are somewhat insulated from market forces. Therefore, their actual pay may not be comparable with what it would be under perfect competition. From the employer's standpoint, new blood is discouraged from entering the organization, thereby stifling creativity. There are also disadvantages from a societal viewpoint because internal labor markets may inhibit societal goals. For example, they can retard the rate at which women and minorities move into managerial, professional, and technical jobs within organizations.

One noteworthy example of how internal labor markets have an effect on movement into higher jobs can be taken from the court case of *Weber v. Kaiser Aluminum*.[13] Kaiser Aluminum had an internal promotion system that allowed employees, on the basis of seniority, to go through an apprenticeship training program, after which they could move from unskilled to skilled jobs. Because mostly white men held the highest seniority, minorities would not qualify for the apprenticeship training program. To overcome this problem, Kaiser and the union agreed to an Affirmative Action Plan in which minorities qualified at a rate equal to nonminorities. One employee, Brian F. Weber, believed this was reverse discrimination and filed suit. The U.S. Supreme Court decided that Kaiser Aluminum could legally change its internal labor market system to give this type of preferential treatment to minorities.

### Emergence of Internal Labor Markets

How do internal labor markets emerge in the first place? Most grow out of the sociotechnical system of a specific organization.[14] For example, a large gas station sells gasoline, tires, batteries, and accessories, as well as provides tune-ups and other mechanical service. The owner of the station uses a certain technology in servicing customers. The owner at first may decide that all employees will do all the duties (that is, be completely cross-trained). At this point, the owner of the station would probably pay all the employees the same wage rate.

But, some employees may lack the skills to perform mechanical work or perform grease jobs whereas others have these skills. In a large station, there may be enough work for employees to specialize. Before long, employees who work on engine repair may decide that they are making larger contributions to the organization than others, and they will argue that they deserve more pay. The owner may grant a pay differential so that engine mechanics earn more than anyone else. Over time, the employees who grease cars and change exhaust systems may believe that they too deserve more pay than the employees who pump gas. They do not deserve as much as the engine mechanics (probably even in their own minds), but they deserve more pay than the general station attendant. Over time, three different jobs evolve in the gas station: pump attendant, general mechanic, and engine mechanic. These three jobs are differentiated in the amount of pay, and over time, qualified employees will be allowed to move up the progression ladder of jobs as vacancies in higher jobs occur.

Internal labor markets change over time as technology and the business change. Today, an engine mechanic must be much more highly skilled than 30 years ago, and the other two jobs of attendant and general mechanic may have undergone numerous changes as well so that the internal labor market no longer exists in the old sense. There may now be three job families (a job family is a set of jobs grouped together by technology, custom, or administrative unit).

Any time there is technologic change within the organization, a new sociotechnical system may emerge that will restructure the internal labor market.[15] For example, the advent of the diesel engine in the railroad industry eliminated the need for the job of fireman (although this job still exists in some railroad companies). Another example is the advent of more sophisticated instrumentation in modern jet airliners that has resulted in a reduction of the flight crew from three jobs (captain, first officer, and flight engineer) to two jobs (captain and first officer).

Chapter 3 showed that equity considerations are important to workers. The gas station example above points out the fact that within organizations some jobs require more contributions than other jobs. For people to feel equitably treated relative to other employees in the organization, there must be different rates of pay for different jobs. The compensation decision maker's discretion regarding specific wage rates will be influenced by the employer's perception of the internal labor market. The administrative process for determining these different rates of pay (a wage structure) requires conducting a job evaluation and then pricing the jobs. *Job evaluation* can be defined as "the process of determining the relative worth of jobs to the organization and its employees." *Job pricing* is the process of fitting the evaluated jobs to market data. Job pricing and job evaluation are important activities linked to internal and external equity considerations.[16] In terms of the internal labor market, the process of job evaluation is the process of capturing the relationships that are believed to be fair among jobs within an internal labor market.

## Interindustry Wage Structure

Internal equity is certainly a more easily achievable goal than external equity—especially when wage comparison is made across industries. As compensation decision makers attempt to fairly exercise the discretion afforded them by the internal labor market, they may look to the broader labor market, beyond their own organization and their own industry. What they discover will be wide variations in pay for equal work.

### Interindustry Relationship to Wages

Interindustry wage structure is defined as wage differentials between employees of different industries who have comparable skills. Research has found that manufacturing organizations pay a 20 percent premium over service organizations for similar work.[17] For example, a manufacturing organization may pay an employee $12 per hour, whereas an employee in a service organization will receive $10 per hour for a job that requires similar skills.

Research on the interindustry wage structure supports the existence of a wage differential. This differential holds true historically and internationally and applies to employees of different race, sex, age, and occupation. Viewed historically, the differential remained relatively constant in a comparison of data from 1923 to 1984.[18] Research has found that the transportation industry is a high-wage industry in both the United States and Japan and the apparel and textile industries are low-wage industries.[19] The wage differential, although it may still exist, is not as prevalent in less-developed nations or in socialist and communist countries. Does the quality of the workers employed explain the differences between interindustry wage structure? The correlation between industry wage differentials with and without controls is .95. The workers' characteristics controlled were age, sex, marital status, race, education, location, and job tenure. Although the interindustry differential is reduced when worker characteristics are controlled (most of reduction attributed to sex and occupation), a large difference still remains.[20]

## Causes of Wage Differentials

There are several reasons for wage differentials that are not associated with the specific skills or abilities of individual employees. The following are factors that are related to interindustry wage differentials: characteristics of the industry product market, profitability of the industry, degree of capital intensity, and level of union density.

Part of the wage differential comes from the market an industry operates within. Generally, industries operating in less-competitive product environments pay higher wages because of higher profit due to higher concentration ratio, entry barriers, and less foreign competition.[21] This relationship, however, is affected by the quality of labor (for example, education) a firm may have in place.

The profitability of the industry can be used as another determinant of an industry's ability to pay high wages and, therefore, as a prediction for the existence of a wage differential. Several studies found that industries with higher profitability pay all employees a relatively high wage rate.[22] In essence, they share some of the wealth with all employees and are thus able to be more selective in the labor market.

The ratio of capital to labor is also a determinant of interindustry wage differentials. The more capital-intensive industries pay a higher average wage than less capital-intensive industries.[23]

*Union density* is defined as the proportion of employees covered by a union contract. The higher the union density, the greater the number of unionized employees, and according to research, the larger the wage differential. Union density is positively related to the wage of both union and nonunion workers.[24] The positive influence of union density is greater for nonunion workers of large organizations than those working for small organizations.[25] The perceived threat of unionization for the large nonunion organizations is believed to be the main reason for their high-wage policy.

Union density as a cause of interindustry wage differentials should be approached cautiously. Research has not yet shown whether union density is a cause of wage differentials or just related to it. This caution can be illustrated by the presence of relatively high wages in the automotive industry before the industry became predominantly unionized.

Research on the interindustry wage structure is extensive. Generally, the conclusions drawn from the research support the existence of a wage differential; employees in different industries receive different pay for jobs that are comparable.[26] The specific reasons for the presence of wage differentials are more difficult to establish. But whatever the reasons behind them, these wage differentials impact on the compensation decision makers. They must take into account the industry within which they operate and the industries with whom they compete in the external labor market as they attempt to exercise their discretionary power.

# Labor Unions and Compensation Process

While the exact relationship of unions to wage differentials may not be known, no one questions that, overall, labor unions are among the most significant institutional forces influencing compensation in this country. Unionism is a critical constraint in the compensation decision-making process for firms with unions. And even though less than 18 percent of the U.S. labor force is currently unionized, many nonunionized firms are influenced by the mere presence of unions in the U.S. economy. These firms are concerned about potential unionization as well as about the effect of competing with unionized firms. The process of negotiations between the labor union and the organization is called *collective bargaining,* and through these negotiations, the compensation of employees is determined.

Understanding the negotiation process in a unionized environment is essential for understanding the limitations compensation managers face in establishing wage and benefit levels for unionized workers. The organization's freedom to set wage and benefit level, the method of payment (base pay versus incentive), the percentage of total compensation that goes to benefits or wages, and the wage structure are all constrained by the presence of the union. Even in nonunion situations in which the supply of skilled workers is less than the demand, the workers will find themselves in a favorable bargaining position and will be able to negotiate a better package than workers of equal skill who are in a situation in which there are ample workers available to meet demands.

## Issues in Collective Bargaining

National labor law sets the framework for what can be bargained over. There are three general categories of bargaining issues: (1) prohibited issues, (2) permissive issues , and (3) mandatory issues.[27] *Prohibited issues* are prevented statutorily. For example, it is illegal for a union to negotiate an apprenticeship program that discriminates against women and minorities. *Permissive issues* are those issues that labor and management can negotiate if they both want to, but the parties are not bound by law to negotiate them (bargain in good faith). For example, they may negotiate whether the union should have a say in the firm's product advertising program. *Mandatory issues* are those issues that the parties by law are required to negotiate.

Wages and employee benefits are both mandatory items, and there are many other mandatory items that are less directly related to compensation and yet have an impact on labor costs. Prohibiting supervisors from doing the work of bargaining unit members is a mandatory issue that could affect total labor costs; it could, for example, result in the need to hire an additional worker.

## Collective Bargaining Committee

Once a union is certified to represent a group of employees within an organization (the bargaining unit), the members of the bargaining unit typically elect a bargaining committee. This committee is normally composed of elected rank-and-file members plus the union president. If the local union is affiliated with a national union organization, such as the United Auto Workers, the national union may provide a staff person who is adept at contract negotiations. (If the contract to be negotiated is a precedent-setting contract, the national union will want very much to have a person on the bargaining committee.) The local union often has its lawyer on the bargaining committee, and there may be other union officials as the local union sees fit.

Management also formulates its bargaining committee. Typically, the committee includes a high-level member of management (such as, the vice-president of production), the manager of the plant in which the union members work, the company attorney, and one or more labor relations specialists. In a larger company such as General Electric or McDonnell Douglas, the bargaining committee may consist of 25 to 30 members or more. However, at a small company, the bargaining committee may consist of the president and an attorney.

## Bargaining to a Settlement

**Settlement Ranges** Exhibit 4.2 presents a diagram to illustrate the process of bargaining to a settlement. The dollar amounts in Exhibit 4.2 represent all labor costs—the wages, benefits, and other labor costs are expressed as an average rate for members of the bargaining unit. The points in the exhibit are not known to the opposite sides (and sometimes not to the parties themselves).

As Exhibit 4.2 shows, both labor and management have a settlement range in mind. In the case of management, this range falls along a continuum from A to C. Similarly, labor has an acceptable settlement range from D to E. As the bargaining process starts, each party presents its initial demand or offer. Labor makes the initial demand that it would like to win—point E in Exhibit 4.2. Although it is often true that labor makes the initial demand, it is becoming more common today for management to make an initial take-back counter-offer (for example, point A). A take-back counter-offer can be defined as an initial offer by management that is actually below the current compensation package being received by the workers. Such take-back counter-offers have been seen in recent bargaining in the manufacturing industry, for example, and represent situations in which the organization must cut labor costs to remain competitive.[28] Point B in Exhibit 4.2 is the wage value of the present wage package for the union members.

**Range Overlap** Points C and D in Exhibit 4.2 represent management's and labor's respective sticking points. At point C, management is no longer willing to negotiate, because point C is management's maximum offer. Above this point, management will consider a lockout. The lockout is management's ultimate weapon in bargaining with labor. Under labor law, management has the right to close down its plant—lock out the employees—if it determines in good faith that the parties cannot arrive at an agreement.

Similarly, labor has a minimally acceptable offer that it is willing to take, point D in Exhibit 4.2. All settlements to the left of point D are unacceptable to members of the bargaining unit and may result in a strike. Just as the lockout is management's ultimate weapon, the strike is considered to be labor's ultimate weapon.[29] By law, labor in the private sector has the right to withhold its services—or strike against the employer—if it determines in good faith that further talks will be fruitless.

Point C in Exhibit 4.2 is to the right of point D; management's sticking point is to the right of labor's sticking point. The area of overlap between points D and C is the range of feasible settlements, as represented by the area F. There may not always be an overlap between the two parties' settlement ranges. Point D could lie to the right of point C. In this case, there would not be an acceptable settlement range for the two parties, and either a strike or lockout would occur. However, little of all work time available is lost to a strike or lockout, which indicates there is usually an overlap in the bargaining range.

**Bargaining Deadlock**   Using Exhibit 4.2 to illustrate the bargaining process, assume that labor opens the negotiations by making demands equal to point E. Management makes a counter-offer at point A, citing hard economic times for the organization. The two parties, if they are bargaining in good faith, now begin to concede toward agreement. This process may not be smooth or conflict-free and can take anywhere from days to months, depending on how far apart the parties were in the first place and how hard a bargain each side wants to drive. The goal of bargaining is to move toward the other side's position and at the same time to find the other side's sticking point. For example, in the process of negotiating toward agreement, labor might think that management's sticking point is at point H in Exhibit 4.2. Labor will now be committed to point H and will try to convince management that the union will take a lockout or go on strike before it will move from point H. Point H is to the right of point C, however, and management will not accept a settlement at point H.

---

**EXHIBIT 4.2**   CONCEPTUAL THEORETIC BARGAINING SITUATION

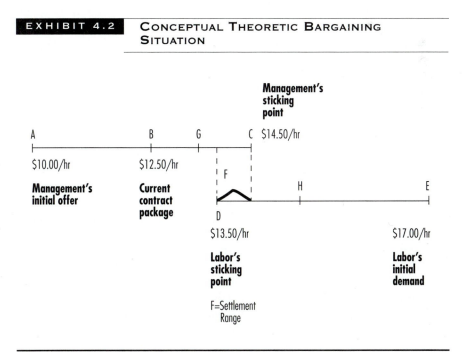

**Reopening Negotiations**   What happens when one of the two parties commits to a demand or offer that is outside the range of settlement for the other party? There will be a strike or lockout unless the other party is willing to move.[30] The party who is committed to a position finds it difficult to bargain again for fear of losing face with the other side—being perceived as bluffing and thereby losing credibility in future negotiations. One solution to this problem is provided by a neutral third party, such as the Federal Mediation and Conciliation Service.[31] If labor and management agree, a representative of the Federal Mediation and Conciliation Service can enter the bargaining process to help the parties get moving again on negotiations without a loss of face for either party.

**Settlement**   Once the negotiations are moving again, the two parties can once more attempt to find the settlement range. Management would like to find labor's minimum sticking point (point D) to know the best deal that management can get at the table. Labor would like to find point C, management's maximum sticking point, because that would give labor the best deal. Once the parties' demands and offers get between points D and C, the first one to be committed will end up with the best deal. At this point, a strike or lockout will not occur because all settlements within the range are acceptable to both parties.

The bargaining process depicted in Exhibit 4.2 is simplistic in that it deals only with compensation issues. Many bargaining issues are noneconomic in nature, such as the seniority system (plant-wide versus department seniority), union security provisions, and superseniority (superseniority awards artificial seniority to, for example, low-seniority union officials who may be let go under layoff conditions). Despite its oversimplification, Exhibit 4.2 aids in understanding the bargaining process.

**Special Case of Public Sector Unions**   Unions that represent public sector employees are faced with a different situation than private sector unions. These unions, by law, are often not allowed to strike.[32] The problem created by the loss of the right to strike is serious. Without the right to strike, labor finds it difficult to drive much of a bargain with management.

In many states, this loss of right to strike is counterbalanced with interest arbitration. Under interest arbitration, if the parties cannot reach agreement, they submit their final offers and demands to a neutral third party (an arbitrator) who makes a decision on the merits of the positions.[33] The arbitrator's decision may be advisory or binding on one or both parties depending on that state's particular law. Interest arbitration is an attempt to rebalance the relative power of labor and management when the right to strike has been denied.

Interest arbitration should not be confused with rights arbitration. *Interest arbitration* involves an arbitrator deciding the terms of a contract, whereas *rights arbitration* involves an arbitrator deciding on interpretation of the respective parties' rights and responsibilities within the context of an existing contract.[34]

# Labor Union Influence on General Compensation Issues

## Labor's Share of National Income

One way to look at the question of the impact of unions on wages is to look at the impact that unions may have had on labor's share of the national income. The data in Exhibit 4.3 suggest that between 1930 and 1990 labor's share of the national income has varied, usually below the early 1930s level.

It is difficult, therefore, to infer that the labor movement in the United States has had substantial influence on labor's share of national income.

## Influence on Wage Levels

Can the influence of the labor movement on wages be seen in the differences between union and nonunion wage rates? One of the problems with examining the wages of union and nonunion employees is that they are affected by industry and ability to pay. For example, some industries are highly unionized whereas others are not. At the same time, ability to pay varies among industries. The lathe operator in unionized industry A may make more than the lathe operator in nonunionized industry B; but industry A may also have a higher ability to pay. Nevertheless, data from a series of studies conclude that unions raise wages of union workers in the range of 7 to 10 percent relative to the wages of nonunion workers.[35] Findings showing the differentials by industry and occupation are presented in Exhibit 4.4.

H. G. Lewis, in a 1986 analysis of 114 studies of the wage gap between union and nonunion wages, found a positive effect in the range of 9.6 to 16.4 percent;

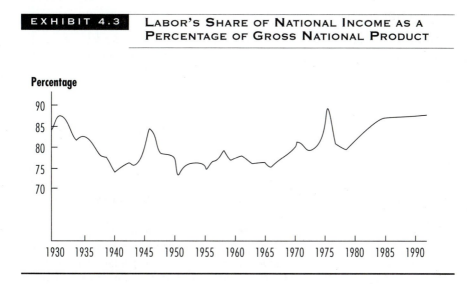

**EXHIBIT 4.3**     **LABOR'S SHARE OF NATIONAL INCOME AS A PERCENTAGE OF GROSS NATIONAL PRODUCT**

Adapted from *The Survey of Current Business Statistics*, vol. 63; p. 93.

| EXHIBIT 4.4 | USUAL WEEKLY EARNINGS OF FULL-TIME WAGE AND SALARY WORKERS, 1991 |

| Occupation | Union/Nonunion Earnings Ratio |
|---|---|
| All occupations | 1.41 |
| Managerial and professional specialty | 1.01 |
| Technical, sales, and administrative support | 1.24 |
| Service occupations | 1.73 |
| Precision production, craft, and repair | 1.38 |
| Operators, fabricators, and laborers | 1.53 |
| Farming, forestry, and fishing | 1.58 |

| Industry | Union/Nonunion Earnings Ratio |
|---|---|
| All industries | 1.19 |
| Mining | 0.98 |
| Construction | 1.16 |
| Manufacturing | 1.14 |
| Transportation and public utilities | 1.18 |
| Wholesale and retail trade | 1.27 |
| Finance, insurance, and real estate | 1.01 |
| Services | 1.12 |
| Government workers | 1.20 |

SOURCE: U. S. Bureau of Labor Statistics, "News: United States Department of Labor," February 10, 1992.

however, a reanalysis by Jarrell and Stanley revised the figures to 8.9 to 12.4 percent and concluded that the range varied with the national unemployment rate.[36] One study examining union wage premiums by industry found that the gap increased significantly across industries from 1973 to 1986. Nevertheless, in some industries, the premium remained constant or even declined; thus looking only at aggregate data can be misleading.[37] A study examining the wage premium across selected industrial countries (United States, United Kingdom, West Germany, Austria, Australia, and Switzerland) found that unions have a positive effect in all countries, but the magnitude of difference in the United States is two and one-half times greater (unweighted average difference) than the other five countries.[38] In general, union density is positively related to wage rates.[39]

A different view of union influence on wages is in the area of wage concessions. Many of the highly publicized wage concessions have occurred in the unionized sector (for example, steel, auto, and rubber), which may be a result of the relatively high premium that employees in these industries have enjoyed in comparison with the average manufacturing wage level. Wage concessions have taken the form of a wage reduction, less rigid work rules, back loading the contract, a lump sum (one time) bonus with no wage increase added to the employee's wage base, and either reduced benefit coverage or the employee paying more of the cost of the fringe benefits. The presence of the union requires that management meet and negotiate any changes being proposed. In a nonunion organization, management may unilaterally impose the new compensation without input from labor. Under that circumstance, labor can blame management, but when negotiations end in concessions, labor may blame union as well as management. It is essential for the political life of the union to attempt to resist concession bargaining. If concessions are needed, the compensation manager must carefully review the existing contract to identify where the concessions will provide the organization with the greatest return but be the least painful for labor to accept. The compensation manager must also be emotionally prepared for very painful negotiations.

## *Influence on Wage Structure*

A stream of research has focused on the influence of unions on the variation in wages. The data suggest that unions narrow the overall wage structure both within an organization and for the workers within a bargaining unit.[40]

Organizations that are unionized are more likely to pay employees in the same job a single wage rate instead of using wage ranges and are less likely to use merit pay as part of their compensation program.[41] The unions will negotiate different wages for different classifications of a job and special compensation for the skilled classifications.[42] Also, unions in the United States have been found to reduce the wage dispersion among hourly male workers (15 to 20 percent), among female workers, and among public sector employees.[43] In a study of six industrial countries, the dispersion among unionized workers was smaller than among nonunionized workers, but unlike the wage premium results mentioned earlier, the magnitude of the United States wage dispersion was similar to the other five countries.[44]

In the past few decades, organizations have used a two-tier wage and benefit payment plan. In a two-tier compensation system, one group of employees (usually newer) will receive less wages and benefits than the rest of the workers, even though they perform the same work. The approach is not new; however, it gained in popularity during the 1970s and 1980s when organizations were attempting to reduce per unit labor costs. The use of two-tier compensation plans reached 11 percent in 1985 but declined to 6 percent by 1989.[45] Unions initially viewed two-tier wage plans as less damaging to the union and its members than a wage freeze or wage reduction. The union has, however, found that the presence of two classes of employees within the same bargaining unit is a potentially explosive situation, especially as the percentage of lower-wage earners increases. For this reason, the union prefers to negotiate a two-tier plan in which employees are only temporarily paid at the lower level and move to the higher level based on a predetermined time schedule.

### Influence on Nonwage Benefits

Empirical evidence supports the belief that unions in the United States have a significant effect on the level of fringe benefits, especially pensions.[46] The positive effect of unions on fringe benefits is also present in other countries. Studies show unionized workers in Great Britain receive higher fringe benefits, Canadian and Australian union workers have higher probability of receiving pensions, and unionized Japanese workers receive higher bonuses and severance pay.[47]

Review of General Accounting Office data shows that unionization did not eliminate the ability of organizations to innovate. In the area of compensation, there was no significant difference in the use of gainsharing and Employee Stock Ownership Plans whether the employees were unionized or nonunionized, but profit sharing was used significantly more in nonunion settings.[48]

### Influence on Productivity (as Indicator of Ability to Pay)

The effect of unions on productivity (ability to pay) is inconclusive. Many studies show that unions have a positive influence on productivity, but a significant number of other studies do not support that positive influence. It is generally agreed that the labor relations climate has more of an effect on productivity than does the presence of a union and collective bargaining.[49] There is agreement that unionized organizations are less profitable than nonunionized organizations.[50] This lower profitability may have an effect on the organization's ability to pay and its ability to invest in new equipment. Research in other countries tends to support the findings of lower profitability of unionized organizations.[51]

### Influence on Compensation Packages of Nonunion Employees

It has been shown that the union has a positive impact on the compensation packages of its members, but the union also has an impact on the compensation packages of nonunion employees (spillover effect). This influence is felt by nonunion employees of the same organization and also by nonunion employees of other organizations in the relevant labor market. When the organization negotiates a combination of wage and benefit improvements for its unionized employees, it will often grant the same compensation improvements for its nonunion employees. The organization wishes to keep the compensation package of union and nonunion employees identical or very similar. The process of adjusting nonunion wages and benefits to those granted unionized employees is called *tandem wage adjustment*. The authors have even heard managers express pleasure in a benefit negotiated for union employees because they expected to receive the same benefit. Nonunionized organizations will carefully review settlements of their main unionized competitors in the labor market and make any adjustment they believe is economically practical that will reduce the probability of unionization and keep them competitive in attracting qualified workers.[52] Even though their wage cost may be similar to the unionized organization, the nonunionized organization may have lower unit labor cost because of increased flexibility, ability to make faster adjustments, and the lower administrative cost of not dealing with the union as an institution.

### Influence on the U.S. Trade Deficit

It is popular to put a significant part of the blame for the U.S. trade deficit on the contracts negotiated by American labor unions. This blaming is partially due to the reduction in market share and the corresponding loss of employment in several high-visibility unionized industrial sectors such as autos, steel, and rubber. Generally, however, the data do not support the conclusion that labor unions are a significant cause of the U.S. trade deficit. In examining data from the United States and 13 other countries, it was found that only 2 countries, South Korea, 10 percent and Hong Kong, 15 percent, had lower unionization rates than the United States (18 percent). Also, the wage rate of the United States was the fourth highest ($13.90), with West Germany, Switzerland, and Sweden surpassing the United States. Trade with the high-wage countries of Japan ($13.14), Canada ($13.58), and West Germany ($18.07) accounted for 63 percent of the deficit in 1988, whereas the 5 low-wage countries of Taiwan, South Korea, Hong Kong, Mexico, and Brazil only accounted for 28 percent.[53] The above data from a macro analysis do not support a conclusion that unionization is a main cause of the U.S. trade deficit.

Because the evidence that unions are a major cause of the overall U.S. trade deficit is not strongly supported by a macro analysis, what is their effect at the industry level? One study found that high unionization rate was not related to high import levels (except primary metals) or to low export levels.[54] A contrary finding resulted from a 1987 study by the U.S. Federal Trade Commission (FTC), which found unions were positively related to imports.[55] The FTC study included wage rates as a variable (called human capital), and some scholars believe that it biases the results. When the wage rate is replaced with median years of education (some believe a more valid measure of human capital), the union effect disappears.[56] For example, in a study of the steel industry (lost 200,000 production jobs and 20 percent of its market), wage rates were only responsible for 3 percent of the loss in employment from 1976 to 1983,[57] whereas other factors accounted for the remaining loss.

## Labor Union Influence on Specific Compensation Decisions

Unions influence the compensation decision-making process in many ways. Besides influencing wages and benefits and, therefore , direct labor costs , unions also influence many indirect labor costs. For example, a union may negotiate over the length of rest breaks. Because rest breaks are usually with pay, the results of the negotiation affect indirect costs. Labor unions will participate in decisions over virtually any issue that has an impact on their membership.

This section discusses the main ways in which unions influence both direct and indirect costs of labor, as well as the main issues in which unions seek involvement.

## Influence on Wage and Benefit Decisions

One of the main goals of a union is to increase the average wage and benefit levels of its members. This happens in several ways. First, the union attempts to increase the real wage level of its members over time. *Real wages* can be defined as the buying power of money; they take into account the cost of living. To this end, the union will want to negotiate wage increases that are larger than the increase in the cost of living (although this is not always possible) at the time contracts are negotiated.[58]

One of the ways unions protect real wages in contracts of multiple-year duration is through *cost-of-living adjustment clauses* (COLAs). A COLA clause provides for an automatic increase in wages anytime the cost of living (as measured by the Consumer Price Index) goes up by an agreed amount.[59] These clauses are popular with unions because they achieve labor's goal of maintaining real wages. The COLA clauses are, however, problematic for management because they assume that management can pass the additional costs on to the consumer. Management tends to resist COLA clauses because of the uncertain impact on labor costs and product costs. Evidence shows that there is a positive relationship between the length of a contract and the existence of a COLA provision.[60]

Unions would also like to see the average wage level of their members increase relative to that of other workers. Between 1987 and 1989, wage increases for union employees were significantly less than for nonunion employees when comparing all workers, but unionized manufacturing workers did better than nonunionized manufacturing workers.[61] It should not be surprising that unions want to justify their existence to members, and one way to do this is to show that members of the union are better off than other employees by virtue of their union membership. The union wage premium may, in reality, have an adverse effect on union membership; unionized employers may lay off workers because of a declining market share which they blame on higher labor costs. One study reviewing current population survey data found a significant relationship between union wage premiums and loss of union membership.[62]

Unions would also like to enhance the benefits their members receive relative to other groups.[63] Thus it is reasonable to expect unions to ask for a pension plan, severance pay, and more liberal vacation policies for union members relative to other employees. Whether unions are successful at these endeavors is likely to be dependent on the organization's ability to pay, the history of previous settlements, and the economic outlook for the employer in the future.

## Influence on Wage Structure Decisions

Labor unions are probably as concerned about negotiating wage and benefit structure decisions as they are about negotiating wage and benefit level decisions. Wage and benefit structure issues concern what share different members get from the item that is bargained. In most cases, not all jobs held by union members are considered equal by the union membership, and the union may wish to negotiate a certain percentage differential in wages between particular jobs. For example, the union might represent lathe operators and machine attendants. The union might want the machine attendant to make 80 percent of what the lathe operator makes, whereas management may want the machine attendant to make only 60 percent of what the lathe operator makes. This issue must be negotiated at the bargaining table.

Unions will usually prefer to negotiate a set wage rate rather than a wage range. A *wage range* is defined as the variation in pay that is available in a job. If a wage range is to be used, the unions normally bargain strongly for movement through the range to be based on seniority, not merit. Because of the competitive nature of most product markets, many firms desire to relate employees' wages to some performance index. By relating pay to performance, the companies are better able to control labor cost and remain competitive. Unions are concerned with any subjective performance assessment system because they believe such systems permit personal feeling to be more a determinant of an employee's wage increase than the employee's actual performance. There is considerable controversy over how to assess an employee's contribution to an organization effectively; performance assessment is discussed in Chapter 11.

Just as unions want to negotiate the distribution of wages among jobs in the bargaining unit, they wish to negotiate the distribution of employee benefits. As an example, it is common practice to allocate the vacation time that an employee is to receive on the basis of seniority; the longer the employee works for the company, the more days of vacation will be provided. If labor and management have agreed that 1 additional day of vacation will be granted each year (the benefit level decision), the next issue is how will that vacation day be distributed among union members (the benefit structure decision). Management may want to allocate the additional day across the board—all union employees will get the additional day. However, the union members may want to increase the vacation time for only those union members with 10 or more years of service. The union might bargain for those with less than 10 years of service to get no extra days of vacation, those with 10 years of service to get 2 extra days of vacation, those with 15 years of service to get 3 extra days, and those with 20 years of service to get 5 extra days. The total days would add up to 1 additional day of vacation on average for all employees in the union.

The distribution of the wage and benefit package can have considerable impact on the direct labor costs of the firm. In the vacation allocation example, wages will be higher for more senior employees because of both their seniority and the jobs that they hold. If the employees with greater seniority also possess greater skills and knowledge, replacing them during vacation time with workers who have similar skills will require higher wage rates than replacing a person in a lower-skilled position. Thus the union's preferred distribution of the additional vacation day may result in higher labor costs than management's preferred distribution. For this reason, compensation decision makers should be concerned about both the apparent change in wage level negotiated and the real wage level change that results from the distribution of wages and benefits.

### *Influence on Income Security*

In the past 20 years, unions have been interested in protecting the income of their members through several mechanisms. One of these mechanisms is the *Supplementary Unemployment Benefit* (SUB). A SUB plan is set up to entitle employees to supplemental benefits over and above the normal unemployment benefits that they would receive should they be laid off from work. The fund for SUB is typically established by management out of current operating funds. When employees are laid off, they collect from the fund. For example, one plan allows for SUB payments to supplement unemployment insurance up to 80 percent of the employee's base pay. Benefits stop when the employee returns to work or when the fund is exhausted.[64]

A second approach by unions to income security is the *Guaranteed Annual Wage*. Under this plan, labor and management agree to a guaranteed annual wage (for example, 80 percent of annual base wage). In this situation, an employee who works zero hours during a year would receive 80 percent of normal pay.[65]

Both plans and Guaranteed Annual Wage plans are generally resisted by management. Such plans increase income security for union members at the expense of increased financial pressure on management. Few companies in today's economy are likely to be receptive to these financial burdens, especially because the burden falls at a time when organizations are themselves struggling to remain healthy. A minority of all labor and management agreements in effect have provisions for these plans.

## Labor Union Involvement in Compensation Decision Making

In general, unions wish to participate in any decisions that influence the terms and conditions of employment for their membership. The obvious decisions are wages and benefits, and often these are negotiated at the bargaining table. However, labor–management contracts cannot anticipate all the events that might disrupt a contract over its lifetime. As a result, labor and management often establish permanent or *ad hoc* joint committees to deal with issues relevant for union members and the organization. Committees most relevant to compensation issues will be briefly discussed.

### *Job Classification Committee*

Job evaluation is the process of determining the relative worth of jobs. (Chapter 8 in the text is devoted to job evaluation.) Very often labor and management set up a job classification (evaluation) committee to reanalyze the worth of jobs.

During the course of a contract, it is not uncommon for the jobs in which union members work to change. This change can result from new technology, new work processes, or both. When such changes occur, there is a need to reassess the value of jobs. One way to do this would be to reopen the contract. This, of course, has the potential of leading to a strike or lockout over a dispute.

Many unions and organizations, therefore, have adopted joint job evaluation committees to deal with job evaluation issues in lieu of contract reopening. Exhibit 4.5 is a union–management contract clause that provides for such a committee.

Such committees result in indirect cost increases to the firm because they are likely to consume considerable management time and require union members to be away from their work stations, thereby increasing labor costs. The impact of such committees on direct labor costs probably depends on the nature of the changes in jobs. Whether re-evaluation of jobs will result in higher or lower wages is an empirical question.

## Wage and Benefits Survey Committee

Many times employers act unilaterally in gathering survey data for making compensation decisions. Unions often conduct their own surveys. In other cases the two parties jointly seek out survey data for comparative wage purposes. Both labor and management will initially wish to use comparative survey data that are most favorable to their position and most unfavorable (probably) to the other side's position. However, joint committees might discuss the different types of data that are available and establish criteria for the acceptance of particular data. (A later chapter discusses the types and sources of data that are available to management and, in some cases, labor.)

As with job evaluation committees, the largest costs of such committees are likely to be the costs associated with employee time away from normal job duties and the administrative costs for management.

## Incentive Plan Committee

Employers may set up an incentive plan to encourage employees to work at higher levels of productivity. Such plans are subject to negotiation at the bargaining table. Incentive plans must also be managed on a day-to-day basis, and unions may wish to participate in this process. Exhibit 4.6 presents a labor–management contract clause providing for a joint committee.

Joint committees for the management of such plans are probably desirable.[66] In a later chapter, the issue of employee resistance to incentive plans is discussed. Part of that resistance has to do with fears that management will manipulate the plan to the employees' disadvantage. Joint participation probably helps reassure employees that the plan is fair. Joint decision making also will allow union input into daily management of the plan. The cost to management of such joint action is, again, the time that it may require employees to be away from their normal duties.

## Health Care Benefits Committee

Both labor and management are concerned with the ever increasing costs of health care and related benefits. Labor desires at the very least to maintain the existing benefits and hopefully increase the level of health care coverage. Management, experiencing cost increases in the double digits, is constantly

| EXHIBIT 4.5 | C. DESCRIPTION AND CLASSIFICATION OF NEW OR CHANGED JOBS |
|---|---|

**Section A**

1. Description and Classification of Jobs

   In the interest of the effective administration of the Job Description and Classification procedures as set forth in the May 6, 1950 Agreement between the parties, a plant union committee on job classification (hereinafter called the plant union committee) consisting of three employees designated by the Union shall be established in each plant.

   The job description and classification for each job in effect as of the date of this Agreement shall continue in effect unless (1) Management changes the job content (requirements of the job as to training, skill, responsibility, and working conditions) to the extent of one full job class or more; (2) the job is terminated by Management or not occupied during a period of one year; or (3) the description and classification are changed in accordance with mutual agreement of officially designated representatives of the Company and the Union.

   When and if from time to time the Company, at its discretion, establishes a new job or changes the job content (requirements of the job as to training, skill, responsibility, and working conditions) of an existing job to the extent of one full job class or more, a new job description and classification for the new or changed job shall be established in accordance with the following procedure:

   a. Management will develop a description and classification of the job in accordance with provisions of the May 6, 1950, Agreement between the parties hereto.

   b. The proposed description and classification will be submitted to the plant union committee for approval, and the standard salary scale rate for the job class to which the job is thus assigned shall apply in accordance with the provisions of Subsection B of this Section. At the same time copies of the proposed description and classification shall be sent to a designated representative of the International Union. If the job involves new-type facilities or a new-type job, special designation of this fact shall be made.

   c. The plant union committee and Management shall discuss and determine the accuracy of the job description.

   d. If Management and the plant union committee are unable to agree upon the description and classification, Management shall install the proposed classification, and the standard salary scale rate for the job class to which the job is thus assigned shall apply in accordance with provisions of Subsection B of this Section. The plant union committee shall be exclusively responsible for the filing of grievances and may at any time within 30 days from the date of installation file a grievance with the plant management representative designated by the Company alleging that the job is improperly described and/or classified under the provisions of the May 6, 1950 Agreement. Thereupon the plant union committee and Management shall prepare and mutually sign a stipulation setting forth the factors and factor codings which are in dispute. Thereafter such grievance shall be referred by the respective parties to their Third Step Representative for further consideration. In the event the Third Step Representatives are unable to agree on the description and classification within 30 days, they shall prepare and mutually sign a stipulation (which may amend the stipulation set forth by the plant union committee and Management) setting forth the factors and factor codings which are in dispute and a summary stating reasons for the respective positions of the parties at both the plant committee and the Third Step levels, copy of which shall be sent to a designated representative of Management and the aforementioned representative of the International Union. The receipt by the Union's Third Step representative of such stipulation and summary shall be deemed to be receipt of the minutes for the purposes of time limit requirements in making an appeal to arbitration.

e. In the event the parties fail to agree as provided, and no request for review or arbitration is made within the time provided, the classification as prepared by the Company shall be deemed to be approved.

f. In the event Management does not develop a new job description and classification, the plant union committee may, if initiated promptly, process a complaint under the complaint and grievance procedure of this Agreement requesting that a job description and classification be developed and installed in accordance with the provisions of the May 6, 1950 Agreement. The resulting classification shall be effective as of the date when the new job was established or the change or changes installed.

---

Excerpted from "Agreement between USS Division of USX Corporation and the United St of America," *Salaried Employee*, February 1, 1987.

searching for ways to contain health care costs. Management's goal is not so much to reduce coverage but to control the cost to remain competitive in the product market. Companies have formed joint committees with labor to study the health care issue and to make recommendations that will maintain the level of coverage but provide the benefits through a lower cost delivery system. For example, the 1990 UAW and General Motors Corporation agreement provides for funds up to $2,250,000 that can be spent over the 3-year contract on mutually agreed studies, pilot programs, and consultants.

## Interpreting Contract Rights Related to Compensation Issues

Once a labor–management contract has been bargained at the table and ratified by the membership, the two parties must live by that agreement for its life. During the life of the contract, many questions as to the rights of the respective parties under the contract are likely to arise. Compensation issues that may lead to contract interpretation questions include the following: Does a supervisor have the right to order an employee to work overtime? Can a pay increase be denied an employee because of poor attendance?

Even though the contract might address such issues as how overtime is to be allocated or what standards are to be used in giving pay increases, often the wording of the contract is unclear or vague or the parties may have different interpretations of what the words mean. When this occurs, there is a strong likelihood of a strike or lockout if there is no method to deal with the dispute. Most labor–management contracts provide for a grievance procedure that allows the specific issue to be aired.

Typically, if the two parties cannot agree about the issue, the grievance process ultimately requires that a neutral third party arbitrate the issue. That is,

**EXHIBIT 4.6**    ILLUSTRATE WAGE INCENTIVE PLANS

### Allis Chalmers Corporation, West Allis Plant and Auto Workers

### Expires January 31, 1986

Section 14. An employee having a question concerning an established Incentive Standard or the revision of an Incentive Standard on a work assignment to which he has been assigned may present it to his Foreman after having worked on the assignment for a sufficient length of time to insure that the Incentive Standard has been given a reasonable trial.

If the work assignment in question is within a group of work assignments, the employee at that time may request the isolation of that work assignment in order to identify performance for purposes of investigation and resolution of the question.

If the question is not resolved by the Foreman to the employee's satisfaction, the question may be referred to the Industrial Engineering Department. If necessary, the Industrial Engineering Department shall conduct a floor review or timestudy and promptly report the results to the Steward.

If the question remains unresolved, it may be processed as a grievance through the steps of the grievance procedure short of arbitration. A representative of the industrial engineering department will be present at second step grievance meetings where the issues being discussed require his presence. The exclusive procedure for further processing of an unresolved question which has arisen under this Article and is arbitrable shall be as provided in paragraphs 170-179.

Section 15. If the question is not satisfactorily adjusted within 10 work days after discussion in the third step of the Grievance Procedure, the Union may certify it to the Impartial Referee selected in accordance with the procedure provided in Article VIII, Section H, within 30 work days after the third step discussion for a special Impartial Referee hearing. The provisions of paragraph 235 shall apply at this point. If the assignment in question (or one sufficiently similar to make a review of it relevant) is not performed in this time period, and the Union desires to study it prior to processing the grievance further, the 30 work days shall be extended until one week, or more by mutual agreement, after there has been an opportunity for such a study. The special hearing procedure is as follows:

    1. The parties shall make every effort to select an independent Industrial Engineer and notify him and the Impartial Referee of its certification of the question for a special Impartial Referee hearing.

If the parties are unable to select an independent Industrial Engineer within 2 weeks after certification of the question, they shall by joint letter request the Federal Mediation and Conciliation Service to submit to them a list of names of 7 qualified and experienced Industrial Engineers.

    2. If the parties cannot agree upon one of the persons named on the list, the Company and the Union shall strike a name alternately beginning with the Company until one name remains. Such remaining person shall act as the Industrial Engineer.

    3. Immediately following the selection of the Industrial Engineer or Industrial Engineering firm, a meeting among appropriate Company and Union representatives and the Industrial Engineer shall be arranged at the Plant. This meeting shall be for the purpose of presenting all necessary facts of the dispute to the Industrial Engineer.

    4. In addition to hearing pertinent statements by the Union and the Company, the Industrial Engineer may make such observation and study of the operation in

question as is necessary to enable him to make accurate findings of fact in the case and shall have access to information pertinent to the dispute, including Standard Data and any time recording of the operation.

5. Upon completion of his study the Industrial Engineer shall send a report of his findings to the Union, the Company and the Impartial Referee.

6. Upon receipt of the Industrial Engineer's report the Union, the Company and the Impartial Referee shall meet to present their positions, including written summaries thereof, to the Impartial Referee on the question. At the instance of the Impartial Referee, the Industrial Engineer shall also be present.

7. Thereafter the Impartial Referee shall render his decision which shall be binding upon the Union, the employees and the Company, provided it is within the scope of his jurisdictional authority.

8. The jurisdictional authority of the Impartial Referee is restricted to the determination of questions which have been submitted to him by the parties concerning compliance with the provisions of this Article.

---

both parties will make their case to the arbitrator, and the arbitrator will make a determination for one of the parties. Usually, the arbitrator's decision is final and binding (binding arbitration), and the parties must live by the decision. Only if the issue is renegotiated at the next contract renewal will the decision change.

The grievance procedure is one more example of joint decision making between the union and management. As indicated earlier, the due process system can involve issues of compensation. In such cases, the compensation decision maker should be included. For example, an employee may interpret the contract to find the total number of paid vacation days was incorrectly calculated. If this issue is grieved, which it most likely would be, the compensation decision maker should be included to ensure that both employees and management interpret the contract properly from the compensation expert's viewpoint. The compensation decision maker also needs to ascertain the implications of differing interpretations for the compensation cost structure. Immediate costs of grievance procedures are the cost of staff time and the lost labor of union members who are away from their normal duties.

# Summary

This chapter addresses two important constraints on the compensation decision-making process: labor markets and labor unions.

Internal labor markets require organizations to focus on equity in pay relationships among jobs within the organization. The process for doing this is job evaluation. Inferences drawn from the operation of the internal labor market also suggest that organizations may have some degree of latitude in establishing the wage payments for higher-level jobs, but wage payments to low-level (entry-level) jobs are probably most sensitive to competitive wage rates in the external labor market. Organizations, as a result, are probably most concerned about being wage competitive in the market for these entry-level jobs.

Internal labor markets arise out of the sociotechnical system of the organization. They persist over time because the advantages for both employees and employers apparently outweigh the disadvantages. Internal labor markets as a phenomenon hold implications for compensation decision making. The analysis of the internal labor market concept suggests that (1) organizations may have considerable discretion over wage payments for certain jobs; (2) organizations should be concerned that certain jobs (entry-level) are wage competitive in the labor market; and (3) there may be a greater concern about perceived fairness in wage payments between certain jobs (internal equity) than about fairness relative to the external labor market (external equity).

Interindustry wage structure was defined. Evidence generally supports the presence of an interindustry wage differential. That is, the same job will be paid proportionately more or less depending on the industry in which it is located. The general causes of interindustry wage differentials are based on the industry's product market, competitive profitability, level of employment, degree of capital intensity, and the level of union density.

Labor unions are also an important constraint faced by organizations. The constraint is most severe for those organizations that have a union representing some, or all, of their employees. This chapter discusses the main issues that unions bargain over. It presents a conceptual framework for understanding the bargaining process. Unions attempt to influence the terms and conditions of employment for their members. In the case of compensation, unions attempt to influence wages and benefits through collective bargaining. Labor–management negotiations cover wage, benefit level, wage structure, and nonwage issues that have an effect on labor costs. Several of the more common ways in which unions share in joint decision making over compensation issues range from joint decisions at the bargaining table to standing or *ad hoc* joint committees to the grievance procedure itself. In the unionized context, compensation decision makers can expect to have unions involved in the compensation decision-making process.

## Discussion Questions

1. Identify how a job you have worked at fits into the internal labor market in that organization.

2. What variables would influence a person high in a firm's internal labor market not to quit a job even though he or she does not like the work?

3. Discuss the bargaining process that labor and management go through in arriving at a contract. When would it pay one side to bluff at the table?

4. Discuss the limitations faced by an employer who might want to have a preventive labor relations strategy of paying a wage premium.

5. How does the presence of the union influence the compensation decision-making process?

## EXERCISE

An employer has 20 union employees working in the shop. These employees are allocated among three jobs as follows:

Machine operator: 10 employees
Machine attendant: 5 employees
General laborer: 5 employees

The employees currently receive the following pay rates per contract:

All machine operators make $9.20 per hour.
All machine attendants make $8.00 per hour.
All general laborers make $6.00 per hour.

A. In contract negotiations the employer and the union agree: (1) to a 10 percent wage increase for machine operators, (2) that the machine attendants new wage will be 90 percent of the machine operator's rate, and (3) that the general laborer wage rate will be 70 percent of the machine operator's rate.

   1. Calculate the current hourly wage bill for the employer.
   2. Calculate the new contract hourly wage bill for the employer.
   3. What effective percentage increase is the new wage bill relative to the old wage bill?
   4. Calculate the current wage level (average wage ) for the employer.
   5. Calculate the new wage level (average wage) for the employer.
   6. What effective percentage increase in the wage level (average wage) will the employer realize?
   7. Is the percentage wage bill increase equal to the percentage wage level increase? Why or why not?
   8. Discuss your findings in class. Does the real percentage increase in labor costs depend on how one calculates the numbers?
   9. Which job got the largest percentage wage rate increase?

B. In part A, did you use. the current or new machine operator wage in calculating the rate differential (wage structure) for the machine attendant and general laborer wage rates? Using the alternate that you did not use in Part A, reanswer questions 1 to 9.

C. Does contract language interpretation make a difference in effective costs?

## References

[1] For further elaboration and development of the internal market concept, see P. B. Doeringer and M. I. Piore, *Internal Labor Markets and Manpower Analysis* (Lexington, MA: D.C. Heath, 1971).

[2] L. G. Reynolds, *Labor Economics and Labor Relations*, 6th ed. (Englewood Cliffs, NJ: Prentice-Hall, Inc., 1974), 112–140.

[3] *Ibid.*

[4] T. J. Bergmann and F. S. Hills, "Internal Labor Markets and Indirect Pay Discrimination," *Compensation Review* 14 (1982), 41–50.

[5] Doeringer and Piore, *Internal Labor Markets and Manpower Analysis.*

[6] H. G. Heneman III and M. G. Sandvar, "Markov Analysis in Human Resource Administration: Applications and Limitations," *Academy of Management Review* 2 (1977), 22–23.

[7] For a general discussion of the isolation hypothesis, see F. S. Hills and R. E. Hughes, "Salaries and Fringe Benefits in an Academic Labor Market: Internal/External Labor Markets and Geographic Differentials" (paper presented at the 37th annual Academy of Management meeting, Orlando, FL, August 1977).

[8] Doeringer and Piore, *Internal Labor Markets and Manpower Analysis.*

[9] *Ibid.*

[10] K. M. Rowland and M. G. Sovereign, "Markov Chain Analysis of Internal Manpower Supply," *Industrial Relations* 9 (1969), 88–99.

[11] J. Ford et al., "Internal Labour Market Processes," *Industrial Relations Journal* (Summer 1984), 42.

[12] *Ibid.*

[13] 415 F. Supp. 761.

[14] Doeringer and Piore, *Internal Labor Markets and Manpower Analysis.*

[15] M. J. Piore, "On the Job Training and Adjustments to Technological Change," *Journal of Human Resources* 3 (Fall 1968), 435–449.

[16] R. W. Beatty and J. R. Beatty, "Some Problems with Contemporary Job Evaluation Systems" in *Comparable Worth and Wage Discrimination: Technical Possibilities and Political Realities*, ed. Helen Remick (Philadelphia: Temple University Press, 1984), 59–60.

[17] A. B. Krueger and L. H. Summers, "Reflections on Inter-Industry Wage Structure" in *Unemployment and the Structure of the Labor Market*, eds. K. Lang and J. S. Leonard (New York: Basil Blackwell, 1987), 17–47.

[18] *Ibid.*

[19] A. B. Krueger and L. H. Summers, "Efficiency Wages and the Inter-Industry Wage Structure" (mimeo, Harvard University, 1986).

[20] Krueger and Summers, "Reflections on Inter-Industry Wage Structure."

[21] *Ibid.*

[22] *Ibid.*

[23] *Ibid.*

[24] W. T. Dickens and L. F. Katz, "Inter-Industry Wage Differences and Industry Characteristics" in *Unemployment and the Structure of Labor Markets*, eds. K. Lang and J. S. Leonard (New York: Basil Blackwell, 1987), 48–49.

[25] M. Podgursky, "Union, Establishment Size, and Intra-Industry Threat Effects," *Industrial and Labor Relations Review* 39 (1986), 277–284.

[26] K. Lang, J. S. Leonard, and D. M. Lilien, "Labor Market Structure, Wages and Unemployment," in *Unemployment and the Structure of Labor Markets*, eds. K. Lang and J. S. Leonard (New York: Basil Blackwell, 1987).

[27] J. A. Fossum, *Labor Relations*, 4th ed. (Homewood, IL: BPI/Irwin, 1989).

[28] L. Uchitelle, "Blue-Collar Compromises in Pursuit of Job Security," *New York Times* C x LI (April 19, 1992), Y1, 13.

[29] J. R. Hicks, *The Theory of Wages*, 2d ed. (New York: St. Martin's, 1966).

[30] Fossum, *Labor Relations.*

[31] J. R. Stepp, R. P. Baker, and J. T. Barret, "Helping Labor and Management Solve Problems," *Monthly Labor Review* (November 1982), 22–28; H. E. Myer, "The Decline of Strikes," *Fortune* 104 (February 1981), 66–84 N2.

[32] D. J. B. Mitchell, "Collective Bargaining and Compensation in the Public Sector," in *Public-Sector Bargaining*, 2d ed., eds. B. Aaron, J. M. Najita, and J. L. Stern (Washington, DC : The Bureau of National Affairs, Inc., 1988), 124–159.

[33] Mills, *Labor–Management Relations* (New York: McGraw-Hill, 1978).

[34] *Ibid.*

[35] D. J. B. Mitchell, *Unions, Wages, and Inflation* (Washington, DC: Brookings Institute, 1980), 80–83.

[36] S. B. Jarrell and T. D. Stanley, "A Meta-Analysis of the Union-Nonunion Wage Gap," *Industrial and Labor Relations Review* 44 (October 1990), 54–67.

[37] P. D. Linneman, M. L. Wachter, and W. H. Carter, "Evaluating the Evidence on Union Employment and Wages," *Industrial and Labor Relations Review* 44 (October 1990), 34–53.

[38] D. G. Blanchflower and R. B. Freeman, "Unionism in the United States and Other Advanced OFCD Countries," *Industrial Relations* 31 (Winter 1992), 56–79.

[39] D. L. Belman and P. B. Voos, "Wage Effects of Increased Union Coverage:

Methodological Considerations and New Evidence," *Industrial and Labor Relations Review* 46 (January, 1993), 368–380.

[40] For recent research on these issues, see Richard B. Freeman, "Is Declining Unionization of the U.S. Good, Bad or Irrelevant?" in *Unions and Economic Competitiveness,* eds. L. Mishel and P. B. Voos (Armonk, NY: M. E. Shape, Inc., 1992), 143–169; B. T. Hirsch, "The Interindustry Structure of Unionism, Earnings, and Earnings Dispersion," *Industrial and Labor Relations Review* 36 (October 1982), 22–39.

[41] C. Brown, "Firms' Choice of Methods of Pay," *Industrial and Labor Relations Review* 86 (February 1990), 165–182; R. B. Freeman and M. Kleiner, "The Impact of New Unionization on Wages and Working Conditions," *Journal of Labor Economics* 8 (January 1990), 8–25.

[42] Agreement between UAW and the General Motors Corporation , September 17, 1990.

[43] R. B. Freeman and M. M. Kleiner, "Employer Behavior in the Face of Union Organizing Drive," *Industrial and Labor Relations Review* 43 (April 1990), 351–365; D. Macpherson and J. Stewart, "Union and the Dispersion of Wages Among Blue Collar Workers," *Journal of Labor Research* 8 (Fall 1987), 395–495; R. B. Freeman, "Unionism Comes to the Public Sector," *Journal of Economic Literature* 24 (March 1986), 41–86.

[44] D. G. Blanchflower and R. B. Freeman, "Unionism in the United States and Other Advanced OFCD Countries," *Industrial Relations* 31 (Winter 1992), 56–79.

[45] K. Jennings and E. Traynham, "The Wage of Two-Tier Pay Plans," *Personnel Journal* 67 (March 1988), 56–63; Augsti, K. F., "Non Wage Benefits as a Limited Dependent Variable: Implications for the Impacts of Unions," *Journal of Labor Research* 14 (Winter, 1993), 29–40.

[46] S. Allen and R. Clark, "Unions , Pension Wealth , and Age-Compensation Profiles," *Industrial and Labor Relations Review* 42 (April 1988), 342–359.

[47] Blanchflower, and Freeman, "Unionism in the United States and Other Advanced OFCD Countries."

[48] A. E. Eaton and P. B. Voos, "Unions and Contemporary Innovations in Work Organization, Compensation, and Employee Participation," in *Unions and Economic Competitiveness,* eds. L. Mishel and P. B. Voos (Armonk, NY: M. E. Sharpe, 1992), 15–37.

[49] Blanchflower and Freeman, "Unionism in the United States and Other Advanced OFCD Countries."

[50] *Ibid.*

[51] *Ibid.*

[52] L. Solnick, "The Effect of the Blue Collar Unions on White Collar Wages and Benefits," *Industrial and Labor Relations Review* 38 (1985), 23–35.

[53] T. Karier, "Trade Deficits and Labor Unions: Myths and Realities," in *Unions and Economic Competitiveness,* eds. L. Mishel and P. B. Voos (Armonk, NY: M. E. Shape, 1992).

[54] *Ibid.*

[55] *Ibid.*

[56] *Ibid.*

[57] *Ibid.*

[58] S. Aronowitz, *False Promises* (Durham, NC: Duke University Press, 1992).

[59] R. H. Ferguson, *Cost-of-Living Adjustments in Union Management Agreements* (New York: Cornell University, 1976).

[60] K. J. Murphy, "Determinants of Contract Duration in Collective Bargaining Agreements," *Industrial and Labor Relations Review* 45 (January 1992), 352–365.

[61] K. E. Anderson, P. M. Doyle, and A. E. Schwenk, "Union–Nonunion Pay Differences," *Monthly Labor Review* 113 (June, 1990), 26–38.

[62] P. D. Linneman, M. L. Wachta, and W. H. Carter, "Evaluating the Evidence on Union Employment and Wages," *Industrial and Labor Relations Review* 44 (October, 1990), 34–53.

[63] Fossum, *Labor Relations.*

[64] J. S. Rosenbloom and G. V. Hallman, *Employee Benefit Planning* (Englewood Cliffs, NJ: Prentice-Hall, 1981).

[65] H. A. Young and M. F. Dougherty, "Influence of the Guaranteed Annual Wage upon Labor Relations and Productivity: National Sugar Refinery's Experience," *Management of Personnel Quarterly* (Winter 1971), 27.

[66] M. J. Wallace, Jr., "Work Design, Teams and Rewards at Saturn Corporation," *ACA Journal* 2 (Spring/Summer 1993), 6–13.

# 5

# The Legal Environment

## Learning Objectives

**To review the major legislation that influences compensation decision making.**

**To learn what each law requires and to whom the law applies.**

**To learn the main provisions of each law.**

**To learn which agency enforces each law.**

**To learn how each law affects compensation decision making.**

## Introduction

Societies have been regulating wage and salary payments for most of recorded history. During the Middle Ages, for example, the Church and State of England regulated wages through the *Just Wage Doctrine*. The doctrine was based on the idea that occupations can be rank ordered according to the value they provide to society. Consequently, a just wage for members of an occupation is one that is consistent with the occupation's value to society. The Just Wage Doctrine is an example of an early attempt to establish relative pay differentials between occupational groups and between jobs within a given organization.

This chapter examines main federal legislation that influences compensation decision making. The chapter discusses (1) wage and hour laws, (2) income continuity protection laws, (3) mandatory retirement security law, (4) laws regulating voluntarily provided pension and welfare benefits, and (5) other regulation.

## Wage and Hour Laws

The laws discussed in this section were passed to ensure that the employment agreement (exchange) between the employer and employee is not based on the employee's desperation for paid work but on a "fair" exchange between the work provided and the pay received for that work. These laws are the Fair Labor Standards Act of 1938 (FLSA) and the Equal Pay Act of 1963 (EPA), which amended the FLSA. Also included in this category are federal laws which apply to federal government contractors and which govern their employees' wages and hours of work. These laws contain requirements that are similar or related to the requirements of the FLSA. The main contractor laws discussed in this chapter are the Davis-Bacon Act of 1931, the Copeland Act of 1934, the Walsh-Healy Public Contracts Act of 1936, and the McNamara-O'Hara Services Act of 1965. Nearly all states also have laws governing minimum wages and maximum hours of work, patterned after federal wage and hour law. Because of space constraints, state wage and hour laws are not discussed in this book.

## Fair Labor Standards Act (FLSA) of 1938

The FLSA[1] regulates minimum wage, child labor, and overtime pay; it also prohibits pay differentials based on sex. The act requires employers to keep specific records of time worked and pay received by each employee. The record-keeping requirement is used as evidence in determining compliance with the law.

The original intent of the FLSA was to protect workers from two main problems caused by the Great Depression: deflation and unemployment. The act's minimum wage provision fought deflation by increasing the purchasing power of low-paid workers. The child labor and overtime pay provisions reduced unemployment of adults by prohibiting or restricting employment of children and by mandating overtime pay. These provisions eliminated the practice of hiring children at $.10 per day when adults had to be paid $1.00 per day. It also encouraged expansion of work forces by making it cheaper to hire additional workers than to pay existing workers overtime pay.

Currently, the FLSA covers about 50 million workers. It requires extensive record-keeping and provides substantial penalties for violators. The act applies equally to citizens, legal aliens, and illegal aliens. Some employers for a time avoided compliance to FLSA and other employment laws by arbitrarily calling their alien workers "independent contractors." The 1986 Immigration Reform and Control Act (IRCA) ended that loophole; it requires treatment of most alien workers as employees, rather than as independent contractors.[2] Despite the above qualifier, not all employees or employers are covered by the FLSA. Exhibit 5.1 defines the FLSA's categories of covered employee and covered enterprise.

---

**EXHIBIT 5.1**    **FAIR LABOR STANDARDS ACT'S DEFINITIONS OF COVERED EMPLOYEE AND COVERED ENTERPRISE**

---

A covered employee is one who is

    (a)   engaged in interstate commerce; or

    (b)   engaged in the production of goods for interstate commerce; or

    (c)   employed by an "enterprise" that is either engaged in interstate commerce or in the production of goods for interstate commerce; or

    (d)   a private household domestic service worker.

An employer is a covered "enterprise" if it has

    (a)   two or more employees engaged in interstate commerce or in the production of goods for interstate commerce.

        "Engaged in" includes handling, selling, or working on goods that have been produced for commerce by anyone, or working on goods that have moved in commerce.

        Some industries must also meet a $500,000 volume of business tests, but not hospitals.

        Enterprise coverage is not based on activities of individual employees; if there is coverage, then all individuals meeting FLSA requirements are covered.

---

**Minimum Wage Provision**   This provision requires covered employers to pay a minimum hourly wage specified by the act, to covered employees, regardless of whether employees are paid hourly, by salary, or on an incentive basis. Since 1938, the minimum wage has been raised a number of times, most recently in 1991. At that time, Congress also established a *training wage* which, subject to some constraints, allows employers to pay 85 percent of the minimum wage as a training wage for the first 3 months of employment.[3]

**Child Labor Provision**   This provision sets forth standards for employing children between the ages of 14 and 18 years. Under very restricted conditions, 14 and 15 year olds may be employed in nonmanufacturing and nonhazardous manufacturing jobs. Less stringent conditions apply to minors between the ages of 16 and 18 years. Within the established restrictions, children employed in covered enterprises are included in the FLSA's minimum wage and overtime pay provisions.

**Overtime Pay Provision**   Certain employees within a covered group may be exempted from FLSA's overtime provision. The overtime exemptions are complicated, and the burden is on the employer to establish that one or more of the 34 total or partial exemptions applies. Unless exempt, employees must be paid at one and one-half times their "regular hourly rate" for all hours worked in excess of 40 in a work week. Hospitals and nursing homes (profit and nonprofit)[4] are examples of a group that is subject to a special provision that allows employers to enter into a prior agreement with their employees to compute pay on the basis of a 14-consecutive-day "work week," with overtime paid for all hours over 8 in a day and over 80 in the 14-day period. Coverage also extends to institutions connected with the operation of a hospital, such as schools for mentally or physically handicapped and rehabilitation centers. Exhibit 5.2 describes five of the most common exemptions from the FLSA's overtime pay provision.

**Equal Pay Provision**   Enacted in 1963 as an Amendment to the FLSA, the EPA makes it unlawful for an employer to discriminate

> between employees on the basis of sex by paying wages to such employees [of one sex]...at a rate less than the rate at which he pays wages to employees of the opposite sex...for equal work on jobs the performance of which requires equal skill, effort and responsibility, and which are performed under similar working conditions, except where such payment is made pursuant to (i) a seniority system; (ii) a merit system; (iii) a system which measures earnings by quantity or quality of production; or (iv) a differential based on any other factor other than sex.

Although the above excerpt from the EPA seems straightforward, many court cases were needed before the court established that the equal work standard does not require that the jobs being compared are identical, only that they are "substantially equal" with respect to the actual work performed. For an employer

| EXHIBIT 5.2 | FIVE OF THE MOST COMMON EMPLOYEE EXEMPTIONS FROM THE FLSA'S OVERTIME PROVISION |
|---|---|

## Motor Carrier Exemption

If the Department of Transportation has the authority, whether or not exercised, to regulate hours of work, then FLSA overtime does not apply. Thus, medical service delivery personnel who transport body fluid specimens to an airport for flight to out-of-state laboratories are exempt from FLSA overtime; normal ambulance and emergency medical service personnel are not exempt.

## White Collar Exemption

Any employee employed in a *bona fide* executive, administrative, or professional capacity is exempt from the wage and hour provisions of the act. Also exempt are certain computer workers.

**An executive** is a person whose primary duty is management and who customarily and regularly supervises two or more employees and works in the exempt capacity at least 80 percent of the time and has a salary of at least $250.00/week. If the salary is less than $250.00/week but more than $154.00/week, then to be exempt the individual must also have the authority to hire, fire, or effectively recommend hiring, firing, or promoting of other employees and to use discretionary powers regularly.

**An exempt administrative employee** is one who makes at least $250.00/week and whose work consists primarily of office or nonmanual work directly related to management policies or general business operations; or one who makes more than $154.00/week and who works as above and regularly exercises discretion and independent judgment; one who directly assists a *bona fide* executive or administrative person; who works with little supervision; and who devotes at least 80 percent of time to administrative duties (other requirements also apply to educational and retail service establishments).

**A professional** is an employee whose primary duties (more than 80 percent of time) require advanced knowledge in a field of science or learning customarily acquired by a prolonged course of specialized intellectual instruction and study, as distinguished from a general academic education or apprenticeship; who consistently exercises discretion and judgment; whose output is not standardized; and who makes more than $250.00/week or holds a valid license to practice law or medicine and is engaged in that practice or is an intern or resident.

**Skilled computer-related exemption** applies to employees who are paid either a salary of not less than $170.00/week or six and one-half times the minimum wage if hourly ($27.63/hour) and whose primary duties consist of

1. Application of systems analysis techniques and procedures, including consulting with users to determine hardware, software, or system specifications; or

2. The design, development, documentation, analysis, creation, testing, or modification of systems or programs, including prototypes, based on and related to user or system design specifications; or

3. The design, documentation, testing, creation, or modification of programs related to machine operating systems; or a combination of 1 through 3.

to support a claim of pay difference due to unequal work requires showing that the male job's skill, effort, and responsibility requirements are substantially greater than those required in the female's job; the tasks involving the extra skill, effort, and responsibility consume a significant amount of time for all employees whose additional wages are in question; and the extra skill, effort, and responsibility must have a value commensurate with the questioned pay differential, as determined by the employer's own evaluation system.[5] Working conditions are considered a measure in determining equal work.

**Record-Keeping Provision**    The FLSA requires employers to keep various records on each employee. The purpose of these records is to ensure that there is adequate documentation if an investigation is necessary. For employees covered by both the minimum wage and overtime FLSA provisions, the following records are required:

1.   Personal information including employee's name, home address, occupation, sex, and date of birth (if younger than 19 years of age).

2.   Hour and day when work week begins.

3.   Total hours worked each work day and each work week.

4.   Total daily or weekly straight-time earnings.

5.   Regular hourly pay rate for any week when overtime is worked.

6.   Total overtime pay for the work week.

7.   Deductions from or additions to wages.

8.   Total wages paid each pay period.

9.   Date of payment and pay period covered.

Records, including original time cards or other time-keeping records, should be maintained for 3 years because of possible claims invoking a 3-year statute of limitations. Failure to have the required records available for inspection by Wage and Hour investigators is itself a violation of the act. If records are not available, it is presumed that they would have supported the claim of the employee or the government.

### *Wage and Hour Laws for Federal Contractors*

The contractor laws use local labor market surveys to identify the "prevailing wage" in the area and that wage becomes the minimum wage for work performed on projects contracted with the federal government. These laws vary on the dollar amount expenditures they target for coverage, the pay aspects they cover, and whether or not they apply to manufacturing or service contracts. The main government contractor compensation related laws include the following:[6]

**The Davis-Bacon of 1931** and related acts require payment of prevailing wage rates and fringe benefits on federally financed or assisted construction.

**The Copeland Act of 1934** prohibits contractors from requiring their employees to pay back some of the pay they received as a condition for continuing employment. The act was passed after it became evident that some contractors were circumventing the Davis-Bacon Act's prevailing wage provision by requiring employee kickbacks of wages paid.

**The Walsh-Healey Public Contracts Act of 1936** extended the Davis-Bacon Act to all government contract work. It requires payment of minimum wage rates and overtime pay on contracts to provide goods to the federal government.

**The McNamara-O'Hara Service Contract Act of 1965** extended labor standards to employers holding contracts or subcontracts that provide services to federal agencies. This act requires payment of minimum wage rates and overtime pay.

**The Contract Work Hours Standard Act of 1962** established uniform overtime standards that apply to the three acts discussed above. It requires all federal contractors to pay overtime to employees working on federal contracts at a rate of one and one- half times for all hours over 40 hours in a week.

**Executives orders** are issued by the President of the United States. Although these orders are not law, they have the force of law and apply to government contractors and subcontractors. **Executive Orders 11246** and **11375** prohibit discrimination on the basis of race, color, religion, sex, or national origin. **Executive Order 11141** prohibits age discrimination. **Executive Order 11914** prohibits handicap discrimination. Generally, violation of the antidiscrimination prohibitions increases the threat of losing the government contract. These orders, then, have an impact on compensation decision making which is similar to the impact made by the laws already discussed in this chapter.

## *Administration of the Wage and Hour Laws*

The Wage and Hour Division of the Department of Labor administers FLSA's minimum wage, child labor, overtime pay, and record-keeping provisions as well as the contractor laws. The division has local offices in federal buildings throughout the United States.

The FLSA's minimum wage, overtime pay, and record-keeping provisions are enforced by both private employee suits and by the Secretary of Labor acting through regional solicitors. Violators can be subject to civil, criminal, and injunctive actions. Violation of a wage and hour injunction may result in contempt of court proceedings, which may involve additional fines and/or imprisonment. Penalties for violating child labor provisions may further include personal liability of owners and managers.

FLSA's equal pay provision is enforced by the Equal Employment Opportunity Commission (EEOC). This agency is authorized to investigate charges and to bring suit for violations. Employee remedies now include receipt of compensatory and punitive damages, within limits determined by the size of the employer's work force. There is a three-year statute of limitations for "willful" violations, but the normal limitation period is two years. Although EPA complaints are frequently combined with other equal employment violations under Title VII of the 1964

Civil Rights Act, the plaintiff does not have to pursue the two avenues of recourse jointly or sequentially.

With respect to contractor laws, employers with federal contracts must post the wages of the jobs used in the contract work in a conspicuous place for their employees to see. Employers are also required under the acts to pay wages on a weekly basis. Finally, contractors must agree to allow the government to withhold accrued contract payments for the purpose of compliance with the wage provisions of the acts. Should an employee complain, the division will investigate the complaint. The division also has the power to use any portion of the withheld accrued contract payments to pay any back pay that an employee might have coming under one or more of the contractor acts. The division may also prevent an employer from holding government contracts for up to three years if found guilty of violating any contractor law.

## *Wage and Hour Laws and Compensation Decision Making*

With the exception of the equal pay provision, employer responses to the other FLSA's provisions and to the contractor laws are a clerical task. Consequently, employers should not look at the Wage and Hour Division as an adversary. Most division investigators are more interested in ensuring compliance than in prosecuting violations. As a result, most division offices are extremely helpful in aiding employers, in interpretation of the law. Compensation decision makers should, therefore, make full use of this resource in questions of FLSA interpretation.

With respect to the equal pay provision, the courts have provided some direction for compensation decision makers. First, pay policy should contain an equal pay for substantially equal work provision. Second, the equal work determination must be based on the actual work performed (content of the job) and must reflect the job's skill, effort, and responsibility requirements as well as its working conditions. Third, it is legal to pay men and women who perform substantially equal work differently if the pay system is designed to differentially recognize performance, seniority, quality or quantity of results produced, or factors other than sex. Of these four defenses, the "factors other than sex" provision is clearly ambiguous, thus the legality of its operationalization is likely to be determined through court interpretations.

The EPA amendment to the FLSA is a mandate by the federal government not to discriminate in wage and salary payments between men and women. From a compensation decision-making perspective, this means that the organization should study jobs carefully by conducting a thorough task-oriented job analysis and a subsequent job evaluation. Furthermore, the pay system should be audited regularly to determine if there are differences in pay that cannot be justified by the four exceptions under the law.

To highlight the pay system audit, suppose that an organization has a data entry clerk job in which both men and women work. Men in the job earn on average $350 per week, whereas women in the same job earn on average $300 per week. Would this be an example of illegal pay discrimination under the EPA? There may be legitimate reasons for the difference in average pay. For example, the organization may find that when it began hiring people for the job, it hired more men than women. If subsequently the organization gave pay increases as a function of length of service, the difference in average pay may be justified.

Like the FLSA, compliance with the contractor laws is largely a clerical task. The acts, nevertheless, may pose several management-related problems for contractors. For one, the acts require employers to comply only with respect to employees who work on the government contracts. Those same employers need not apply the contractor acts to employees who do not work on the government contract. If the contractor is able to pay all employees the required government contractor wages, overtime, and benefits, the potential problem of wage inequity does not exist. However, some contractors may not be financially able to maintain that pay equity. In these cases, the contractor must assess the problems that may be caused by the situation of paying different wages to workers performing the same job. Although this situation may be a candidate for the equal pay allowance of differential pay for "factors other than sex," the legality of differential pay may have to be tested in the court of law, even if based on government contract requirements. Another potential problem is the reduction of wages once the contract term expires. If the employer is unable to keep paying the previous wage rate, how will employees react to the pay cut? Obviously, the answer to this question will depend on several factors, such as availability of other jobs in the area, whether money is the primary reason for working at the current firm, and how the employer treats the employees. In any event, several potentially negative consequences may occur from severe wage reductions. These include increased absenteeism and turnover, decreased productivity, and openness to unionization.

## *Regulation of Pay Garnishment*

When do employees relinquish the rights to the wages they have earned? Prior to 1968, State law regulated a process known as garnishment. Garnishment involves the issuance of a court order requiring an employer to deduct money from an employee's paycheck to repay a bad debt that the employee has accrued.[7] State laws, although highly variable, generally worked in favor of the debt holder who asked for the court order. In some states, the law allowed the court to take 100 percent of the employee's net pay until the debt was paid off, placing a considerable burden on the employee who relied on the paycheck for food and lodging. The employer of a person whose pay was garnished often terminated that employee, creating even greater financial hardship.

**The Consumer Credit Protection Act of 1968** was designed in part to alleviate some of those problems. It established national garnishment regulation. The act applies to all employers in private employment as well as state and local governments. Federal employees' wages are exempt from garnishment. Under the act, the amount of money subject to garnishment is related to a worker's take-home pay. If a worker's take-home pay is less than a prescribed amount, no garnishment can be made. If the take-home pay is within the range of a prescribed amount, only that portion above the minimum of the range is subject to garnishment. If the take-home pay is above the maximum of the prescribed range, a maximum of 25 percent of total pay is subject to garnishment.

Under the act, wages can be garnished only by court order. Also, the employee must be given advance notice by the employer and is entitled to appear in court to argue against the garnishment. If one garnishment does not cover all the bad debt, a second garnishment or multiple garnishments may be obtained. However, a separate garnishment must be obtained for *each* pay period. The act also makes it illegal for employers to terminate employees for garnishments that result from any one bad debt.

The Consumer Credit Protection Act is enforced by the Wage and Hour Division of the Department of Labor. Violations of the law may be reported to the division.

Basically, there is little compensation-related decision making regarding garnishment law. Compliance with this law is largely a clerical task.

# Income Continuity Protection Laws

The laws discussed in this section are labeled income continuity protection laws because they were passed to ensure a flow of income during periods of intermittent unemployment or on permanent disability. The main laws that provide income continuity are Social Security, workers' compensation, and unemployment compensation.

## Social Security Act of 1935

The Social Security system is a pay-as-you-go system. Employers and employees alike are taxed equally through the Federal Insurance Contribution Act's (FICA)-specified tax payments. Social Security provides a basic floor of continuing income to ill and disabled workers, dependents of disabled workers, retired workers, and survivors of workers.

## Workers' Compensation

Workers' compensation laws are state laws, intended to continue the flow of income, for a prespecified period, for workers whose injuries are job-related (that is, arise "out of and in the course of…employment"). Although seemingly straightforward, the concept of job-relatedness is very broadly defined. Frequently, workers have been awarded compensation for injuries occurring off the job premises or after working hours or even for injuries having occurred after the worker left employment with the firm. Although injuries caused by acts of God are not generally covered, an exception exists when the employee's work requirement increases the risk of such injury. For example, a utility pole worker who is struck by lightning when working is covered because the work increases the risk of such an injury. Also covered are injuries that either lead to a disability or aggravate a pre-existing disability. An example of the former injury is a hearing loss resulting from repeated exposure to high noise levels. An example of the latter injury is a diabetic who dies from a bruise when accidentally hit by a soft object.[8]

The origin of workers' compensation laws can be traced to the Industrial Revolution. Before the Industrial Revolution, workers had personal ties with their employers, and when injury or illness kept a worker away from the job, the employer voluntarily assumed some responsibility for support of the worker and the worker's family. After the Industrial Revolution, business ownership became separated from management, the worker-management relationship became impersonal, and the worker lost assurance of care in time of need. The only legal remedies for victims of occupational injuries and illnesses came through time consuming and costly lawsuits—lawsuits that were often fruitless. Common law excluded an employer from liability if it could be shown that the worker voluntarily took the job knowing its risks, or if the worker's negligence contributed to the injury. Also, the employer was not liable to the extent that the injury was caused by the action of a fellow worker. Ironically, common law stated that only the injured worker had the right to file a lawsuit. If the worker died, the surviving dependents could not receive compensation.[9]

All these problems surfaced at the end of the nineteenth century when journalists publicized the inability of workers to gain legal redress for work-related injuries. As a result, several states passed laws designed to provide relief. In 1911, Wisconsin passed the first workers' compensation law. By 1948, every state had its own law. Such a major development would not have taken place if employers had not seen benefits to the laws. The most important benefit is that the laws exempt employers from being sued by their employees and provide a ceiling on the employers' liability.[10]

With respect to employers, workers' compensation coverage is compulsory in all states except South Carolina, New Jersey, and Texas. In these states, employers electing not to be covered can be sued by workers. In defending such suits, however, the employers are prohibited from using the previously noted common law defenses (knowledge of job risk, contributory negligence, and injury caused by action of a fellow employee). Six states (Nevada, North Dakota, Ohio, Washington, West Virginia, and Wyoming) require that employers participate in state-administered workers' compensation insurance programs. The remaining states use private insurance programs. Also, all states except North Dakota, Texas, and Wyoming permit employers to self-insure against workers' compensation claims.[11]

With respect to workers, states vary in amounts paid for permanent disabilities, the ceilings on amount of income replaced, the likelihood that a disputed worker's claim will be resolved in favor of the claimant, and the ease with which workers can collect for occupational illnesses. Despite those differences, workers' compensation laws share common features:[12]

1. **Income Loss resulting from total disability.** Typically, workers receive weekly cash payments after a brief waiting period, usually 3 to 7 days. Most cash payments are at least 66-2/3 percent of weekly pay. When added to social security, the payments cannot exceed 80 percent of weekly pay.

2. **Income loss resulting from a permanent partial disability.** Receipt of income is based on a schedule of lump-sum payments defined for permanent partial disabilities. In most states, the payments are an *addition* to the total disability benefits workers are entitled to receive.

3. **Medical expense payments.** The laws provide unlimited coverage for medical expenses resulting from injury or illness.

4. **Rehabilitation expense payments.** All states attempt to help injured or impaired workers return to the labor force. This help may include payments for tuition, meals, lodging, travel, and maintenance while obtaining vocational training.

5. **Income loss resulting from death.** Most states provide a burial allowance and also income benefits to surviving spouses and dependent children. The spouse receives the benefits until remarriage; the children receive them up to a specified age.

Also common to virtually all workers' compensation laws are the following features:[13]

1. All job related injuries and illnesses are covered.

2. Coverage is provided regardless of whose negligence caused the injury or illness.

3. Payments are usually made through an insurance program financed by employer-paid premiums.

4. There is an element of co-insurance. Co-insurance is insurance under which the beneficiary of the coverage absorbs part of the loss that is covered. Thus, the worker's loss is usually not fully covered by the workers' compensation payments.

**Administration of Workers' Compensation**   In most states, the state workers' compensation board administers the law. The board's main function is to decide disputed claims. In some states, that decision is made by the courts. Another component of the administrative system is the insurance system that pays the compensation. The company's premium rates for workers' compensation insurance are based on the company's claim experience. The rates are intended to be an incentive for employers to improve safety and health conditions on the job. Toward this goal, workers' compensation insurance carriers offer different safety program services to employers they cover.

**Workers' Compensation and Compensation Decision Making**   Although improvements in workers' compensation coverage have been made over the years, the coverage is not uniform or adequate across states. Furthermore, some states continue to have statutes of limitations for occupational disease claims. This can severely limit the claims of workers who suffer the latent effects of exposure to toxic substances and radiation. Asbestosis and black lung are two common occupational diseases with long latency periods. Although Congress has not enacted federal workers' compensation standards, employee benefit specialists think that the probable reform of state workers' compensation laws is a variable to consider in benefits planning.

## Unemployment Compensation

Unemployment compensation[14] provides income to a subset of workers who are temporarily unemployed and searching for suitable employment. Suitable employment is defined as any employment that is (1) in the worker's customary occupation, (2) located at a reasonable distance from the worker's residence, and (3) free from risk to health and safety. Like the workers' compensation system, the unemployment compensation system is based on state laws and is funded by employers. Unlike workers' compensation, it is carried out under federal supervision. Employers are subject to a federal payroll tax (FUTA), but they can get most of the tax back as a credit if they pay it into a federally approved state unemployment compensation program. To qualify for the FUTA credit, states must also comply with the following stipulations:

1. Workers earn a certain amount of pay or work a certain amount of time before becoming eligible for unemployment compensation.

2. Workers who receive compensation register at a public employment office and prove that they are available for work.

3. Compensation is denied to workers who refuse suitable offers of employment.

4. Workers may appeal through an impartial hearing process in the event that unemployment benefits are initially denied by the state.

The groundwork for unemployment compensation laws was laid by the 1935 Social Security Act. Title IX of the act provided for federally controlled unemployment insurance programs administered by the states. If states chose not to pass such laws, all covered employers in the state would have had to pay the full FUTA tax to the federal government. Needless to say, all states and the District of Columbia enacted federally approved unemployment compensation laws within two years after the passage of the Social Security Act.

All states allow workers to receive unemployment compensation whenever they are unemployed because of lack of *suitable* employment. All states deny benefits for the following six reasons:

1. Voluntary quits without a good cause.

2. Discharges for misconduct (that is, just cause).

3. Discharges for different types of fraud.

4. Failure to seek or accept suitable employment.

5. Receipt of certain other forms of unemployment benefits such as severance pay, workers' compensation, pension benefits, and social security.

6. Unemployment caused by labor disputes that cause work stoppages.

Although the above reasons sound straightforward, states vary considerably in their interpretation of these criteria and thus in the unemployment compensation paid to unemployed workers. As examples of how the criteria may be interpreted, consider the following: Some states accept quitting a job to accompany a relocated spouse as "good cause." If there is evidence that a worker was harassed into quitting, the termination may be viewed as a *constructive discharge* (that is, superficially voluntary but for all practical purposes involuntary). One of the more important unemployment compensation questions concerns discharge for disciplinary reasons. Most states agree that a discharge for incompetence does not prevent the discharged employee from collecting unemployment compensation. Generally, only misconduct can cause denial of unemployment compensation. The distinction between discharge for incompetence and discharge for misconduct centers on the employee's ability to control behavior. Incompetence is normally not under the control of the individual. Consequently, if employees can convince the compensation board that they were working to the best of their ability, their claims are usually granted. However, if the termination is due to misconduct, the compensation board will view it as another variety of voluntary termination and thus not grant unemployment compensation.

The disallowance of unemployment compensation claims which result from labor disputes is intended to maintain the government's neutrality in the labor–management conflict. One may surmise, therefore, that any labor dispute resulting in a work stoppage would disqualify workers from claiming unemployment compensation. This is not true. Only three states (Alabama, Arizona, and Minnesota) even define the term *labor dispute*. Some states also distinguish between source of work stoppage. Whereas workers on strike may not be entitled to unemployment compensation, fellow workers who are prevented from crossing the picket line might qualify. Some states also allow unemployment compensation claims if the employer locks out the workers but not if the workers walk out in a strike.

**Administration of Unemployment Compensation**   Each state is responsible for financing and administering its unemployment compensation plan. States base the financing on the FUTA tax and an experience rating system. FUTA requires employers to pay 6.2 percent on the first $7,000 of each employee's annual wage. The employer can receive a credit of 5.4 percent on the tax paid if the state system meets federal guidelines.

All states see to it that their systems meet or exceed those guidelines. Currently, Puerto Rico and eight states (California, Florida, Indiana, Maryland, Mississippi, Nebraska, New York, and South Carolina) base their unemployment taxes on the FUTA standards of $7,000 and 6.2 percent. The remaining states use either a base greater than $7,000, a percentage greater than 6.2 percent, or both.

The fact that the employer's tax rate is also based on the experience rating system produces great variability in taxes paid by employers within a state. The general principle behind the experience rating system is that each employer should contribute enough tax payments to cover all claims outstanding against the employer and to build up a reserve balance in the state's fund. Consequently, employer tax rates may vary dramatically. For example, using a standard tax rate of 6.2 percent, the tax rates for two employers, located in the same state, with same size work forces but with good versus poor experience ratings may vary from $6,750 to $69,750.

**Unemployment Compensation and Compensation Decision Making**
Keeping in mind the potential variance in tax rates, compensation specialists must monitor their organizations' turnover rates to control experience ratings. Some organizations with very high turnover rates actually contract with claims control specialty firms to identify errors in their systems to decrease their taxation dollars. Employers should also maintain accurate termination records to assist appeals of the state's decision for granting benefit eligibility to some employees.

Equally important is the organizations' obligation to protect workers from income discontinuity when they are terminated through no fault of their own. This is a particularly important issue during economic downturns, as neither the benefit nor the time frame may be adequate to allow for re-employment.

The duration of unemployment compensation benefits is a function of length of employment before termination. The standard maximum period for payments is 26 weeks, although Congress can extend the period when deemed necessary. Like workers' compensation, unemployment compensation incorporates a co-insurance component in that states set ceilings on the maximum benefits employees may receive. Those state-set benefit ceilings penalize higher-paid employees (salary exempt, professional, managerial) in that the percentages of income replacement allowed is smaller for higher-paid workers than it is for lower-paid workers. For the higher-paid workers, the 26-week maximum period of unemployment is often too short to cover the time needed to find a comparable job. In reality, in cases of permanent job loss and wide-scale organizational downsizing, a 26-week maximum period of unemployment benefits is too short for most workers.

Due to the above worker problems, employers design supplementary unemployment benefit (SUB) packages. SUB benefits have to be integrated with unemployment compensation and with other benefits that protect employees in case of unemployment. To retain tax advantages for providing added unemployment assistance benefits, benefits specialists must also ensure that the SUB benefits offered do not favor the highly paid.

# Laws Regulating Pension and Welfare Benefits

The pension portion of the Social Security Act of 1935 is the only mandatory retirement protection law. It provides a minimal flow of income to retired workers, their spouses, and their dependents. Also provided is a basic insurance program that covers the cost of hospital and related care (Medicare) and a supplementary medical insurance plan that pays for various medical services. As discussed earlier, the Social Security system is a pay-as-you-go system, which requires the employer and employee equally to contribute the prespecified amount, as a FICA tax. Consequently, compliance with this law is a clerical task.

Many companies go beyond the mandatory social security. As of 1989, 81 percent of employees in medium and large firms were covered by some additional pension or capital accumulation retirement plan and 92 percent of full-time employees had medical care coverage.[15] These and other benefits, voluntarily provided by employers, include all forms of income security, capital accumulation, and service programs. The main categories of benefits voluntarily provided by employers are (1) payments for time not worked, (2) health, welfare, and survivor (HWS) income protection, (3) pension income protection, and (4) capital accumulation plans.

Since the passage of the 1935 Social Security Act and the National Labor Relations Act, the government has enacted many laws that encourage certain benefit practices and discourage others. The main vehicle used for this purpose is tax law. As a means of furthering the social and economic interests of the United States, Congress regularly grants favored tax treatment to certain forms of benefits. For example, giving tax advantages for employer-provided health care coverage minimizes destitution caused by unexpected large medical bills. Giving tax advantages for employer-provided pension plans lowers the risk that the elderly will become fully dependent on the government.[16]

Two tax policy criteria for minimizing or eliminating tax obligations have the greatest impact on benefit practices: (1) doctrine of constructive receipt and (2) antidiscrimination rule.[17]

The doctrine of constructive receipt states that cash income and goods that have monetary value are taxable at the time the individual receives them. Thus, anyone who receives anything of monetary value, such as cash, property, stock, products, or services, will be taxed at the time of receipt.

The antidiscrimination rule states that employers can obtain tax advantages only for those benefits that do not discriminate in favor of highly compensated employees. Currently, the highly compensated individual is defined as one who at any time during the current or previous year was in at least one of the following categories:

1. Owned at least 5 percent of the stock/partnership rights.

2. Acted as a company officer earning more than $45,000 per year.

3. Earned more than $75,000 per year.

4. Earned more than $50,000 per year and also was among the highest paid 20 percent of the work force.

Besides being subject to the antidiscrimination rule, benefit plans must also meet the Employee Retirement and Income Security Act's (ERISAs) criteria to qualify for tax advantaged status. Those benefits that meet the criteria for tax advantaged status are called *qualified plans* and those that do not are called *nonqualified plans.* Needless to say, most companies try to assure that their benefit plans, with the exception of some executive benefits, are qualified plans.

### Employee Retirement and Income Security Act of 1974 (ERISA)

The ERISA is the most important comprehensive law governing the operation of private-sector employee benefit plans. Although there have been many attempts to extend ERISA or pass parallel legislation to the public sector, government employee benefit plans remain exempt from this type of law.

Under ERISA, a benefit plan is one that provides either benefits affecting well-being, such as health care and disability protection, or pension benefits.[18] Although ERISA preempts state laws, states retain control over insurance plans. This is a significant exception to ERISA as insurance coverage includes some time-off with pay practices, holiday observances, and state-required minimum benefit levels, employee rights, and services within health care insurance plans.[19] Given the state control over insurance plans, ERISA's main focus is pension plan regulation.

In the generic sense, a pension plan is any form of income accumulation that will provide income continuity after retirement. That definition can be further differentiated by two types of pension plans: defined benefit and defined contribution plans.

*Defined benefit plans* are what people normally think of as pension plans. These plans either guarantee the retiree a specific amount of income on retirement or they specify the method for determining the benefits the retiree will receive. For example, pension plans may specifiy (1) a fixed benefit—a stated percentage of compensation that the individual will receive per month, (2) a flat benefit—the actual dollar amount per month, or (3) a unit benefit—a monthly income based on a combination of a stated percentage of compensation multiplied by years of service. The funding of defined benefit plans is based on the organization's payroll costs and the employer's contributions; contributions are determined actuarially on the basis of anticipated retirement income obligations for the work force as a whole.

*Defined contribution plans* include all forms of capital accumulation that do not allow withdrawal of funds until retirement. Examples include retirement-focused profit-sharing plans, employee stock ownership plans, and many salary reduction strategies. Unlike the defined benefit plans, the retirement income from defined contribution plans is not guaranteed. Rather, it is a function of the fund's investment growth. Unlike defined benefit plans, the employer's contribution is guaranteed. Thus, in contrast to the defined benefit plans, defined contribution plans are, by definition, fully funded, and the participants in those plans are immediately vested. With this distinction in mind, ERISA's pension provisions apply to defined benefit plans and not to defined contribution plans.

ERISA's passage was motivated by two pension-related problems. The first problem was the high rate of pension plan forfeitures. At the time ERISA was being debated, the rate of pension plan forfeitures was more than 50 percent. One cause of the problem was the very strict and complicated rules, called *vesting rules,* that governed employee rights to pension benefits. The second problem was that companies often terminated pension plans when they went out of business, shut down operations at a facility, or were acquired by other companies.[20]

With respect to defined benefit pension plans, ERISA establishes minimum standards regarding coverage and funding:[21]

1.   Who must be covered by the plan (participation requirement). The basic standard is that a plan cannot deny eligibility for participation

beyond the time the employee reaches age 21 years and completes 1 year of service. Generally, 1 year of service means at least 1,000 hours of service during a 12-month period. Partial year credits do not have to be granted, except in absences resulting from pregnancy, childbirth, and adoption. In those cases, at least 501 hours of service must be credited to employees taking maternity and paternity leaves of absence. Plan participants who incur 5 consecutive 1-year breaks in service forfeit all previous credited years of service and benefits unless they had already vested.

2. How long the person must work to be entitled to the benefits (vesting requirement). These rules have been amended over the years. The current basic standards are

   full vesting after 5 years of service (or 10 years in multiemployer plans), or

   20 percent after 2 years of service and 20 percent for each year thereafter (100 percent after 7 years of service), and

   full vesting on reaching the plan's normal retirement age regardless of number of years of service.

Those basic minimum standards apply to plans that do not discriminate in favor of the "highly compensated" as defined in the statutes. Special vesting rules apply when the benefits of the highly compensated exceed 60 percent of the accrued benefits for all participants. In these cases, common in smaller organizations, participants must vest at least as rapidly as:

   100 percent after 3 years of service, or

   20 percent after 2 years of service and 20 percent for each year thereafter (100 percent vesting after 6 years of service).

3. How much money the employer must set aside each year to fund the benefit plan. Before ERISA, the Internal Revenue Service (IRS) had already issued rules requiring that pension plans be funded on an annual basis. ERISA set forth the requirement that past service liabilities and plan improvements be amortized over a period not to exceed 30 years. It provides for actuarial determination of funding, monitoring, and periodic adjustment of funding. ERISA also provides rules and penalties for dealing with issues of plan underfunding.

ERISA further requires that the plan be handled in the best interests of the participants and their beneficiaries (fiduciary requirement) and that participants are informed of their rights under the benefit plan (communication requirement).

## Post-ERISA Legislation

As noted previously, benefit offerings are motivated primarily by tax incentives and disincentives written into revenue acts. Since 1974, all major tax laws have affected employee benefit plans. Exhibit 5.3 summarizes the post-ERISA laws that have affected employee benefit plans. Note that a number of these laws could be considered antidiscrimination laws.

As seen from Exhibit 5.3, little significant benefits legislation has been passed since 1990. In 1991 and 1992, ERISA activity seemed to focus on change in regulations to ensure that qualified plans do not discriminate in favor of the highly paid. Several ERISA-related court cases have also been heard. In the 1991 *Hamilton v. Air Jamaica* case, the court found the airline's reserved right to alter its pay policy to be valid. The issue was whether the provision for 4 weeks of severance pay defined in the employee handbook was binding on Air Jamaica. The court ruled that the provision was not binding because the handbook also included a provision reserving Air Jamaica's right to amend its pay practices and any other employment policies or benefits.[22] The ruling in the *Hamilton* case was consistent with labor law's reserved rights doctrine.

A potentially more significant question relates to the 1992 *McGann v. H&H Music Company* case.[23] In that case, the plaintiff filed suit under section 510 of ERISA, claiming that H&H Music's group medical plan reduced benefits for AIDS and related illnesses. The district court ruled that an employer has an absolute right to alter the terms of medical coverage available to plan beneficiaries. The ruling was affirmed by appellate court. The issue, however, is bound to resurface, as the 1990 Americans with Disabilities Act (ADA) specifically prohibits discrimination in compensation for AIDS-related disability.

Exhibit 5.3 also shows that post-ERISA legislation subjects compensation plans to antidiscrimination law requirements. The Age Discrimination in Employment Act (ADEA) of 1976, the 1978 Pregnancy Act amendment of Title VII of the 1964 Civil Rights Act, the pregnancy provision of the 1991 Civil Rights Act, and the 1990 ADA specifically regulate benefits and apply to pay-related discrimination.

The **1976 Age Discrimination in Employment Act** prohibits employment discrimination against workers older than the age of 40 years. In case of benefits, the Department of Labor issues specific guidelines that generally permit reduction in group term life insurance coverage for those who work past age 65 years. Other reductions may also be allowed if they can be justified on the basis of cost. The U.S. Supreme Court, for example, approved a plan that made employees ineligible for disability retirement benefits once they attained the age of 60 years.[24]

The **1978 Pregnancy Act** forbids discrimination in employer-provided health care benefit packages. The act mandates that pregnancy-related expenses and disabilities be treated in the same way as other health problems. Furthermore, any employer-provided health care benefit package that covers the wives of male employees must provide pregnancy benefits for them.

**Title VII of the 1964 Civil Rights Act** prohibits discrimination in terms and conditions of employment on the basis of race, color, religion, sex, or national origin. Thus, this law applies to both pay and benefit practices.

Two kinds of discrimination claims may be filed under Title VII:

1. **Disparate treatment** claims assert than an employee or employees have been treated less favorably than other similarly qualified employees because of their protected status.

| EXHIBIT 5.3 | SUMMARY OF POST-ERISA LEGISLATION THAT AFFECTED EMPLOYEE BENEFIT PLANS |

<u>1978</u> **Revenue Act** added section 125 covering cafeteria plans and section 401(k) covering cash or deferred income arrangements to the Internal Revenue Code.

**Age Discrimination in Employment Act Amendments** extended benefit projections for most employees from age 65 to 70 years.

**Pregnancy Amendments to Civil Rights Act of 1964** required employers to treat disabilities caused by pregnancy the same as other disabilities covered under group benefit programs.

<u>1980</u> **Miscellaneous Revenue Act** made it possible for employees to be given a choice among benefits, cash, and deferred income as part of a section 125 cafeteria plan.

<u>1981</u> **Economic Recovery Tax Act (ERTA)** created payroll-based tax credit employee stock ownership plans (ESOPs), extended eligibility for individual retirement accounts to all wage earners, and made employer-provided child care programs nontaxable for employees.

<u>1982</u> **Tax Equity and Fiscal Responsibility Act (TEFRA)** imposed tax withholding requirements on pension plan payments and placed many limitations on tax-qualified plans, including lowered maximum benefit accruals and employer contribution levels.

<u>1984</u> **Retirement Equity Act (REA)** extended employee benefit rights and protections by amending ERISA pension plan provisions regarding plan participation, vesting, survivor provisions, and break-in-service rules.

**Deficit Reduction Act (DEFRA)** included a variety of restrictions on benefit plans as part of a comprehensive effort to lower a large budget deficit.

<u>1986</u> **Consolidated Omnibus Budget Reconciliation Act of 1985 (COBRA)** required employers to offer extended group health plan participation for up to 36 months to employees and dependents whose coverage would otherwise end due to certain qualifying events, such as termination of employment.

**Tax Reform Act of 1986** contained the most sweeping legislative changes affecting benefit plans since ERISA. Major themes were (1) more uniform provisions for controlling discrimination in favor of highly paid employees under different types of plans, (2) firmer guidelines to make tax-advantaged plans more equitable, and (3) tighter pension plan standards and tax penalties to ensure use of deferred income for retirement purposes.

**Age Discrimination in Employment Act Amendments** established that, effective January 1, 1987, mandatory retirement based on age would no longer be permitted for most employees.

**Omnibus Budget Reconciliation Act of 1986 (OBRA)** required, starting in 1988, pension accruals and pension participation beyond a plan's normal retirement age (usually 65 years) for employees in company pension plans.

<u>1987</u> **Omnibus Budget Reconciliation Act of 1987 (OBRA '87)** substantially raised and extended Pension Benefit Guarantee Corporation pension insurance premium provisions and made the existing level of group term life insurance coverage which is includable in income for federal income taxes further subject to FICA tax.

<u>1988</u> **HMO Amendments of 1988** relaxed rules governing federally qualified health maintenance organizations and repealed the dual choice mandatory requirement, effective October 24, 1995.

*(Exhibit 5.3, continued)*

**Medicare Catastrophic Coverage Act of 1988** provided for a series of additional benefits to be phased in over a 5-year period (1989 to 1993) along with higher premiums for participants and a special surtax for Medicare eligibles. Note: This law was repealed at the end of 1989.

**1989 P.L. 110–140** repealed section 89, nondiscrimination rules contained in the Tax Reform Act of 1986. These rules had been designed to control abusive discrimination in favor of highly paid employee participants within group welfare benefit plans. Agreeing retrospectively that they were needlessly complex and unnecessary, Congress repealed the rules at the end of 1989.

**1990 Omnibus Budget Reconciliation Act of 1990 (OBRA '90)** raised the excise tax for pension asset reversions, the taxable wage base for Medicare payroll tax, and PBGC premium rates, and modified and clarified the status of miscellaneous nontaxable benefits and services.

**1990 Americans With Disabilities Act (ADA)** prohibited discrimination in employee benefits for qualified individuals with a disability that substantially limits major life activities. The act specified covered and uncovered disabilities. Its prohibitions removed the employers' ability to exclude from benefit coverage the pre-existing conditions covered under ADA.

**1992 Unemployment Compensation Amendments of 1992 (P.L. 102–318)** extended unemployment benefits and also required a 20 percent mandatory income tax withholding on qualified benefit plans.

SOURCE:  Robert M. McCaffery, *Employee Benefit Programs*, Boston, MA: PWS-Kent Publishing, 1992, pp. 70–71 (data through 1990 OBRA Act).

2. **Disparate impact** claims assert that a particular practice or policy, neutral on its face, nonetheless has an unjustifiable disproportionate negative impact on the protected group.

The **1991 Civil Rights Act,** like Title VII, applies to both pay and benefit practices, although it specifically regulates some benefits. This act was a Congressional response to 1989 Supreme Court rulings under Title VII, which were unfavorable to civil rights advocates. The *Wards Cove* ruling, for example, held that plaintiffs always retained the burden of persuasion in overt discrimination cases.[25] The *Price Waterhouse v. Hopkins* ruling involved a woman who was turned down for a senior partnership for a mixture of sexist and legitimate reasons. The Court upheld the firm's decision and, by so doing, communicated the message that employers could avoid Title VII liability by showing that the same decision would have been made even in the absence of the illegal motive.[26] Other 1989 Supreme Court rulings applied a stringent standard of review to preferential treatment of minority contractors, reduced the damage awards available in certain EEO lawsuits, and limited the time period during which plaintiffs could challenge a seniority system under Title VII.[27]

Like Title VII, the 1991 Civil Rights Act covers employers, employment agencies, and labor organizations in an "industry affecting commerce." Employers with

15 or more employees are covered by the act. Exceptions are tax-exempt private clubs, aliens employed by American companies outside the United States, and Indian tribes who are employers.

With limited exceptions, the act outlaws discrimination based on race, color, religion, sex, or national origin in every aspect of the recruitment, hiring, and employment process. The exceptions are

1.  Wages may be based on a *bona fide* seniority system, merit, and quantity or quality of production.

2.  Religion, sex, or national origin may be a qualifier for employment if it is a *bona fide* occupational qualification.

The "wages" exception allows for the same defenses for unequal pay practices as allowed by the EPA. Thus, for practical purposes, the equal pay for equal work provision is extended to all classes protected by the 1991 Civil Rights Act. The 1991 Civil Rights Act also specifies that sexual orientation is not a protected category.

Consistent with the 1983 Supreme Court ruling on the Pregnancy Act of 1978,[28] the 1991 Civil Rights Act establishes that "spousal" benefits, such as medical insurance, must be made available to male and female employees. The act also requires that pregnancy and childbirth be treated as are other disabilities under health care plans.

The 1990 ADA prohibits discrimination against disabled individuals in private employment, public employment, public accommodations, public transportation, state and local government services, and telecommunications. The employment-related issues are addressed in title 1 of the act. Although ADA explicitly prohibits pay and benefits discrimination the act's provisions are currently more relevant to benefit eligibility issues.

ADA applies to employers with 15 or more employees. Section 102 of the act states that

> No covered entity shall "discriminate" against a "qualified individual with a disability" because of the "disability" of such individual in regard to job application procedures, the hiring, advancement, or discharge of employees, employee compensation, job training, and other terms, conditions, and privileges of employment.

ADA defines *disability* as meaning

1.  A physical or mental impairment that substantially limits one or more major life activities;

2.  A record of such an impairment; or

3.  Being regarded as having such an impairment.

The following are considered disabilities because they "substantially" limit major life activities such as caring for one's self, performing manual tasks, maintaining personal relations, and being able to work:

Epilepsy

Diabetes

Heart disease

Cancer

Orthopedic, visual, or speech impairment

Drug addiction (rehabilitated drug user)

Alcoholism

HIV, AIDS

ADA specifically excludes from protection current drug users and certain sexual disorders such as transvestism, exhibitionism, and pedophilia. ADA also excludes from protection homosexuality, gambling disorders, kleptomania, pyromania, and psychoactive substance use disorders resulting from current drug use.

Under ADA, a "qualified" individual is one who has a disability and with reasonable accommodation can perform the *essential* functions of the job. Furthermore, essential job functions are to be determined by the employer and written into a job description. Written job descriptions are evidence of which tasks are essential. Findings of discrimination may include the behaviors listed in Exhibit 5.4.

## Administration of ERISA and Antidiscrimination Laws

**ERISA Regulation and Benefit Protection**   ERISA's enforcement is the responsibility of two federal agencies. The IRS oversees compliance with ERISA's participation, vesting, and funding standards. The Department of Labor oversees compliance with the fiduciary standards and reporting and disclosure requirements.

Pension plan protection is guaranteed by a third government agency, the Pension Benefit Guarantee Corporation (PBGC). The PBGC administers an insurance program for private defined benefit pension plans and guarantees the payment of basic retirement benefits to participants of terminated pension plans. The PBGC is chaired by the Secretary of Labor, with the Secretaries of Commerce and Treasury as board members. It is authorized to borrow up to $100 million from the Treasury to make payments, up to a statutory maximum, to individuals whose retirement plans were terminated by their employers.

**Regulation of Antidiscrimination Laws**   The EEOC administers all antidiscrimination laws except the IRCA, whose administration it shares with five other federal as well as state agencies. The EEOC investigates charges of discrimination and determines whether there is "probable cause" to believe the charge. It first seeks to resolve the claim through conciliation. If conciliation fails, the EEOC may bring suit in federal court and/or notify the claimant that he or she may sue. The suit may encompass any discrimination discovered in the course of its investigation, whether or not that discrimination was included in

---

**EXHIBIT 5.4** BEHAVIORS THAT MAY LEAD TO FINDINGS OF DISCRIMINATION UNDER ADA

---

1. Limiting, segregating, or classifying a job applicant or employee in a way that adversely affects the opportunities or status of such employee or applicant because of the disability.

2. Participating in contractual or other relationships that have the effect of subjecting qualified applicants or employees with disabilities to prohibited discrimination.

3. Utilizing standards, criteria, or methods of administration that have the effect of discrimination on the basis of disability or that perpetuate the discrimination of others who are subject to common administrative control.

4. Excluding or denying equal jobs or benefits to a qualified individual because of the known disability of an individual with whom the qualified individual is known to have a relationship or association.

5. Not making "reasonable accommodations" to the known physical or mental limitations of an otherwise qualified individual with a disability, unless employer can demonstrate that the accommodation would impose an undue hardship on the operation of the business.

6. Denying employment opportunities to an otherwise qualified individual with a disability if such denial is based on the need of the employer to make "reasonable accommodation."

7. Using qualification standards, employment tests, or other selection criteria that screen out or tend to screen out individuals or a class of individuals with disabilities unless the standard, test, or criteria is shown to be job-related and consistent with business necessity.

8. Failing to select and administer tests in the most effective manner to ensure that when such tests are administered to individuals with impaired sensory, manual, or speaking skills, the results accurately reflect what the test is supposed to measure rather than reflecting the impaired sensory, manual, or speaking skills of such individuals (except where such skills are a factor that the test purports to measure).

---

the original charge. Employees may also sue employers in state or federal court. Furthermore, the Civil Rights Act of 1991 provides for a jury trial and the payment of compensatory and punitive damages, within limits determined by the size of the employer's work force.

### Additional Laws Regulating Health Care Plans

Besides the laws listed in Exhibit 5.3 and state-controlled health care insurance programs, some additional legislation exists to regulate medical care delivery sources and flexible benefit plans.

**Medical Care Delivery**  Medical care is typically provided through five sources: (1) insurance companies, (2) nonprofit Blue Cross/Blue Shield Associations (BCBS), (3) self-funding arrangements, (4) health maintenance organizations (HMOs), and (5) preferred provider organizations (PPOs).[29]

Insured medical care plans, including BCBS plans are subject to state regulation. Self-funding plans need to satisfy ERISA requirements only, which generally are less comprehensive than most state regulations. Laws regulating HMOs and PPOs require further explanation.

HMOs are community-based health care centers that provide members with health care services for a fixed monthly fee. HMO plans are subject to the Health Maintenance Organization Act of 1973. This act specifies that if an employer is petitioned by a qualified HMO and at least 25 employees live within the HMO's service area, the employer is required to offer the HMO as an alternative to the existing insurance plan. If employees choose to participate in the HMO, the employer is obligated to pay the cost of HMO participation in an amount equal to that expended for health care insurance. Federal regulations also require that employers provide for at least 10 working days each calendar year for group enrollment. During that time, employees may transfer between alternative health plans without penalties or limitations based on their health status.

The PPO is a cross between HMOs and the traditional doctor/patient arrangement. PPOs are groups of health care providers that contract with employers, insurance companies, or third-party payers to provide medical care services at a reduced fee. PPOs differ from HMOs in that employees are not obligated to use the PPOs services. They are free to go where they like for medical services, but if they choose to go to a PPO, the fee for the service is lower and they pay the PPO when they receive the service. PPOs are relatively unregulated with respect to rate setting and requirements for employers. One potential obstacle for future PPO growth is its antitrust status. For example, in 1982, the U.S. Supreme Court ruled that two medical groups in Maricopa County, Arizona, had engaged in price fixing by setting physician fee standards.[30]

**Flexible Benefit Plans**    Besides being subject to statutory law requirements, flexible benefit plans are also subject to common law, the body of precepts handed down by judges and juries.

A flexible benefit plan differs from the traditional plan in that it allows employees to choose among the different types of benefits that the employer is willing to provide. Sometimes called "cafeteria plans," flexible benefits were first implemented in the early 1970s. The passage of ERISA, however, briefly ended their development, as section 2006 of ERISA permitted existing plans to continue but forbade the development of new plans that gave employees choices. The Revenue Act of 1978, by adding section 125 to the Internal Revenue Code (IRC), allowed employers to offer choices between cash and benefits without causing the benefits to become taxable. The Miscellaneous Revenue Act of 1980 strengthened the foundation for flexible benefit offerings by sanctioning inclusion of a tax deferral arrangement per IRC 401(k) and by 1984 and 1989 issuances of proposed regulations for IRC section 125.[31]

Statutory law now permits flexible benefit offerings and allows those plans to include deferred compensation as an employee option. Current law defines a flexible benefit plan as one that allows employees to choose among nontaxable benefits or to take part of the benefit in the form of four taxable benefit options: cash, group term insurance in excess of $50,000, dependent life insurance in excess of $2,000, and extra vacation days. The employee can defer paying taxes on the cash only if the cash is placed in a stock, bonus, or profit-sharing retirement plan.[32]

Regarding common law, the courts have held that there is an implied contract between the employer and employee and that the benefits available to similarly classified employees are part of that contract. Employers who violate the implied contract may be sued by the employee. Furthermore, employers who counsel employees in benefit selection may be held responsible for the quality of the counseling.[33]

### Pension and Welfare Benefits and Compensation Decision Making

In his book, *Employee Benefit Programs: A Total Compensation Perspective*, McCaffery notes that

> Today it would be sensible and appropriate for employee benefit managers to accept government as a major partner in the business of managing company plans. (p.73).

McCaffery further notes that benefit executives can influence the laws affecting company benefit plans through direct contact with sponsoring legislators and key legislative staff members. Memberships in organizations such as the U.S. Chamber of Commerce also serve as vehicles for transmitting employers' views to legislators.

Because new benefit regulation is incorporated in tax laws almost yearly, benefit planners must monitor pending legislation and audit company plans for compliance requirements, impact on taxation, legal liability, and administrative costs. The success of these activities is highly dependent on the accuracy and completeness of relevant employee records. Employers should also communicate benefit coverage to employees as well as the legal requirements for benefit offerings, as such information will enable employees to understand the reasons for benefit changes, which otherwise may be negatively perceived.

Compensation specialists must also ensure that the pay plan components (actual and relative pay, job worth, and pay adjustment practices) do not discriminate against any protected group. Antidiscrimination laws specify consideration of certain groups. Effective management practice, however, requires fair treatment of all employees, whether or not they are members of a "protected" group. Of all the discrimination laws, the ADA appears to suggest the most specific compensation-related activities. First, ADA suggests that the practice of disallowing employee benefits for specified "preconditions" may be no longer valid. Second, ADA specifies the use of a task-oriented job analysis to determine essential job functions and explicitly states that the job description is assumed to detail only the functions that are essential to job performance. Employers whose compensation systems are managed by knowledgeable professionals will find that they need not make any changes to their job analysis and job description procedures. Many organizations, however, will need to ensure that the job analysis is task-oriented and that job descriptions reflect the actual essential tasks required for job performance.

As with benefits regulated by statutory law, flexible benefit plans can involve taxation, legal liability, and administrative costs; employers are cautioned to evaluate the potential impact of those plans. Cockrum[34] offers the following suggestions to minimize vulnerability to common law implied contract violations:

1.  Provide minimum health care benefits to reduce antidiscrimination problems. Such problems can lead to loss of tax advantage status for the benefit offering.

2.  Limit flexible benefit plans to choices among nontaxable benefits. This will reduce administrative costs associated with valuing each taxable benefit for IRS income reporting.

3.  Omit options for additional payments that an employee could make to a qualified retirement plan. Such payments could bring flexible plans under quasi-ERISA jurisdiction.

4.  Give the human resources department strict instructions to provide factual information about each benefit but never guide, assist, or counsel employees in benefit selection.

## Summary

This chapter reviews the main federal legislation that influences the compensation decision-making process. The FLSA is important principally because of its minimum wage, overtime pay, and equal-pay-for-equal-work provisions. Certain wage and hour laws pertain specifically to federal contractors. These include the Davis-Bacon Act, The Walsh-Healy Act, the McNamara-O'Hara Act, and the Contract Work Hours Standard Act. Violation of the regulations set forth by these acts can jeopardize federal contracts. Federal contractors and subcontractors may also place their contractual agreements with the federal government at risk if they violate executive orders.

Workers' compensation and unemployment compensation laws are important considerations for the compensation decision maker. Providing adequate employee protection from income discontinuity while exercising cost control requires careful decisions and detailed record keeping. Perhaps the greatest government constraint on compensation decision making is in the area of voluntarily provided pension and welfare benefits. Benefit offerings are subject to specific federal and state statutes, common law, and antidiscrimination law regulations.

Besides reviewing the major legislation affecting compensation decision making, the chapter discusses the agencies that enforce each of the laws and how the laws affect compensation decision making.

## Discussion Questions

1.  What are the main wage and hour laws? Why were these laws passed? How do they affect compensation decision making?

2. What are income continuity protection laws and why were these laws passed? Characterize the main provisions of these laws.

3. If state workers' compensation and unemployment compensation laws have common provisions, why are workers in different states treated differently with respect to these laws?

4. What are the implications of workers' compensation and unemployment compensation laws on compensation decision making?

5. How does the government encourage employers to provide various benefits to their workforces? To what extent is government successful in this effort? Speculate on the extent to which government success may correlate with firm size and other factors.

6. Do any of the equal employment laws allow reduction in compensation for a particular employee group? Explain.

7. Why shouldn't employers counsel employees on benefits selection?

8. What are the implications of voluntarily provided benefits on compensation decision making?

9. It has been suggested that the Americans with Disabilities Act contains the most specific compensation related requirements among all antidiscrimination laws. Explain.

### References

[1] U.S. Department of Labor, *Handy Reference Guide to the Fair Labor Standards Act;* "FLSA of 1989 (HR2) Part 1—Text of House Passed Bill, Part II—Text of House Committee Report," *Labor Law Reports,* Commerce Clearing House, March 31, 1989, part 2 #119, 11, 12.

[2] *Legislative History of the Immigration Reform and Control Act* (Public Law 99-603) (Washington, DC: Government printing Office, 1980); J. Ledvinka and V. Scarpello, *Federal Regulation of Personnel and Human Resource Management* (Boston, MA: PWS-Kent Publishing, 1991).

[3] "FLSA of 1989 (HRs) Part 1—Text of House Passed Bill, Part II—Text of House Committee Report," *Labor Law Reports,* Commerce Clearing House, March 31, 1989, part 2 #119, 12.

[4] See 1965 Health Care Amendments to the FLSA.

[5] See U.S. Department of Labor, *Women Workers Today* (Washington, DC, 1976); U.S. Department of Labor, *The Earnings Gap Between Men and Women* (Washington, DC, 1976); U.S. Department of Labor, Interpretative Bulletin, *Equal Pay for Equal Work under the Fair Labor Standards Act* (Washington, DC, August 31, 1971); U. S. Department of Labor, *Brief Highlights of Major Federal Laws and Orders on Sex Discrimination in Employment* (Washington, DC, February 1977); E. A. Cooper and G. V. Barrett, "Equal Pay and Gender: Implications of Court Cases for Personnel Practices," *Academy of Management Review* 9 (1984), 84–94.

[6] E. I. Manger, "Administration of the Davis-Bacon Act," *Construction Review* 11 (1965): 4–6; V. Scarpello and J. Ledvinka, *Personnel/Human Resource Management: Environments and Functions* (Boston, MA: PWS-Kent Publishing, 1988).

[7] U.S. Department of Labor, The Federal Wage Garnishment Law, WHD Publication 1324 (Washington, DC: U.S. Government Printing Office, 1978), 5.

[8] Ledvinka and Scarpello, *Federal Regulation of Personnel and Human Resource Management.*

[9] *Ibid.*

[10] *Ibid.*

[11] R. M. McCaffery, *Employee Benefit Programs: A Total Compensation Perspective* (Boston, MA: PWS-Kent Publishing, 1992).

[12] Ledvinka and Scarpello, *Federal Regulation of Personnel and Human Resource Management.*

[13] *Ibid.*

[14] See McCaffery, *Employee Benefit Programs;* Ledvinka and Scarpello, *Federal Regulation of Personnel and Human Resource Management; Unemployment Insurance: Trends and Issues* (Washington, DC: Tax Foundation, 1982); *Compensation,* BNA Policy and Practice series #842, April 1981, p. 356:75; *Compensation,* BNA Policy and Practice Series #973, July 1986, p. 365:25; W. Corson, A. Hershey, and S. Kerachsky, *Nonmonetary Eligibility in State Unemployment Insurance Programs. Law and Practice* (Kalamazoo, MI: W.E. Upjohn Institute for Employment Research, 1986); "Tax Rate Tables," *Compensation,* BNA Policy and Practice Series #1043 (May 1989) 356: 41–45.

[15] U.S. Department of Labor, Bureau of Labor Statistics, *Employee Benefits in Medium and Large Firms,* 1989 (Washington, DC: U.S. Government Printing Office, June 1990).

[16] Scarpello and Ledvinka, *Personnel/Human Resource Management: Environments and Functions.*

[17] *Ibid.*

[18] R. Schmitt, "Private Pension Plan Reform: A Summary of the Employee Retirement Income Security Act of 1974 (ERISA)," *Congressional Research Service,* Report No. 81–247 EPW (1981).

[19] McCaffery, *Employee Benefit Programs.*

[20] Ledvinka and Scarpello, *Federal Regulation of Personnel and Human Resource Management.*

[21] See Schmitt, *Private Pension Plan Reform;* Ledvinka and Scarpello, *Federal Regulation of Personnel and Human Resource Management;* McCaffery, *Employee Benefit Programs.*

[22] *Hamilton v. Air Jamaica, Ltd.,* 945 F.2d 74 (3d Cir. 1991).

[23] *McGann v. H&H Music Co.,* 946 F.2d 401 (5th Cir. 1991), petition for cert. filed, 60 U.S.L.W. 3582 (1992) [cert. was denied].

[24] *Public Employees Retirement System of Ohio v. Betts,* ____U.S.____, 109 S.Ct. 2854, 50 FEP Cases 104 (1989).

[25] *Ward's Cove Packing Co. v. Atonio,* ____U.S.____, 109 S.Ct. 2115 (1989).

[26] *Price Waterhouse v. Hopkins,* ____U.S.____, 109 S.Ct. 1775 (1989).

[27] See Ledvinka and Scarpello, *Federal Regulation of Personnel and Human Resource Management,* 183.

[28] *Newport News Shipbuilding and Dry Dock Co. v. EEOC,* 103 S.Ct. 2622 (1983).

[29] See McCaffery, *Employee Benefit Programs.*

[30] *Arizona v. Maricopa County Medical Society,* 102 S.Ct. 2466 (1982).

[31] See Scarpello and Ledvinka, *Personnel/Human Resource Management;* McCaffery, *Employee Benefit Programs.*

[32] See Scarpello and Ledvinka, *Personnel/Human Resource Management;* Newkirk Associates, *Current Comment 84–44: The Tax Reform Act of 1984.* (Indianapolis, IN: The Research and Review Service of America, 1984).

[33] Scarpello and Ledvinka, *Personnel/Human Resource Management,* 449.

[34] R. B. Cockrum, "Has the Time Come for Employee Cafeteria Plans?" *Personnel Administrator* 27 (1982), 68.

# 6

# Compensation Decision Making: A Strategic Perspective

## Learning Objectives

**To learn the meaning of strategy and its levels within the context of compensation decision making.**

**To learn about the basic compensation strategy of the past and the reasons for the evolution of today's contingency approach to compensation decision making.**

**To learn about the important organizational contingencies that may influence compensation decision making.**

**To learn about the characteristics of the external environment that influence selection of compensation strategies.**

**To learn about the levels of the organization that may be more or less appropriate for different aspects of compensation decision making.**

**To become familiar with two other perspectives on the relationship between compensation and organization contingencies.**

## Introduction

Ten years ago, compensation texts did not have a chapter on the topic of strategic compensation decision making. Does this mean that strategic compensation is a new phenomenon? We think not. The changes in the competitive environment, however, have changed the basic business strategy and its related compensation strategy.

There are many perspectives about how compensation decision making has changed, but all agree that the organization's external environment is the basis for change. Because strategies are formulated in response to the external environment, this chapter focuses on explaining the characteristics of the environment that influence selection of compensation strategies. By understanding environment contingencies, human resource executives will be able to select those strategies that best meet the organization's performance and social responsibility requirements and also provide synergy across interrelated human resource management programs. Furthermore, by understanding environment contingencies, new strategies as well as changes in strategies can be systematically devised.

## Strategies—What Are They?

The term *strategy* has been defined in a variety of ways. Common to all perspectives is the view that strategy is the means of achieving future goals. Also common to all perspectives is the view that strategies are the chosen means of interacting with the external environment. Sometimes, the term *strategic planning* also refers to a particular type of planning process. For example, a long-range planning process may be defined as a process that entails plotting a course from *A* to *B*. In contrast, strategic planning refers to a more sophisticated planning process, which includes assessing anticipated changes in competitor behaviors and developing alternative or contingent plans to deal with potentially variable competitor actions.

This book defines strategic compensation decision making as decision making focused on ensuring that compensation plan design, implementation, and control activities relate directly to the achievement of the organization's performance goals, within the constraints of societal expectations and mandates. This definition of strategic compensation decision making suggests that compensation strategies are constrained by strategies formulated at higher levels.

Strategies affecting compensation decision making may be formulated at four levels: societal, corporate, business, and functional. Societal level strategies are formulated by governments and focus on achievement of social, economic, and political goals of a society. The primary strategic issues are to decide the best ways of solving particular problems that threaten society. Organizational strategies are formulated by organizational managers. In single-product or service organizations, the responsibility for corporate- and business-level strategies usually resides with the organization's top management. In diversified organizations, those strategic responsibilities are divided between corporate and business unit managers. At the corporate level, the primary strategic issues are to decide which set of businesses the corporation should pursue and what relative emphasis to give to each. The main task is to manage the corporation's financial portfolio. At the business unit level, strategies deal with how to compete in a particular industry or in a particular product market segment. Two primary strategic issues are determination of the organization's distinctive competencies and assessment of the business's potential and actual performance in the marketplace.[1] The distinctive competence focus is particularly relevant to human resource managers because the knowledge, skills, and abilities of the work force represent the organization's distinctive competencies. Responsibility for functional strategies resides with functional managers. Functional strategies focus mainly on maximizing productivity within the function by achieving synergy across its activities. Human resource strategies cross strategic levels. For example, compliance with society's demands for workplace justice is a concern at the corporate level. It is also a concern at the business and functional levels. Ensuring human resource productivity is a concern at the business level of strategy formulation, as the organization's managers are responsible for producing the product or service offered by the organization. The human resource department is responsible for developing systems of managing people and for ensuring that the function's activities are coherent and consistent with one another and with the goals and strategies of the organization. This means that compensation decisions must support the performance goals of the organization, be consistent with the organization's societal mandates, and be consistent with other human resource management activities such as staffing, training, development, labor relations, and employee safety and health.

Strategies formulated at different levels are distinct, but all are intended to fit together to form a coherent and consistent whole. With respect to human resource strategies, societal demands constrain the subsequent three levels of strategy formulation: corporate, business, and functional.[2] Within constraints, however, many decision-making options exist. Consider, for example, how a societal strategy such as a legislated change in minimum wage constrains compensation decision making. The organization is bound by law to comply with such a change. Nevertheless, the strategy it may use to implement the minimum wage mandate is likely to be influenced by the competitiveness of the product and labor markets in which the firm operates and the proportion of its work force paid minimum wage rates. If an organization has multiple product or service lines and separate business locations, compliance with the new minimum wage mandate might require consideration of many other organizational factors. For example, some organizations may wish to maintain wage rate consistency across their locations. Other organizations may be already paying wages above the mandated minimum in some locations and not in others. In high-wage locations where wages are already in compliance with the new minimum wage rate, some organizations may decide to increase their wage rates by an amount proportional to the minimum wage increase, whereas others may decide simply to maintain their current wage rates, thereby changing their wage-level policies. Internally, organizations will also have to decide how to deal with many related issues such as whether the change in minimum wage has implications for changes in pay structures of supervisors of minimum wage workers and other employees whose jobs are more complex but whose pay rates no longer differ significantly from the new minimum wage rates.

Some societal strategies may or may not have strategic compensation implications. For example, consider possible influences of revenue acts on benefit packages. Revenue acts, passed yearly, often contain tax incentives as means of motivating employers to provide certain benefits to employees. Granting tax advantages for different benefits practices is a strategy the American government uses to deal with numerous social and economic problems. To obtain or retain tax-advantaged status for benefits provided to employees, firms normally revise their benefits offerings when revenue acts motivate them to do so. In these cases, there is little compensation strategy. However, tax policy also specifies that employers can obtain tax advantages only for those benefits that do not discriminate in favor of highly compensated employees. That "antidiscrimination" rule may constrain some companies from giving their executives more benefits than they give other employees. Other companies, however, may decide that providing executives with higher benefit levels than those provided to other employees will result in significant improvement in the firm's performance, even though both the company and the executives receiving the benefits will have to pay taxes on the benefits.

The above examples illustrate how societal strategies may relate to compensation strategies. The examples also indicate that the organization normally has choices of how it will implement government mandates and whether it will take advantage of government incentives. The next section of the chapter describes past business and compensation strategies. The description should alert the reader to the fact that strategies, although interrelated, are not always explicitly planned or formally stated. Rather, strategies may be the result of piecemeal and fragmented decisions that come together to shape future behavior.

## Past Business and Compensation Strategy

Although not formally stated, in the past, the overriding business strategy in the United States was to take the labor factor of production out of competition.[3] That strategy was based on the view that employers within an industry had similar product markets, similar ways of working (technologies), and priced their products similarly to their competition. They also tended to use the same sources for acquiring needed employees.[4] Because of those similarities, the costs of production were similar for employers within an industry. Although there were no official strategies that stated the compensation goal was to take labor out of competition, the effect of such a strategy could be observed across American industries. Employers within an industry tended to offer similar compensation for the skills they demanded. Competitive advantage, therefore, came from nonwage practices rather than from significant differences in compensation practices. Because different industries are constrained by different cost factors, we also saw compensation policies and practices differ across industries. Some industries paid more than others for equivalent skills.[5] These practices were illustrated in Chapter 4, which showed the interindustry wage patterns that have maintained themselves over the years.

The grand strategy of taking labor out of competition motivated compatible "me too" compensation strategies with respect to pay level (average wages paid), pay mix (proportion of fixed wages and salaries to incentives) , and pay adjustment policies and practices, within industries. Furthermore, the "me too" strategy was reinforced through compensation packages designed by compensation consulting firms for managerial and other nonunionized employee groups; through collective bargaining agreements, because unions recognized it was in their interest to bargain similar compensation for similar workers across labor markets; and through legislation such as prevailing area wage requirements for government contractors, discussed in Chapter 5.

Involvement of these external forces in compensation decision making made the strategy of taking labor out of competition quite effective within the United States. Employers could ensure that their compensation offerings were consistent with those of their product and labor market competitors and workers could benefit from increased income and thus an increasing standard of living. The strategy was also effective within the context of U.S. trade because trade was primarily conducted with Western European countries, which were relatively similar in their evolution of production processes and employment patterns.[6]

Notice that strategies, whether formulated formally or informally, explicitly or implicitly, direct implementation tactics and operations. The grand strategy of taking labor out of competition and its related "me too" compensation strategies resulted in centralization of compensation decision making and in viewing all human resource activities as implementation problems which could be performed by middle- or lower-level human resource specialists. "Me too" compensation strategies also motivated those human resource administrators to protect and preserve the pay systems they were administering.

## Current Business and Compensation Strategy

The business strategy of taking labor out of competition is no longer a viable strategy for many firms operating in the United States. During the past two decades, global markets have opened up and previously underdeveloped countries have industrialized. With increased global competition, American firms have begun expanding trade and production in these countries. The worldwide dissemination of computer and information technologies also has significantly altered dependence on large, reliable, and full-time work forces for productivity gains. With the new technologies, productivity gains have become increasingly dependent on the firm's ability to distribute work in flexible ways and thereby to control fixed costs.[6] The worldwide dissemination of computer and information technologies also has altered U.S. trade relations and has changed the nature and scope of competition for U.S. firms. The global economy has further produced multicountry ownership of businesses within many countries. It has been reported, for example, that foreign ownership of American companies increased more than 300 percent since the 1950s.[7] Along with foreign ownership, employment of America's workers by foreign-owned firms continues to increase. For instance, by the late 1980s Japanese-owned firms employed about 350,000 workers in the United States and were projected to employ 1 million by the year 2000.[8]

Given the presence of global competition and the heterogeneity of nations competing in any one country, it becomes obvious that the traditional American strategy of taking labor out of competition is no longer a feasible strategy for many firms. The expansion of competition to Second and Third World nations requires a compensation strategy that is more flexible and tailored to the specific market in which the business unit operates. Thus, the approach of standardized, centralized, and industry-specific compensation practices no longer satisfies the needs of our society, its organizations, and its labor force.[9]

The newly evolving compensation strategy is a contingency strategy. Like the contingency theory of organizations, which proposes that the more effective organizations match their structures to environmental conditions, the evolving strategy for compensation decision making is to match the organization's compensation plan to environmental conditions. The need to control fixed costs and to distribute work in flexible ways suggests also that the newly emerging compensation strategy is a two-dimensional strategy. The first dimension requires deciding the relative criticality of skills demanded by the organization. This decision alerts the organization to the possible interrelationships between compensation strategy and staffing strategy and compensation strategy and training strategy. The second dimension requires deciding how to match compensation offerings, for the skills demanded, to the organization's performance goals. This alerts the compensation decision maker to the importance of understanding the environment in which the organization functions and its implications for compensation decision making.

# Compensation Strategy and Other Human Resources Strategies

## Compensation Strategy and Staffing Strategy

Economists explain that the demand for labor is derived from the demand for products or services offered by the organization. Furthermore, the interaction between labor demand and available supply determines how many people can be hired at a particular wage rate. Consequently, compensation strategy cannot be formulated without regard for the skill group whose labor the organization demands. Reduced dependence on the size of work forces for increasing productivity also introduces another variable in the skill-compensation relationship. As global competition produces uncertain demand for the organization's products and services and fluctuating input costs, incentives to control fixed costs increase.

One of the evolving strategies for controlling fixed costs is to depart from the traditional staffing concern of obtaining large, reliable, and full-time work forces. The staffing trend seems to be dominated by two interrelated strategies. The first strategy is to limit permanent, full-time employment to a core group of employees who possess skills that are critically needed to meet customer demand; such employees are not readily available in the labor market and their skills take substantial time to acquire. The second strategy is to use contingent workers on an "as needed" basis.[10] Other strategies may include organizational restructuring and work redesign. Companies using different strategies for controlling fixed costs will also have to devise compatible strategies for paying their employees or subcontractors.

As available information and technologies change the nature of skills and which skills are demanded across industry lines, labor market boundaries will change. In the past, employers tended to use industry-nonspecific markets for the cheaper, entry-level labor and industry-specific markets for experienced professionals and managers; in the future, competition for experienced workers, whose skills are demanded across industries, will cross industry-specific labor market boundaries. This will be particularly evident for jobs in which performance does not require possession of firm-specific and industry-specific knowledge and skill.[11] For example, managers who have demonstrated the ability to develop effective teams will be sought out by organizations outside their industry because the skill they have transcends the narrowness of a specific industry. As skill competition crosses industries, compensation decisions will need to be integrated with staffing and retention concerns. Experts have noted that integrating staffing and retention strategies with compensation strategies may be particularly important for labor intensive firms that require employees with firm-specific knowledge and skills but that operate in highly uncertain and competitive markets and experience variable but highly predictable demand for goods and services. Consumer product industries have these characteristics and are already accommodating the personal and family needs of their critically skilled employees.[12]

### Compensation Strategy and Training Strategy

Surveys of training practices show that U.S. firms either train or pay for the training of between one-quarter and one-third of the civilian labor force yearly.[13] Furthermore, through the rest of the decade, technological changes are expected to have a greater impact on training activities than political, economic, demographic, or social changes.[14] Compensation strategy needs to consider the cost implications of training. One issue to consider is whether to pay workers when they are away from their jobs for training. Another issue is whether training costs can be offset by lower starting wages.

Technological change has also produced economic displacement of large segments of unionized workers. These displacements have motivated unions to bargain for training and retraining of current workers. Because compensation is a mandatory issue for bargaining, compensation and training issues need to be integrated into a cohesive and coherent bargaining strategy by both management and union.[15]

## Organizational Environments and Compensation

In today's competitive environment, assessment of the complexity of the firm's environment is necessary to selection of organizational niches, effective organization structures, and effective reward systems. Indeed, analysis of the organization's environment is extremely important for choosing the organization's pay-level and pay-mix strategies[16] and the criteria for evaluating the pay plan's effectiveness.[17] The organization's environment is also important for anticipating government incentives to provide various benefits and, in some cases, to actively influence benefit legislation.

The contingency approach to compensation decision making recognizes that compensation is a key strategy for achieving business objectives.[18] It also alerts decision makers that organizations function in heterogeneous environments. Understanding the type of environment in which the organization functions, the levels of environment, and the stability or instability of environmental sectors is basic to matching the organization's performance goals to compensation. Environmental analysis also helps to suggest the organizational levels most appropriate for compensation decision making related to the organization's performance and social responsibility goals.

### Types of Organization Environments

A useful characterization of heterogeneity with respect to the environments in which organizations function is provided by Emery and Trist. Terryberry also related organizational planning processes to the organization's environment.[19] These relationships are graphically presented in Exhibit 6.1.

*Placid Randomized Environment:* This environment is the simplest type because the environmental sectors of relevance to the organization are relatively unchanging in themselves, and when change occurs, the change is random. Because environmental changes occur in a random fashion, the organization cannot anticipate those changes or plan for future events. Rather, it must react when changes occur. In these organizations, characteristic of firms in a pure competition or regulated situation, the primary way to increase performance is to become internally efficient.

*Placid Clustered Environment:* This environment is also a relatively simple and stable environment and is characteristic of imperfect competition. Although competitors exist, their behavior is not a significant factor in the firm's decision making. The placid clustered environment is characterized by relatively unchanging environment sectors; the changes that occur are not randomly distributed but can be observed to cluster together in ways that allow for analysis of positive and negative trends. Consequently, long-range planning processes can be profitably implemented.

*Disturbed Reactive Environment:* This type of environment is characterized by the presence of a number of similar organizations, each wishing to move in the long run in the same direction as their competitors. Competition in limited-growth markets characterizes the disturbed reactive environment. Such competition motivates use of a more sophisticated planning process than necessary for less complex environments. The term *strategic planning* is used to define such a planning process. In this context, strategic planning refers to a planning process that includes specifying a variety of possible changes in different environment sectors and developing contingent plans to deal with the changes that may occur.

*Turbulent Environment:* This type of environment is extremely dynamic. There are continuous changes in the relevant environment sectors and the sectors are

| EXHIBIT 6.1 | RELATIONSHIP BETWEEN ENVIRONMENTAL UNCERTAINTY AND ORGANIZATION'S PLANNING PROCESS |
| --- | --- |

| Environment Type | Corresponding Planning Process |
| --- | --- |
| Placid randomized | None |
| Placid clustered | Long-range |
| Disturbed reactive | Strategic |
| Turbulent | Adaptive |

not changing independently. Examples of changes include sudden changes in market demand, unanticipated moves by competition, unpredictable technological advances, and currency and stock market fluctuations. The key factor is that the changes cannot be anticipated in advance, not even in the short run. Changes in turbulent environments are "surprises." Given such surprises, long-range or strategic planning is useless. To survive the changes, the organization needs to adapt quickly. Thus, adaptive short-range strategies may be implemented.

Emery and Trist introduced their environment categorization scheme in 1963. At that time, most businesses located in the United States were primarily in placid randomized and placid clustered environments. In such environments, the "me too" compensation strategy is effective. Today, businesses function across all four Emery and Trist classifications. Equally important, the nature of the competition has changed for many industries. For example, consider the dominance of the automobile industry by the "big three" American auto manufacturers (General Motors, Ford, Chrysler). In the 1960s, the "big three" still dominated the automobile industry. That dominance produced a disturbed reactive environment for the other manufacturers. For example, if one of the "big three" companies introduced a 30,000-mile warranty, others followed. The "big three" also led the industry in pricing and other decisions. At that time, U.S. auto trade relations were also based on competition in quality and design rather than in price. Because of those factors, the automobile industry could continue to use the strategy of taking labor out of competition.[20] Unions also benefited from that strategy because the size of the contract was not a key factor in negotiations with the auto companies. With all of the domestic auto companies unionized, the unions developed a corresponding "me too" strategy called *pattern bargaining*, in which the terms settled with one major auto manufacturer became the bases for negotiations with the other major manufacturers. Pattern bargaining resulted in establishment of similar wage levels and structures across the major automobile competitors and removed wages and benefits from the competitive process. Although pattern bargaining prevailed through the early 1980s,[21] that strategy is less feasible today. Besides competing on quality, Japan's auto manufacturers also compete on price.[22]

The entry of price competitors in global markets moves a firm's environment from the placid categories to the more dynamic disturbed reactive or turbulent fields. Japan's auto industry behavior also points to the importance of assessing not only the character of the organization's external environment but also the basis of competition among its product or service market competitors when making strategic compensation decisions. The latter assessment will enable the organization to evaluate the similarity of its cost structure to the cost structures of its major competitors and, by so doing, provide insights into the type of strategies that may be best for the organization to pursue.

## *Levels of Environment*

The organization theory and strategic management literature define two levels of environment: general and task. The *general environment* consists of economic, social, and demographic sectors that indirectly affect the organization. The *task environment*, however, consists of those environmental sectors that have a direct affect on the organization through their influence on operations and goal attainment.[23] For the purpose of organizational structuring, the relevant environment is viewed as consisting of those sectors that directly affect the goal attainment of the specific firm or business unit. These task environment sectors include all or several of the following: customers, suppliers, government regulations, labor supply, technology, unions, and the nature of the economy that directly affects the operations of the firm.[24] Organizations with multiple product lines are therefore likely to have as many task environments as divisions (units) in their organizational structures.[25]

With respect to pay plan design, task environment is the critical environment to consider because it is this environment that has a direct effect on goal attainment and hence performance of the firm. For example, the general environment may exhibit a high rate of unemployment, suggesting that the organization may be able to hire highly qualified people at low wages. However, the task environment may require personnel with scarce skills, and therefore, the unemployment rate may be of little relevance to compensation decision making. Similarly, the general environment may show that union membership is at an all-time low and that unions had been bargaining concessions in recent years just to maintain employment security for their members. However, the union that represents employees of a particular firm may prove to be a strong partner in decisions regarding wages, hours, and terms and conditions of employment for the workers it represents. Although one may suggest that the pay rate offered to the workers with scarce skills may be lower during periods of high unemployment than during periods of low unemployment and even a strong union may not be as militant during economic downturns as during economic prosperity, it is also obvious that organizations hire and pay people because they need people to do certain work to achieve the organization's performance goals. Consequently, performance-related human resource activities can be said to be more influenced by developments in the task environment sectors than by the general environment. It therefore follows that decisions about the pay plan should be made at the business unit level.

### Environmental Stability/Instability

Writers have categorized task environments along two dimensions: (1) homogeneity or heterogeneity of environment sectors that the organization has to manage and (2) the relative changeability of the environment sectors. The first dimension reflects the relative complexity of the organization's overall environment. The environment is said to be complex when multiple elements have to be dealt with within the relevant environment sectors. Exhibit 6.2 provides an example of a relatively simple and complex characterization of an environment. Exhibit 6.2 shows that environmental complexity is associated with the presence of multiple constituents within each of the environment sectors. The second dimension reflects the uncertainty or lack of predictability decision makers face when they interact with the task environment

| EXHIBIT 6.2 | EXAMPLES OF RELATIVELY SIMPLE AND COMPLEX ENVIRONMENT SECTORS | |
|---|---|---|
| **Environment Sector** | **Simple Environment** | **Complex Environment** |
| Customers | One type of customer (for example, adult men) | Many different types of customers |
| Suppliers | Limited number of suppliers | Multiple suppliers within multiple industries |
| Government regulations | Limited number and limited variety of product, environment, financial, and human resource regulatory requirements | Large number and large variety of regulatory requirements |
| Technology | Routine, limited in scope | Variable in number and scope |
| Economy | Little effect on operations | Variable effect on operations |
| Labor supply | Homogeneous, ample supply | Heterogeneous, variable supply |
| Unions | Not a factor or limited in number and influence | Ranges from not a factor to highly influential, moderate in number |

sectors. Exhibit 6.3 shows that environmental uncertainty is associated with rate of change in the task environment sectors.

At the level of the corporation, these two environment dimensions (complexity and rate of change in task environment sectors) characterize the amount of information available about the environment for organizational decision makers and hence influence executive perceptions of environmental uncertainty. The main reason that multiple product organizations modify their structures is that the rates

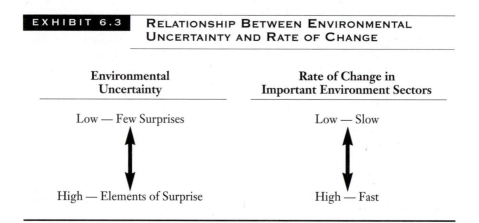

| EXHIBIT 6.3 | RELATIONSHIP BETWEEN ENVIRONMENTAL UNCERTAINTY AND RATE OF CHANGE |
|---|---|
| **Environmental Uncertainty** | **Rate of Change in Important Environment Sectors** |
| Low — Few Surprises | Low — Slow |
| ↕ | ↕ |
| High — Elements of Surprise | High — Fast |

of change in heterogeneous environment sectors produce decision bottlenecks within the organization and reduce its ability to meet market demands in a timely fashion. Consequently, firm performance suffers. By organizing multiple product lines into self-contained units, or divisions, the organization decentralizes decision making by allowing each unit to deal with its own task environment and thus respond to its unique task environment in a timely fashion. At the level of the business unit, the instability or rate of change in the task environment sectors characterizes the organization's environmental uncertainty, as there is only one primary task environment with which the organization interacts. Finally, although an organization's task environment may be uncertain, the importance of the task environment sector to organizational performance is the necessary condition for motivating attention to selected environmental sectors.[26]

Because executives are responsible for the organization–environment alignment,[27] uncertainty of environmental sectors and their importance have been suggested as key determinants of executive planning, decision making, and strategy formulation. Given that pay plan design is an outcome of a planning process oriented toward motivating performance behaviors, Rockmore and Scarpello[28] proposed that the organization's pay plan design should also be aligned with the perceived uncertainty of the firm's task environment. Furthermore, pay plan designs that fit the perceived uncertainty of the firm's task environment should show a more positive relationship to firm performance than do pay plans that do not fit the perceived uncertainty of the firm's task environment. Exhibit 6.4 shows the environmental uncertainty model of pay plan design.

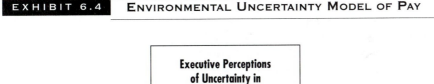

**EXHIBIT 6.4**    **ENVIRONMENTAL UNCERTAINTY MODEL OF PAY**

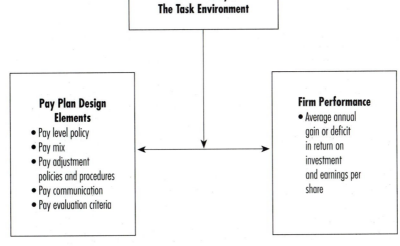

SOURCE: Rockmore and Scarpello, *The Environmental Uncertainty Model of Pay Plan Design.*

To date, the environmental uncertainty model of pay presented in Exhibit 6.4 was supported in two studies. Using a heterogeneous sample of 130 business units within 66 four-digit SIC codes, the studies found that the business units could be categorized into two environments: "more" and "less" certain. Six pay plan characteristics were also found to differentiate the pay plans of salaried exempt professionals across the two environments. The differentiating variables are shown in Exhibit 6.5. Of significance was the finding that a match between pay plan design and environmental classification category was related to a 5-year annual average gain in firm performance as measured by return on investment (ROI) and earnings per share (EPS). In contrast, a mismatch between the pay plan design and environmental classification category was related to a 5-year average annual deficit in firm performance.[29]

## Levels of Compensation Decision Making

Writers on compensation frequently describe compensation decision making as centralized (decisions made at the top of the corporation) or decentralized (decision made at the business unit level). Furthermore, although there seems to be some general agreement that pay plan design decisions are best decentralized, writers also suggest *ad hoc* reasons for centralizing those decisions.

In this text, both levels of the organization (corporate level and business unit or division level) are viewed as relevant to compensation decision making. However, these levels correspond to two different decision-making categories: the corporate level is appropriate for equity and social responsibility

---

**EXHIBIT 6.5** PAY PLAN CHARACTERISTICS THAT DIFFERENTIATE PAY PLANS BETWEEN MORE AND LESS UNCERTAIN ENVIRONMENTS

| Firms in Less Uncertain Environments Show: | Firms in More Uncertain Environments Show: |
| --- | --- |
| Greater use of market-lag pay-level policy | Greater use of market-match pay-level policy |
| Greater emphasis on seniority awards | Greater emphasis on performance awards |
| Greater use of lump-sum pay adjustments | Greater use of distributive pay adjustments |
| Greater use of cash bonus awards | Greater use of stock bonus awards |
| Greater emphasis on creating competition among individuals | Greater emphasis on creating cooperation within teams of employees |
| Greater use of internal standards for evaluating pay plan effectiveness | Greater use of external comparisons for evaluating pay plan effectiveness |

related decisions, and the business unit level is appropriate for firm performance-related decisions.

At the corporate level, activities focus on managing the financial portfolio of the business or of multiple businesses within the corporation and on managing the organization's responsibilities to society. At the business unit level, activities focus on managing the operations to ensure achievement of stated performance goals. In a single- or dominant-business company, the corporate and business unit level decisions are made at the same organizational level; therefore, decision making is said to be centralized at the top of the organization. In multiple- product or service firms, the decisions regarding corporate and business unit issues are made at their appropriate organizational levels. Therefore, decision making is said to be decentralized.

Traditionally, pay *and* benefit plans have been centralized at the corporate level. That centralization was largely due to the fact that through the 1950s, most American corporations were single-product or dominant-product corporations and not multiple-product corporations as they are today. In multiple product organizations, the question of whether to centralize decision making regarding pay and/or decision making regarding benefits is largely answered if we relate pay and benefit offerings to their purposes: organizational performance and fulfillment of societal responsibilities.

Other than being in compliance with legally required minimums, pay systems are designed primarily to provide the necessary incentives to influence individual performance. Directors of compensation note that pay plans of diversified companies must be tailored to meet the specific performance needs of the individual businesses that comprise the diversified company.[30] Indeed, business units can be expected to have their own unique environments with respect to stage of development of their products or services and with respect to their industry competitors, customers, suppliers, regulatory agencies, technologies used to produce the products, skills demanded of their work forces, and the economy's effects on operations. Because of potential differences in environment sector importance to firm performance, the current view is that pay plans should be designed to support the performance goals of the single or dominant business.[31] Thus, within multi-product organizations, pay plans should be designed for single businesses or business units. Besides environmental uncertainty, the culture and value milieu in which a firm operates influence pay practices through the organization's ability to attract, retain, and motivate the quality and quantity of employees needed to perform the organization's jobs. These influences are normally factored into the design of pay plans and the development of human resource policies that flow from the broader human resource and compensation strategies.

There are, however, aspects of compensation (namely, benefits) that do not directly relate to the firm's performance goals. Rather they relate to the firm's societal obligations for fair and impartial treatment of employees and organizational responses to societal mandates or incentives to provide particular benefits to employees. Logic suggests that decision making related to the non-performance aspects of compensation should be centralized rather than decentralized. By centralizing decisions about societally mandated regulations or inducements, the organization can concentrate expertise in one location, experience substantial savings from economies of scale, minimize its vulnerability to charges of employment and compensation law violations, and provide employees with recourse should they experience unfair treatment within individual employing units.

By decentralizing pay decisions and centralizing decisions about benefits and employment and compensation law compliance issues, the organization motivates performance and complies to societal and cultural expectations for employee treatment. Obviously, the costs associated with pay and benefit offerings must be accounted for as total compensation cost. The integration of performance and nonperformance aspects of compensation can take place at the corporate level, as done with comparable financial and legal decision making. Thus, at the corporate level, employee compensation focuses on financial and legal issues. Even so, certain operational aspects of this decision making remain decentralized. These relate to compliance with state wage and hour laws and state fair employment practice requirements, as well as accommodation to local customs. With respect to custom, for example, in certain areas of Wisconsin, it is not unusual for the opening week of deer hunting season to be a scheduled week of vacation. This practice reduces absenteeism and overtime costs which could be substantial in an area where deer hunting is a time-honored ritual.

## Alternative Proposals of the Relationship Between Compensation Decision Making and Organizational Contingencies

This section of the chapter introduces two additional contingency perspectives that have been related to pay plan designs: product life cycle and Miles and Snow typology. In contrast to the external orientation of the environmental uncertainty perspective discussed throughout the chapter, the contingency perspectives discussed below are internally focused.

### Product Life Cycle

The product life cycle (PLC) model attempts to explain organizational development through assignment of discrete stages of product or service evolution: birth to introduction, growth, shakeout/turnaround, maturity, and decline.[32]

The PLC model was first used in executive compensation as a vehicle for relating the organization's cash-flow concerns at different PLC stages to means of attracting, retaining, and motivating executives at different PLC stages. Ellig[33] proposed that cost-efficient and cost-effective executive pay plans should vary in pay level and pay mix by the organization's PLC stage. At the executive level, pay level refers to the executive's base salary and thus is the "fixed" portion of the executive's pay. Executives are also provided different incentives (for example, stock options), which they have to earn on a yearly basis and thus remain "variable" portions of pay. Ellig proposed the following relationships between PLC stage and executive pay level and pay mix.

*Introductory PLC Stage:* During this stage, the main concern of the business is to reinvest earnings into marketing and into development of the production process. To conserve the limited cash flow, executive pay plans offer lower than market salaries and high long-term growth-oriented incentive opportunities such as stock option or stock purchase plans.

*Growth PLC Stage:* During this stage, the business is in a position to improve executive salaries. However, to realize the desired profit, it must continue both capital investment and expansion of the product's distribution channels. To motivate executives toward those goals, executive plans continue the emphasis on variable over fixed pay. However, there is a change in the type of incentives offered. Short-term incentives are implemented as motivators of operational efficiency. Long-term incentives continue as a means of rewarding growth in market share.

*Shakeout/Turnaround PLC Stage:* Ellig did not propose a relationship between this PLC stage and executive pay, but logic suggests that, in this stage, executive compensation would be similar to that in the introductory PLC stage.

*Maturity PLC Stage:* At this stage, the organization has achieved its market potential. The primary business concern is to maximize short-term earnings and to generate a positive cash flow to enter new ventures. As a means of improving earnings, cost containment strategies are implemented. Consistent with cost containment, executive pay plans reduce the incentive portion of pay and increase emphasis on fixed salary, benefits, and perquisites. Short-term incentives continue to be provided and long-term incentives may also be provided. However, consistent with the cost containment goal, long-term incentives reward operational (nonmarket) performance rather than market performance.

*Decline PCL Stage:* During this stage, the organization's goal is to maximize cash-flow generation. To accomplish this goal, executive pay plans provide high salaries and benefits and deemphasize the incentive portion of pay. When incentives are used, they are usually short-term cost reduction incentives and long-term operational efficiency incentives.

The PLC concept suggests that pay plans are designed to reward the degree of risk taking the organization needs to ensure some level of performance. Compensation researchers have suggested that the PLC model may be applicable to compensation of employee groups below the executive level. To date, however, there is little support for that premise.[34] It may be that PLC is a viable model for some organizations and some employee groups but not for others. For example, the PLC model suggests that pay level and pay mix decisions may be dependent on the amount of control the organization has over its product's market penetration, production, and distribution. When control is low (introductory, growth PLC stages), organizations design pay plans to motivate discretionary performance. When control is high (maturity and decline PLC stages), organizations design pay plans to motivate maintenance of established markets, production, and distribution processes. Control, however, is not the only variable to consider. Another key variable is the nature of work performed. For example, if the work performed is routine, the employees have little opportunity for discretionary performance, and even if opportunity exists, the impact of the performance is unlikely to affect the organization's productivity significantly. Similarly, the more routine the work is, the more people there are who can perform the work without training. Performance of routine work by individuals with low human capital investments is likely to translate into low wage offerings, typically, minimum wage. Organizations at the introductory PLC stage, requiring performance of routine work by minimum wage workers, are not likely to add to their wage bill by providing incentives to earn more than minimum wage because they may not have the ability to pay more than minimum wage. Creative compensation plans, however, can be developed for even minimum wage workers. Attendance can be rewarded with "time off" during slow periods. Special performance may be rewarded by periodic tickets to a concert or sporting event. These and other incentives may be within the expense budgets of even the most budget-constrained employers and may result in high productivity and loyalty from the incentive recipients.

## Miles and Snow Typology

Writers have argued that the compensation strategy of a business unit depends on the way the firm interacts with its environment. Miles and Snow typology proposes four ways that organizations interact with their environments.[35] This typology has been related to pay mix decisions of three organizations: Hewlett Packard, Texas Instruments, and Lincoln Electric.

*Prospectors:* These firms operate within a broad product-market domain that undergoes periodic redefinition. Through either strategic or adaptive planning, prospector firms respond quickly to perceived opportunities in their external environment, with new product development and market introduction. These organizations value being first in new products and market areas, even if not all of these efforts prove to be highly profitable. Miles and Snow showed that prospector firms place heavy emphasis on incentive pay to reward risk-taking behavior.

*Defenders:* These firms attempt to locate and maintain secure niches in relatively stable product or service areas. The firms generally offer a more limited range of products or services than their competitors and try to protect their domains by offering high quality, exemplary service, low prices, and other customer incentives. Often, these types of organizations are followers rather than innovators in their respective industries. They tend to ignore industry changes that have no direct influence on current areas of operation and concentrate instead on doing the best job possible in a limited area. Miles and Snow showed that defender firms emphasize fixed pay to ensure internal operating efficiency and maintain stability in their operations.

*Analyzers:* Like the defenders, the analyzers attempt to maintain a limited but stable line of products or services. However, unlike the defenders, analyzers monitor developments in their markets and follow the leaders into related markets with cost-efficient improvements. Because analyzers are oriented toward both market performance and product stability, their pay plans have been shown to contain a combination of fixed and variable pay components.

*Reactors:* These firms are not oriented toward the market in ways that require planning. Indeed, they operate in response to randomly occurring external events that threaten their operations. For these reasons, reactor firms are not studied by strategic management scholars, and writers have not related this typology to pay plan design.

Like the PLC concept, the Miles and Snow typology focuses on internal responses to environmental contingencies. As noted, the PLC concept suggests that pay plans are designed to reward the degree of risk taking the organization needs to ensure some level of performance. The Miles and Snow typology takes the view that the risk-taking propensity of organizational decision makers motivates their behavior with respect to product or service market interactions and with respect to design of reward systems, the latter of which are intended to maintain the firm's market interaction orientation. With respect to compensation, researchers have not yet investigated whether there is a relationship between PLC stage or Miles and Snow classification and firm performance. Nevertheless, these models are included in the chapter as heuristic aids in compensation decision making.

## Summary

This chapter defines strategic compensation as decision making focused on ensuring that compensation plan design, implementation, and control activities relate directly to the achievement of the organization's performance goals, within the constraints of societal expectations and mandates. The chapter notes that the past American strategy of taking labor out of competition, along with its "me too" compensation strategy, is no longer feasible for many companies. The chapter also points out that although strategies may be formulated formally or informally, explicitly or implicitly, they direct implementation tactics and operations. Just as yesterday's strategies are no longer feasible for many firms, yesterday's implementation tactics and operations must also be re-evaluated. The chapter discusses four levels of strategy and how those levels are interrelated. The chapter also suggests that the performance and social responsibility goals of compensation may be best achieved if pay decisions are decentralized and fair employment and benefits decisions are centralized. The chapter suggests that the contingency approach to compensation decision making recognizes that compensation is a key strategy for achieving business objectives. Because the development of contingency approaches requires understanding of the characteristics of the external environment with which the organization interacts, a large segment of the chapter discusses environmental concepts and how these relate to compensation decision making. Several internally focused contingency models are also described.

## Discussion Questions

1. What is the meaning of strategy within the context of compensation decision making, and what levels of strategy are relevant to such decision making?

2. Is strategy a new concept in compensation decision making? Explain your position.

3. What are the important organizational contingencies that may influence compensation decision making. Discuss both external and internal contingencies.

4. What are the two broad goals of compensation, and what levels of the organization should have the primary responsibility for the achievement of those goals? Why does it make sense for responsibility to be placed at the levels you specified? Can you make a case for other solutions?

5. Are there situations in which the "me too" compensation strategy continues to be a viable strategy? Explain.

6. Is it true that variability in compensation strategy is likely to influence other human resource activities? Explain.

*References*

[1] C. W. Hofer, "Toward a Contingency Theory of Business Strategy, *Academy of Management Journal* 18 (1975), 784–810.

[2] For information about how governments influence organizational strategies, see C. K. Prahalad, "Developing Strategic Capability: An Agenda for Top Management," *Human Resource Management* 22 (1983), 237–254; for information about how different levels of organizational strategy constrain other levels, see C. W. Hofer and D. Schendel, *Strategy Formulation: Analytical Concepts* (St. Paul, MN: West Publishing, 1978).

[3] See D. L. Leslie, "Labor and Anti-Trust Laws," *Labor Law in a Nutshell* 8 (1986), 236–270.

[4] R. B. Freeman, *Labor Economics* (Englewood Cliffs, NJ: Prentice-Hall, 1972); L. G. Reynolds, *The Structure of Labor Markets* (New York: Harper, 1951).

[5] See A. B. Krueger and L. H. Summers, "Reflections on Inter-Industry Wage Structure," in *Unemployment and the Structure of Labor Markets*, eds. K. Lang and J. S. Leonard (New York: Basil Blackwell, Inc., 1987), 17–47; J. Dunlop, *Wage Determination Under Trade Unions*, (New York: McGraw Hill, 1944); J. Dunlop, "The Tasks of Contemporary Wage Theory" in *New Concepts in Wage Determination*, eds. G. Taylor and F. Pierson (New York: McGraw Hill, 1957), 117–139.

[6] See S. Christopherson, "The Mobile Work Force" in *High-Flex Society Working Papers* (Washington, DC: Roosevelt Center for American Policy Studies, 1987); V. Scarpello and S. Motowidlo, "Workforce 2000: Assumptions, Trends and Staffing Implications," *IRRA, 42nd Annual Proceedings* (1989), 518–516.

[7] L. R. Gomez-Mejia and T. M. Welbourne, "Compensation Strategy in a Global Context, *Human Resource Planning* 14 (1991), 29–42.

[8] J. R. Beatty, J. T. McCune, and R. W. Beatty, "A Policy Capturing Approach to the Study of U.S. and Japanese Managers' Compensation Decisions," *Journal of Management* 14 (1988), 465–474.

[9] L. A. Berger, "Trends and Issues for the 1990s: Creating a Variable Framework for Compensation Design" in *The Compensation Handbook*, eds. M. L. Rock and L. A. Berger (New York: McGraw-Hill, 1991), 12–23.

[10] V. Scarpello and S. Motowidlo, "Workforce 2000"; S. Christopherson, *The Origins of Contingent Labor Demand in Changing Production Organizations* (Washington, DC: Women's Bureau, U.S. Department of Labor, 1988).

[11] V. Scarpello and S. Motowidlo, "Workforce 2000."

[12] See K. Chin, "Home Is Where the Job Is," *Infoworld* 6 (1984): 17; S. Christopherson, *The Origins of Contingent Labor Demand in Changing Production Organizations*; E. Appelbaum, "Technology and Work Organization in the Insurance Industry," *ILR Report* 23 (Cornell Univ.) (Fall 1985), 21–26.

[13] See J. Gordon, "Where the Training Goes," *Training* 27 (1990), 41, 50-68; E. Bowen, "Schools for Survival," *Time* (February 11, 1985), 74–75.

[14] See L. T. Ralphs and E. Stephan, "HRD in the Fortune 5OO," *Training and Development Journal* 40 (October 1986), 69–76.

[15] See S. Deutsch, "Successful Worker Training Programs Help Ease Impact of Technology," *Monthly Labor Review* 110 (1987), 14–20.

[16] B. B. Overton and W. T. Steele, *Designing Management Incentive Plans: An Approach to Developing a Short-term Incentive Plan for Managers* (Scottsdale, AZ: American Compensation Association, 1992).

[17] B. W. Rockmore and V Scarpello, *The Environmental Uncertainty Model of Pay Plan Design: An Empirical Investigation* (Georgia State University working paper, 1993).

[18] For writers noting that compensation is the means for achieving business objectives, see L. B. Gomez-Mejia and D. B. Balkin, *Compensation, Organizational Strategy and Firm Performance* (Cincinnati, OH: South-Western Publishing Co., 1992); B. Gerhart and G. T. Milkovich, "Employee Compensation: Research and Practice" in *Handbook of Industrial and Organizational Psychology* 3, 2d ed., eds. M. D. Dunnette and L. M. Hough (Palo Alto, CA: Consulting Psychologist Press, 1992), 481-569; B. C. Ellig, "The Compensation Function: From the Chief Personnel Officer's Perspective," *Compensation and Benefits Review* 22 (January/February 1990), 30–35.

[19] For environment types see F. E. Emery and E. L. Trist, *The Causal Texture of Organizational Environments.* (A paper read at the XVII International Congress of Psychology, Washington, DC, August 20–26, 1963); also appeared in *Human*

*Relations* 18 (1965), 21–32. For relationship between environment type and planning, see S. Terryberry, "The Evolution of Organizational Environments," *Administrative Science Quarterly* 12 (1968), 590–613.

[20] R. Marshall, *Unheard Voices* (New York: Basic Books, 1986).

[21] K. J. Ready, "Is Pattern Bargaining Dead?" *Industrial and Labor Relations Review* 43 (1990), 272–279.

[22] R. Marshall, *Unheard Voices*.

[23] See J. D. Thompson, *Organizations in Action* (New York: McGraw-Hill, 1967); R. L. Daft, J. Sormunen, and D. Parks, "Chief Executive Scanning, Environmental Characteristics, and Company Performance: An Empirical Study," *Strategic Management Journal* 9 (1988), 123–139.

[24] W. R. Dill, "Environment as an Influence on Managerial Autonomy," *Administrative Science Quarterly* 2 (1957–58), 409–443; R. L. Daft et al., "Chief Executive, Scanning, Environmental Characteristics, and Company Performance"; R. L. Tung, "Dimensions of Organizational Environments: An Exploratory Study of their Impact on Organization Structure," *Academy of Management Journal* 22 (1979), 672–693; L. J. Bourgeois, "Strategy and Environment: A Conceptual Integration," *Academy of Management Review* 5 (1980), 29–39.

[25] P. Lawrence and J. Lorsch, *Organization and Environment* (Homewood, IL: Irwin, 1969).

[26] See D. A. Aaker, "Organizing a Strategic Information Scanning System," *California Management Review* 25 (1983), 76–83; J. Pfeffer and G. R. Salancik, *The External Control of Organizations* (New York: Harper & Row, 1978).

[27] R. G. Ritvo, P. Salipant, Jr., W. W. Notz, "Environmental Scanning and Problem Recognition by Governing Boards: The Response of Hospitals to Declining Birth Rates," *Human Relations* 32 (1979), 227–235.

[28] Rockmore and Scarpello, *The Environmental Uncertainty Model of Pay Plan Design*.

[29] *Ibid.*; B. W. Rockmore and V. Scarpello, *Are the Determinants of Pay Plan Effectiveness the Same for American and Foreign Owned Business Units?* (Georgia State University working paper, 1993).

[30] B. A. Weitz and R. Wensley, eds., *Readings in Strategic Marketing* (Chicago, IL: The Dryden Press, 1988).

[31] Overton and Steele, *Designing Management Incentive Plans and Approach to Developing a Short-term Incentive Plan for Managers*.

[32] For PLC discussion, see E. E. Chaffee, "Three Models of Strategy," *Academy of Management Review* 10 (1985), 89–98; Hofer, "Toward a Contingency Theory of Business Strategy," *Academy of Management Journal* 18 (1975), 784–810; C. W. Hofer and D. Schendel, *Strategy Formulation: Analytical Concepts* (St. Paul, MN: West Publishing Company, 1978); B. R. Ellig, *Executive Compensation: A Total Pay Package* (New York: McGraw-Hill Publishing Co., 1982).

[33] B. R. Ellig, *Executive Compensation: A Total Pay Perspective* (New York: McGraw-Hill Publishing Co., 1982).

[34] D. D. Balkin and L. R. Gomez-Mejia, "Toward a Contingency Theory of Compensation Strategy," *Strategic Management Journal* 8 (1987), 169–182.

[35] For writers relating Miles and Snow classifications to type of compensation strategy pursued, see S. J. Carroll, "Business Strategies and Compensation Systems," in *New Perspectives on Compensation*, eds. D. B. Balkin and L. R. Gomez-Mejia (Englewood Cliffs, NJ: Prentice-Hall, Inc., 1987); D. C. Hambrick and C. C. Snow, "Strategic Reward System," in *Strategy Organization Design, and Human*

*Resource Management*, ed. C. C. Snow (Greenwich, CT: JAI Press, Inc., 1989); M. Wallace, *Rewards and Renewal: America's Search for Competitive Advantage Through Alternative Pay Strategies* (Scottsdale, AZ: American Compensation Association, 1990).

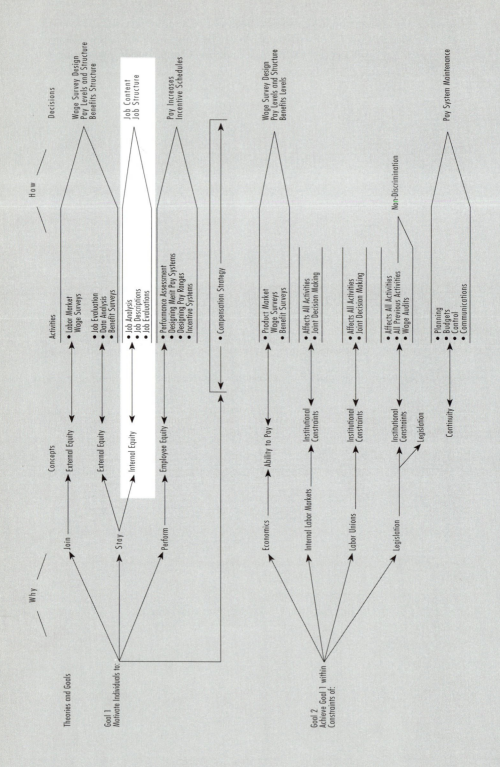

# III

# Internal Equity Determination

# 7

# Job Analysis and Job Descriptions/Specifications

## Learning Objectives

**To learn that the job is the basic unit of analysis in compensation decision making.**

**To learn that job analysis is a fundamental activity for compensation decision making.**

**To learn the process or steps in conducting job analysis.**

**To learn the commonly accepted approaches and techniques that organizations use in conducting job analysis.**

**To learn how to build a job analysis program for compensation decision making.**

## Introduction

Chapters 1 through 6 introduce the subject of compensation decision making and address some of the main theoretic concerns surrounding compensation decision making. This chapter begins the transition from the theoretic framework to the administrative practices that compensation decision makers use and begins the development of the compensation specialist's basic skills. In this chapter, the focus is on job analysis and job descriptions, including the meaning of these terms, the uses of job analysis data, the methods of collecting job analysis information, the use of specific techniques, and the writing of job descriptions, specifications, and standards.

## Definition and Purpose of Job Analysis

### What Is Job Analysis?

Job analysis is a systematic process of gathering information about the job. The job information normally gathered will include (1) the activities performed in that job (for example, what tasks are performed); (2) which job the analyzed job reports to; (3) the tools, materials, and equipment required for the job; (4) the outcomes of the job (for example, nails driven, walls built, engines assembled , or reports written); (5) the knowledge , skills, and abilities needed to perform the job; (6) the job environment (such as the working conditions); and (7) what constitutes good, poor, and superior performance on the job.

### Purpose of Job Analysis

The data obtained from the job analysis process are used to assist decision makers in making a variety of human resource decisions. This information is usually codified in a job description and a job specification. A *job description* can be defined as a narrative essay that details what the job is all about in terms of information noted in the previous paragraph. Frequently, these data are used to construct other documents as well (for example, job specifications). A *job specification* is a statement of the job requirements (for example, the job requires typing skills, a college degree, or legal training). The data may be used to set performance standards (discussed later in the text). Exhibit 7.1 shows the relationship between job analysis and job descriptions, performance standards, and job specifications.

Job analysis is usually designed for a specific purpose. The organization may do job analysis to clarify reporting relationships, to clarify responsibilities among jobs, or for many other reasons. The multitude of uses for job analysis

**EXHIBIT 7.1**   RELATIONSHIP BETWEEN JOB ANALYSIS AND OTHER HUMAN RESOURCE AND COMPENSATION ACTIVITIES

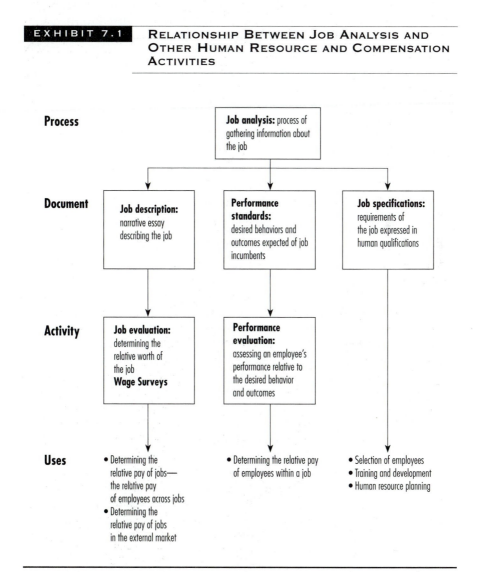

**Process**

**Job analysis:** process of gathering information about the job

**Document**

**Job description:** narrative essay describing the job

**Performance standards:** desired behaviors and outcomes expected of job incumbents

**Job specifications:** requirements of the job expressed in human qualifications

**Activity**

**Job evaluation:** determining the relative worth of the job **Wage Surveys**

**Performance evaluation:** assessing an employee's performance relative to the desired behavior and outcomes

**Uses**

• Determining the relative pay of jobs— the relative pay of employees across jobs
• Determining the relative pay of jobs in the external market

• Determining the relative pay of employees within a job

• Selection of employees
• Training and development
• Human resource planning

data is revealed in Exhibit 7.1. As organizations continue to adjust staffing levels and carry out job restructuring due to increasing product market competition, more emphasis will be placed on job analysis to identify essential job elements.[1] Some of the uses identified in Exhibit 7.1 are beyond the compensation area but are pertinent in the broader human resource management area. The uses specific to the compensation field are to provide information for conducting job evaluation and to gather performance standards information.

**Job Analysis and Job Evaluation**    Job evaluation is briefly discussed here and in more detail in Chapter 8.

Job evaluation is the process of establishing the relative worth of jobs. To decide if some jobs should ultimately be paid more than others, the organization needs to have information about each of the jobs in question so that it can establish their relative value to each other. To establish the relative worth of jobs, it is absolutely critical that the information collected about the jobs allows the analyst to make meaningful distinctions between them. These distinctions are based on the compensable factors that are important to the organization.

A *compensable factor* can be defined as any standard or criterion that the firm wishes to use in distinguishing among jobs for pay purposes. Examples of compensable factors are (1) the degree of responsibility, as measured by the number of subordinates supervised; (2) the amount of knowledge required, as measured by the years of schooling or related experience needed to do the job; and (3) the working conditions, as measured by the degree of physical discomfort (such as heat, cold, and noise) associated with the job. In a future chapter, the types of compensable factors used by organizations are developed more completely. For now, however, it is sufficient to know that compensable factors and their identification are important for job analysis when the purpose is job evaluation.

When an organization wishes to link the internal hierarchy of jobs determined by job evaluation to the external labor market, it will need to obtain external wage data. One method is to conduct a wage and benefit survey of relevant competitors in the labor and product market. To obtain accurate data, it is essential that, for each job surveyed, the organization supply a short description of the duties, responsibilities, and qualifications associated with the job. This enables the responding organization to provide valid information on the jobs requested. Across organizations, the same job titles may be attached to jobs that have significantly different duties, responsibilities, and qualifications, and thus job titles alone are inadequate to identify similar jobs.

**Job Analysis and Performance Standards**    In conducting a job analysis, information is often obtained on the level of performance expected of each individual doing that job. A job standard (performance standard) is the level of desired behaviors and outcomes expected of job incumbents. This information is used in the evaluation of the performance of each job incumbent. Establishing performance standards is the subject of Chapter 11. The job standard is the level of expected performance against which actual performance is compared. This is very important for organizations that have a merit pay policy because it will be the primary criterion on which the size of the merit increase will be based.

Even for those firms that do not have merit pay, performance standards must be identified if the organization is going to view employees as a human resource and attempt to develop that resource through a coaching and counseling philosophy. Many organizations view the assessment of performance both from an evaluative and a developmental perspective and thus carry on both continuously throughout the year.

Besides the above compensation-specific reasons for conducting a job analysis, there are legal reasons to have trained professionals conduct a systematic analysis of all jobs. The decisions made in job evaluation and performance assessment may incur legal challenge for alleged wage and benefit discrimination. In general, the following should be a guide for conducting a job analysis that can withstand legal challenges: (1) Hire trained professionals to conduct the analysis, (2) provide documentation, (3) focus on important duties, responsibilities, and qualifications, (4) provide an adequate sampling of incumbents in the jobs being analyzed, (5) ensure that the demographics of the incumbents included are similar to the population, and (6) use a systematic method of data collection, summarization, interpretation, and reporting because this may be construed as a test.[2] Provision of a complaint process to handle disagreements relating to job analysis also reduces the incidence of legal challenge.

## *Tasks, Jobs, and Positions*

Any discussion of jobs and job analysis assumes a knowledge of certain definitions. What are tasks, jobs, and positions; how are they alike and how are they different? A task can be defined as an activity that a person performs. For example, washing a wall, typing a letter, and starting an engine are all tasks that an employee might perform. A job is a collectivity of tasks performed by one worker. For example, the job of movie projectionist might include the tasks of unpacking the film, adjusting the carbon arc light, mounting the film on the projector, threading the film, showing the film, focusing the projector, and so on. A position refers to the person performing one job. For example, a company may have 100 truck drivers who operate semitrailer rigs. This company has one job of truck driver, but there are 100 positions for this job.

In talking about a job, it is important to distinguish between collections of tasks that are substantially similar and those that are substantially different. A trucking company may have several different jobs titled "driver." For example, a company might employ over-the-road drivers, short-haul drivers, and dispatch drivers. The distinction between these three jobs might be made on the size of the equipment used (semitrailer trucks, regular trucks, and vans) or on the basis of differences among the jobs in terms of working conditions. (Over-the-road drivers may be gone from home regularly for a week at a time, short-haul drivers may be out usually no more than one night per week, and dispatch drivers may never have to be gone from home.)

In this example the company has three types of driver jobs and a series of positions for each job. Each job has a slightly different set of tasks. One of the main issues in studying jobs is deciding when two jobs are alike enough to be considered the same job and when they are different enough to be considered distinct jobs.

The issue of similarities and differences among jobs is important from several standpoints. First, when organizations engage in job evaluation, they are determining the relative worth of jobs. A key element in determining the relative worth of jobs is to identify how jobs differ from each other. Second, differences and similarities among jobs hold legal implications under the Equal Pay Act of 1963, the Civil Rights Act of 1964, and the Fair Labor Standards Act of 1938. Under each of these acts, the employer must be able to meet certain legal requirements to ensure that the compensation system does not violate the law. For example, under the Equal Pay Act the employer must show that men and women earn equal wages if the jobs they perform are substantially equal in terms of skill, effort, and responsibility and if they are performed under similar working conditions. The Civil Rights Act imposes similar requirements in wage payments regardless of race, color, creed, sex, or national origin. Under provisions of the Fair Labor Standards Act, employers must determine which jobs must be paid overtime (nonexempt jobs) and which jobs do not require overtime payments (exempt jobs).

# Steps in Conducting Job Analysis

The procedures for conducting job analysis are examined here in a step-by-step process, which is summarized in Exhibit 7.2.

## *Preparation for Job Analysis*

The first step in doing job analysis is to determine the uses for the job analysis information. As indicated in Exhibit 7.1, many uses of the data go beyond the compensation area. As with any data collection process, the analyst must balance the information needed with the length of the process.[3] Only the information actually needed for decision making should be collected because resistance will increase from employees and supervisors if the process is unduly long. All the information that will be used within a reasonable time should be collected at one time to minimize interruptions.[4] Compensation decision makers will play a part in the job analysis when they intend to use the collected data for pay decisions. To this end, the job analyst will be interested in an analysis technique that allows distinction among jobs or distinction among performance levels within jobs.

The job analyst must be sure that high-level management gives active and visible support to the project if real cooperation throughout the organization is to be obtained. Also, the analyst must review the organizational chart, analyze the actual work flow, be aware of both the formal and informal power structure within the organization, check for potential seasonal or other variations in the operational process that must be taken into consideration, consult with outside sources (for example, the union, the Dictionary of Occupation Titles, trade groups, professional associations), and thoroughly review the current job descriptions and specifications.

The frequency of conducting job analysis is dependent on the stability of the job environment. If an organization is going through restructuring, job analysis must be performed unless it was completed recently. Organizations operating in the growth stages of product life cycle will require more frequent job analysis than those in a

**EXHIBIT 7.2**

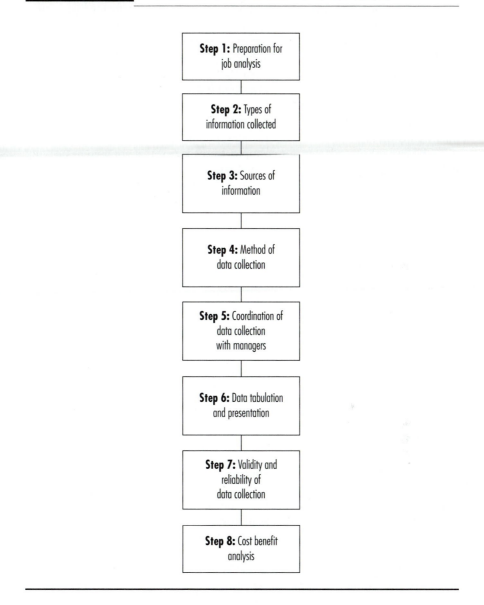

mature life cycle stage. An organization with operating divisions at different product life cycle stages will have each division operate on a different time table.[5]

## *Types of Information Collected*

**Activities Performed**   The information requested under work activities would include such things as a list of all significant activities, the frequency and amount of time each activity takes, the job objective that the activity would assist in accomplishing, how the activity is performed, who the activity is performed with, who reports to this job—number of people and the kind of work they perform, the level of responsibility (for example, hiring, assessing performance), who this job reports to, what other jobs are dependent on the output of this job, what level of external interface this position requires along with the degree of importance of these contacts, and the frequency and level of independent judgments made.

**Equipment, Tools, Materials, and Other Work Aids**   The analyst must also identify any mechanical devices (for example, computer), tools (for example, socket wrench), and other work aids (for example, Lotus 1-2-3) that are used in carrying out the work activities. Identification should include the amount of time the device is used in carrying out the job. The analyst also notes the employee responsibilities for maintaining, setting up, and breaking down equipment and specifies if the job requires handling of any special materials (for example, expensive raw material such as gold).

**Performance Expectations**   The analyst identifies the level of performance required of employees on each activity, citing the normal level of proficiency expected in operating each piece of equipment, work aid, or tool and describing the appropriate level of performance for the efficient and effective use of materials. Industrial engineering may be helpful in designing this section to provide insights into obtaining accurate and reliable data.

**Job Context**   The conditions under which the job is performed are important. This includes both physical and psychological environmental factors that make the job more difficult, dangerous, or stressing. This may include such factors as physical extremes (for example, stooping, climbing), poor conditions (for example, heat, noise, cold), and unique job demands (swing shifts, travel, interpersonal stress interactions, very tight time demands). The analyst must clearly and precisely identify these conditions and note the frequency and duration of their existence.

**Individual Characteristics**   Identification of individual characteristics helps to pinpoint the specific skills required to perform the job satisfactorily and the means to acquire those skills. For example, the job may require knowledge of Lotus 1-2-3 and a specific keyboard speed. The analyst determines how this knowledge is obtained, through formal training (school) or experience, and identifies the amount of experience required with the specific package. If physical (for example, lifting 100 lbs.) or mental (for example, ability to handle upset customers) skills are part of the job, the skill level and means of attainment are also important data.

### Sources of Job Analysis Information

**Secondary Sources**   Several secondary sources may be available to the analyst as the job analysis process begins. These are sources that provide background information regarding the job.

*Technical manuals* are particularly useful if the new job being created or being revised is due to a technologic change. If the purchase price of the new equipment is large enough, it is reasonable to expect a detailed manual to accompany it. Often the manuals will describe the activities to be performed, the level of output expected, the kinds of personal qualifications needed to operate it, the unique kinds of materials needed for the equipment, and other information that may be related to typical information collected through job analysis. The manual will not provide all necessary information but may provide an excellent starting point and significantly reduce the information that must be personally collected.

The **Dictionary of Occupational Titles** is published by the Department of Labor and contains thumbnail job descriptions and job specifications for thousands of jobs across the country. This is an excellent starting place for any compensation specialist who wants some general information on a job new to the organization. This source is only a starting spot because the information presented in it is inadequate for compensation decision making.

**Primary Sources**    The two primary sources of job analysis information are job incumbents and the immediate supervisor. Based on the authors' experience and past research, it is recommended that information be obtained from both sources whenever possible because the two sources at times provide conflicting information.[6] This may seem expensive, but because this information is used in multiple human resource decisions, it seems to be a wise investment of time and money. The use of these two groups as subject matter experts (SMEs) will provide support if employees challenge the outcomes either internally or externally through the courts or Equal Employment Opportunity Commission. The concept of using SMEs involves the completion of thorough questionnaires and the utilization of statistical analysis to arrive at the job analysis information.[7]

The supervisor's input may be weighted more in the areas of reporting relationships, amount of supervision received, and performance standards, whereas the employee's input may be weighted more in such areas as activities performed, equipment used, working conditions, and individual qualifications. The decision rule used in weighting should take into consideration who is in the best position to provide valid information and whether the person has anything to gain personally by providing inaccurate information. Ideally, it would be best to have all incumbents and supervisors participate, but that is often not economically or practically possible. In those situations in which many positions are associated with the jobs under analysis, a random or stratified random sampling technique can be successful. As mentioned previously, the data obtained by subject matter experts can be statistically combined to provide summary data. If sampling is used, a random or stratified random sample may be drawn. One study provides some insights into selection of sources for job analysis information. That study found that experience was significantly associated with task ratings; race and education were also related but to a much lesser extent.[8] More information on sampling is provided in Chapter 9.

## *Methods of Data Collection*

There are many methods the analyst can use to collect the job analysis information identified earlier. The following subsections present the most common methods. Once the purpose and the kind of information to be collected is decided, the analyst is in a position to decide on the method for data collection. One consideration in selecting the technique is the purpose and the kind and amount of data required. A second consideration is the nature of the jobs under study. For example, routine jobs that have clearly defined indicators of success are more amenable to study using a work methods approach than jobs that require nonroutine work with less clearly defined indicators of success. A third consideration is the amount of time and money that the organization is willing to commit to the job analysis program. Cost considerations may constrain the quality of the job analysis activity.

This text presents each method of data collection as if an organization uses only one method to collect data, but that is not always the case. An organization may use a combination of methods to obtain more valid and reliable information. It may use the interview method for one group of jobs but a questionnaire for a different group. Within a group, it may start with technical manuals that accompany the new technology because they provide information useful in designing questions for the interview or the questionnaire.

**Direct Observation**     To conduct a job analysis by direct observation, the analyst might start with a basic recording form like the one in Exhibit 7.3.

The analyst would then gather the job information data at the work area. In the case of a job with a short cycle time (all tasks are performed within an hour or so), the analysis might take only a few hours. If the cycle time of the task is very long (it takes several days before all the tasks in the jobs can be observed), the amount of time required for analysis is longer.

The direct observation method of job analysis may be useful for identifying health and safety hazards of jobs, but it also has certain limitations.[9] First, direct observation does not capture the mental aspects of jobs, including such things as decision making or planning, and second, observation provides little information on the personal requirements for performing jobs. A third problem with direct observation is that the behaviors observed may not comprise the total set of behaviors that should be performed on the job. The worker may not perform all the tasks that the job requires during the time of observation. The job analysis system should include a built-in check against this happening. Two potential checks involve observing more than one employee at the same job and reviewing the observed results with the supervisor or job incumbent to be sure that the analysis includes all activities.

A fourth limitation of many observation methods is the problem of rater bias. Most people have perceptual biases; analysts can disagree on what they think they saw in observing workers. One way around this type of bias is to have several analysts observe each job and then discuss their results. Collectively, they may arrive at a more accurate picture of what the job entails.

Several of the more common direct observation techniques follow:

*Work methods analysis* is a direct observation technique for studying jobs. A job analyst watches the employee perform the job in the work setting.

| EXHIBIT 7,3 | RECORDING FORM FOR DIRECT OBSERVATION JOB ANALYSIS |
|---|---|

Job title: _____

Job reports to: _____

Job interfaces with (other jobs): _____ _____ _____

Tools/equipment/materials used: _____ _____ _____

Tasks performed in the job: _____
_____
_____

Outcomes expected: _____
_____
_____

Skills required of job incumbents: _____
_____

Job environment: _____
_____

The analyst may be an industrial engineer who times the employee in different phases of the job. For example, a work methods analyst who is studying the job of lathe operator first identifies all the different physical activities that go into processing a part on a lathe—obtaining a piece of unprocessed metal, mounting the metal in the lathe, starting the lathe, turning down the part, turning off the lathe, loosening the part from the lathe, and placing the part in the finished products bin. After identifying each step in the process of producing a finished part, the analyst then uses a stopwatch to record the amount of time to complete each discrete step in the process. Based on large numbers of observations, the analyst arrives at an average time for each discrete step in the production process and an average time for producing a finished product.

The type of information obtained from the work methods approach to job analysis is often used for job redesign, determining if there is a better or more efficient way of doing the job, or for establishing the production standards for a piece rate incentive system. *A piece rate incentive system* is a pay system based on the number of units made. If the job analyst finds that an average worker could make 20 units of product per hour, the piece rate might be set at $0.40 per unit. An average employee would make $8 per hour, but above- and below-average employees would make more or less per hour. Work methods analysis is an important job analysis technique when the employer wants to pay on a piece rate system.[10]

Work methods analysis is also appropriate when the employer wishes to establish a performance evaluation system. For example, the analyst, by studying many employees performing the same job, could arrive at production levels for superior performance, average performance, and below-average performance. Work methods, however, are not concerned with studying differences between jobs and are not useful for job evaluation purposes.

*Critical incident techniques* are another type of direct observation.[11] In the critical incident approach, the job analyst observes the actual behavioral incidents exhibited by an employee on the job and records them. For example, in a critical incident analysis of the job of carpenter, it would be possible to identify those behaviors that are particularly good or poor. The analyst might identify such positive behaviors as driving a nail straight, making a square cut on a board, and erecting a straight wall and such negative behaviors as damaging the wood while driving a nail, ruining a board because of an incorrect cut, and not having a straight wall.

After deciding what the desired and undesired work outcomes are, the analyst looks at the behaviors that are critical in attaining those desired and undesired outcomes. In the carpenter example, if a smoothly finished wooden wall is desired, then one of the critical incidents that goes into the desired outcome is to "strike the head of each nail squarely with the hammer"; the critical incident associated with the undesired outcome is to miss the head of the nail and hit the board itself. Considerable time and effort go into the job analysis to identify all the critical incidents that are likely to result in desired and undesired outcomes. Once each of the outcome's dimensions and the critical incidents are identified, then the analyst goes over the information with those who are to use the data to make sure that employees know what the incidents mean. The purpose of this step is to be sure that the incidents are expressed in terms of the users' language.

In recent years, there has been a growth in the number of variations of critical incident methods. Techniques such as behaviorally anchored rating scales and behavioral observation scales have been suggested.[12] The data indicate that when these techniques are used for assessing performance, they are probably no more accurate than other, more traditional performance appraisal techniques.[13]

Critical incident techniques probably have their greatest uses in the human resource area of performance appraisal, because the techniques focus on important incidents within a job and not across jobs. With regard to pay decisions, this method is probably useful in establishing wage differences between job incumbents within a given job but is probably less valuable for establishing wage differences between jobs. This method would be appropriate for input into performance evaluations but not useful for input into job evaluation.

Because of the need to study many incumbents to ensure that all job components are observed, the need to use multiple analysts to get analyst reliability, and the need to observe the entire job cycle, observation methods are time consuming and costly. For this reason, many employers resort to other methods of data collection.

**Questionnaire**   A paper-and-pencil questionnaire can be constructed to cover the information needed as input to compensation decision making. Great care must be taken to construct the question stems because the respondent will have to answer based on the written question. If no one in the organization is familiar with questionnaire design, it is essential that a consultant be hired to construct a valid and reliable instrument. It is essential that the questionnaire is piloted on a small sample of employees to increase the probability that the vocabulary used is appropriate. Also, a debriefing session should be held with the employees participating in the pilot to answer questions they may have, to clarify ambiguous areas, to determine if any key areas are being overlooked, and to thank them for their time and effort. The advantages of the questionnaire method are (1) information can be obtained from many respondents in a relatively short time and at a reasonable cost, (2) the same questions are asked of all participants in the same order, (3) bias of the analyst is removed from the recording of the data, and (4) if scales are used for responses, it is easy to analyze the data statistically. There are several disadvantages: (1) It is costly to develop; (2) it may not be psychometrically sound; (3) there is no assurance the questions are being interpreted correctly; (4) response rate may be low; (5) codifying open-end responses is difficult; and (6) there is no control over condition under which the questionnaire is completed. Even with the above-mentioned disadvantages, it is a popular method of data collection. If an organization is going to use an interview technique, it would likely use a structured interview in the data collection process and thus the organization would have to do much of the same work required for a questionnaire. The section on specific job analysis techniques identifies several standardized questionnaires.

In large organizations, a task inventory may be developed for a group (cluster) of jobs, and incumbents can select those tasks that pertain to their job. This inventory can be put on a computer, and the respondents can enter their selections directly into the computer, which can then tabulate and summarize the results. This is especially efficient if there are many jobs in the group and/or many incumbents.[14]

**Interviewing**   Another important method of job analysis is to ask people what they do. The job analyst interviews one or more job incumbents to find out what is involved in the job. There is wide variation in how structured these interviews are. The interview may be very informal, or the analyst may undertake the interview with a detailed and highly structured questionnaire. The structured interview has a greater likelihood of ensuring coverage of all components of the job and inclusion of common information across all jobs under analysis, and it is generally preferable to the informal interview. The job analyst may interview one job incumbent or more than one at a time, depending on the total number to be interviewed.

This section covers the interview process and some of the standardized structured interview procedures.[15]

*Opening the interview* is an important part of the process. A job incumbent may consider the analyst a stranger in the work environment. The employee is likely to be unsure of the analyst and the motives for studying the job. The analyst should work to overcome these apprehensions.

First, the analyst should make an effort to develop rapport with the employee by calling the employee by name when meeting for the first time. The analyst should also allow for a "warm-up" period of 5 to 10 minutes to talk about something of interest to the employee and put the person at ease.

Second, the analyst needs to make clear to the employee the purpose of the interview, what the analyst expects to accomplish, and how the interview will help in determining fairer human resource practices. It should not be assumed that the employee's immediate supervisor has informed the employee of any of these points. This second step allows the analyst to reinforce the supervisor's message if the supervisor did communicate with the employee.

Third, the analyst should encourage the worker to talk by listening intently and not interrupting but allowing the employee to finish a line of thought. This will also facilitate putting the employee at ease.

Fourth, the analyst must not forget the purpose of the interview and must develop questions that will yield complete information. For example, if the job requires lifting, then questions pertaining to how much is lifted, the percentage of time, the kinds of work aids provided, and so on, are essential. Also, some questions may be better asked of the supervisor for the job under discussion rather than the job's incumbent, depending on who is in the best position to provide valid information.

*Directing the interview* is the analyst's job, so that minimal time investment results in maximum information gain. First, the interviewer should consider the best procedure for getting job information from the incumbent. If the worker normally performs a routine task or set of tasks, it is probably appropriate to have the worker describe the work cycle, beginning with the first task and moving to the last task. The worker will then be able to describe the natural flow of tasks in the work cycle. However, a worker may perform a nonroutine job or a job in which duties are not performed in any regular order. In this case, the analyst would probably want the worker to describe the tasks, beginning with the most important task performed and moving to the least important task performed. The employee should also describe those nonroutine but nonemergency duties that are performed. For example, an employee may only occasionally set up a machine or handle finished inventory. The goal of the interview is the discovery of all the dimensions of the job.

Second, the interviewer should ask the worker only one question at a time and allow sufficient time for a complete answer before moving on. Third, questions that call for a yes or no answer should be rephrased to require more explanation by the employee. Fourth, the worker should be allowed to answer questions in his or her own words.

Fifth, as the interview proceeds, the analyst should follow the interview questionnaire to keep the interview on track. If the incumbent strays from the subject at hand, the analyst might summarize the point up to where the employee strayed and then continue.

Sixth, the language of the interview should be easily understood. For example, the analyst may be interested in identifying the amount of a certain compensable factor in a job. Because the term *compensable factor*, for example, may not mean much to the incumbent in the interview, the analyst instead could ask the incumbent how much time it takes to become competent to perform the job without excess supervision. (There is no need to use the term *compensable factor*.) The analyst should always be aware of professional terminology because the employee may not have a correct understanding of the term.

Seventh, the job incumbent may be uneasy or nervous during the interview. If some portion of the interview makes the employee nervous, the analyst should gently lead him or her through that portion and allow adequate time to answer. The employee should never feel pressured by the analyst.

*Some basic approaches for interviewing* may make the process easier. It is difficult to anticipate everything that may arise during the course of an interview, but some suggestions to smooth the interview follow:

1. Be polite and courteous during the interview. Always afford complete respect for the employee and his or her statements.

2. Do not talk down to an employee. Say nothing to denigrate the employee or the job.

3. Do not permit notes or responses to be influenced by personal likes or dislikes. Be as neutral and objective as possible.

4. Talk to the worker only with permission of the immediate supervisor.

5. Take notes in as nondisruptive a fashion as possible. A standardized data collection sheet should facilitate this.

6. Do not assume that the worker will know all the information that is requested. For example, a worker may not know all the job titles of the jobs that his or her job interfaces with. The worker may also not know the training times for the job. It may be necessary to interview several people (including the supervisor) to get complete information.

7. Do not assume that employees can follow written questions (if handed out before the interview). It is better for the analyst to ask the questions verbally.

8. Do not assume that all employees have good verbal skills and can readily describe their jobs. Patience is critical in helping many employees describe their work. Be prepared to ask the question in more than one way because some employees may need it worded differently. Be prepared to use open-end questions and probing questions (for example, why do you do that?) to obtain desired information.

9. When asking questions regarding qualifications or performance standards, be aware that the employees may respond based on what they have or how well they do, not what is required for satisfactory performance. Be sure your questions clearly indicate the difference and specify what you actually want.

10. Leave until the end of the interview questions that are sensitive or threatening so they do not interfere with collection of the other information.

11. Do not become argumentative with the employee. Take statements at face value. If there is a question about the accuracy of a statement, check the facts later with another employee or with a supervisor.

12. Do not show partiality to statements made by the employee that concern the employee and employer relationship. For example, an employee might protest that a required duty is unfair or inappropriate.

Do not take sides on this type of issue. Explain that your job is to find out what is done, not whether it should or should not be done.

13. Do not discuss the wage classification of the job.

14. Verify the information that is obtained by interviewing more than one job incumbent, by checking the responses with supervisors, or both.

15. End the interview with a general question that permits the employee to add information he or she believes is important but that was not asked for.

16. Thank the employee for his or her time and cooperation.

When more than one employee is interviewed at the same time, the interviewer must take special precautions to ensure that accurate and valid information is obtained. First, ensure that all participants have equal chance to provide input so no single employee dominates the meeting. Second, guard against going in one direction, thus have questions developed ahead of time to cover a broad array of areas. Third, keep the size of the group small so all feel free to participate. Fourth, provide adequate time for the interview because it may take some members a short period of time to feel comfortable enough to participate fully.

**Diaries**   In this approach, each job incumbent maintains a narrative description of work activities during a specified period of time and records any other relevant information (for example, the kinds of equipment used, when it is used, the level of performance required, and any maintenance or set-up required). The diary offers several advantages: the employee provides the information in his or her own words and records the events at the time they actually take place. But this approach also has disadvantages: it is very difficult for the analyst to identify relevant information, the analyst must interpret what is meant by the employee, the data provided often lack reliability, there may be lack of adequate detail in the entry to be useful in decision making, and the large amount of entries may overwhelm the analyst.[16]

## Coordination of Data Collection with Managers

The compensation analyst must be sure that whatever method is used to collect the information does not interfere with each operating unit's ability to operate effectively and efficiently. For example, if data are to be collected through interviews, the analyst carefully coordinates scheduling of the interviews with the line managers so the disruptions within the department are minimized. Thus if the line manager has peak periods during the day or seasonal variation within the department, interview scheduling would revolve around those key times. It is also important that managers are kept well informed during the planning stages and kept up to date as the process is executed so that they know about events that have an effect on them well in advance and so that they can provide additional input to the process.

## Data Tabulation

Data tabulation is a significant undertaking, especially in organizations that have many jobs being analyzed or many employees working in a few jobs. When the number of respondents is large, it is essential that the data tabulation issue is addressed in the early stages of job analysis design. The number of actual correspondents affects the amount of information collected and the method used to collect the data. If the number of respondents is going to be large, it is essential that the requested information is limited to that which will actually be used in compensation decision making. With many respondents, the cost and time consuming nature of interviewing may preclude the use of this method as the major data collection technique. Instead, the organization may decide to use a questionnaire to collect data and only use interviews to deal with inconsistent responses. Different employees may respond differently to the same questions, or supervisor and employee may respond differently. It is important that such differences are examined and the correct information recorded for future decision making.[17] If many employees will be responding, it may be advantageous to construct the questionnaire so that the respondents are restricted to a limited number of choices to which they respond numerically. The responses can then be quantified and tabulated by the computer. This can save enormous amounts of time and energy and reduce the problems at this stage.

### *Validity and Reliability of Data Collection*

Reliability is the consistency of the data obtained. Reliability can refer to consistency of data between analysts or within an analyst's data. Consistency of data between analysts compares the data obtained by different analysts who are studying the same jobs. Consistency within an analyst's data compares the data obtained by the same analyst at different times or for different employees performing the same jobs. Researchers have found inconsistencies when comparing responses from supervisors to those of incumbents, whereas job analysts using different methods of data collection on the same jobs are relatively reliable.[18] The evidence supports the necessity of having both supervisor and employee participate because they each have a different perspective on the job, and the multiple data sources enable the analyst to look for inconsistencies. One of the main problems in measuring reliability is that much of the data cannot be easily quantified. Often determining reliability becomes more of a judgmental decision than a quantitative decision. Some job analysts rely heavily on standard techniques such as the Position Analysis Questionnaire because by their design they lend themselves to quantitative measures of reliability.

Validity refers to the accuracy of the data collected. The data collected can be very reliable without being valid. The same analyst may collect the same erroneous data at two different times, or two different analysts may collect the same erroneous data. In both cases, there would be consistency but not validity. The best method to guard against invalid data is to have multiple sources of data collection and to compare information systematically to determine if it is the same. Also, the data collected can be compared against industry norms through a professional association or through organizations employing similar jobs sharing data bases with each other. It is essential that job analysis follow all professional standards because it is a human resource activity reviewed in most discrimination cases.[19]

## Cost Benefit Analysis

The organization must calculate the total cost of its proposed job analysis process and compare it with the perceived benefits. If several key human resource decisions are to be made from the data collected, it is easier to justify significant expenditures. Refer to Exhibit 7.1 for an indication of the kind of human resource decisions that use job analysis information. If compensation decisions are the sole purpose for data collection, then a conservative analysis should be performed.

The cost should include the cost of the time that the human resource department must allocate to the project and the time that supervisors and job incumbents must spend on the project. The amount of employee and supervisor participation in the design of the process and the method of data collection may significantly affect the cost of the project. If the organization wishes to include employees in all steps of the job analysis as part of a total employee involvement philosophy, the cost may increase significantly but final product acceptance should also increase. Whatever the level of involvement, it is essential that the organization estimate both direct cost (for example, copying, computer) and indirect cost (for example, employees', supervisors', and compensation specialist's hours) to obtain an accurate total cost of the project. The cost of a custom-designed job analysis may run between $350,000 and $500,000, making the already developed techniques seem relatively inexpensive by comparison.[20]

# Standardized Structured Approaches to Job Analysis

Over the years, several fairly standardized approaches to job analysis have been developed. Several of the more commonly accepted approaches are discussed below.

## Functional Job Analysis

Functional job analysis is a method developed by the Training and Employment Service of the U.S. Department of Labor. It combines observation and interview methods.[21]

In functional job analysis, the analyst collects job information in five categories: (1) worker functions, (2) work fields, (3) machines, tools, equipment, and work aids, (4) materials, products, subject matter, and services, and (5) worker traits. The first category, worker functions, refers to how people relate to three aspects of work: data (mental aspects), people (social aspects), and things (physical aspects), as shown in Exhibit 7.4. A job might carry a code of Data=4 (computing), People=8 (taking instructions—helping), and Things=0 (setting up).

The work fields category consists of 99 subcategories encompassing use of the tools, equipment, and machines or techniques designed to fulfill the job. An example of a subcategory is "drafting, riveting, and sawing." The third category identifies the particular machines, tools, equipment, and work aids required to perform the job. Jobs are coded in the fourth category into one or more of 580 subcategories for materials, products, subject matter, and services. Finally, the analyst records worker traits for each job. The dimensions of worker traits recorded are (1) training time for the job, (2) aptitudes needed for the job, (3) interests tapped by the

| EXHIBIT 7.4 | WORKER FUNCTIONS |
|---|---|

| Data | People | Things |
|---|---|---|
| 0 Synthesizing | 0 Mentoring | 0 Setting up |
| 1 Coordinating | 1 Negotiating | 1 Precision working |
| 2 Analyzing | 2 Instructing | 2 Operating—controlling |
| 3 Compiling | 3 Supervising | 3 Driving—operating |
| 4 Computing | 4 Diverting | 4 Manipulating |
| 5 Copying | 5 Persuading | 5 Tending |
| 6 Comparing | 6 Speaking—signaling | 6 Feeding—offbearing |
| | 7 Serving | 7 Handling |
| | 8 Taking instructions— helping | |

SOURCE: U.S. Department of Labor, Manpower Administration, *Handbook for Analyzing Jobs* (Washington, DC: U.S. Government Printing Office, 1972), p. 73.

job, (4) temperaments necessary for the job, (5) physical demands of the job, and (6) the working conditions of the job.[22]

The functional job analysis approach is incorporated into the *Dictionary of Occupational Titles*.[23] From the compensation decision maker's viewpoint, probably one of the best features of this type of analysis is that it is extremely comprehensive, although some of the dimensions it measures are probably not useful for job evaluation purposes. It is an approach the job analyst should review when designing a job analysis system because it can provide ideas of what to look for in jobs. Some of the dimensions are very consistent with the types of compensable factors frequently used by employers. For example, two of the worker trait dimensions—training time for the job and working conditions of the job—are standard compensable factors used in many job evaluation plans. Unfortunately, the breakdown of these factors in functional job analysis may not provide the level of refinement needed for job evaluation. Functional job analysis is not very useful for performance evaluation systems because it provides for taxonomy (classification) of jobs rather than distinguishes between good and poor performers within a job.

## Structured Job Analysis Questionnaires

**Position Analysis Questionnaire**    The position analysis questionnaire (PAQ) approach uses an extremely lengthy and sophisticated standardized questionnaire designed by Ernest J. McCormick and associates.[24] It identifies 187 job elements related to six main divisions of work. These main divisions and examples of the job elements associated with them are depicted in Exhibit 7.5.

The PAQ, probably the most widely known standard questionnaire, was used to analyze thousands of jobs in McCormick's research program.[25] An organization can obtain the questionnaire from PAQ Services, Inc., along with a training manual and computer packages to analyze the large volume of data generated with the questionnaire.[26]

---

**EXHIBIT 7.5**     JOB ELEMENTS FROM THE POSITION ANALYSIS QUESTIONNAIRE[a]

---

1. Information input (where and how the worker gets information used in performing the job)
   a. written materials
   b. behaviors
   c. touch

2. Mental processes (reasoning, decision making, planning, and information processing activities involved in performing the job)
   a. reasoning in problem solving
   b. analyzing information or data
   c. using mathematics
   d. estimating speed of moving objects

3. Work output (physical activities the worker performs and the tools or devices used)
   a. precision tools
   b. foot-operated controls
   c. assembling/disassembling
   d. finger manipulation

4. Relationships with other persons (relationships with other persons required in performing the job)
   a. entertaining
   b. coordinates activities
   c. supervision received

5. Job context (physical and social contexts in which the work is performed)
   a. indoor temperature
   b. noise intensity
   c. frustrating situations

6. Other job characteristics (activities, conditions, or characteristics, other than those described above, relevant to the job)
   a. specific uniform/apparel
   b. irregular hours
   c. working under distractions
   d. travel

---

[a]PAQ further specifies job elements in questionnaire.
SOURCE: Ernest J. McCormick, P. R. Jeanneret, and R. C. Mecham, *Position Analysis Questionnaire*, © 1969, 1989, Purdue Research Foundation. Reprinted with permission.

The authors of the PAQ claim it may be used for human resource selection, job evaluation, performance evaluation, job profile matching, and the development of job families. Whether the information from this questionnaire has real value to the compensation decision maker for performance evaluation is questionable. The information collected is again designed more as a taxonomic (classification) device for jobs rather than as a means to determine variations in performance within a job. However, the PAQ may be highly useful in the job evaluation context. McCormick and associates report that compensation rates can be predicted with considerable accuracy by using specific job elements in the questionnaire.[27] Similar results were observed by another researcher,[28] suggesting that the position analysis questionnaire holds considerable promise in job evaluation programs. Compensation decision makers must remember that pricing directly from the PAQ will tie pay to the market but may not represent the appropriate internal structure for their organization.

The Professional and Managerial Position Questionnaire (PMPQ) has been developed specifically for use for professional, managerial, and other related positions. It is similar to the PAQ (consists of only 98 items) and is accompanied by much of the same software.

**Task Inventory Questionnaire**   Another common type of questionnaire is a task inventory. Task inventories typically measure job characteristics and worker characteristics. Exhibit 7.6 displays information from an inventory that assesses job characteristics.

One of the best-known task inventories is the Comprehensive Occupational Data Analysis Program (CODAP) developed by the U.S. Air Force and used in both the military and public sector.[29] The incumbents in the jobs are asked to indicate from a list which tasks they perform, time spent performing the tasks, the importance of each task, and the training time required to learn the tasks. The incumbents themselves, supervisors, or others who are familiar with the positions being analyzed usually create the task lists. Task inventory questionnaires are often completed at a computer terminal, which permits immediate scoring of all responses and quick summarizing of employees' responses. In studies, this technique and PAQ were rated highest for the purpose of job evaluation.[30]

These worker-oriented inventories can also measure worker attributes such as skills needed, education required, strength needed, manual dexterity, and so forth. Task inventories probably have use for job evaluation purposes, but little use for performance evaluation purposes.

**Job Analysis Questionnaire**   The job analysis questionnaire is another lengthy questionnaire that analyzes jobs along three dimensions: job tasks, job environment, and job knowledge. In a study conducted by Newman and Krzystofiak,[31] the questionnaire yielded 60 underlying factors among 1,700 jobs.

Like other standardized job analysis questionnaires, the job analysis questionnaire holds promise for job evaluation purposes.[32] However, it probably has limited use for performance evaluation purposes.

## Custom-Designed Job Analysis

From a compensation decision maker's viewpoint, no one standard approach seems to satisfy adequately all the data requirements for both job evaluation and performance evaluation. The most practical resolution is either to combine many approaches and adapt them to the organization or to design a job analysis program

**EXHIBIT 7.6**    **TASK-ORIENTED JOB CHECKLIST**

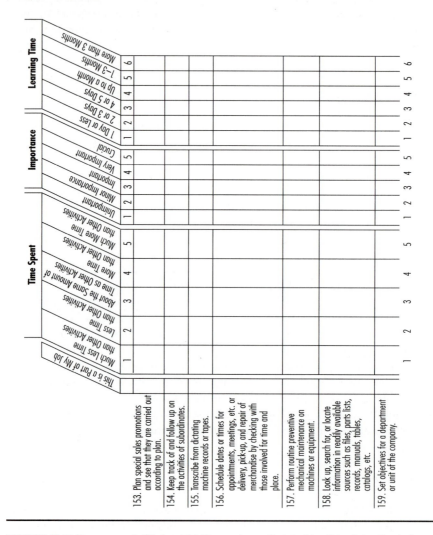

SOURCE: M. D. Dunnette, et al., "Task and Job Taxonomics as a Basis for Identifying Labor Supply Sources and Evaluating Employment Qualifications," *Human Resource Planning* 2 (1979), p. 1. Used for describing nonexempt level clerical, maintenance, warehousing, selling, and foreman jobs in a retail organization. Copyright by Personnel Decisions Research Institute, 1977. All rights reserved.

tailored to the needs of the organization. Designing a plan should revolve around its intended purpose. The organization will probably never do one comprehensive job analysis; instead, it will undertake several different job analyses, each adapted to the needs at the time.

From a compensation perspective, the data obtained from a job analysis must have two characteristics. First, it must include information about jobs that distinguishes between jobs. For this characteristic, a standardized procedure such as the PAQ might be used. Conversely, the organization might design its own job analysis system based on the particular compensable factors it wishes to use. Appendix 7.1

provides an example task analysis worksheet used by a small company to gather relevant job analysis information. The second characteristic is that the information must distinguish between different performance levels within the job. This information is necessary for performance evaluation and is usually gathered through a custom-designed system.

## Job Analysis Outcomes

Three primary documents are developed based on the information collected through job analysis. The three documents are job descriptions, job specifications, and job standards. It is possible to combine all three documents into one document or have three separate documents. The discussion to follow is based on three separate documents. The top of each document should contain the following information: (1) job title, (2) date information collected, (3) date information last revised, (4) job status (for example, full- versus part-time exempt versus nonexempt), (5) who wrote it, (6) who approved it, (7) location, (8) department, (9) wage range, and (10) immediate supervisor.

### *The Job Description*

As indicated earlier, job analysis information is used in many human resource decisions, and thus its accuracy and reliability is essential. The data collected in any job analysis are usually codified in one or more documents, such as a job description. A job description can be defined as a narrative essay that communicates information about the job. The information collected dictates what is said about a job in the description. Two jobs are depicted in Exhibit 7.7.

Job description (also called position description) is a critical document to aid managers in human resources decision making. The Americans with Disabilities Act is placing increased emphasis on writing job descriptions that focus on essential and nonessential job tasks.[33] The layout of the job description can follow the types of information obtained through job analysis. There can be a separate section covering activities performed; equipment, tools, materials, and other work aids; and job context. Because all this information is not used in every human resource decision, the organization may wish to begin each section on a separate sheet, and thus managers only retrieve that which is needed. Each sheet of the job description should include the job title, date the information was collected, and date of last revision. Because job descriptions are revised more frequently than complete job analysis is performed, both dates are essential so the decision maker is aware of the recency of the information. The first part of the job description provides a general description of the job duties and responsibilities. The writing of the job description should follow these guidelines: (1) Use terse statements, (2) use the present tense, (3) use common terminology whenever possible, (4) use action words to describe such things as duties, responsibilities, reporting relationships, interdependencies, and accountabilities, (5) list important activities, not every activity, (6) precisely identify equipment, tools, materials, or other work aids used on the job and the level of minimum performance expected, and (7) include, as the last statement on the activity list, "other activities may be assigned based on organizational need."

The first job description in Exhibit 7.7 is taken from the *Dictionary of Occupational Titles;* the second description was established using the PAQ. They demonstrate the difference in job descriptions that can result from different approaches to job analysis and different ways of summarizing the data.

## Job Specifications

Job specifications are the minimum qualifications required to perform the job successfully. They represent those qualifications needed to perform the job, not the level of qualifications held by current job incumbents. Job specifications might note that a job requires typing, the ability to maintain an accounting ledger, and so forth. Sometimes the specifications will be more

---

**EXHIBIT 7.7** | **TWO JOB DESCRIPTIONS**

---

**Job Description from the *Dictionary of Occupational Titles***

Title: Keypunch Operator
DOT: 213582010

Operates alphabetic and numeric keypunch machine, similar in operation to electric typewriter, to transcribe data from source material onto punchcards, paper or magnetic cards, and to record accounting or statistical data for subsequent processing by automatic or electronic data processing equipment: attaches skip bar to machine and previously punched program card around machine drum to control duplication and spacing of constant data. Loads machine with decks of tabulating punchcards, paper or magnetic tape, or magnetic cards. Moves switches and depresses keys to select alphabetic or numeric punching, and transfer cards or tape through machine stations. Depresses keys to transcribe new data in prescribed sequence from source material into perforations on card, or as magnetic impulses on specified locations on tape or card. Inserts previously processed card into gauge to verify registration or punches. Observes machine to detect faulty feeding, positioning, ejecting, duplicating. skipping, punching, or other mechanical malfunctions and notifies supervisor. Removes jammed cards using prying knife. May tend machines that automatically sort, merge, or match punchcards into specified groups. May verify accuracy of data, using verifying machine. May perform general typing tasks.

**Job Description from the Position Analysis Questionnaire**

A. Title: Keypunch Operator
   DOT: 213582010

B. Duties:
   General description

Under general direction, performs clerical and/or related activities, has a nontypical schedule and/or optional apparel style, operates machines and/or equipment. To a lesser extent, performs routine and/or repetitive activities, works other work schedules.

---

SOURCE: PAQ Users Manual (System II), p. 43. Copyright by PAQ Services, Inc., Purdue Research Foundation, Lafayette, IN. Reprinted with permission.

general and indicate that job incumbents should have two years of business school training or equivalent experience, for example. Sometimes the job specifications are included as part of the job description. An example of a job specification appears in Exhibit 7.8.

---

**EXHIBIT 7.8**     **JOB DESCRIPTION AND SPECIFICATION FOR A HUMAN RESOURCE MANAGER**

---

## Job Description

### General description

Performs responsible administrative work managing human resource activities of a large state agency or institution. Work involves responsibility for the planning and administration of a human resource program that includes recruitment, examination, selection, evaluation, appointment, promotion, transfer, and recommended change of status of agency employees, and a system of communication for disseminating necessary information to workers. Works under general supervision, exercising initiative and independent judgment in the performance of assigned tasks.

### Example of work performed

Participates in overall planning and policymaking to provide effective and uniform human resource services.

Communicates policy through organization levels by bulletin, meetings. and personal contact.

Interviews applicants, evaluates qualifications, classifies applications.

Recruits and screens applicants to fill vacancies and reviews applications of qualified persons.

Confers with supervisors on human resource matters, including placement problems, retention, or release of probationary employees, transfers, demotions, and dismissals of permanent employees.

Supervises administration of tests.

Initiates human resource training activities and coordinates these activities with work officials and supervisors.

Establishes effective service rating system, trains unit supervisors in making employee evaluations.

Maintains employee personnel files.

Supervises a group of employees directly and through subordinates.

Performs related work as assigned.

## Job Specification

### General qualification requirements

Experience and training: Should have considerable experience in human resource administration.

Education: Graduation from a 4-year college or university, with a major in education and human resource management.

Knowledge, skills, and abilities: Considerable knowledge of principles and practices of human resource administration; selection and assignment of human resources job evaluation.

| EXHIBIT 7.9 | PERFORMANCE STANDARDS FOR SALESPERSON |
|---|---|

### Quantity of Sales

Superior performance: $50 thousand gross/month

Above-average performance: $40 to $49 thousand gross/month

Average performance: $30 to $39 thousand gross/month

Below-average performance: $20 to $29 thousand gross/month

Unacceptable performance: less than $20 thousand gross/month

### Sales Quality

Superior performance: 95 percent repeat business from first-time accounts

Above-average performance: 90 percent repeat business from first-time accounts

Average performance: 85 percent repeat business from first-time accounts

Below-average performance: 80 percent repeat business from first-time accounts

Unacceptable performance: Less than 80 percent repeat business from first-time accounts

## *Performance Standards*

Performance standards can be defined as the desired employee behaviors or performance outcomes. A set of performance standards, expressed in terms of performance outcomes, is presented in Exhibit 7.9. Performance standards are important for assessing the performance of employees in their jobs; Chapter 11 is devoted to performance assessment.

## Summary

This chapter focuses on the process of job analysis and the outcomes associated with job analysis. The terms *job analysis, task, job, position, job evaluation, job description*, and *job specification* are defined.

Job analysis is the process of studying jobs. Although job analysis is an important activity for human resource management in general, it is particularly important to the compensation decision maker because it serves as the cornerstone for job evaluation and performance evaluation.

Most job analysis approaches use some combination of observation and interviews. It is important to conduct a thorough and complete job analysis and to get cooperation of others in the organization. Gathering data from employees builds acceptance of the process and the results of job analysis. If these are accepted by the employees, programs built on the job analysis are more likely to be accepted.

There are many standardized job analysis approaches. Among these are work methods analysis, functional job analysis, position analysis questionnaires, job analysis questionnaires, and task inventories. The discussion focuses on the use of these for the compensation decision maker. No one standard approach to job analysis seems to collect the data necessary for a good job evaluation system and a good performance evaluation system. A custom-designed job analysis system would seem to have the most overall use.

The main outcomes of a job analysis are a written job description, performance standards, and job specifications. The first two of these are particularly important to the compensation decision maker because they serve as inputs into job evaluation and performance evaluation, respectively.

## Discussion Questions

1. Define the terms *job analysis, job description, job specification,* and *performance standard.* What is each of these used for; how are they related to each other?

2. What is a job; a task; a position?

3. Some job analysis techniques seem to be more useful for performance evaluation purposes than other techniques. Which ones are these, and why are they better?

4. Suppose a job analyst only collected information on how jobs related to each other (that is, the horizontal and vertical relationships among jobs were identified). Would this data be useful in conducting a job evaluation? Why or why not?

5. Discuss the steps in conducting a job analysis.

6. Refer to the suggestions for job analysis interviewing. Why is each of these important?

## Activities

1. You are to go to the student union and, by the observation method of job analysis, collect information about the job identified by your instructor. From that information, write a detailed job description that you will share with another student in your class.

2. You are the human resource manager for a large multistore retailer. Your boss has requested that you start hiring only college graduates for all management trainee positions. The purpose is to upgrade the quality of management trainees because these positions have been experiencing high levels of voluntary and involuntary turnover. What action would you suggest to your boss?

## *References*

[1] M. Messmer, "Rightsizing, Not Downsizing," *Industry Week* 241 (August, 1992), 23–26.

[2] S. E. Bemis, A. H. Belenky, and D. A. Soder, *Job Analysis* (Washington, DC: Bureau of National Affairs, 1983).

[3] S. Gael, *The Job Analysis Handbook for Business, Industry and Government* (New York: Wiley, 1988).

[4] N. R. Lange, "Job Analysis and Documentation," in *The Compensation Handbook*, eds. M. L. Rock and L. A. Berger (New York: McGraw-Hill, 1991), 49–71.

[5] *Ibid.*

[6] R. D. Gatewood and H. S. Field, *Human Resource Selection* (Hinsdale, IL: Dryden, 1990).

[7] F. J. Landy and J. Vasey, "Job Analysis: The Composition of SME Samples," *Personnel Psychology* 44 (1991), 27–50.

[8] *Ibid.*

[9] T. H. Stone, *Understanding Personnel Management* (Hinsdale, IL: The Dryden Press, 1982), 122.

[10] Methods study evolved out of the scientific management movement, of which Frederick W. Taylor is considered to be the father. For a development of this subject and its contribution to human resources management, see Daniel A. Wren, "The Origins of Industrial Psychology and Sociology," in *Classics of Personnel Management*, ed. Thomas H. Patten, Jr. (Oak Park, IL: Moore Publishing, 1979), 4–12.

[11] J. C. Flanagan, "The Critical Incident Technique," *Psychological Bulletin* 51 (1954), 28–35.

[12] For examples of these techniques, see H. John Bernardin and Patricia Cain Smith, "A Clarification of Some Issues Regarding the Development of Behaviorally Anchored Rating Scales (BARS)," *Journal of Applied Psychology* 66, no. 4, (1981), 458–463; Kevin R. Murphy et al., "Do Behavioral Observation Scales Measure Observation?" *Journal of Applied Psychology* 67 (1982), 562–567.

[13] D. P. Schwab et al., "Behaviorally Anchored Rating Scales: A Review of the Literature," *Personnel Psychology* 28 (1975), 549–562.

[14] Lange, "Job Analysis and Documentation."

[15] U.S. Department of Labor, Manpower Administration, *Handbook for Analyzing Jobs* (Washington, DC: Government Printing Office, 1972).

[16] Bemis et al., *Job Analysis.*

[17] C. A. O'Reilly III, and D. F. Caldwell, "The Impact of Normative Social Influence and Cohesiveness on Task Perception and Attitudes: A Social Information Processing Approach," *Journal of Occupational Psychology* 58 (September, 1985), 193–206.

[18] P. Sackett, E. T. Cornelius III, and T. J. Carron, "A Comparison of Global Judgement v. Task-Orientated Approaches to Job Classification," *Personnel Psychology* 34 (1981), 791–804.

[19] W. F. Cascio. and H. J. Bernardin, "Implications of Performance Appraisal Litigation For Personnel Decisions," *Personnel Psychology* 34 (1981), 211–226.

[20] G. T. Milkovich and J. M. Newman, *Compensation* (Homewood, IL: BPI/Irwin, 1990).

[21] U.S. Department of Labor, Manpower Administration, *Handbook for Analyzing Jobs.*

[22] *Ibid.*

[23] U.S. Department of Labor, *Dictionary of Occupational Titles*, 4th ed. (Washington, DC: Government Printing Office, 1977).

[24] E. J. McCormick et al., *Position Analysis Questionnaire* (West Lafayette, IN: Purdue University, 1969).

[25] *Ibid.*

[26] E. J. McCormick et al., *PAQ: Job Analysis Manual* (Logan, UT: PAQ Services, 1977).

[27] E. J. McCormick, "Job and Task Analysis," in *Handbook of Industrial and Organizational Psychology*, ed. M. D. Dunnette (Chicago: Rand-McNally, 1976), 651–696; P. R. Jeannert, "Equitable Job Evaluation and Classification with the Position Analysis Questionnaire," *Compensation Review* 12 (Winter, 1980), 32–42; R. C. Mechan, "Quantitative Job Evaluation Using the Position Analysis Questionnaire," *Personnel Administrator* 28 (June, 1983), 82–86, 88, 124.

[28] R. M. Madigan and D. J. Hoover, "The Effects of Alternative Job Evaluation Methods on Decisions Involving Pay Equity," *Academy of Management Journal* 29 (1986), 84–100.

[29] R. Christal and J. Weissmuller, "Job-Task Inventory Analysis," in *The Job Analysis Handbook for Business, Industry and Government*, ed. S. Gael (New York: Wiley, 1988).

[30] E. L. Levine, R. A. Ash, H. Hall, and F. Sistrunk, "Evaluation of Job Analysis Methods by Experienced Job Analysts," *Academy of Management Journal* 26 (1983), 339–348.

[31] J. Newman and F. Krzystofiak, "Quantified Job Analysis: A Tool for Improving Human Resource Management Decision Making." Paper presented at the Academy of Management Meeting, Orlando, FL, August 15, 1977.

[32] *Ibid.*

[33] G. Carmean, "Tie Medical Screening to the Job," *HR Magazine* 37 (July, 1992), 85–87.

<table>
<tr><td>**APPENDIX 7.1**</td><td>**TASK ANALYSIS WORKSHEET**</td></tr>
</table>

Job Title _____   Employee's Name _____

Department _____   Supervisor's Name _____

Hours Worked _____   Date Completed _____

Status:     Full Time _____     Part Time _____

Please answer the following questions as completely and honestly as possible and return it to the Human Resources Director.

> *Note:* When referring to "your supervisors," please consider this to be the person to whom you report directly.

### JOB DUTIES SECTION

1. Purpose of the job. _____

   _____

   _____

2. Use this section to list and thoroughly describe the major task activities that are required to perform your job. Be sure to assign numbers to each specific task activity being described.

| Task Identification No. | Description of Task | Time: D=Daily W=Weekly O=Other | Importance to Overall Job Performance 1=Critical; 2=Moderate; 3=Little |
|---|---|---|---|
|  |  |  |  |
|  |  |  |  |
|  |  |  |  |
|  |  |  |  |
|  |  |  |  |
|  |  |  |  |
|  |  |  |  |
|  |  |  |  |
|  |  |  |  |

*Continue on back of page if necessary.

3. Are you now performing unnecessary duties? If yes. please explain.

   _____

   _____

   _____

4. Indicate the number of days of out-of-town travel that is required of your job each month? _____

5. What percentage of time (of a day) does your job require you to exercise independent judgment?_____ Please give specific examples of the kind of judgment required.

_____

_____

_____

6. My supervisor checks my work:

_____ Constantly        _____ Weekly

_____ Hourly            _____ Less than weekly

_____ Daily

7. What kinds of errors can occur in your job? _____

_____

_____

8. How and by whom are these errors identified?_____

_____

_____

9. List all people from whom you normally take directions. (Titles only)

_____

_____

_____

_____

10. *Education:* Check the blank that indicates the educational requirements for the job, *not your own educational* background.

   (a) ____ No formal education required     (d) ____ 2-yr. certificate
                                                  (college or technical school)

   (b)____ Less than high school diploma

   (c) ____ High school diploma or equivalent  (e)____ 4-yr. college degree

11. Indicate the education or *experience* you had when you began working this job.

_____

_____

_____

_____

12. *Training:* Check the amount needed to perform your job.

    (a) _____ Basic orientation is sufficient (less than 1 week)

    (b) _____ 1 week to less than 1 month

    (c) _____ 1 month to less than 3 months

    (d) _____ 3 months to less than 6 months

    (e) _____ 6 months or more

13. Indicate the length of the training period you had when you were placed on this job._____

14. How long did it take you to become comfortable at this job? _____

15. Describe the kinds of interpersonal skills required to perform your job.

    _____

    _____

    _____

    _____

    _____

    _____

    _____

    _____

    _____

    _____

16. *Skill:* Describe the skills required in the performance of your job and indicate how often these skills are used. Also indicate which tasks the skills are used to perform. Use the same number of given tasks to identify them as given in the job duties section (example, amount of accuracy, math, verbal, artistic).

| Skills | Rarely | Occasionally | Frequently | Task Identification No. |
|---|---|---|---|---|
|  |  |  |  |  |
|  |  |  |  |  |
|  |  |  |  |  |
|  |  |  |  |  |
|  |  |  |  |  |
|  |  |  |  |  |
|  |  |  |  |  |

17. *Physical Demands:* Describe undesirable physical demands of your job and indicate the frequency of their occurrence. Also identify which tasks (from the job duties section) are performed under these conditions (for example, handling heavy materials, cramped positions). Use back of this page if additional space is required.

| Description of Physical Demand | Daily | Weekly | Occasionally | Task Identification No. |
|---|---|---|---|---|
|  |  |  |  |  |
|  |  |  |  |  |
|  |  |  |  |  |
|  |  |  |  |  |
|  |  |  |  |  |

18. *Emotional Demands:* Describe undesirable emotional demands placed on you by your job and indicate the frequency of their occurrence. Also identify which tasks (from the job duties section) are performed under these emotional demands (for example, time pressure, jam-ups).

| Description of Emotional Demand | Daily | Weekly | Occasionally | Task Identification No. |
|---|---|---|---|---|
|  |  |  |  |  |
|  |  |  |  |  |
|  |  |  |  |  |
|  |  |  |  |  |
|  |  |  |  |  |

19. *Environmental Conditions:* Describe objectionable conditions under which you must perform your job and indicate the frequency of their occurrence. Also identify which tasks (from the job duties section) are performed under these environmental conditions (for example, temperature, ventilation).

| Description of Environmental Condition | Daily | Weekly | Occasionally | Task Identification No. |
|---|---|---|---|---|
|  |  |  |  |  |
|  |  |  |  |  |
|  |  |  |  |  |
|  |  |  |  |  |
|  |  |  |  |  |

20. What changes (if any) would you make to your job duties? _____

_____

_____

_____

_____

21. Describe dependencies on other people or departments that make your job difficult. Offer suggestions for improvement.

_____

_____

_____

_____

_____

22. Are there specific traits and/or abilities that would benefit a person in your job? If so, list them.

_____

_____

_____

_____

_____

_____

### For Supervisors, Managers, and Directors Only

Describe your supervisory responsibilities below. Only respond based on positions for which you are held directly accountable.

| Job Title | Number Supervised | Check Area (x) of Responsibilities | | | | | | | | Describe consequence of error by individual in the position |
|---|---|---|---|---|---|---|---|---|---|---|
| | | Hiring | Termination | Training | Assigning of Work | Evaluation of Work | Quality of Work | Quantity of Work | Timeliness of Work | |
| | | | | | | | | | | |
| | | | | | | | | | | |
| | | | | | | | | | | |
| | | | | | | | | | | |
| | | | | | | | | | | |

What percentage of your time (daily) is spent on the above supervisory responsibilities? _____ percent

# 8

# Job Evaluation: Determining Internal Equity

## Learning Objectives

To learn what job evaluation is and to review the reasons for conducting job evaluation.

To learn the evolution of job evaluation.

To learn what compensable factors are and how and why they are used in job evaluation.

To learn the ranking method of job evaluation, including the steps an organization follows.

To learn the job classification method of job evaluation and the steps to follow.

To learn the factor comparison method of job evaluation and the steps used by organizations to implement the method.

To learn the point method of job evaluation including the steps to follow in implementing the method.

To learn the main advantages and disadvantages of these four methods of job evaluation.

To become familiar with other job evaluation methods used by organizations.

To recognize the concept of relative goodness regarding these methods.

# Introduction

The previous chapter described job analysis, the process which provides the information needed as input for determining a job hierarchy based on internal equity. This chapter deals with job evaluation. Job evaluation is the process used to actually establish that hierarchy—to determine the relative value of jobs to the organization without taking into consideration the pay of those jobs or the individuals performing the jobs.

# Background on Job Evaluation

## *Origin and Growth of Job Evaluation*

Job evaluation has been traced back to the early 1900s when Frederick W. Taylor conducted a systematic study to establish piece rate pay systems for jobs. The scientific management movement gave job evaluation its first great push. Subsequently, job evaluation became part of the pay system in American industry.

Two other important factors reinforcing the use of job evaluation were the wage–price freezes during World War II and the development of labor and management relations in general. During World War II, the federal government, concerned about inflation in the economy, instituted wage and price freezes. However, employers wanted permission to make wage adjustments to alleviate inequities in pay that existed before the implementation of the freeze. The federal government permitted employers to adjust wages where the employer could demonstrate an inequity—employers were required to demonstrate differences in jobs to justify wage adjustments. The administrative vehicle for adjusting pay rates was job evaluation.

The other factor, development of labor and management relations, continues to contribute to job evaluation growth.[1] A contract between labor and management typically has a no-strike and no-lockout clause. Problems may emerge regarding how to settle rights disputes that arise over interpretation of the parties' rights under an existing contract.[2] A grievance procedure may be established to resolve these disputes. Often, one component of that grievance system is a labor and management job evaluation committee. This committee is most likely to be needed when jobs change during the period of the contract and require re-evaluation.

Although in many situations labor and management use job evaluation to solve rights disputes under the terms of a contract, not all unions support job evaluation.[3] Sometimes labor views job evaluation as a management ploy to manipulate wages. Job evaluation also may not be consistent with the union's philosophy about wage rates. For example, some unions believe that all workers in the bargaining unit should make the same wage regardless of the work performed. Under this philosophy of equal pay for a day's work, a union is likely to be resistant to management's attempts to distinguish among jobs in terms of pay rates.[4] Also, labor unions may be resistant to job evaluation programs if they do not see themselves as having meaningful input into the decisions that are made. Some managements may structure the job evaluation process to give the union only a rubber stamp role in the decision process. Without meaningful joint decision making, unions can be expected to resist the program. Nevertheless, job evaluation as an administrative activity to determine equitable pay relationships among jobs is now a widespread practice. One study showed that 86 percent of the surveyed firms used some form of job evaluation.[5]

## Theoretic Basis for Job Evaluation

In Chapter 3, which covered the importance of equity in employee retention, it was argued that job evaluation is an administrative technique to maintain feelings of internal equity by assessing the relative worth of jobs. Equity theory is very important in explaining why organizations engage in job evaluation. Equity theory addresses both distributive and procedural justice, which are critical in obtaining employee acceptance of the job evaluation process and outcomes.

Evidence supports the belief that employees compare the outcomes/inputs ratios of their job to other employees within the firm and, based on these comparisons, feel equitably or inequitably treated.[6] This comparison of outcomes/inputs ratios is based on the notion of distributive justice. In procedural justice, the focus is on the process and procedures used to arrive at the decision. The theory holds that the amount of involvement and participation that employees perceive they have in the process of determining the value of their job will influence their perception of fairness and satisfaction with both the evaluation process and its outcomes.[7] There has been little research regarding procedural justice as it relates to perceived equity. Intuitive reasoning does support the need to involve employees in the job evaluation process and has resulted in widespread use of job evaluation committees. In job evaluation, the firm is attempting to identify those inputs that are most valuable to the organization and to develop a job hierarchy based on which jobs have more or less of those relevant dimensions.

## Criteria for Choosing Compensable Factors

The concept of compensable factors (factors that the firm values) was defined earlier, but because it lies at the heart of job evaluation, additional elaboration is warranted. Discussion of appropriate compensable factors for an organization is a complex undertaking. Compensable factors are not chosen for each job; rather, they are chosen for a group of related jobs. For example, one set of compensable factors may be established for clerical jobs; another set may be established for production jobs. The following criteria for selecting compensable factors are general; they are intended to help a company determine what can legitimately be considered as compensable factors. The final decision regarding specific factors must be business-unit specific.

First, compensable factors ought to be acceptable to all the parties involved. They must be acceptable to management, employees, and union leaders if there is a union. This constraint is crucial because the heart of job evaluation is to establish an internal pay system that is perceived as equitable. Only if the compensable factors are perceived as relevant will the job evaluation plan itself be perceived as equitable.

Second, compensable factors must validly distinguish among jobs.[8] They must capture the important differences among jobs to ensure that the job evaluation is valid and to ensure that they satisfy legal requirements and are not challengeable in court.[9]

Third, compensable factors must be relevant. If a factor does not apply to the group of jobs under consideration, the factor obviously cannot aid in differentiating among those jobs. For example, if the factor innovation is applied to all clerical jobs and there really is no opportunity for innovation involved in any of those jobs, this factor is actually irrelevant.

Fourth, and related to the above point, jobs must vary on the factors chosen. Different jobs must possess different amounts of the compensable factor. For example, if the factor working conditions is applied to all clerical jobs, and all have the same working conditions, this factor is useless.

Fifth, the compensable factors must be measurable.[10] If working conditions are chosen as a factor, the organization must be able to measure the differences in working conditions within jobs. It might be applied as "length of time exposed to extreme temperatures" or "length of time exposed to noxious fumes." If the factor cannot be measured, it will not be useful for establishing the relative worth of jobs.[11]

Sixth, compensable factors should be independent of each other. Two factors should not measure the same dimension. If they do, double weight is given to the same construct. Either one alone would give the relative worth of the jobs. Application of these six criteria when selecting compensable factors helps an organization achieve a meaningful job evaluation system.

## Who Selects Compensable Factors?

Closely related to the criteria for selecting compensable factors is the issue of who selects the compensable factors. Because the job evaluation plan will ultimately result in a hierarchy of jobs within the organization, management needs a voice in determining what criteria will be compensated.

There are also sound reasons for including first-line managers and rank-and-file employees, as well as minority employees, in the factor selection process. Supervisors have an intimate understanding of the jobs they supervise and will probably have insight into the important ways that these jobs differ. Supervisors are a potentially rich source from which to identify useful compensable factors. Employees are the ones who perform the jobs and have feelings about equitable pay among jobs. It makes sense to determine what employees see as the important criteria that distinguish among jobs. Inclusion of minority representatives in this process can eliminate the inequity that is sometimes perceived simply because of lack of input. Despite the apparent theoretic importance (procedural justice) of considering employee views in the selection of compensable factors, it is seldom done. One study found that only 7.5 percent of all job evaluation plans in existence within the surveyed companies involved employee committees.[12]

Finally, if a labor union has representational rights over the jobs that are to be evaluated, union representatives should be included in the factor selection process. Because the determination of wages will rest in part on the result of the evaluation, management and union will need to bargain in good faith over the compensable factors.

## Criteria for Selection of Key Jobs

The use of key jobs (or benchmark jobs) is critical in all job evaluation techniques except the ranking method. Because of the important role of key jobs, they should satisfy several criteria. The criteria are shown in Exhibit 8.1.

First, key jobs should be selected from the range of all jobs to be evaluated; that is, the key jobs should constitute a sample of all jobs from high to low in the hierarchy of jobs.

A second criterion for key jobs is that they must be important jobs. Importance can be assessed in several ways. For example, key jobs may employ relatively large numbers of workers, which means they contribute substantially to

---

**EXHIBIT 8.1**     CRITERIA FOR KEY JOBS

---

1. Key jobs should be selected from the total range of jobs to be evaluated.

2. Key jobs should be important. (They should have large numbers of employees in them or contribute substantially to organizational goals.)

3. Key jobs should be clearly defined in terms of job descriptions and job specifications.

4. Key job content should be relatively stable.

5. Key jobs should be comparable in content across many organizations and industries so that a correct wage can be established.

6. Key jobs should be acceptable to labor and management.

---

labor costs. Or key jobs may be important in terms of their contributions to the organization, financial or otherwise.

Third, key jobs should also have clear and well-defined job descriptions/specifications and performance standards written for them. Such clear definitions and standards are important because market rates for these jobs will be determined by comparing each to a nearly identical job in other organizations.

A fourth criterion for key jobs is that the content of these jobs should be fairly stable over time. Use of this criterion helps ensure stability of the job evaluation system itself and suggests that the jobs chosen are probably stable in other organizations as well.

Fifth, key jobs should be those that are comparable across many organizations and industries. Normally, the organization will have conducted a wage and salary survey for the key jobs and determined the pay rates generally considered correct for those jobs. This criterion also means that the same key jobs in many other organizations can be surveyed to determine fair wages.

Finally, key jobs (benchmark jobs) should satisfy the criterion of acceptability: management, employees, and the labor union must believe that the key jobs are important and are useful in setting the pay of other jobs in the organization. Without this criterion, the parties are not likely to have much faith in the results of the job evaluation process.

### Single versus Multiple Plans

The organization will have to determine if it wishes to design one plan for all jobs or to design a separate system for each main job cluster. A *job cluster* is the grouping of similar jobs (for example, production, office/clerical, maintenance) for the purpose of administrative actions such as job evaluation. The Academy of Science has suggested that organizations use only one plan as a technique to reduce the chance of sex discrimination in job evaluation. Recent litigation suggests that use of a single plan to reduce discrimination may, in fact, point to discrimination where none really exists. In the case of *Briggs v. City of Madison*,[13] that city maintained a job evaluation system in which both predominantly male jobs and predominantly female jobs were graded into the same pay grade, and both jobs carried the same pay rates. However, the city faced a shortage of employees in the male-dominated jobs and was forced to offer a higher wage to attract and retain employees in the male-dominated occupation. At trial, the judge found that the predominantly male and female jobs were similar and should be paid the same; however, the judge also recognized that a market defense for paying higher rates to employees in the predominantly male jobs was legitimate. The point is that the whole issue may have been avoided had the city never attempted to equate the jobs in the first place. Some legal scholars[14] advise the use of multiple plans to avoid litigation:

> Different systems should be used for different job families, so that no direct comparison in the system is possible.... (p. 481)

Most organizations have found the concept of one plan impractical because the compensable factors needed to measure one cluster are not needed to measure another cluster. Some organizations as a compromise have developed a core set of compensable factors that are used in doing job evaluation across all job clusters. These permit unique factors to be added as needed for each specific job cluster within the organization. As organizations attempt to position themselves strategically in the product market they serve, the likelihood of their not adopting one system for the total organization increases. It will become increasingly critical for each business unit within the organization to design a compensation system that supports its strategic objectives. This will include compensable factors (identification and weighting) that are tailored to fit what is most important to a specific business unit marketplace. For example, a business unit that is competing in a very mature market may legitimately value one set of compensable factors, whereas, a business unit in the high-tech area may value another. Innovation would probably not be an expected part of any job in the mature market, whereas in the high-tech market, it might well be required. Innovation then would be an important compensable factor in the high-tech market but not even taken into account in the mature market. In the future, as the product market changes dramatically and quickly, it may be necessary to redo job evaluation systems frequently.

## Creating or Buying Job Evaluation Plans

Organizations can create their own job evaluation system or purchase a modified system from an external consulting firm (for example, Hay and Associates; Cole). The advantages of developing a system internally are (1) potential for a better fit to the firm's needs, (2) ability to tie in directly to the firm's strategies, and (3) knowledge that the individuals in charge of the system truly understand it and that responsibility rests with a specific unit within the organization. The disadvantages include (1) time, (2) cost, and (3) a possible lack of technical expertise, which may result in a flawed system. In contrast, the advantages of buying the system from a consulting firm are (1) speed, (2) vast wealth of expertise in specialized areas, (3) ability to convert the internal hierarchy into a wage structure using market wage data collected by the consulting firm, and (4) avoidance of internal political problems. The disadvantages include (1) cost, (2) difficulty of finding a firm that understands your product market, (3) possibility of getting one of the consulting firm's canned packages (with minor modifications) rather than a system tailored to your firm's needs, and (4) possible dependency on outside expertise to monitor and update the system.

## Selecting the Evaluator of the Jobs

The evaluator can be one person (manager or compensation specialist) or it can be a committee made up of a cross section of the organization. Use of a committee approach is recommended whenever politically and practically feasible. Those who serve on the committee should satisfy several criteria. First, they should be familiar with the jobs in question. As the ranking exercise at the end of this chapter illustrates, it is difficult to evaluate jobs if the evaluator does not know what the job is about. Good job descriptions help solve this problem. To increase familiarity, it may be necessary to have guests (current job incumbent and supervisor of the job) attend certain meetings to provide additional information and answer questions (of the committee members).

Second, committee members should be selected from management and from the employees whose jobs are being evaluated. To gain the acceptance of both managers and employees, it is essential that they both have representation. It is also recommended that minorities be included on the committee in proportion to those present in the current or near-term composition of the organization's work force.

The perception by the work force of the quality of committee members and their actual qualifications are equally important. It is essential that those selected are respected within the organization as fair, honest, thorough, and competent. The personality mix of the people on the committee must be considered so as not to build in personality conflicts.

Third, raters should be trained in the concept and objectives of job evaluation. They should have a good grasp of what job evaluation is about and what they will be doing in their committee work. Among those selected, there should be someone knowledgeable in compensation practices (compensation specialist) and financial analysis (spread sheet and statistical analyst–compensation specialist/financial specialist).

The chair of the committee is a key position because this person provides leadership for the process. The chair could be someone from the Human Resource Department or an outside consultant who acts as the technical specialist (compensation specialist), arranges meetings, establishes agendas, obtains information from throughout the organization as needed, schedules guests, keeps the committee on target, ensures open forum for discussion, and resolves conflicts as they arise. Some organizations use a consultant as the committee chair to increase objectivity and permit all key organization people to participate fully.

Often compensation decision makers rely on such outside consultants to assist in the implementation of a job evaluation program. One study found that this is done about 55 percent of the time.[15] The use of outside consultants does not negate the importance of having managers and employees involved in the job evaluation committee. Reliance on outside consultants places even greater importance on the need for the organization to ensure that managers and employees know the system and how it works.

The committee carries out two functions. First, it is heavily involved in the design of the job evaluation plan. Second, it functions as an appeal body to those employees who believe their jobs may have been incorrectly evaluated. This must be done in all the job evaluation techniques that will be discussed.

## Ranking Method of Job Evaluation

The ranking method of job evaluation is the simplest of the job evaluation approaches and compares one job with another.[16] The steps in conducting job evaluation with the ranking method are summarized in Exhibit 8.2.

EXHIBIT 8.2     STEPS IN THE JOB RANKING METHOD

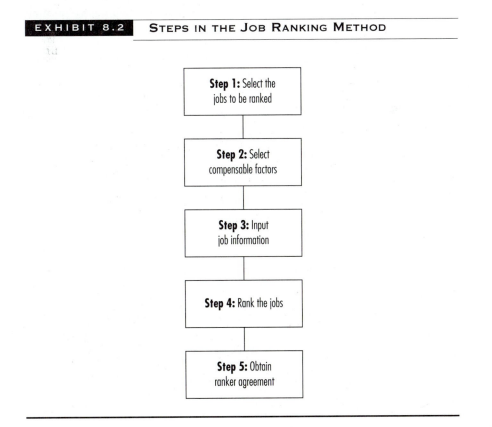

**Step 1:** Select the jobs to be ranked

**Step 2:** Select compensable factors

**Step 3:** Input job information

**Step 4:** Rank the jobs

**Step 5:** Obtain ranker agreement

## Steps in the Job Ranking Method

**Step 1: Select the Jobs to Be Ranked**   Several items must be considered in selecting the jobs to be ranked. First, because the job ranking method can be difficult to work with if there are many jobs, it may be useful to conduct ranking within departments. This method is sometimes called the *departmental order of importance method*.[17] Conducting ranking within departments is similar to evaluating by job cluster (by job families). A *job cluster* can be thought of as a set of jobs that are linked together by administrative unit, by technology, or by custom.[18] For example, within a factory the jobs of lathe operator, machine attendant, stock handler, and maintenance mechanic may all be located within one department and be considered a job cluster. Within a hospital, the jobs of nurse, nurse's aide, orderly, and housekeeping aide may all be linked together by geographic proximity (a hospital wing). Even though several of these jobs report to different functional units (housekeeping aide to the housekeeping department, orderly to the admissions department, and so on), they may all be considered part of one group or cluster for wage determination purposes.

If jobs are ranked by subset, organizations must decide whether they want an overall ranking as well. Some choose to ignore the question of relative worth between or across job clusters. This is often the case and it is one reason that some organizations have more than one job evaluation system.[19] There may be an evaluation system for each job cluster within the organization. There is no problem with this so long as job clusters are anchored to different labor markets—job pricing is carried out within job clusters.

A different approach is needed if the organization wishes to integrate the departmental rankings and develop an overall ranking scheme. In this case, it may be necessary to conduct a second ranking among dissimilar jobs across organizational units to find out the relative value of those jobs.

**Step 2: Select Compensable Factors**   The committee members determine the criteria on which they will base the relative worth of jobs. In the ranking method, only one or two compensable factors are usually chosen. The evaluation process becomes unwieldy if there are too many factors in the ranking method. Instead of one or two compensable factors, a whole job method of job ranking may be used, which ranks jobs based on their overall importance to the organization. Once the factors are chosen, the committee must then decide how to measure them. If responsibility is the compensable factor, it must be defined so that all members know what responsibility means as a compensable factor. Responsibility could be defined in terms of the dollar cost of errors in workmanship, dollar value of equipment used on the job, supervision of others, or in some other way. The actual definition given to the factor is probably less important than committee member agreement and consistent application of that definition. If the committee does not agree and apply the same definition across jobs, it is unlikely that its members will arrive at the same relative rankings for the jobs.

**Step 3: Input Job Information**   The information used is normally contained in job descriptions and job specifications.

**Step 4: Rank the Jobs** There are many techniques to rank the jobs. Two of the most common are the deck of cards method and the paired comparison method. In the deck of cards method, the ranker starts with the job title and relevant job description and specification information on a separate card for each of the jobs to be ranked. The ranker then goes through the entire deck to identify the most highly ranked job. This card is set aside, and the balance of the deck is gone through a second time until the next highest ranked job is identified. This card is then set aside and the deck is gone through again. This process continues until the original deck is exhausted.

An alternative deck of cards approach is to rank the cards in alternate order (that is, identify the most important job and then the least important). This results in easy ranking at the extremes and more difficult decisions for a few jobs that fall in the middle. The evaluators can concentrate on those few difficult decisions and focus on the differences between a relatively small number of jobs.

The paired comparison method of ranking is probably the most commonly used approach. In this method, the ranker compares each job to all other jobs. One way to do this is with a comparison table, such as the one labeled Exhibit 8.3.

To use the paired comparison method as shown in Exhibit 8.3, the ranker compares the job title (description/specification) at the beginning of a row with the job title beginning each column. If the job is worth more than a job in the column, an *X* is made in the cell. If the job is worth less than a job in the column, the cell is left blank. This process is continued for each job that begins a row. After all the jobs have been compared with all other jobs, the evaluator adds up the *X*s for each job across the row. The total number of *X*s for a job will establish its worth relative to other jobs. In Exhibit 8.3, the mailroom clerk job is worth the least, and the data processing manager job is worth the most.

**Step 5: Obtain Ranker Agreement** After the committee members have conducted independent assessments of the jobs, they discuss their rankings and seek agreement on the overall relative rankings.[20] This discussion should reveal any different perceptions of jobs or different applications of the compensable factors. If discussion does not resolve discrepancies, one approach is to average the rankings of the committee members. Such averaging should occur only as a last resort because it does not address the underlying reasons for the disagreement.

## *Advantages and Disadvantages of the Ranking Method*

The simplicity of the ranking method is one of its main advantages. Because of its simplicity, it is also the fastest method to implement, requiring a minimum amount of time to form a committee, define factors, and rank the jobs. It is also, without a doubt, the least costly method in terms of staff time and involvement. In a small organization or organization with a few jobs, these advantages probably outweigh the disadvantages.

There are, however, important disadvantages with the ranking method. First, if there are many jobs involved, it can be extremely difficult to compare all jobs with each other. For example, 15 comparisons need to be made if there are 6 jobs ($6 \times 5/2$), whereas 66 comparisons need to be made if there are 12 jobs ($12 \times 11/2$).[21] As

EXHIBIT 8.3

## PAIRED COMPARISON RANKING TABLE

| Columns / Rows | Mailroom Clerk | Data Processing Manager | Data Entry Clerk | Executive Secretary | Computer Operator | Systems Analyst | Control Clerk | Programmer | File Clerk | Assistant Manager | Total |
|---|---|---|---|---|---|---|---|---|---|---|---|
| Mailroom Clerk | — | | | | | | | | | | 0 |
| Data Processing Manager | X | — | X | X | X | X | X | X | X | X | 9 |
| Data Entry Clerk | X | | — | | | | | | X | | 2 |
| Executive Secretary | X | | X | — | X | | X | X | X | | 6 |
| Computer Operator | X | | X | | — | | X | | X | | 4 |
| Systems Analyst | X | | X | X | X | — | X | X | X | | 7 |
| Control Clerk | X | | X | | | | — | | X | | 3 |
| Programmer | X | | X | | X | | X | — | X | | 5 |
| File Clerk | X | | | | | | | | — | | 1 |
| Assistant Manager | X | | X | X | X | X | X | X | X | — | 8 |

a result, the method is limited to smaller organizations, or organizations in which fewer jobs are ranked in job clusters.

A second disadvantage is, because only a few compensable factors are chosen, the method may not capture important differences among jobs. Third, because the method does not require careful specification of the factors and careful documentation of the procedures used, it can appear to be arbitrary to those not involved in the original evaluation process. Finally, and perhaps most importantly, the ranking method does not allow one to determine how much more one job is worth than another. Although one might know that job X is more valuable than job Y, the magnitude of the differences between these jobs is not known.

# Job Classification Method

The job classification method compares the job with a predetermined standard.[22] The job classification method establishes job value categories (also called grades) with descriptions for each category, and jobs are slotted into them based on descriptive matches. This approach is like a ladder: Each rung represents a value category (the space between one rung and another is the grade range) and jobs are hierarchically ordered and must then be slotted onto one rung only. This is the method used by the federal government for assigning civil service jobs to pay categories. Its use outside the government is limited.

The steps for implementing this method are summarized in Exhibit 8.4.

## *Steps in the Classification Method*

**Step 1: Select the Jobs to Be Evaluated**   The jobs that are to be included in the job evaluation program are normally predetermined. The determination of jobs will have been decided by management and reflected in the instructions given to the job evaluation committee, if one is used. At this point, it must be decided whether the jobs will be treated as one job cluster (or family) for which general descriptions will suffice or if they will be broken down into narrower clusters (or families). This decision must be made to facilitate step 5 of the procedure, developing job grade descriptions. There may be enough diversity among the jobs to be evaluated that category (grade) descriptions should be expressed in the language of different job (or occupational) clusters.

Exhibit 8.5 presents both a general and occupational-specific factor degree description from the federal government's job evaluation plan.

The exhibit shows the primary description for the first two degrees of the factor "knowledge required by the job." It also shows the same two degrees for that factor worded for the occupation of mail and file clerks.

When job evaluation is conducted across job clusters (families), the job grade structure encompasses several job clusters. An example of combining jobs across clusters into one classification system appears in Exhibit 8.6.

**EXHIBIT 8.4** STEPS IN THE JOB CLASSIFICATION METHOD

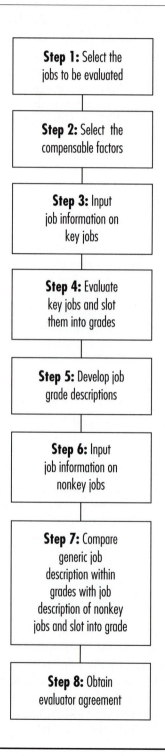

**Step 1:** Select the jobs to be evaluated

**Step 2:** Select the compensable factors

**Step 3:** Input job information on key jobs

**Step 4:** Evaluate key jobs and slot them into grades

**Step 5:** Develop job grade descriptions

**Step 6:** Input job information on nonkey jobs

**Step 7:** Compare generic job description within grades with job description of nonkey jobs and slot into grade

**Step 8:** Obtain evaluator agreement

| EXHIBIT 8.5 | GENERAL (PRIMARY) AND OCCUPATIONAL-SPECIFIC FACTOR DEGREE DESCRIPTIONS FOR THE FACTOR: KNOWLEDGE REQUIRED BY THE JOB |

## Primary[a]

Factor 1 measures the nature and extent of information or facts that the worker must understand to do acceptable work (steps, procedures, practices, rules, policies, theory, principles, and concepts) and the nature and extent of skills/abilities necessary to apply these knowledges.

### Degree A
Knowledge of simple, routine, or repetitive tasks, processes, or operations that typically includes following step-by-step instructions; operating simple equipment (for example, date stampers and mailing machines) or equipment that operates repetitively (for example, reproduction machines); or equivalent knowledge.

### Degree B
Knowledge of basic or commonly used rules, procedures, or operations that typically require some previous training or experience; basic knowledge of switchboard equipment; or equivalent knowledge.

## Occupational-Specific: Mail and File Grade-Level Standard[b]

This series grade-level standard shows the application of the Primary Grade-Level Standard to the Mail and File Series. It describes degrees of factors typically found in the mail and file occupation. There may be some positions, however, that do not fall into the typical pattern.

### Degree A
Knowledge of filing or sorting in alphabetical, numerical, chronological, or other logical sequence. Skill in operating simple equipment such as date or time stampers or equipment that operates repetitively, such as copy machines and power mail openers.

### Degree B
In addition to knowledges described at Degree A, positions at Degree B of this factor require knowledge of functions or work flow of operating units; knowledge of classified categories and security precautions or regulations; extensive knowledge of modes of transportation and related schedules; extensive information concerning postal regulations; or similar knowledges.

---

[a]Primary factor degree descriptions are from C. H. Anderson and D. B. Corts, "Development of a Framework for a Factor Ranking Benchmark System of Job Evaluation," U.S. Civil Service Commission, December 1973, p. 77.

[b]U.S. Civil Service Commission, "Report of Project to Develop, Test and Evaluate an Improved Approach to the Evaluation of Non-Supervisory Positions at $GS_1$ through $GS_{15}$," July 1974, p. 122.

In Exhibit 8.6, a fire chief and director of nursing both fall within grade 20, whereas fire captain, ward director, and administrative assistant fall within grade 19.

If the decision is made to keep job clusters separate, separate job grading systems are created for each job cluster. This results in multiple job evaluation systems within the organization.

| EXHIBIT 8.6 | EXAMPLE OF JOB GRADE ACROSS JOB CLUSTERS (FAMILIES) |
|---|---|

| | Job Clusters | | |
|---|---|---|---|
| Grade | Fire Department | Nursing | Secretarial |
| 20 | Fire chief | Director of nursing | — |
| 19 | Fire captain | Ward director | Administrative assistant |
| 18 | — | — | Legal secretary |
| 17 | — | Registered nurse | Department secretary |

**Step 2: Select Compensable Factors**   The job evaluation committee decides which factors are to be used. It is possible to use one or many factors in the classification method. Five to seven factors are normally used. The more factors that are used, the more lengthy each grade description will be. The compensable factors should be clearly defined and included only if necessary for each grade.

**Step 3: Input Job Information on Key Jobs**   Job data are obtained by job analysis (job descriptions/specifications). Collection and documentation of this data should be carried out with the concept of compensable factors (either explicit or inferred) from the job in mind.

**Step 4: Evaluate Key Jobs and Slot Them into Grades**

**Step 5: Develop Job Grade (Categories) Descriptions**   After the compensable factors are known, it is important to attach a category level to each amount of a compensable factor. For example, responsibility for equipment valued at from $500 to $2,000 may cause a job to be graded at category III. The requirement to know company procedures may require the job to be graded at category III also. If only one or the other of these requirements is necessary for a category III slotting and if the two in combination do not qualify a job to be moved to a higher category, this must be stated explicitly. Thus, consistent with the example, the grade III grade description might read in part: "Jobs that require responsibility for $500 to $2,000 of equipment and/or which require knowledge of company procedures…are assigned to this grade."

A second approach to the grading scheme in the classification method is to use grading rules. In this approach, a series of grading rules is established, based on the compensation factors. This results in a job being assigned to only one grade. The exercise at the end of this chapter uses grading rules. Whether actual job grade descriptions or grading rules are written, both are predicated on the same compensable factors and should yield identical results.

It is not an easy task to write clear grade descriptions that are mutually exclusive and collectively exhaustive of all the combinations of compensable factors, as the classification exercise at the end of this chapter illustrates. It is partly because of this difficulty of writing grade descriptions that grading rules are developed. However, it is also difficult to write grading rules that are readily interpretable by individuals not involved in their development. New employees involved in grading should be well trained in how the job evaluation scheme was developed, what each grading rule means, and how it was established.

**Step 6: Input Job Information on Nonkey Jobs, Same as Step 3 but for Nonkey Jobs**

**Step 7: Compare Generic Job Description Within Grades with Job Description of Nonkey Jobs**    In this step, committee members grade the jobs under evaluation. It is recommended that individual members initially conduct independent evaluations. Part of the reason for this is to determine if the grade descriptions or grade rules are sufficiently clear to ensure accurate classification of jobs.

**Step 8: Obtain Evaluator Agreement**    When multiple evaluators are used, it is possible they may not agree on the same grade (category) assignment for a particular job. The grades or grading rules may not be clear. Important compensable factors may have been omitted, or the process itself may not have yielded distinctions among jobs that are actually known to exist. Rater agreement serves to check on the validity of the job classification approach. If no solutions can be reached after thorough discussion and if the variation in grade assignment is not major (for example, one evaluator puts it at grade II and another puts it at grade III), one way to resolve discrepancies is to allocate the job to the grade most commonly assigned by the evaluation committee members.

### Advantages and Disadvantages of the Classification Method

Probably the greatest advantage of the classification approach to job evaluation is that it causes both managers and employees within the organization to think in terms of job groupings. A hierarchy of jobs is considered as soon as the method is introduced to the organization. A second advantage of the classification method is that it often produces the same results as a more elaborate and costly system. Often jobs are grouped even if some other method of job evaluation is initially used. For example, if the point method is used and jobs carry point values of between 400 and 1,000 points, the organization may assign jobs with point values 400 to 460 to grade I, jobs with point values of 461 to 520 to grade II, and so on. It is, therefore, argued that one can skip all the steps involved in developing a point system and just work directly with the job classification method.

There are two main criticisms of the classification method. First, job grades tend to combine factors in ways that are not readily apparent based on reading the grade description. It may appear that a job fits into more than one grade. This typically happens because the amount of a factor required in a job to qualify for a particular grade may not be clear in the grade description. A second related disadvantage of the classification method is that it is extremely time consuming and difficult to construct clear grade descriptions. Some organizations deal with this problem by constructing grading rules instead of grade descriptions. A grading rule system specifies the grade value a job will carry for having certain amounts of a compensable factor.

## Factor Comparison Method of Job Evaluation

The factor comparison method of job evaluation is a refinement of the ranking method. The method uses a process of comparing jobs and ranking them in relation to each other. Two aspects of the process make the factor comparison system more complex than the ranking method. First, the method almost always entails a set of universal factors for defining job value.[23]

Second, the method begins with the assumption that key jobs, which are evaluated first, have a fair price already assigned to them. Job pricing for key jobs is therefore completed before the internal relationships among all other jobs are established.[24] Other job evaluation methods price the jobs after the internal job structure is determined (after job evaluation is completed).

The steps to implement the factor comparison method are summarized in Exhibit 8.7.

### Steps in the Factor Comparison Method

**Step 1: Select the Job Cluster and the Key Jobs to Be Evaluated**   The selection of appropriate key jobs from the job cluster being evaluated is important in designing a valid factor comparison method.

**Step 2: Select the Compensable Factors**   The job evaluation committee has a wide range of choices in selecting compensable factors. Usually, about five factors are chosen. The committee may create factors or it might use compensable factors that have been developed by others for job evaluation systems. Refer to Exhibit 8.8 for a summary of some of the more common universal factor systems.[25] The factors developed by Benge[26] are used in the factor comparison exercises at the end of this chapter.

**Step 3: Input Key Job Information**   This step is the same as in other job evaluation methods. The only additional point to be stressed is that often the job descriptions are written in terms that help establish the compensable factors for use in the job evaluation plan. Because of the frequent occurrence of certain factors and their repeated use in job evaluation plans, they are sometimes referred to as universal factors. (Exhibit 8.8, showing sets of compensable factors, is provided so that the reader can see the high overlap in factors between different plans.)

**Step 4: Rank Key Jobs by Factor**   This step, in particular, demonstrates that the factor comparison method is a refinement of the ranking method. The job

EXHIBIT 8.7    STEPS IN THE FACTOR COMPARISON METHOD OF
JOB EVALUATION

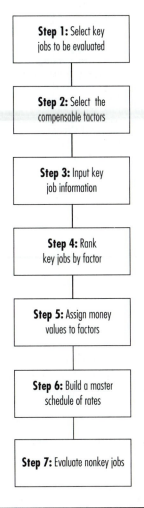

**Step 1:** Select key
jobs to be evaluated

**Step 2:** Select the
compensable factors

**Step 3:** Input key
job information

**Step 4:** Rank
key jobs by factor

**Step 5:** Assign money
values to factors

**Step 6:** Build a master
schedule of rates

**Step 7:** Evaluate nonkey jobs

evaluation committee members rank the key jobs on each compensable factor. Exhibit 8.9 is an example of the ranking scheme applied to several jobs.

Each of the key jobs is ranked on one factor at a time. That is, there should be an independent ranking of jobs for each of the compensable factors. Because different factors are likely to result in different rank orderings of jobs, if the evaluator does not rank jobs on each factor independently, there is a chance that the ranking on one factor will bias the overall ranking. Ranking of jobs within factors is important to reduce this potential bias.[27]

Once all members of the committee have ranked the jobs on each of the factors independently, the results should be compared. The committee will need to

---

| EXHIBIT 8.8 | COMMONLY USED UNIVERSAL COMPENSABLE FACTORS |
| --- | --- |

| Bass | Benge | NEMA–NMTA |
| --- | --- | --- |
| Skill | Mental requirements | Skill |
| Responsibility | Skill requirements | Effort |
| Working conditions | Physical requirements | Responsibility |
| | Responsibility | Job conditions |
| | Working conditions | |

| FES | Hay and Purves | Equal Pay Act |
| --- | --- | --- |
| Knowledge required by the position | Know-how | Skill |
| Supervisory controls | Problem solving | Effort |
| Guidelines | Accountability | Responsibility |
| Complexity | | Working conditions |
| Scope and effect | | |
| Personal contacts | | |
| Physical demands | | |
| Work environment | | |

---

come to agreement where there are differing results. One method is to take the average ranking on a factor across committee members. Another approach is to take the modal ranking. Probably the best approach in case of a dispute is for the committee to first discuss the reasons for their rankings, which may explain the disparity and lead to reconciling the differences.

---

| EXHIBIT 8.9 | RANKING OF KEY JOBS BY FACTOR |
| --- | --- |

| Key Job | Mental Require- ment | Skill Require- ment | Physical Require- ment | Respon- sibility | Working Conditions |
| --- | --- | --- | --- | --- | --- |
| Patternmaker | 1 | 1 | 7 | 2 | 9 |
| Machinist | 3 | 2 | 5 | 3 | 7 |
| Pipe fitter | 4 | 4 | 4 | 4 | 4 |
| Poleman | 8 | 8 | 2 | 8 | 2 |
| Painter | 5 | 5 | 6 | 6 | 5 |
| Substation operator | 2 | 3 | 10 | 1 | 10 |
| Drill-press operator | 6 | 6 | 9 | 5 | 6 |
| Rammer | 10 | 9 | 1 | 9 | 1 |
| Carpenter helper | 7 | 7 | 8 | 7 | 8 |
| Laborer | 9 | 10 | 3 | 10 | 3 |

Disagreement on the rankings of key jobs within factors can usually be attributed to one or more of the following causes. First, the job descriptions or specifications may be ambiguously written so that it is difficult to reach consensus on how much of a compensable factor is present in a job. Second, the compensable factors may be written so that there is ambiguity in the application of a factor. Third, committee members may not understand the job evaluation process and what is being done. For example, committee members, through lack of good training, may confuse the credentials of job incumbents with the requirements of the job. Finally, the committee might be made up of the wrong people. For example, committee members should have some first-hand knowledge of the job—no matter how good the job descriptions or compensable factor definitions, there is no substitute for first-hand knowledge of the job and what is required of incumbents.

**Step 5: Assign Money Values to Factors**    Once the relative rankings within all factors have been assigned, the committee must allocate the current wages across the compensable factors (horizontal comparison). This step involves deciding the relative contributions (weight) of each compensable factor for total pay for each job. This can be done either logically or mathematically (by weighting each factor). In the allocation of wage rate among factors, two constraints must be satisfied. First, the total wage for a job must be allocated among the factors. Exhibit 8.10 shows allocation of wages to the jobs ranked in Exhibit 8.9. For example, in Exhibit 8.10 the patternmaker job carries a wage rate of $8.40 per hour and is divided up as shown.[28] Second, the dollar amounts allocated among factors for jobs must also be consistent within factor rankings. The allocation of dollars across factors for a specific job should be done independently of the rank ordering in step 4. That is, a #1 ranking on two different factors does not require equal dollar amounts. The order of the dollar amounts within a factor, however, should match the rank order done in step 4. That is, because the patternmaker job

---

**EXHIBIT 8.10**    **WAGE ALLOCATION BY FACTOR AND JOB**

| Key Job | Mental Require-ment | Skill Require-ment | Physical Require-ment | Respon-sibility | Working Conditions | Total Wage |
|---|---|---|---|---|---|---|
| Patternmaker | $2.46 | $3.04 | $0.94 | $1.44 | $0.52 | $8.40 |
| Machinist | 1.50 | 2.26 | 1.28 | 1.34 | 0.72 | 7.10 |
| Pipe fitter | 1.18 | 2.08 | 1.40 | 1.18 | 1.12 | 6.96 |
| Poleman | 0.74 | 1.18 | 2.48 | 0.90 | 1.60 | 6.90 |
| Painter | 1.12 | 2.04 | 1.26 | 1.12 | 1.06 | 6.60 |
| Substation operator | 1.80 | 2.10 | 0.24 | 1.62 | 0.24 | 5.90 |
| Drill-press operator | 1.04 | 1.86 | 0.76 | 1.16 | 0.98 | 5.80 |
| Rammer | 0.34 | 0.50 | 2.52 | 0.56 | 1.68 | 5.60 |
| Carpenter helper | 0.94 | 1.72 | 0.88 | 1.04 | 0.62 | 5.20 |
| Laborer | 0.64 | 0.36 | 2.10 | 0.50 | 1.40 | 5.00 |

is ranked highest on mental requirements and receives $2.46 for this factor, no other job in the key group could receive more than $2.46 for mental requirements because no other job is ranked as high. If the numeric rankings and the dollar allotments are not consistent, the process needs to be repeated until there is internal consistency. If there are disagreements, the same questions addressed in step 4 should be reviewed here. Also, the evaluators should stop and ask if this job is a true key job. If it is not, the job may have to be dropped from the process at this stage and evaluated later as a nonkey job.

**Step 6: Build a Master Schedule of Rates**   Once internal consistency has been achieved among jobs and within factor ranks, the committee can build a master schedule of rates for the key jobs. The master schedule lists the jobs as they are ranked within compensable factor and the associated monetary value assigned to the job.

Two types of master schedules can be constructed that differ only in the way the information is presented. One master schedule is portrayed in Exhibit 8.10, which lists the jobs in the left column, the compensable factors at the top, and the wage allocated for each factor and each job in the body of the schedule.

A second way to arrange the data is portrayed in Exhibit 8.11. Here the wage values appear in the left-hand column, the compensable factors across the top, and the jobs within the body of the schedule. In this method, the jobs are entered into the schedule according to their ranking within each compensable factor. This type of master schedule shows the relative ordering of jobs within compensable factors and is generally preferred.

**Step 7: Evaluate Nonkey Jobs**   The establishment of the master schedule of key jobs and their wage values by factor allows the job evaluation committee to evaluate the nonkey jobs. The committee slots each of the remaining jobs into the master schedule. For example, the nonkey job of tool crib attendant can now be evaluated. The committee first decides where this job ranks relative to the other jobs on each of the compensable factors and then assigns a monetary amount for each factor. The factor monetary values totals to the wage rate for that job. If the tool crib attendant job ranks higher in mental requirements than the pipefitter job but lower in mental requirements than the machinist job, it might be assigned a dollar value for mental requirements of $1.48, between those of the two key jobs. This process is repeated for the tool crib attendant job for each of the compensable factors. Once the dollar value is established for each factor, the total across all factors is the total wage for the tool crib attendant job. In Exhibit 8.12, the tool crib attendant job is evaluated using the data in the master schedule in Exhibit 8.11. By adding up the dollar value across factors, Exhibit 8.12 shows that the job will be paid $5.00.

This slotting process continues for all nonkey jobs, and they are slotted into the master schedule as they are evaluated. Subsequent jobs are compared not only against key jobs but also against previously evaluated nonkey jobs. When all jobs have been evaluated, all jobs will be recorded in the master schedule.

| EXHIBIT 8.11 | MASTER SCHEDULE |
| --- | --- |

| Rates ($) | Mental Requirement | Skill Requirement | Physical Requirement | Responsibility | Working Conditions |
| --- | --- | --- | --- | --- | --- |
| 3.04 | | Patternmaker | | | |
| | | | | | |
| 2.52 | | | Rammer | | |
| 2.51 | | | | | |
| 2.50 | | | | | |
| 2.49 | | | | | |
| 2.48 | | | Poleman | | |
| 2.47 | | | | | |
| 2.46 | Patternmaker | | | | |
| | | | | | |
| 2.26 | | Machinist | | | |
| | | | | | |
| | | Substation | | | |
| 2.10 | | operator | Laborer | | |
| 2.09 | | | | | |
| 2.08 | | Pipefitter | | | |
| | | | | | |
| 2.04 | | Painter | | | |
| | . | . | . | . | |
| | . | . | . | . | |
| | . | . | . | . | |
| | | | | | |
| 0.65 | | | | | |
| 0.64 | Laborer | | | | |
| 0.63 | | | | | |
| 0.62 | | | | | Carpenter helper |
| | | | | | |
| 0.56 | | | | Rammer | |
| 0.55 | | | | | |
| 0.54 | | | | | |
| 0.53 | | | | | |
| 0.52 | | | | | Patternmaker |
| 0.51 | | | | | |
| 0.50 | | Rammer | | Laborer | |
| | | | | | |
| 0.36 | | Laborer | | | |
| 0.35 | | | | | |
| 0.34 | Rammer | | | | |
| | | | | | Substation |
| 0.24 | | | | | operator |

Note: This is a partial schedule. A full schedule would include every wage rate from lowest to highest and would include each job in its appropriate position in each column.

| EXHIBIT 8.12 | SLOTTING IN THE TOOL CRIB ATTENDANT JOB |
|---|---|

**Factor 1: Mental Requirements**

Tool crib attendant (TCA) job demands considerably more
mental requirements than pipefitter (ranked 4 = $1.18)
but slightly less mental requirements than machinist
(ranked 3 = $1.50). Therefore, allocate $1.48 to TCA:                    $1.48

**Factor 2: Skill Requirements**

TCA job requires considerably more skill than rammer job
(ranked 9 = $0.50) but somewhat less than poleman job
(ranked 8 = $1.18). Therefore, allocate $1.10 to TCA:                    1.10

**Factor 3: Physical Requirements**

TCA job requires more physical effort than drill-press operator
(ranked 9 = $0.76) but somewhat less effort than carpenter's helper
(ranked 8 = $0.88). Therefore, allocate $0.80 to TCA:                    0.80

**Factor 4: Responsibility**

TCA job requires considerably more responsibility than
poleman (ranked 8 = $0.90) and nearly as much as
carpenter helper (ranked 7 = $1.04). Therefore, allocate $1.02 to TCA:    1.02

**Factor 5: Working Conditions**

TCA job has slightly better working conditions than carpenter's
helper (ranked 8 = $0.62) but definitely poorer conditions than
patternmaker (ranked 9 = $0.52). Therefore, allocate $0.60 to TCA:        0.60

Total pay for tool crib attendant                                        $5.00

## Examples of Factor Comparison

The cooperative wage survey (steel industry) has developed, through a joint
union–management committee, two job evaluation plans which they identify as
factor comparison plans: one for hourly production and maintenance jobs in
the plant, and one for clerical and technical jobs. The production and maintenance plans have 12 factors: pre-employment training, employment training and
experience, mental skill, manual skill, responsibility for material, responsibility
for tools and equipment, responsibility for operators, responsibility for safety of
others, mental effort, physical effort, surroundings, and hazards. The salaried
clerical and technical have 7 factors: pre-employment training, employment
training and experience, mental skills, responsibility for performance, responsibility for contacts, working conditions, and responsibility for direction.

## Advantages and Disadvantages of the Factor Comparison Method

Advocates of the factor comparison method argue that a custom-made job evaluation plan results because the master schedule reflects only the jobs in the

organization. Furthermore, they argue that the method is relatively easy to use once it is set up. That is, even relatively untrained evaluators can slot jobs into the master schedule and come up with the total wage for a job. And finally, advocates suggest that the relative value of a job is expressed in terms that everyone can understand.

Critics of the approach suggest that the use of dollar values can bias the assessment of jobs. Because evaluators may know the relative wage of a job, they may assign more money to a factor than the job is actually worth. A second main criticism focuses on the assumption that key jobs are available throughout the total range of jobs to be evaluated. Often key jobs are entry-level jobs, and there are no good benchmark jobs at higher levels. As a consequence, the fairness of the wage rates assigned to higher level jobs is in question. Third, although the method is relatively easy to use, it is not easily set up. Some critics assert that, because of the complexity of establishing the master schedule, many employees will not understand how the plan was conceived and operationalized. Employees may have little faith in an evaluation approach that they do not understand. If this happens, the purpose in conducting job evaluation in the first place is defeated. Finally, it is often argued that when actual dollars are used to assess jobs, the master schedule becomes more obsolete every time wage rates change for key jobs. As inflation or other factors cause the value of the dollar amounts in the master schedule to change, the organization will need to change the master schedule itself. This is one reason some organizations use a measurement scheme independent of dollars.[29]

## Point Method of Job Evaluation

In the point method (also called point factor) of job evaluation, the organization identifies the compensable factors and breaks them down into degrees. The organization must also weight the factors, determine the number of scales for each factor, and assign points. The result is that the evaluator assigns a numeric score to a job for each factor based on how much of that factor appears in the job. The job's total worth is then determined by adding up the numeric scores across all factors. This procedure, when conducted across all jobs, will result in a relative ordering of jobs based on the number of points that each job earns.

Although the point method allows an organization to develop one job evaluation scheme for all jobs in the organization, this is rarely done for several pragmatic reasons. First, it is difficult to identify one set of compensable factors that is applicable for all jobs. For example, the use of working conditions may distinguish among shop jobs, but there is not likely to be any variance among office jobs on that compensable factor. Second, creating single definitions of factors in language easily understood by all employees would be nearly impossible. Different operational definitions would be needed for the same compensable factor for different clusters of jobs. Third, the fact that different job groups are often anchored to different labor markets cannot be ignored.[30] In an equity sense, comparison with job families (clusters) within an organization may be less relevant than comparison with a job family in the relevant labor market.

Even with point methods of job evaluation, organizations usually have a series of job evaluation plans. For example, there may be one plan for skilled shop jobs, another plan for unskilled assembly work, and still a third plan for office and clerical. The discussion that follows is valid regardless of the employee population on which the point method is used.

The steps for implementing the point method of job evaluation are summarized in Exhibit 8.13.

## Steps in the Point Method

**Step 1: Select the Job Cluster and the Key Jobs to Be Evaluated**   This is the same as in other methods of job evaluation.

**Step 2: Input Key Job Information**   As with all job evaluation approaches, the jobs must be analyzed and job descriptions/specifications prepared.

**Step 3: Select Compensable Factors**   Just as with the factor comparison method, the point method generally uses a set of factors that have been developed by others (refer back to Exhibit 8.8). It has long been accepted that three to five factors are sufficient to capture a desired criterion structure.[31] Additional factors may be merely redundant and do not explain unique variation in the job structure. However, it is also important to remember that job evaluation plans are rationalizations for job relationships and the pay structure. Therefore, if employees and management believe that additional factors are important for job worth purposes, they should be included to provide "face validity" to the plan.[32] Basically, the job evaluation committee should select those factors that are viewed within the organization as most important in rewarding work and distinguishing among jobs.

**Step 4: Define Compensable Factors**   In this step, once factors are chosen, the committee must clearly define what each factor will mean in the context of the job evaluation plan.

The more specific a factor is, the narrower the definition tends to be, and frequently, the easier the factor is to use. One of the important criteria in determining whether factors are broadly or narrowly defined is related to the types of jobs covered. If the jobs are from a narrow job cluster, the factor might be correspondingly narrow. However, if the jobs are from a range of job clusters, factors will need to be correspondingly broader with more subfactors to capture variability in all the jobs.[33]

As an example of this point, suppose an organization is defining the factor of working conditions for a narrow job cluster of shop jobs. In this case, the subfactor definitions might include only noise and temperature. If the firm wishes to use one job evaluation plan to cover office workers as well, another subfactor for working conditions might be necessary, such as visual concentration (to cover staring at video terminals).

Some organizations use factors and subfactors as illustrated in Exhibit 8.14A and B. Exhibit 8.14A allots the total percent to the factor; whereas

EXHIBIT 8.13    STEPS IN THE POINT METHOD OF JOB
EVALUATION

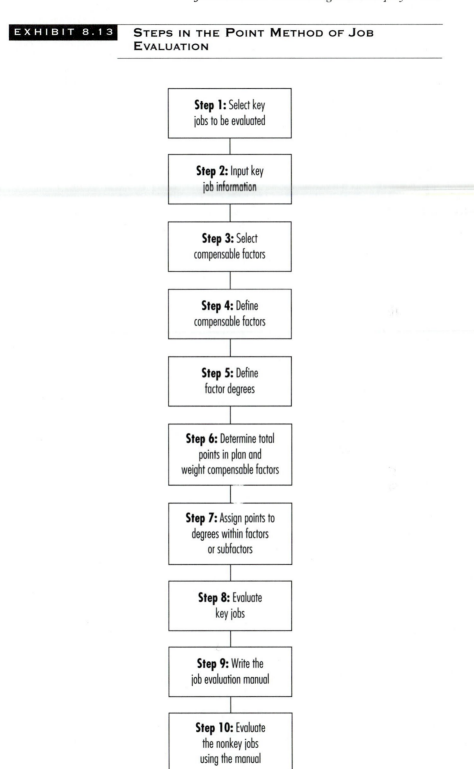

**Step 1:** Select key
jobs to be evaluated

**Step 2:** Input key
job information

**Step 3:** Select
compensable factors

**Step 4:** Define
compensable factors

**Step 5:** Define
factor degrees

**Step 6:** Determine total
points in plan and
weight compensable factors

**Step 7:** Assign points to
degrees within factors
or subfactors

**Step 8:** Evaluate
key jobs

**Step 9:** Write the
job evaluation manual

**Step 10:** Evaluate
the nonkey jobs
using the manual

Points

| Factor | Percent | First Degree | Second Degree | Third Degree | Fourth Degree | Fifth Degree | Sixth Degree |
|---|---|---|---|---|---|---|---|
| Job knowledge | 25 | 25 | 100 | 175 | 250 | — | — |
| Training | 10 | 10 | 33 | 55 | 78 | 100 | — |
| Independent judgment | 25 | 25 | 100 | 175 | 250 | — | — |
| Accountability | 20 | 20 | 65 | 110 | 155 | 200 | — |
| Working conditions | 5 | 5 | 20 | 35 | 50 | — | — |
| Mental | 15 | 15 | 42 | 69 | 96 | 123 | 150 |

Note: Total points in plan is 1,000.

EXHIBIT 8.14B FACTORS, DEGREES, AND WEIGHTED POINT VALUES FOR HOURLY EMPLOYEES FOR ORGANIZATIONS USING SUBFACTORS

| Factor and Subfactors | Percent | Points | | | | | | Weight in Percent |
|---|---|---|---|---|---|---|---|---|
| | | First Degree | Second Degree | Third Degree | Fourth Degree | Fifth Degree | Sixth Degree | |
| Skill | 50 | | | | | | | |
| Education and job knowledge | | 12 | 24 | 36 | 48 | 60 | 72 | 12 |
| Experience and training | | 24 | 48 | 72 | 96 | 120 | 144 | 24 |
| Initiative and ingenuity | | 14 | 28 | 42 | 56 | 70 | 84 | 14 |
| Effort | 15 | | | | | | | |
| Physical demand | | 10 | 20 | 30 | 40 | 50 | 60 | 10 |
| Mental or visual demand | | 5 | 10 | 15 | 20 | 25 | 30 | 5 |
| Responsibility | 20 | | | | | | | |
| Equipment or tools | | 6 | 12 | 18 | 24 | 30 | 36 | 6 |
| Material or product | | 7 | 14 | 21 | 28 | 35 | 42 | 7 |
| Safety of others | | 3 | 6 | 9 | 12 | 15 | 18 | 3 |
| Work of others | | 4 | 8 | 12 | 16 | 16 | 20 | 4 |
| Job Conditions | 15 | | | | | | | |
| Working conditions | | 10 | 20 | 30 | 40 | 50 | 60 | 10 |
| Unavoidable hazards | | 5 | 10 | 15 | 20 | 25 | 30 | 5 |
| Total | 100 | 100 | 200 | 300 | 400 | 500 | 600 | 100 |

SOURCE: Herbert G. Zollitsch & Adolph Langsner, *Wage and Salary Administration*, 2nd edition (Cincinnati, OH: Southwestern Publishing Company, 1970), p. 234. Reprinted by permission of Herbert G. Zollitsch.

Exhibit 8.14B divides the percent for the factor over several subfactors. For example, Exhibit 8.14B shows that the skill factor in the context of job evaluation has three subfactors: education and job knowledge, experience and training, and initiative and ingenuity. Each subfactor will have to be operationally defined in specific terms.

Exhibit 8.15 gives examples of three general factor definitions.

**Step 5: Define Factor Degrees**   The committee must decide how many degrees should be on the scale for a given factor, or subfactor. There should be adequate degrees to make meaningful distinctions among jobs. If there are too many degrees, the distinctions may be meaningless. Also, if no job falls within the degree, the steps are probably too narrowly defined. Exhibit 8.16 shows one method of defining factor degrees. All factors or subfactors do not have to use the same number of degrees.

**Step 6: Determine Total Points in Plan and Weight Compensable Factors**   The process for assigning point values to factors begins with a decision as to how many total points the job evaluation plan will have. There is no magic number of points that a plan should have. A general rule is to have enough total points in the plan to differentiate adequately among the jobs to be evaluated. One way to arrive at this number is to take the highest paid job covered by the job evaluation plan and divide its wage rate by the wage rate of the lowest paid job. This value is then multiplied by 100.

To illustrate this formula, suppose that the annual wage for the highest paid job is $70,000 and the annual wage for the lowest paid job is $7,000. Dividing the highest wage by the lowest results in 10 ($70,000 ÷ $7,000). Multiplying this value by 100 results in a total of 1,000 points for the job evaluation plan.

---

**EXHIBIT 8.15**    OPERATIONAL DEFINITIONS FOR COMPENSABLE FACTORS

---

**Job Knowledge**

This factor considers the skills necessary to perform the job such as finger dexterity, clerical skills (typing, dictation, filing), human relations skills, and telecommunication skills.

**Training**

This factor considers training the worker must have. It is measured by the number of weeks of on-the-job or formal technical training it will take a worker to be able to perform the job.

**Working Conditions**

This factor considers the requirements of a job concerning the number and severity of unpleasant work context elements present on the job (for example, ventilation, eye strain, temperature).

---

| EXHIBIT 8.16 | DEGREE DEFINITIONS FOR EXPERIENCE AND TRAINING TIME REQUIRED |
| --- | --- |

| Degree | Training Time |
| --- | --- |
| 1 | 1 month or less |
| 2 | More than 1 month but less than 3 months |
| 3 | At least 3 months but less than 6 months |
| 4 | At least 6 months but less than 1 year |
| 5 | 1 year or more |

Under normal conditions this should be enough points to adequately distinguish among the jobs in the organization.

After determining the total number of points that will go into the job evaluation plan, the committee must determine how the points will be divided among the factors or subfactors. Points may be assigned to factors based on committee judgment or based on statistics. Statistical assignment of points is less common partly because of its complexity. Nonetheless, several plans do use regression techniques to find which factors best predict pay rates for jobs.[34] One study found that about 40 percent of the plans used by responding organizations rely on statistical weighing, and the balance rely on judgmental weighting.[35]

The assignment of points to each of the various factors is equivalent to weighting each factor based on its importance. As an example, suppose that an organization has a skill factor in its plan and considers it a very important factor, weighting it at 50 percent. In this case, assuming that the plan carries a maximum of 1,000 points (see Exhibit 8.17A), the skill factor is assigned 500 points (1,000 × 0.50 = 500 points). In this same fashion, points are assigned to subfactors. If skill is composed of several subfactors (such as education and job knowledge; experience and training), then the points are divided among them. If the organization decides that the education and job knowledge subfactor should be weighted 60 percent and experience and training should be weighted 40 percent, then these subfactors would receive 300 and 200 points, respectively. When the organization is not using subfactors, then the total points in the plan (see Exhibit 8.17B) is multiplied by the factor weight to yield the factor points at its highest degree (for example, responsibility—1,000 points × 0.25 = 250 points).

**Step 7: Assign Points to Degree Within Factors or Subfactors**   Once the total number of points and the weight of a factor or subfactor are established, the next step is to assign points to the degrees within the factors. Exhibit 8.17A illustrates one procedure for assigning points to subfactor degrees. First, the highest degree of a subfactor is assigned the maximum points for the subfactor. Using the education and job knowledge subfactor in the above example, the highest degree of this subfactor is assigned 300 points. Second, the number of factor

---

| **EXHIBIT 8.17A** | **ALLOCATING POINTS TO SUBFACTOR DEGREES** |
|---|---|

---

| | |
|---|---|
| Total points in job evaluation plan: | 1,000 points |
| Weight of the factor skill: | 50% |
| Points assigned to skill: | $1{,}000 \times 0.50 = 500$ |
| Weights assigned to skill subfactors of education and job knowledge, and experience and training: | |
|       education and job knowledge: | 60% |
|       experience and training: | 40% |
| Points assigned to education and job knowledge: | $500 \times 0.60 = 300$ |
| Number of degree steps for subfactor education and job knowledge: | 7 |
| Assign points to lowest degree (subfactor: weight × factor weight = $0.60 \times 0.50$; % = point value) | 30 points |
| Highest point value (300) minus the point value for the lowest degree (30) = $300 - 30$: | 270 points |
| Divide the remaining degrees (6) into the remaining points = $270 \div 6$: | 45 point increments |

Education/Job Knowledge Subfactor

Therefore:
    Degree 1 = 30 points
    Degree 2 = 30 + 45 = 75 points
    Degree 3 = 75 + 45 = 120 points
    Degree 4 = 120 + 45 = 165 points
    Degree 5 = 165 + 45 = 210 points
    Degree 6 = 210 + 45 = 255 points
    Degree 7 = 255 + 45 = 300 points

---

degrees is determined, and points are assigned to the lowest degree. The 30 points is arrived at by multiplying the subfactor weight (0.60) by the factor weight (0.50) to determine its relative weight in the overall plan (0.60 × 0.50 = 0.30). This percent is then used as the lowest point value.[36] Thus the lowest point value for the first degree for the subfactor education and job knowledge is 30 points. In the above example, the education and job knowledge subfactor received 300 points; the lowest degree is assigned 30 points. Third, the lowest degree points are subtracted from the highest degree points (300 points - 30 points = 270 points), and this quantity is divided by the number of factor degrees minus 1. This value plus the points assigned to the prior degree (beginning with 30, in this case) gives the number of points to be allocated to each subsequent factor degree. See Exhibit 8.17A for an illustration when factors and subfactors are used and Exhibit 8.17B when only factors are used.

The above procedure assumes that factor or subfactor degrees are equidistant from each other. Usually this procedure gives an adequate distinction between jobs. However, if the committee believes that equidistances between degrees are not satisfactory because the definitions are not equidistant from each other, points can

| EXHIBIT 8.17B | ALLOCATING POINTS TO FACTOR DEGREES |
|---|---|

| | |
|---|---|
| Total points in job evaluation plan: | 1,000 points |
| Weight of the factor responsibility: | 25% |
| Points assigned to responsibility: | $1,000 \times 0.25 = 250$ |
| Number of degree steps for responsibility factor: | 4 |
| Assign points to the lowest degree (equals factor weight because there are no subfactors) | 25 points |
| Highest point value (250) minus the point value for the lowest degree (25) = 250 − 25: | 225 points |
| Divide the remaining degrees (3) into the remaining points = 225 ÷ 3: | 75 point increments |

Therefore:
Degree 1 = 25
Degree 2 = 25 + 75 = 100
Degree 3 = 100 + 75 = 175
Degree 4 = 175 + 75 = 250

be assigned to factor degrees in a manner consistent with committee judgments about differences between degrees.

Some point plans use a geometric progression in assigning points to degrees. Points may be assigned on the basis of 2, 4, 8, 16, 32, and 64. When geometric progressions are used, the committee will need to do log transformations of the point scale to assign degrees. The use of geometric progressions does not alter the relative rank of jobs; it only creates a perception of greater distances between jobs.[37]

Having developed the weighting scale for factors and degrees within factors, the committee must then check the validity of the results by evaluating several key jobs to determine if the point plan as developed results in the expected job hierarchy. This step is critical if the points were developed judgmentally.[38]

**Step 8: Evaluate Key Jobs**   Each key job should be evaluated using the newly designed point method. Compare the hierarchical order of the key jobs with their market pay. If the order is not identical, the compensable factors and the jobs identified as key jobs must be examined. Either some of the jobs are not key jobs or the compensable factors are not defined properly. If the problem is with a key job, you return to step 1; if it is with a compensable factor, return to step 3. This is done to validate the job evaluation; therefore, the wage rate (for example, mean, median) used for comparison with the hierarchical order is not important.

**Step 9: Write the Job Evaluation Manual**   The results of the committee's activities must be written up in a job evaluation manual. Without a well-documented job evaluation plan, the plan is not usable except by the original committee. Documentation of the committee's work should include the rationale for the factors chosen, the rationale for weighting the factors, the rationale and procedures for assigning points to factor degrees, and finally, a description of the factors, sub-factors, and the degrees assigned to each.

Committee members should remember that other employees who were not involved in development of the plan may have to use it. The documentation of the committee's work should be clear enough so that other employees using the job evaluation manual could retrace the decisions. It is recommended that non-committee members review the manual and that the committee make any nec-essary revisions based on their comments.

**Step 10: Evaluate the Nonkey Jobs Using the Manual**   Once the manual is complete and all the documentation is in place, the committee must evaluate all the jobs. Each committee member should independently evaluate each job based on how much of each compensable factor that job possesses. It is recom-mended that each job be evaluated on one factor at a time to increase consistency of application. The outcome of this process will be a numeric value assigned to each job.

As with all job evaluation methods, it is quite possible for the committee members to disagree on the points to be assigned for a given factor. As with other methods, the committee members should compare their independent assess-ments of the job and seek agreement. Discussion should resolve any discrepan-cies among evaluators. Significant amounts of disagreement and an inability to resolve differences suggest that the factor definitions and degree definitions are not precise enough or that individual evaluators perceive the job in radically different ways. In either case, efforts must be made to clarify the cause of the discrepancies.

### *Examples of Point Method*

Two examples of point-type plans are the National Position Evaluation Plan (NPEP) and the Hay Guide Chart Profile Method.

**Multifactor Methods**   The NPEP originated with the National Metal Trades Association (NMTA) and the National Electrical Manufacturers' Association (NEMA), but it is now known as NPEP.

Because there are organizations still using the original version, a short expla-nation will be provided. The NEMA originally identified the four general factors of skill, effort, responsibility, and working conditions. Each of these factors was then divided into subfactors. NMTA designed a similar method to evaluate jobs. For example, NMTA defines five factors (training, initiative, responsibility, job conditions, and supervision) for clerical, technical, and service positions. The subfactors for each factor are as follows: training (knowledge, experience), ini-tiative (complexity of duties, supervision received), responsibility (errors, contact with others, confidential data), job conditions (mental/visual demands, working conditions), and supervision (character of supervision, scope of supervision). The NPEP has a separate plan for manufacturing, maintenance, warehousing, distri-bution, and service jobs (unit 1); one for nonexempt clerical, technical, and ser-vice jobs (unit 2); one for exempt supervisory, professional, sales, and administrative jobs (unit 3); and one for executive jobs (unit 4). Interested parties are able to purchase manuals from the NMTA that provide factors, factor definitions, and factor degree definitions.[39]

**Hay Guide Chart Profile Method**    The Hay method of job evaluation probably has been the most popular proprietary job evaluation system available.[40] The system was developed for use on predominantly white-collar, managerial, and professional jobs. It is actually a variation on the factor comparison and point methods of job evaluation. As developed by Hay and associates, the Hay plan uses three universal factors to compare all jobs: know-how, problem solving, and accountability. When appropriate, a fourth factor—working conditions—can be added.[41] Know-how is the total of all skills and knowledge required to do the job; it measures the interrelationship between the three subfactors of specialized and technical knowledge, managerial relations, and human relations. Problem solving is the amount of original thinking required to arrive at decisions in the job; it is composed of the two subfactors of thinking environment and thinking challenge. Accountability is the answerability for actions taken on the job; it is composed of freedom to act, impact on end results, and magnitude of impact.

To use this method, the evaluator needs the Hay guide chart for each of the three factors. The job is then assigned a point value for each factor/subfactor. The total of points across all of the factors is the point value for the job. Each job evaluated requires a profile that shows the relative weights of the three compensable factors. The weight assigned to problem solving cannot be greater than that given to know-how, based on the belief that you cannot use knowledge that you do not have.

The traditional Hay system (guide chart method) is based on an idea that there are universal compensable factors which are applicable across industries and companies. Currently, the guide chart method makes up only a small amount of compensation system design work performed by Hay Management Consultants. Hay has developed an approach called the Hay Dynamic Pay concept[42] which is consistent with the philosophy of this text. The Hay Dynamic Pay concept is based on the fact that organizations operate in a dynamic world; and therefore, they must be adaptable. These organizations need pay programs that are integrated with the organizational culture, that correspond to the organizational strategy and structure, and that respect the nature of the organization's employees. In this approach, greater emphasis is placed on the value of the individual, not just on the value of the job.

Hay has identified four basic models for classifying organizations. The *functional model* focuses primarily on reliability and consistency of operations. Traditional management hierarchies are established to control and monitor the organization's operations. The *process model* is a result of the recent emphasis on quality and customer satisfaction. It emphasizes employee empowerment, formal and informal communication, and the integration of planning, execution, and control to increase the firm's ability to respond to customer needs. The *time-based model* "emphasizes the ability to dominate markets in their high profitability phases, and then move toward a new opportunity as those markets reach a mature, lower-return stage."[43] These organizations are generally finance- and manufacturing-driven. The *network model* emphasizes flexibility and responsiveness to customer and market needs. Traditional management structures and long-term alliances are replaced by temporary alliances and a high level of flexibility and adaptiveness. Hay suggests that the compensation mix between base pay, variable pay, and benefits varies based on the organizational model under which the organization is operating. Since most organizations do not fit nicely into one of the above four models, it is essential that the compensation program be tailored uniquely for each organization.

### Advantages and Disadvantages of the Point Method

Probably the greatest single advantage of the point method is that once factors and degrees are defined, the job evaluation plan should be highly stable over time. The compensable factors should be valid for several years unless there is radical change in the way the organization does business. Second, given the amount of work that goes into a carefully defined job evaluation manual, the plan is likely to be perceived as valid by the users, thus enhancing employee perceptions of equitable treatment. Third, because factors and degrees are carefully defined, if job descriptions are equally accurate, there is likely to be high agreement within the committee in assessing jobs. A fourth advantage of the point method is that it provides ample data to explain to employees why their jobs fall where they do in the overall pay structure or to prepare a case in appeals that may be brought forward by employees, the union, or governmental agencies. Finally, the point method has found acceptance by employees, union officials, and managers.

Probably the greatest disadvantage to the point plan is the time, effort, and money required to set up the plan. Implementation of the point method requires careful definition and weighting of factors, careful definition and assignment of degrees to factors, and careful development and documentation of the evaluation manual. The compensation decision maker must weigh the benefits of this approach against the costs. A second disadvantage is that the organization will typically end up building pay grades even after going through the point method. For example, an organization with a 1,000-point plan may end up with ten pay grades (discussed later in chapter), each 100 points in width. If the organization is going to revert to a job classification method anyway, why should it go to the trouble and expense of developing a point method? Finally, as with the factor comparison method, the point method relies heavily on key jobs for which valid wage rates can be determined. Unless such key jobs and correct pay rates exist, the point method may not be valid.

## Other Job Evaluation Techniques and Variations

The four methods of job evaluation reviewed in this chapter are the most commonly used methods. However, there are other approaches to job evaluation. The following methods are briefly discussed because a number of companies use these specific techniques.

## Single Factor Job Evaluation Methods

One of the more intriguing job evaluation methods was suggested by Elliott Jaques.[44] Jaques argued that all jobs can be evaluated in terms of their time span of discretion. Jaques defined time span of discretion as the longest period of time an employee is permitted to exercise discretion without review of his or her actions by a supervisor.

Although this approach is interesting, there is not a great deal of empirical work to substantiate it. Where research has been conducted, researchers have found that organizations have difficulty administering such a program. The principal problem seems to be getting an accurate description of the time span for any given job. Another problem is that time span of discretion amounts to a single-factor method of job evaluation, and most employees would probably prefer to have several important job dimensions reflected in the evaluation process.

There are other single-factor job evaluation methods besides Jaques's approach, such as the popular problem-solving compensable factor method.[45] This approach amounts to a ranking method using the problem-solving factor as the criterion for ranking jobs. A third single-factor method that uses decision making as the compensable factor was developed by Arthur Young International and called Decision Band Method.[46] It was based on the belief that all jobs (regardless of level) require some level of decision making, and this provides a common yardstick on which to evaluate them. The method uses the following six bands on which jobs are compared: corporate policy making, programming, interpretive, process, operational, and defined. Bands D, E, and F are "adaptive" bands (that is, related to planning), whereas the three lower bands (A, B, C) are "instrumental" and are related to the execution of decisions made in bands D, E, and F. Each band is subdivided through a subgrading process using factors related to the decision-making criteria .[47]

Similar to Young's Decision Band Method is the new management banding program recently introduced by AT&T.[48] According to this program, management salary grades are grouped into management bands to provide business units and divisions with more flexibility in managing their operations. It provides managers more opportunity for professional and career development. Management banding focuses on the years ahead and the wide range of skills that will be required.

Salary grades 1–5 are grouped into A band; separate grades such as A1, A2, A3, A4, and A5 exist within A band. These grades are retained to support the current proficiency plans and movement of managers from entry positions to higher level management. Salary grades 6–11 are consolidated into three bands B, C, and D. Managers in these bands have greater opportunity to enhance current responsibilities, explore different jobs, and work as teams. Salary grades 12–14 are grouped into an E band.

There are several advantages of the management banding program. First, banding helps business units and divisions easily adapt to changing business conditions. Second, it makes operations work more smoothly. Third, banding facilitates the use of cross-functional teams. Fourth, managers are able to move more easily across groups and business units/divisions. Fifth, banding supports

AT&T's strategy to reduce management layers and increase teamwork. Lastly, managers have greater flexibility in rearranging responsibilities without requiring promotion or demotion.

### Position Analysis Questionnaire

The advent of the computer has made it possible to integrate job evaluation into other decision-making activities. The Position Analysis Questionnaire, as discussed in Chapter 7, was designed for job analysis; however, in combination with known key job market wage rates, it has also been used for job evaluation.[49] This method relies on a statistical association between the various jobs' scores on the questionnaire's dimensions and known equitable market rates for those key jobs (obtained from a market survey of key job rates). This policy-capturing approach is not unique to this method but has been used to capture pay and point associations in other quantitative job analysis systems as well.[50]

# End-Products of Job Evaluation

The end result of job evaluation depends on the method used to conduct the job evaluation. Ranking methods produce simple rank orderings of whole jobs from highest to lowest value. Classification methods place jobs of equivalent values into slots called "grades" and rank order the job grades according to value. Jobs within each grade are therefore treated as equal in value. Point methods assign total point values to the evaluated jobs. This suggests that one-point differences between jobs reflect differences in job value. Indeed, some companies believe this is true. An example appears in Exhibit 8.18.

The practice cannot be justified because methods of job evaluation are simply not capable of making such fine job value distinctions. Employers who recognize that fact group jobs with similar points into grades and treat the jobs within each grade as equivalent in value. There are several reasons for clumping jobs of similar values into grades.

### Reasons for Job Grades

First, the continuum of points may be too refined a measurement system, and the differences between jobs may have been overmeasured. Although two jobs may vary from each other by three or four points, when the jobs themselves are examined it may be difficult to actually distinguish between them based on compensable factors.

A second argument suggests that because jobs on a continuum must be re-evaluated whenever their duties change, considerable administrative effort can be saved by forming broad groups of jobs. Jobs can then be changed in minor ways within the group without need for re-evaluation.[51]

A third reason for forming job grades is to allow for meaningful differences for rates of pay. If each point is worth 5 cents and one job is worth 100 points and another is worth 101 points, then presumably the first job would be paid $5.00 per hour and the other job would be paid $5.05 per hour. This point distinction may be meaningless, and the organization may just as well pay both jobs at the same rate. Broader grades would allow larger pay differences between grades.

A fourth consideration is the desired relationship among jobs that is naturally present. Specifically, the decision maker needs to take into account the natural breakdown of jobs.[52] Within a job family, both management and employees may distinguish between a subset of jobs such as clerk typist, file clerk, and typist. If there is a perceived meaningful distinction between these jobs, then the grade system should be designed to reflect these distinctions, even though there may not be much difference among these jobs on a point basis.

**EXHIBIT 8.18**  **JOBS AND THEIR ASSOCIATED JOB EVALUATION POINTS**

| Job Number | Points | Midpoint Wage | Job Number | Points | Midpoint Wage |
|---|---|---|---|---|---|
| 1 | 306 | $5.50 | 61 | 456 | $7.60 |
| 5 | 312 | 5.65 | 62 | 462 | 7.80 |
| 8 | 318 | 5.65 | 65 | 468 | 7.80 |
| 10 | 324 | 5.80 | 67 | 474 | 8.00 |
| 13 | 330 | 5.70 | 69 | 480 | 8.20 |
| 14 | 336 | 6.00 | 70 | 486 | 8.00 |
| 17 | 342 | 6.20 | 73 | 492 | 8.15 |
| 20 | 348 | 6.15 | 74 | 498 | 8.35 |
| 21 | 354 | 6.30 | 77 | 504 | 8.50 |
| 24 | 360 | 6.40 | 78 | 510 | 8.40 |
| 26 | 366 | 6.50 | 80 | 516 | 8.60 |
| 29 | 372 | 6.55 | 81 | 522 | 8.65 |
| 30 | 378 | 6.65 | 84 | 528 | 8.65 |
| 33 | 384 | 6.80 | 87 | 534 | 8.90 |
| 35 | 390 | 6.65 | 90 | 540 | 8.85 |
| 38 | 396 | 6.70 | 92 | 546 | 9.00 |
| 39 | 402 | 7.00 | 93 | 552 | 9.00 |
| 41 | 408 | 7.05 | 95 | 558 | 9.15 |
| 45 | 414 | 7.15 | 98 | 564 | 9.05 |
| 47 | 420 | 7.30 | 99 | 570 | 9.45 |
| 50 | 426 | 7.20 | 103 | 576 | 9.30 |
| 51 | 432 | 7.35 | 104 | 582 | 9.50 |
| 53 | 438 | 7.50 | 107 | 588 | 9.60 |
| 56 | 444 | 7.60 | 110 | 594 | 9.70 |
| 59 | 450 | 7.55 | 117 | 600 | 9.75 |

A fifth consideration is the internal labor market for promotion. If employees and the organization perceive a set of jobs as related in a promotional sequence, then it would be appropriate for the job evaluation system to assign this set of jobs to different grades.

The above arguments ultimately come back to the fact that it is administratively appropriate to collapse jobs within a range of point values into a reduced set of grades. If this were done for the jobs in Exhibit 8.18, a series of grades could be established such as that in Exhibit 8.19.

This might seem to be circular reasoning—if the job evaluation system did not make significant distinctions among jobs, then maybe the jobs are the same. But what is important here is the perceived relationship among jobs. Perceived

---

**EXHIBIT 8.19** | PAY GRADES BASED ON JOB EVALUATION POINT RANGES

| Grade | Job Number | Points | Midpoint Wage | Grade | Job Number | Points | Midpoint Wage |
|-------|-----------|--------|---------------|-------|-----------|--------|---------------|
|   | 1 | 306 | $5.50 |   | 61 | 456 | $7.60 |
|   | 5 | 312 | 5.65 |   | 62 | 462 | 7.80 |
| 1 | 8 | 318 | 5.65 | 6 | 65 | 468 | 7.80 |
|   | 10 | 324 | 5.80 |   | 67 | 474 | 8.00 |
|   | 13 | 330 | 5.70 |   | 69 | 480 | 8.20 |
|   | 14 | 336 | 6.00 |   | 70 | 486 | 8.00 |
|   | 17 | 342 | 6.20 |   | 73 | 492 | 8.15 |
| 2 | 20 | 348 | 6.15 | 7 | 74 | 498 | 8.35 |
|   | 21 | 354 | 6.30 |   | 77 | 504 | 8.50 |
|   | 24 | 360 | 6.40 |   | 78 | 510 | 8.40 |
|   | 26 | 366 | 6.50 |   | 80 | 516 | 8.60 |
|   | 29 | 372 | 6.55 |   | 81 | 522 | 8.65 |
| 3 | 30 | 378 | 6.65 | 8 | 84 | 528 | 8.65 |
|   | 33 | 384 | 6.80 |   | 87 | 534 | 8.90 |
|   | 35 | 390 | 6.65 |   | 90 | 540 | 8.85 |
|   | 38 | 396 | 6.70 |   | 92 | 546 | 9.00 |
|   | 39 | 402 | 7.00 |   | 93 | 552 | 9.00 |
| 4 | 41 | 408 | 7.05 | 9 | 95 | 558 | 9.15 |
|   | 45 | 414 | 7.15 |   | 98 | 564 | 9.05 |
|   | 47 | 420 | 7.30 |   | 99 | 570 | 9.45 |
|   | 50 | 426 | 7.20 |   | 103 | 576 | 9.30 |
|   | 51 | 432 | 7.35 |   | 104 | 582 | 9.50 |
| 5 | 53 | 438 | 7.50 | 10 | 107 | 588 | 9.60 |
|   | 56 | 444 | 7.60 |   | 110 | 594 | 9.70 |
|   | 59 | 450 | 7.55 |   | 117 | 600 | 9.75 |

equity is the compensation decision-maker's goal. In any event, decision makers will want to be aware of these considerations in establishing pay grades.

## Determining the Number of Job Grades

No absolute answers exist regarding how many pay grades will suffice for a pay structure. Each organization must examine its own situation and consider its own goals in establishing pay grades.

As noted earlier, one very important consideration is the number of pay grades necessary to achieve perceived internal equity. Employees and management may perceive meaningful differences among jobs even though those differences are not large from a job points perspective. These differences should be reflected in the job grade system.

An organization must also take into account its own policies. If the organization desires to associate salary increases with promotion, then a larger number of grades will be used. Thus, almost every time a person receives a promotion, the increase in duties and responsibilities will increase points sufficiently to move the person to the next higher grade.

A third consideration is the number of jobs and the variety of jobs being evaluated. If the organization is using only one plan to cover all jobs within the organization, then it will need to use more job grades or have very wide grade ranges (for example, grade 2 = 306 to 396 points) to handle the jobs. Whereas if the same organization was developing different plans for each job family, it could deal with those jobs with fewer grades and/or narrower grade spread (for example, grade 1 = 306 to 330 points).

There is a more mechanical approach to determining the number of pay grades.[53] This approach uses three variables to establish the number of grades. First, the company must know the midpoint wage rate for the lowest paid job in the structure. Second, it needs to know the midpoint wage rate for the highest paid job. Third, the desired percentage increase from grade to grade must be determined. The decision maker then looks at the total percentage increase from lowest to highest paid job and asks: How many times must the lowest paid job's rate be compounded at the given percentage rate between grades to achieve the highest wage rate? The percentage set by the organization will reflect its underlying pay philosophy.

For example, suppose the lowest paid job in the structure receives $10,000 per year and the highest paid job receives $20,000 per year. The desired midpoint difference between grades is 5 percent. Because the grade system will result in a wage structure with 100 percent increase in pay from lowest to highest job and because the midpoint difference between grades is 5 percent, there will need to be about 15 grades. The way to solve for the number of grades is to take the value of 1.00 plus the known percentage increase between grades (in this case, 5 percent) and raise this value (1.05) to the power that will equal the ratio of the highest to lowest wage rate. That is, 1.05 raised to the 15th power will give a value of about 2.0, which is equal to the ratio of the highest to lowest paid job ($20,000 ÷ $10,000 = 2). In this case, it would take about 15 pay grades with midpoint increments of 5 percent to move smoothly from a grade with a $10,000-a-year job to a grade with a $20,000-a-year job.

# Relative "Goodness" of Job Evaluation Methods

Which job evaluation method is best for a particular organization? The research on this issue is mixed, and conclusions are contingent on the criteria used. Some of those criteria are reviewed here, along with some general conclusions.

## Simplicity and Cost

Job ranking is the simplest of the plans, with job classification, factor comparison, and point plans following in advanced order of complexity.[54] This same continuum reflects relative cost from inexpensive to expensive. Smaller organizations, which frequently have fewer different jobs to deal with and greater limitation of funds, may, therefore, find job ranking superior to the point method.

## Acceptability

Plan acceptability is not as easily determined. Employers must be able to understand the plan and be able to communicate it to those who work under its rules. Thus, plan clarity is critical. There is a lack of evidence regarding which plans are superior from an acceptability standpoint. Experience suggests that the care with which plans are implemented may have as much to do with plan success as the type of plan chosen.[55]

## Plan Defensibility

Another criterion for selection would certainly be the "defensibility" of the method. With employee groups challenging wage equality and questioning comparable worth, organizations may now have to defend their job evaluation plan not only to their employees but also to the Equal Employment Opportunity Commission (EEOC) and the federal judiciary. In this light, the more rational and systematic the plan is, the more likely it will withstand legal scrutiny. Because the point method is the most highly explicit approach, this is also probably the most readily defensible. For example, point pay systems are commonly used in comparable worth pay plans in the public sector. One study examined how point systems have treated state government jobs, which are held disproportionately by women, minorities, and union members. The findings indicated that female jobs gain from comparable worth pay proposals; however, unionized and minority workers tend to lose both proposed and actual pay. In addition, the dispersion of points and pay narrowed for jobs covered by collective bargaining agreements.[56] It is important to recognize that the Equal Pay Act has articulated the compensable factors of "skill," "effort," "responsibility," and "working conditions" as criteria for wage differences. Therefore, any plan that uses these factors should, in theory, be defensible.

## Plan Reliability and Validity

Conventional wisdom has held that the job evaluation method does not matter and that different methods produce the same results. This conclusion is based on several studies using correlational analysis.[57] Examination of several point method plans and factor comparison plans revealed that they produced highly similar results in terms of job hierarchy. These findings have been replicated many times[58] with basically similar findings. Even more recently, one study analyzed the interchangeability of 16 job evaluation methods for supplying information on a single job series and obtained average intercorrelations of 0.90 between plans.[59] Interestingly, these correlational results were found despite the fact that all 4 generic methods of job evaluation discussed above were in the study and the plans used widely diverse compensable factors. From this viewpoint, plans are substitutable for each other.

However, correlational analysis alone is an inadequate test of whether job evaluation plans are equivalent. One important study looked at the degree to which six different plans resulted in classification agreement.[60] That is, what percentage of the time do different plans result in jobs being assigned to the same pay grade? When comparing plans with each other, Madigan and Hoover's study (1981) found agreement among grade assignments as often as 73 percent of the time in the case of 2 plans but only 23 percent of the time between 2 other plans. Based on this analysis, all job evaluation plans are clearly not the same, because different plans assign jobs to different grades. Because real dollars result from grade assignments, there are going to be real dollar differences in pay for jobs as a function of whether the plan puts the job in a higher or lower grade. These discrepancies cast doubt as to the equivalency of plans for achieving internal equity. Furthermore, different plans can have substantially different impacts on the total wage bill.[61] In short, from a compensation decision-making standpoint, all job evaluation plans are not equivalent to each other, and they should not be treated as such for compensation purposes. Many of these issues assume a relatively sophisticated knowledge of job evaluation; we encourage you to reread this section after reading the balance of the next two chapters.

## Summary

The first part of the chapter presents the evolution of job evaluation and addresses the criteria for determining both the compensable factors and the composition of the evaluation committee.

The remainder of this chapter examines the different methods of job evaluation (that is, ranking, job classification, factor comparison, and point). It concludes with a brief presentation of other job evaluation methods and the end-product of job evaluation and discusses in general the relative goodness of all the methods.

## Discussion Questions

1.  Identify and discuss the steps in conducting the ranking, job classification, factor comparison, and point methods of job evaluation.

2.  Why is it so important to have employees or their representatives involved in the job evaluation process?

3.  Discuss the advantages and disadvantages of the ranking, job classification, factor comparison, and point method of job evaluation.

4. Distinguish between job assessment and people assessment. Why is it so important?

5. Develop three operational measures of the following compensable factors: (a) working conditions, (b) skill level, and (c) responsibility.

6. Why is the factor comparison method also called the job pricing method?

7. A job evaluation plan has a maximum of 750 points. Factor A is to be weighted 20 percent and will have 6 degrees. Assign the point values to each degree.

8. What are the criteria for identifying compensable factors, and who should select and define the factors?

9. What factors must be considered in determining which method of job evaluation is best for an organization?

### EXERCISES

1. Using one of the techniques identified under the Ranking Method of Job Evaluation section, establish the relative worth of the following hospital jobs and briefly present your rationale for the rankings you establish.

*Floor Finisher:* Operates 19-in. floor scrubbing machine. Uses various chemicals to remove old finishes from floors and to clean carpets. Uses mops and buckets to clean up residue from floor stripping and to apply new finishes. Must have ability to examine old finishes, identify their type, and mix chemical solutions to desired strength to remove old finishes without ruining floor surfaces. Must be able to identify various types of terrazzo and tile flooring composition and use appropriate cleaning agents. Must know several types of polymeric floor finishes and appropriate application to floor surfaces.

*Checkout Aide:* Cleans patient's room after the patient checks out of the hospital. Must know procedures for properly cleaning patient room. Must know procedures for stripping off old linen, cleaning bed frame, and remaking patient bed. Must coordinate cleaning with check-in desk so that rooms are ready for next scheduled patient. Must be able to use routine germicidal products to ensure safe patient environment.

*Housekeeping Aide:* Must know procedures and germicidal products for cleaning patient rooms. Works on a routine schedule established by department supervisor.

*Projects Aide:* Engages in nonroutine labor tasks within hospital. Must be capable of working under general supervisor. Typical projects are moving furniture, cleaning up nonrecurring messes (for example, water puddle caused by broken water pipe), and moving equipment.

*Flatiron Attendant:* Works at finishing end of flatiron in hospital laundry. As pressed sheets and other flat linen emerge from flatiron, folds linens and places them on laundry cart. Pushes full carts to linen wareroom.

*Washer/Extractor Operator:* Operates commercial washers of up to 3,000-lb. capacity and extractors of up to 1,000-lb. capacity. Must know how to load and unload washer and extractor. Centrifugal force extractor requires judgment in loading so that loads are not out of balance, thereby causing damage to equipment or hazards to employees. Must know appropriate washing formulas to ensure that linens are clean. Must know special procedures for assuring that difficult-to-clean stains are handled to salvage the linens. Oversees work of assistant washer/extractor operator.

2. From the job descriptions below, extract the basic abilities required and use the job classification method to evaluate the jobs. The basic abilities system to be used as the basis for the job classification follows the job descriptions.

## Job Descriptions

*Mail Clerk:* Sorts mail and runs postage meter. Takes mail to post office. Picks up supplies from supply houses. Picks up and delivers mail within the office. Takes photostats to photographer. Drives mail truck. Reports to mailroom supervisor.

*IBM Clerk:* Operates IBM machines to perform tabulating, sorting, bookkeeping, and reproducing functions. Wires control panels from diagrammed instructions. Performs miscellaneous clerical duties. Reports to data processing supervisor.

*Keypunch Operator:* Operates keypunch to record written and typed information on IBM cards. Verifies work of other keypunch operators. Reports to data processing supervisor.

*File Clerk:* Sorts, arranges, and files documents and correspondence. Finds and pulls needed information and documents from files. Picks up and delivers filing from and to other departments. Reports to department secretary.

*Clerk Typist:* Types, files, and performs miscellaneous clerical duties. Reports to department secretary.

*Advertising Manager:* Meets salespersons and advertising solicitors. Escorts visitors through office. Composes, edits, and prepares layout for copy. Assists in preparing newspaper, radio, and magazine advertising. Acts as chairman of annual supervisors' meeting. Prepares weekly bulletin for supervisors. Answers correspondence. Composes letters and ads for agents. Supervises marketing department in the absence of department head. Formulates advertising policy. Meets with advertising agency representatives. Attends policy-making meetings. Reports to marketing department head.

*Assistant Purchasing Agent:* Supervises supply and service department. Keeps inventory of supplies. Processes orders from departments. Orders office supplies. Provides for service calls from suppliers of office equipment. Supervises mailroom. Reports to purchasing agent.

*Secretary:* Takes and transcribes dictation on confidential matters. Sets up and maintains necessary files and records. Relieves superior of minor administrative details such as reports and requisitions. Makes appointments. Meets and directs callers. Answers routine correspondence. Reports to department manager/head.

## Grading Rules Used in the Basic Abilities System

*Rule 1:* Classifications that require a basic skill or knowledge that can be acquired in only 3 to 6 months shall originally be graded to salary grade III, whereas classifications that require a basic skill or knowledge that takes 1 year or more to acquire shall originally be graded to salary grade V.

*Exercise 2* (*continued*)

Rule 2:   Classifications that do not require the ability to exercise independent judgment shall be moved up one salary grade if in addition to basic skills or knowledge they require one of the following:

a.  Knowledge of department or company procedures

b.  Ability to work under unpleasant conditions

c.  Ability to act as a group leader, directing two to four employees

d.  Ability to get along with people and meet people

Rule 3:   Classifications that do not require the ability to exercise independent judgment shall be moved up two salary grades if in addition to basic skills and knowledge they require one of the following:

a.  Knowledge of company procedures and products

b.  Ability to work under hazardous conditions

c.  Ability to organize and direct the work of four or more employees

Rule 4:   Classifications that because of some combination of grading rules 1, 2, and 3 are in salary grade V shall be moved up two salary grades to grade VII whenever the requirement to exercise independent judgment is added. No job classification shall be graded to VII or above unless it requires the ability to exercise independent judgment and no classifications in the first six salary grades can possess this requirement.

Rule 5:   Classifications that are in salary grade VII, because of rule 4, shall be moved up one salary grade if in addition to basic skills or knowledge and independent judgment they require one of the following:

a.  Knowledge of company procedures and products

b.  Ability to work under hazardous conditions

c.  Ability to plan, organize, and direct the work of others

d.  Ability to create or design company procedures or products

Rule 6:   Supervisory classifications must be graded at least one salary grade above most of the classifications supervised. For purposes of this rule, the lead worker who is ordinarily the senior member of a group of three to five workers is not considered a supervisor. With this elimination, the three supervisory classifications are

a.  Group leaders, who direct the work of from two to four employees engaged in the same type of work as their own

b.  Group supervisors, who organize and direct the work of from four to eleven employees engaged in the same general type of work

c.  Supervisors, department heads, and assistant department heads, who plan the work of other employees as well as organize and direct it. All employees in this group must exercise independent judgment.

**Exercise 2** (*continued*)

As a result of the operation rules 2 through 5, group leaders will commonly be graded one grade above the employees supervised, and higher supervisors classed two or more grades above the employees supervised. Rule 6 has an independent effect only in those cases in which the condition that it states is not already met as a result of rules 2 through 5.

---

SOURCE: Ralph W. Ellis, *The Basic Abilities System of Job Evaluation* (Madison, WI: University of Wisconsin, Madison School of Business, 1951).

3. Using the grading rules from problem 2, write grade descriptions that reflect the compensable factors. *Hint:* You might want to draw a decision tree to reflect all the branches in the decision process for moving a job to a particular grade.

4. A set of job descriptions and job specifications follows the exercises, along with the known fair wage rate for the key jobs in this group.

   1. Using the factor comparison method, evaluate the key jobs and construct a master schedule. Evaluate the remaining jobs and assign a final pay rate to them.

   2. Develop a job evaluation plan using the point method. After developing the job evaluation manual, evaluate all the jobs using the manual and write up a final report.

   The report is to contain:

   - Factors selected for compensation

   - Rationale for these factors

   - Factor definitions

   - Degrees within each defined factor

   - Total points allocated to the plan

   - Weights assigned to the factors and the reason the weights were assigned as they were

   - Points distributed to the factors and the factor points distributed to the degrees within each factor

   - The final point value assigned to each job

---

### Job Specifications

---

1. *Universal Teller:* Requires occasional direction and checking of work. Does not require frequent exercise of independent judgment. Demands substantial public contact, but infrequent intrabank contact. Offers few physical demands and few unpleasant working conditions. Requires a high degree of concentration. Requires 2 to 3 months of on-the-job training. Requires use of general banking equipment, pneumatic units, and teller machines; calls for typing, finger dexterity, and human relations skills.

2. *Deposit Services Representative:* Requires occasional independent judgment and some direction and checking of work. Demands substantial public contact but

*Exercise 4* (*continued*)

infrequent intrabank contact. Requires a high degree of concentration; however, has few physical demands and few unpleasant working conditions. Requires about 2 to 3 months of on-the-job training. Involves use of general banking equipment, and calls for typing and human relations skills.

3. *File Clerk:* Requires little independent judgment and infrequent direction and checking of work. Demands little public or intrabank contact. Calls for a high degree of concentration, but has light physical demands with little or no unpleasant working conditions. Requires 1 week of on-the-job training. Requires use of general banking equipment, and demands finger dexterity skills.

4. *Coin Processor:* Necessitates little exercise of independent judgment. Requires infrequent direction; however, work is frequently checked. Demands little public or intrabank contact. Requires a moderate degree of concentration with moderate physical demands and few unpleasant working conditions (some machinery noise). Requires 1 month of on-the-job training to perform the job at an acceptable level. Calls for operation of general banking equipment, coin wrapper, and postage machines.

5. *Document Sorter:* Requires occasional direction, but work is infrequently checked. Calls for infrequent exercise of independent judgment. Demands little public or intrabank contact. Requires a high degree of concentration, with light physical demands (occasional heavy lifting) and moderate amount of unpleasant working conditions (machine noise). Calls for 1 to 3 months of on-the-job training to perform the job at an acceptable level. Requires the necessary finger dexterity skills to operate the document sorter, proof machine, and general banking equipment.

6. *Statement Bookkeeper:* Requires occasional direction and checking of work; entails infrequent independent judgment and little public or intrabank contact. Demands moderate degree of concentration with little physical demand or unpleasant working conditions. Requires training period of 1 to 3 months. Calls for typing skills and use of general banking equipment and teller machines.

7. *Secretary (Trust):* Requires infrequent exercise of independent judgment, and requires occasional direction and checking of work. Demands some public and intrabank contact. Requires a moderate degree of concentration. Offers few physical demands and few or no unpleasant working conditions. Requires 2 to 3 months of on-the-job training. Involves the use of general banking equipment and transcribing equipment. Calls for general secretarial skills, including shorthand.

8. *Switchboard Operator:* Requires little independent judgment on the part of the employee. Calls for little direction and infrequent checking of work. Demands substantial public contact but infrequent intrabank contact. Demands little or no extraordinary concentration. Makes few physical demands with little or no unpleasant working conditions. Requires less than 1 month of training. Calls for use of general banking equipment and the PBX. Requires telephone communication skills.

9. *Supervisor, Universal Tellers:* Requires occasional independent judgment and needs occasional direction and checking of work. Demands frequent public contact but little intrabank contact beyond the tellers. Requires high degree of concentration, but makes few physical demands and offers few or no unpleasant

**Exercise 4** (*continued*)

working conditions. Requires about 2 to 3 months of training. Involves working with general banking equipment, pneumatic units, and teller machines. Demands typing, finger dexterity, and human relations skills.

10. *Staff Accountant:* Requires occasional independent judgment and needs occasional direction and checking of work. Demands little public or intrabank contact. Demands a high degree of concentration, but has few physical demands and little or no unpleasant working conditions. Requires about 3 to 6 months of training. Calls for use of general banking equipment and requires typing skills.

---

## Job Descriptions

---

Position title:  Universal Teller                    Market Rate:  $5.90
Division:  Deposit Services
Department:  Main Office, Drive-In, Branch
Title of immediate supervisor:  Branch Manager, Branch Supervisor
Date Issued:  9–1–92

1.  Provide banking services to all customers in a friendly, efficient, and professional manner
2.  Verify and control the payment and receipt of cash assigned to you
3.  Balance all cash assigned to you and prepare a balance sheet
4.  Accept and verify demand deposit, savings, and time deposit transactions
5.  Accept and verify installment, charge card, ready reserve, and real estate loan transactions
6.  Process night depository and bank by mail transactions
7.  Process armored car transactions
8.  Process Series E bonds, travelers' checks, and bank money order transactions
9.  Accept and issue receipts for collection items
10.  Process loose coin and verify coin machine totals
11.  Prepare cash item report
12.  Accept and verify miscellaneous payments such as federal taxes and utilities
13.  Prepare volume and activity reports
14.  Assist other employees within the department whenever possible
15.  Perform other duties that are approved or assigned by your superiors

Position title:  Deposit Services Representative
Division:  Deposit Services
Department:  Main Office, Drive-In
Title of immediate supervisor:  Deposit Services Supervisor (Main Office), Drive-In Manager
Date issued:  9–1–92

1.  Provide banking services to all customers in a friendly, efficient, and professional manner
2.  Open all types of demand deposit accounts
3.  Open all types of savings and time deposit accounts
4.  Issue travelers' checks and Series E bonds
5.  Open night depository accounts
6.  Provide general information pertaining to bank services available in other departments and banking locations

*Exercise 4* (continued)

7. Process and sell bank promotional and premium items
8. Process check and deposit ticket orders and reconcile billings
9. Distribute and explain Ready Reserve and charge card applications
10. Establish file for the proper follow-up on missing social security numbers, incomplete account resolutions, and unsigned signature cards
11. Process special agreement forms for such services as direct deposit, IRA accounts, and funeral trusts
12. Approve specific savings withdrawals, checks, cash paybacks, and cash advances
13. Process volume and activity reports
14. Assist other employees within the department whenever possible

Position title:  File Clerk                                    Market Rate: $5.34
Division:  Deposit Services
Department:  Deposit Accounting, Main Office
Title of immediate supervisor:  Deposit Accounting Supervisor
Date issued:  9–1–92

Minimum responsibilities:
1. Provide banking services to all customers in a friendly, efficient, and professional manner
2. File checks and deposit tickets
3. Review items on specified accounts for proper signatures, endorsements, dates, etc.
4. File bank money orders and payroll and interest checks
5. File signature cards on closed accounts
6. Assign numbers to new accounts
7. Assist other employees within the department whenever possible
8. Perform other duties that are approved or assigned by your supervisor

Additional responsibilities that may be assigned:
1. File daily computer reports
2. File corporate resolutions
3. Balance and maintain files for payroll account monthly
4. Maintain money order audit sheets
5. File money orders daily and balance weekly
6. Relieve other desks as needed

Position title:  Coin Processor
Division:  Deposit Services
Department:  Main Office—Customer Services, Main Office
Title of immediate supervisor:  Customer Services Supervisor
Date issued:  9–1–92

1. Provide banking services to all customers in a friendly, efficient, and professional manner
2. Operate the coin wrapping machine
3. Balance all processed coin
4. Deliver documents to and from other banks
5. Deliver daily transactions to the proof department from all bank locations
6. Assist in opening the main office cash vault
7. Deliver coins to all bank locations
8. Assist as a teller

*Exercise 4* (*continued*)

9. Check the security cameras and record the frame numbers daily
10. Deliver specified commercial account statements
11. Assist the Internal Services Department whenever possible
12. Assist other employees within the department whenever possible
13. Perform other duties that are approved or assigned by your superiors

Position title:  Document Sorter Operator
Division:  Deposit Services
Department:  Proof and Adjustments, Main Office
Title of immediate supervisor:  Proof and Adjustments Supervisor
Date issued:  9–1–92

1. Provide banking services to all customers in a friendly, efficient, and professional manner
2. Microfilm all transactions and cash letter tapes
3. Operate document sorters and proof machines
4. Prepare and deliver cash letters
5. Prepare proof balance worksheets and appropriate entries
6. Prepare recap totals and deliver all items for application updates
7. Assist other employees within the department whenever possible
8. Perform other duties that are approved or assigned by your superiors

Position title:  Statement Bookkeeper
Division:  Deposit Services
Department:  Deposit Accounting, Main Office
Title of immediate supervisor:  Deposit Accounting Supervisor
Date issued:  9–1–92

1. Provide banking services to all customers in a friendly, efficient, and professional manner
2. Microfilm all processed items
3. Review items on specific accounts for proper signatures, endorsements, dates, etc.
4. Organize and prepare demand deposit account statements
5. Prepare all computer reports for distribution
6. Balance item counts for demand deposit accounts with list postings
7. Review all processed microfilm
8. Assign numbers to new accounts
9. Assist other employees within the department whenever possible
10. Perform other duties that are approved or assigned by your superiors

Position title:  Secretary—Trust Department
Division:  Trust
Department:  Trust, Main Office
Title of immediate supervisor:  Vice President and Senior Trust Officer
Date issued:  9–1–92

1. Provide trust services to all customers in a friendly, efficient, and professional manner
2. Perform general secretarial duties such as typing, taking shorthand, acting as receptionist, and filing

*Exercise 4 (continued)*

3. Prepare all checks and deposits for trust customers
4. Prepare and verify computer entries
5. Maintain all paying agency accounts
6. Prepare month-end computer filing and mail customer statements
7. Maintain all authentication accounts
8. Post and balance debenture and corporate accounts
9. Maintain all files
10. Assist other employees within the department whenever possible
11. Perform other duties that are approved or assigned by your superiors

Position title: Switchboard Operator            Market Rate: $5.22
Division: Financial Services
Department: Internal Services, Main Office
Title of immediate supervisor: Internal Services Officer
Date issued: 9–1–92

1. Provide banking services to all customers in a friendly, efficient, and professional manner
2. Operate the switchboard
3. Open incoming mail and disperse to the proper departments
4. Maintain the copy machine and record daily usage
5. Coordinate the usage of the bank-owned vehicles
6. Receive information for the daily bulletin
7. Receive and deposit all rental income
8. Maintain petty cash and prepaid postage funds
9. Receive and deposit milk machine money
10. Verify and record Internal Services time cards and attendance records
11. Provide specific copy machine reproductions for all bank locations
12. Assist other employees within the department whenever possible.
13. Perform other duties that are approved or assigned by your superiors.

Position title: Supervisor, Universal Tellers—Main Office  Market Rate: $7.38
Division: Deposit Services
Department: Universal Tellers—Main Office
Title of immediate supervisor: Vice President and Cashier
Date issued: 9–1–92

1. Supervise and coordinate all daily functions of the tellers and safe deposit receptionists
2. Organize and prepare work and vacation schedules and approve requests for days off
3. Review, discuss, and explain all operational policies, procedures, and related changes to all department personnel through scheduled meetings
4. Review, approve, and maintain employee time cards and attendance records
5. Review, approve, and complete reports for all teller variations within the department
6. Prepare all salary increases, requests for additional staff, terminations, promotions, demotions, transfers, and employee grievances
7. Assist in planning and developing training and cross-training programs for all employees in the department
8. Provide relief for peak periods, lunch breaks, vacations, and absentees

**Exercise 4** *(continued)*

9. Manage the collection function including land contracts, sight drafts, bonds, coupons, checks, and any other transactions requiring special handling
10. Process all foreign currency, coin, and travelers' checks transactions
11. Daily balance of the collection desk for travelers' checks, issued and redeemed U.S. Series E bonds, credit card cash advances, and Treasury, tax, and loan deposits
12. Approve checks, savings withdrawals, cash back on deposits, cash advances, cashed certificates, and closed accounts
13. Prepare reports for all phases of the collection functions
14. Assist other employees within the department whenever possible
15. Perform other duties that are approved or assigned by your superiors

Position title:  Staff Accountant I—General Accounting
Division:  Financial Services
Department:  General Accounting
Title of immediate supervisor:  Senior Staff Accountant
Date issued:  9–1–92

1. Provide banking services to all customers in a friendly, efficient, and professional manner
2. Prepare reconciliation of various accounts
3. Verify and obtain approvals on all invoices and review all accounts payable
4. Verify purchasing orders and maintain expense control ledgers
5. Prepare annual closing entries for all income and expense accounts
6. Prepare requisitions for major recurring expenditures
7. Prepare Branch and Trust Profitability reports
8. Perform a physical inventory of all fixed assets
9. Verify and process changes and generate current listing of fixed assets
10. Prepare inventory listings and returns for personal property taxes
11. Assist bank examiners and auditors
12. Assist other employees within the department whenever possible
13. Perform other duties that are approved or assigned by your superiors

---

## Wage Data (Product Market)

---

Hourly rates are converted to monthly rates using 173 hours in an average work month. Rate ranges are calculated using 30 percent.

1. Universal Teller

Averages calculated using 40 employees:

| Number of Employees | Hourly Rate | Monthly Rate |
|:---:|:---:|:---:|
| 4 | $5.60 | $ 968.80 |
| 4 | 5.67 | 980.91 |
| 10 | 5.81 | 1,005.13 |
| 15 | 5.95 | 1,029.35 |
| 4 | 6.16 | 1,065.68 |
| 3 | 6.37 | 1,102.01 |

*Exercise 4* (*continued*)

Average hourly rate: $5.90
Average monthly rate: $1,021.48 ($5.90 × 173)
Hiring rate: $5.60/hour, $968.80/month
Rate range: $5.60/hour – $7.28/hour ($5.60 × 1.30 = $7.28)
$968.80/month – $1,259.44/month

2. File Clerk

Averages calculated using 39 employees:

| Number of Employees | Hourly Rate | Monthly Rate |
|:---:|:---:|:---:|
| 10 | $5.11 | $884.03 |
| 9 | 5.25 | 908.25 |
| 4 | 5.32 | 920.36 |
| 12 | 5.53 | 956.69 |
| 4 | 5.60 | 968.80 |

Average hourly rate: $5.34
Average monthly rate: $923.82 ($5.34 × 173)
Hiring rate: $5.11/hour, $884.03/month
Rate range: $5.11/hour – $6.64 hour ($5.11 × 1.30 = $6.64)
$884.03/month – $1,148.72/month

3. Switchboard Operator

Averages calculated using 33 employees:

| Number of Employees | Hourly Rate | Monthly Rate |
|:---:|:---:|:---:|
| 12 | $5.11 | $884.03 |
| 8 | 5.18 | 896.14 |
| 4 | 5.25 | 908.25 |
| 4 | 5.34 | 923.82 |
| 5 | 5.41 | 935.93 |

Average hourly rate: $5.22
Average monthly rate: $903.06 ($5.22 × 173)
Hiring rate: $5.11/hour, $884.03/month
Rate range: $5.11/hour – $6.64/hour ($5.11 × 1.30 = $6.64)
$884.03/month – $1,148.72/month

4. Supervisor, Universal Tellers

Averages calculated using 10 employees:

| Number of Employees | Hourly Rate | Monthly Rate |
|:---:|:---:|:---:|
| 3 | $7.21 | $1,247.33 |
| 2 | 7.32 | 1,266.36 |
| 1 | 7.39 | 1,278.47 |
| 2 | 7.49 | 1,295.77 |
| 1 | 7.56 | 1,307.88 |
| 1 | 7.63 | 1,319.99 |

**Exercise 4** *(continued)*

Average hourly rate: $7.38
Average monthly rate: $1,276.74
Hiring rate: $7.21/hour, $1,247.33/month
Rate range: $7.21/hour – $9.37/hour ($7.21 × 1.30 = $9.37)
$1,247.33/month – $1,621.01/month

## References

[1] J. Zalusky, "Job Evaluation: An Uneven World," *American Federationist* 88 (April 1981), 11–20.

[2] For a discussion of the distinction between rights arbitration and interest arbitration, see J. A. Fossum, *Labor Relations Development, Structure, Process*, rev. ed. (Dallas: Business Publications, 1989).

[3] H. D. Janes, "Union Views on Job Evaluation: 1971–1978," *Personnel Journal* 58 (February 1979), 80–85.

[4] T. A. Mahoney, *Compensation and Reward Perspectives* (Homewood, IL: Irwin, 1979).

[5] S. Rynes, B. Rosen, and T. Mahoney, *Comparable Worth: Summary Report of Survey* (paper presented to the American Compensation Association, 1983).

[6] J. S. Adams, "Inequity in Social Exchange," in *Advances in Experimental Social Psychology*, vol. 2, ed. L. Berkowitz (New York: Academic Press, 1965), 267–299.

[7] J. Greenberg, "Organizational Justice: Yesterday, Today, and Tomorrow," *Journal of Management* 16 (1990), 399–432.

[8] J. A. Lee and J. L. Mendoza, "Comparison of Techniques Which Test for Job Differences," *Personnel Psychology* 34 (Winter 1981), 731–758.

[9] The analogy to selection settings is inevitable. We know of no cases challenging the validity (or job-relatedness) of compensable factors in a compensation setting. However, for a review of the problem in selection settings, see *Griggs v. Duke Power Co.* (401 U.S. 424, 3 FEP 175, 1971) for a case dealing with educational requirements, and *Weeks v. Southern Bell Telephone & Telegraph Co.* (408 F.2d, 1 FEP 656, 5th Cir. 1969) for a case dealing with weightlifting requirements.

[10] J. T. Brinks, "The Comparable Worth Issue: A Salary Administration Bombshell," *Personnel Administrator* 26 (November 1981), 37–40.

[11] K. E. Foster, "Measuring Overlooked Factors in Relative Job and Pay," *Compensation Review* 15 (1983), 44–55.

[12] Rynes et al., *Comparable Worth*.

[13] *Briggs v. City of Madison*, 436 F. Supp. 435, W.D. of Wis., 1982.

[14] B. L. Schlei and P. Grossman, *Employment Discrimination Law*, 2d ed. (Washington, D.C.: Bureau of National Affairs, 1983).

[15] Rynes et al., *Comparable Worth*.

[16] J. D. Bexson, "A System for Job Ranking," *Personnel Management and Methods* 30 (March 1964), 28–29, 38.

[17] J. S. McCleod, "Dual Job Evaluation Systems: EEO Hazard," *EEO Today* 6 (1979), 45–48.

[18] J. T. Dunlop, "The Task of Contemporary Wage Theory," in *New Concepts in Wage Determination*, eds. G. W. Taylor and F. C. Pierson (New York: McGraw-Hill, 1957), 127–139.

[19] Rynes et al., *Comparable Worth*.

[20] R. D. Arvey, S. E. Maxwell, R. L. Gutenberg, and C. Camp, "Detecting Job Differences: A Monte Carlo Study," *Personnel Psychology* 34 (Winter 1981), 709–730.

[21] The general formula for determining how many comparisons must be made is $[N(N-1)]/2$, where $N$ is equal to the number of jobs to be compared or ranked.

[22] R. B. Pursell, "R&D Job Evaluation and Compensation," *Compensation Review* 4 (2nd quarter 1972), 21–31.

[23] The reader should not be overly concerned with the concept of a universal factor. The term is used because the factors used in factor comparison plans are commonly accepted factors. That is, they have widespread acceptability among those who design

and implement job evaluation plans. Table 8.4 presents some of the more common universal factor job evaluation plans. Some of the factors are so universally accepted that they have even been written into the Equal Pay Act of 1963.

[24]In recent years, some firms have attempted to separate the pricing of key jobs from the design of the factor comparison system by substituting arbitrary units in the place of dollars. This has been done partly to eliminate problems in keeping master schedules up to date during inflationary times. For ease of discussion, however, the factor comparison method is discussed as it was originally developed.

[25]Discussion of the universal factors listed in Table 8.4 can be found in the following sources: A. W. Bass, Jr., "Applying the Point Method of Job Evaluation," *Iron Age* (October 8, 1936), 58–60; E. J. Benge, *Job Evaluation and Merit Rating* (New York: National Foreman's Institute, 1946); American Association of Industrial Management, *Job Rating Manual (Shop)*, (Melrose Park, PA: AAIM, 1969); U.S. Office of Personnel Management, *Factor Evaluation System* (Washington, DC: Government Printing Office, 1977); E. N. Hay and D. Purves, "The Profile Method of High-Level Job Evaluation," *Personnel* 28 (September 1951), 162–170; *Equal Pay Act of 1963*, 23 U.S.C. Sec. 206(d) (1).

[26]Benge, *Job Evaluation and Merit Rating.*

[27]D. J. Chesler, "Reliability and Comparability of Different Job Evaluation Systems," *Journal of Applied Psychology* 32 (October 1948), 465–475.

[28]The reader should not forget where this wage rate came from. The job of pattern-maker is a key job. The organization is going to pay key jobs wages that are *a priori* determined. These wage rates were established through some process that usually involves a wage survey of other organizations. The factor comparison method assumes that fair wage rates for key jobs have already been determined.

[29]For two different computational methods, see W. D. Turner, "The Percent Method of Job Evaluation," *Personnel* 25 (May 1948), 476–492 and E. N. Hay, "Creating Factor Comparison Key Scales by the Percent Method," *Journal of Applied Psychology* 32 (October 1948), 456–464.

[30]The practice of using more than one job evaluation plan and anchoring each plan to separate labor markets is part and parcel of the comparable worth pay discrimination debate. For implications of these practices, see D. J. Thomsen, "Eliminating Pay Discrimination Caused by Job Evaluation," *Personnel* 55 (September/October 1978), 11–22.

[31]C. H. Lawsche, Jr., "Studies in Job Evaluation 2. The Adequacy of Abbreviated Point Ratings for Hourly Paid Jobs in Three Industrial Plants," *Journal of Applied Psychology* 29 (June 1945), 177–184. C. H. Lawsche, Jr., and R. F. Wilson, "Studies in Job Evaluation 6. The Reliability of Two Point Rating Systems," *Journal of Applied Psychology* 31 (August 1947), 355–365. C. H. Lawsche, Jr., E. E. Dudek, and R. F. Wilson, "Studies in Job Evaluation 7. A Factor Analysis of Two Point Rating Methods of Job Evaluation," *Journal of Applied Psychology* 32 (April 1948), 118–129.

[32]D. P. Schwab, "Job Evaluation and Pay Setting: Concepts and Practices," in *Comparable Worth Issues and Answers*, ed. E. R. Livernash (Washington, DC: EEAC, 1980), 49–77.

[33]See, for example, J. A. Lee and J. L. Mendoza, "Comparison of Job Evaluation Techniques Which Test for Job Differences," *Personnel Psychology* 34 (Winter 1981), 731–758.

[34]In the simplest case, multiple regression could be used to weight the factors. This procedure calls for the investigator to know acceptable pay rates for key jobs and then to regress each job's relative standing on each factor onto the pay rates for the key jobs. Through approximation (exploring alternate weighting schemes), the weighting scheme that best predicts the desired pay rates for key jobs could be discovered and used. For an examination of the weighting of factors, see Luis R. Gomez-Mejia, R. Page, and W. Tornow, "Development and Implementation of a Computerized Job Evaluation System," *Personnel Administrator* 24 (February 1979), 46–54.

[35]Rynes et al., *Comparable Worth.*

[36]D. Belcher, *Compensation Administration* (Englewood Cliffs, NJ: Prentice-Hall, 1967).

[37] On this point and on the general observation that the relative ranking of jobs depends less on the weighting of factors than the variability of the distribution of factor scores, see D. P. Schwab, "Job Evaluation and Pay Setting: Concepts and Practices," in *Comparable Worth Issues and Alternatives*, ed. E. R. Livernash, (Washington, DC: Equal Employment Advisory Council, 1980), 51–77.

[38] If statistical weighting is performed, the weights for factors will by definition capture the market rates of key jobs and reflect the desired hierarchy. See Schwab, "Job Evaluation and Pay Setting."

[39] NIMA, *The National Position Evaluation Plan*. (Westchester, IL: MIMA The Management Association and the NMTA Network Unit II of IV, 1980).

[40] Hay Associates, *The Guide Chart Profile of Job Evaluation* (Philadelphia: Hay Associates, 1981).

[41] E. N. Hay and D. Purves, "A New Method of Job Evaluation," *Personnel* 61 (July 1984), 72–80.

[42] _____, *Dynamic Pay for a Changing World of Work* (Dallas, TX: Hay Group, May 1993).

[43] *Ibid.*

[44] E. Jaques, *Time-Span Handbook* (London: Heinemann Educational Books, 1964).

[45] A. W. Charles, "Installing Single-Factor Job Evaluation," *Compensation Review* 3 (1st quarter 1971), 9–17.

[46] T. T. Paterson and T. M. Husband, "Decision Making Responsibility: Yardstick for Job Evaluation," *Compensation Review* 2 (2nd quarter 1970), 21–31.

[47] A. Young, *The Decision Band Method* (New York: Arthur Young International, 1982).

[48] _____, "Salary Grades to Management Bonds," *Compensation and Benefits Update*, Special Edition (Piscattanay, NJ: AT&T, November, 1992), 1–6.

[49] E. J. McCormick, "Job and Task Analysis," in *Handbook of Industrial and Organizational Psychology*, ed. M. D. Dunnette (Chicago: Rand-McNally, 1976), 651–696.

[50] See, for example, W. Tornow and P. Pinto, "The Development of a Managerial Job Taxonomy: A System for Describing, Classifying, and Evaluating Executive Office Positions," *Journal of Applied Psychology* 61 (1976), 410–418.

[51] H. G. Heneman, III, D. P. Schwab, J. A. Fossum, and L. D. Dyer, *Personnel/Human Resource Management*, 3d ed. (Homewood, IL: Irwin, 1986).

[52] E. R. Livernash, "The Internal Wage Structure," in *New Concepts in Wage Determination*, eds. G. W. Taylor and F. C. Pierson (New York: McGraw-Hill, 1957), 143–172.

[53] R. C. Smyth and M. J. Murphy, *The Guide Line Method of Job Evaluation* (Rhinebeck, NY: Smyth and Associates, 1974).

[54] F. S. Hills, "Internal Pay Relationships," in *Compensation and Benefits*, ed. L. R. Gomez-Mejia (Washington, DC: Bureau of National Affairs, 1989), 29–69.

[55] *Ibid.*

[56] P. F. Orazen, J. P. Martila, and S. K. Weikum, "Comparable Worth and Factor Point Pay Plans," *Industrial Relations* 31 (Winter 1992), 195–215.

[57] D. J. Chesler, "Reliability and Comparability of Different Job Evaluation Systems," *Journal of Applied Psychology* 32 (1948), 465–475.

[58] A. B. A. Boshoff, "A Comparison of Three Methods for the Evaluation of Managerial Positions," *Psychologia Africana* 12 (1969), 212–221; D. L. Peters and E. McCormick, "Comparative Reliability of Numerically Anchored Versus Job Task Anchored Rating Scales," *Journal of Applied Psychology* 50 (1966), 92–96; D. D. Robinson, O. W. Wahlstrom, and R. Mecham, "Comparison of Job Evaluation Methods," *Journal of Applied Psychology* 59 (1974), 633–637; R. C. Rogers, "Analysis of Two Point Rating Job Evaluation Plans," *Journal of Applied Psychology* 30 (1974), 579–585.

[59] R. J. Snelgar, "The Comparability of Job Evaluation Methods in Supplying Approximately Similar Classifications in Rating One Job Series," *Personnel Psychology* 36 (1983), 371–380.

[60] R. M. Madigan and D. J. Hoover, "Effects of Alternate Job Evaluation Methods on Decisions Involving Pay Equity," *Academy of Management Journal* 29 (1981), 84–100.

[61] R. M. Madigan and F. S. Hills, "Job Evaluation and Pay Equity," *Public Personnel Management* 17 (1988), 323–330.

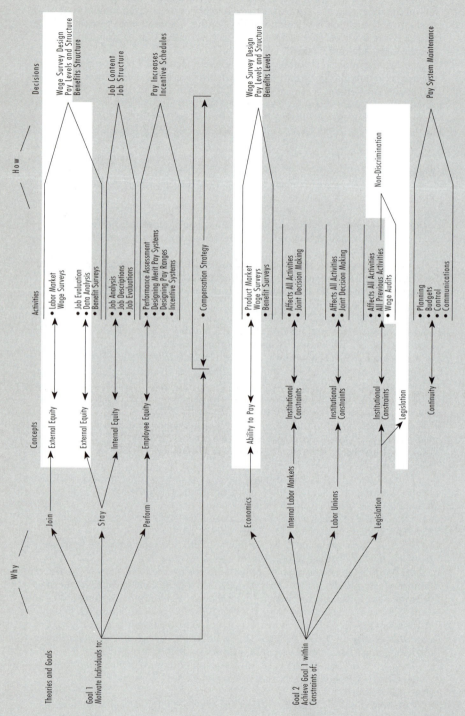

# IV

## *Pay Structure Decisions*

# 9

# Job Pricing: Surveying Labor and Product Markets

# Learning Objectives

In general, to learn about how organizations price jobs in the marketplace.

To learn that labor market surveys are conducted with external equity considerations in mind.

To learn that product market surveys are conducted with ability to pay constraint considerations in mind.

To learn how to design a survey for wages and benefits.

To learn how to decide which firms should be included in a product market survey.

To learn about third-party sources of labor and product market data.

To learn about the more commonly used methods of summarizing survey data.

# Introduction

As discussed in Chapter 8, the purpose of job evaluation is to determine the relative worth of jobs to the organization, resulting in a structure of jobs, from high to low, that is internally equitable. The job structure should be perceived as equitable by both employees and management within the company.

The next step in establishing a wage system is pricing the jobs that have been evaluated. Job pricing is the subject of this chapter. Job evaluation focuses primarily on the relative position of jobs with respect to each other; job pricing is a decision as to absolute wage rates in dollars for specific jobs in the job structure. When all jobs are priced, the wage structure that results should reflect the job structure.

## *Reasons Behind Wage and Benefits Surveys*

Job pricing is carried out to elicit desired behaviors from individuals: to motivate them to join the organization and to motivate them to stay. These behaviors must be achieved, however, within the organization's ability to pay. *Job pricing*, then, is the process of attempting to achieve external pay rate equity within the organization's ability to pay constraint.[1] To accomplish this, job pricing involves conducting wage and benefits surveys. These surveys are normally conducted in labor or product markets. The organization uses labor market data to achieve external equity with respect to the labor market[2] and uses product market data to price jobs within the economic constraints of the organization.[3]

## *Labor and Product Market Constraints*

Chapter 3 discussed equity theory as it related to compensation decision making. Organizations must have pay systems that are perceived as equitable if they are going to be able to accomplish the goal of attracting and retaining employees. Organizations usually conduct wage and benefit surveys to ensure that they are competitive in their wage and benefits payments to employees. In one sense, then, the wages paid in the labor market are indicators of what any single organization will have to pay to foster perceptions of equity. These rates operate as one constraint in compensation decision making.

Chapter 2 discussed marginal revenue productivity theory as it relates to compensation decision making. Organizations are constrained by their ability to pay. If an organization is going to survive in the long run, its costs (including labor costs) must not be so high that they put the employer at a competitive disadvantage in the product market.[4] Employers, especially labor-intensive employers whose product demand is elastic with respect to price, are likely to conduct wage and salary and benefits surveys among the firms with which they compete for consumers of their good or service. Ability to pay is an important constraint faced by the organization.

The distinct goals of labor and product market wage and benefit surveys are summarized in Exhibit 9.1.

Chapters 2 and 3 also considered what happens when these two surveys give conflicting results. That is, wages in the product market may be above or below wages in the labor market, and this fact constrains compensation decision making. The reader may wish to refer back to these earlier chapters to examine the employer's options under varying combinations of these constraints.

Labor market and product market surveys are management tools to accomplish different purposes. Understanding the nature of labor and product markets will aid in designing a wage and benefits survey.

## Labor Market Surveys

An organization conducts a labor market survey to assess its wage and benefits practices relative to its competitors. The objective is to determine whether its

| EXHIBIT 9.1 | SUMMARY OF GOALS FOR LABOR AND PRODUCT MARKET SURVEYS |
|---|---|

| Type of Survey | Goals |
|---|---|
| Labor market wage and benefit survey | To ensure equitable wages and benefits so that individuals are motivated to join and stay with the organization. |
| Product market wage and benefit survey | To ensure that wage and benefit costs do not exceed the firm's ability to compete in its industry. |

wage and benefit package is competitive enough in the labor market to allow it successfully to attract and retain labor. Firms that underpay raise the risk of lower morale and increased turnover.[5] Firms that overpay establish a pattern that is difficult to change, a pattern that ultimately may cost the organization its competitive edge in the marketplace and its profitability.

Why should other firms help an organization to gather this data? Participating organizations must perceive that the benefits for them are greater than the costs. The greatest benefit is usually a summary of the results of the survey. Thus, the participants recognize that they can achieve the same objective from the survey as the surveying organization. This is a significant benefit only if the results are reported back to the organizations in a form that is usable in decision making but does not reveal information regarding any specific organization. Also, the report must be timely to be beneficial. Receiving the summary report nine months later does not provide the information on a timely basis for decision making. The surveying organization can minimize the costs for participants: first, by designing the method of data collection to minimize the amount of time it takes to provide the information; second, by asking only for information that will be used; third, by designing the process so that the participating organization can schedule completion of the questionnaire or interview without disrupting business; fourth, by providing adequate information regarding the key jobs being surveyed so accurate matches can be made; and fifth, by ensuring the use of safeguards to protect the identity of the firm providing the information. Organizations should be contacted before requesting the specific survey information. At that time, the surveyor should request participation in the survey and identify within each firm a contact position from whom the data will be gathered. That first call is also the ideal time to spell out the benefits of participation and explain how costs will be kept to a minimum.

### Occupational Level and Labor Markets

In an examination of the relevant labor market, the occupational levels of the jobs are an important consideration.[6] Different occupational groups have different labor markets. As a general rule, the geographic area for the relevant labor market varies directly with the skill level of the occupation. For example, the relevant labor area for unskilled laborers may be a 20-mile radius; the relevant labor area for highly skilled employees, such as middle managers, may be regional or even national. The precise relevant labor area for any given occupational group is an empirical question subject to study. It can vary from organization to organization, and compensation decision makers should carefully determine the labor areas for occupational groups for their organizations. In general, it is worth asking if the organization's present human resource policies and programs (pay levels, recruiting efforts, training and development, and so on) allow the organization to attract an adequate quantity and quality of applicants. Then, what geographic areas do these employees come from?

The fact that labor markets have a geographic dimension and an occupational dimension suggests that it is inappropriate to think of the labor market survey as a single survey. The labor market survey is really a series of surveys.

In other words, because the geographic area of labor markets varies as a function of occupational level, the organizations to be surveyed will vary also. For example, the subset of organizations included in a survey of wage rates for operatives will be different from the subset of organizations in a survey of wages for managers.

## Geographic Scope of Labor Markets

It is important to survey organizations from the relevant geographic labor market. To determine the boundaries of the geographic labor market, the commuting distance of employees must be examined. For example, an employer of office and clerical employees may discover that 50 percent of those employees come from a 10-mile radius of the office complex, that 75 percent come from a 20-mile radius, and that fully 95 percent come from a 30-mile radius. In this case, the geographic scope of the relevant labor market for office and clerical employees would be 30 miles or less, as depicted in Exhibit 9.2.

**EXHIBIT 9.2**   CONCEPTUAL ANALYSIS OF RELEVANT LABOR AREA FOR OFFICE AND CLERICAL EMPLOYEES

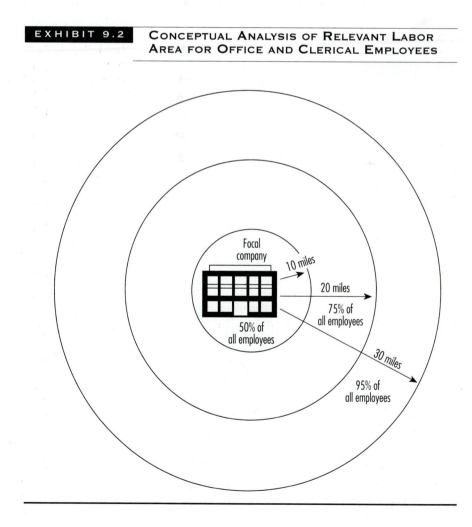

Actually, it is a misconception to think of an employer as located at the geometric center of a labor area because most employees may come from only one direction—from the north, southwest, or so on. Because of this phenomenon, some labor market analysts have suggested that employers use isobar analysis. Isobars (lines of equal distance) are like the contour lines on a map that show changes in elevation. Exhibit 9.3 is an example of isobar analysis.

To use *isobar analysis* for a labor market, the employer might draw a continuous line around a plant (or other operating site) to represent the area from which 20 percent of the employees come. A second line is drawn around the area from which 30 percent of the employees come, a third line for 40 percent, and so forth until a line is drawn to show the area from which 100 percent of all employees come. The areas within the concentric lines define the geographic labor area for a given group of employees. Isobar analysis shows more precisely where employees come from and in what concentrations. This type of analysis has also been supported as valid in a court of law when there was concern over possible discrimination in hiring of minorities.[7]

The specific steps to follow in doing the geographic labor market analysis are (1) analyze the address of all current employees and recent applicants,

---

**EXHIBIT 9.3**     **ISOBAR ANALYSIS OF RELEVANT LABOR AREA FOR OFFICE AND CLERICAL EMPLOYEES**

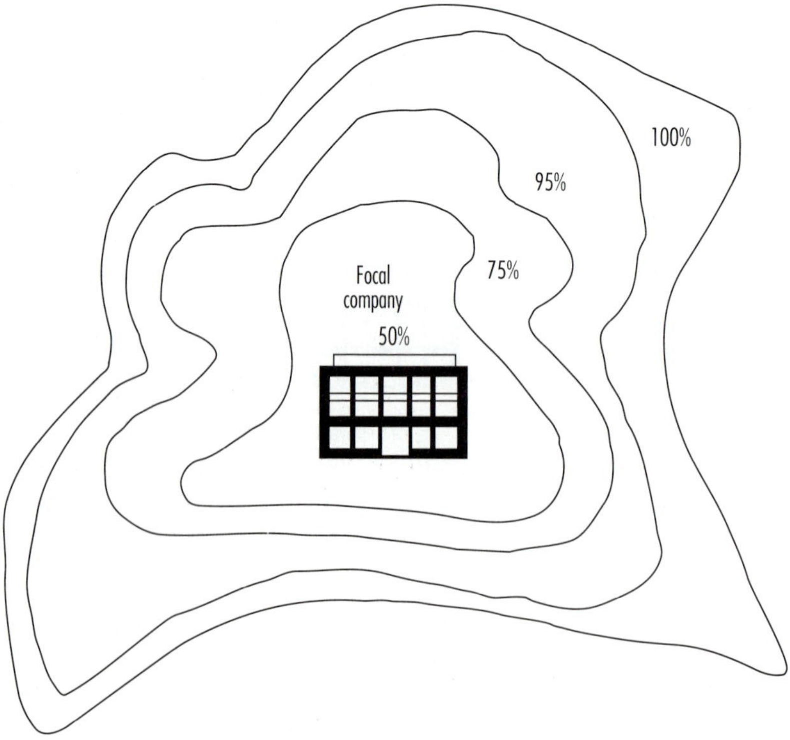

(2) analyze the traffic patterns to determine the commuting times and mileage from employees' (applicants') homes to the firm's location, and (3) take the home location of the employees (applicants) and determine the distance they would commute in the opposite direction of your firm to identify other potential labor market competitors.[8]

## Selecting the Organizations to Survey

The compensation decision maker must decide which organizations to include in the labor market survey. Probably the simplest approach uses a labor market analysis to identify all the organizations in each of the relevant labor markets. The number of employers in the relevant labor markets may be so large, however, that it is not practical to survey all of them.

In this case, the surveying organization may wish to survey a subset of these firms. A general rule of thumb is to survey a cross section of between 10 and 30 competitor employers.[9] There are two common methods of determining a subset of firms: the random sample and the stratified random sample.

Random sampling involves selecting a sample of organizations from a larger population. If the sample is to be a true *random sample*, then each organization should have an equally likely probability of being selected for the sample. If the sampling procedure does not ensure that each organization is equally likely to be chosen, then the sample is said to be biased.[10] Biases in sampling are important to the extent that they cause mistakes in inferring attributes of the larger population of organizations. For example, to make an inference about the average height of student athletes, it would be unwise to sample only those people observed playing basketball in an NCAA tournament.

In the context of wage and salary surveys, an organization wishing to make an inference about the average wage for a job normally should obtain the survey data from an unbiased sample. It is important that firms are chosen for the survey on a random basis. To do so, the organization could use procedures ranging from very simple to very complex. For example, suppose that there are 500 possible firms in the labor market. Perhaps the organization wishes to have 50 firms in the final sample (for a 10 percent sampling rate). The organization could write the names of all 500 firms on cards, and draw 50 cards out of a barrel. Alternately, the firm could assign each firm a number and then use a table of random numbers to identify the 50 firms.[11]

There may be times when an organization would want to intentionally bias the survey data. For example, if an employer considered it important to sample by size of firm or if an employer wished to place particular weight on firms with a particular technology, then it could introduce this known bias into the sampling using *stratified random sampling*.[12]

As an example, the organization might have identified 500 firms within the population to be surveyed. Half of those firms have fewer than 250 employees, 25 percent have 251 to 500 employees, and another 25 percent have more than 500 employees. If the surveying organization places heavy emphasis on being competitive with the firms that have 251 to 500 employees, then the survey sample could be weighted accordingly. The organization might want 50 percent of the responding firms to be from this group and 25 percent of the respondents from each of the other two groups. If the total sample is to be 50 organizations, the composition of that sample would be 12.5 firms with 1 to 250 employees, 25 firms with 251 to 500 employees, and 12.5 firms with more than 500 employees. (The fractions could constitute a twenty-sixth firm in the 251- to 500-employee-size group.) If the employer wanted this ratio of firms from all firms identified, it could then determine the sampling rate by firm size. The calculations for doing this are shown in Exhibit 9.4.

Conscious bias should be well grounded in some rationale. Conscious bias might be used to ensure that one type of company that is a small percentage of the total labor market gets extra weight to assess wages accurately in that industry, to place extra emphasis on one geographic area of the market, or to place more or less stress on companies that use certain types of equipment (such as electronic spreadsheets as opposed to accounting ledgers).

Another approach to selecting the organizations to survey involves determining the organization's position in the labor queue through such means as employee résumés (to determine prior place of employment) and through exit interviews (to learn about employment plans of employees who leave the organization). If the organization can determine its position, then surveying the organizations above and below it in the labor queue will allow the organization to price its jobs to remain at the same relative standing in the labor queue.

Frequently, organizations decide that conducting their own survey is not practical or necessary. These employers use wage and benefits data gathered by third parties (such as, government agencies, professional associations, or consultants) to establish a pay policy relative to the median. Although this approach is often followed, it has the disadvantage that the wage data often is

---

| EXHIBIT 9.4 | CALCULATIONS FOR DETERMINING THE SAMPLING RATE OF FIRMS TO SURVEY IN A STRATIFIED SAMPLE | | | |
|---|---|---|---|---|
| | **No. of Firms in Labor Area** | **Desired Weighting of Firms in Survey (%)** | **No. in Desired Final Sample[a]** | **Sampling Rate by Firm Size** |
| Less than 251 employees | 250 | 25 | 12 | 12 ÷ 250 = 4.8% |
| 251 to 500 employees | 125 | 50 | 26 | 26 ÷ 125 = 20.8% |
| More than 500 employees | 125 | 25 | 12 | 12 ÷ 125 = 9.6% |
| Total | 500 | 100 | 50 | |

[a]Rounding adds one firm to the 251 to 500 employee group and deletes 0.5 from the other two groups.

not from a particular employer's relevant labor market. This disadvantage is discussed in the section on third-party data.

## Product Market Surveys

Just as with labor market surveys, compensation decision makers must make a series of decisions about whom to include in the product market wage and benefits survey.

Firms surveyed in the product market should satisfy three criteria. First, they should be in the relevant product market; second, they should use similar technology; and third, they should be of similar size as measured by number of employees. Ideally, a compensation decision maker would conduct a survey among those firms that meet these criteria. Unfortunately, it is not always easy to attain this ideal. For example, an organization may use one technology to produce a series of products, some of which the surveying organization may not make. These two firms are not totally similar in terms of products made and the allocation of labor costs to those products. Further, costs outside the production process may not be similar. For example, differences in shipping costs may offset labor savings. A brewery in Eden, North Carolina, with a relatively low wage rate will incur large shipping costs to send its product to Detroit, whereas a brewery in Detroit with higher labor costs will incur low shipping costs to sell its product there. These additional costs must be considered.

Compensation decision makers should aim for the ideal product market survey; however, they must be creative as well as analytical in interpreting survey data, because seldom will competitors be surveyed under the ideal conditions outlined here.

### Geographic Scope of the Product Market

Like labor markets, the product market also has a geographic scope. That is, an organization typically markets its product in a particular geographic area. To determine which organizations to survey in the product market, the first general rule is to determine which organizations are its product market competitors. They can be identified by observing which companies' products are next to the organization's on the supermarket shelf or in hardware stores. Similarly, a brewery in Eden, North Carolina, may be interested in knowing wage rates paid by a brewery in Detroit and a brewery in Williamsburg, Virginia, if it is considering expanding its product into that market. However, it would not need to know the wages paid at a brewery in Phoenix, Arizona, if it does not compete in that product market. The relevant product market can be seen in the same sense as the relevant labor market, in that both have a definable geographic scope.

### Technology and Product Market Surveys

Product markets also have a technologic dimension that may or may not perfectly correlate with occupational skill levels and transferability of those skills. Specifically, the surveying organization will want to include those competitors who have similar technologies and are of about the same size.[13] The organization is trying to ensure that its labor costs will not vary significantly from its competitors', putting it at a competitive disadvantage in the product market. An employer can estimate the wage level of the production unit of its competitors if the competitors use a similar technology.

Exhibit 9.5 is a diagram that illustrates this dimension. The organization depicted in the diagram is assumed to make a product with a given technology. The production unit of this firm has three job levels as depicted in Exhibit 9.5. The weighted average of the wage rates across job levels for this production unit is $6.48 per hour. The organization also has a key job at each of the three job levels. If the organization wants to know the wage level paid by its competitors, it could survey the three key jobs among its competitors. Assuming that its competitors use similar technology (and apply labor to technology in roughly the

---

| EXHIBIT 9.5 | THEORETICAL PRODUCTION ORGANIZATION AND ASSOCIATED KEY JOB PRODUCT MARKET RATES |
| --- | --- |

| **Average Key Job Rate (Product Market)** | **Job Level as Proportion of Total Weighting** |
| --- | --- |
| Job 3 = $11.00 | 5/255 = 2.0%  $ 0.22 |
| Job 2 = $ 7.80 | 50/255 = 19.6%  1.53 |
| Job 1 = $ 6.10 | 200/255 = 78.4%  4.78 |
| | Wage Level  $6.53 |

Wages = $10.50 / , *N*=5

Wages = $ 8.00 / , *N*=50

Wages = $ 6.00 / , *N*=200

Key job 3    Key job 2    Key job 1

Wage level = $6.48

same ratio), the employer will have a good estimate of the wage level of these competing firms. Exhibit 9.5 shows at the top that given the wage rate for the three key jobs and the job level of each key job relative to total employment, the wage level in the product market is $6.53 per hour. This is a favorable comparison with the organization's rate of $6.48.

Because managers, support staff, and so on, tend to be employed in roughly similar ratios to production employees for employers of similar size, similar estimates can be made for the wage levels of these groups and finally for the organization as a whole.

# Wage and Benefit Custom-Designed Surveys

The organization primarily has two options for securing wage and benefit survey data: It may create a custom-designed survey, or it may use survey results provided by a third party. It is recommended that organizations do both. By using both sources, it can cross check the information obtained through its own survey with that provided by the third parties. When the various sources have similar findings, the decision maker can have more confidence in making decisions based on the results. When they do not converge, further investigation is essential to identify the reasons and clarify the results.

## Custom-Designed Surveys

An organization that chooses to collect its own wage and benefit data may select written questionnaires, personal visits, or telephone interviews as its data collection method. It is customary to use all three in varying degrees to collect valid and reliable information.

## Written Questionnaires

A written questionnaire is the most commonly used method of collecting data. The frequency of administration of the survey is dependent on the degree of instability in the labor market. In the design of the survey, it is essential to consider how the data will be finally presented and what kind of statistical information is required. If quantitative reports are to be compiled, as is usually done, it is essential that the questions be designed in a format that lends itself to later quantification. The designer will have to either provide questions that can be answered by use of a scaled format or develop a scoring scheme to deal with open-ended responses. These issues should be addressed in the design stage to reduce *post hoc* decision making. Similarly, the organization may wish to design a survey that will provide data in key areas that most third-party surveys omit or handle poorly and then use the traditional third-party sources for standard, less critical areas. This approach will save the company both design time and tabulation time.

An example of a custom-designed survey appears in Appendix C. The sample survey has five parts: a letter of transmittal, followed by sections on organizational policy, employee benefits, merit review data, and job data.

**Letter of Transmittal**    Each survey questionnaire should have a letter of transmittal attached. This letter should include

> A reference to the earlier phone call in which the organization agreed
> to participate
>
> A statement of purpose
>
> A desired response date
>
> An overview of the survey content
>
> An assurance of anonymity, if desired
>
> A commitment to share the results with the surveyed organization
>
> The name of the specific contact person at the surveying organiza-
> tion
>
> A specific date on which the contact person will telephone to clarify
> any items on the survey
>
> An expression of appreciation for participation

The last item is desirable, not just from a courtesy standpoint, but to ensure
as high a response rate as possible. The commitment to share survey results will
also enhance response rates, as will the assurance of anonymity. It is desirable to
contact each company by telephone, in advance of sending out the survey, to
solicit its participation verbally.

**Organizational Policy**    Specific questions regarding organizational policy are
essential because of the considerable variance among employers on general policies.[14] This variability seems to be greatest across industries; responses in a labor
market survey would probably vary more than in a product market survey.[15]

Organizational policies should be solicited for different groups of employees.
In the sample survey form in Appendix C, the breakdown is provided for exempt
(not subject to FLSA minimum wage and overtime provisions) and nonexempt
(subject to FLSA) jobs. Further breakdowns may be desirable. For example,
office and clerical nonexempt jobs are typically treated the same as managerial
jobs for workweek periods and hours of work. However, in some settings they
may not be treated the same. Assuming that an organization follows the typical
practice can lead to inaccurate conclusions. Similarly, although nonexempt union
and nonunion employees are usually treated the same for overtime purposes, this
is not always the case. There seems to be no sure way of knowing where these
exceptions occur except to have a first-hand knowledge of employee practices in
one's industry and geographic area. The wage survey form should be constructed
to allow for identification of such differences.

The extent of the policy section depends on the date of the last survey that
included policy information and the kind of problems the organization has been
experiencing. For example, if an organization is not having difficulty attracting
employees but does have difficulty retaining employees in the 2- to 3-year range,
it may be a result of the pay progression policy of the organization. Knowledge

of pay progression policy of other organizations should be sought; the discovery, for example, that competing organizations are moving new people through the wage range in 1 year, but the surveying firm is taking 3 years is invaluable information. The organization learns employees are leaving after obtaining experience because they do not wish to wait the additional time to reach the maximum wage rate, nor do they have to wait if they change organizations.

**Employee Benefits**    Employee benefits have grown over the years until today they represent about 28 percent of total compensation for small and large employers.[16] Employee benefits are a main component of the total compensation package, and failure to obtain employee benefits data could threaten the validity of the survey results. One industry study found that benefits and wages tend to vary together.[17] High-paying firms within the industry also had higher benefit levels. This study, besides demonstrating the importance of employee benefits in general, found that both employee wages and benefits are determined by ability and willingness to pay. These results are consistent with a main theme of this textbook, that wages are constrained by a firm's ability to pay.

Surveying organizations about benefits data is problematic in that the formulas used for computing the employers' contributions to such things as the group health insurance plan vary considerably from one plan to another. Also, the absolute benefits vary considerably from one plan to another.[18] Knowing the percentage employees contribute to a plan says nothing about the relative costs of this benefit for the employers. If, particularly in the case of a product market survey, the surveying organization is basically interested in the contribution of benefits to labor costs, it may be more appropriate to ask the surveyed organizations to report the cost of all benefits as a percentage of payroll or as a percentage of base pay. Many organizations are now doing this, and in the future this information should be more readily available in most firms.[19] A firm that is concerned about compensation in the product market is less concerned about the structure of benefits (such as paid holidays off versus longer vacations) and more concerned about the total costs of the benefits package.[20] The sample survey in Appendix C in the employee benefits section asks for the cost of benefits as a percentage of total labor costs or base pay.

If, however, the organization is concerned about benefits from an employee equity standpoint, then the earlier questions in the employee benefits section of the same survey are crucial. Because employees may compare their pension, vacation, or paid holiday schedule with those offered by other organizations, the surveying organization may be concerned about how the structure of its benefits package compares with the structure of benefits packages of other firms within the relevant labor market.[21]

**Merit Review Data**    The surveying organization will want to know how employees qualify for pay increases within their jobs. Are pay raises based on merit, on seniority (such as time in grade), or on a combination of merit and seniority? It is also important to know if employees qualify for annual bonuses; often an employer will offer slightly lower wages but will provide an annual bonus of 5 to 10 percent. For example, a study by Towers, Perrin, Foster, and Crosby found that executive pay increased only 6 to 7 percent from one year to the next, but when total compensation was included it increased between 9 and 13 percent.[22]

**Job Data**   The job data section of the survey form asks the responding organization to provide data about specific key jobs. In Appendix C, the form is presented for only one job. There would be as many of these forms as there are key jobs being surveyed. One source has recommended that at least 30 percent of the surveying organization's jobs should be included in the wage survey to achieve an appropriate level of confidence in the data.[23] Identification of that many key jobs for surveying may be impossible, or it may have such a negative impact on response rate that it would be inadvisable. In general, it is worthwhile to provide the job title in use by the surveying organization, alternate job titles, and a brief job description and job specifications. The responding organization can then determine which of its jobs is closest to the key job in the survey.

Besides providing this information, the surveying organization should provide wage data about its own organization to the respondent. This is one more way to increase the likelihood of a response.

Finally, the job data section asks for both wage information as it might appear in policy statements and wage behavior actually engaged in by the firm. This distinction is an important one. Often an employer's pay behaviors are different than its stated policy.[24] If an employer is paying more or less than its stated policy, using only the stated policy data will place the surveying organization at a disadvantage when it makes its own pay decisions. If, for example, the responding organization's pay is actually higher than its policy but the surveying organization follows the policy statement, then the surveying organization has underpriced its jobs relative to the responding organization. Compa-ratio, a control mechanism, can help an organization determine if its pay practices are following its pay policies; this will be discussed later in the text. In the case of wage behavior relative to the product market, underpricing may result in wage savings; however, if the data is from the labor market, then the organization may be hurt in its ability to compete for employees. Overpayment relative to the product market will result in a cost disadvantage for the organization; whereas overpayment relative to the labor market should work to the organization's advantage in attracting labor supplies. In any event, it is critical to obtain information on actual pay practice as well as stated pay practice so that compensation decision makers are relying on valid data.[25]

## *Comprehensive and Abbreviated Surveys*

The survey form in Appendix C is a comprehensive custom-designed survey form used to ascertain considerable information from the surveyed organization. Mailed surveys are generally much briefer in format. In all likelihood, an organization will not regularly ask for all this information in every survey for several reasons. First, one of the problems of surveys is obtaining cooperation. Although there may be many reasons for a lack of willingness to participate in surveys, one main reason is the length of the survey. The shorter the survey form can be kept, the greater the likelihood that others will cooperate in filling it out.[26]

A second reason for using a shorter survey questionnaire is that many employment policies do not change rapidly over time. For example, there are rarely changes in vacation policy or number of paid holidays.[27] Firms probably do not have to gather most benefits data any more frequently than every 3 to 5 years; the same is true for data on general policies and merit policies. There are some benefits areas such as health care that should perhaps be tapped each year because many organizations are trying different methods of cost control and because many different programs are becoming available to them. The questions dealing with wage rates for key jobs definitely need to be sent to respondents on an annual basis. Using streamlined survey forms, especially in follow-up years, may increase the probability of respondents returning the completed questionnaires.

## Personal Visitation

The personal visit to the cooperating organization is the most costly and time-consuming method to collect wage and benefit data but provides the organization with the most valid information. The interviewer will normally have prepared a detailed questionnaire before the visit and use the interview to collect data and clarify ambiguous survey areas. The interviewer can interview the appropriate compensation specialist at the surveyed organization. Alternatively, the interviewer can personally collect the relevant information from payroll data and obtain clarification of unusual data before leaving the cooperating organization. This technique is primarily used for jobs that are particularly important to the surveying organization. The interviewer must be knowledgeable about the jobs being surveyed, have a good grasp of the compensation field, and have excellent interpersonal skills.

## Telephone Surveys

Telephone surveys are useful when the surveyor is seeking a limited amount of data in a short time span.[28] For example, the organization may be concerned about the wage rate for a particular entry-level job or the number of paid holidays provided by other firms. In these cases, the compensation manager may call several labor or product market competitors to determine their current practices. If this process is repeated often enough (it frequently is in many firms) and the information is properly maintained, then a mail survey may never be undertaken because piecemeal data collection over time has made it unnecessary. The telephone survey is also used when there is a need to get a quick estimate of a job's market price and when clarification of other data is desired.

# Third-Party Wage and Benefit Surveys

Much of the information organizations want regarding their labor market is available without the organization having to conduct its own surveys. This information, referred to as third-party data, is available from three sources: government agencies, professional associations, and consultants. Third-party surveys provide useful supplements to the organization's own wage and benefit survey data.

## Federal Government Surveys

The U.S. government conducts several surveys that are available to private and public sector organizations. Of the four main federal government surveys discussed here, three are conducted by the Bureau of Labor Statistics. The fourth survey is conducted by the Federal Reserve System.

**Area Wage Surveys**    Area wage surveys are conducted throughout the United States in the largest of the standard metropolitan statistical areas. The surveys cover many clerical and operative occupations in both manufacturing and non-manufacturing sectors of the economy. They present results in the form of pay data for classes of jobs and indicate mean, median, and pay range data for the jobs. These surveys also provide information on employee benefits, such as vacation practices, health insurance and pension plans, shift differentials, and weekly work schedules.

**Industry Wage Surveys**    Industry wage surveys cover 50 manufacturing and 20 nonmanufacturing industries within the economy. The surveys provide data on wages for select jobs and also on hours worked per week and employer contributions to insurance and pension plans. Many of the industries in the survey are relatively low-wage industries, suggesting that the government is subsidizing product market surveys for certain firms in the economy.

**Professional, Administrative, Technical, and Clerical Surveys**    The professional, administrative, technical, and clerical surveys are conducted in metropolitan areas among employers with 2,500 or more employees. Types of occupations surveyed include accounting, legal services, personnel management, engineering, chemistry, buying, clerical supervisory, drafting, and clerical. The survey data report straight-time earnings, bonuses, commissions, and cost-of-living increases.

**Federal Reserve System**    The Federal Reserve System conducts wage surveys in each of its respective districts to ensure that its employees' pay is at market within the district. Summaries are generally available through the Federal Reserve System.

## Professional Association Surveys

Many professional associations at both the local and national level conduct one or more wage and benefit surveys of their membership. For example, the Society for Human Resource Management in conjunction with a private firm conducts wage and salary surveys for human resource and industrial relations executives. Many local chapters of this association also conduct wage and benefit surveys for select key jobs within their local labor areas.

Appendix A presents a partial list of professional associations that conduct wage and benefit surveys. Such professional associations provide useful sources of wage and salary information for the compensation decision maker. Awareness of the professional association data is particularly important to organizations because individuals in the surveyed professions often review these surveys to determine whether they are equitably paid.

## Consultants

Another main source of data for compensation decision makers is consulting firms. Several large consulting firms conduct wage and benefit surveys for clients and others wishing to purchase the data. Many of these firms operate exclusively within an industry. Others specialize in a particular occupational segment. For example, Appendix B shows that Towers, Perrin, Forster, and Crosby specialize in top- and middle-management surveys.

## Advantages and Disadvantages of Third-Party Surveys

There are both advantages and disadvantages to the use of third-party surveys. One of the main advantages is that the data can be obtained relatively cheaply. This is particularly true of government data and may be true of data from consultants if it is provided as part of a larger package, such as implementation of a comprehensive compensation system. A second advantage of third-party surveys is the summary form of data presentation. The organization does not have to manipulate the data into usable form. Third, this type of collection is usually based on large numbers of organizations and jobs. From a statistical sampling standpoint, the user can put greater faith in the data as being truly representative of prevailing wage practices.

Despite the above advantages, there are several drawbacks to third-party data. First, especially in the case of government survey data, the data may be out of date by the time the survey reports are made available to an organization. It is essential to find out from the government agency when the data collection actually occurred rather than to rely on the date of publication. If the information is old, an estimated update of the wage data can be made.

Second, the user has no way of knowing the relevance of the wage and benefit data reported in the survey to its own key jobs. Because mailed surveys of organizations provide much of the data, it may not be clear whether the jobs for which pay rates are reported are the same jobs that the organization would like pay data for.

Third, the usual summary form of the data may make it difficult for the user to determine if the pay rates reported are relevant for the organization's labor area or industry. If, for example, organization size and broad industry groupings are the summary categories for a job, there is no way to be sure that the organization can rely on that data as the appropriate reference base for its pay system. For example, the survey may report a job's wage data for the state as a whole or for a region within a state. If an organization's particular labor area or product market is not surveyed, then the survey results will have little use for assessing pay equity or checking pay constraints. Also, the provider of the data may not provide the sample size for each job and the variance around the mean wage. If the data look unusual, it is advisable to ask the provider to verify the data or do a spot check to verify it personally.

Finally, the ready-made survey results may not inquire into the important issues from the user's standpoint. For example, the survey data may give no information on health insurance or retirement plans. In short, users of ready-made surveys are in the position of taking whatever is given them.

## Summarizing Survey Data

There are almost as many ways to summarize wage data as there are people who do the summarizing.[29] The basic rule to follow, however, is to choose a format that is useful for the surveying organization. This issue is a moot one for those organizations that rely on third-party data; they must use the data as it is summarized for them. The following discussion pertains to data collected in a custom-designed survey. Note that determination of the data summary format should precede the design of the data collection method so that the data can be collected in a manner conducive to summarizing.

### Wage Data

The purpose of wage data is to determine going rates in the labor or product market, data should be summarized in terms of ranges (minimum, maximum), mean, and median of actual pay rates. The standard deviation should be provided so that those using the survey data are aware of the dispersion in the data. An employer may also be interested in the averages of these pay rates.

By examining the average of the minimum rates, maximum rates, and the mean, the compensation decision maker can identify the parameters surrounding the organization's own pay practice to make decisions about changes in current pay rates. It would be beneficial if an appendix included the individual pay for each position to provide the decision maker with the specific data dispersion for each job. To include this, the questionnaire would have to be designed to ask for individual values, not summary values. The specific rate paid per individual within a job would provide information on how the data actually lay out and may be helpful in showing how pay policies are actually being implemented by the responding organization. Gathering this data could, however, present a new problem if the information is perceived as being used to violate antitrust laws.

### Summary Statistics and Wage Data

The reporting of wage rate data can take many forms. As noted above, means, medians, and modes are one set of summary statistics. The *mean* of a set of wage rates is the arithmetic average of all the wage rates reported. The *modal* wage rate is the most common wage rate reported, and the *median* wage rate is the middle wage rate reported. Each of these may be important in its own right, and they will be equal only when the distribution of wage rates is normal.

More often than not, what is more interesting than the simple mean wage or modal wage is the mean, median, or mode of other characteristics of the wage data. For example, 20 employers might report the minimum pay, the median pay, and the maximum pay for a given job. It may be of interest to look at the mean of each of these three measures. Specifically, the compensation decision maker may be interested in the average minimum wage rate for the job, the average median rate, and the average maximum rate. These three wage rate values would provide for stability in the statistics being analyzed.

Another way to report the data is by quartiles. This summary would include the wage rate below which 25 percent of the reported rates fall, the rate below which 50 percent of the reported rates fall, and the wage rate below which 75 percent of the wage rates fall. From these data, the interquartile range can be reported. The *interquartile range* is the range between the 25th percentile wage rate and the 75th percentile wage rate. This is a commonly accepted indicator of central tendency.

An alternative method to summarize the data is to examine *weighted average wage rates*. That is, the analyst could take the actual wage rate paid to employees, multiply it by the number of employees at each rate, sum this value, and divide by the total number of employees working in the job (see Exhibit 9.6). This weighted average provides information about the average actual pay level in the survey group, a figure that could be different than the average wage rate across surveyed companies.

Several of the summary statistics discussed above can be seen in Exhibit 9.7, which reports survey results from a local government survey for the job of clerk steno II. It is important that the compensation manager use a consistent wage measure (for example, weighted mean) in making wage decisions. The compensation manager, when using third-party survey data, should verify with the

---

| EXHIBIT 9.6 | MEANS USING WEIGHTED AND UNWEIGHTED PAY RATES | |
|---|---|---|

| Survey Organization | No. of Executive Assistants | Average Rate (per hour) |
|---|---|---|
| Ajax Information | 1 | $15.00 |
| Venture Technologies | 8 | $10.00 |
| Dynamic Images | 10 | $12.00 |
| | 19 | $37.00 |

Unweighted mean $= \dfrac{37.00}{3} = 12.34$

Weighted mean $= \dfrac{215.00}{19} = 11.31$

EXHIBIT 9.7 SUMMARY ANALYSIS SHEET: CLERK STENO II

| | Minimum | | | Midpoint | | | Maximum | | | Average/Actual | | |
|---|---|---|---|---|---|---|---|---|---|---|---|---|
| | Rate | No. Employed | Agency | Rate | No. Employed | Agency | Rate | No. Employed | Agency | Rate | No. Employed | Agency |
| | $15,048 | 14 | V | $18,150 | 14 | V | $21,252 | 14 | V | $19,728 | 14 | V |
| | 13,624 | 2 | S | 16,224 | 2 | S | 18,824 | 2 | S | 16,102 | 11 | U |
| | 12,792 | 21 | T | 15,600 | 11 | U | 18,720 | 11 | U | 15,652 | 2 | S |
| | 12,480 | 11 | U | 14,900 | 4 | M | 17,772 | 4 | M | 13,865 | 21 | T |
| | 12,028 | 4 | M | 14,394 | 21 | T | 16,046 | 1 | N | 13,520 | 4 | D |
| | 11,690 | 0 | L | 13,520 | 4 | D | 15,995 | 21 | T | 13,454 | 1 | N |
| | 10,962 | 15 | C | 13,454 | 0 | L | 15,964 | 9 | P | 13,262 | 4 | M |
| | 10,861 | 1 | N | 13,454 | 1 | N | 15,620 | 4 | D | 13,137 | 2,414 | R |
| | 10,816 | 9 | P | 13,130 | 9 | P | 15,350 | 0 | L | 12,871 | 15 | A |
| | 10,706 | 8 | J | 12,606 | 2,414 | R | 14,639 | 4 | I | 12,810 | 9 | P |
| | 10,656 | 2,414 | R | 12,515 | 4 | I | 14,556 | 2,414 | R | 12,802 | 15 | C |
| | 10,580 | 15 | A | 12,383 | 8 | J | 14,196 | 15 | A | 12,383 | 8 | J |
| | 10,566 | 4 | D | 12,256 | 15 | A | 14,060 | 8 | J | 12,102 | 4 | I |
| | 10,440 | 4 | Z | 12,086 | 15 | C | 13,991 | 15 | C | 11,972 | 32 | H |
| | 10,391 | 4 | I | 11,972 | 32 | H | 13,673 | 32 | H | 11,785 | 4 | Z |
| | 10,271 | 32 | H | 11,764 | 4 | Z | 13,468 | 13 | B | 11,690 | 0 | L |
| | 10,072 | 7 | E | 11,463 | 7 | E | 13,128 | 4 | Z | 11,572 | 13 | B |
| | 9,776 | 13 | B | 11,076 | 13 | B | 12,853 | 7 | E | 11,457 | 7 | E |
| | 8,189 | 1 | G | 9,320 | 1 | G | 10,451 | 1 | G | 9,953 | 1 | G |

| | |
|---|---|
| Respondents | 19 |
| Mean range | $11,155 - $15,293 |
| Mean midpoint | $13,172 |
| Q1 range | $10,416 - $13,832 |
| Median range | $10,706 - $14,639 |
| Q3 | $11,859 - $16,021 |

| | |
|---|---|
| Respondents | 19 |
| Mean | $13,164 |
| Q1 | $11,972 |
| Median | $12,841 |
| Q3 | $13,520 |
| No. employed | 192 |

Weighted average actual $13,412

## Clerk Steno II

This is responsible clerical work involving the performance of a variety of secretarial and office manager duties. The Clerk Steno II exercises considerable judgment in establishing or adapting work procedures to new situations. Work is reviewed on completion, but frequently no check is made of the data compiled or the records prepared. May exercise supervision over the general operations of an office and over other clerical personnel. Requires graduation from high school and considerable experience (usually 2 to 5 years) in clerical and stenographic work. (Grade 23) supply organization what kind of mean is being reported if it is not identified in the report.

## Benefits Data

There are many ways to summarize the survey benefits data and the policies relating to those benefits. Only an example is presented here. In the case of numbers of holidays granted with pay, several questions may be of interest. First, the organization may wish to know the total number of holidays with pay provided by surveyed organizations. In this case, the appropriate summary of data would be a distribution of the number of holidays with pay, along with relative and cumulative frequency distributions. The data table might show (relative frequency graph) that 15 firms (30 percent) provide 8 paid holidays per year, and ten firms (20 percent) provide 9 paid holidays per year; it might also show (cumulative frequency graph) that 25 firms (50 percent) provide 10 or more paid holidays per year, and 35 firms (70 percent) provide at least 9 paid holidays per year; and so forth. An example of this data presentation is shown in Exhibit 9.8.

A second question may be which holidays are granted with pay each year. Thus, the data may show that 100 percent (all 50) of the firms grant the Fourth of July off with pay, but that only 50 percent (25 firms) grant the employee's birthday off with pay, and so forth. One way of presenting the data is displayed in Exhibit 9.9.

A third issue may be the firm's policy regarding work requirements the day before and after the holiday to be eligible to receive holiday pay: What percentage of organizations require the employee to work the day before or the day after or both to qualify for holiday pay? Again, this could be presented quite simply, in bar graph form.

An organization should not attempt to provide every possible type of data summary for holidays or for any other benefit. Rather, it should choose methods of summary that provide the most clear and concise answers to the questions which are pertinent to that organization.

## Reporting Data to Management

It is easy to overkill with numbers and to confuse rather than clarify. A good way to report data to management is by job. A summary sheet might look something like the one in Exhibit 9.10 (on page 286).

Exhibit 9.10 shows the wage data from 14 organizations that participated in a survey. The top of the figure contains the raw data reported by the responding organizations. If the number of participants is very large, this information should be left off the report. The information at the bottom of Exhibit 9.10 is most relevant. It shows the average minimum wage, average median wage, average maximum wage, and the weighted average wage in these organizations. As presented, this information is relatively easy to understand and could be presented clearly to management.

Some sources consider survey data as a yardstick[28] to assess, in general, how an organization's pay practices relate to other organizations. Because of sampling

RELATIVE AND CUMULATIVE FREQUENCY DISTRIBUTIONS FOR PAID HOLIDAYS AMONG FIRMS SURVEYED

## Relative Frequency

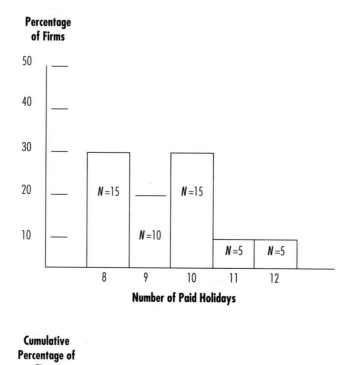

Percentage of Firms

Number of Paid Holidays

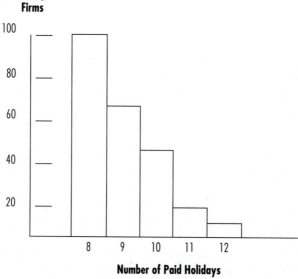

Cumulative Percentage of Firms

Number of Paid Holidays

| EXHIBIT 9.9 | FREQUENCY DISTRIBUTION OF FIRMS PROVIDING SELECT HOLIDAYS WITH PAY |

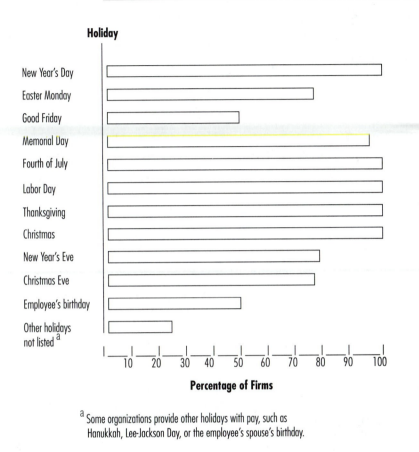

a Some organizations provide other holidays with pay, such as Hanukkah, Lee-Jackson Day, or the employee's spouse's birthday.

problems, sample sizes, and lack of participation, they argue that survey data are too unstable for making fine distinctions about wage payments; they conclude it should be used only to make rough comparisons about relative pay equity. These arguments have some validity; but if the data collection from the appropriate organizations is carefully accomplished, it can be argued that the resulting information could be considered a micrometer used for fine-tuning the pay system. Results that can be used to fine-tune wages can generally be obtained only from custom-designed surveys.

## Wage and Benefit Survey Data and Antitrust Law

One potentially serious concern with compiling and using wage data is whether the data lead to collusion in wage setting. If organizations act in a way that could be regarded as a conspiracy to restrain the free pricing of labor, courts could view

EXHIBIT 9.10   SUMMARY OF WAGE SURVEY DATA

| Organization | Pay Policy Rates | | | Average/Actual Rate | |
|---|---|---|---|---|---|
| | Minimum | Midpoint | Maximum | Rate | No. of Employees |
| D | $12,251 | $15,620 | $18,096 | $14,913 | 15 |
| P | 11,908 | 14,482 | 17,602 | 14,144 | 2 |
| H | 11,848 | 13,814 | 15,783 | 13,814 | 4 |
| K | 10,780 | 13,004 | 16,439 | 13,628 | 40 |
| A | 11,112 | 12,871 | 14,909 | 14,549 | 26 |
| C | 11,510 | 12,690 | 14,690 | 14,306 | 16 |
| I | 10,391 | 12,515 | 14,639 | 14,249 | 3 |
| M | 9,896 | 12,259 | 14,621 | 10,911 | 5 |
| G | 10,451 | 11,895 | 13,339 | 12,598 | 3 |
| Z | 9,960 | 11,544 | 13,128 | 12,557 | 28 |
| E | 10,072 | 11,463 | 12,853 | 12,029 | 9 |
| J | 9,692 | 11,203 | 12,714 | 11,203 | 4 |
| R | 8,911 | 10,543 | 12,175 | 11,451 | 2,268 |
| B | 8,476 | 9,776 | 11,648 | 10,526 | 14 |

Average of minimum = $10,518
Average of midpoint = $12,406
Average of maximum = $14,474
Weighted average for actual = $11,579

Interquartile range for midpoint is $11,463 to $13,004.

that action as a violation of antitrust law. At least one employer association has signed a consent decree with a court after a labor union in the Boston area raised questions about the antitrust implications of conducting wage surveys.[30]

Employers can probably protect themselves from such charges by making wage decisions independently and by not acting in concert with other organizations.

There are some things the organization can do to protect itself from appearances of collusion.[31] First, if the employer has face-to-face encounters with other employers while sharing survey data, it would be prudent to have an independent third party monitor the discussions to ensure that they do not involve anything that could be considered collusion. Second, the organization should not imply in any way that its behavior is contingent on a specific behavior of other survey participants. For example, to imply that the organization will not raise wages more than 5 percent if other survey participants do not raise wages by more than a specified percentage would probably be considered illegal. Third, unless it can present a defensible use for data on individuals, the organization may want to collect and report the data in such a way that limits the ability to identify individual employee pay rates.[32]

## Summary

This chapter focuses on wage and benefits surveys. The first part of the chapter reviews the importance and nature of such surveys of the labor and product market. It focuses on identification of appropriate labor and product markets for implementing wage and benefit surveys.

The second portion of this chapter examines survey data sources. There are two main ways to collect wage and benefit data: custom designed surveys and third-party surveys. There are three ways to collect data by a custom-designed survey: written questionnaire, personal visitation, and telephone. A sample survey form is presented and used to show the importance and purpose of each of the components of a wage and benefits survey. There are three main sources of third-party survey data: government agencies, professional associations, and consulting firms. Strengths and weaknesses of third-party data are discussed, along with custom-designed surveys and their attendant strengths and weaknesses. Finally, approaches for summarizing survey results are presented.

## Discussion Questions

1. Discuss the relative advantages and disadvantages of third-party and custom-designed survey data.

2. A college wants to conduct a labor market survey for (a) office clerical employees; (b) maintenance employees; (c) administrators; and (d) faculty. Identify the relevant labor market for each of these occupational groups.

3. Is a college concerned about relevant product market surveys? Might it be concerned about such surveys for one or more occupational groups but not others? If so, which groups and why?

4. What are the relevant dimensions of a labor market and a product market?

5. Explain why product market surveys are intended to reflect the wage level of product market competitors.

6. Why is it important to collect actual wage and benefits data as opposed to stated wage and benefits policies?

7. After conducting labor and product market surveys, a nonunionized truck manufacturer in rural Virginia finds that it is paying about $4 per hour above the going market rate, but about $1 per hour below the product market rate (where other employees are unionized and represented by the UAW). Discuss this phenomenon. What do you suspect led to this situation, and what advantages and disadvantages would you associate with this wage position in the marketplace?

8. A hospital in a small university-dominated community (population 35,000, with 23,000 students) pays at the bottom of the wage rate for all occupational groups except doctors relative to other hospitals in the area and relative to other firms in the area. Total population in the relevant labor and product market area is 300,000. This hospital has no trouble attracting qualified applicants. Why?

9. What can an organization do to increase participation in a wage and benefits survey it is conducting?

10. You are the Compensation Manager for Leinies Inc. and must prepare a presentation to the key management group regarding the results of the wage and benefits survey conducted in your product market. What will you include in your report?

## EXERCISES

1. The Busti National Bank has just decided to open a branch in Bemus Bay, an exclusive resort located about 20 miles from Arkwright, a large city. There is no bank there at present.

Busti is anxious to determine the appropriate wage for the clerical staff it expects to hire. Clerks in the bank's offices in Arkwright receive a starting wage of $150 a week, but through promotions they can work up to $200. As a matter of company policy, these wage rates have been set at the midpoint of other bank's rates in Arkwright.

A survey of the local businesses at Bemus Bay, primarily realty and insurance offices and local stores, indicates that the going rate for qualified clerical personnel is $225 to $250 a week. The higher rates in Bemus Bay may be attributed in part to the higher cost of living in this resort town, the limited number of young people seeking employment, and the fact that there currently are no other banks in Bemus Bay. Banks in Arkwright have traditionally paid lower wages than other businesses, on the grounds that banks offer better working conditions and higher prestige.

a. What should the Busti Bank establish as its hiring rate for clerical personnel? What factors should be considered in making the decision?

b. Could the bank justify to its Arkwright employees the fact that it was paying higher wages in Bemus Bay?

2. Below are the results of labor and product market survey data for one job.

a. Calculate summary statistics for these data.

b. Recommend a pay rate for this job.

### Survey of Labor Market Wages

| Organization | Minimum | Midpoint | Maximum | Rate | No. of Employees |
|---|---|---|---|---|---|
| S | $16,432 | $19,552 | $22,672 | $19,344 | 2 |
| U | 15,200 | 19,000 | 22,800 | 20,300 | 2 |
| V | 15,444 | 18,909 | 22,374 | 19,728 | 14 |
| T | 13,832 | 15,564 | 17,295 | 16,328 | 18 |
| M | 12,028 | 14,900 | 17,772 | 13,262 | 6 |
| W | 11,336 | 14,200 | 17,056 | 14,200 | 2 |
| D | 10,566 | 13,520 | 15,620 | 13,520 | 5 |
| N | 10,861 | 15,454 | 16,046 | 13,454 | 1 |
| P | 10,816 | 13,130 | 15,964 | 12,974 | 5 |
| A | 11,112 | 12,871 | 14,909 | 13,518 | 13 |
| H | 11,022 | 12,854 | 14,686 | 12,854 | 10 |

### Survey of Product Market Wages

| Organization | Minimum | Midpoint | Maximum | Rate | No. of Employees |
|---|---|---|---|---|---|
| L | $11,157 | $12,837 | $14,644 | $13,328 | 2 |
| K | 10,286 | 12,408 | 15,686 | 13,004 | 21 |
| Z | 10,920 | 12,324 | 13,728 | 12,431 | 18 |
| J | 11,115 | 12,105 | 13,094 | 12,105 | 2 |
| C | 10,962 | 12,086 | 13,991 | 13,455 | 20 |
| Y | 9,588 | 11,988 | 14,388 | 15,444 | 1 |
| I | 9,888 | 11,916 | 13,944 | 9,888 | 2 |
| R | 9,749 | 11,529 | 13,309 | 11,808 | 1,509 |
| G | 9,953 | 11,329 | 12,704 | 12,099 | 1 |
| E | 9,605 | 10,914 | 12,222 | 9,890 | 1 |
| B | 8,476 | 9,776 | 11,648 | 9,343 | 14 |

SOURCE: Leonard R. Sayles and George Strauss, *Managing Human Resources*, 1977, p. 390. Reprinted by permission of Prentice-Hall, Englewood Cliffs, N.J.

3. You are the supervisor for the shipping department of Smith Manufacturing. You have received a memo from the firm's compensation manager that the salary survey of the local labor market for positions under your supervision has been tabulated and there is concern that wages paid within your department are 25 percent above the market. Below is the printout provided with the memo:

|  | Smith's Wage | Market Wage |
|---|---|---|
| Material mover | $7.50 | $6.00 |
| Picker | 6.56 | 5.25 |
| Labeler | 5.94 | 4.75 |
| Packing | 6.25 | 5.00 |
| Helper | 5.63 | 4.50 |

The average age of your work force is 43 years; 80 percent have been with the company for more than 10 years. The productivity of your work force in your eyes is outstanding, which was verified by a study that shows that your crew produces at 105 percent of standard. What would you do to prepare for the meeting you are to have in 2 weeks with the compensation manager and the plant manager to discuss this situation?

### References

[1] G. J. Meng, "Compensation: Link Pay to Job Evaluation," *Personnel Journal* 69 (March 1990), 98–104.

[2] R. J. Sokol, "Seven Rules of Salary Surveys," *Personnel Journal* 69 (April, 1990), 82–87.

[3] S. L. Rynes and G. T. Milkovich, "Wage Surveys: Dispelling Some Myths About the 'Market Wage,'" *Personnel Psychology* 36 (Spring, 1986), 71–90.

[4] *Ibid.*

[5] R. J. Sokol, "Seven Rules of Salary Surveys."

[6] W. Fogel, "Occupational Earnings: Market and Institutional Influences," *Industrial and Labor Relations Review* 32 (October 1979), 24–35.

[7] See H. R. Bloch and R. L. Pennington, "Measuring Discrimination: What Is a Relevant Labor Market?" *Personnel* 57 (July/August 1980), 21–30.

[8] C. E. Tate, J. F. Cox, F. Hay, V. Scarpello, and W. W. Steward, *Small Business Management and Entrepreneurship* (Boston: PWS-Kent, 1992).

[9] B. R. Ellig, "Solar Survey: Design to Application," *Personnel Administrator* 22 (1977), 41–50.

[10] R. L. Ackoff, *Scientific Method* (New York: Wiley, 1962).

[11] *Ibid.*

[12] *Ibid.*

[13] R. Lester, "Pay Differentials by Size of Establishment," *Industrial Relations* 6 (October 1967), 57–67; G. A. Syer, "The Exempt Salary Survey, Part 1: Collecting Information," *Personnel* 63 (June, 1986), 45–49.

[14] H. Heneman, III, D. P. Schwab, J. A. Fossum, and L. D. Dyer, *Personnel/Human Resource Management* 3d ed. (Homewood, IL: Irwin, 1986).

[15] T. A. Pugel, "Profitability, Concentration and the Interindustry Variation in Wages," *Review of Economics and Statistics* 62 (May 1980), 248–253.

[16] U. S. Chamber of Commerce, *Employee Benefits 1990* (Washington, DC: U. S. Chamber of Commerce, 1991).

[17] F. S. Hills and R. E. Hughes, "Salaries and Fringe Benefits in an Academic Labor Market: Examining Internal and External Labor Markets, Explaining Geographic Differentials" (Presented at National Academy of Management Meetings, National Academy of Management, San Francisco, CA, 1978).

[18] E. C. Smith, "Strategic Business Planning and Human Resources: Part 1," *Personnel Journal* 61 (August 1982), 606–610.

[19] J. Rosenbloom and G. V. Hallman, *Employee Benefits Planning* (Englewood Cliffs, NJ: Prentice-Hall, 1981).

[20] R. W. McCaffery, *Managing the Employee Benefits Program* (New York: American Management Association, 1972).

[21] T. Easton, "Bargaining and the Determinants of Teacher Salaries," *Industrial and Labor Relations Review* 41 (January 1988), 263-278.

[22] B. Liebtag, "New Challenges For Compensation," *Journal of Accountancy* 164 (November 1987), 79–82.

[23] Sokol, "Seven Rules of Salary Surveys."

[24] M. Dyekman, "Take the Mystery Out of Salary Surveys," *Personnel Journal* 69 (June 1990), 104–106.

[25] G. A. Syer, "The Exempt Salary Survey, Part 2: Analyzing and Reporting Data," *Personnel* 63 (July 1986), 24–31.

[26] G. A. Syer, "The Exempt Salary Survey, Part 1: Collecting Information," *Personnel* 63 (June 1986), 45–49.

[27] U.S. Chamber of Commerce, *Employee Benefits 1980* (Washington, DC: U.S. Chamber of Commerce Survey Research Center, 1981).

[28] M. Dyekman, "Take the Mystery Out of Salary Surveys."

[29] D. W. Belcher, N. Bruce Ferris, and J. O'Neill, "How Wage Surveys Are Being Used," *Compensation and Benefits Review* 17 (September-October 1985), 34–51.

[30] See In the Matter of the Boston Survey Group, Superior Court of Massachusetts, CA No. 56341, August 2, 1982.

[31] G. D. Fischer, "Salary Surveys—An Antitrust Perspective," *Personnel Administrator* 30 (April 1985), 87–97+.

[32] *Ibid.*

**Administrative Management Society**—4622 Street Road, Trevose, PA 19047; (215) 953-1040; clerical, management, and electronic data processing compensation; regional breakdown; $150–250.

**American Association of Engineering Societies**—345 East 47th Street, New York, NY 10017; (212) 705-7840; engineering salaries including government and education; $55–$225.

**American Chemical Society**—1155 16th Street, NW, Washington, DC 20030; (202) 872-4600; members' salaries and starting salaries for chemists and chemical engineers; geographical and industrial breakdown; $20–$75.

**American Compensation Association**—P.O. Box 1176, Scottsdale, AZ 85252; (602) 951-9191; management compensation, salary budget survey; geographical breakdown; free–$10.

**Bank Administration Institute**—60 Gould, Rolling Meadows, IL 60008; (312) 228-6200; compensation for all positions in banking; geographical breakdown; $50 for members, $75 for nonmembers.

**Battelle Institute**—505 Kings Avenue, Columbus, OH 43201; (614) 424-6424; research and development, salary and compensation; across industries; price varies, available to participants or government contractors.

**Chamber of Commerce**—1615 H Street, NW, Washington, DC 20062; (202) 659-6000; manufacturing and nonmanufacturing benefits; geographical breakdown; $17.50.

**College and University Personnel Association**—11 Dupont Circle, Suite 120, Washington, DC 20036; (202) 462-1038; compensation for administration and faculty in higher education; geographical breakdown; $25 for participants, $75 for non-participants.

**College Placement Council, Inc.**—65 East Elizabeth Avenue, Bethlehem, PA 18018; (215) 868-1421; starting salaries of all college graduates; industrial and geographical breakdown; free to members, $150 per year to nonmembers.

**The Conference Board, Inc.**—845 Third Avenue, New York, NY 10022; (212) 759-0900; compensation of top executives and outside directors; breakdown by industry and company size; $25–$150.

**The Dartnell Institute**—4660 Ravenswood Avenue, Chicago, IL 60640-9981; (312) 561-4000; sales personnel compensation; industrial breakdown; $115.50.

**The Endicott Report**—Northwestern University, Evanston, IL 60201; (312) 492-3709; salaries offered to college graduates; $10.

**Executive Compensation Service, Inc.**—Two Executive Drive, Fort Lee, NJ 07024; (201) 585-9808; top, middle, and supervisory management, professional and scientific, clerical and sales compensation; industrial and regional breakdown; $110–$495.

**Health Insurance Institute**—1850 K Street, NW, Washington, DC 20006; (202) 862-4000; health insurance benefits; free.

**Institute of Management and Administration, Inc.**—29 West 35th Street, 5th Floor, New York, NY 10001-2299; (212) 244-0360; to set compensation for executives, managers, supervisors, and office staff; $245.

**International Foundation of Employee Benefits Plans**—P.O. Box 69, Brookfield, WI 53005; employee benefits, regional and asset size breakdowns; free.

**National Association of Mutual Insurance Companies**—P.O. Box 68700, Indianapolis, IN 46268; (317) 875-5250; executive sales in insurance industry; geographical breakdown; free to participants, $20–$30 for nonparticipants.

**National Society of Professional Engineers**—1420 King Street, Alexandria, VA 22314; (703) 684-2800; salaries of engineers; breakdowns geographically and by industry; $30 to members, $55 to nonmembers.

**National Telephone Cooperative Association**—2626 Pennsylvania Avenue, NW, Washington, DC 20037; (202) 298-2300; all telephone jobs; breakdown by region; $20 to members, $40 to nonmembers.

**New York Chamber of Commerce**—200 Madison Avenue, New York, NY 10016; (212) 561-2020; salaries and benefits for all office jobs in New York City; $165 for members, $196 for nonmembers.

**Scientific Manpower Commission**—1776 Massachusetts Avenue, NW, Washington, DC 20036; (202) 223-6995; salaries of scientists, engineers, and technicians; industrial and regional breakdown; $30.

**Tool and Die Institute**—77 Busse Highway, Park Ridge, IL 60068; (312) 825-1120; trade compensation in the Chicago area; some by industry; free to members, $75 for nonmembers.

CONSULTING ORGANIZATIONS PROVIDING WAGE
AND BENEFIT SURVEY DATA

**Abbott, Langer and Associates**—548 First Street, Crete, IL 60417; (708) 672-4200; wage surveys of many occupations; geographical and industrial breakdowns; $100–$475.

**Arthur Young and Company**—277 Park Avenue, New York, NY 10017; (212) 407-1500; executive compensation and compensation for board of directors; industrial breakdowns; $95–$195.

**Cole Survey**—100 Summer Street, Boston, MA 02110; (617) 547-3341; compensation in financial organizations; geographical breakdown; $300–$5,000.

**Compass International**—338 Beacon Street, Boston, MA 02116; (617) 536-2333; worldwide compensation; $1,000/year.

**D. Dietrich Associates, Inc.**—P.O. Box 511, Phoenixville, PA 19460; (215) 935-1563; technical compensation and compensation of some others; geographical breakdown; $60–$130.

**ECS – A Wyatt Company**—Two Executive Drive, Fort Lee, NJ 07024; (201) 585-9808; professional and scientific personnel, $580; middle management positions, $690.

**Educational Research Services, Inc.**—1800 Kent Street, #1020, Arlington, VA 22209; (703) 243-2100; salaries and compensation for professionals in teaching; geographical breakdown; three volumes at $30/volume.

**Ernst & Young**—1400 Pillsbury Center, Minneapolis, MN 55402; (800) 827-4575; office, technical skilled trades, and custodial jobs.

**Hay Associates**—229 South 18th Street, Philadelphia, PA 19103; (215) 875-2300; both exempt and nonexempt wages; all industries and some by geographic region; price varies by client.

**Heidrick and Struggles**—125 South Wacker Drive, Chicago, IL 60606; (312) 867-9876; outside director and committee service compensation; breakdown by industry and company size; $20.

**Hewitt Associates**—100 Half Day Road, Lincolnshire, IL; (312) 295-5000; top and middle management compensation; geographical breakdown; free for participants, $25 for nonparticipants.

**Hospital Compensation Services**—115 Watchung Drive, Hawthorne, NJ 07506; compensation for all positions in nursing homes and salaries for executives in hospitals; regional breakdowns; $105.

**KPMG Peat Marwick**—345 Park Avenue, New York, NY 10154; (212) 872-5770; wide range of areas such as foreign banks, university administrators; fee depends on survey.

**Mercer Incorporated**—The National Survey Group, 1417 Lake Cook Road, Deerfield, IL 60015; (800) 333-3070 or (212) 345-7584; human resource management: $275 participants, $525 nonparticipants; executive compensation: $650 participants, $1,300 nonparticipants; finance, accounting, and legal: $450–925; information systems/telecommunication: $750–1,400; materials and logistic management: $250–500.

**Reggio and Associates, Inc.**—547 West Jackson Boulevard, Suite 505, Chicago, IL 60606; (312) 236-1840; many salary surveys covering various occupations; dependent on survey, geographical, and industrial breakdowns; price varies with survey.

**Robert Half International**—552 Fifth Avenue, New York, NY 10036; (212) 221-6500; financial and data processing starting salaries; free.

**Towers, Perrin, Forster and Crosby**—600 Third Avenue, New York, NY 10016; (212) 309-3400; top and middle management and some nonexempt positions; $500–$1,200.

Ms. Compensation Manager
XYZ Corp.
Anytown, USA ZIP

Dear Ms. Jones:

Thank you for agreeing to participate in ABC Company's wage and benefits survey. The requested information is very important to us for our annual survey of key jobs, and as we agreed on the phone, I will look forward to a return of the information in the enclosed self-addressed, stamped envelope no later than February 15, 19__.

I would like to take just a second to acquaint you with the survey itself. The survey has four basic parts. First, we would like information on general policy issues. Second, because benefits are becoming such a major component of pay, we ask that you provide benefits information to us. Third, we have included a separate sheet for each of _____ key jobs. Please provide us with information on the jobs that seem (based on the enclosed descriptions) to be most like our key jobs. The fourth and final section asks for information on merit and bonus systems in your organization.

I also want to reiterate our assurances to you that we will not identify your company individually in reporting the survey results. As is true of all our surveys, we are interested in assessing wage payments across a number of employers. However, we would like your permission to use your name as one of the respondents to the survey. Thus, although your individual pay practices will not be identified, we would like participants who receive the results to know which firms were included in the survey. If you would agree to allow us to use your company name, please indicate so at the appropriate place on the survey form. If you do not wish your company name identified with the survey, we will not do so.

As has been our policy for the past 15 years, we continue to provide the results of this survey free of charge to all of those who participate. If you would like a copy of these results, please indicate so at the appropriate place on the survey form.

Finally, you might note that we are providing you with our current pay practices for each of the key jobs. Although this may not be as useful as summary data, we feel that you may be interested in knowing OUR pay practices at the present time for these key jobs.

Ms. Analyst is coordinating this survey for our company. She will be contacting your company on December ___ to determine if you have any questions on the survey. If, before that time, you have questions on the survey, please call her at (XXX) YYY-ZZZZ.

Thank you again for your participation in the survey. If you can have your results back to us by February 15, 19__, we should be able to share these results with you by April 1.

Sincerely,

## Organizational Policy

### I. Staff and Hours

Exempt = E and Nonexempt = NE

Number of employees?   E_____   NE_____

How many hours per week do your employees normally work?   E_____   NE_____

How much time allotted for lunch?   E_____   NE_____

Is it paid lunch (circle appropriate response)   E: Yes   No        NE: Yes   No

How much time alloted for breaks?   E_____   NE_____

How much daily time alloted for them?   E_____   NE_____

Do you have a 4-day week?   E: Yes   No        NE: Yes   No

Do any of your employees work on shifts? (E only)   Yes   No
  If "Yes," answer below:

| SHIFT | Shift hours | % premium pay |
|-------|-------------|---------------|
| Evening (2nd) | _____ | _____ |
| Late (3rd) | _____ | _____ |
| Other | _____ | _____ |

Do you have any form of flextime (allows employees to choose working hours)?

  Managerial: Yes   No        Other Exempt: Yes   No        NE: Yes   No

If "Yes," please provide a sheet explaining how your flextime system works.

### II. Salary Payment Policies

If your standard number of hours worked per week is less than 40, do you pay overtime for hours in excess of the normal workweek but less than 40?   Yes   No

Do you pay overtime for time worked in excess of 8 hours in a day?   Yes   No

If certain groups within the organization have less than a 40-hour workweek, please list them:

| GROUP | HOURS |
|-------|-------|
| _____ | _____ |
| _____ | _____ |
| _____ | _____ |

What is overtime rate for individuals required to work on regularly scheduled holidays?

_____ None        _____ 1½        _____ Double time        _____ Other

What is rate for individual required to work regularly on Saturdays and Sundays?

_____ None        _____ 1½        _____ Double time        _____ Other

Have you granted any general across-the-board adjustments in wages or salary within the past 24 months?   Yes   No   If "Yes":

|  | Date | Approximate % Adjustment |
|---|---|---|
| 1. | _____ | _____ |
| 2. | _____ | _____ |

Are these adjustments linked to the Bureau of Labor Statistics Consumer Price Index? Yes   No

Please provide equation used for such adjustments: _____

If linked to any other price index, please indicate _____

## III. Starting Salaries of College Graduates

What is your average starting salary for a college graduate with a Bachelor's degree in Business Administration, Accounting, Finance, Economics, Management, etc., pursuing a nontechnical occupation in your firm?   $_____

What is your average starting salary for a college graduate with a Bachelor's degree in Engineering, Mathematics, Statistics, etc., pursuing a technical occupation in your firm? $_____

## IV. Employment Policies

Do you pay employment agency fees for noncollege graduates?   Yes   No

If "Yes," do you pay the fee at the time of employment?   Yes   No   If "No," when? _____

Do you require aptitude tests be passed before employment?   Yes   No

If "Yes," for which jobs do you require those tests?

### Employee Benefits

## I.   Paid Vacations

What paid vacations are allowed?

| Years of service inclusive: | Weeks of Vacation Allowed | | |
|---|---|---|---|
|  | Nonexempt | Exempt | Executive |
| 0-1 | _____ | _____ | _____ |
| 1-4 | _____ | _____ | _____ |
| 5-9 | _____ | _____ | _____ |
| 10-15 | _____ | _____ | _____ |
| more than 15 | _____ | _____ | _____ |

Can unused vacation time be carried over to the following year?   Yes   No   If "Yes," how many days? _____

## II. Paid Holidays

How many paid holidays do you grant? _____

| | | | | | |
|---|---|---|---|---|---|
| Christmas Day | E____ | NE____ | Independence Day | E____ | NE____ |
| New Year's Day | E____ | NE____ | Labor Day | E____ | NE____ |
| Washington's B'day | E____ | NE____ | Veterans' Day | E____ | NE____ |
| Good Friday | E____ | NE____ | Thanksgiving Day | E____ | NE____ |
| Memorial Day | E____ | NE____ | Employee's B'day | E____ | NE____ |

Other (specify)

_____E____      NE____

                E      NE,

Are employees required to work day before? _____, day after _____, or both _____
                                          Yes/No          Yes/No          Yes/No

## III. Sick Leave

Do you have an official sick leave plan?   Yes   No

How many days sick leave are granted per year?   E_____      NE_____

Do you have a waiting period before an employee is eligible for sick leave?
E: Yes   No      NE: Yes   No

What happens to such time not used? _____

## IV. Other Leaves

Do you grant leave with pay for any of the following reasons? (If yes, please indicate the number of days.)

| | | | | | |
|---|---|---|---|---|---|
| Jury Duty | E_____ | NE_____ | Death (Family) | E_____ | NE_____ |
| Marriage | E_____ | NE_____ | Dental Appt. | E_____ | NE_____ |
| Family Illness | E_____ | NE_____ | Other _____ | E_____ | NE_____ |

## V.  Insurance Benefits

Do you have a group hospitalization or surgical plan?   Yes   No    If "Yes," what percent is paid by the employer? _____

What is the monthly cost to the employee?        Single Plan $_____
                                                 Family Plan $_____

Is there a major medical additional to the regular insurance plan?   Yes   No

If "Yes," what is the one-time illness maximum?   $_____

What is the lifetime illness maximum?   $_____

At what amount of "out-of-pocket" employee cost per illness does the major medical plan assume full responsibility?   $_____

Do you have a group dental plan?   Yes   No    If "Yes," what percent is paid by the employer? _____

What are the main limitations to this plan?

_____

Do you have a group life insurance plan?   Yes   No

If "Yes," is it contributory?   Yes   No

If "Yes," what percent does the employer pay? _____

Is the amount of insurance made available as a percentage of annual salary? (Circle appropriate figure.)

        1.5      2.5      3.5      other

Is there a base to your insurance plan?   Yes   No    If "Yes," what is that base?
$_____

Is there a cap to your insurance plan?   Yes   No    If "Yes," what is that cap?
$_____

What is the company payment to any of the above insurance benefits for its retirees? If yes, please explain: _____

_____

## VI. Pension Plan

Do you have a pension plan?   Yes   No

Does it include all employees?   Yes   No

If "No," which groups are excluded?

Is it integrated with Social Security?   Yes   No

How do you determine average salary for pension purposes? (Please circle your method.)

    Salary, final 3 years    5 years    10 years    career average    other _____

Is it a defined benefit plan?   Yes   No

If "Yes," what formula do you use for determining final pension benefits?

_____

Is it a defined contribution plan?   Yes   No

If "Yes," how do you determine contributions?

Which vesting plan are you using? _____

What is your normal retirement age? _____

Do you have an early retirement eligibility?   Yes   No

If Yes," how do you determine it? Age, service, age and service, other _____

Have you provided a pension plan supplement for retirees in the past 5 years?
  Yes   No

Do you provide death benefits for retirees?   Yes   No

Do the retirees contribute to the death benefit premiums?   Yes   No

**General**

Do you provide a cafeteria service for your employees?   Yes   No

If "Yes," percent subsidization? _____. What is average cost per employee per year? _____

Do you provide parking for all employees or subsidize parking fees?   Yes   No
Cost _____

Are your clerical employees represented by a labor union?   Yes   No

Are your nonclerical employees represented by a labor union?   Yes   No

Do you have an education benefit?   Yes   No

If "Yes," for what employee groups?

    E_____    NE_____    Exec_____

If "Yes," for what programs?

    G.E.D.    Undergraduate    Graduate    Vocational    Other _____

If "Yes," what percent of tuition is reimbursed? _____. What is average cost per employee, per year? _____

Does your organization calculate the total cost of fringe benefits as a percentage of payroll or base pay?   Yes   No

If "Yes," what is the percent?  _____

What components go into this percentage? (Check all that apply.)

    Employer contributions to Social Security _____

    Employer contributions to private pension plan _____

    Employer contributions to group health insurance_____

    Employer contributions to group dental plans _____

    Unemployment compensation insurance_____

    Workers' Compensation insurance_____

    Other _____

## Merit Review Plan

Do you have a merit pay plan?   E:  Yes   No    NE:  Yes   No    Exec:  Yes   No

Briefly describe:

Do you have an annual bonus plan?   E:  Yes   No    NE:  Yes   No
Exec:  Yes   No

For each group indicate date of last bonus _____    % of salary _____

## Job Data

Job Title:   Switchboard Operator

Thumbnail Job Description:

1. Provide banking services to all customers in a friendly, efficient, and professional manner.

2. Operate the switchboard.

3. Open incoming mail and disperse to the proper departments.

4. Maintain the copy machine and record daily usage.

5. Coordinate the usage of the bank-owned vehicles.

6. Receive information for the daily bulletin.

7. Receive and deposit milk machine money.

8. Verify and record internal services time card and attendance records.

9. Provide specific copy machines reproductions for all bank locations.

10. Assist other employees within the department whenever possible.

11. Perform other duties that are approved or assigned by your superiors.

Job Specifications Switchboard Operator

The job requires little independent judgment on the part of the employee. Little direction is needed, and the work is infrequently checked. There is substantial public contact but infrequent intrabank contact. The job demands little or no extraordinary concentration. There are few physical demands with little or no unpleasant working conditions. Less than a month of training is required. General banking equipment and the PBX are used. Telephone communications skills are necessary.

Please complete this form for your comparable job:

Job Title: _____

Minimum Pay: _____ (or entry-level hiring rate)

Median Pay: _____ (or average of the range)

Maximum Pay: _____ (or maximum longevity rate)

Total Number of Employees in this Job: _____

Minimum Actual Pay:  _____ Number of Employees:  _____

Maximum Actual Pay:  _____ Number of Employees:  _____

Average Actual Pay:   _____ Number of Employees:  _____

Medium Actual Pay:   _____ Number of Employees:  _____

# 10

# Pay Structure Design: Integrating Job Evaluation and Pay Structure Data

## Learning Objectives

To learn how to integrate information from job evaluation with information from wage surveys to build a wage policy line.

To learn the reasons for balancing internal and external equity.

To learn how to develop a wage policy line with the freehand method and with the multiple regression method.

To learn why and how to construct pay grades.

To learn about pay ranges and how they can be used in compensation decision making.

To learn how to implement a comprehensive pay structure.

## Introduction

This chapter is, in some ways, a summary and integration of the activities of the compensation decision makers as discussed in the previous chapters. Chapter 8 discussed job evaluation and how to conduct such an evaluation. Job evaluation is a process to establish a hierarchy of jobs in terms of their relative worth to the company. Chapter 8 noted that this relative worth is often established in terms of compensable factors, which are selected in the context of a job evaluation committee composed of employees and management. This committee, through job evaluation, determines that one job is worth more than a second job, which in turn is determined to be worth more than a third job—but how much more in terms of dollars is not determined at this point. Job evaluation establishes an internal relationship among jobs that is perceived as equitable by members of the organization. Enhanced feelings of internal equity may result in higher motivation to remain with the organization. Chapter 9 discussed labor and product market wage and benefits surveys. The data obtained through these wage surveys give the organization an understanding of the broader picture—an idea of what is occurring externally.

This chapter discusses how that data is used to develop a pay structure—an array of hierarchical-arranged pay rates. The pay structure should advance the compensation goals of internal equity (to motivate staying), external equity (to motivate joining and staying), and reward for individual performance and other job contributions. The pay structure should be constructed to support strategic goals of the organization as well.[1]

## Determining Internal Equity

The first step in establishing an equitable pay structure is to examine internal wage relationships in the light of the jobs that have been evaluated and the relative relationships among those jobs. This process focuses entirely on internal equity and says nothing about external equity. A typical example of this appears in Exhibit 10.1.

Exhibit 10.1 depicts a bivariate plot (two variables plotted, one on the "x" axis and the other on the "y" axis) of present midpoint wage rates (y axis) against the evaluated number of points allotted to each of these jobs (x axis) for a hypothetical company. Examination of the relationship between current pay rates and the job evaluation points in Exhibit 10.1 indicates that current pay rates reflect considerable inequity. For example, jobs evaluated at 200 points have midpoint wage rates ranging from about $4.85 to $5.20. In an equitable situation, all jobs worth 200 points would have the same pay rate. Further examination of Exhibit 10.1 shows that although one job evaluated at 200 points is currently paid at $5.20, another job evaluated at 205 points is currently being paid a rate of $4.95. Because higher point jobs should have higher relative pay rates, this further demonstrates internal inequity.

### Line of Best Fit

The compensation decision maker's need to make judgments shows up at this stage when an effort is made to determine what the wage rate should be for jobs of varying points. One way to achieve equity within jobs of equal point value and across jobs of different point values is to find a line of fit that best captures

---

**EXHIBIT 10.1** BIVARIATE PLOT OF CURRENT MIDPOINT WAGE RATES AND JOB POINTS

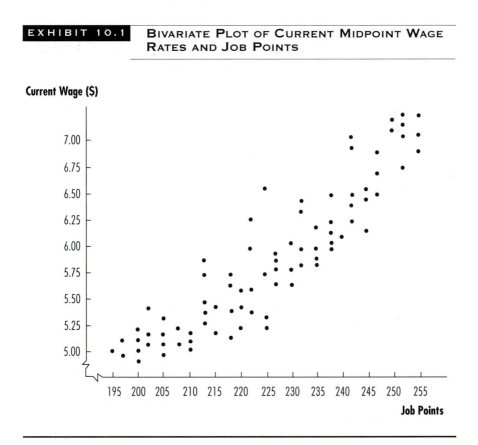

the central tendency or trend among all these data points on the figure. Several approaches are used in practice. One is to inspect the data points and simply draw a line to best capture the relationships among and within jobs. Exhibit 10.2 offers an example of such a freehand line.

It is a trend line that captures wage and points combinations. A variation of the total freehand approach is the anchor approach. In this method, the highest and the lowest wage rates in the entire scatterplot are connected, which yield the trend line.

The decision maker can then determine the wage rate to be paid to all jobs that have the same point value. This is done by dropping a line straight down (for those above the line) or straight up to the already established trend line and then drawing a horizontal line to the $y$ axis. The location on the $y$ axis is the wage for that point value and the appropriate internal wage for all jobs that have earned that job evaluated point value.

Alternately, the decision maker can determine wage rates by establishing an algebraic equation for this trend line. The trend line can be defined algebraically by using the equation for a straight line. The equation for a straight line is

$$y = a + bx,$$

where
$y$ is the wage rate for a job,
$a$ is the $y$ intercept,
$b$ is the slope of the line, or the money value per point, and
$x$ is the number of points which the job carries.

Any two points on the trend line can then be used to create two equations. Using the data in Exhibit 10.2, a job worth 205 points that is paid at the trend line receives $5.25 per hour. A job having 225 points receives $6.00 per hour if paid on the trend line. The two equations are

$$\$6.00 = a + 225b$$
$$\text{and}$$
$$\$5.25 = a + 205b$$

Solving these simultaneously reveals that the slope of the line (b) is equal to 0.0375. In other words, according to this freehand line, jobs are paid an additional 3.75 cents per hour for each additional job evaluation point. The $y$ intercept (where the line crosses the $y$ axis) in this case is −$2.43, and the full wage equation for this freehand trend line is

$$y\ (\text{wage}) = -\$2.43 + \$0.0375 \times x\ (\text{job points})$$

### Regression Line Analysis

A second, commonly used method of determining a line of best fit is to use least-squares regression methods.[2] This is the approach used in this text. The

| EXHIBIT 10.2 | FREEHAND TREND LINE OF CENTRAL TENDENCY AMONG WAGE RATES AND JOB POINTS |

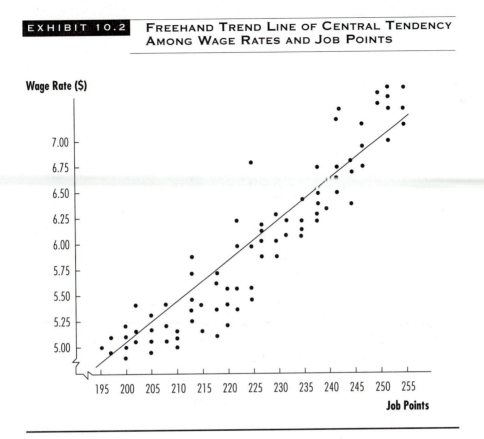

least-squares method for a line of best fit involves the use of a statistical procedure known as regression analysis. In regression analysis, the investigator,
in this case the compensation decision maker, again uses the equation for a
straight line to empirically derive a line of best fit between the ordering of the
jobs and the wage rates for the jobs.

Usually a firm pays a job a constant amount plus so many cents per job evaluation point. If, for example, the firm decides to pay every job the equivalent of
$1.50 (the constant is equal to $1.50), plus $0.05 per point (the slope of the line
is 0.05); then actual pay for jobs of different point values can be found. For example, a job worth 200 points would then carry a pay rate of

$$y = a + bx, \text{ or}$$
$$\text{Wage rate} = \$1.50 + \$0.05 \times \text{points, therefore,}$$
$$\text{Wage rate (at 200 points)} = \$1.50 + \$0.05 \times 200, \text{ or}$$
$$\text{Wage rate (at 200 points)} = \$11.50$$

Similarly, a job worth 240 points would be paid $13.50 per hour, and a job
worth 190 points would be paid $11.00 per hour. This pay line is depicted in
Exhibit 10.3.

| EXHIBIT 10.3 | HYPOTHETICAL PAY LINE |

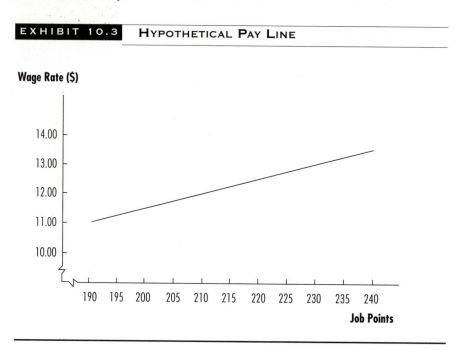

But how does the compensation decision maker decide on the equation for the pay line? Estimating the equation for the pay line is what regression analysis is used for.

With computers, pocket calculators, and more recently the advent of miniprocessors of various types, using (and misusing) regression has become relatively easy. The computational equations for determining the constant $a$ and the slope $b$ of a line are

$$ b = \frac{n(\sum xy) - (\sum x)(\sum y),}{n(\sum x^2) - (\sum x)^2} $$

$$ a = \frac{\sum y - b(\sum x)}{n} $$

The regression procedure treats the data as though a straight line is the best way of expressing the relationship between the $y$ and $x$ variables (in this case, between pay rates and job evaluation points). The procedure minimizes the sum of squared deviations around the line. The computer calculates an infinite array of equations with the goal of finding a line of best fit for the data with the minimum (least) sums of squared deviations. This line, when derived, is the best expression of a linear relationship between pay rates and job points. Once the equation is derived, if the organization adjusts wage rates to the line (bringing all deviations to zero), then there would be a theoretically equitable and continuous array of job and pay rate combinations. Using the data in Exhibit 8.18 produces this equation:

$$y = \$1.19 + 0.014x$$

This line can be plotted on the data from Exhibit 8.18 as shown in Exhibit 10.4.

## Nonlinear Wage Lines

Most organizations that have a systematic job evaluation system do rely on a linear model, but this practice is reflective more of custom than any scientific reason or rationale. A firm may use nonlinear wage lines for various reasons (such as, to conform with a particular market's practice or to allow for compatibility among job families.) Two hypothetical examples of nonlinear wage lines sometimes used in designing a pay structure appear in Exhibit 10.5.

**EXHIBIT 10.4**  REGRESSION LINE FOR LINE OF BEST FIT

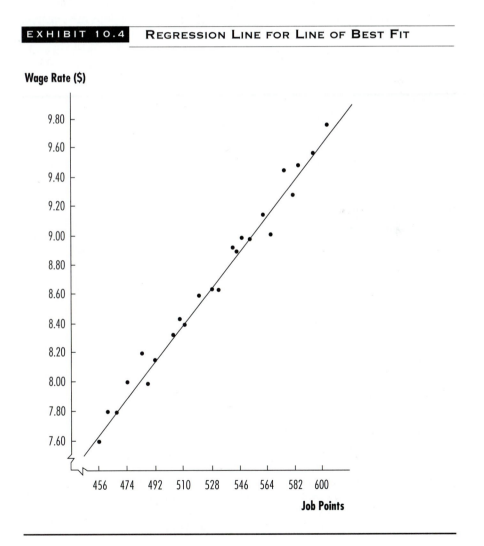

Curve A in Exhibit 10.5 is an exponential curvilinear wage line. This curve might result from the actual wage relationships in the labor or product market. That is, this curvilinear relationship may capture more accurately the relationship between job points and wage rates than a straight line. If so, then an organization using a trend line established with linear regression would tend to overpay jobs in the midrange of the distribution of jobs and underpay jobs at the high and low ends of the distribution of jobs. Use of the curvilinear line may reduce the total wage bill relative to the wage bill under a linear trend line, because wage rates will rise more slowly for jobs of lower point values, which typically have the most job incumbents.

Curve B in Exhibit 10.5 may result from a pay structure when wage pressure is exerted from another job family below the lower jobs in the evaluated job groups.[3] For example, the cluster (family) of jobs represented in the curve may be managerial, technical, and professional, with the 100-point jobs held by first-line supervisors. The supervisors lead unionized workers, and the union pushes its wages up for highly skilled bargaining unit members (the top jobs in a separate job hierarchy). To provide compatibility between the two job clusters and not have supervisors' pay below that of the employees being supervised, the supervisory jobs may pay higher than what the market dictates. This would result in a more gradually sloped pay line for the first series of jobs in the managerial, professional, and technical job cluster.

### Internal Equity as a Sole Criterion

The calculations to derive the wage rate and job point combinations in Exhibit 10.4 are based on data that reflect current wage rates in the organization. The first step

---

**EXHIBIT 10.5    TWO NONLINEAR PAY LINES**

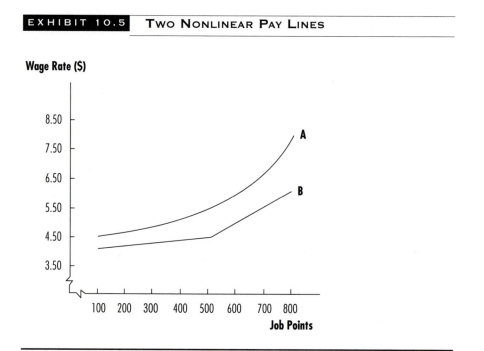

in balancing internal and external equity is to examine present wage rates against the evaluated job points. This process says nothing about external equity but focuses instead on the internal equity issue. This preliminary step gives the wage line for an internally consistent set of wage rates regardless of external equity considerations. The calculations revealed that the pay line should be

$$y = \$1.197 + 0.014x$$

If only internal equity is considered, the organization should pay the wage rate and point combinations on the regression line depicted in Exhibit 10.4. Pay rates for some jobs would need to be adjusted upward to the line, whereas pay rates for other jobs should be adjusted downward. (Organizations rarely decrease the wage rates of jobs that have too high a pay rate. Procedures for handling these jobs are discussed later in this chapter.)

## Determining External Equity

A second important question in wage setting is how current wage rates for jobs in the organization compare with labor market rates. The procedure for determining external equity is similar to that for internal equity. The wage rates used in the analysis of pay rate and job point relationships are the market rates obtained from the labor market survey of key job wage rates. Each of these key jobs has a predetermined point value. Creating a trend line for these key jobs relative to market rates allows the organization to infer what its pay structure should look like if market rates were the determining factor. A set of key job rates appears in Exhibit 10.6, and a corresponding line of best fit superimposed on a bivariate plot of the wage rate and points combinations appears in Exhibit 10.7. The regression line (or line of best fit) for these data is

Wage rate $(y) = \$3.54 + 0.0089$ job points $(x)$

| EXHIBIT 10.6 | LABOR MARKET KEY JOB RATES |
|---|---|

| Job Number | Points | Midpoint Wage |
|---|---|---|
| 1 | 306 | $6.25 |
| 8 | 318 | 6.30 |
| 14 | 336 | 6.52 |
| 24 | 360 | 6.82 |
| 29 | 372 | 6.90 |
| 47 | 420 | 7.29 |
| 62 | 466 | 7.73 |
| 80 | 522 | 8.26 |
| 93 | 552 | 8.44 |
| 107 | 588 | 9.01 |

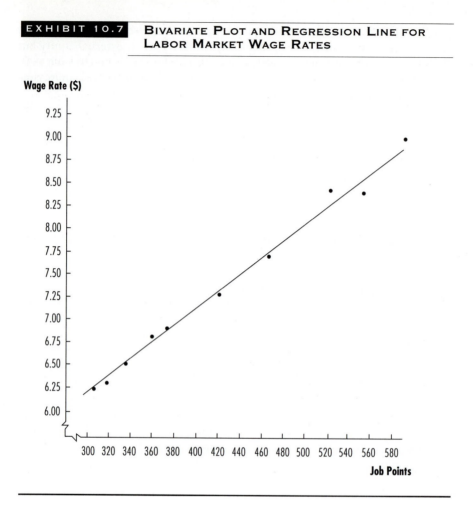

**EXHIBIT 10.7** BIVARIATE PLOT AND REGRESSION LINE FOR LABOR MARKET WAGE RATES

## Wage Rates

The wage rate data in Exhibits 10.6 and 10.7 need to be analyzed by the decision maker. The rates reflect the actual average current pay per key job for each of the ten firms surveyed. The calculated regression line is a reflection of labor market rates across a diverse group of organizations with which the surveying organization competes for labor. If the organization pays according to this line of best fit, its wages will be reflective of rates for key jobs in the market and still maintain an internally equitable wage structure.

## Slotting in Nonkey Jobs

If the organization decides to pay according to the wage line in Exhibit 10.7, then it can use the wage line equation to slot in other, nonkey jobs. The organization will calculate the pay rate for jobs of various point values using the regression equation based on external labor market rates.

### Product Market Constraints

Just as a wage line can be calculated for key jobs and their associated labor market rates, a wage line can also be calculated for key jobs and their associated rates in the product market. Sample data and an associated wage line appear in Exhibit 10.8. The individual data points are not included in Exhibit 10.8, only the corresponding line of best fit. Once again, the compensation decision maker can examine the association between key job points and product market rates to determine the wage line with respect to the product market.

## Labor Costs and Decision Making

To be effective, compensation decision makers must be concerned about motivating employees to join and stay with the organization within the economic

---

| EXHIBIT 10.8 | REGRESSION LINE FOR PRODUCT MARKET WAGE RATES |
|---|---|

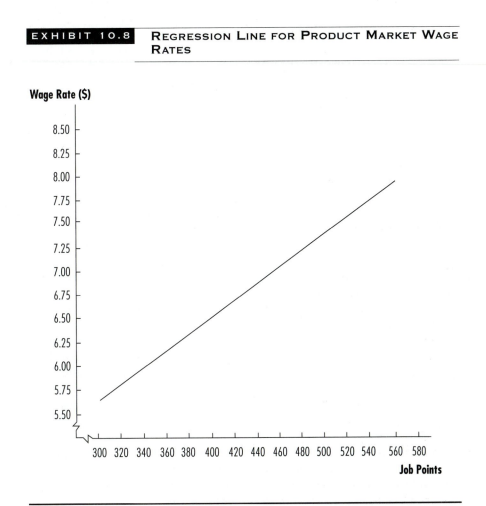

constraints faced by their organization. In one sense, the purpose of pay structure calculations is to assess the impact of alternatives on labor costs and to determine what the organization can achieve within its economic constraints.[4] The decision maker must examine the wage lines based on current rates, labor market rates, and product market rates to determine the impact each would have on the organization's labor costs.[5]

What will be the wage bill cost if the organization attempts to achieve internal equity by establishing a systematic pay line among its current internal rates? The cost is the difference between the current wage bill and the wage bill that would result if the organization would pay to a standard line. What would be the wage bill if the organization uses a wage line reflective of labor market rates? The compensation decision maker can compare this wage cost both with its present pay practice and with a wage bill based on internal equity alone.

An estimated wage bill can also be calculated with the product market data. This information is critical because it represents the wage bill constraint that the organization does not want to exceed under normal assumptions of product market competition (such as similarity of costs for competitors).

Using these calculations, the decision maker can recommend or take action on the organization's pay structure. For example, if the current wage bill and the projected wage bill using the labor market wage line are both below the wage bill calculated with product market data, the organization can choose to adjust its wage rates upward to stay competitive with the product market. However, if calculations reveal that the wage bill is above the product market line but below the labor market line, the decision maker may discover that the organization is not competitive in the labor market and, because of labor cost being higher than product competitors, its market share is shrinking. This situation requires the organization to examine its overall organizational goals carefully.

## Constructing Ranges and Grades

The discussion up to this point has focused on establishing individual pay rates for evaluated jobs. The organization may, however, decide that a pay rate structure is appropriate. The majority of an organization's jobs are nonkey jobs, and the process to be discussed enables the organization to systematically determine an appropriate wage for those jobs.

Establishing pay rate structure requires the development of job grades. A job grade is the clustering together of jobs that have similar values. Thus, instead of each job having a corresponding wage, jobs of similar value will be treated as being identical for wage determination decisions. Plotting all jobs on a scattergram is helpful in obtaining a visual picture of the value distribution of jobs. The organization must determine if a flat wage rate or wage ranges are to be used. A *flat wage rate* pays all individuals who occupy a job with identical points or jobs with the same grade the same pay regardless of the employee's length of service or individual contribution (for example, $5.00 for all workers). A *pay range* provides a range of pay for each job or grade based on seniority or individual's performance (for example, $4.50 to $5.00 per hour). The pricing is the process of integrating the relative value of jobs to their pay in the external labor market.

## Flat Rate Systems

In a flat rate pay system, because there is only one pay rate for a job in a given grade, the wage rates for job grades are the wage rates on the trend line. Flat rate systems are typically used for jobs covered by labor union contracts in which the wage structure is renegotiated at each contract renewal date. However, an organization may find that its situation requires a more complex pay structure. The organization may wish to establish job grades and wage ranges for the grades. This requires decisions regarding the size of the range, range overlap, how employees progress through the ranges, and how job grades are priced.

## Designing Pay Ranges

Once the wage trend line is determined, the next step in building the pay structure is to establish the pay range for jobs if that is desired by the organization. A *wage range* can be defined as the variation in pay that is available in a job. Important considerations for determining the width of pay ranges include whether the expected length of service of job incumbents is long enough and whether the pay increases are large enough to be meaningful. The precise use of ranges is dependent on management policy and philosophy. Decisions about pay ranges should reflect these considerations. Use of a wage range gives the organization four options, or a combination of the four.

First, wage ranges for a job can be used to pay different amounts of money to different employees in the same job depending on their relative performance levels. The use of pay ranges for this purpose allows the organization to reward performance. The establishment of pay ranges can be thought of as an administrative mechanism to motivate performance.

Second, pay ranges can allow salary growth based on differences in seniority. When wage ranges are used for this purpose, an employee will typically move up in pay for each fixed interval of time on the job. For example, an employee might receive a 5 percent raise at the end of the first 6 months of employment, another 5 percent raise at the end of 1 year of employment, and 5 percent at the end of each subsequent year of employment, up to the maximum of the range. Use of the pay range in this fashion will probably not motivate performance, but such seniority-based raises should motivate employees to stay with the organization.

Third, pay ranges can allow variation in pay among employees during probationary employment. For example, it may take time for employees to become minimally proficient in their jobs. The organization may wish to pay lower wages during the time employees are learning the job and to increase wages once they are proficient at the job.

Fourth, pay ranges can permit the organization to start a new employee who has had similar job experience in another organization at a higher rate than it would start an inexperienced employee. This would enable the organization to attract a different quality of individual and permit greater selectivity.

Some pay plans use a combination of merit increase, seniority increase, and probationary or proficiency increases.

## *Ranges for Merit*

Before discussing the technical aspects of wage ranges to reward meritorious performance, a few questions seem pertinent. Does pay for performance really fit with the organizational culture? Will performance increase if merit pay is used, or will it result in long-term mediocrity? What is the objective of merit ranges: Is it to make the organization more attractive, to improve retention, to motivate the worker? The basic purpose of these questions is not to imply that merit ranges should not be used. Rather, it is to point out that when wage ranges based on performance are used, their use should increase the ability of the organization to reach its strategic objectives and fit within the management style and organizational culture.

For an organization to consider the use of pay ranges to reward employees for differential performance on jobs, several criteria must be met. First, the performance variance possible within a job must be sufficient for merit to be used as a criterion for pay allocations. Many jobs have little room for performance variation. For example, an assembly line worker who mounts a seat in a car either does or does not install the seat correctly. There is little room for superior performance in terms of doing an excellent installation. There is also no opportunity for this worker to increase his or her productivity because the speed of work is dictated by the movement of the line.[6] If there is little room for performance variance, there is little sense in distinguishing between performance levels. Thus, some organizations may have only 20 percent range ($4.50 to $5.40 per hour) for jobs low in the hierarchy (for example, receptionist) but ranges in the neighborhood of 60 percent plus ($20,000 to $32,000 salary per year) in the higher levels (for example, managerial).[7] One study found an average range of 50 percent for white collar occupations.[8]

Second, the performance variance of jobs must be measurable if the organization hopes to pay for performance. It is extremely difficult to measure differences in performance in many jobs. In these cases, the organization may be better off not using performance as a pay criterion because improper measurement may create either an inequitable situation or one that could be perceived as inequitable.

Third, employees must want to be assessed on the basis of either relative or absolute job performance.[9] Even if performance variance exists and can be measured, employees must accept performance as a valid pay criterion. If the employees do not want pay for performance, then it will be resisted, as occurs on some production line jobs.[10] This is also why unions often negotiate a single rate for their members and often resist two-tier wage systems.[11]

## *Policy Considerations for Merit Ranges*

Pay policy decisions about pay ranges should be consciously made to reflect several considerations. An important consideration is the expected length of service for employees in these jobs. For example, if the organization expects employees to stay in a job for 8 to 10 years, then ranges need to be relatively wide so the organization can continue to reward high performance. Without reasonably wide ranges, high performers will reach the top of the range early and there will not be room for future salary growth. The size of the range is also influenced by the size of the annual increases that the firm wishes to grant to employees. The larger the merit increase, the faster the range is exhausted by a high performer. For example, if superior performance can result in a 10 percent pay raise above the general increase granted an average employee, then a high performer will be at the top of a 30 percent range within 3 years and a 20 percent range in 2 years. This may be acceptable if it is expected that high performers will be promoted within these time frames, but it would be unacceptable if promotions come at a slower rate. Because most organizations do not provide this size premium to higher performance, it may take longer than illustrated but the issue is still germane.

In fact, a different problem develops if the premium size is quite small. Often the gap between general wage structure increase (increase in whole structure) and merit increase is only 1 to 2 percent. This small difference may create serious problems for the organization.[12] For example, an employee is hired at the bottom of the range and the salary range for the position is 50 percent. If this employee performs above average and obtains a merit performance rating such that he or she earns the maximum 2 percent allocated to merit, it will take many years (in excess of 11 years) to reach the midpoint. The wider the salary range and the smaller the amount of the overall wage increase that is allocated based on merit, the longer it takes to move from minimum to midpoint. This can result in a very demoralized employee. The situation can be further complicated by the organization's hiring practices. If the company needs an experienced person to fill a vacancy in the area, it will often have to hire a person with a salary near the midpoint (market rate) of the range for that job. The salary level of the new hiree will likely be above current employees who are performing above average and who have more experience than the new hiree because of the long time period it takes to move from minimum to midpoint.[13]

There are a number of possible solutions to this problem.[14] First, the firm can reduce the salary range so that the move from minimum to midpoint takes less time. This, however, reduces the ability of the organization to reward long-term performance and runs contrary to most current thinking. Second, the firm can provide equity adjustments to move the person to their appropriate position within the range. This raises questions of why the inequity was allowed to develop. A third approach is to use *time targeting*. In this technique, the midpoint is replaced by a "control point" wage, which is the level of performance expected of an average competent employee for that job. The minimum is determined based on how long it takes the average worker to reach competency.[15] For each year of experience required, a 3 percent differential is subtracted from the control point to set the beginning wage rate. Thus, if a control point is set at \$21,000 and it takes 4 years to reach competency, the minimum would be approximately 18,658 ($21,000 \div 1.03^4$). Once the control point is established, the organization must decide how much it wants to provide to reward performance above the competency level. If the organization wants a 25 percent differential above the competency level, it merely multiplies the control point by the differential

$(21,000 \times 1.25 = 26,250)$. Organizations should permit employees who learn faster than normal to move from minimum to control point faster than scheduled if their "real" performance dictates such. All the above discussion only looks at changes in wages caused by learning the job and meritorious performance. The whole wage structure normally increases to reflect a basic general increase granted to employees performing at the normal level of performance. Often this is done to maintain equity with the external labor market.

### Ranges for Seniority

Because the criteria for pay ranges based on merit (sufficient and measurable performance variance and employee desire for assessment) are often not met, many organizations use pay ranges only for seniority. It is typical for ranges to reward seniority when performance is not a consideration or when employees want seniority pay. Seniority pay ranges may be desirable as a matter of policy. One example of this would be a situation in which management knows that job performance varies with length of service but performance itself is extremely costly to measure. In this situation, it may be desirable to reward on seniority because performance is assumed to increase with seniority.

A second situation in which a seniority pay policy may be appropriate occurs when it is highly desirable to encourage employees to stay with the company. If turnover is extremely costly to the organization, it may be cheaper in the long run to reward for seniority and realize reduced turnover costs.[16] This is especially true for jobs that require long and costly training times or other extensive investment in labor resources.

### Examples of Merit and Seniority Pay Ranges

An example of three pay ranges—a merit range, a seniority range, and a combination range—is presented in Exhibit 10.9. (A training step range design is not presented because it is a special case of a seniority pay range policy.)

Part A in Exhibit 10.9 depicts a pay range established to reward performance. One of the primary considerations in setting pay ranges for merit is how large the spread of the pay range should be. From a decision-making standpoint, two primary variables in setting the range are the average length of time an employee remains in a job in that range and the size of the pay increases that are expected to be granted. In terms of length of tenure, the concern is with how many pay increases will have to be allowed for the typical employee. Actual increases may vary from the average, but an average increase for the average employee should allow the employee to reach the top of the range at about the end of the expected tenure period for the job. If the organization wishes to give pay increases that average 5 percent, and average tenure is about 5 years, the organization would need to establish a pay range slightly greater than 25 percent (to allow for the compounding effect of adding one increase onto the other). An alternative approach is to have the average employee wages stop at the midpoint of the range. To move beyond the midpoint, the employee would have to exceed the performance of the average performer on a continuous basis.

**EXHIBIT 10.9** **PAY RANGES AND THEIR USES**

### A. Pay Ranges for Performance Rewards

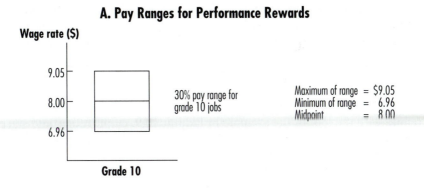

30% pay range for
grade 10 jobs

Maximum of range = $9.05
Minimum of range = 6.96
Midpoint = 8.00

### B. Pay Ranges for Membership Reward (Seniority)

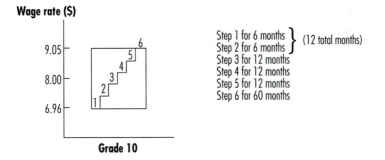

Step 1 for 6 months ⎫
Step 2 for 6 months ⎬ (12 total months)
Step 3 for 12 months
Step 4 for 12 months
Step 5 for 12 months
Step 6 for 60 months

### C. Pay Ranges for Rewarding Membership and Performance

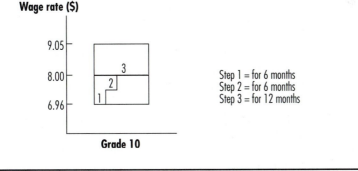

Step 1 = for 6 months
Step 2 = for 6 months
Step 3 = for 12 months

Movement from the minimum to the midpoint is based on how the employee performance is progressing as compared with the level of performance that should be expected of an average performer during that time period.

The second variable of considerable importance is the size of the increase. Some literature suggests that increases that are not large enough may not even be perceived by the employee.[17] For wage increases to have any value in rewarding performance, they should at least be between 5 and 6 percent, which requires a pay range of 25 to 30 percent if average tenure is 5 years.

One formula for setting the minimum and maximum pay rates is to divide the wage rate from the trend line (the midpoint rate for the range) by 100 percent plus one-half the desired percentage range. The midpoint of $8.00 would be divided by 1.15 percent in part A of Exhibit 10.9. The base wage for this range is $6.96, and 30 percent above this is $9.05.

A typical pay range for rewarding long membership is displayed in part B of Exhibit 10.9. This pay system provides for a pay increase at fixed intervals of tenure with the job. In the example in Exhibit 10.9, employees would start at the minimum rate, move up a step after six months, move up another step at the end of one year, and move up in consecutive steps until they reach the top of the grade after four years in the job.

### Ranges for Combination of Merit and Seniority

Organizations may combine seniority with merit as shown in part C in Exhibit 10.9. Here the organization allows for seniority increases after six months and one year.

The philosophy behind this approach is that all employees who are capable of performing the job at a satisfactory performance level should make the average pay (midpoint of range) for the job. The example assumes an employee should be able to perform at a satisfactory level after two years in the job and the wage will be automatically adjusted based on months of service. A secondary issue here is the question: Should employees who are learning faster than most be able to progress through the seniority levels at a faster rate than the average employee?

### Reasons for Multiple Pay Structures

Although an organization may develop one wage structure for the entire organization, it is more realistic to think in terms of an organization having multiple wage structures. Organizations employ many types of labor (such as managerial, clerical, operative, and sales talent). For several reasons, the organization may not want to or be able to integrate all these occupational job families into one wage structure. One reason why this may not be practical is that it is difficult to find compensable factors that are appropriate for distinguishing among jobs across job families. For example, working conditions are not an appropriate factor to distinguish among managerial jobs, nor is decision-making authority appropriate to distinguish among operative jobs.

A second reason for having many wage structures is that jobs are usually anchored to a specific labor market. Clerical talent may come from a relatively narrow labor market, whereas sales talent may be drawn from a broader market. Wage structures across jobs families may pose problems when it comes time to price those jobs.

A third reason for multiple structures is the labor union. Unions are more concerned about equity for jobs in the bargaining unit (the jobs held by union members) than about equity for jobs in general. Where wage structure considerations are under the joint decision of management and labor, only the union jobs are considered.[18]

Fourth, technology may influence which jobs are included in a given wage structure. Although it is true that technology tends to be constant within an industry, there is also variation in technology to some extent. For example, there is considerable variation in technology between a fast-food hamburger stand and the neighborhood deli. One might also expect these differences to influence the relationships among jobs within these respective organizations.[19]

Given these forces that have an effect on the way jobs are combined and organized, it should not be surprising that multiple wage structures may be administratively convenient. The compensation decision maker may decide, for example, to have one wage structure for the operative jobs (production jobs), another for jobs in the warehouse, another for the engineering staff, and a fourth wage structure for the managerial and office staff.

## Multiple Wage Structure Relationships

If an organization uses multiple wage structures, then balancing equity perceptions among the various wage structures may become an important compensation decision-making issue. An obvious situation that challenges interstructure equity is the union's negotiation of a wage (or benefit) increase for bargaining unit members. Nonunion employees in the other wage structures may wonder why they too are not eligible for more money. Organizations will often adjust the wage structure upward for these other groups as well, particularly if there is strong concern about interstructure equity. Wage adjustments between union and nonunion wage structures have been referred to as *tandem wage adjustments*.

A similar situation can exist for any two wage structures. For example, the firm may adjust the wage structure of engineers. If it does so, it has the problem of deciding whether to adjust the other wage structures as well to eliminate perceptions of inequity.

In many regards, the comparable worth issue discussed in Chapter 5 is related to multiple wage structure equity questions. Some job clusters are female- (usually clerical) or male- (usually maintenance) dominated. Because there are often large differences between wage rates for clerical and maintenance jobs (maintenance jobs generally pay higher), questions arise as to the fairness of these differences. This inequity is being challenged by comparable worth advocates.

## Pricing Job Grades

If the organization has made a policy decision to group jobs together and use job grades, then it will price the job grades and consider all jobs that fall point-wise within the job grade similarly in regard to wages. Often bivariate distribution will show natural clusterings of jobs that can be used in pricing the job structure. Exhibit 10.10 illustrates how job grades are priced. The jobs being priced here are low-level and service job cluster; thus, the lowest job grade will start at minimum wage and have an overlap of 40 percent and a range of 30

| EXHIBIT 10.10 | PRICING OF JOB GRADES (RANGE = 30%; OVERLAP = 40%) | | | | |

|  | Minimum | Midpoint | Maximum | Max–Min | 1-Overlap |
|---|---|---|---|---|---|
| Grade 1 (Points 100–200) | $4.25 | $4.89 | $5.53 | $1.28 × | 0.60 = $0.77 |
| Grade 2 (201–300) | $5.02 | $5.78 | $6.53 | $1.51 × | 0.60 = $0.91 |
| Grade 3 (301–400) | $5.93 | $6.82 | $7.71 | $1.78 × | 0.60 = $1.07 |
| Grade 4 (401–500) | $7.00 | $8.05 | $9.10 | $2.10 × | 0.60 = $1.26 |
| Grade 5 (501–600) | $8.26 | $9.50 | $10.74 | $2.48 × | 0.60 = $1.49 |
| Grade 6 (601–700) | $9.75 | $11.21 | $12.67 | | |

percent. The starting wage for grade 1 is set at minimum wage, and the maximum is the minimum multiplied by the range and added to the minimum ($4.25 × 0.30 = $1.275). Thus, the maximum for grade 1 is $4.25 + $1.28 = $5.53 per hour. To have a 40 percent overlap between grades 1 and 2, the minimum of grade 2 will start 60 percent (1 - 0.40 = 0.60) through grade 1. Thus, take the per-hour range of grade 1 ($1.28) and multiply it by 60 percent ($1.28 × 0.60 = $.77) to arrive at the cents per hour that must be added to the minimum of grade 1 to yield the per-hour starting rate for grade 2 ($4.25 + $0.77 = $5.02). This method yields a 40 percent overlap, a range of 30 percent and an approximate 18 percent increase from each midpoint to the midpoint of each subsequent higher grade.

An alternate approach is to use the following procedure. First, plot a bivariate distribution of all key jobs. Second, calculate a line of best fit for the data points in the distribution. Third, develop your job grades. For example, using data in Exhibit 10.10, there will be 6 job grades, grade 1 starting at 100 points with each additional grade being 100 points in width. Fourth, find the midpoint of the job grade points (that is, for grade 1 it would be 150 points) and move directly above to intersect the least-squared regression line and proceed horizontally to the y axis, which will provide the wage dollar rate. Fifth, determine your minimums and maximums from that point on the least-squared line. That is, if the organization wishes the spread to be 15 percent above and below the anchor point ($4.89), it would yield a maximum of $5.63 and a minimum of $4.25 per year for grade 1. As one can see, this provides a slightly different minimum and maximum than the first approach.

## Range Overlap

In an integrated pay structure, the overlap in the ranges from one job grade to another is generally considered to be no threat to internal equity because it allows incumbents in lower jobs to make as much as or more than incumbents in higher jobs under conditions of greater seniority or higher performance. Employees generally consider these conditions valid reasons for pay differences. It is possible, however, to have a set of jobs (such as those hierarchically adjacent in promotion ladders), in which too much overlap is dysfunctional. For example, if there is 70 percent overlap between two jobs, and an incumbent in the lower-grade job at the top of the range is promoted to the higher job, then there is only a small opportunity to continue to reward that person on the new job. When jobs in one grade are feeder jobs for the next higher grade, the organization may want to have less overlap. Some experts note that there should be no more than a 50 percent overlap in ranges. Others suggest that the top of the lower-level job's range should be below the midpoint of the next higher graded job.

# Implementing and Maintaining a Systematic Pay Structure

Beginning with the discussion of job analysis in Chapter 7 and ending with the discussion of pay ranges in this chapter, this text has traced the components and the administrative activities necessary to create a comprehensive wage structure. These components and activities can now be put together for the pay structure to emerge. Exhibit 10.11 is a graphic representation of a completed pay structure. Once the pay structure is completed, its implementation becomes the key consideration.

## Linking Pay Structure to Policy

Once the organization knows what the relationship is between the internal and external value of jobs, it must decide on the desired pay policy. The organization, in its pricing, must determine if it desires to pay less (lag), pay greater (lead), or pay at (follow) the product or labor market pay rates. For example, if the firm is going to lag the market and the market is paying a specific job $25,000 per year, the organization may have a policy of paying 90 percent of the market and thus would price the job at $22,500.

## Updating Total Wage Pay

After the new wage structure is in place, several procedures should be implemented to maintain it. The organization should conduct periodic labor and product market surveys to ensure that the wage structure remains current in its relationship to practices in other organizations. Normally it is sufficient to resurvey key jobs every 12 to 24 months. Instability in labor market demand/supply ratios and high rates of inflation, however, will motivate more frequent surveying.

| EXHIBIT 10.11 | A PAY STRUCTURE AND ITS ELEMENTS |

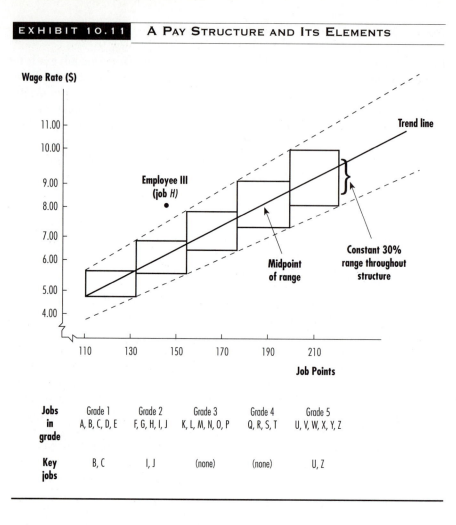

| Jobs in grade | Grade 1 A, B, C, D, E | Grade 2 F, G, H, I, J | Grade 3 K, L, M, N, O, P | Grade 4 Q, R, S, T | Grade 5 U, V, W, X, Y, Z |
| --- | --- | --- | --- | --- | --- |
| Key jobs | B, C | I, J | (none) | (none) | U, Z |

A secondary issue is the updating of the pay structure from year to year. Organizations normally adjust the total pay structure annually (general increase; excluding merit) after they have obtained new product and labor market rates. It is also important when collecting this data to know when the surveyed organizations last adjusted their pay structure and the expected increase for the next year. This should be done so that adjustments to the pay structures for the upcoming year will maintain the position the organization wants to be in, in comparison with its competitors, throughout the year. For example, if the organization's pay policy is to pay at the midpoint of the market, and the pay structure is adjusted to reflect market data, it may fall quickly behind that midpoint if the surveyed organizations provide data which is 11 months old. The surveyed organizations would increase their wages almost immediately, and the surveying organization would be paying below the midpoint and thus not complying with its own pay policy. Organizations that know when the pay increase of surveyed firms is scheduled to take place and what that increase will be are better able to schedule their wage increases to maximize wage policy compliance. They may give half the general increase immediately and the other half at the end of the next 6 months.

Existence of an ongoing job evaluation committee also helps to maintain the pay structure. This practice is common in union and management settings. The purpose of such committees is to re-evaluate those jobs that have changed substantially since the implementation of the program or to evaluate new jobs. Changes in jobs occur as technology changes, work processes change, and management decides to redesign jobs. In non-unionized settings, job evaluations may also be conducted by committees or by professional job analysts. An appeal procedure should be designed to address employees who believe their job has been unfairly paid. The specifics of the appeal procedure should be custom-designed to fit the organization's culture and to deal with the grievance in a timely manner.

## Initial Adjustment of Rates

When a new pay plan is introduced, there are likely to be many employees whose wages are below or above the ranges dictated by the new program. Wages paid employees below the dictated rates are said to have *"green circle"* pay rates. In theory, these employees' rates would be increased to the minimum of their grade immediately on implementation of the new plan. However, this may not be practical. For example, an employer may be locked into long-term contracts for products whose cost is based on the lower wages. In such cases, implementation of the new wage program might be delayed until the organization can afford to bring all green-circle rates to the minimum of the new structure. A formal time schedule of wage increases should be developed and communicated to affected employees.

A problem arises when jobs or incumbents are above the pay range for the job. For example, in Exhibit 10.11 one employee's pay rate is above the range for job H given the job's pay grade. What should be done in this situation?

Many solutions to this problem have been suggested. The most practical one is known as "red-circling" the job incumbent's pay. *Red-circling* means that the incumbent's pay is kept at its present level, but the job itself is brought into line within the pay structure. Thus, although the incumbent's pay will stay at the higher rate, all new individuals hired into the job will be paid according to the pay policy dictated by the internal wage structure—the range for that job. Red-circling the incumbent's pay rate may also mean that further pay raises will not be granted until the wage structure overtakes the current rate. This will happen gradually as inflation causes the entire wage structure to shift upward. Extreme care must be taken in explaining to the affected employee why this action was taken.

A slight variation to this policy is to red-circle the rate of incumbents whose jobs are out of line and to attempt to transfer them to jobs whose wage rates are consistent with the employees' current pay. If an employee refuses the transfer, the current pay is reduced in accordance with the pay range for the job. The reduction in pay could be the total amount or it could be done over time to permit the employee to adjust to a different standard of living.

These approaches are preferred over direct pay reduction, which will generate employee resistance to a new systematic wage structure. At the start of the process of designing a pay system, to allay fears of the new program, management usually communicates to employees that no one's pay will be reduced as a result of the new pay policies.

Two points should be emphasized. First, red-circling concerns job incumbents and not jobs. That is, the red circle applies to the rate that an incumbent is paid, not to the job itself. This distinction is important because new entrants into the job are paid the rate as established by the new pay structure. Second, it is not sufficient for an individual in a job just to be in the appropriate range; the appropriate position within that range must also be determined. The first step, then, may be to get the individual's rate within the range; but once that is accomplished, where the individual's actual wage rate should fall must be determined based on past seniority and performance. It may be that additional adjustments will have to be made to ensure internal equity.

## Communicating with Employees

Communication with employees at each stage of the pay structure process is critical. At the time the decision is made to proceed with the design of a new pay system, employees should be informed that a reanalysis of current pay policies is under way. This communication should be both written and verbal. It should stress the goals of a new pay structure (including the organization's continued concern over fairness of wage payments) and assure employees that no one's pay will be reduced by a new pay structure. This is important to overcome possible resistance to the new program.

Communication should continue, both verbally and in writing, regarding the status of the project as it progresses. Employees are going to expect change, and it is helpful and settling to know when the changes are likely to occur.

At the time the program is put into place, employees should be told where their individual jobs fit into the new program (which grade). It is also appropriate to educate employees on how certain decisions were made (such as explaining that the method used to arrive at the median wage rate for the grades was to use the 50th percentile of the labor or product market). The criteria (merit, seniority) for moving through the grades should be clearly explained.

Employees should also be told if their individual pay rate is above their job's pay grade and what policy the company will follow to deal with this: to freeze the wage in the future or to transfer the employee to more highly valued work.

In general, it is desirable to keep employees as informed as possible about the new program. If the objective of the program is a more equitable wage system, both in an internal and external sense, then the value of the program is not likely to be fully appreciated unless it is communicated effectively.

## Training Managers

Ultimately, managers and supervisors throughout the organization are the people who will use the new wage structure. If they fail to implement the system properly on a day-to-day basis, the system is likely to fail regardless of how well it is designed.

Managers should be trained in several areas. They should understand the new pay system in terms of how it was developed and what it is attempting to achieve. They should be comfortable with its implementation and able to explain it to the employees. If merit pay is to be a part of the plan, the decision-making role of managers becomes even more important. Managers need to know the goals of the merit pay plan and how it was conceived (performance appraisal is the subject of Chapter 11). For continued implementation of the plan, they also need to be trained in how to conduct effective performance appraisals; this includes training in the recognition of biases, the legal considerations in performance appraisal, the purposes and workings of the organization's performance appraisal system, the importance of accurate appraisal, the importance of employee acceptance, and the role of performance appraisal from a strategic management perspective. Failure to train managers in these important areas can result in useless or counterproductive appraisals, which in turn may mean that the organization's goal of rewarding merit may not be realized and behaviors may not be channeled to increase the organization's effectiveness and efficiency in reaching its long-term goals.

## Wage Compression

Wage compression is one potentially serious problem compensation decision makers must handle. It is defined as the narrowing of the wage differential between positions. For example, the wage differential between Jobs A and B in the past might have been $1.00, but over a few years, for several different reasons, it was reduced to $0.35. (If the wage of a lower valued job actually surpasses the wage of a higher valued job, it is called *wage inversion*.)

The causes of wage compression can be of internal or external origin. Wage compression occurs due to internal causes when flat wage increases upset the pay structure or when there are weaknesses in the pay structure itself: when excessive overlaps exist between pay grades, when too few pay grades lump dissimilar jobs together, or when small pay ranges do not permit significant room to reward different contribution.[20] There are several significant external causes that need elaboration. First, an external tight labor market may require the organization to set the pay of new employees at a higher level than the internal wage structure allows already employed workers to receive. To solve this problem, some firms lower the hiring standards of new hirees so wage differentials between the positions do not narrow. Some organizations pay a hiring bonus but increase wages only equal to that of the total wage structure. This policy may cause serious turnover problems in the future as these employees learn their wage is significantly below the market. But current employees may believe there is compression if the wage differential and the lower hiring standards do not correspond. Second, compression may occur each time there is a change in the Fair Labor Standards Act; the firm may be required to raise the wage of minimum wage positions beyond the level of the increase allowed in the wage structure. If an organization has many employees at or near minimum wage level, this could have significant impact on the employee perception of the degree of fairness of the compensation. Wage structures rarely increase in a given year by as large a percentage as changes in minimum wage. To off-set this compression caused by a new minimum wage, organizations will often keep increases for the jobs at the minimum wage level to a lower percentage than the general increase for a number of years until the previous differential is restored. A third external cause of compression is union activity. Unions, because of their bargaining power, may obtain a higher wage increase or a more lucrative overtime provision for their members than the non-unionized employees. This may cause serious supervisory–subordinate compression. Many organizations provide the non-union employees the same package they provide unionized workers (defined earlier as tandem wage adjustment). For supervisors, they may pay the supervisor 15 percent more than the highest paid employee or pay overtime after a set number of hours (for example, 48 hours). Fourth, geographic wage premiums are usually offered to employees who work in a higher cost-of-living area. This can cause problems when the employee is returned to a lower cost area. Employers are often reluctant to reduce wages equal to the reduced cost of living, and thus the transferred employee's wage may be out of position in the new location.[21] It is probably best to reduce the wage to the local market level, and if this is not acceptable, some other employee should be given the opportunity to relocate.

The best solution to wage compression is to design the compensation system properly and to monitor it continuously so that it remains both equitable and competitive. A properly designed system provides a range of wages with an adequate difference between midpoints of pay grades. It includes well-defined levels of performance which an employee must achieve for movement within a grade or promotion into the next grade. Even the best system can face compression problems. Managers must establish a formal method of review to monitor the systsem. They may use compa-ratios to reveal the distribution and concentration of wages within a range. *Compa-ratio* is defined as the ratio of actual wages to the midpoint of the wage range for a given wage range. They may study the present employees in each quartile of the wage range. They may focus on relationships between seniority and wages, watching for normal rates of movement. No matter how well the system is designed, carried out, and monitored, there is no perfect defense against compression. Managers must always attempt to balance the monetary costs of preventing compression with the psychological costs (employee dissatisfaction) of allowing it to occur.

## A Structureless System

The traditional methods of determining pay levels create a definite structure by which managers must abide. This structure is intended to ensure that pay is equitable, that it is competitive, and that it is reasonable (in terms of the organization's ability to pay).

Some authors advocate the use, instead, of a structureless system—one in which line managers determine what to pay their people. Under this approach, managers would establish pay levels for new employees and determine the amount and the timing of raises. In a 1992 article, A. W. Smith explained the benefits of this structureless salary approach.[22] First, since managers set the pay levels, pay is more closely linked to performance. Second, this closer link between pay and performance strengthens the motivational effect of the pay program. And, third, time is better used; thus, productivity is increased.

Obviously, this rather radical departure from the traditional approach would not work everywhere. Smith suggests its implementation only in companies with decentralized management systems and autonomous business units. Line managers must have clear profit responsibilities for a structureless pay system to be successful. The structureless system is not likely to replace the more traditional approach in most organizations.

## Summary

By this point in the text, all the necessary tools and skills to implement a systematic wage structure have been discussed. Also, the goals of a compensation system and the theoretic foundations for the administrative practices that are a part of the compensation decision-maker's job have been presented in detail.

This chapter focuses on designing an integrated pay structure. Job evaluation data and labor and product market data on key jobs are employed to develop a trend line of wage rates that reflects both internal and external equity. The chapter explains the use and establishment of pay ranges, the reasons for multiple pay structures, and the actual pricing of pay grades. It handles some of the problems associated with implementing the pay structure, and it stresses the continual need for communicating with employees and monitoring and updating the system. In subsequent chapters, the remaining components of a total compensation program are discussed.

## Discussion Questions

1. Should an organization put wage caps on the wage potential of any position? If it did, would it hurt the ability of the organization to attract, retain or motivate employees?

2. Suppose an organization finds that the wage structure in its product market is less steeply sloped than the wage structure in its labor market. What implications would this have for designing a wage structure, and how would this affect the wage bill? (Assume that the two trend lines intersect about halfway through the job hierarchy.)

3. Discuss the concept of a red-circle rate and discuss why red-circling is preferable to other approaches of adjusting wages.

4. What are pay ranges used for, and what influences the percentage spread in the range?

5. Discuss the concept of a flat-rate pay system. Why might an organization use a flat-rate system?

6. Should the pay ranges be of equal percentage? If yes, why? If not, why?

## EXERCISES

Following are information and data about the current pay practices of the Olson Company, along with labor and product market wage data, job evaluation data, and limited financial information. Based on these data, design a comprehensive wage structure for the Olson Company that is consistent with the goals and objectives of a compensation program as outlined in this text. Be sure to make recommendations and support each recommendation with the appropriate reasoning consistent with the known parameters that are critical for shaping a wage structure. Also, demonstrate your mastery of the techniques used in designing a wage structure. Do one analysis with A data for turnover and product market information, and then repeat the analysis with B data.

## Exercise 1

The Olson Company, located in a large metropolitan area, is a distributor of sand and gravel. The company employs 140 unskilled laborers and 20 exempt employees.

The Olson Company is an old and venerated supplier to individual homeowners and major construction companies. The company provides sand and gravel to homeowners doing self-repair work on driveways and self-built garages and other buildings. This was their main business until 1961. Since 1961, the company's principal market has been major construction companies. They provide sand and gravel to these companies for driveways and foundations, and occasionally they provide extensive concrete contracts on large commercial buildings.

During the early 1970s, the company's wage level was competitive in the labor market. As the general wage level began to rise, the Olson Company failed to adjust its wage level accordingly. The company soon found that it was paying only the minimum federal wage, which resulted in a heavy turnover of personnel, but management was not worried because the labor market was fairly loose, and they were able to keep an adequate work force.

As the labor market got tighter, management experienced increasing problems with maintaining a work force of sufficient quality and quantity to operate the company. With great reluctance, management adjusted the wage level enough to reduce turnover to about 45 percent.

Years passed, during which management made no additional wage adjustments. General wage levels increased considerably, and although the labor market is currently quite loose, the company has considerable turnover and is experiencing an inability to attract new workers.

In response to these problems, the company hired a dynamic human resource manager with particular expertise in compensation. The human resource manager immediately undertook a systematic analysis of the problems faced by Olson, spending long days and weeks amassing data to guide recommendations to the president. Some of these data are contained in the following tables. Also, the following human resource policies were already in effect.

The company has a single flat-rate system of pay for each job; hiring rates and any pay changes are negotiated by the individual employee with management.

All jobs throughout the unskilled job family tend to be filled from outside the company through newspaper ads or walk-ins.

Some turnover is good (as a matter of policy) because it discourages too stable a work force and, therefore, unionization.

On average, it costs $400 to recruit, train, and process onto the payroll one nonexempt employee.

The company has a modest profit-sharing plan (10 percent net profit) but no other employee benefits.

The new human resource manager was stricken with a heart attack after collecting all the data and will be completely incapacitated for 8 months. The Olson Company, not wanting to let their turnover problem deteriorate further, has retained you as a consultant to analyze and make recommendations on the data gathered by the human resource manager.

## Revenues from Sources of Business

| Year | Individuals | Contractors |
|------|-------------|-------------|
| 1960 | $0.12 million | $ 0.01 million |
| 1965 | 0.16 million | 0.09 million |
| 1970 | 0.22 million | 0.22 million |
| 1975 | 0.30 million | 0.42 million |
| 1980 | 0.48 million | 0.72 million |
| 1985 | 0.72 million | 1.30 million |
| 1990 | 0.90 million | 1.44 million |

## Results of Job Evaluation

| Job No. | Points | Current Flat Hourly Rate |
|---------|--------|--------------------------|
| 1 | 195 | $5.30 |
| 2 | 200 | 5.30 |
| 3 | 200 | 5.40 |
| 4 | 205 | 5.60 |
| 5 | 205 | 5.40 |
| 6 | 210 | 5.20 |

*(continued)*

**Exercise 1** *(continued)*

**Results of Job Evaluation** *(continued)*

| Job No. | Points | Current Flat Hourly Rate |
|---|---|---|
| 7 | 210 | 5.50 |
| 8 | 210 | 5.60 |
| 9 | 215 | 6.00 |
| 10 | 215 | 6.35 |
| 11 | 215 | 6.45 |
| 12 | 220 | 6.15 |
| 13 | 220 | 6.15 |
| 14 | 220 | 6.55 |
| 15 | 230 | 6.65 |
| 16 | 235 | 6.65 |
| 17 | 240 | 6.75 |
| 18 | 240 | 6.95 |
| 19 | 250 | 6.85 |
| 20 | 250 | 7.05 |
| 21 | 250 | 7.15 |
| 22 | 255 | 7.05 |
| 23 | 255 | 6.95 |
| 24 | 260 | 7.45 |
| 25 | 260 | 7.15 |
| 26 | 270 | 7.25 |
| 27 | 270 | 7.50 |
| 28 | 280 | 7.70 |
| 29 | 280 | 7.80 |
| 30 | 290 | 8.00 |

**Results from Labor Market Wage and Salary Survey (N = 15 Firms)**

| Job No. | Low[a] | Median[a] | High[a] |
|---|---|---|---|
| 1 | $5.20 | $5.40 | $5.60 |
| 3 | 5.50 | 5.70 | 5.90 |
| 7 | 5.80 | 5.90 | 6.00 |
| 13 | 5.90 | 6.25 | 6.55 |
| 15 | 6.45 | 6.85 | 7.30 |
| 17 | 6.65 | 6.95 | 7.30 |
| 20 | 6.85 | 7.15 | 7.50 |
| 24 | 7.30 | 7.70 | 8.10 |
| 26 | 7.70 | 8.10 | 8.50 |
| 29 | 8.00 | 8.50 | 9.00 |

[a]The average of the five lowest, five median, and five highest wage rates for each job.

***Exercise 1*** *(continued)*

### "A" Data for Product Market Wage and Salary Survey

| Job No. | Average Hourly Rate |
|:---:|:---:|
| 1 | $5.35 |
| 3 | 5.44 |
| 7 | 5.87 |
| 13 | 6.07 |
| 15 | 6.58 |
| 17 | 6.65 |
| 20 | 7.25 |
| 24 | 7.40 |
| 26 | 7.96 |
| 29 | 8.08 |

### "A" Data for Analysis of Turnover for Olson Company Jobs

| Job No. | No. of Positions | Annual No. of Voluntary Quits |
|:---:|:---:|:---:|
| 1 | 10 | 13 |
| 2 | 10 | 14 |
| 3 | 5 | 7 |
| 4 | 5 | 8 |
| 5 | 6 | 8 |
| 6 | 6 | 11 |
| 7 | 6 | 9 |
| 8 | 6 | 9 |
| 9 | 6 | 8 |
| 10 | 6 | 3 |
| 11 | 5 | 1 |
| 12 | 5 | 7 |
| 13 | 5 | 6 |
| 14 | 5 | 1 |
| 15 | 5 | 2 |
| 16 | 5 | 2 |
| 17 | 5 | 2 |
| 18 | 5 | 2 |
| 19 | 4 | 3 |
| 20 | 4 | 0 |
| 21 | 3 | 0 |
| 22 | 3 | 1 |
| 23 | 3 | 1 |
| 24 | 3 | 0 |
| 25 | 3 | 3 |
| 26 | 3 | 4 |
| 27 | 2 | 0 |
| 28 | 2 | 1 |
| 29 | 2 | 0 |
| 30 | 2 | 0 |

*(continued)*

*Exercise 1* (*continued*)

## "B" Data for Product Market Wage and Salary Survey

| Job No. | Average Hourly Rate |
|---------|---------------------|
| 1       | $5.65               |
| 3       | 5.90                |
| 7       | 6.00                |
| 13      | 6.40                |
| 15      | 6.50                |
| 17      | 6.70                |
| 20      | 7.05                |
| 24      | 7.15                |
| 26      | 7.50                |
| 29      | 7.60                |

## "B" Data for Analysis of Turnover for Olson Company Jobs

| Job No. | No. of Positions | Annual No. of Voluntary Quits |
|---------|------------------|-------------------------------|
| 1       | 10               | 7                             |
| 2       | 10               | 5                             |
| 3       | 5                | 3                             |
| 4       | 5                | 2                             |
| 5       | 6                | 5                             |
| 6       | 6                | 6                             |
| 7       | 6                | 4                             |
| 8       | 6                | 3                             |
| 9       | 6                | 2                             |
| 10      | 6                | 0                             |
| 11      | 5                | 1                             |
| 12      | 5                | 3                             |
| 13      | 5                | 3                             |
| 14      | 5                | 0                             |
| 15      | 5                | 1                             |
| 16      | 5                | 0                             |
| 17      | 5                | 2                             |
| 18      | 5                | 0                             |
| 19      | 4                | 3                             |
| 20      | 4                | 7                             |
| 21      | 3                | 5                             |
| 22      | 3                | 7                             |
| 23      | 3                | 12                            |
| 24      | 3                | 5                             |
| 25      | 3                | 6                             |
| 26      | 3                | 12                            |
| 27      | 2                | 5                             |
| 28      | 2                | 5                             |
| 29      | 2                | 5                             |
| 30      | 2                | 7                             |

## Exercise 2

Assume the role of the compensation manager for Aero manufacturing company. On your desk is a recommendation for the promotion of Jim Zep. Jim currently occupies a job that falls into grade 4 and is being recommended for promotion to a grade 5 job. Jim has been an outstanding performer in his current position, and therefore, his current salary is at the top of grade 4. Because of the overlap in pay grades, even if he is given no salary increase when promoted, his salary would be beyond the minimum of grade 5. It is normal policy for those being promoted to start near the bottom of the salary range because training is necessary to become proficient on the job. It is also customary for the employee to receive some salary increase when a promotion is earned. If Jim were granted the normal percentage increase that corresponds to a promotion, his salary would be near the midpoint of grade 5. This may cause an inequity problem with some current job holders in this grade who have not reached the midpoint themselves.

You will be meeting with Jim's present and future supervisors to determine what to do in this situation. Before the meeting, you prefer to have several alternatives to suggest for dealing with this salary issue. It is very important that this case is handled well because this is the first promotion since the company has instituted job grades and formal job ranges.

## Exercise 3

You have just completed formal job evaluation and corresponding pricing of the job structure. For the jobs that are underpaid, you are recommending immediate wage increase to the appropriate position within the salary range. For those jobs above the maximum, you are recommending a phased-in reduction to the maximum of the range. You have one problem position that is giving you a dilemma. The position most overpaid is the secretary to the president and owner, who has been with the firm for 15 years. What are your suggestions to the president, who must approve all the above recommendations?

### References

[1] S. E. Gross, "Customizing Compensation: The Right Diagnostic Tools," *Compensation and Benefits Review* 21 (November/December 1989), 24–33.

[2] C. H. Fay, "External Pay Relationships," in *Compensation and Benefits*, Luis R. Gomez–Mejia, ed. (Washington, DC: Bureau of National Affairs, 1989), 3–70, 3–97.

[3] F. S. Hills, "Comparable Worth: Implications for Compensation Managers," *Compensation Review* 14 (1982), 33–43.

[4] G. S. Crystal, "The Reemergence of Industry Pay Differentials," *Compensation Review* 15 (1983), 29–32.

[5] C. H. Fay, "External Pay Relationships."

[6] Task Force to the Secretary of Health, Education, and Welfare, *Work in America* (Cambridge, MA: MIT Press, 1973).

[7] J. D. England and D. A. Pierson, "Salary Ranges and Merit Matrices: The Time Targeting Approach," *Compensation and Benefits Review* 22 (July/August 1990), 36–47. See complete article for a detailed explanation.

[8] M. E. Personick, "White-Collar Pay Determination Unclear Range-of-Rate Systems," *Monthly Labor Review* 107 (October/December 1984), 25.

[9] C. Brown, "Firms' Choice of Method of Pay," *Industrial and Labor Relations Review* 43 (February 1990), 165–182.

[10] L. S. Festinger and K. Back, *Social Pressures in Informal Groups* (New York: Harper and Row, 1950).

[11]D. B. McFarlin and M. R. Frone, "A Two-Tier Wage Structure in a Non Union Firm," *Industrial Relations* 29 (Winter 1990), 145–154.

[12]England and Pierson, "Salary Ranges and Merit Matrices."

[13]*Ibid.*

[14]*Ibid.*

[15]*Ibid.*

[16]D. R. Dalton, W. D. Todor, D. M. Krackhardt, "Turnover Overstated: The Functional Taxonomy," *Academy of Management Review* 7 (1982), 117-123.

[17]See, for example, L. A. Krefting and T. A. Mahoney, "Determining the Size of a Meaningful Pay Increase," *Industrial Relations* 16 (February 1977), 83–93.

[18]R. B. Freeman, "Union Wage Practices and Wage Dispersion within Establishments," *Industrial and Labor Relations Review* 36 (October 1982), 3–21.

[19]E. R. Livernash, "The Internal Wage Structure," in *New Concepts in Wage Determination*, G. W. Taylor and F. C. Pierson, eds. (New York: McGraw-Hill, 1957), 143–172.

[20]T. J. Bergmann, M. A. Bergmann, D. Roff, and V. Scarpello, "Salary Compression: Causes and Solutions," *Compensation and Benefits Management* 7 (Fall 1991), 7–16.

[21]*Ibid.*

[22]A. W. Smith, "Structureless Salary Management: A Modest Proposal," *Compensation and Benefits Review* 24 (July/August 1992), 22–25.

# 11

# Performance Assessment

# Learning Objectives

**To learn the relationship between merit pay and subjective performance assessment systems.**

**To learn the process of conducting employee performance reviews.**

**To learn the major types of errors, biases, and problems that enter into the performance review process.**

**To learn the major ways in which performance assessment systems come under legal scrutiny.**

**To learn some of the more common approaches to performance assessment.**

**To learn how performance assessment information is linked to pay decisions.**

# Introduction

This chapter deals with the process of performance assessment, examining such assessment in the light of (1) its objectives, (2) the major methods involved, (3) the legal parameters, (4) the more important biases that interfere with its accuracy, and (5) the application to pay determination.

This chapter provides an appreciation for performance assessment, an understanding of the assessment techniques available, and the means to design a performance assessment system to accomplish compensation objectives.

## People Assessment versus Job Assessment Revisited

Chapter 8 described job evaluation as a process used to establish the relative worth of jobs. Job evaluation results in a hierarchy of jobs; it does not deal with a person's worth, but with job worth.

Performance assessment is the process of determining the relative worth of employees within a given job. Performance assessment, therefore, determines how well a person is doing in a job. If the organization does not have pay ranges and pays one set amount for a job, it cannot have performance-based pay (unless the firm uses a technique such as a lump sum bonus to reward yearly perfor- mance). Pay ranges, as indicated in an earlier chapter, permit pay for perfor- mance. Performance assessment determines the individual's position within the wage range based on his or her performance when compared with the established job standards. In other words, performance assessment establishes which people in a certain job are superior performers, which people are average performers, and which are poor performers.

Job evaluation and performance assessment differ in their purposes. Both are important in pay determination. Job evaluation establishes the relative worth of jobs and is used to determine job pay, whereas performance assessment establishes relative pay within jobs (that is, individual equity). This chapter deals with assessing employees' performance relative to their jobs.

## Purpose of Performance Assessment

Performance assessment is a process of identifying, measuring, evaluating, and developing human resources within the organization. The purposes of performance review are

To provide and receive adequate feedback to and from the employee regarding the employee's past performance

To communicate and discuss organizational, departmental, and individual goals

To mutually identify the employee's developmental needs

To demonstrate commitment by the organization and the supervisor to the employee's developmental needs. This will usually require a commitment of time on the part of the supervisor and resources on the part of the organization

To identify and discuss with the employee the criteria used to allocate organizational rewards (for example, promotion, salary)

To provide proper documentation of the basis of human resource decisions

To receive feedback from the employee regarding what the supervisor is doing that aids and hinders performance on the job

## Uses of Performance Assessment Information

Performance assessments play an important role in most human resource decisions made in organizational settings. The assessment provides the data necessary to evaluate selection and training programs and to make transfer, termination, layoff, promotion, and salary decisions; thus, the assessment determines what kind of investment will be made in an employee. In one study, 91 percent of the firms surveyed used performance assessment in merit increases; 90 percent, in developmental feedback; 82 percent, in promotion decisions; 64 percent, in termination or layoff decisions; and 62 percent, to determine the potential of employees.[1] As the data illustrates, uses of performance assessment extend far beyond determination of merit pay. These assessments have significant influence in human resource decision making, and every effort should be made to increase their reliability, validity, and acceptability.

## Why Managers Dislike Performance Assessment

While performance assessment is critical to organizations, publications such as *The Wall Street Journal* note that employees dislike and mistrust the assessment process. Likewise, many supervisors admit uneasiness with the process and often conduct assessments only after pressure from the human resource department. The authors have presented performance assessment workshops for nearly 20 years; supervisors attending these workshops have repeatedly listed the following reasons for not liking the process:

> Enormous amount of time required to complete the paper work, prepare for the interviews, and conduct the interviews

> Fear of subjectivity in evaluating the employee (performance is hard to measure and outside factors may be having an effect on employee performance)

> Lack of training in how to document performance, what is to be documented, how to complete the forms, and how to handle the performance appraisal interview

> Strong desire to be liked by employees and fear that an honest evaluation may hinder that

> Feeling of conflicting roles — being a boss and a co-worker at the same time

> Inadequate forms to use in evaluation process

> Memories of poor past experiences regarding the whole process

> Knowledge that carrying out quality performance assessment is not included as a job standard on which the supervisor's own performance is evaluated

> Sense that recommendations are ignored, reversed, or changed by higher-level managers

> Lack of input into the design of the assessment system

> Knowledge that not all managers do performance assessment

> Perception that behaviors do not improve but at times deteriorate after the assessment

This chapter attempts to provide the reader with information that allows the design of a performance assessment system that reduces the intensity of the above complaints.

## Theoretical Foundation

The basic theories that are briefly related to performance assessment in this section are expectancy theory, reinforcement theory, equity theory (procedural and distributive justice), goal-setting theory, and implicit contract theory. Not only are these theories relevant to performance assessment but they form the basis for incentive pay (discussed in Chapter 12).

## *Expectancy Theory*

Performance assessment as an activity can be linked to several theories developed earlier in this text. Chapter 3 discussed expectancy theory and showed that before a pay system is likely to motivate high levels of performance, it must meet many conditions.[2] These and other conditions that are necessary for the success of a merit or performance pay system are summarized in Exhibit 11.1.

## *Reinforcement Theory*

Reinforcement theory as developed by Skinner and discussed in detail in Chapter 3 is also relevant to shaping employee performance. From a compensation perspective, reinforcement theory proposes that the outcomes (for example, pay, promotions) of the employment exchange should be closely tied to the behavior of the employee. Through performance assessment, the organization is attempting to strengthen the stimulus-response bonds of appropriate employee responses and weaken the stimulus response bonds of inappropriate responses. Recall that one of the purposes of performance assessment is to identify and discuss with the employee the criteria used to allocate organizational rewards. For example, the supervisor gives strong positive feedback at the quarterly performance review session to an employee who has performed very well during the past quarter. That is not to say that the supervisor does not provide positive feedback on a more frequent basis, but the performance review session permits a summarization and more formal recognition of the appropriate behavior. It also reinforces the association of any rewards with performance. However, if an employee is engaging in inappropriate or inadequate performance, the organization withholds any wage increase to extinguish that behavior. Here, again, the performance assessment should reinforce the association of poor performance with the absence of a wage increase. A more forceful way to eliminate

---

**EXHIBIT 11.1**   **CONDITIONS FOR A SUCCESSFUL MERIT OR PERFORMANCE PAY SYSTEM**

1. Employees must have the ability to perform at high levels.

2. Employees must believe they have the ability to perform at high levels.

3. Employees must value the receipt of more money.

4. Employees must value more money relative to other outcomes.

5. Employees must believe that level of pay is associated with level of effort.

6. There must be a method to measure performance.

7. The organization must be willing to discriminate on the basis of performance.

8. The performance assessment method must capture real and meaningful differences in performance.

an inappropriate behavior is through punishment; when performance is very inadequate or inappropriate, the organization may use a wage reduction to shock the employee into realizing that the behavior cannot continue. This practice, however, is not the suggested approach due to the long-term negative consequences of such action (for example, quitting, reduced effort).

### Equity Theory—Distributive and Procedural Justice

Early research in equity theory focused primarily on distributive justice (that is, fairness of outcomes); whereas the new interest in procedural justice focuses on methods (processes and procedures) used to arrive at outcomes.[3] See Chapter 3 for an explanation of equity theory.

Researchers have thoroughly studied distributive justice based on the concept of equity theory. Results indicate a small positive relationship between overpayment and increased outputs,[4] and between underpayment and decreased outputs.[5] A main limitation of this research is that distributive justice addresses the outcome of compensation decisions but does not address the process within which these decisions are made. To address that issue, researchers are focusing on the concept of procedural justice to examine the relationship between employees' views of the processes leading to outcomes and their attitudes and behaviors.[6]

Procedural justice identifies the concepts of *process control* and *decision control*.[7] Process control is the amount of input that participants have in the process of resolution of a dispute in which they are involved; decision control is the amount of influence they have in the outcomes. In subsequent studies, there has been strong evidence that individuals who are permitted process control (in a variety of situations) believe the procedure is fairer than those denied such input.[8] Specifically, in performance assessment, the degree of procedural input by employees appears critical in influencing the employees' perception of the firm's compensation program. Research to date has shown that employees perceive performance assessment as fairer when they are involved in the evaluation process.[9] One study found that employees perceived the performance assessment procedure, the rater, and the outcome as fairer when they participate in the evaluation.[10] Another study showed that procedural justice is related to employees' perception of fairness of the performance evaluation and satisfaction with pay raises.[11]

Seven elements have been identified as being important in influencing an individual's perception of the fairness of the decisions made.[12] Applying this to the performance assessment decision, employees who have some control or input regarding the following procedural elements will perceive the situation as fairer: (1) selection of the evaluation tool or technique; (2) establishment of performance assessment ground rules; (3) establishment of the procedures for gathering performance data; (4) structuring of the decision procedures; (5) existence of a procedure to appeal evaluation decisions—one recent study found that about 85 percent of *Fortune* 100 companies have either a formal or informal appeal procedure;[13] (6) establishment of procedures to ensure appropriate use of power by the manager making the assessment; and (7) existence of a mechanism to make an adjustment of the evaluation decision if the decision is deemed unfair.

Four interpersonal communication dimensions may also influence the employees' perception of the fairness of the performance assessment. The four procedural justice criteria are truthfulness, respect, propriety of questions, and justification.[14] Two studies have found a relationship between interpersonal communication and procedural justice.[15] Because a significant part of performance assessment revolves around the performance review interview, it is logical that a relationship between interpersonal communication and procedural justice is relevant to the performance assessment process.

### Goal-Setting Theory

The theory of goal setting indicates that employees work behavior is a result of attempting to reach pre-established goals.[16] When an employee successfully accomplishes (or surpasses) these goals, that employee is evaluated as being successful. The performance standards established for all employees occupying the same job can be considered common goals for that job. Besides common goals, most assessment systems require each employee to establish unique goals for each evaluation period, and the individual employees are evaluated separately against those individual goals.

The most direct application of goal setting is a technique called *management by objectives*, which is discussed later in this chapter. Research has shown that goal setting can improve performance if the goals are specific, challenging, attainable, and relevant.[17] The research on procedural justice tends to support the concept that employees should be involved in the setting of goals and that goals should not be given to them without their involvement.

### Implicit Contract Theory

Implicit contract theory is similar to marginal productivity theory in that it proposes that workers be paid based on their marginal contribution to productive capacity, but it differs from marginal productivity theory in that it assumes productivity varies among workers and, consequently, suggests that pay should vary correspondingly. Thus, if the organization does not vary pay based on performance, it will overpay some workers while underpaying others. Not only does this increase labor costs but also sends the wrong signal to both the underpaid and overpaid group of workers. As with any performance-based pay system, the measurement of actual employees' contributions becomes critical. Performance assessment is a process whereby performance variations can be identified and the various levels of rewards distributed based on the individual's measured performance.

## Performance Assessment Paradox

### Overview

Research has empirically found that both an administrative and a developmental dimension to the performance assessment interview exist.[18] However, use of the same performance assessment situation for both pay purposes and developmental purposes can be problematic. The differences between performance assessment in a developmental setting and performance assessment for pay purposes are summarized in Exhibit 11.2.

Some years ago, researchers at General Electric observed that performance assessment systems used for both pay determination and for developmental purposes seemed to break down.[19] General Electric was not successfully achieving these two goals with one assessment system, perhaps because the goals are so radically different. For example, if the performance review is to be used for both development of employees and for determining pay, then employees are not likely to be very open to discussion of their weaknesses because they know that pay is also an outcome of the performance assessment. The employees are apt to find external reasons for their poor performance and may not be responsive to suggestions for performance improvement.

Based on the research at General Electric, organizations should operate two separate performance assessment programs: one for employee development purposes and the other for pay determination purposes. That idea seems logical and has had continued support. In a 1991 article, H. H. Meyer[20] stated explicitly, "Based on my experience, I still maintain very strongly that appraisal for two different purposes should be separated." Nevertheless, some research has found that salary discussion during performance appraisal has little impact on the appraisal. When it does have an impact, that impact is positive.[21] At this point, insufficient research has been completed to draw definitive conclusions on the issue.[22]

Some managers view performance assessment as how well a person conforms relative to the general work rules of the organization, and others view it as how well a person performs relative to the performance standards of the job. *Work rules* are defined as the general rules of conduct that apply to all employees. Examples of work rules are rules governing absenteeism, consumption of alcoholic beverages on the job, dress and grooming, and tardiness. Most organizations have explicit or implicit work rules governing the conduct of employees

---

**EXHIBIT 11.2**　**PERFORMANCE ASSESSMENT FOR DEVELOPMENTAL AND PAY PURPOSES CHARACTERISTICS**

| Goal | Characteristics |
|---|---|
| Developmental | Continuous<br>Can be informal<br>Emphasis on growth and change<br>Forward looking (what is wanted to happen)<br>Improve performance in future |
| Performance pay | Set intervals<br>A snapshot of performance over the period<br>Formal<br>Backward looking (what has happened)<br>Judgmental of past performance |

over many subject areas.[23] Organizations often assess employees on compliance with these rules for pay purposes, but it is the position of this text that performance based pay should not be dependent on these criteria.

When wage payments are involved, the performance criteria of relevance should be the performance standards of the job itself. Examples of job-related performance standards are numbers of dowels turned on a lathe per hour, number of dollars of insurance policies sold, and percentage of parts made that pass quality control tests. *Performance standards* can be defined as the levels of performance expected of an employee in each major activity for which that employee is held accountable. A specific example of performance standards for typing follows:

| | |
|---|---|
| Superior performance: | 120 or more words per minute (error free) |
| Above-average performance: | 90 to 119 words per minute (error free) |
| Average performance: | 60 to 89 words per minute (error free) |
| Below-average performance: | 30 to 59 words per minute (error free) |
| Unacceptable performance: | less than 30 words per minute (error free) |

Pay raises based on performance levels communicate to employees that their relative productivity will influence their pay. In the remainder of this chapter, the discussion of performance assessment relates specifically to job-related performance standards and not to work rule behaviors.

## *Job Outcome versus Behavioral Outcome Dimensions*

Job outcome dimensions of performance are those that measure performance in terms of some product. Examples of job outcome dimensions are number of units produced and error rates per number of units produced. Job outcome dimensions tend to measure a tangible outcome of performance.

Another type of performance assessment focuses on measuring employee behaviors. The following example distinguishes between job outcomes and behaviors. An organization wishes to establish performance standards for a lathe operator. Job outcomes that might be identified include number of units turned out in an hour and percentage of units passing quality control. Both of these measures are readily observable. It would also be relatively easy to specify behaviors for this job. Examples of behaviors might be properly inserting raw material onto the lathe bench, selecting the appropriate cutting tool for the job at hand, periodically checking the tolerances on the machine, and reporting machine wear to maintenance staff in a timely way. It would be inferred that if the lathe operator did all the behavioral things that good lathe operators do, then she or he should be a good performer. When behaviors are assessed, there is an assumption that the employee who does the right things should be rewarded for that behavior. As this example shows, job outcome measures are a more direct and objective assessment of performance than behavior measures are. Because job outcome measures objectively and directly measure performance, they are usually preferable.

However, some jobs do not lend themselves to outcome measurement. For example, job outcomes from a manager's job are not objectively and directly measurable. When this happens, behaviors must be measured. A problem develops when an employee engages in the right behavior but the job outcomes prove unsatisfactory.

A meta analysis examining the relationship between behavioral ratings and job outcome measures concluded that they are not substitutes for each other. The correlation between the supervisor's rating and the performance dimension was low (0.27), with the lower limit actually being negative at the 90 percent confidence interval.[24] The author suggested, however, that readers be very careful in generalizing the results of one study and applying them to their current situations. The author also suggested that to improve the convergence between behavioral and performance outcomes, clear job standards must be used and organizations must simplify the processing of information by the evaluator.

Whether job outcome and/or behaviors are used, it is essential to develop appropriate and useable measures of performance. Both the economic and behavioral theories discussed earlier require adequate measures of performance from not only the organization's but also the employee's perception. Adequate performance measures require that the standards must be tied into the strategic objectives of the department and the organization. Second, the standards must be specific and measurable. This enables the employees to evaluate their own performance and also increases the objectivity of the evaluation. Third, employees should provide input into the development of the standards. Depending on the organizational philosophy, employees may only provide comments on the standards or they may participate fully in the identification and defining of the performance standards. Research has shown that employee participation results in employees being more satisfied with the assessment and more willing to change. Employee participation also leads to perceptions of the pay system as more effective.[25] Fourth, workers must be able to achieve the performance level within each standard. If the top performance level is not reachable, it will not have a positive effect on performance and may actually be dysfunctional. Fifth, the organization cannot evaluate employees on a performance standard that is beyond their control. Each employee's ability to perform must be independent of the performance of others. Sixth, particularly for employees who do not participate in the development of the job standards, the supervisor must communicate to each employee the standards and the kinds of outcomes or behaviors that are expected for each performance level within a job standard.

# Who Conducts Performance Assessment?

Most often in evaluating an employee for a compensation decision, the final decision rests with the immediate supervisor.[26] Before a recommendation is made, the immediate supervisor may wish to use other sources to verify his or her evaluation, fill in gaps, or add a different perspective. Each of the sources of potential performance data is discussed below.

## *Immediate Supervisors*

Estimates are that immediate supervisors perform 95 percent of all employee assessments.[27] This makes sense from several perspectives. First, an employee's supervisor is the person most directly responsible for ensuring that the employee performs at an acceptable level. Assessment provides the supervisor with a tool to ensure acceptable performance.[28]

Second, and probably more important, the employee's immediate supervisor is usually the person most familiar with both the job that the employee is supposed to perform and the employee's performance level. It is highly desirable that a supervisor with first-hand knowledge of the job requirements and with knowledge of the employee's performance conduct the evaluation.[29] In *Brito v. Zia* (1973), the courts were disturbed when raters did not have substantial contact with the evaluatees and their performance.[30] In *Signal Construction Corporation v. Stanbury*, the District of Columbia Court upheld a $250,000 award to an employee when an employer gave a poor job reference based on second-hand information.[31] The prospective employer was led to believe the performance data being supplied was based on first-hand knowledge, whereas it was based on second-hand information.

## *Self-Appraisal*

The popularity of self-appraisal has increased over the years. In this process, the employee evaluates his or her own performance based on the same performance standards used by the supervisor. In many circumstances, the supervisor and employee may actually use the same forms and share their evaluation. When the authors started doing performance assessment training for managers some 20 years ago, few supervisors asked their employees to conduct self-appraisals, but now from 35 to 50 percent of the managers attending these training sessions routinely request that their employees conduct formal self-appraisal. The advantages of having employees do self-appraisal are as follows: (1) employees' self-worth increases; (2) the manager becomes a coach/counselor and not just an evaluator; (3) employees' commitment increases; (4) employees pay closer attention to what they are doing on the job; (5) discussion is based partially on what employees perceive; (6) employees feel involvement and participation in a process that has significant impact on the work environment;[32] and (7) issues that in the past would continue to fester are put on the table and addressed.[33] There are some disadvantages to self-appraisal. First, the supervisor must deal with the employees' perceptions because the employees likely have no documentation to support their self-evaluations. Second, the employees and possibly the supervisor may not possess the interpersonal skills to handle this kind of interview. Third, some managers believe it will undermine their authority if they enter into this kind of dialogue. Fourth, some subordinates have a tendency to evaluate themselves higher than the supervisor, and this discrepancy must be dealt with directly.[34] Fifth, employees may lack interest or be fearful of the consequences of complete honesty and thus may not do a good job of self-appraisal. Most of these disadvantages can be reduced or eliminated if adequate training takes place.

Research has also shown that the supervisor can influence new employees' self-appraisal, but when the supervisor attempts to influence the self-appraisal of experienced employees, these employees often react in ways contrary to what the supervisor desired. It is important that employees are trained and encouraged to increase documentation of their behavior to reduce the potential differences in rating between supervisor and subordinate.[35] In the past, organizations have increased training of supervisors in performance assessment, but they have done little to formally train subordinates who are being requested to be increasingly active partners in the assessment process. It would seem logical to include employees in performance assessment training if the organization wants them to be active participants.

## Peer Evaluations

There are cases in which peers conduct the evaluations. Peer evaluations are used when it is difficult for a supervisor to observe the specific contributions of individuals.[36] For example, loosely supervised team projects might necessitate peers' evaluating each other's performance.

Peers may serve as evaluators when the assessment requires the evaluators to have technical knowledge of performance. For example, in universities, faculty peers evaluate other faculty for promotion and tenure. It is assumed that faculty are better informed of a colleague's academic performance than are administrators.

Even though peer evaluation has been discussed for years, there has been little business adaptation of the technique.[37] Use of peer assessments remains rare primarily for the following reasons: (1) bias — same group, similar personal characteristics, friends, (2) inadequate view of the big picture, (3) harmful to teamwork, and (4) harmful to morale. Even though research has shown that peer evaluation may be valid and reliable, it does not generate high levels of support from employees. One study revealed that it was more acceptable when used for a developmental purpose rather than for an evaluative purpose, when employees' past experience with peer rating was good, and when confidentiality of ratings was maintained.[38]

## Subordinate Evaluations

Another approach to performance assessment is to have an employee's subordinates evaluate performance. In university settings, a departmental faculty may evaluate the performance of the department head. This approach is sometimes taken in business and industry as well when top management wishes to know if lower level and middle managers are performing well in the eyes of their subordinates. Firms such as IBM, Ford, RCA, and Syntax have supposedly experimented with subordinate evaluations.[39]

Subordinate assessments of performance seem to be appropriate under at least two conditions. First, subordinate evaluation can be useful when a great deal of importance is placed on voluntary compliance with the supervisor's directives. In this case, subordinates must look positively on the supervisor before they will comply with requests. A second situation in which subordinate evaluation may be useful is when top management wants to be sure that supervisors are fair to their employees. In this case, getting subordinate input into the evaluation is important. However, subordinate evaluations of an employee rarely constitute the sole performance assessment. Even though it is viewed as a noble and democratic process, there is little evidence that subordinate assessment is a widespread practice. In a study of 140 organizations, only 10 reported using subordinate assessments of managers. Nevertheless, when such assessment was used, it received relatively positive marks.[40] A recent study of managers (organizations not using subordinate assessments) found that about 70 percent approved of subordinate assessment for developmental purposes; however, 71 percent did not believe subordinate evaluations should count as heavily as supervisory ratings. Approval of subordinate assessments was based on manager beliefs that subordinates are in better positions to evaluate the supervisor's interpersonal type behaviors (for example, communication, leadership) but not the task performance criteria (e.g., budgeting, planning).[41] Possible pitfalls to such assessments revolve around subordinates' limited information or their self-interest. Subordinates may not know the whole job of the supervisor. They may want to discredit the supervisor to reduce the supervisor's influence. Possibly a subordinate may even have designs on the supervisor's job.

### Other Evaluators

Sometimes, an employee's immediate supervisor has too little information on actual performance to make a sound judgment. For example, it may be difficult for a sales manager to spend much time watching a salesperson close a deal. Furthermore, the behavior observed on one occasion may not be typical for the salesperson (who may know that he or she is being observed). In these cases, it may be appropriate to query customers for their assessments of the salesperson.

Using customers to evaluate performance is also common in the hotel and restaurant industry. Customers may fill out evaluation forms to determine if they are pleased with the performance of cleaning staff and food servers. Students' evaluations of faculty is another version of customer evaluation of the quality of service. As with subordinate evaluations, organizations may use customer evaluations as one form of input into a larger assessment.

### Multiple Evaluators

Accurately assessing employee performance is often a monumental task. Because performance assessments can be subject to many biases (as discussed in the next section), multiple assessments are often desirable.[42] Based on *Brito v. Zia*, the use of multiple raters can reduce the likelihood of bias.[43]

As noted above, the immediate supervisor is often primarily responsible for employee performance assessment. Team reviews, however, are increasing in popularity. The managers at the same level all meet together to review the performance of all people who report to them. This approach should increase objectivity, fairness, consistency, and comprehensiveness of the evaluation. It may also increase acceptability of the evaluation because the evaluation results from group consensus.[44] Most performance assessment systems used for pay purposes have at least one check against the immediate supervisor. The immediate supervisor's evaluation must also be acceptable to the evaluator's superior. Similarly, in universities, faculty members evaluate other faculty for promotion and tenure; but this peer evaluation must be reviewed by several levels of university administration. Multiple-level reviews provide for checks and balances in the review session so that no one person can bias the evaluation. Multiple observations of performance provide information from individuals who may have observed different dimensions of the job performance.[45] For example, a meta analysis revealed that the correlation between peer and supervisor ratings was relatively high (+0.62), but moderate for self-peer (+0.36) and self-supervisor (+0.35).[46] Finally, multiple review processes improve the organization's ability to defend its action if legal action is taken by an unhappy employee.[47]

The remainder of this chapter discusses performance assessment from the immediate supervisor's perspective, although the issues are valid for any kind of assessment.

## Problems with Performance Standards

At least part of the difficulty in performing fair and accurate performance assessment stems from problems with developing the standards against which the employee will be judged. Evaluating performance in one dimension (such as number of units produced) may not be difficult, but as a practical matter, performance is usually multidimensional.[48] For a lathe operator, performance is more than turning out a certain number of dowels; it is turning out that number of dowels that also meet quality control standards a given percentage of the time, with a minimally acceptable materials waste rate, and with acceptable levels of wear and tear on the lathe itself. A main objective in designing a performance assessment system is to identify the important performance dimensions for the job through job analysis.

### Standards Beyond Employee Control

It is inappropriate to evaluate employees using standards over which they lack control. An employee's performance may be dependent on the performance of an outside agent or on someone else within the organization. If that other person's performance is poor, it produces a negative evaluation for the employee who is hindered but who has no control over the situation. Management must deal directly with this kind of problem.

### Criterion Deficiency and Contamination

Proper identification of performance dimensions can eliminate or at least reduce two common biases that enter into performance assessment: criterion deficiency and criterion contamination. Criterion deficiency and criterion contamination are illustrated in the diagram in Exhibit 11.3.

In Exhibit 11.3, the circle on the left, circle A, can be thought of as the true domain of job performance. The lined area is unmeasured job performance. To

| EXHIBIT 11.3 | CRITERION DEFICIENCY AND CRITERION CONTAMINATION |

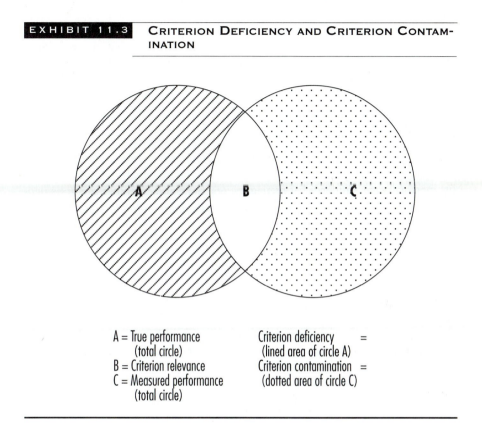

A = True performance (total circle)
B = Criterion relevance
C = Measured performance (total circle)

Criterion deficiency = (lined area of circle A)
Criterion contamination = (dotted area of circle C)

the extent that the performance assessment system fails to measure a large part of circle A, the assessment device is deficient. The lined area, known as criterion deficiency, can be defined as true job performance that is unmeasured.

The circle on the right, circle C, depicts the domain of job performance that is being measured. There is some overlap between true job performance and measured job performance, which is area B in the exhibit (sometimes called criterion relevance). The dotted area in the exhibit represents criterion contamination. That is, there are aspects of performance that are measured but that do not overlap with the true domain of performance. To the extent that a performance assessment device has dimensions that do not overlap with the true domain, there is criterion contamination.

Criterion deficiency occurs when an important performance standard is omitted in the process of conducting a performance assessment on an employee.[49] For example, if a lathe operator's performance is based on an evaluation that does not consider the number of units produced on the lathe in some period of time, then the assessment has criterion deficiency. An example of criterion contamination is assessing a lathe operator on typing speed. Because typing performance has nothing to do with performance as a lathe operator, this criterion is contaminated.

Job analysis is the main method of guarding against both deficiency and contamination problems. Job analysis is also a necessary requirement for a performance assessment system to withstand a legal challenge under equal employment opportunity litigation.[50] Literature clearly documents the need for professionally conducted job analysis, but according to one study, only 37 percent of its respondents attend to that need.[51]

### Measurability of the Criteria

A related problem in establishing performance standards is the issue of their measurability. It may be relatively easy to determine performance standards for operative employees, for example, but it can be extremely difficult to establish performance standards for managers, teachers, and customer relations people. Thus, measurement is often a problem for many jobs. In a later section, some techniques are discussed that attempt to assess performance standards in behavioral rather than job outcome terms.

### Combining Performance Dimensions

Another problem with performance standards involves determination of how the standards should be combined into a total overall score for an employee. That is, given the multidimensionality of performance, how are the various dimensions weighted into a composite score for the employee? This decision relates directly to the final decision on an employee's pay raise. One writer suggests three bases for combining various standards into one overall measure.[52] The three bases are judgmental (what individuals think is the relative importance of the criteria); statistical (whether dimensions are correlated or not); and economic (which dimensions are most important in terms of economic contribution to the organization). Ideally, the weighting of dimensions should be based on their economic contribution, but because that is not always practical, the judgmental approach is often used.

### Lack of Employee Participation

An area that may become more problematic in the future is the lack of participation by the employees in the establishment of performance standards. As organizations turn increasingly to participative management in operational aspects of the job, employees will likely expect increased participation in identifying and defining the standards on which evaluation takes place. Either organizations will have to increase the involvement of employees or communicate a good rationale for their nonparticipation.

## Rater Biases and Errors in Performance Assessment

Even with the best standards established, the performance assessment system will be only as good as those who use it. Many errors and biases that arise in performance assessment are directly attributable to the rater. Some of the more common biases and recommended procedures for their reduction are reviewed in this section and summarized in Exhibit 11.4. Many of these are mutually

| EXHIBIT 11.4 | PROBLEMS AND SOLUTIONS OF PERFORMANCE APPRAISAL |
|---|---|

| Problem | Solutions |
|---|---|
| Halo or horns bias | Evaluator training for bias<br>Clearly defined performance dimensions<br>Evaluators evaluated by superior |
| Excessive strictness or leniency bias | Evaluator training for bias<br>Clear performance standard<br>Evaluators evaluated by superior |
| Central tendency bias | Evaluator training for bias<br>Clear performance standards for each dimension<br>Evaluators evaluated by superior |
| Recency tendency bias | Employee performance log over time<br>Evaluators evaluated by superior |
| Primacy bias | Employee performance log over time<br>Evaluators evaluated by superior |
| Similarity or difference bias | Reference to clearly defined performance dimensions<br>Evaluators evaluated by superior |
| Order effect or contrast bias | Reference to clearly defined performance dimensions for each employee<br>Evaluators evaluated by superior |
| Spillover | Do not review past evaluation forms before current evaluation<br>Evaluators evaluated by superior |
| Range restriction | Clear and precise job standards<br>Training<br>Evaluators evaluated by superior |
| Unwillingness to discriminate | Training in philosophy and objectives of performance assessment<br>Evaluators evaluated by superior |

exclusive. For example, an evaluator cannot be guilty of excessive strictness and excessive leniency at the same time. Although this text offers suggestions for reducing biases and errors, there are no known methods to completely eliminate them in performance assessment.

## *"Halo or Horns" Bias*

The halo or horns bias occurs when an evaluator allows one positive or negative performance dimension to influence the assessment of the employee on other performance dimensions.[53] For example, if the assessor is guilty of the halo bias in evaluating a secretary, a high score on typing performance may influence the evaluator to give a high score on filing performance as well, even though the secretary actually does poorly on the filing performance dimension. The horns effect would result in a poor score on typing performance based on the poor filing dimension score. Training assessors to be aware of the potential bias and designing assessment techniques that clearly separate performance dimensions can reduce the halo or horns bias.[54] Research shows that halo rating errors can be substantially reduced if the job standards are internally homogeneous and clearly and specifically written.[55] It would seem that any attempt to design one performance assessment form for use across multiple job or job clusters would increase the likelihood of rating errors such as the halo effect. One practical solution when a form is used across job clusters is to require behavioral or job examples that lead the evaluator to rate the employee at the appropriate level. Also, the training techniques of group discussion, practice and feedback, and lecture have been effective in reducing the halo effect error, with group discussion as the most effective.[56] There are also statistical techniques that can control for the halo as well as other errors.[57]

Some researchers believe that halo "error" is a legitimate evaluation of employee behavior because it focuses on an overriding attribute rather than overemphasizing what may be infrequent behavior of an employee.[58] Contextual factors may affect the measurement of observed halo.[59] Likewise, the global measure of an individual's performance may not be identical to the value of a mean computed for a set of specific performance standards used in the assessment. This seems to suggest that global measures of employee behavior are more relevant for evaluative decisions and specific measures are more relevant for developmental feedback.

### Excessive Strictness or Leniency

A second type of rater bias is the tendency of some evaluators to rate all employees either too leniently or too strictly.[60] A manager who rates all employees leniently might rate all employees as above average in performance. Conversely, a manager who evaluates all employees too strictly might rate all performances as below average. Probably the best way to reduce this bias is to make the standards extremely clear for what is expected at each level of performance. Training should make evaluators aware of this bias. Human resource managers should track all supervisors' evaluations and compare those ratings to see if the department's performance parallels that of its employees' ratings. In a review of studies that examined the effect of various training techniques (group discussion, practice and feedback, lecture) to reduce leniency error, group discussion was the most successful, followed by practice and feedback. Use of a lecture provided little help.[61]

### Central Tendency

Just as some managers are guilty of excessive leniency or strictness in evaluating employees, other managers have a tendency to evaluate most employees in the middle. In this type of bias, called central tendency, a manager might assess most employees as having satisfactory performance regardless of their actual performance levels. Again, the two best methods to reduce this bias are performance standards expressed in behavioral or job outcome terms and training to raise evaluator awareness of the problem. The organization through its policies may actually encourage this problem. For example, we are familiar with one organization that required a comments section filled in on any employee not evaluated as average (3 on 5-point scale). The organization should not have been surprised to find a disproportionate number of employees rated as "3." The organization was actually rewarding supervisors for this tendency.

## Recency Tendency

Another bias is the tendency of assessors to remember the most recent performance behaviors and to forget performance behaviors that occurred earlier. Recency bias can influence the performance assessment because it prevents an assessment of the employee's performance over the entire evaluation cycle, concentrating instead on just the recent past. Research has shown that the rating of employees is less accurate when it is delayed (thus, once a year evaluations are totally inadequate) and when it is based on a small amount of information.[62] One effective way to reduce this bias is to keep a log of employee behaviors or performance outcomes over the entire assessment period. When it is time to conduct the assessment, the assessor can refer to the log to determine a weighted overall performance level during the period for each performance dimension. One study has shown that raters can increase their accuracy by keeping an employee log for each individual who must be evaluated.[63]

## Primacy Bias

Many people are guilty of allowing first impressions to taint their judgments. This phenomenon is known as primacy bias. As an example, an employee might perform some part of a job exceedingly well or poorly the first time he or she attempts the task, and the evaluator may carry this first impression into future assessments of performance. In some ways, this bias is the reverse of the recency bias. A performance log is also useful in guarding against primacy bias.

## Similarity or Difference Bias

In similarity or difference bias, an evaluator may use a stereotype and then compare other employees with this stereotype. In some cases, this stereotype may be the evaluator. The assessor judges the employee's performance based on whether the stereotype is a good or poor performer and on the assessor's perception of the employee as unlike or like the stereotype. The best way to avoid this bias is to use the job requirements, not other employees, when assessing performance.

## Order Effect and Contrast Bias

In the process of evaluating the performance of one employee, the assessor may be influenced by the performance assessment of another employee who was recently evaluated. This phenomenon is known as order effect and contrast bias. In this type of bias, a superior performer may be evaluated first. When the performance of other employees is assessed, it seems poor in comparison with the superior performance. A prior assessment of a poor performer may result in the next employees being rated higher than their performance would justify. This effect works against an employee if the previous employee was superior in performance and for the employee if the previous employee was an inferior performer. Bias caused by order and contrast can be reduced by evaluating employees against predetermined standards rather than against each other.

## Spillover Effect

Spillover effect occurs when the evaluation of the employee during the previous evaluation period influences the evaluation during the current period. If the evaluator uses the previously completed evaluation form to review how the person did on each job standard before rating the person for the current evaluation period, this bias is likely to occur. There is a tendency to make current ratings similar to previous ratings. The best solution to this error is to delay review of the old evaluation until the current evaluation is completed. If special performance goals have been established, they must be reviewed before the evaluation. For this reason, special performance goals should be listed on a separate sheet so that they can be removed from the file and reviewed independently.

## Range Restriction

Range restriction refers to ratings that are confined to a narrow portion of the rating scale, stemming from a rater's apparent reluctance to use the entire scale. Range restriction assumes a natural midpoint that may or may not coincide with a scale's actual midpoint.[64] An example may be central tendency, strictness, or leniency bias as discussed earlier.

## Unwillingness to Discriminate

Some evaluators may be reluctant to differentiate on the basis of performance. Such managers often produce biased and invalid assessments.

Many factors contribute to unwillingness to differentiate on the basis of performance. Managers may not want to have to justify different performance ratings to the employees. They may find it easier to give all employees similar evaluations. Managers may also not want to have to defend their decisions about people to their own supervisors. For example, because of the financial ramifications of performance-based pay, a supervisor may insist that any superior rating be validated; the manager may then have to provide detailed documentation to support the rating. This manager may find it easier to give the employee a slightly above-average rating and save the additional work involved in defending a superior rating.

A third reason why managers do not discriminate on performance is an unwillingness to play God, so to speak. Many managers do not like being put in the position of judging others and resist doing so. Managers with this attitude are likely to evaluate all employees at least average and to give similar evaluations to all employees.

## Training Suggestions

Few managers actually understand their organization's performance assessment system, including how the system was developed, what the system is expected to accomplish, and how it works. It should not be surprising that assessments by these managers may be biased.

Better training of managers should result in more valid assessment systems. Every organization should develop a training program to teach managers these fundamentals:

1. The organization's policy on performance assessment and that the policies are to be enforced[65]

2. The purpose of the organization's performance assessment system

3. Background on the development of the performance assessment system

4. The appropriate procedure for conducting an assessment interview[66]

5. The biases that each manager may bring to the assessment interview and ways to reduce them[67]

6. A mechanism to increase consistency between evaluations[68]

7. The need to inform employees clearly of their level of performance and, if inadequate, the degree to which it is deficient and the consequences if the deficiency continues[69]

8. The need to inform employees of the procedure if they want to appeal the evaluation

9. The need for documentation on which the evaluation was based

# Legal Considerations in Performance Assessment

Whenever employee procedures are involved, particularly in regard to hiring and pay, legal considerations are extremely important. Misinterpretation of the existing laws or court rulings can cost companies dearly.

## Adverse Impact Discrimination under Title VII

Adverse impact occurs whenever a performance assessment system used by an organization results in lower performance assessment scores for one protected group under the Civil Rights Act of 1964 compared with the scores for other groups. If the scores are then used for determining employment outcomes (in this case, pay outcomes), the organization could face a discrimination suit under Title VII of the Civil Rights Act. Although there are no hard and fast rules for determining the properties of a performance assessment system that will survive legal challenge when there is adverse impact, at least one court case has given some guidance on the subject. In the case of *James v. Stockham Valve and Fittings Co.*, the court found that the performance assessment system used for pay determination was not discriminatory, even though black employees earned less than white employees.[70] The evidence showed that

1. Each job in the plant was studied and evaluated in terms of job functions (job analysis).

2. The defendant's procedure allowed an employee to file and simultaneously maintain applications on any number of jobs in the plant regardless of whether a vacancy existed.

3. When a vacancy occurred, all pending applications were reviewed.

4. The performance evaluation was undertaken by the manager having first-hand knowledge.

5. The standards for ratings were defined in written terms.

6. The evaluative instrument was of fixed content and called for the recording of discrete judgments.

7. Each employee's performance was rated on seven factors: quality, quantity, job or trade knowledge, ability to learn, cooperation, dependability, industry, and attendance.

8. The evaluations were graded under standardized conditions.

9. The rating form was weighted according to a predetermined numerical table. The rating manager was unaware of the weights assigned.

10. An employee who did not receive a pay increase because of the merit rating could ask for a meeting with the manager, the superintendent, and a committee member to discuss the failure to qualify for an increase.

The *Stockham* case has several interesting features. First, job analysis was critical to identify the important job components on which performance was determined. Second, the factors were weighted, not arbitrarily, but beforehand, and the manager doing the rating did not know the weights so that there was no opportunity to bias the scores. Third, the manager who knew the employee's performance did the evaluating.[71] Fourth, the evaluations were conducted under standardized conditions, which meant that every employee was assessed by an identical process. Finally, the employee had several levels of appeal to resolve a disagreement with the manager's assessment. This last point is particularly important in unionized and public sector organizations in which failure to provide due process to an employee can be a violation of the contract or the employee's Fourteenth Amendment rights to due process.[72]

## *Equal Pay Act Considerations*

In Chapter 5 one of the important pieces of legislation mentioned was the Equal Pay Act of 1963. That act is important in this discussion as well because it provides for specific exceptions to an equal pay policy.

The act allows for differences in pay between men and women in similar jobs if the difference is attributable to a merit system, a system that measures earnings by quantity or quality of production, a seniority system, or any factor other than sex. The first exception is directly applicable to performance assessment.

For example, suppose that an employer uses a merit pay system that bases pay increases on supervisors' judgments of absolute performance. Women, on average, score poorer on the performance assessment form than men. If pay is based on merit, women on average would be expected to be paid less than men. This pay system would be legal so long as there were true differences in real performance between men and women. However, if the difference in average scores between men and women is due to one or more biases (perhaps some of the biases identified earlier), then the merit system itself would be discriminatory. In turn, the pay system would also be discriminatory. The excerpt from one court case presented in Exhibit 11.5 identifies pay differentials that are legal and illegal.

The second exception permits a pay system based on quantity or quality of production. If an employer establishes pay on one or both of these criteria, then the pay plan is permissible under the act, subject to the requirements that such a pay plan is not designed to, nor does it in fact, discriminate against one sex or the other. As an example, suppose that an employer pays employees 20 cents for each 100-lb bag of material taken from a loading dock and stacked in a storeroom. Both men and women work at this job. Men, on average, move 60 bags per hour, while women, on average, move 40 bags per hour. In this situation, men earn, on average, $12 per hour, while women earn $8 per hour. This difference in pay is legitimate because it is based on true differences in production quantity. However, if there were errors in measuring production quantity, then this pay difference could be illegal.

Studies have revealed, at various times, a pro-male, pro-female, and no bias, but the studies showing a pro-male bias in performance are predominant.[73] Due to sex stereotyping, the probability of gender bias in performance assessment increases as the amount of measurable and objective performance data decreases. The performance assessment form may aid in reducing gender bias if the form requires objective measures of performance, systematic analysis of each individual's behaviors and outcomes, dialogue between the employee and the evaluator, and specific documentation of behaviors or outcomes on which the evaluation is based.[74]

| EXHIBIT 11.5 | LEGITIMATE DIFFERENCES IN PERFORMANCE LEVEL |
| --- | --- |

Maureen S. Bullock
v.
PIZZA HUT, INC. and Pizza Hut
of Louisiana, Inc.
Civ. A. No. 75-176
United States District Court,
M. D. Louisiana
March 30, 1977

[5-7] Defendant argues that the higher salaries paid to the male Unit Managers were based on characteristics which these men possessed that made them more valuable as managers. With one exception, we do not agree. The defendants established that Paul Grace had seven years experience in Florida and Texas as a Pizza Hut Unit Manager and Area General Manager. He was also personally known to Gerald York, defendants' Area General Manager for Baton Rouge. We think that these facts justified the wage differential between plaintiff and Grace. As to the other two managers in the Baton Rouge area, defendants argue that Clyde Martin's higher salary was based on his three years of college education and extensive experience in dealing with the public. However, we note that the plaintiff's application for employment with defendants shows she had at least as much experience in dealing with the public as did Martin, having occupied positions as either manager or manager trainee in other food service establishments at least as far back as 1965. Furthermore, while not discounting the value of a college education, we do not believe it justifies the wage differential in this instance.

While we might have found the evidence of a broader educational background as justifying a disparity in wages during an initial period of employment, we think that in light of plaintiff's repeated high performance in profitability it cannot provide justification for her wage differential during the entire period prior to the standardization of wages. We derive support for this position from the fact that Charles Naquin, the manager who was hired at almost exactly the same time as plaintiff, at all times prior to the standardization of wages earned as much as $150 per month more than the plaintiff. No justification is offered for this, other than defendants' assertion that this disparity was due to Gerald York's personal assessment of Naquin's worth as a manager. We have previously discussed the factors that York used in evaluating the salaries of potential employees. We can see no justification for the difference in salaries other than the plaintiff's gender. The defendant argues that plaintiff's gender was a valid consideration because of cultural distinctions which would inhibit the plaintiff's development in learning leadership qualities and mechanical skills. A short answer to this contention is that this was not shown to be the case here. The defendants' stereotyping of the plaintiff in this manner is merely a round-about way of saying that the plaintiff is being paid less because in our society women are willing to work for less. This is clearly an inappropriate factor under the law. *Brennan v. Prince William Hospital Corp.*, 503 F.2d 282 (4th Cir. 1974); *Hodgson v. Brookhaven General Hospital*, 436 F.2d 719 (5th Cir. 1970).

## Age Discrimination in Employment Act of 1967

Employers must continually be alert to the possibility of discrimination charges under the Age Discrimination in Employment Act of 1967 in addition to the Equal Pay Act and Title VII of the Civil Rights Act. Very few managers may consciously make pay decisions on the basis of age; however, built-in biases about age and productivity may cause an organization to discriminate on the basis of age. For example, some managers assume that you "can't teach old dogs new tricks." Such a belief is apt to result in older employees receiving lower scores in a judgmental performance rating. One study found that supervisors rated older subordinates lower than younger subordinates performing the same job.[75]

There is nothing wrong with paying older employees less than younger employees if the differences in pay are legitimate; that is, older employees must, in fact, be less productive than younger employees. To be sure that the pay system does not discriminate illegally against older workers, the organization should compare the merit ratings of both groups to determine if older employees systematically receive lower evaluations. If they do, the organization should make sure that the ratings are, in fact, valid and defensible.

## Grievance Discrimination

There is some evidence that supervisors will evaluate employees lower who have previously filed a grievance against them[76] despite the fact that the National Labor Relations Act prohibits discrimination against employees who exercise their rights as union members. The strength of the negative reaction by the supervisor is dependent on the levels at which the grievance is resolved and whether the decision is for or against the supervisor. If the grievance is resolved at a level above the supervisor and the supervisor loses, the probability of negative reaction by the supervisor is increased. This type of bias not only discredits the grievance process but also damages the credibility of the performance assessment system. The organization may reduce this problem by educating managers that the grievance procedure is not a win–lose contest but a tool for solving problems.

## Summary for Legal Compliance

To increase the probability that the organization's performance assessment system is in legal compliance, the following should be accomplished. First, formalize and standardize the assessment procedure. Second, establish performance criteria that are job-related, preferably behavioral- or outcome-based. Third, use formal job analysis that is professionally done and current. Fourth, limit subjective evaluation to no more than part of the evaluation process. Fifth, train all evaluators. Sixth, ensure that the evaluators have substantial contact with the employees they are evaluating. Seventh, use multiple evaluators whenever possible. Eighth, provide a mechanism for employees to appeal their evaluation. Ninth, be sure that performance assessment files are secure from individuals not requiring access. Tenth, have detailed documentation of specific behaviors or outcomes impacting on the employee's evaluation. Eleventh, recognize that the human resource department has an obligation to review all evaluations to see if any rating errors (for example, halo) or biases (for example, age, sex) are present. Twelfth, be sure that all evaluations are performed in a timely manner.

# Performance Assessment Techniques

## *Ranking Methods*

Over the years, several performance assessment techniques have been put forth. Some of the earliest methods of assessment involved ranking systems. Ranking systems provide a relative value for each employee by comparing employees with each other rather than with precisely defined performance standards.

The simplest of the ranking approaches is the *rank order method*. In this approach, the evaluator ranks all the employees working in a job from best to worst. A second approach is an *alternate ranking method*. In this method, the evaluator identifies the best performer, then the worst performer, then the second best, the second worst, and so forth. The basic idea behind this approach is to make distinctions by constantly contrasting good and poor performance.

Most ranking methods, although not all, use a single performance dimension, such as quantity or quality of work. Often the performance criterion is not defined by the organization but is left to the discretion of the evaluator. If this is done, the ranking system is subject to the biases of criterion contamination and deficiency. Further, if individual performance dimensions are not identified and each employee is ranked separately, there is a real possibility of halo or horns bias entering into the assessment.

Another problem with simple ranking approaches is that, although the process gives a distribution of employees from best to worst, it does not address the question of how well employees perform relative to absolute performance standards. In other words, the worst employee might actually be performing well above average, or the best might be well below average.

A third ranking method is the *forced distribution method*, which is used in only about 10 percent of organizations based on one study[77] and in 27 percent of *Fortune* 100 organizations according to a second study.[78] In this method, the evaluator assigns a predetermined percentage of the employees to each of several categories, such as superior, above average, average, and so on. This approach is predicated on the assumption that employee performance varies according to some predetermined distribution, which may not be true. Further, just as with the rank order and alternate ranking methods, this method often identifies only one performance dimension. This approach is subject to many of the biases noted earlier.

A fourth approach to ranking is the *paired comparison method*. In this approach, the evaluator compares each employee with every other employee. The employee receives a point for each time she or he is ranked higher than another employee. After all comparisons are complete, the evaluator determines the ranking by totaling the points. Again, the approach does not really address the question of how well an employee performs relative to absolute performance standards, but only how well the employee performs relative to other employees.

A fifth ranking approach is the *forced choice method*. In this method, the evaluator must choose between a positive and negative performance statement to describe the employee and assign points. After assigning points for an extensive list of paired statements, the assessor adds the points to determine a performance score for the employee. All employees can then be ranked according to their total scores. This approach, more thorough than any other ranking approach, incorporates various performance dimensions into the evaluation.

### Graphic Rating Scales

The most frequently used performance assessment technique is the graphic rating scale method. An example of a graphic rating scale appears in Exhibit 11.6.

Several features of Exhibit 11.6 are important. The Factors column, which outlines performance dimensions, identifies five important factors: job knowledge, technical skills, quality of work, work volume, and initiative. Although the example is a good first attempt to identify the important performance dimensions, the factor degrees as listed in the evaluations column are not defined in clear enough detail to identify the standard used. For example, for the job knowledge factor, the highest possible evaluation is a five: "exceptional understanding of all phases of the job." This evaluation is likely to result in considerable bias because there is no operational definition of what is exceptional understanding. That is, what are the job behaviors or performance outcomes that result if an employee exhibits exceptional understanding of the job? None of the evaluations possible for the individual factors are anchored in employee behaviors or job outcomes. The Remarks column provides a place for behaviors or outcomes to be documented that caused the evaluator to rate the employee the way he or she did. The information in the Remarks column is critical to the assessment. By requiring the Remarks column to be completed in all evaluations, specific performance or outcome dimensions are documented.

The next section of the form in Exhibit 11.6 allows evaluation of overall performance levels. Several features of this section are also worthy of comment. There are six possible levels of performance, but again, they are not anchored in job behaviors or job outcomes. Completion of the earlier remarks sections will provide the key behaviors or outcomes that caused the overall performance rating. Each assessor must determine what outstanding, commendable, and so forth, should mean. The example in Exhibit 11.6 also attempts to combine a forced distribution technique with the overall rating: it suggests only 5 percent of the employees will be outstanding, only 5 percent unsatisfactory, and so forth. As noted earlier, one should be very careful about making assumptions about the distribution of employee performance. If an organization desires a forced choice evaluation, it may be best to have that in addition to overall ratings of each employee based on an absolute performance standard. This would guard against such situations as an employee's only overall rating being lowest among all the workers supervised by a supervisor, and thus having a negative impact on the employee's pay when in absolute terms that employee is above average.

The remaining sections of the form provide space for any employee development plans (meaning that this assessment is used for more than pay purposes), for both supervisor and employee comments, and for the signatures of the evaluator and employee (these last two sections protect the company legally).

The graphic rating scale method is the most commonly used performance assessment system. Despite its popularity, there are many problems with the system: (1) a lack of job outcome or job behavior anchors for the degrees within dimensions; (2) a failure to combine the various performance dimensions into a

| EXHIBIT 11.6 | A GRAPHIC RATING SCALE |
|---|---|

## Nonexempt Performance Review

| Name | Employee number | Date of hire |
|---|---|---|
| Department name | | Job title |

| Salary grade | Time on present position | Years _____ | Months _____ | Date of review | Date of prior review |
|---|---|---|---|---|---|

**Performance Appraisal Statement and Comments**: This form provides a suggested format in which to comment on the employees' performance against job requirements. Please consider all statements carefully. You should check one of the suggested comments on the scale and write in your own statement or status of the incumbent's performance within the "Remarks" section. This enables you to provide an overall rating on each factor, as well as to comment on specific characteristics of the position of the individual evaluated.

| Factors | Evaluations | Remarks |
|---|---|---|
| **Job knowledge**<br>Consider knowledge of own job and department's function; the understanding of principles, methods, or processes used. | ☐ 5. Exceptional understanding of all phases of the job.<br><br>☐ 4. Full knowledge of all job duties; exceptional understanding of some phases of the job.<br><br>☐ 3. Full knowledge of the job.<br><br>☐ 2. More knowledge is needed for fully effective performance. Knowledge is adequately improving.<br><br>☐ 1. Lacks adequate comprehension of job; adequate improvement is not observed. | |
| **Technical skills**<br>Consider degree of proficiency and strengths or weaknesses in such technical skills as clerical, secretarial, technician, or paraprofessional. | ☐ 5. Exceptionally proficient in all technical skills.<br><br>☐ 4. Fully competent technical skills; exceptionally proficient in some technical skills.<br><br>☐ 3. Fully competent technical skills.<br><br>☐ 2. More skills are needed for fully effective performance. Skills are improving adequately.<br><br>☐ 1. Lacks adequate job skills; adequate improvement is not observed. | |

*Exhibit 11.6* (continued)

| Factors | Evaluations | Remarks |
|---|---|---|
| **Quality of work**<br>Consider accuracy, thorough-ness, neatness of work, and ability to make improvements. | ☐ 5. Work quality is consistently excellent.<br><br>☐ 4. Work quality consistently meets job standards; in some areas, work quality is excellent.<br><br>☐ 3. Work quality generally meets job standards.<br><br>☐ 2. Work quality is below acceptable standards but is improving adequately; work must be regularly checked.<br><br>☐ 1. Work quality is not adequate; errors are extensive; adequate improvement is not observed. | |
| **Work volume**<br>Consider the quantity of acceptable work accomplished and promptness in completing assignments. | ☐ 5. Unusually high work output; consistently exceeds job standards.<br><br>☐ 4. Work output consistently meets job standards; in some areas, work output exceeds job standards.<br><br>☐ 3. Work output generally meets job standards.<br><br>☐ 2. Work output is adequate; adequate improvement is observed.<br><br>☐ 1. Work output is not adequate; adequate improvement is not observed. | |
| **Initiative**<br>Consider ingenuity, self-reliance, abilty to originate ideas and actions, degree of supervision required. | ☐ 5. Consistently performs job duties independently; initiates improvement that increases in job performance. Also makes sound recommendations that improve departmental efficiency.<br><br>☐ 4. Consistently performs normal duties without detailed instruction; initiates work improvements that increase effectiveness in job performance.<br><br>☐ 3. Consistently performs normal duties without detailed instruction. | |

*Exhibit 11.6 (continued)*

| Factors | Evaluations | Remarks |
|---|---|---|
| | ☐ 2. In some cases, must be given detailed, repeated instruction. Adequate improvement is observed. | |
| | ☐ 1. Must consistently be given detailed instruction even on repeated assignments; adequate improvement is not observed. | |

**Overall Performance Level**

☐ Outstanding — Far above competent performance—a high degree of excellence (approximately 5 percent of all people perform at this level). Overall rating is "5."

☐ Commendable — Noticeably better than competent (required) job performance (approximately 10 to 15 percent of all people perform at this level). Overall rating is "4."

☐ Competent — At or somewhat above required job performance (approximately 60 percent of all people perform at this level). Overall rating is "3."

☐ Learning/competent — Learning the job assignment; in training and performance is consistently improving (most persons recently assigned to a new job perform at this level). Overall rating is "2."

☐ Satisfactory improvement/marginal — Below competent (required) job performance; however, improvement to meet job requirements is expected (approximately 15 percent of all people perform at this level). Overall rating is "2."

☐ Unsatisfactory — Unacceptable job performance; improvement is unlikely and transfer or termination should be considered (approximately 5 percent of all people perform at this level). Overall rating is "1."

**Plans for Future Action**

(What action do you plan to take to continue this employee's development? For example, cross-training, transfer, eductaion.)

**Supervisor Comments**                    **Employee Comments**

Employee's signature _____

Supervisor's signature _____     Title _____

Approval signature _____     Title _____

Personnel manager approval _____     Title _____

global assessment; and (3) the opportunity for various forms of bias to enter the assessment process.[79] Partly because of these problems with graphic rating scales, other approaches have been suggested. One of these approaches is behaviorally anchored rating scales.

## Behaviorally Anchored Rating Scales

The behaviorally anchored rating scales approach to performance assessment is actually an outgrowth of the critical incidence method. Under a critical incidence method of assessment, evaluators keep track of job behaviors that are exceptionally good and lead to high performance, or exceptionally bad and lead to poor performance.[80]

The evolution of the critical incidence method into a behaviorally anchored rating scale involves five steps. First, individuals with first-hand knowledge of the job describe specific examples of exceptional, good, poor, and average performance. Second, these individuals cluster the behavioral descriptions into five to ten performance dimensions that are considered important for overall job success. Third, independent of the first group, a second group of individuals who also have first-hand knowledge of the job allocates the behavioral descriptions among the performance dimensions. This step acts as a check on the reliability of the behavioral descriptions for capturing a performance dimension. Any behavioral descriptions or incidents over which the two groups have main disagreements are then dropped. Fourth, the second group of individuals assigns the behavioral descriptions along a continuum in terms of how much the behaviors or incidents contribute to performance variation. Fifth, based on this assignment of descriptors or incidents, a final instrument is developed to assess employees. An example of one dimension for a behaviorally anchored rating scale appears in Exhibit 11.7.

Behaviorally anchored rating scales are quite expensive to develop because of the enormous time involvement they require from many individuals. This fact has caused inquiry into their economic feasibility. At least one set of writers, after comparing the literature on this approach with that on other performance assessment techniques, has concluded that it is not sufficiently more accurate to make it worth the additional cost. It has also been suggested that, regardless of the assessment method used, the reliability and validity of assessment scores are determined by the evaluator, the employee, and the intent of the assessment. Thus, apparently, there is no such thing as a bias-free assessment.[81]

Despite these limitations, behaviorally anchored rating scales should withstand legal scrutiny. They are developed using individuals with first-hand knowledge of the job and are based on observed job behaviors, so they are in essence based on a thorough job analysis. The very process of developing a scale can be advantageous to the organization in that individuals come to appreciate the importance of accurate performance assessment. Performance assessment standards are written in language that both job incumbents and evaluators readily understand.[82] However, behaviorally anchored rating scales are not likely to be cost-effective unless many job incumbents are involved.

| EXHIBIT 11.7 | EXAMPLE OF A BEHAVIORALLY ANCHORED RATING SCALE |
|---|---|

| | | |
|---|---|---|
| Extremely good performance | 7 | This checker would organize the order when checking it out by placing all soft goods [such as] bread, cake, etc., to one side counter; all meats, produce, frozen foods, to the other side, thereby leaving the center of the counter for canned goods, boxed goods, etc. |
| Good performance | 6 | When checking, this checker would separate strawberries, bananas, cookies, cakes, and breads, etc. |
| Slightly good performance | 5 | You can expect this checker to grab more than one item at a time from the cart to the counter. |
| Neither poor nor good performance | 4 | After bagging the order and customer is still writing a check, you can expect this checker to proceed to the next order if it is a small order. |
| Slightly poor performance | 3 | This checker may be expected to put wet merchandise on the top of the counter. |
| | | This checker can be expected to lay milk and by-product cartons on their sides on the counter top. |
| Poor performance | 2 | This checker can be expected to damage fragile merchandise [such as] soft goods, eggs, and light bulbs on the counter top. |
| Extremely poor performance | 1 | |

SOURCE: Lawrence Fogli, Charles Hulin, and Milton R. Blood, "Development of First-level Behavioral Job Criteria," *Journal of Applied Psychology* 55, no. 7 (February 1971). Copyright 1971 by the American Psychological Association. Reprinted by permission of the author.

## Management by Objectives

Management by objectives means many things to many people. To some, it is a total management philosophy, whereas to others it is a performance assessment process.[83] Because the concern here is performance assessment, the discussion covers only those features of management by objectives most relevant to that narrower topic.

The management by objectives process involves several steps. First, the subordinate and the superior agree on a set of objectives to be accomplished by certain dates. This step of establishing objectives can be thought of as a negotiating and role clarification process in which both parties understand more clearly what the subordinate's job is and what needs to be achieved. These objectives should have completion dates stated in terms of results (outcomes) and, wherever possible, should be expressed quantitatively.

In the second step, the subordinate works on the established objectives. As time passes, the superior and subordinate communicate with each other in terms of how much progress the subordinate is making and whether they should adjust the target date or objectives. As events modify objectives, new objectives should be immediately set. During this time, the superior may engage in extensive coaching and counseling to develop the potential of the employee.

In the third step, the assessment stage, the superior and subordinate review the extent to which the subordinate has accomplished the earlier objectives. At this stage, the level of performance may tie back into the merit pay system to determine the pay increase for the person. After the assessment stage, the process is repeated with a new objective-setting stage, and so on.

Management by objectives is very difficult to implement. For example, employees must trust their supervisors. Lack of trust will cause subordinates to set easy objectives so that they will look good at the assessment stage. Another difficulty is that it takes a long time for employees to identify and commit to objectives. There is also a tendency for managers to assign employees their objectives. This goes against one of the fundamental goals of management by objectives, to have employees participate in the establishment of their objectives.

Despite such difficulties, management by objectives can be an effective performance assessment technique, especially for jobs in which it is difficult to define performance in the first place. In those jobs, it can be helpful in obtaining agreement among levels of management on what performance levels (objective attainments) are acceptable.

One of the main problems with management by objectives as it relates to compensation is that it sets objectives for individual employees. This causes problems when it comes time to allocate money based on the performance review.

For example, suppose that a manager has two subordinates: subordinate A is a superior performer in all regards, and subordinate B is average in all respects. The manager works with both employees on setting goals. Subordinate A sets goals that will result in a very small improvement in performance but that require high levels of ability and effort (subordinate A is already a superior performer). Subordinate B sets objectives that will result in a considerable improvement in performance, but because subordinate B is currently putting forth little effort, a small increase in effort will be sufficient to meet these objectives. At the end of the assessment period, subordinate A has failed in the objectives, but subordinate B has succeeded. Even so, subordinate A is still a better performer than subordinate B. According to the assessment, the manager should recommend a larger pay increase to subordinate B than to subordinate A. However, subordinate A is the one who deserves a larger increase.

The above example points out some of the problems of using objectives designed for individuals as a basis for pay. Unless the organization is able to translate each person's achievements back into a common metric across all employees, inequities are likely to result. Therefore, although management by objectives can be highly useful for the development of employees, its use in a compensation context is problematical at best.

# Performance Assessment Interview

The performance assessment interview will have significant impact on how the employee perceives the evaluation process because this is often the only formal meeting of the parties regarding the employee's performance.[84] Even though an in-depth discussion of the performance interview is beyond the scope of this book, a brief discussion is pertinent. The performance interview is special because it enables the employee and supervisor to meet face to face to discuss how each perceives the employee is doing, what their goals and aspirations are, and what can be done to build on the employee's strengths and to improve areas of deficiency. Coaching and counseling of employees is a continuous process and not a once- or twice-a-year event, but the need for a formal meeting(s) is essential because it enables both parties to review events that have occurred and to provide the other party feedback on how each perceives the situation. If the organization has all employees evaluated at the same time, it requires an excessive amount of work by supervisors who have many employees. This can possibly lead to poor preparation on the supervisor's part, which can result in inaccurate assessments. In response to this problem, some organizations have supervisors evaluate each employee on his or her anniversary date of hire, thus spreading the workload out over the year.

## *Preparing for the Interview*

Both the evaluator and evaluatee must prepare for the interview. The evaluator must clearly establish what the interview should accomplish. The evaluator (supervisor) must review the employee's performance for the current period, including the organization's performance records, evaluator's employee performance log, and goals established for this period of time. After reviewing all behavioral and job outcome performance data, the evaluator must evaluate the employee using the appropriate form. A proposed developmental plan must be prepared to correct employee's deficiencies so that the evaluator can provide suggestions to the employee during the interview. The evaluator may wish to identify what is available both internally (training, resources) and externally (workshops, seminars, classes) before the meeting so that a positive commitment can be made to the employee during the interview. But the evaluator must view any evaluation and developmental plans as tentative because information provided by the employee during the interview may necessitate changes.

The evaluator should schedule the interview where interruptions are minimal, privacy is guaranteed, and neither will feel intimidated (neutral setting). The employee should have ample advance notice to prepare for the discussion. If the evaluator wishes the employee to do a self-assessment, the employee should be provided data to do an adequate evaluation and some training on the purpose of assessments, rating errors, and use of assessment forms. Because of the move toward increased employee participation in the assessment process, it is essential that organizations take on more systematic training of employees for the assessment interview. The research on procedural justice strongly indicates that employees' participation in all dimensions of the performance assessment process will increase their perception of procedural and outcome fairness.

### Feedback

With organizations putting increasing pressure on evaluators to enter into serious two-way communication, a few additional comments should be made regarding feedback during the performance assessment interview. It is a generally accepted belief that feedback and performance are related and that evaluators must provide ample feedback to their employees.[85] There are two basic aspects to performance assessment feedback: the amount of feedback and the quality of that feedback. For real flow of information to take place during the interview and over the course of the evaluation period, both aspects must be present to appropriate degrees. If an evaluator requests a lot of feedback but provides little to the employee, the likelihood of receiving feedback is sharply reduced. Frequent feedback is usually more effective than infrequent, but there is some feeling that feedback can be overdone. For example, continuous positive feedback may lose its usefulness as a motivator; continuous negative feedback may lead to despondency.[86]

The quality of the feedback is equally critical. First, in giving feedback during the interview, the evaluator should start with descriptive feedback without labeling it good or bad until later in the discussion. Evaluative feedback early in an interview tends to increase employee defensiveness, which can take many forms such as denial, aggression, withdrawal, and rationalization. Second, the evaluator should offer specific rather than general feedback, providing specific examples. Third, feedback should satisfy not only the evaluator's needs but the needs of the employee. Thus, it is important to be supportive and helpful, especially in the developmental areas. Fourth, the evaluator should direct comments to aspects of the job over which the employee has control. Fifth, feedback should be carefully timed so that the employee is receptive and looking for assistance. Sixth, the evaluator should anticipate employee reactions to feedback by carefully preparing for each individual based on how that person has reacted in past interviews.

The source of the feedback can influence the perception of the receiver. A recent study found that a supervisor's rating had a stronger relationship to performance than did feedback from peers, self, or the task.[87]

## Performance Assessment and Compensation Decision Making

Once the performance assessment process is complete, the compensation decision maker must translate the results into pay increases for employees. Regardless of the performance assessment system used, the assessment data must be translated into dollar increases. Like performance assessment itself, this process becomes difficult in practice, and there are problems associated with the distribution of pay increases.

The performance assessment process should result in the overall rating of each employee's performance; the rating may be a global rating or a composite of multiple dimensions. If the overall performance rating is valid, it should make a fair and equitable pay distribution possible. But, unfortunately, it is not that simple.

One reason for difficulty in allocating pay is that not all employees in a given job (for example, operatives, data entry clerks, or machinists) work in the same organizational unit or report to the same manager. This may result in inconsistencies, which can be very demoralizing to employees. If evaluators who are evaluating the same jobs meet and get agreement on specific outcomes and behaviors at each performance level for each performance standard, they can increase the probability that similar outcomes/behaviors will yield similar evaluations. This should increase employees' perception of the fairness of their pay raises.

### Allocating Pay Increase Budgets

The common organizational method of equalizing assessment is to allocate an average percentage increase of the payroll of a department to that department for distribution among employees within a job group.[88] There are problems with this approach. Such action assumes a normal distribution of employees across departments. This may not be a valid assumption. A fairer allocation rule would be to allocate pay increase budgets based on unit performance. This would result in more productive units having more dollars to distribute as merit pay increases.

### Percentage Increases to a Department

If a fixed percentage pay increase budget is allocated to each department, the manager must grant increases to employees without exceeding the dollar total available. Administratively, the manager can easily accomplish this if all employees are reviewed for a pay increase at a given time in the fiscal year. New employees, however, may receive unfair assessments based on only a short work history; their salary will be set for the next 12 months based only on that short period. A fairer approach has organizations review employees for pay increases on the employees' individual anniversary dates of employment. Under this approach, the budgeting of pay increases is a bit more complicated.[89] For example, if the supervisor gets a percentage amount for the year and evaluates employees at different times throughout the year, there may not be adequate dollars available at the time an evaluation takes place (late in the budget year) to reward an employee appropriately. The supervisor would have to make a special case to obtain extra dollars, but the supervisor may be unwilling to approach his or her supervisor for an additional allocation.

Knowing the performance level of employees relative to the job standards and the average percentage increase available for distribution, the supervisor can make recommended pay increases. Assuming that merit is the only criterion for a pay increase, the supervisor needs to translate the performance assessment outcome into a dollar outcome. This is usually done by deciding on the percentage or dollar increase that the supervisor wishes to recommend based on performance.

Although the supervisor recommends the pay increase to be allocated, he or she usually does not have unilateral authority to make this decision. Normally, the decision must be reviewed by the supervisor's superior, and typically the compensation manager will also have to agree on the recommendation. This process is important as a check in the compensation control system.

## Guidecharts

Most recommendations for pay increases are subject to one more constraint. The recommended increase should not bring the employee's total pay rate above the maximum rate for that employee's job. If the recommended increase would bring the employee above that maximum, the compensation manager may have to disapprove it. Some organizations use guidecharts to assist supervisors in making pay decisions. A typical guidechart appears in Exhibit 11.8.

The guidechart in Exhibit 11.8 might be used for pay increases based on merit. Using the guidechart, the pay increase is dependent on two variables: the employee's current status within the pay range, and the performance rating. According to the guidechart, the higher the employee moves up the pay range, the smaller the pay increase available while holding performance constant. Most perplexing is the fact that two employees (or the same employee at two different points in time) can earn different percentage increases for the same level of performance or the same percentage increase for different levels of performance.

Guidecharts are necessary because maximum pay rates for jobs cannot be exceeded if the organization hopes to achieve a consistent pay policy. However, guidecharts probably contribute substantially to the confusion about whether there is any association between pay and performance levels. It is quite difficult to convince an employee that there is a pay for performance system in effect

---

**EXHIBIT 11.8**    **GUIDECHART FOR MERIT INCREASES**

| Current Pay Quartile | Performance Rating (%) | | | |
|---|---|---|---|---|
| | **Superior** | **Above Average** | **Average** | **Below Average** |
| Maximum[a] | | | | |
| 4th | 4 | 2 | 0 | 0 |
| 3rd | 6 | 4 | 2 | 0 |
| 2nd | 8 | 6 | 4 | 0 |
| 1st | 10 | 8 | 6 | 0 |
| Minimum | | | | |

[a]Percentage increase cannot put the employee above the maximum for the job.

when another employee who is paid less and is no higher a performer receives a larger increase because there is more room in the pay grade. Nevertheless, one study found all employees who were under guidechart programs were satisfied with their pay, except for the lowest (below average) performers.[90] Some writers have suggested that merit pay increases not be built into the base pay but rather that they be one-time allocations. Under such a system, an employee may qualify for up to a 30 percent performance pay bonus each year, but each new year the employee would revert to the base rate and would have to qualify anew for a performance-based pay bonus.[91] However, one study did not find a difference in a merit bonus system versus the traditional system in influencing the pay–performance relationship.[92]

## Summary

This chapter focuses on performance assessment for pay increases. It discusses the theoretical bases for performance assessment and focuses attention on the various evaluators in the process of performance assessment.

Different types of errors and biases enter the assessment process, including criterion deficiency, criterion contamination, halo or horns bias, excessive strictness or leniency bias, central tendency bias, and recency bias. The chapter presents these errors and biases and offers suggestions for reducing them.

Concerns about adverse impact discrimination are also handled as they relate to performance assessment. One court case is included that gives some guidance as to the characteristics of performance assessment systems that are likely to withstand court challenge. The chapter presents the traditional ranking and rating methods of performance assessment, along with an explanation of their shortcomings, and a brief discussion of the performance assessment interview.

Accurate performance assessment based on job performance variance is fundamental to an effective merit pay system. Unless employees believe that different performance is rewarded differently, they are not likely to be motivated by the promise of differential monetary increases. The chapter concludes by discussing how performance assessment data translates into pay increases.

## Discussion Questions

1. Discuss how the different theories support the goals of performance assessment.

2. Should employee evaluation and development be carried out in the same interview?

3. Distinguish between the simple ranking, alternate ranking, paired comparison, and forced choice methods of performance assessment.

4. Describe the graphic rating method of performance assessment and discuss the limitations of this method.

5. Discuss behaviorally anchored rating scales as a performance assessment method along with their strengths and weaknesses.

6. Describe the management by objectives process as it relates to performance assessment and its use for making pay decisions.

7. Identify a set of performance dimensions for any job. Once you have identified the important performance dimensions, develop a scaling system for each dimension. Do this exercise first using job outcome dimensions and then using behavioral outcome dimensions.

8. Discuss the characteristics of a performance assessment system that is likely to withstand legal challenge. Why are each of these components necessary in defending the system?

9. Discuss the rationale for basing merit pay on performance variation within a job rather than on work rule behavior.

10. Identify the types of bias that tend to disrupt the link between actual performance and measured performance.

11. What must a manager consider before the actual performance assessment interview?

12. Discuss how performance appraisal data are translated into pay increases for employees. What are the problems in this process? How are these problems likely to influence the employee's perceptions of a pay for performance system?

## EXERCISES

1. Below are some data on employees from two departments within a textile firm. Based on the information, make recommendations for pay increases for these employees. How would you justify your decisions to your boss? To the employees? Were you fair? Note: Assume all information is valid — there is no bias in performance assessment.

2. Rework Exercise 1, except this time use as your allocation guidelines the guidechart from Exhibit 11.8. Again, make your recommendations and defend your decisions both to your boss and to the employees. What do you think the conversation would be like if Bob Scott and Linda Nelson discussed their current pay and your recommended increase for them? What would the conversation be like if Steve Hooper and Sally Boone discussed their current pay and recommended pay increases? How about Sheila Rowe and Moe Hill? Tina Lund and Michelle Gowan?

*Exercise 1*

| Job Titles | Name | Current Pay | Company Seniority (years) | Job Seniority (years) | Performance Evaluation Score |
|---|---|---|---|---|---|
| **Department A** | | | | | |
| Systems analyst | Joe Hage | $37,600 | 14 | 8 | 4 |
| Systems analyst | Sally Boone | 38,100 | 23 | 12 | 8 |
| Systems analyst | Billy Carper | 34,500 | 6 | 5 | 8 |
| Programmer | Linda Nelson | 32,200 | 21 | 1 | 7 |
| Programmer | Karl Figgs | 34,000 | 10 | 5 | 5 |
| Programmer | Tina Lund | 28,500 | 8 | 7 | 3 |
| Data entry clerk | Moe Hill | 13,700 | 2 | 2 | 6 |
| Data entry clerk | Phyllis Hardy | 11,000 | 3 | 3 | 8 |
| **Department B** | | | | | |
| Systems analyst | Steve Hooper | $38,700 | 18 | 14 | 4 |
| Programmer | Mike Veil | 32,800 | 9 | 3 | 8 |
| Programmer | Al Marks | 33,600 | 3 | 1 | 7 |
| Programmer | Michelle Gowan | 30,000 | 10 | 7 | 6 |
| Programmer | Bob Scott | 36,500 | 14 | 12 | 8 |
| Data entry clerk | Mabel Kavid | 12,500 | 4 | 4 | 6 |
| Data entry clerk | Sheila Rowe | 12,500 | 8 | 8 | 6 |
| Data entry clerk | Allison Wade | 12,500 | 6 | 6 | 6 |
| Data entry clerk | Becky Stone | 12,500 | 1 | 1 | 6 |

Merit increase budget for the current year is 6 percent based on the total department labor budget.

**Wage Data**

| Job | Pay Range | |
|---|---|---|
| Systems analyst | Maximum: | $40,000 |
| | Midpoint: | 35,000 |
| | Minimum: | 30,000 |
| Programmer | Maximum: | $36,000 |
| | Midpoint: | 32,000 |
| | Minimum: | 28,000 |
| Data entry clerk | Maximum: | $14,000 |
| | Midpoint: | 12,500 |
| | Minimum: | 11,000 |

3. Role-Playing Performance Appraisal Situation.

## THE BLACKSTONE COMPANY CASE
### Background: Company and Personnel

The Blackstone Company, located in Los Angeles, sells off-the-shelf electronic equipment nationwide. Although some of their sales effort is done by a field sales force, a certain

*Exercise 3* (*continued*)

portion of sales occurs through the efforts of in-house sales personnel working out of the Los Angeles office who handle sales made by telephone contact only with the customer. Because of the need to deal with customers on the east coast, the in-house sales force begins work at 7 A.M. to accommodate the 3-hour time difference. The technical nature of the product means that in-house sales personnel require approximately 2 years experience before they have sufficiently learned the product to be considered fully effective. There are three in-house sales people at the company: John Dixon, Luis Sanchez, and Lou Brown. All have been with the company between 4 and 6 years.

Up until a month ago, there were four in-house sales people, the fourth being Ann Wilson. However, when the company was reorganized last month, it was decided that Ann Wilson would be promoted to manager of in-house sales and that three sales people were sufficient to handle the business under reorganization. Previously all four sales people had reported directly to Bob Strand, Vice President of Sales. However, under the new structure, the three sales people report to Ann Wilson, who in turn reports to Bob Strand.

Sue O'Meara, an executive secretary who previously worked for Bob Strand, became the secretary to Ann Wilson. Sue is 35 years old, married, a graduate of Los Angeles Secretarial College, and has been on the same job for the past 10 years. It is accepted by everyone that Sue O'Meara, because of her longevity in the position of working with in-house sales, has an excellent knowledge of this segment of the company and had "almost run" the in-house sales department on behalf of Bob Strand (as is often the case with an excellent secretary). Sue's hours had been 8 A.M. to 4:30 P.M. but were changed to 8:30 A.M. to 5 P.M. 3 weeks ago.

When the company was reorganized a month ago, it was common knowledge that the two primary contenders for the position of in-house sales manager were Ann Wilson and John Dixon. John Dixon had been with the company longer. Most people expected that John would be the person promoted because his house is on the same block as Bob Strand's and they frequently play golf together. There was considerable speculation among the sales staff that Ann was promoted because of an effort to promote women to positions of greater responsibility within the company. John appeared to take Ann's promotion rather well, although people speculated that he did not fully support the decision.

Ann Wilson is a very attractive, very professional 28-year-old single woman. She graduated from New York University with a degree in history and came to the Blackstone Company on graduation. Her performance evaluations have always been exceptional in selling and in her ability to maintain rapport with the customer. Her evaluations indicate that she is average in interpersonal skills in areas not dealing with customer relations.

John Dixon is a 29-year-old graduate of Stanford who majored in psychology as an undergraduate. He started an MBA program at Stanford but dropped out after the first semester. He then took a position with the Blackstone Company and has been with them ever since. John has been a very good employee who has had exceptional sales productivity and has consistently been the top sales person in in-house sales. He is well liked by customers and by other people in the Blackstone Company. Eight weeks ago, John's wife and father were injured. John's two little boys, ages 2 and 4 years old, fortunately were not in the car at the time of the accident. Although John seemed very

*Exercise 3 (continued)*

shook-up in the first several weeks after the accident, he appears to have adjusted well. He also had been looking in poor health the past few months but recently has been looking better.

Luis Sanchez has been a very consistent performer within the sales department. He is 50 years old and has been with the company all his working life. Luis is always very adaptable to whatever position he is in and is always willing to put out that extra effort that is so valued in an employee. Although Luis did not go to college, his personal qualities have enabled him to be very successful within sales. He cooperates with everyone in the company and is exceedingly loyal to the organization.

Lou Brown has had an excellent sales record. His productivity ranked behind John Dixon and Ann Wilson but ahead of Luis Sanchez. While Lou is generally very personable, he has an abrasive manner that comes out at times with certain customers. There have been several complaints about Lou's relationships with certain customers, and it has become necessary to transfer some customers from Lou to other sales people. The same was true for Ann Wilson, and it is sometimes joked about among employees that Lou and Ann are two of a kind, "typically aggressive, abrasive New Yorkers."

Two weeks ago, John Dixon started coming to work late, typically arriving between 7:10 and 7:25 rather than before the 7 A.M. starting point for Ann Wilson and the other two in-house sales people. There had never been a problem with John coming in late before.

### Information for John Dixon

You have just received a note from Sue O'Meara indicating that an appointment has been scheduled for you to see Ann Wilson at 2 P.M. Because your sales performance this past quarter has been tremendous, 20 percent greater than any of the other 3 in-house people, you anticipate that you will receive rather substantial praise.

You are looking forward to this opportunity to get together with Ann Wilson because you also want to explain why you have been late for the past two weeks. You heard a snide remark from Lou Brown the other day related to your late arrivals at work, and you are concerned that Ann might be upset about the few minutes tardiness involved. Eight weeks ago your wife and father were injured in an automobile accident, and this caused your 2-year-old some psychological problems. Your 4-year-old was not affected. Since that time, you and your wife have not gotten along as well as before the accident. In the past month, on your doctor's advice, you have developed a highly structured exercise program, which requires 1 hour of work at the local health center; this is resulting in your late arrival. This is the only time available at the center, and the evening slots have been reserved for years. There are no other centers available within the area. This exercise program was developed because of a health problem, and you believe you are a more productive employee because of the program. The other free time you have available is taken up by your church and family.

You have not explained your circumstances to anyone at work. You believe that it is your business and your responsibility to handle your problems well without burdening other people; as a result, you have tried to deal with it as best you can. You have not

*Exercise 3* (*continued*)

even told Bob Strand, Vice President of Sales, about your problems during your golfing expeditions. However, you believe that he would be very understanding of your circumstances, and accordingly, you have not deemed it to be a big problem. Bob told you to do whatever is necessary to get your life back in order after the accident.

You also wish to bring up another matter during your meeting with Ann Wilson: the schedule for Sue O'Meara, the secretary. Her new 8:30 starting time is an hour and a half after the sales force arrive, and this has complicated their efforts in terms of getting paperwork processed, channeling phone calls, etc. You think that for the sales people to adequately do their jobs, they must receive support from above, and part of that entails having secretarial help available before 8:30. In fact, you believe 7:30 would be a better starting time for the secretary.

### Information for Ann Wilson

You are exceedingly pleased about being named manager of in-house sales. You know that John Dixon had outperformed you in sales, and you were somewhat surprised that you had been promoted. Because you are not the leading sales person, you have concerns that some of the sales people view you to be a "token." As a result, you want very much to establish your credibility with your staff and have them respect you and like you. You also know that you are viewed as an abrasive Easterner, and you have made every effort to try to maintain good relations with your staff.

Because this would be your first supervisory position, you knew you would have a lot to learn about how to manage the in-house sales department. You knew Sue O'Meara would be invaluable because of her vast experience in running this department as the secretary to Bob Strand. As you had anticipated, you immediately found Sue tremendously helpful, and you have told her that you could not have gotten through without her. You know there is still much you need to learn from her; your job would be much more difficult if she were no longer available. You feel that without her help, your success in the position may be questionable.

When Sue came to you three weeks ago and asked to move her hours back by half an hour so that she could attend aerobics classes in the morning, you asked her why that was necessary. She indicated that she was very stressed out from the job. The reorganization had meant a lot of additional work for her, and she would have no choice but to seek a transfer within the company if she was not able to attend aerobics classes to release her tension. Because you did not want to lose the benefit of Sue's contribution, you had hesitantly agreed that Sue could change her hours. Just this morning you were thinking how glad you are that you had agreed to do that because you now have a report to complete within the next two weeks for which Sue's presence is going to be instrumental. The report (which is due to Bob Strand) requires a great number of calculations using data with which only Sue is experienced. Without Sue there to do it, there is no way you could get the report completed in six weeks, to say nothing about within the two-week deadline Bob Strand set.

You have had Sue schedule a meeting with John Dixon for this afternoon. Although his performance has been 20 percent higher than any of the other sales people, you are very upset about his absences during the past two weeks. The primary reason for your displeasure has been that you have been getting pressure from two of the other

*Exercises 3, 4, and 5 (continued)*

sales people about his late arrivals. Luis Sanchez and Lou Brown have both complained to you about John's tardiness. Although Lou is more of a complainer, it is the expression of concern from Luis that particularly concerns you because he does not complain unless he sincerely feels that a complaint is necessary.

The two sales people have been able to handle any incoming calls for John while he has been tardy. However, this morning you noted that three calls from customers were referred to you by the sales people. You believe the sales people are referring these calls to you from John's customers to make it evident that the sales people face a problem because of John's tardiness. Accordingly, you have determined that it will be necessary to speak to John about his tardiness at the meeting this afternoon.

**OBSERVER'S INSTRUCTIONS**
**(Role-Playing Observer)**

1. How was the interview handled?

2. Did the manager

    get all the relevant facts?

    find out how the employee perceived the situation?

    get his or her goal accomplished?

    have control of the interview?

    get a commitment from the employee to change behavior by a particular time?

    communicate to the employee the specific consequences if the problem continues?

3. Will the manager have problems with the rest of the work team as a result of the handling of this situation?

4. What was the tone of the performance assessment interview?

4. Case Analysis: Confused Supervisor

You (Mary Jones) have been a supervisor in this department for the past 15 years and are in the process of evaluating all your employees. John Smith transferred from another department 9 months ago where he was performing the same job. You have just completed his evaluation and rated him a poor (4 of 5) on all 8 performance standards. You have felt this way about his performance from the beginning, but at first you thought it was the transfer (his request) and hoped his performance would improve. You have been tactful in approaching John over the past 9 months, but that has not resulted in any positive change. In the past few months, you have increased your feedback and have become more pointed in your comments. The puzzling aspect of all this is what you found when you reviewed his past evaluations (after you finished yours) by his previous supervisor. In each of the past 8 evaluations (8 years), his previous supervisor had rated him very good (2 of 5). As you sit here, a few issues come to mind:

1. Why would this be?

2. Is my evaluation of "poor" that different than other supervisors?

3. Who should I talk to?

4. How do I prepare for this interview?

5. Case Analysis: Compensation Specialist Dilemma

One of your jobs is to review the evaluations of all employees to check for any systematic bias or unusual evaluations. Mary Jones' evaluations have always been well done, complete, and on time. In reviewing her evaluations, you came across John Smith's. You have reviewed John Smith's evaluations in the past and are surprised by the low evaluation. He is usually rated as very good (2 of 5) but under Mary Jones he is rated poor (4 of 5). In your analysis, you found that John transferred to Mary's department about 9 months ago but is doing the same job. You believe you must look into this situation further.

1. What additional data do you analyze?

2. How do you deal with both Mary Jones and John Smith's previous supervisor?

## References

[1] C. J. Fombrun and R. L. Laud, "Strategic Issues in Performance: Appraisal Theory and Practices," *Personnel* 60 (November/December 1983), 23–81.

[2] V. H. Vrodom, *Work and Motivation* (New York: Wiley, 1964).

[3] J. Greenberg, "Organizational Justice: Yesterday, Today, and Tomorrow," *Journal of Management* 16 (1990), 399–432.

[4] I. R. Andrews, "Wage Inequity and Job Performance: An Experimental Study," *Journal of Applied Psychology* 51 (1967), 39–45; E. E. Lawler, "Equity Theory as a Predictor of Productivity and Work Quality," *Psychology Bulletin* 70 (1968), 596–610; J. Greenberg, "Approaching Equity and Avoiding Inequity in Groups and Organizations" in *Equity and Justice in Social Behaviors*, eds. J. Greenberg and R. L. Cohens (New York: Academic Press, 1982).

[5] Andrews, "Wage Inequity and Job Performance: An Experimental Study"; R. D. Pritchard, M. D. Dunnette, and D. O. Jorgenson, "Effects of Perception of Equity and Inequity on Worker Performance and Satisfaction," *Journal of Applied Psychology* 56 (1972), 75–94.

[6] Greenberg, "Organizational Justice Yesterday, Today and Tomorrow."

[7] J. Thilbaut and L. Walker, *Procedural Justice: A Psychological Analysis* (Hillsdale, N.J.: Lawrence Erlbaum, 1975).

[8] E. A. Lind and T. Tyler, *The Social Psychology of Procedural Justice* (New York: Plenum, 1988); R. J. Bies and D. L. Sharpiro, "Voice and Justification: Their Influence on Procedural Fairness Judgements," *Academy of Management Journal* 31 (1988), 676–685; T. R. Tyler and R. Folger, "Distributional and Procedural Aspects of Satisfaction with Citizen-Police Encounters," *Basic and Applied Social Psychology* 1 (1980), 281–292.

[9] J. Greenberg, "Organizational Performance Appraisal Procedures: What Make Them Fair?" in *Research on Negotiation in Organizations*, Vol. 1, eds. R. J. Lewicki, B. H. Sheppard and M. H. Bazerman (Greenwich, CT: JAI Press, 1986), 25–41.

[10] J. Greenberg, "Using Diaries to Promote Procedural Justice in Performance Appraisal," *Social Justice Research* 1 (1987), 219–234.

[11] R. Folger and M. Konovsky, "Effect of Procedural and Distributive Justice on Reactions to Pay Raise Decisions," *Academy of Management Journal* 32 (1989), 115–130.

[12] G. S. Leventhal, "What Should Be Done with Equity Theory?" in *Social Exchange: Advances in Theory and Research*, eds. K. J. Gergen, M. S. Greenberg, and R. H. Willis (New York: Plenum, 1980), 27–55.

[13] R. D. Bretz, Jr., and G. T. Milkovich, "Performance Appraisal in Large Organizations: Practice and Research Implications" (Working Paper no. 89–17), Center for Advanced Human Resource Studies, Ithaca, NY, 1989.

[14] Bies and Sharpiro, "Voice and Justification: Their Influence on Procedural Fairness, Judgements."

[15] *Ibid*; Greenberg, "Using Diaries to Promote Procedural Justice in Performance Appraisal."

[16] E. A. Locke, "Toward a Theory of Task Motivation and Incentives," *Organizational Behavior and Human Performance* 3 (1968), 157–189.

[17] A. J. Mento, R. P. Steel, and R. J. Karren, "A Meta-Analytic Study of the Effects of Goal Setting on Task Performance: 1966–1984," *Organizational Behavior and Human Decision Processes* 39 (1987), 52–83.

[18] W. Dorfman, W. G. Stephan, and J. Loveland, "Performance Appraisal Behaviors: Supervisor, Perception and Subordinate Reaction," *Personnel Psychology* 39 (1986), 579–596.

[19] H. H. Meyer, E. Kay, and J. R. P. French, Jr., "Split Roles in Performance Appraisal," *Harvard Business Review* 43 (1965), 123–129.

[20] H. H. Meyer, "A Solution to Performance Appraisal Feedback Enigma," *Academy of Management Executive* 5 (1991), 68–76.

[21] Dorfman, Stephan, and Loveland, "Performance Appraisal Behaviors: Supervisor Perception and Subordinate Reaction."

[22] J. B. Price and E. E. Lawler III, "Does Salary Discussion Hurt the Developmental Performance Appraisal," *Organizational Behavior and Human Decision Process* 37 (1986), 357–375.

[23] J. Wollenberger, "Acceptable Work Rules and Penalties," *Personnel* 40 (1963), 23–29.

[24] R. L. Heneman, "The Relationship Between Supervisory Ratings and Results-Oriented Measures of Performance: A Meta-Analysis," *Personnel Psychology* 39 (1986), 811–826.

[25] B. A. Friedman and E. T. Cornelius, "Effect of Rater Participation on Scale Construction on the Psychometric Characteristics of Two Rating Scale Format," *Journal of Applied Psychology* 61 (1976), 210–216; S. B. Silverman and K. N. Wexley, "Reactions of Employees to Performance Appraisal Interviews as a Function of Their Participation in Rating Scale Development," *Personnel Psychology* 37 (1984), 703–710.

[26] E. Lawler, "Managers' Attitude Toward How Their Pay Is and Should Be Determined," *Journal of Applied Psychology* 50 (1966), 273–279.

[27] B. L. Davis and M. K. Mount, "Design and Use of a Performance Appraisal Feedback System," *Personnel Administrator* 29 (March 1984), 91–95.

[28] A. H. Lochner and K. S. Teel, "Performance Appraisal—A Survey of Current Practices," *Personnel Journal* 56 (1977), 245–254.

[29] H. Levinson, "Appraisal of What Performance," *Harvard Business Review* 54 (1976), 30–36.

[30] *Brito v. Zia Co.* (428 F.2d 12001[10th Cir.1973]).

[31] *Signal Construction Corp. v. Stanbury* (D.C. Appeal No. 89-866, Feb 5, 1991).

[32] R. Folger and J. Greenberg, "Procedural Justice: An Interpretive Analysis of Personnel Systems," in *Research in Personnel and Human Resource Management* 3, eds. K. M. Rowland and G. R. Ferris (Greenwich, CT: JAI Press, 1985), 141–183.

[33] Meyer, "A Solution to Performance Appraisal Feedback Enigma."

[34] *Ibid;* L. M. Shore and G. C. Thornton III, "Effect of Gender on Self and Supervisor Rating," *Academy of Management* 29 (1986), 115–129.

[35] R. W. Eder and D. B. Fedor, "Priming Performance Self-Evaluation: Moderating Effect of Rating Purpose and Judgment Confidence," *Organizational Behavior and Human Decision Process* 44 (1989), 474–493.

[36] E. Lawler III, *Pay and Organizational Effectiveness: A Psychological View* (New York: McGraw-Hill, 1971).

[37] G. M. McEvoy and P. F. Buller, "User Acceptance of Peer Appraisals in an Industrial Setting," *Personnel Psychology* 40 (1987), 785–797.

[38] *Ibid.*

[39] H. J. Bernadin, "Subordinate Appraisal: A Valuable Source of Information About Managers," *Human Resource Management* 25 (1986), 421–439.

[40] H. J. Bernadin and L. A. Klatt, "Managerial Appraisal Systems: Has Practice Caught up to the State of the Art?" *Personnel Administrator* 32 (March 1987), 79–86.

[41] G. M. McEvoy, "Evaluating the Boss," *Personnel Administrator* 35 (September 1988), 115–120.

[42] *Ibid.*

[43] *Brito v. Zia Co.*

[44] Meyer, "A Solution to Performance Appraisal Feedback Enigma."

[45] R. L. Henderson, *Performance Appraisal* (Reston, VA: Reston Publishing Company, 1984).

[46] M. M. Harris and J. Schaubroeck, "A Meta-Analysis of Self-Supervisor, Self-Peer, and Peer-Supervisor Rating," *Personnel Psychology* 41 (1988), 43–62.

[47] H. J. Bernardin and R. W. Beatty, *Performance Appraisal: Assessing Human Behavior at Work* (Boston, MA: Kent Publishing Company, 1984).

[48] For a discussion of the multidimensionality of criteria, see P. C. Smith, "Behaviors, Results, and Organizational Effectiveness: The Problem of Criteria," in *Handbook of Industrial and Organizational Psychology*, M. D. Dunnette, ed. (Chicago: Rand McNally, 1976), 745–775.

[49] For a more detailed discussion of criterion continuation and deficiency, see M. L. Blum and J. C. Naylor, *Industrial Psychology: Its Theoretical and Social Foundations* (New York: Harper and Row, 1968), 176–177.

[50] B. L. Schlei and P. Grossman, *Employment Discrimination Law* (Washington, D.C.: Bureau of National Affairs, 1976).

[51] Bernardin and Klatt, "Managerial Appraisal Systems."

[52] Smith, "Behaviors, Results and Organizational Effectiveness," 746–747.

[53] R. M. Guion, *Personnel Testing* (New York: McGraw-Hill, 1965).

[54] D. E. Smith, "Training Programs for Performance Appraisal: A Review," *Academy of Management Review* 11 (1986), 22–40.

[55] W. H. Cooper, "Internal Homogeneity, Descriptiveness, and Halo: Resurrecting Some Answers and Questions about the Structure of Job Performance," *Personnel Psychology* 36 (1983), 489–502.

[56] D. E. Smith, "Training Programs for Performance Appraisal: A Review," *Academy of Management Review* 11 (1986), 22–38.

[57] F. E. Saal, R. G. Downey, and M. A. Lahey, "Rating the Ratings: Assessing the Quality of Rating Data," *Psychological Bulletin* 88 (1980), 413–428.

[58] B. R. Nathan and N. Tippens, "The Consequences of Halo 'Error' in Performance Ratings: A Field Study of the Moderating Effect of Halo on Test Validation Results," *Journal of Applied Psychology* 75 (1990), 290–296.

[59] K. R. Murphy, R. A. Jako, and R. L. Anhalt, "Nature and Consequences of Halo Error: A Critical Analysis," *Journal of Applied Psychology* 78 (1993), 213–218.

[60] R. J. Vance, P. S. Winne, and E. S. Wright, "A Longitudinal Examination of Rater and Ratee Effects in Performance Rating," *Personnel Psychology* 36 (1983), 609–630.

[61] Smith, "Training Programs for Performance Appraisal."

[62] R. L. Heneman and K. N. Wexley, "The Effects of Time Delay in Rating and the Amount of Information Observed on the Performance Rating Accuracy," *Academy of Management Journal* 26 (1983), 677–686.

[63] A. S. DeNisi, T. Robbins, and T. P. Cafferty, "Organization of Information Used for Performance Appraisals: Role of Diary Keeping," *Journal of Applied Psychology* 74 (1989), 124–129.

[64] A. S. Tsui and B. Bruce, "Interpersonal Affects of Rating Error," *Academy of Management Journal* 29 (1986), 586–597.

[65] P. S. Eyres, "Legally Defensible Performance Appraisal Systems," *Personnel Journal* 68 (1989), 58–62.

[66] L. L. Cummings and D. P. Schwab, *Performance Organizations* (Glenview, IL: Scott Foresman, 1981).

[67] S. J. Carroll and C. E. Schneir, *Performance Appraisal and Review Systems* (Glenview, IL: Scott Foresman, 1981).

[68] Eyres, "Legally Defensible Performance Appraisal Systems."

[69] Ibid.

[70] *James Stockham v. Valves and Fittings Co.*, 294 F. Supp. 434 (N.D.Ala. 1975).

[71] G. V. Barrett and M. C. Kernan, "Performance Appraisal and Terminations: A Review of Court Decisions Since Brito v. Zia with Implications for Personnel Practices," *Personnel Psychology* 40 (1987), 489–503.

[72] Schlei and Grossman, *Employment Discrimination Law.*

[73] E. R. Auster, "Task Characteristic as a Bridge Between Macro- and Micro-Level Research on Salary Inequity Between Men and Women," *Academy of Management Review* 14 (1989), 173–193.

[74] Ibid.

[75] B. S. Lawrence, "New Wrinkles in the Theory of Age: Demography, Norms, and Performance Ratings," *Academy of Management Review* 31 (1988), 309–337.

[76] B. S. Klass and A. S. DeNisi, "Managerial Reactions to Employee Dissent: The Impact of Grievance Activity on Performance Ratings," *Academy of Management Journal* 32 (1989), 705–716.

[77] C. Peck, "Pay and Performance: The Interaction of Compensation and Performance Appraisal," No. 155 (New York: The Conference Board, 1984).

[78] Bretz and Milkovich, "Performance Appraisal in Large Organizations."

[79] Auster, "Task Characteristics as a Bridge Between Macro- and Micro-Level Research on Salary Inequity Between Men and Women."

[80] W. C. Borman and M. D. Dunnette, "Behavioral Based Versus Trait-Oriented Performance Ratings: An Empirical Study," *Journal of Applied Psychology* 60 (1975), 561–565.

[81] D. P. Schwab, H. G. Heneman III, and T. A. DeCotis, "Behaviorally Anchored Rating Scales: A Review of the Literature," *Personnel Psychology* 28 (1975), 549–562.

[82] H. J. Bernardin and P. C. Smith, "A Clarification of Some Issues Regarding the Development and Use of Behaviorally Anchored Rating Scales (BARS)," *Journal of Applied Psychology* 66 (1981), 458–463.

[83] M. L. McConkie, "A Clarification of the Goal Setting and Appraisal Processes in MBO," *Academy of Management Review* 4 (1979), 29–40.

[84] J. Greenberg and C. L. McCarty, "Comparable Worth: A Matter of Justice," in *Research in Personnel and Human Resource Management*, Vol. 8, eds. K. M. Rowland and G. R. Ferris (Greenwich, CT: JAI Press, 1990).

[85] T. E. Becker and R. J. Klimoski, "A Field Study of the Relationship Between Feedback Environment and Performance," *Personnel Psychology* 42 (1989), 343–358.

[86] *Ibid.*

[87] *Ihid*

[88] Peck, "Pay and Performance."

[89] S. D. Beggs, "The Lead-Lag Problem: Adjustments Needed for Salary Comparison," *Compensation and Benefits Review* 18 (November/December 1986), 44–54.

[90] F. S. Hills, R. M. Madigan, K. D. Scott, and S. E. Markham, "Tracking the Merit of Merit Pay," *Personnel Administrator* 32 (1987), 50–57.

[91] F. S. Hills, "The Pay for Performance Dilemma," *Personnel* (September/October 1979), 23–31.

[92] D. P. Schwab and C. A. Olson, "Merit Pay Practices: Implications for Pay-Performance Relationships," *Industrial and Labor Relations Review* 43 (1990), 237–255.

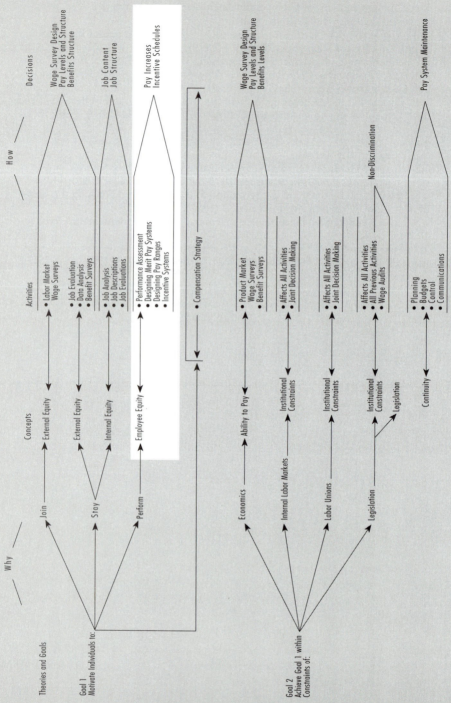

# V

# *Individual Equity*

# 12

# Individual and Group Incentives

# Learning Objectives

To learn that incentive plans must be integrated with corporate strategic plans.

To reinforce that all incentive plans are efforts to motivate high levels of job performance.

To learn in detail about individual incentive plans.

To learn when to use individual or group incentive plans.

# Introduction

This chapter focuses on individual and group incentive plans. After studying the chapter, the reader should be able to identify the main forms of incentive plans, discuss conditions under which incentive plans are likely to work, and design an incentive plan.

# Incentive Plans Tied to Corporate Strategy

All incentive plans must be tied to the organization's long- and short-term goals and objectives. The increasing global competition is forcing U.S.–based firms to look for methods that will positively shape employee behavior.[1] Because of the organization's presence in this relatively new environment of increased risk, uncertainty, and competition, the compensation manager must not only look at the traditional incentive systems but must also be innovative in modifying existing approaches and be open to the use of new and creative approaches.[2]

Incentive plans focus on human behavior and how behavior changes based on the reward system of the organization. It is essential that the incentive system actually result in behaviors that aid the organization in the accomplishment of its corporate goals. If this is not well integrated into the design stage, the incentive system may motivate behaviors that are harmful to the organization but beneficial to the individual or group.

As the term *incentive* implies, all incentive plans share the common objective of promoting and retaining the highest performance in employees.[3] Whether they accomplish this goal is partially dependent on a set of boundary conditions. These boundary conditions are the underlying conditions necessary to predict high performance when money is used as a reward, and the assumptions about human motivation and the work environment.

# Theoretical Foundation

As discussed in Chapter 2, for monetary rewards to motivate high performance, expectancy theory requires satisfaction of a number of conditions.[4] Eight basic conditions are summarized in Exhibit 12.1.

| EXHIBIT 12.1 | CONDITIONS OF AN INCENTIVE SYSTEM |

1. Employees must be capable of performing at high levels.
2. Employees must believe they can perform at high levels.
3. Employees must believe that performance will result in more money.
4. Employees must value money.
5. Jobs must allow for performance variation.
6. Performance must be measurable.
7. The process of evaluation must be viewed as fair and equitable.
8. The plan must be compatible with the nature of work (individual versus group output).

The first condition for all incentive plans is that employees are capable of performing at high levels. Unless the work force has the capability to perform at high levels, there will be no potential for high performance. A second condition is that employees believe that they can perform at high levels if they expend the effort (expectancy). Even if individuals have the capability, unless they recognize their capability, they are unlikely to perform highly.

A third condition is that individuals perceive a link between high performance (instrumentality) and money and believe they will be rewarded for high performance. There must be a strong demonstration that the level of reward varies directly and systematically with the level of performance. Because money acts as a secondary reinforcer, the organization must be able to convince employees that the level of monetary reward will vary based on level of job performance. The strength of the bond between job performance and reinforcer (money) is a summation of the employees' perception of past experience (current and past organizations and their managers) and the employees' perception that the situation will be similar or different than the past. If an organization's past incentive plans had not worked, when new plans are introduced, employees may perceive rewards as not relating to performance and thus not be motivated to increase effort.[5]

A fourth condition is that individuals value money as a reward. Not all individuals value money equally, but money must have enough value to motivate behavior. For example, people may value acceptance from peers more than they value money. In this case, money alone is not likely to be adequate incentive for encouraging high performance if there is the possibility of antagonizing peers in the process.[6] Money, however, may satisfy multiple needs within the individual. For some, money not only satisfies physiological needs but also achievement and recognition needs. Employees may view monetary rewards as a way to objectively keep track of their accomplishments and their career progress. This is analogous to gunfighters in the Old West cutting notches in the handles of their guns to indicate the number of times they won gunfights. Thus, the identification of the need structure and the importances attached to specific needs (especially money) is critical in the design of an effective system.

The fifth condition for an incentive system is that the job allows room for performance variation.[7] For there to be a change in rewards as a result of performance, the job must permit a large enough variance to be able to adequately relate rewards to those performance changes. If the employees' performance level is mostly driven by technology or outside sources (for example, component parts from an outside vendor), it may be better not to use an incentive system.

The relatively objective measurement of performance variation is a sixth condition.[8] When organizations use loose measures of performance, employees often question the fairness of reward distribution and trust can break down quickly. Closely related to this is the seventh condition. The employees must believe the process is fair; they must perceive procedural justice.

The eighth condition is compatibility of the incentive plan with the nature of work. The organization must determine whether successful performance is a group or an individual effort.[9] An example of individual contribution to success would be the number of insurance policies sold. This outcome can usually be attributed to one person. An example of group-determined success might be when a team of eight people constructs a building. In this case, the success is a function of every one of the eight contributing his or her best.

## Reasons for Incentive Systems

The use of incentive systems is not new. Incentive systems were used to influence the behavior of workers in ancient times and became more popular with the Western Industrial Revolution.[10] Now, with productivity as a main issue in the search for a competitive edge, organizations are increasingly looking at variable pay that is tied to performance dimensions.[11] A survey conducted by the American Productivity and Quality Center found that at least 75 percent of those surveyed used a variable pay plan and that most were started in the 1980s.[12]

The basic question is why do organizations use incentive systems to motivate employees' behavior. First, competition has forced employers to find ways to control their labor cost. By switching from an hourly rate to an incentive plan, a larger percentage of wage cost becomes variable instead of fixed.[13] The sum of hourly wage rate and incentive rate must at least equal the level of minimum wage to be lawful. Second, the need to control labor cost is tightly coupled with the need to increase productivity of labor. This is particularly relevant to the service sector of the economy, which lags the manufacturing section in productivity. Third, deregulation has forced organizations (for example, communication, trucking, banking) that previously did not have to examine cost structures seriously to review their cost and institute programs to reduce the cost of the product or service they provide. Fourth, organizations that have executive bonus plans in place are looking at expanding them to include lower organizational levels because of pressures from ineligible workers who believe their inability to participate makes such plans inequitable.[14] A study of 630 companies revealed that 53 percent of those surveyed provide variable incentives to workers below the executive level.[15] Fifth, organizations see incentive systems as a means to increase congruence between the goals of the organization and those of the individual.[16] Sixth, organizations use incentive systems because other organizations do. Thus, the systems help retain key people who would otherwise leave for other organizations that provide incentive plans for both financial and nonfinancial growth.[17] Seventh, organizations view group incentives as a means to facilitate the building of effective teams.

## Individual Incentive Plans

Individual incentive plans give employees greater control over their compensation in any work period. The employees know clearly what the organization expects. They can increase their individual performance and thus increase their rewards. The incentive offers both motivation and feedback.

There are two basic types of individual plans for employees: piece rate plans and standard hour plans. In *piece rate incentive plans*, the employee is paid a given rate for each unit produced, each service provided, or each item sold. In *standard hour plans*, the bonus pay is based on performing the work task in less time than required by the standard.

### Establishing a Piece Rate Plan

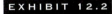

There are three steps in establishing a piece rate incentive system. These steps are summarized in Exhibit 12.2.

**Step 1: Establish Output Standards for the Job**    This first step usually requires industrial engineering input. An industrial engineer will study the job in minute detail, often using time and motion study methods to determine the average amount of time it will take a fully trained employee with average ability to complete the task.

Time and motion study involves two distinct although highly related parts. *Motion study* analyzes different ways to do the same task or activity. That analysis identifies the most efficient movements for completing the task or activity.

**EXHIBIT 12.2    PIECE RATE INCENTIVE PLAN PROCESS**

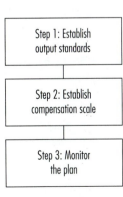

Step 1: Establish output standards

Step 2: Establish compensation scale

Step 3: Monitor the plan

*Time study* determines the average time to perform a task or activity when a particular motion is used. Time study is based on the assumption that raw materials are always available and that finished goods are removed so they do not interfere with future output.[18] A simplified example of the process that industrial engineering uses to design a piece rate compensation plan is presented in Exhibit 12.3.

As a result of time and motion study, an output standard is set for a given unit of time. The standard serves as the average output rate per hour (or some other unit of time) and is applied to all the employees on the job.

**Step 2: Establish Compensation Scale** Several considerations go into establishing the incentive rate for a piece rate system: desired base pay, whether fixed or variable incentive rates will be used, and desired maximum pay. These three issues are interrelated, but they are discussed separately to highlight the key decisions in each issue.

*Base Pay Rate* Every piece rate system must establish the job's base pay. This can be done in two ways, as shown in Exhibit 12.4. One popular way to do this is to equate the output standard with the minimum or base rate of pay that the organization wishes to pay (option A—Exhibit 12.4). The organization may use traditional job evaluation and job pricing procedures, discussed in earlier chapters, to determine this base pay. In this approach, every employee is guaranteed the base rate whether or not the output standard is met. For example, the employer may want average wages to be $5.00 per hour. If the production standard is 100 units per hour, then the piece rate would be $0.05 and the average worker would earn $5.00 per hour. An employee who does not meet the production standard will still be guaranteed the $5.00 minimum. Not meeting the production standard could be caused by employee problems or by other problems (such as a shortage of raw material or machine downtime).

A second approach makes average pay equivalent to the output standard, but the base rate guaranteed to those who do not meet the output standard is lower (option B—Exhibit 12.4). That minimum base may be the legal minimum wage rate. In this approach, the output standard is the midpoint of the job's pay range. For example, the employer might set the equivalent wage at $5.00 and use a lower minimum or base wage of $4.25. The piece rate would remain at $0.05, and the average worker could earn $5 for meeting the output standard of 100 units per hour. Employees who do not meet the standard in any given hour

---

**EXHIBIT 12.3** **IE PROCESS FOR ARRIVING AT A STANDARD TIME**

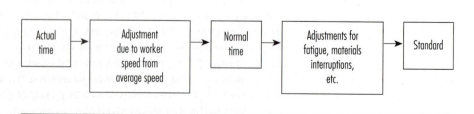

| EXHIBIT 12.4 | SETTING BASE PAY IN AN INCENTIVE PLAN |
| --- | --- |

### Option A

| | |
| --- | --- |
| Guaranteed average pay base | $5.00 |
| Piece rate | $0.05 |
| Standard production based on time study | 100 units/hour |
| Average pay | $5.00/hour |

### Option B

| | |
| --- | --- |
| Guaranteed minimum wage base | $4.25 |
| Piece rate | $0.05 |
| Standard production based on time study | 100 units/hour |
| Average pay | $5.00/hour |

receive the minimum wage of $4.25 for that hour.[19] Option B in Exhibit 12.4 results in lower labor costs across all employees who cannot meet the standard. In industries that must control costs closely, this may be a necessary step.

***Fixed or Variable Incentive Rates*** The incentive rate scale is the pay rate per unit produced over the entire productivity schedule. There are three variations on incentive rate scales: fixed rates, increasing rates, and decreasing rates. Examples of the three variations appear in Exhibit 12.5.

The data in Exhibit 12.5 demonstrate several features of incentive rate scales. For example, if overhead is $100 per hour (for machine maintenance, electricity), any increases in productivity will reduce the hourly overhead costs per unit of output in column 4. Overhead per unit produced goes down as productivity goes up.

A second feature is that fixed-, increasing-, and decreasing-rate scales allow employees to earn more based on their increased productivity. Under the fixed-rate schedule, employees do not share in the cost savings; they are paid the same per unit of output regardless of the productivity level. With increasing-rate scales employees share in the savings caused by their greater productivity in that they earn more per unit as their productivity goes up. At the same time that employees are sharing the productivity gains, per unit production costs are still decreasing for the employer.

With decreasing-rate scales, employees do not share in productivity gains. In this case, employees are wealthier only because of their own productivity increases, because the rate scale is decreasing as a function of productivity. Employees still make more per hour, and decreasing-rate scales result in the greatest decrease in per unit costs.

Under the decreasing-rate scale presented in Exhibit 12.5, employees can make up to 135 percent of the standard pay rate (assuming a standard rate of

| EXHIBIT 12.5 | FIXED, INCREASING, AND DECREASING INCENTIVE SCALES |
|---|---|

### Fixed Incentive Rate Scale

| (1) Number of Units | (2) Rate | (3) Total Earnings | (4) Overhead Unit | (5) Total Unit Cost |
|---|---|---|---|---|
| 100 | $0.050 | $5.00 | $1.00 | $1.05 |
| 110 | 0.050 | 5.50 | 0.91 | 0.96 |
| 120 | 0.050 | 6.00 | 0.83 | 0.88 |
| 130 | 0.050 | 6.50 | 0.77 | 0.82 |
| 140 | 0.050 | 7.00 | 0.71 | 0.76 |
| 150 | 0.050 | 7.50 | 0.67 | 0.72 |

### Increasing Incentive Rate Scale

| (1) Number of Units | (2) Rate | (3) Total Earnings | (4) Overhead Unit | (5) Total Unit Cost |
|---|---|---|---|---|
| 100 | $0.050 | $ 5.00 | $1.00 | $1.050 |
| 110 | 0.055 | 6.05 | 0.91 | 0.965 |
| 120 | 0.060 | 7.20 | 0.83 | 0.890 |
| 130 | 0.065 | 8.45 | 0.77 | 0.835 |
| 140 | 0.070 | 9.80 | 0.71 | 0.780 |
| 150 | 0.075 | 11.25 | 0.67 | 0.745 |

### Decreasing Incentive Rate Scale

| (1) Number of Units | (2) Rate | (3) Total Earnings | (4) Overhead Unit | (5) Total Unit Cost |
|---|---|---|---|---|
| 100 | $0.050 | $ 5.00 | $1.00 | $1.050 |
| 110 | 0.049 | 5.39 | 0.91 | 0.959 |
| 120 | 0.048 | 5.76 | 0.83 | 0.878 |
| 130 | 0.047 | 6.11 | 0.77 | 0.817 |
| 140 | 0.046 | 6.44 | 0.71 | 0.756 |
| 150 | 0.045 | 6.75 | 0.67 | 0.715 |

$0.05 per unit at 100 units per hour = $5.00 per hour). That is, at 150 units of output per hour, and a standard rate of $0.045, a worker can make $6.75 per hour, which is a 35 percent increase over the desired base pay rate.

Decreasing-rate scales do not always result in this relationship, however. The precise relationships are a function of the range in performance variability, the magnitude of the overhead costs, and the interaction of the two. The organization would need to know its own productivity variability potential and overhead rates and experiment with the two to determine the precise rate scale that would enable a 35 percent growth opportunity in wages while still controlling costs.

For obvious reasons, an increasing-rate scale should be more motivating than either a fixed- or decreasing-rate scale, and a fixed-rate scale should be more motivating than a decreasing-rate scale.[20]

***Maximum Pay Rate***   The third main consideration is the maximum pay an employer is willing to pay an employee under a piece rate incentive system. Although in theory there is no limit to how much an employee can earn under a piece rate system, practicality does limit the amount. For one thing, if piece rate workers earn too much relative to other employees in the plant, including their supervisors, feelings of inequity may result.[21] Thus, some practical limit on the total amount that can be earned may be established.

One way to limit incentive pay is to decide the percentage above the average pay rate equivalent that will be allowed and to scale the piece rate along a continuum that corresponds to that maximum. Administratively, this could be accomplished as follows. First, the organization decides the maximum pay for the job. Next, it determines the maximum output rate that could be achieved by no more than 5 percent of the employees, for example. The piece rate is then scaled accordingly. As in the example used for decreasing rate, an employer may decide that employees can earn a premium up to 35 percent of base pay. An incentive scale is then determined that takes into account the productivity opportunities of technology and is compatible with the above goals.

**Step 3: Monitor the Plan**   Successful piece rate plans must have a good administrative system behind them to tabulate performance levels of employees accurately and to provide wage payments on a timely and routine basis. As in merit plans, the incentive plans should also recognize the potential multidimensionality of performance. The two most important dimensions may be quantity and quality of output. Where pay is determined by quantity of output alone, there may be a strong tendency on the part of employees to ignore quality issues. The organization needs to establish quality standards to back up the quantity standards.[22] For example, an organization may specify that productivity levels must be achieved with less than 2 percent of the parts produced rejected by quality control or less than 0.05 percent waste of raw materials. One of the problems frequently associated with piece rate systems is that incentive pay may lag behind performance. For example, the employer may pay the standard rate for the current period but delay the performance pay by one or more periods. This is a legitimate delay that permits the employer to adjust the employee incentive pay for quality problems that are not identified by internal quality control programs. Unfortunately, this procedure often results in confusion among employees about whether they are actually paid relative to their productivity level and weakens the link between performance and rewards. Organizations must continuously review the behavioral outcomes the incentive program is generating.

There are times that incentive plans are very effective in changing behavior, but the new behavior is counterproductive to the organizational goals and objectives. Close monitoring is essential therefore to ensure incentive programs actually contribute to organizational strategy and effectiveness.[23]

## Examples of Piece Rate Plans

Over the years, many individuals and organizations have developed piece rate incentive plans. Such plans are common in the rubber, textile, and apparel industries.

**Straight Piecework**    Straight piecework plans are common. In these plans, the financial incentive is the same at all points on the individual's production curve. For example, truck farms often use piecework plans to pay employees a particular amount for each pint of strawberries picked. The textile industry also uses straight piecework plans, paying employees a certain amount for each towel they fold and package. Piecework plans also are common in the apparel industry, in which employees may be paid a fixed amount for sewing pieces of a garment. Ramada Renaissance Hotel in Atlanta uses a piece rate plan for housekeeping staff. Before the piece rate system, employees received $4.50 an hour; since the program has been installed, the average rate has been $6.00 per hour based on $2.22 per room. If an employee does not reach minimum wage through the piece rate system or when employees are not doing incentive work, the organization guarantees them minimum wages.[24] Sales people often work on a basic commission with a base. Sales associates often receive a percentage of dollars sold, which may have a guaranteed base associated with it or not. More detailed discussion of sales incentives occurs in Chapter 15.

Piece rate plans for operation employees are popular in industries that have highly competitive product markets and are labor-intensive. These firms must keep labor costs at a minimum because of the impact of labor costs on total costs and the competitive nature of product markets. Piecework systems allow for this; employees who do not produce may not be paid, subject to minimum wage limitations.

**Differential Piece Rate—the Taylor Plan**    Frederick W. Taylor developed a piece rate plan at the end of the nineteenth century that provided two different piece rates for the same work.[25] The criterion used to determine which rate applied was the employee's productivity level. An employee who performed below the predetermined standard was paid at the lower rate. An employee who performed at or above the predetermined standard received the higher rate. This higher rate was normally about 20 percent more than the lower rate. Exhibit 12.6 demonstrates the value to the worker on reaching the level of production needed to activate the premium pay.

This differential provides a large financial incentive to employees to meet at least a minimum level of production of 100 units. Even though it does not guarantee that all employees will reach the 100 level of production each hour, it does increase significantly the probability that at least 100 units of output will be attained by most employees. This has significant positive value to managers scheduling delivery to customers: It increases the ability to promise delivery dates

| EXHIBIT 12.6 | TAYLOR DIFFERENTIAL PIECE RATE PLAN |
|---|---|

### Piece Rate

| | |
|---|---|
| Production less 100 units per hour | $0.06 per unit |
| Production 100 units or more per hour | $0.072 per unit |

### Employee A

| | |
|---|---|
| Production Rate | 98 units per hour |
| Piece Rate | $0.06 per hour |
| Hourly Rate | (98)($0.06) = $5.88 |
| Weekly Pay | (40)($5.88) = $235.20 |

### Employee B

| | |
|---|---|
| Production Rate | 110 units per hour |
| Piece Rate | $0.072 per hour |
| Hourly Rate | (110)($0.072) = $7.92 |
| Weekly Pay | (40)($7.92) = $316.80 |

and to honor these promises. This relative assurance that a maximum production level will be maintained is more critical as more organizations adapt the just-in-time inventory approach (maintaining minimum inventory levels). These organizations will not have much of a surplus inventory to use if a delivery is missed.

**Stage Differential Piece Rate—the Merrick Plan** The Merrick plan, developed by D. W. Merrick in the early twentieth century, is similar to the Taylor plan. The main difference between the two is that the Merrick plan uses three different pay rates.[26] The highest rate is used for employees who exceed the predetermined standard. These employees receive 120 percent of the lowest rate. A middle rate is used for employees who achieve at least 84 percent of the standard but do not exceed the standard. These employees receive 110 percent of the lowest rate. The lowest rate is paid to those at or below 83 percent of the standard (see Exhibit 12.7). This plan will not be illustrated because of its close similarity to the Taylor plan.

Both the Taylor and Merrick plans vary the pay rate as a function of productivity level. This relationship is direct so that in effect both plans have an increasing rate scale that permits employees to share in their productivity gains.

## Establishing a Standard Hour Plan

Standard hour plans are very similar to piece rate incentive plans. The steps for establishing a standard hour plan are identical to those used in setting up a piece rate system. First, industrial engineering identifies the standard times

| EXHIBIT 12.7 | MERRICK PIECE RATE PLAN |
|---|---|

| | |
|---|---|
| Production at 83 percent of standard | $ 0.06 per unit |
| Production between 84 to 100 percent of standard | 0.066 per unit |
| Production greater than 100 percent of standard | 0.072 per unit |

for each task or job; second, the organization decides the desired standard hour rate of pay; and third, the organization monitors the plan and the quality of work.

The main difference between the two types of plans is that, in standard hour plans, the production standard is expressed in time units. Under this type of plan, industrial engineering uses time study methods to analyze a job and establishes a fixed unit of time for completion of the job. The employee who is assigned to the job receives the standard rate of pay for the job, whether he or she finishes the job in the standard time frame or takes a shorter or longer time.

An example of a standard hour plan is a task that is determined through time study to carry a standard time of 0.40 hours (24 minutes). If the standard pay rate is $5.00 per hour, then the employee receives $2.00 (0.40 × $5.00 = $2.00) for completing the task, whether it required 0.40 hours or 0.20 hours or 0.50 hours.

In most cases, the actual time to do the job is expressed relative to the standard time. In the above example, if the employee completed the job in 0.20 hours, the employee is working at 200 percent of standard time (0.40 hours divided by 0.20 hours × 100 percent = 200 percent). Expressing actual output as a percentage of standard output tells the employee how much of the standard hourly rate is earned. In this example, if the employee performs 5 tasks at the above rate, she or he has worked at 200 percent of standard time for 1 full hour, and the actual pay would be twice the standard time rate, or $10.00 (2 × $5.00 standard rate).

### Examples of Standard Hour Plans

The preceding discussion is based on the assumption that standard hour plans use a fixed-rate schedule of pay for standard time units. Just as a piece rate incentive rate may vary with output, so can a standard hour rate. The following discussion considers three of the better known standard hour plans in which the rate varies with production level.

**Halsey Plan**   The Halsey plan, established by Frederick Halsey at the end of the nineteenth century, allows both employees and management to share in any direct labor savings.[27] Under the Halsey plan, employees are guaranteed a predetermined hourly wage. When the worker performs the task, the amount of time it took to perform the task is compared with the standard time. Employees and management share any savings. The plan originally established a 33⅓ employee and 66⅔ employer share of the savings.[28] In practice, the percentage that goes to the employees varies between 30 percent and 70 percent of the time saved, with most at around the 50 percent level.

For example, an employee who is paid $7 per hour (the minimum rate) performs a task with a standard time of 4 hours but completes the task in only 3 hours. For this task, the worker is 25 percent more productive than the standard. Under the Halsey plan, the employee receives a bonus for the savings as a percentage of the base pay. Exhibit 12.8 illustrates the above assuming a 50/50 sharing. The employee is entitled to 50 percent of the time saved because of his or her efficiency.

**Rowan Plan**    The Rowan plan is similar to the Halsey plan.[29] A basic difference is that, whereas management and labor share in the labor cost savings at a fixed rate in the Halsey plan, in the Rowan plan the employees realize a larger proportion of the savings as their productivity increases. Also, while the Halsey plan calculates its bonus on the time saved, the Rowan plan calculates the bonus on the time worked.

Exhibit 12.9 illustrates how an employee might receive 15 percent of the direct labor savings for completing the job within 85 percent of standard time, but 30 percent of the labor savings if the task is completed within 70 percent of standard time. The bonus percentage applied to base pay is a direct function of the percentage of time saved under the Rowan plan.[30]

---

**EXHIBIT 12.8    HALSEY PLAN**

---

Hourly Wage Rate = $7.00
Time to Complete Job = 4 hours
50/50 Sharing between Employer and Employee

**Employee A**

---

Complete Job in 3 Hours
Savings = 1 hour
Normal Pay = $7.00/hour

$$\text{Actual Pay Due to Efficiency} = \quad \$7.00 \times 3 \text{ hours} = \$21.00$$
$$.50 \times \$7.00 \times 1 \text{ hour} = \underline{\quad 3.50}$$
$$\$24.50$$

Actual Pay for Job (3 hours worked) = $24.50

$$\text{Actual Hourly Pay Rate} = \frac{\text{Job Pay}}{\text{Actual Hours Worked}} = \frac{\$24.50}{3} = \$8.17$$

Differential = Actual − Standard ($8.17 − $7.00 = $1.17 per hour)

---

| EXHIBIT 12.9 | ROWAN PLAN |
| --- | --- |

Hourly Rate            =   $7.00
Time to Complete Job   =   6 hours
Sharing Schedule:      15 percent for 85 percent of standard
                       30 percent for 70 percent of standard

### Employee A

Completes job in 5.1 hours (85 percent of standard)
Sharing Schedule   = 15 percent
Actual Hourly Rate = ($7.00)(1.15) = $8.05
Actual Pay for Job = ($8.05)(5.1) = $41.06

### Employee B

Completes job in 4.2 hours (70 percent of standard)
Sharing Schedule   = 30 percent
Actual Hourly Rate = ($7.00)(1.30) =   $9.10
Actual Pay for Job = ($9.10)(4.2)  = $38.22

**Gantt Plan**    A third version of a standard hour plan is the Gantt plan. First introduced in a large machine shop at Bethlehem Steel Company, it is a variation of the Halsey and Rowan plans.[31] The Gantt plan sets the initial standard time to demand high employee effort. All employees are guaranteed a base wage, and a bonus is paid at the rate of 120 percent for employees who meet or exceed the standard. Thus an employee not reaching standard receives the guaranteed hourly rate. Those employees who complete the task in the allowed time or less receive the bonus. In this system, the organization often grants the supervisors a bonus based on the productivity of their workers. This is meant to encourage supervisors to do all in their power to increase the efficiency of each worker. In addition to sharing in each worker's efficiency, the supervisors might earn an additional 50 percent bonus if all workers under their supervision earn an incentive.

## Problems with Individual Incentive Plans

There are a host of problems associated with installing and operating incentive plans, ranging from engineering problems to problems with managerial and employee attitudes and behaviors. These problems are summarized in Exhibit 12.10 and discussed in this section.

## Engineering-Related Problems

The first step in an incentive plan is for an industrial engineer to conduct a time and motion study of one or more employees to determine the average number of pieces that can be produced per unit of time, or the average time to complete a job or task. This process can be difficult. Many factors contribute to the problem of setting standards.

**Finding Typical Employees**   An alternative to finding a typical employee would be to study many employees doing the same task or job and to average the results. There may be a question of whether employees are performing at their normal work rate in the study or if they are working more slowly so that a lower standard will result.[32] Employees could also work faster than average to impress management during the study. To combat this problem, the rate structure can be varied to reflect the industrial engineer's assumptions about the employees. For example, if employees seem to slow down during the study, the response could be to adjust the standard rate upward, or to pay a larger premium for above–standard output, or to pay a lower premium for below-standard output (as provided by the Taylor and Merrick plan rates discussed above).

**Allowing for Exceptional Work Conditions**   In the short run, there may be spot shortages of raw materials inventory, shortage of storage for finished goods,

---

**EXHIBIT 12.10**   **PROBLEMS WITH INCENTIVE PLANS**

### Engineering-Related

Finding typical employees
Allowing for exceptional work conditions
Establishing accurate allowances for set-up time and machine adjustment
Accurately changing standards as conditions change

### Employee-Related

Lack of understanding and trust
Modest pay desires
Alternative views of fairness
Limited control over outcomes
Negative effects on teamwork

### Managerial-Related

Value conflicts
Incentive budget difficulties
Ability–to–pay constraints

uneven quality of raw materials, or uneven machine performance, to name a few. This comes back to the issue of not making employees responsible for things beyond their control.

**Establishing Accurate Allowances for Set-up and Machine Adjustments**
Standard times may also assume long production runs of the same units and not allow for the set–up time or adjustment times needed for machinery involved in frequent changeovers. These forces mean that in the short run, it may be nearly impossible for an employee to operate at standard. To the extent that these factors are not stable, they cause employees to doubt the validity of the established standards and weaken the belief that high levels of performance can result in more pay.[33]

**Accurately Changing Standards as Conditions Change**    In almost every production process, there are ongoing changes. Each change may be small in and of itself. Examples are switching a bolt system from a four-bolt to a five-bolt assembly, using a new and more pliable raw material, or modifying a machine so that the release mechanism works faster. Each change in the production process may have a minute impact on the standards, but collectively they can cause considerable deviation from standard.[34]

When the collective changes result in extended work cycles, employees have difficulty meeting the standard and may become resentful of the now unrealistic standards. In cases in which work becomes easier, the standards are easily exceeded, resulting in excessive employee bonuses that can destroy internal pay equity relationships.

The only cure for changes is to make time and motion analysis a process that never ceases. As soon as a job or some component of a job changes, the job should be reanalyzed to set a new fair standard rate. Incentive systems require an enormous commitment to industrial engineering if they are to have validity.

### Employee-Related Problems

Employees who work under piece rate systems may often distrust such systems and react negatively toward them. Often this distrust results in peer pressure to conform to certain output levels (the group norm).

**Lack of Understanding and Trust**    Employees may resist incentive plans that they do not understand; it is natural to distrust something that is not understood. The organization may fail to successfully communicate to the employees how and why the standards were set.[35] The solution to this resistance is clear and precise communication of plan intent, content, and operations and feedback during the year on how the plan is doing. If management has no credibility in the first place, however, employees are not likely to receive such messages in the manner intended. Employees may also fear that if they produce at too high a level, management will raise the standard or lay off some employees. These fears, which may result from experience, can result in *soldiering* or working to standard. Employee distrust of management is not easy to overcome.[36]

Management must establish, over time and by example, a belief on the part of employees that they will be dealt with fairly and equitably. If the standards must be changed, management should consider the impact of those changes from the employee perspective to counter employee resistance. Management must also present standard changes to employees with full explanation of what is involved, why the changes are occurring, and what the predicted outcome will be for the organization and for the employees.

**Modest Pay Desires**   It is sometimes argued that even under piece rate systems, employees work only up to a desired income level and then squander time. This might be predicted under an assumption that employees want more from their jobs than money.[37] At many organizations, for example, employees may take care of a football pool or set up a surprise birthday party during work hours, satisfying needs other than money. Employees satisfy multiple needs at work, and money alone may not elicit higher performance on a day in–day out basis.[38]

If money is to be a motivator for higher performance, employees must perceive the level of payout to be worth the increased effort.[39] Often payouts are less than 10 percent to 15 percent, which may not be significant enough to motivate the level of performance required.[40] If the organization does not have the ability to pay an incentive level that will catch the attention of the employee, it may be better not to have a system and save the administrative costs and problems associated with the design and implementation of the plan.

**Alternate Views of Fairness**   In some cases, it is not the incentive level but the existence of an incentive at all that is the problem. Some employees have different attitudes toward work and the rewards associated with work.[41] Although many people hold the attitude that different levels of productivity should result in different levels of pay, this is not universally true. Some employees think that equal work regardless of performance differences should result in equal pay. Although new job candidates may have the opportunity to self-select themselves in or out of an organization based on their views about what is fair pay, incumbent employees do not. When an incentive plan is contemplated, the organization should consider its acceptability in terms of the employees' views of fairness.

**Limited Control over Outcomes**   It is essential that employees have adequate control over their work to produce the desired outcomes.[42] There are times when the performance level of the employee is dependent on other coworkers, other departments, or outside suppliers, customers, or agencies. Any or all of these elements may hinder the employees' attempts to reach the performance levels needed to earn incentive pay. Just because the level of performance is dependent on others does not mean the organization cannot institute incentives. The organization, however, must identify the nature and level of dependencies and ensure that employees are not penalized for something they do not control. Once the organization has identified these hindrances, it must address them from the perspective of reducing or eliminating their regular occurrence, not just living with them. If it is unable to modify the situation (for example, government agency), it might have to eliminate the incentive plan for the affected jobs.

**Negative Effects on Teamwork**  Organizations commonly develop different incentive systems for different hierarchical levels within the organization. The reason normally provided for the differentiation is that duties and responsibilities are different and thus the reward system should vary. The existence of separate plans may be totally justified; however, organizations should recognize that such separation has a tendency to break the work group into separate subgroups and may be counterproductive to developing teamwork—a goal of most organizations today.[43] An example of an incentive plan that is hierarchical in nature and very divisive to developing a loyal and committed work team is the golden parachute. *Golden parachute* is a financial payment to a key member of the management team whose employment is terminated due to merger, acquisition, or dissolution of the company. The purpose of such an incentive program may be sound, but nonrecipient members of the work team usually do not perceive it as such. To motivate a broader range of employee groups, organizations may be wise to consider plans that can be used throughout the organization such as profit sharing, gainsharing, and stock options. When the organization decides to implement special incentive plans, such as the golden parachute for certain groups, it must clearly communicate to all employees why this plan is essential to organizational effectiveness and efficiency.

## Managerial-Related Problems

Just as there are problems associated with engineering and with the employee in designing an effective individual incentive system, there are also problems associated with management.

**Value Conflicts**  Probably the greatest single mistake that management makes is to assume that money alone will motivate high levels of performance. As mentioned in the preceding section, employees value many aspects of work and the workplace other than money.[44] Managers must also remember that not all employees share management's concept of the relationship of individual performance and reward. Instead, some employees may believe in equal pay for equal work (an equal job) and share their output so that it appears they are all working at the same rate.

The differing work orientations between management and employees produce various conflicts. For example, management may see the need to change the performance standard because introduction of better work methods or new technology has made it too easy, whereas employees see that change as an attempt to manipulate them to get higher output or to decrease their pay. Incentive plans must rest on a trust relationship between management and employees. Worker involvement and understanding are necessary for plans to be maximally effective. This is true whether or not a labor union is involved.[45] Finally, it is important to recognize that the needs of both the organization and its employees will change over time. It is therefore important to establish a mechanism that will identify the changes and make adjustments to the incentive system before damage is done to all parties and to their relationship with each other.[46]

**Incentive Budget Difficulties**   If the organization did not comprehend the complexity of the design, implementation, and administration of an effective incentive system, then it may not have budgeted adequate financial resources to carry out the new program appropriately. In today's business world, organizational change is occurring at an ever-increasing rate. The organization should tie its incentive program to its strategies and goals; as they are redefined, it should adjust the incentive system accordingly. The cost of continuous monitoring must be budgeted at the beginning of the plan's design so that the monitoring system is in place when the incentive program is first installed.

**Ability-to-Pay Constraints**   An organization may reach a time when, because of product market conditions, it is unable to continue to pay the incentive that it has been paying. Competition may have caused its profit margins to become so small (or nonexistent) that paying the premium is not financially feasible. This is especially true for incentives that are not tied to profits but to other measures of productivity. Just because productivity increases does not mean that profits will also increase. The competition may cause a price reduction greater than the productivity increase; if this gap is large enough, it may result in the organization having difficulty funding the incentive premium. The organization should always establish a termination date for the incentive program so the changing market conditions can be addressed in a timely manner. Also, the organization must put in place a mechanism to reopen the incentive program if conditions change quickly.

# Group Incentive Plans

Group incentive plans, which operate under the same general assumptions as individual incentive plans, are more practical than individual plans in some instances.

Group plans work when teamwork and cooperation are essential to maximize organizational efficiency and effectiveness. Group plans are also preferred when it is difficult to identify individual performance.[47] Group plans are easier to administer than are individual plans. It takes less time to record group performance than individual performance and employees tend to accept group plans more willingly than they do individual plans.[48]

## Small-Group Incentive Plans

As the term implies, small-group incentive plans are restricted to small work teams.[49] These plans are usually more effective in situations in which there is high interdependence among workers so that productivity is predominantly determined by the contribution of the team as a whole. An example of this might be the construction of a building by a team of equally qualified carpenters. These carpenters may specialize in one part of the building, such as roofers, wall builders, finishing carpenters, bricklayers, and so on. However, if they all work together cooperatively and help with all the different functional tasks, they may be much more productive. To achieve this kind of cooperation, the contractor could use a group incentive plan whereby the carpenters could make extra money as a team for high production.

Just as with individual incentive plans, the two key steps in establishing a group plan are determining the standard production rate and determining the incentive rate. In the case of production standards, the organization must study the work processes and determine the rate to be considered normal (the standard). In the case of the incentive rate, the organization must decide on a minimum rate, a maximum rate, and the rate scale. Each of these, as in individual incentive plans, calls for decisions by compensation decision makers.

### Plantwide Group Incentive Plans

Plantwide group incentive plans are based on the philosophy that an organization is successful only when everybody is contributing to organizational goals. Employees are considered members of a larger team of workers, and despite their various specialized jobs, no one is considered successful unless everybody is successful.[50] For example, Union Carbide has a program that gives bonuses to employees based on return on capital. Shoney's bases some bonus programs on return on sales and others on customer satisfaction reports. DuPont had a program that tied pay increases to profit increases.[51] In fact, the DuPont situation serves as an example of why, even with group plans, monitoring and adjustment procedures must be in place. DuPont entered into a period of falling profits caused by a weak economy. Its employees, who operated on a profit-related incentive plan, became increasingly unhappy as they feared a drop in their earnings. DuPont found it necessary to drop the incentive plan to give its employees greater peace of mind.[52]

Among group incentives, the most often cited approaches are cost reduction and profit sharing. Cost-reduction incentives, also called "gainsharing plans," are designed so that employees share in cost savings caused by group effort. A variety of different cost-reduction plans exist, the best known of which are Scanlon, Rucker, and Improshare plans.

To focus strictly on the incentive nature of these plans is probably erroneous. An elaborate suggestion mechanism for receiving employee input and for processing recommendations accompanies these successful cost-savings plans.[53] They exist in an environment in which both management and labor have made a strong commitment to increased organizational efficiency. The commitment requires a high level of trust, open communication, and a sharing of information. Further, this commitment is reinforced behaviorally: Often the trappings of status (such as separate employee and management washrooms, or executive cafeterias) are notably absent. In short, successful gainsharing plans may be successful because they are only one component of an overall management belief in a company team as opposed to belief that incentives are primarily manipulative devices to motivate high performance.[54]

Graham-Moore and Ross[55] identified the factors that favor gainsharing, dividing them into four main categories. First, favorable organizational factors include manageable size and open climate. Indications are that, as the size of the organization increases, there is a negative impact on gainsharing plans. The effectiveness of the plan also requires an organizational climate of trust and open communication. Second, technologic factors include a high degree of task interdependence, a nonrigid technology, reciprocal work flows, and long work cycles. Third, the financial/market factors needed are good historical cost data, a market for increased output, a stable product such that the cost data are not significantly changing, a mechanism to deal with seasonal variation in product demand if that is present, and a constant review of the capital/labor ratios if capital investment is an ongoing activity. Fourth, labor force factors that aid in gainsharing are moderate to high satisfaction, good union-management relations, flexible and adaptive support services (for example, maintenance), and history of fair and well-administered overtime practices.

**Scanlon Plan**    The Scanlon plan is named for the developer of the plan, Joseph Scanlon of the U.S. Steelworkers.[56] Under a Scanlon plan, a formula determines the employees' share of all cost savings. Exhibit 12.11 contains an example of a Scanlon plan, devised as follows. First, the employer determines the ratio of payroll costs to the value of production. For example, suppose that it took $500,000 of payroll to produce $2 million worth of sales. The ratio of payroll to sales value is 25 percent. Second, the employer determines the amount of savings that results from increased efficiency. For example, if the payroll drops from $500,000 to $400,000 on sales of $2 million, then the savings is $100,000. Third, the employer allocates to a bonus fund the employees' share of this savings. For example, if the employees are to realize 75 percent of the cost savings, then $75,000 would be paid into the bonus fund. Normally, the bonus is paid out at the end of the year, after setting aside a reserve for periods in which labor is less efficient. The bonus is paid to employees as a proportion of their wage to the total wage bill.

Scanlon plans rely on an elaborate suggestion system for employee recommendations for improved efficiency. Usually the employer empowers a departmental committee of one or more workers and one or more managers to review cost-savings suggestions and to act on those below a certain dollar

---

**EXHIBIT 12.11    EXAMPLE OF A SCANLON PLAN COST-SAVING GROUP BONUS**

| | |
|---|---|
| Sales value of production | $2,000,000 |
| Standard labor costs | $500,000 |
| Labor ratio | 25 percent ($500,000/$2,000,000) |
| Current labor costs | $400,000 |
| Actual savings | $500,000 - $400,000 = $100,000 |
| Reserve for deficit | 25 percent = $25,000 |
| Management share | (25 percent of $75,000) = $18,750 |
| Labor share[a] | (75 percent of $75,000) = $66,250 |

[a]This is allocated to each worker based on that worker's earnings as a percentage of total payroll of the period.

cost. A suggestion with a cost above a certain minimum is forwarded for review to a higher-level committee, also composed of managers and workers. All suggestions are either implemented, postponed, or rejected, with reasons communicated to the respective parties. The Scanlon plan requires that the goals of the organization and the personal goals of the employees be congruent. In the ever-changing environment and with the cultural diversity present in many work forces, the organization faces a significant task keeping these goals congruent. Also, there must be a strong commitment by both the organization and the employees to overall equity. The formula developed by the gainsharing plan must fairly share the productivity increases the plan creates.[57]

Like all incentive systems, the integrity of Scanlon plans is rooted in the determination of an accurate standard (the current payroll-to-sales value ratio) and in good labor management relations.[58] Unless accurate base levels are determined, the actual value of cost-savings suggestions cannot be computed. Unless employees trust management, they are likely to see the plan as an attempt on the part of management to manipulate them.

Not many organizations have adopted Scanlon plans. One reason may be that, like all incentive plans, they require a considerable commitment on the part of management to establish the standards and maintain the system.[59] Scanlon plans also require considerable trust between labor and management. If these conditions are not present, an organization is probably wise not to implement Scanlon plans.

**Rucker Plan**   The Rucker plan is similar to the Scanlon plan. The principal difference is in the method of arriving at the labor ratio, which is called the economic productivity index in this plan.

The economic productivity index is determined by dividing the value added by labor's efforts (the sales value of production minus the costs of materials, supplies, and so on) by the costs of labor (payroll for the period). An example of these variables, their definitions, and their relationships is shown in Exhibit 12.12.

Of the $100,000 savings attributable to labor in Exhibit 12.12, one-third might go into a reserve fund and two-thirds would be distributed on a monthly basis. At the end of the accounting period, any reserve not used up by labor cost overruns or accounting adjustments would be distributed to the employees.

**Improshare**   Improshare, developed by Mitchell Fein in 1973, stands for "improved productivity through sharing."[60] Improshare is conceptually and operationally simple and has been developed to apply to either a work team or the whole plant.[61] It is different than the Scanlon and Rucker plans in that it measures work productivity of employees and ignores special adjustments for aspects outside their control. Work standards are an average of past performance calculated from historical data, which include the periods when outside forces slowed production as well as periods of greatest efficiency. See Exhibit 12.13 for an illustration.

The plan makes all comparisons on the basis of hours actually worked to standard hours. Once the standard hours are established for the base period, they are frozen and only change if capital improvements or technologic innovation

| EXHIBIT 12.12 | EXAMPLE OF A RUCKER PLAN BONUS CALCULATION |
|---|---|

### Historical Data

| | |
|---|---|
| Sales value of production | $2,000,000 |
| Cost of material | 1,000,000 |
| Value added (VA) | $1,000,000 |
| Standard cost of labor for $2,000,000 | 500,000 |
| Labor's contribution to value added (LCVA) | 500,000 |

$$\frac{500,000}{\$1,000,000} = 0.5$$

| | |
|---|---|
| Economic productivity index (EPI) | |

$$\frac{1}{\text{LCVA}} = 2.0$$

### Bonus Period Data

| | |
|---|---|
| Sales value of production | $2,000,000 |
| Cost of material | 1,000,000 |
| Value added (VA) | $1,000,000 |
| Cost of labor (COL) | 400,000 |

Actual value of production (AVP) = Sales value of production –
(Cost of material + Cost of labor)
= $2,000,000 - ($1,000,000 + $400,000)

Expected value of production = EPI × COL (for bonus period)
= 2.0 × $400,000
= $800,000

Savings or loss = EVP - AVP
= $800,000 - 600,000
= $200,000

Labor's share = Labor's contribution to value
added × savings

= 0.5 × $200,000
= $100,000

occurs. Most plans are established to calculate the productivity gains and pay the savings on a weekly basis, but some do it monthly. A unit of output in the plan is usually defined as one ready for shipment. This plan's design produces no downside risk for employees. Consequently, even in unionized settings, the organization can implement it without prior union-management negotiation.[62]

## Profit Sharing

Many organizations have profit-sharing plans for their employees. Most profit-sharing plans are pension plans that motivate performance or membership. On

| EXHIBIT 12.13 | EXAMPLE IMPROSHARE CALCULATION (WEEKLY EXAMPLE) |

Total plant employment = 150 (direct and indirect)

Average weekly production = 500 units (based on historical data)

Total plant hours (value output) = 6,000 standard hours (150 employees × 40 hours per week)

Average value of output = 12 hours per unit (6,000 hours ÷ 500 units)

Production per week after Improshare = 650 units

Actual productivity value = 7,800 hours (650 × 12)

Productivity gains 7,800 − 6,000 = 1,800 hours

Sharing (50 percent employee/50 percent company) = 1,800 ÷ 2 = 900 hours savings to employer

New labor costs 6,000 + 900$^*$ ÷ 650 = 10.62 hours per unit

Premium:   900 ÷ 6,000 = 15 percent

Base productivity factor = 7,800 ÷ 6,000 = 1.30

$^*$900 hours are paid to employee and must be added in.

Adapted from *Improshare: An Alternative to Traditional Managing*, Mitchell Fein, Inc., 1981, p. 43.

the one hand, profit sharing implies that because employees will reap the benefits of high profits, they should want to produce at high levels. In this sense, profit sharing is oriented toward performance motivation.

On the other hand, several features of profit-sharing plans work at cross purposes with motivating performance.[63] First, most profit-sharing plans pay out on the basis of total net profit for a given period of time (usually the organization's fiscal year). Employees do not see immediate rewards for high performance. Second, because the payout is a percentage of overall profits, there is no direct relationship between individual performance level and the payout level. Third, profit levels may be a function of variables beyond employee control. For example, in recessionary periods employees may work doubly hard simply to keep the company solvent. The employees may contribute a great deal more than when the organization is riding the crest of an economic recovery. Profits may not correspond to actual levels of performance. Fourth, employees often do not receive the cash value of their profit-sharing accounts until long after they earn their credit. Companies often deposit the funds into a trust, and the employee may be entitled to withdraw the money only under certain emergency conditions or when leaving the company. Many firms use profit-sharing contributions as a part of an employee's retirement program. Because of these and other limitations, profit-sharing plans may be more successful at motivating membership than performance.

## Employee Stock Ownership Plans

Employee stock ownership plans originated in the 1960s and were primarily designed for management personnel. Tax incentives introduced by Congress in 1975 led to extending the plans to a larger group of employees. Organizations use employee stock option plans to fund employee retirement programs and to accumulate capital for plant modernization, product development, and business expansion. In recent years, organizations have increasingly used employee stock option plans to finance acquisitions, to act as a poison pill, and to reduce labor costs of ailing organizations.[64] Currently, 10,000 companies and 10 million employees are covered by employee stock option plans.[65]

An organization on the behalf of the employee purchases stock in the employee's name and deposits the shares in the name of the employee in an employee stock option plan trust. If the money used to purchase the stock is borrowed, the borrower holds the stock as collateral until the loan is paid off. The amount of stock purchased in the name of the employee is based on the salary or seniority of the employee.[66] The shares credited to the employee's account remain there until the employee retires or leaves the organization's employment. If the employee stock option plan is used as a retirement plan, the normal vesting regulations and rights are enforced.

Organizations believed that with stock ownership employees would be more motivated, productivity and profitability would increase, and the price of the stock would also increase. As discussed under profit sharing, the time delays and the lack of a direct relationship between performance and pay interfere with employee stock option plans as performance motivators. Employees were told that, as partial owners through the employee stock option plan, their involvement in decision making would increase. Research has shown that the level of employee involvement is similar to that before the employee stock option plan (for example, job design, working conditions) and has not fulfilled the expectation of most employees.[67]

# Problems with Group Incentive Plans

The use of group incentive plans is not without its problems. Development of group incentive plans is more complex than development of individual plans. Especially for small-group plans, the organization must perform an analysis of the existing work-flow structure to ensure the presence of a significant amount of interdependence among units or of employees within units. That analysis helps identify barriers to realizing the plan's increased efficiency expectations. For example, if interdependencies exist between work groups, the incentive plan should not calculate each work group's incentive separately. It should ensure that all contributors to the intended outcome (supervisors or technical specialists employed in multiple groups) are appropriately rewarded for their contributions to output. If these and similar issues are not addressed in the plan's design stage, serious problems will develop during the implementation stage.

Second, employee preferences for reward distribution will also affect acceptance of group incentives. Some employees would rather receive rewards for their individual performances. If the organization has hired individualists who do not respond positively to group incentives, it has several options, including attempting to modify employee attitudes toward group rewards through training programs, or reassigning these employees to units that reward individual performance. If such adjustments are impractical or unsuccessful, the employer may terminate the employment relationship.

Third, the organizational culture and management style must be congruent with the idea of group incentives. Effectiveness of some plans depends on development of high levels of trust and open communication. If the management style is very authoritarian and nonparticipative, the plan is not likely to be effective. Effectiveness of other plans is less dependent on such human requirements.

Fourth, group peer pressure may become severe, making the group incentive actually counterproductive. The group may develop a need for total group conformity and may not openly analyze suggestions made by group members. This could result in lower overall performance.

## Summary

This chapter focuses on individual and group incentive plans. For incentive plans to be effective, the employer must be able to meet the assumptions of the instrumentality, expectancy, and reinforcement theories developed in Chapter 3: Employees must be capable and believe they are capable of performing at high levels; they must see that high performance results in more pay; they must value money; and they must prefer more money to other employment outcomes. Also, there must be performance variability potential in the jobs, and employers must develop fair and equitable systems that measure that variability and that provide adequate rewards to reinforce appropriate behaviors.

The principal distinction between using a group or an individual incentive plan is whether performance is a group phenomenon or whether performance can be attributed to specific individual behaviors.

Individual incentive plans for production employees are of two basic types: piece rate incentives and standard hour plans. Similarities between the two are noted. Incentive plans can be applied within small groups or on a plantwide basis. Illustrations are provided for the main incentive plans currently being used by industry.

Many problems that tend to mitigate the effectiveness of individual incentive plans are discussed. These include engineering problems as well as attitudinal problems of both employees and managers. Incentive plans require enormous commitment in time and money to be kept current and relevant.

Finally, profit-sharing and employee stock option plans are briefly discussed along with their problems. Although profit-sharing plans are intended to motivate high performance, they probably do not do so because of their design. Employee stock option plans tend to be used to help organizations that are in serious financial trouble and to take advantage of tax benefits rather than to develop true partnership between labor and management.

# Discussion Questions

1. Discuss the assumptions that must be satisfied for instrumentality and expectancy theory to influence employee behavior in desired ways.

2. How is reinforcement theory related to incentive programs?

3. Discuss how corporate strategy and incentive plans are related.

4. Identify the problems that make employees resist piece rate pay systems, and discuss solutions to these problems.

5. Discuss the steps in designing an individual incentive system.

6. Compare and contrast Scanlon and Halsey plans. Discuss why they might have difficulty motivating high performance.

7. Discuss why profit-sharing plans are not likely to motivate high performance.

---

## EXERCISES

1. Do not read this case until directed to do so by your instructor. It has been set up as a prediction case so that you can test your analysis by answering questions before reading the entire case.[68]

**Part I:**

The Hovey and Beard Company manufactured wooden toys of various kinds: wooden animals, pull toys, and the like. One part of the manufacturing process involved spraying paint on the partially assembled toys. This operation was staffed entirely by women.

The toys were cut, sanded, and partially assembled in the wood room. Then they were dipped into shellac, after which they were painted. The toys were predominantly two-colored; a few were made in more than two colors. Each color required an additional trip through the paint room.

For a number of years, production of these toys had been entirely handwork. However, to meet tremendously increased demand, the painting operation had recently been re-engineered so that the eight employees who did the painting sat in a line by an endless chain of hooks. These hooks were in continuous motion, past the line of workers and into a long horizontal oven. Each employee sat at her own painting booth designed to carry away fumes and to backstop excess paint. The employee would take a toy from the tray beside her, position it in a jig inside the painting cubicle, spray on the color according to a pattern, then release the toy and hang it on the hook passing by. The rate at which the hooks moved had been calculated by the engineers so that each employee, when fully trained, would be able to hang a painted toy on each hook before it passed beyond her reach.

The employees working in the paint room were on a group bonus plan. Because the operation was new to them, they were receiving a learning bonus, which decreased by regular amounts each month. The learning bonus was scheduled to vanish in six months, by which time it was expected that they would be on their own—that is, able to meet the standard and to earn a group bonus when they exceeded it.

**Prediction question:** What will the new hook line do to productivity and satisfaction?

## Part II:

By the second month of the training period, trouble had developed. The employees learned more slowly than had been anticipated, and it began to look as though their production would stabilize far below what was planned. Many of the hooks were going by empty. The employees complained that they were going by too fast and that the time study person had set the rates wrong. A few employees quit and had to be replaced with new employees, which further aggravated the learning problem. The team spirit that the management had expected to develop automatically through the group bonus was not in evidence except as an expression of what the engineers called "resistance." One employee whom the group regarded as its leader (and the management regarded as the ringleader) was outspoken in making the various complaints of the group to the foreman: The job was a messy one, the hooks moved too fast, the incentive pay was not being correctly calculated, and it was too hot working so close to the drying oven.

**Prediction question:** What do you believe management will do immediately while it awaits the arrival of the consultant?

## Part III:

A consultant who was brought into this picture worked entirely with and through the foreman. After many conversations with the consultant, the foreman thought that the first step should be to get the employees together for a general discussion of the working conditions. He took this step with some hesitation but took it on his own volition.

The first meeting, held immediately after the shift ended at 4 P.M., was attended by all 8 employees. They voiced the same complaints again: The hooks went by too fast, the job was too dirty, and the room was hot and poorly ventilated. For some reason, it was this last item that they complained of most. The supervisor promised to discuss the problem of ventilation and temperature with the engineers, and a second meeting was scheduled to report back to the employees. In the next few days, the supervisor had several talks with the engineers. They and the superintendent thought this was really a trumped-up complaint and that the expense of any effective corrective measure would be prohibitively high.

The supervisor came to the second meeting with some apprehensions. The employees, however, did not seem to be much put out, perhaps because they had a proposal of their own to make. They believed that if several large fans were set up to circulate the air around their feet, they would be much more comfortable. After some discussion, the supervisor agreed that the idea might be tested. The supervisor and the consultant discussed the question of the fans with the superintendent, and three large propeller-type fans were purchased.

**Prediction question:** What will be the impact of the fan decision on morale and relations with the supervisor?

## Part IV:

The fans were brought in. The employees were jubilant. For several days the fans were moved about in various positions until they were placed to the satisfaction of the group. The employees seemed completely satisfied with the results, and relations between them and the supervisor improved visibly.

The supervisor, after this encouraging episode, decided that further meetings might also be profitable. He asked the employees if they would like to meet and discuss other aspects of the work situation. The employees were eager to do this. The meeting was held, and the discussion quickly centered on the speed of the hooks. The employees maintained that they would never be able to reach the goal of filling enough of them to make a bonus.

The turning point of the discussion came when the group's leader frankly explained that the point was not that they could not work fast enough to keep up with the hooks but that they could not work at that pace all day long. The supervisor explored the point. The employees were unanimous in their opinion that they could keep up with the belt for short periods if they wanted to. But they did not want to because if they showed they could do this for short periods they would be expected to do it all day long. The meeting ended with an unprecedented request: "Let us adjust the speed of the belt faster or slower depending on how we feel." The supervisor agreed to discuss this with the superintendent and the engineers.

The reaction of the engineers to the suggestion was negative. However, after several meetings it was granted that there was some latitude within which variations in the speed of the hooks would not affect the finished product. After considerable argument with the engineers, it was agreed to try out the idea.

With misgivings, the supervisor had a control with a dial marked "low, medium, fast" installed at the booth of the group leader; the speed of the belts could be adjusted anywhere between the lower and upper limits that the engineers had set.

**Prediction question:** What will be the impact of the dial control decision on productivity and satisfaction?

## Part V:

The employees were delighted and spent many lunch hours deciding how the speed of the belt should be varied from hour to hour throughout the day. Within a week, the pattern had settled down to one in which the first half of the shift was run on what the employees called a medium speed (a dial setting slightly above the point marked "medium"). The next 2.5 hours were run at high speed; the half-hour before lunch and the half-hour after lunch were run at low speed. The rest of the afternoon was run at high speed with the exception of the last 45 minutes of the shift, which was run at medium.

In view of the employees' reports of satisfaction and ease in their work, it is interesting to note that the constant speed at which the engineers had originally set the belt was slightly below medium on the dial of the control. The average speed at which the employees were running the belt was on the high side of the dial. Few, if any, empty hooks entered the oven, and inspection showed no increase of rejects from the paint room.

Production increased, and within 3 weeks (some 2 months before the scheduled ending of the learning bonus) the employees were operating at 30 percent to 50 percent above the level that had been expected under the original arrangement. Naturally, the employees' earnings were correspondingly higher than anticipated. They were collecting their base pay, a considerable piece rate bonus, and the learning bonus, which, it will be remembered, had been set to decrease with time and not to function in relation to current productivity. The employees were earning more now than many skilled workers in other parts of the plant.

**Prediction question:** How will other personnel react and why?

**Part VI:**

Management was besieged by demands that this inequity be taken care of. With growing irritation between superintendent and supervisor, engineers and supervisor, superintendent and engineers, the situation came to a head when the superintendent revoked the learning bonus and returned the painting operation to its original status: The hooks moved again at their constant time-studied designated speed, production dropped again, and within a month all but two of the eight employees had quit. The supervisor stayed on for several months but then left for another job feeling aggrieved.

a. What parallels can you see between the case and chapter discussion?

b. What conclusions can be drawn from this case about piece rate incentive systems?

c. Review the problems introduced by the new system and discuss how they might have been avoided.

2. The Henley Brothers Machine Shop performs batch drilling for numerous organizations in its area. Skilled drill press operators at the shop currently earn $10 per hour. Donald Henley, vice president of production, is considering putting drill press operators on a piece rate incentive system when they work on these large batch drilling operations (other work would be straight hourly work).

As a skilled tool and die maker and a trained engineer, Donald Henley has undertaken a time study for these large batch drilling operations. He has observed that his two slowest employees average 60 drilling operations in an hour and the fastest employee to perform the task does 72 drillings in an hour. The average across all employees is 66 drilling operations. If he goes to a piece rate system, Henley would not want maximum pay to exceed $11.20 per hour because of equity considerations for other employees.

a. Would you recommend to Henley that he use or not use a piece rate incentive plan? Why or why not?

b. Design at least two different piece rate incentive plans that Henley might use. Which do you recommend? Why? Which would keep labor costs at a minimum?

c. How would you administer the piece rate plan? Are the costs and troubles worth it?

d. What do you think employees will think of the new plan you propose?

3. Generic Services Inc. is a small company of employees with no fringe benefits other than a two-week paid vacation policy after one year of service. The owner is considering offering a profit-sharing plan to these employees. Five percent of net profits would be distributed to employees as a percentage of their salary to total payroll.

The five-year history of payroll costs and net (after tax) profits appears below:

| Year | Number of Employees | Payroll | Net After-Tax Profit |
|------|------|------|------|
| 19__ | 4 | $40,000 | $60,000 |
| 19__ | 4 | 42,000 | (3,000) |
| 19__ | 4 | 43,500 | 81,000 |
| 19__ | 5 | 55,000 | 42,000 |
| 19__ | 5 | 56,500 | 96,000 |

a. What do you recommend to the owner?

b. In the absence of prior employee benefits, would you recommend initiating some benefits before profit sharing?
Why or why not?

## References

[1] J. T. Rich, "Reincenting America," *Industry Week* 237 (November 21, 1988), 52, 56.

[2] E. E. Lawler III, *Strategic Pay* (San Francisco: Josey-Bass Publishers, 1990).

[3] F. Bartless, "Incentives," *British Journal of Psychology* 41 (1950), 122-128.

[4] J. P. Campbell and R. D. Pritchard, "Motivation Theories in Industrial and Organizational Psychology," in *Handbook of Industrial and Organizational Psychology*, ed. M. D. Dunnette (Chicago: Rand McNally College Publishing Company, 1976).

[5] W. C. Hammer, "Reinforcement Theory and Contingency Management in Organizational Settings," in *Motivation and Work Behavior*, eds. R. M. Steers and L. W. Porter (New York: McGraw-Hill, 1987).

[6] E. E. Lawler III, *Strategic Pay* (San Francisco: Josey-Bass Publishers, 1990).

[7] F. Hills, "The Pay-for-Performance Dilemma," *Personnel* 56 (1980), 23–31; E. Lawler, *Pay and Organizational Effectiveness: A Psychological View* (New York: McGraw-Hill, 1971).

[8] J. L. McAdams and E. J. Hawk, "Capitalizing on Human Assets Through Performance–Based Rewards," *ACA Journal* 1 (Autumn 1992), 60–73.

[9] L. Miller and R. Hambiln, "Interdependence, Differential Rewarding, and Productivity," *American Sociological Review* 28 (1963), 768–778.

[10] C. S. Odell, *Gainsharing: Involvement, Incentives and Productivity* (New York: American Management Association, 1981); P. Shwinger, *Wage Incentive Systems* (New York: Holstad Press Book, 1975).

[11] S. R. Baime, "Incentives for the Masses: A Viable Pay Program?" *Compensation and Benefit Review* 22 (November/December 1990), 50–58; G. W. Florkowski, "Analyzing Group Incentive Plans," *HR Magazine* 35 (January 1990), 36–38.

[12] E. C. Baig, "The Great Earnings Gamble," *U.S. News and World Report* 109 (September 17, 1990), 65, 68.

[13] Rich, "Reincenting America."

[14] *Ibid.*

[15] Baig, "The Great Earnings Gamble."

[16] E. E. Lawler III, "Pay for Performance: Making it Work," *Personnel* 65 (October 1988): 68–71.

[17] J. Greenberg and M. Liebman, "Incentives: The Missing Link in Strategic Performances," *Journal of Business Strategy* 11 (July/August 1990), 8–11.

[18] Historically, piece rate plans used the concept of "task" in designing the standard. Task has to do with various assumptions about how hard employees who are studied are working. That is, are they working at a high, average, or low level of productivity? For a further discussion of task, see Thomas H. Patten, Jr., *Pay: Employee Compensation and Incentive Plans* (New York: The Free Press, 1977), 406–409. In this text, the assumption is made that industrial engineering can determine the average productivity of the average worker under normal work conditions.

[19] Employers using incentive systems for nonexempt employees must be sure that such plans do not violate overtime and minimum wage provisions of the Federal Labor Standards Act. See, for example, Michael Schuster and Gary Florkowski, "Wage Incentive Plans and the Fair Labor Standards Act," *Compensation Review* 14 (second quarter 1982), 34–46.

[20] E. Lawler, *Pay and Organizational Effectiveness* (Reading, MA: Addison-Wesley, 1981).

[21] E. Lawler, "Equity Theory as a Predictor of Productivity and Work Quality," *Psychological Bulletin* 70 (1968), 596–610; R. Opshal and M. Dunnette, "The Role of Financial Compensation in Industrial Motivation," *Psychological Bulletin* 66 (1964), 94–118.

[22] B. G. Posner, "If at First You Don't Succeed," *INC* 11 (May 1987), 132, 134.

[23] Rich, "Reincenting America."

[24] "Piecework Enhances Productivity," *Lodging Hospitality* 46 (September 1990), 54.

[25] F. S. Taylor, "A Piece Rate System," *Transactions of the American Society of Mechanical Engineers* 12 (1891), 755–780.

[26] D. W. Merrick, *Time Studies as a Basis for Rate Setting* (New York: The Engineering Magazine, 1920).

[27] F. A. Halsey, "The Premium Plan of Paying for Labor," *Transactions of the American Society of Mechanical Engineers* 12 (1891), 755–780.

[28] *Ibid.*

[29] Sir William Rowan Thomson, *The Rowan Premium Bonus System for Payment by Results*, 2d ed. (Scotland: McCorquedale and Co., 1919).

[30] P. Shwinger, *Wage Incentive Systems* (New York: John Wiley & Sons, 1975).

[31] H. L. Gantt, "A Bonus System of Rewarding Labor," *Transactions of the American Society of Mechanical Engineers* 12 (1891), 755–780.

[32] Lawler, *Pay and Organizational Effectiveness;* W. F. Whyte, *Money and Motivation* (New York: Harper and Row, 1955).

[33] Shimmin, "Workers' Understanding of Incentive Payment Systems"; P. Daly, "Selecting and Designing a Group Incentive Plan," *Personnel Journal* (June 1975), 322–356; Bentley, "Conversion from Piece Rate to Time Rate Pay for Production Workers"; C. Mace, "Advances in the Theory and Practice of Incentives," *Occupational Psychology* 24 (1950), 239–244.

[34] Shimmin, "Workers' Understanding of Incentive Payment Systems"; Bentley, "Conversion from Piece Rate to Time Rate Pay for Production Workers."

[35] P. Bradley, "Division Management Incentive Plans: Bonus Plans that Really Work," *Compensation and Benefit Review* 23 (January/February 1991), 12–17.

[36] Mace, "Advances in the Theory and Practice of Incentives."

[37] H. Rothe, "Does Higher Pay Bring Higher Productivity?" *Personnel* 37 (1960), 20–27.

[38] Baime, "Incentives for the Masses"; G. W. Florkowski, "Analyzing Group Incentive Plans," *HR Magazine* 35 (January 1990), 36–38.

[39] W. J. Liccione and S. M. Podlogan, "How to Develop Compensation Plans with Incentive Value," *Journal of Compensation and Benefits* 6 (January/February 1991), 37–40.

[40] Liccione and Podlogan, "How to Develop Compensation Plans with Incentive Value."

[41] J. Schuster, "A Spectrum of Pay for Performance: How to Motivate Employees," *Management of Personnel* Quarterly (Fall 1969), 35–38.

[42] Rich, "Reincenting America."

[43] Lawler, "Pay for Performance: Making it Work."

[44] Rothe, "Does Higher Pay Bring Higher Productivity?"

[45] Schuster and Florkowski, "Wage Incentive Plans and the Fair Labor Standards Act."

[46] Rich, "Reincenting America."

[47] J. E. Nickel and S. O'Neal, "Small-Group Incentives: Gainsharing in the Microcosm," *Compensation and Benefits Review* 22 (March/April 1990), 22–29.

[48] D. W. Belcher, *Compensation Administration* (Englewood Cliffs, NJ: Prentice-Hall, 1974).

[49] Nickel and O'Neal, "Small-Group Incentives."

[50] L. Baytos, "Nine Strategies for Productivity Improvement," *Personnel Journal* 58 (1979), 449–456.

[51] Baime, "Incentives for the Masses"; Florkowski, "Analyzing Group Incentive Plans."

[52] A. Thayer, "DuPont Unit Cancels Pay Incentive Plan," *Chemical and Engineering News* 68 (November 5, 1990), 6.

[53] B. Graham-Moore and T. L. Ross, *Gainsharing: Plans for Improved Performance* (Washington, D.C.: The Bureau of National Affairs, 1990).

[54] Rothe, "Does Higher Pay Bring Higher Productivity?"

[55] Graham-Moore and Ross, *Gainsharing.*

[56] B. Moore and T. Ross, *The Scanlon Way to Improved Productivity* (New York: John Wiley & Sons, 1978).

[57] Graham-Moore and Ross, *Gainsharing.*

[58] *Ibid.*

[59] Moore and Ross, *The Scanlon Way to Improved Productivity.*

[60] M. Fein, *Improshare: An Alternative to Traditional Managing* (Hillsdale, NJ: Mitchell Fein 1981).

[61] *Ibid.*

[62] *Ibid.*

[63] Rothe, "Does Higher Pay Bring Higher Productivity?"; O. Dalaba, "Misuses of Compensation as a Motivator," *Personnel* 51 (September/October 1973), 30–37.

[64] R. Brockhardt and R. Reilly, "Employee Stock Ownership Plans After the 1989 Tax Law: Valuation Issues," *Compensation and Benefit Review* 22 (September/October 1990), 27–36.

[65] W. Smith, H. Lazarus, and H. M. Kalkstein, "Employee Stock Ownership Plans: Motivation and Morale Issues," *Compensation and Benefit Review* 22 (September/October 1990), 37–46.

[66] *Ibid.*

[67] *Ibid.*

[68] The following case is abridged from pages 90 to 94, "Group Dynamics and Intergroup Relations" (under the title "Hovey and Beard Company") by A. Bavelas and G. Strauss, *Money and Motivation* by W. F. Whyte, copyright 1955 by Harper and Row, Publishers, Inc. By permission of Harper and Row, Publishers, Inc.

CHAPTER

# 13

# Employee Benefits

## Learning Objectives

To introduce the subject of employee benefits.

To learn the reasons for the growth in employee benefits.

To learn the types of employee benefits offered by organizations.

To learn the benefits that are legally required.

To learn the important variables that influence the employee benefits decision process.

To learn about several important future events that may have a major impact on benefits decision making.

## Introduction

This chapter deals with employee benefits. The objectives of the chapter are to discuss the growth in employee benefits, to identify the main types of benefits that employees receive, to discuss the role of employee benefits in influencing individual employee behaviors, and to discuss trends in benefits.

Employee benefits can be defined as all the indirect economic rewards that the employee receives for continued company membership.[1] Some types of benefits in organizations go to a select group of employees. Examples of these benefits are keys to executive washrooms and lunchrooms, company cars, and the privilege of having mahogany paneling in one's office. These types of benefits (going to a privileged few) are considered prerequisites and should not be confused with employee benefits that accrue to nearly all employees of an organization by virtue of their status as employees. Employee benefits are generally made available to all full-time employees of the organization, and some benefits are available to part-time employees on a prorated basis.

## Theoretical Foundation for Employee Benefits

As Chapter 1 notes, a main goal of any organization's compensation system is to influence individuals to behave as the organization desires. Organizations want to motivate individuals to join and stay with the organization and to perform at high levels. How do employee benefits influence individual behavior? Because most benefits accrue to employees by virtue of membership in the organization, it is doubtful that they contribute to motivating performance. Stated another way, because employees receive most benefits regardless of their performance levels, even if the benefits are highly valued, it is unlikely that they will motivate anything other than minimally acceptable performance (performance adequate to retain a job).

It is also unlikely that employee benefits motivate joining, for several reasons. First, most benefit programs are fragmented and are difficult to compare between organizations. One recent trend among employers is to express benefits as a proportion of direct pay, thereby informing employees of the total economic value of the employee benefit package. To the extent that this becomes standard practice, individuals may become more sensitive to the economic value of the benefits package and perhaps make employment decisions on the basis of relative benefit package worth. However, one study demonstrates that wage levels and benefits levels tend to vary directly with each other.[2] Thus high-wage employers tend to be high-benefit employers as well.

A second reason why benefits probably do not motivate joining is that very often they are noncomparable, although similar on the surface. For example, two organizations may each have a group health insurance plan that will cost an employee the same monthly premium, but one plan may be vastly superior in terms of the coverage. Even though the benefit is the same in one sense (providing health insurance), the plans are noncomparable in terms of the quality of the coverage. In this situation, an individual making a decision to join one of these organizations would probably see the two organizations as equal (both have a health plan) and overlook the qualitative differences in the two plans. The considerable variation in the quality of benefits plans can be seen in Exhibit 13.1. Despite the difficulties of comparison, employees surveyed in one study perceived

**EXHIBIT 13.1**  **COMPARISON OF TWO HEALTH PLANS**

| Plan Attribute | Plan A | Plan B |
|---|---|---|
| Deductible | None | $400 |
| Surgery | 100 percent | 80 percent after deductible |
| Maternity | 100 percent | 80 percent after deductible for the following procedures only:<br>1. cesarean section<br>2. extrauterine pregnancy<br>3. complications requiring surgery after pregnancy termination |
| Hospitalization | 100 percent unlimited days, semiprivate or private room, if medically necessary | 80 percent after deductible for usual and customary rate |
| Dental | 100 percent of preventive care for children, treatment for injuries except for lab charges | 80 percent after deductible for injury or surgery |
| Maximum coverage | No maximum | $20,000 per illness |

that benefits were important to them in attracting them to their current employer.[3]

The same study found that surveyed employees considered benefits as very important in motivating them to stay with their employer.[4] Employee benefits sometimes have been called "golden handcuffs" because they tend to tie the employee to the organization. This effect is particularly true for benefits, such as vacation time and pension benefit levels, that appreciate in value as a function of employment seniority. The role of benefits in achieving compensation's goal of influencing individual behaviors is summarized in Exhibit 13.2.

## Growth in Employee Benefits

There has been tremendous growth in benefits during the past 30 years. Benefits made up only 3 percent of payroll in 1929 and increased continuously to reach 40 percent plus of payroll of large firms in the 1980s according to the U.S. Chamber of Commerce. These figures are not truly indicative of the average benefits level across all employers in the United States; rather they are skewed toward large employers' benefits levels. In review of both small and large employers, the percentage of payroll that is made up of benefits is 28 percent in 1990.[5] There is some evidence that the growth of benefits is over, and the level of benefits may actually be declining. A Bureau of Labor Statistics study of small employers revealed that health care and life insurance benefits were provided by 92 percent and 94 percent of small employers in 1989 compared with 69 percent and 64 percent in 1990.[6] It is likely that changes will occur in small employers before large employers when benefit reduction takes place. If employee benefits do not likely motivate performance or joining behavior, why did benefit levels grow as rapidly as they did? There are many causes for this growth.

### Societal Attitudes

One of the prime contributors to continued benefits growth is the change in attitude that began with the Great Depression of the 1930s. Before the Depression,

---

**EXHIBIT 13.2**  ROLE OF BENEFITS IN ACHIEVING COMPENSATION GOALS

1. Do benefits motivate joining?

   *Answer:* Probably not, because they are fragmented and noncomparable, and there are qualitative differences across organizations.

2. Do benefits motivate staying?

   *Answer:* Yes, because they act as "golden handcuffs," and some benefits grow with seniority.

3. Do benefits motivate superior performance?

   *Answer:* No, because they accrue based on membership, not performance.

both individuals and employers thought it was the responsibility of the individual to face economic adversity. The severity of the Great Depression, however, showed both parties that economic circumstances could be completely beyond an individual's control. Out of this grew a desire to insulate employees from the most severe forms of economic dislocation. Government has provided favorable tax treatments to encourage the growth of private programs and to reduce the pressure for the government to become directly involved. The attitude that employers have responsibilities to their employees continues to grow. The results of one 1991 study found that 80 percent of the respondents believed that employers should provide some form of health insurance coverage to employees.[7]

These attitudinal changes resulted in government intervention in some areas (for example, unemployment insurance programs and workers' compensation insurance) and also resulted in labor and management responding to the challenge in other areas (such as supplementary unemployment benefit).[8] Employer participation in these types of programs, whether required by law or voluntary, contributes to the costs of employee benefits.

## Changing Philosophies about People and Work

Just as attitudes have changed about who should shoulder the responsibility for economic hardship, attitudes are changing about the nature of people and work itself. If organizations believe that people are not lazy, that work is as natural as play, and that people want to contribute to organizational goals, then tying money to performance is not necessary since people will want to perform to the maximum regardless of whether money is an associated outcome. Stated another way, if people receive intrinsic rewards from doing well, there is no reason to think that money is the only vehicle for obtaining high levels of performance.

There are two important features of jobs in this regard. First, on many jobs either there is little room for performance variation or the variation is not measurable. Given these conditions, reward for membership may be the most logical for these jobs. Second, employee turnover can be extremely expensive in and of itself. For example, replacement costs may run more than 100 percent of first year salary.[9] Faced with this economic fact, it would make sense to undertake employee benefit programs that motivate retention.

## Favorable Tax Treatment

One contribution to benefit growth is the favorable tax treatment given to indirect forms of compensation.[10] Benefit plans can be either qualified or nonqualified. A qualified plan is one that meets Internal Revenue Service (IRS) codes and receives favorable tax status. A nonqualified plan is one that lacks favorable tax status. A company cannot take a tax deduction for the expense of a nonqualified benefit, and the employee must pay income tax on the value of the benefit. An example of a qualified benefit would be a health insurance plan designed to protect families from large medical costs. A typical family coverage health insurance plan would cost the employer about $400 per month per employee in 1993. If an employer chose to have the employees maintain such coverage on their own, the employer could increase the employees' pay and let them buy the same insurance. However, since any increases in the employees' paychecks are taxed, the employer would have to pay each employee much more than an additional $400 per month to provide a net of $400 to buy the insurance. The actual cost to the employer would be considerably greater than paying the $400-per-month premium per employee. In recent years, there has been considerable pressure to tax employee benefits as direct income. Should this happen, it is unlikely that benefit programs will be as attractive to individuals or organizations.

Favorable tax treatment requires that benefits do not discriminate in favor of the highly paid employees within an organization. If they do discriminate, the tax advantage may be lost. The IRS in 1991 provided a safe harbor for some employers so they did not have to run a yearly discrimination test, but if the employers desire flexibility in their plans, they would have to do extensive data collection and yearly tests.[11] A high-paid employee is defined as one who owns at least 5 percent of the organization, or earned more than $75,000 per year, or was paid in the top 20 percent of the employees and earned more than $50,000, or was an officer and earned more than $45,000 per year. The dollar amounts will be indexed to inflation to make them moving wage levels. Some benefits in a plan may be qualified—eligible for favorable tax treatment—(for example, health insurance), whereas others may not be, such as deferred compensation plans that exceed normal limits.

The advantages of offering a nonqualified (does not qualify for favorable tax treatment) deferred compensation plan are (1) increased flexibility in plan design, (2) reduced paper work (for example, IRS), (3) deductions based on what is paid out, not what it costs, and (4) Employee Retirement Income Security Act (ERISA) vesting rules do not apply.[12] Due to the ever-changing tax status treatment and regulations regarding benefits, it is best to consult an attorney and tax specialist before making changes. Also, compensation managers are advised to follow tax laws closely because they often affect the tax status of the organization's benefit plan. The passage of such acts as the Tax Equity and Fiscal Responsibility Act (1982), the Deficit Reduction Act (1984), the Consolidated Omnibus Budget Reconciliation Act (1985), and the Tax Reform Act (1986) has caused major revisions in organization's existing benefit plans in the past.

The tax laws do provide the employee with an opportunity to take pretax dollars and have them payroll-deducted and put into an individual employee spending account. The deduction can be made to cover such expenses as health and life insurance and child care expenses. Dollars that have been deducted must be spent on the specified benefits; they cannot be returned to the employee if the plan is to maintain its favorable tax position.

## Employer Self-Interest

The above example demonstrates the clear economic benefit to the employer of providing a health plan. The employer might also provide the health plan out of self-interest. For example, in the above case the employer would have no way of knowing if the employees actually use the additional $400 per month for the health insurance. An employee might use the money toward a new car, for example. Providing coverage directly for the employees limits the actual cost to the actual premium rate. By providing for the health plan directly, the employer protects its own self-interest of having a healthy work force.

Although benefits motivate employees to stay with the organization, at the same time many organizations believe they receive an indirect return from providing certain benefits. In theory at least, employers who provide a health plan might expect to have a healthier work force than employers without such plans, presumably receiving an indirect return on performance and productivity. Similarly, many organizations believe that vacation time should be used not just for recreation, but also for re-creation. These organizations require employees to use vacation time to refresh and rejuvenate themselves. How much of an indirect return firms get from employee benefits is poorly understood, but firms do believe that they receive such benefits.

### Group Coverage Effects

It is also possible for the organization to take advantage of lower rates for programs because of the pooled risk associated with groups of people. In the above example of health insurance, the premium rate for family coverage secured individually would probably not be the $400 cost of the family policy provided by the employer but would be more in the range of $475.

### Employer Paternalism

It is unpopular to talk about organizations that are paternalistic to their employees, acting in a parental role. Some organizations do feel a moral obligation to take care of their employees, and this alone may be a reason for providing certain benefits.

### Bandwagon Effect

Some organizations provide benefits simply because everyone else seems to be doing it. Under an assumption that employees do compare organizations on benefits, their employers may wish to have competitive benefits to attract and retain labor.

### Union Pressures

Labor unions have multiple goals for their members. It is often thought (erroneously) that unions only want larger paychecks for their members. Unions, however, often bargain for benefits as well. They may include in their negotiations expansion of health care benefits or inclusion of dental benefits. Unions also wish to provide for security of members during retirement and in times of unemployment. To these ends, unions often bargain for mandatory retirement programs (after 30 years of service, for example), and for Supplementary Unemployment Benefits, as discussed earlier. Also, unions have pushed for a 4-day workweek for years. One way to achieve this indirectly is to increase the number of days off with pay (holidays, personal days).

# Types of Benefit Programs

There are numerous ways to categorize benefits. The discussion in this text focuses first on legally required benefits, more specifically Social Security, workers' compensation, and unemployment compensation. Then the discussion moves to voluntary benefits, covering pensions, health and welfare, payment for time not worked, and other selected benefits. The most costly benefit to employers is generally the pension plan; however, this is only the case when the federally mandated plan, Social Security, is considered in conjunction with an organization's private pension plan. The cost structure with regard to all benefits may vary considerably among employers since employee benefit plans vary—in number, in type, and in degree—from one employer to another.

# Legally Required Benefits

As noted in the chapter on legal constraints, employers are required to pay into certain mandatory programs. The compulsory programs are Social Security, unemployment compensation, and workers' compensation. These programs cost employers about 8.2 percent of total pay in 1989.[13]

## Social Security

Just as individuals pay a portion of their wages or salaries into Social Security, employers too must contribute to the Social Security funds. Social Security funds (formally titled Old-Age, Survivors', Disability, and Health Insurance) are provided by individual contributions and matching contributions from organizations. The Federal Insurance Contribution Act (FICA) imposes the tax. As of 1992, the amount required by an employer is 7.65 percent to match the individual's contribution of 7.65 percent of the first $55,500 in wages. The Medicare percentage, which is 1.45 percent and is included as part of the 7.65 percent, is now required up to $130,200 of income. Recent trends indicate that, due to an aging workforce, substantial increases will continue in both the percentage rates and the total dollar amount subject to taxation.[14] The maximum dollar amount for Social Security is tied to the average national wage, which cannot be determined years in advance.

Employers typically integrate their private pension plans with Social Security so that employees can be assured of a living income after retirement.[15] Since 1979, employers have had the option of paying not only their share of the FICA tax, but also the employee's share. If the employer pays the employee's share, reducing the employee's gross pay by this amount, it costs the employer less in total wages and taxes on an annualized basis and may also put the employee in a lower tax bracket.[16]

Social security is composed of survivor, disability, and retirement benefits plus hospital and medical insurance (Medicare). Each component has unique requirements and benefits.[17]

**Survivor Benefits**   If a worker dies while insured by Social Security and has earned 21 Social Security credits, the family will be eligible for monthly survivor benefits. A Social Security credit is earned, up to a maximum of 4 credits per year, each time a worker receives a specified dollar amount in wages. Social Security provides a table that identifies the dollar amount needed to earn credits for each year. In 1984, for example, a worker received a credit for each $390 earned, whereas in 1992, the dollar amount was $570. Unmarried children of a deceased eligible worker receive a monthly payment until they reach 18 (or 19 if still in high school), and those over 18 continue to receive benefits if they were permanently disabled prior to turning 22. The children do not lose their benefits due to the surviving parent's remarriage even if they are adopted by their stepparent. The surviving spouse is eligible for benefits at age 60 (50 if disabled) or at any age if caring for a dependent child who is eligible for benefits. Even a divorced spouse is eligible for benefits if he or she was married to the deceased for at least 10 years and cannot obtain equal or higher personal benefits, or if caring for a child who is eligible for benefits. A dependent parent who is 62 or older is also eligible for benefits.

**Disability Benefits**   An employee must have earned 21 Social Security credits, of which 20 must be earned in the 10 years preceding the disability. The employee and dependents can start drawing monthly Social Security benefits 5 months after the employee becomes severely disabled. The employee must be able to provide medical evidence of mental or physical disability that prohibits the performance of substantial work for at least 12 months. The monthly payment is equal to comparable monthly retirement benefits as if the employee had reached retirement. The payments from Social Security are integrated with workers' compensation and other public assistance so that total payments will not exceed 80 percent of prior average earnings.

**Retirement Benefits**   An employee must have earned 40 Social Security credits to be eligible for full benefits at retirement age. Employees who were born in 1937 or earlier can retire at the age of 65 with full benefits. Employees born after 1937 will have to work beyond 65 to retire with full benefits. For example, an individual born in 1954 will have to work until age 66 to receive full benefits, whereas an individual born in 1960 will have to work until age 67. Employees who retire before their eligible retirement time will have a reduction in their monthly retirement payment based on a pre-established formula.

**Medicare Benefits**   Medicare is made up of a hospital (Part A) and a medical (Part B) insurance component. All individuals who have reached legal retirement age, whether they are working or retired, are eligible for hospital coverage if they are eligible for monthly Social Security payments. The hospital component covers hospital care, skilled nursing care, home health service care, and hospice care (for terminally ill patients). Individuals eligible for hospital benefits are automatically eligible for medical benefits. Medical benefits cover a wide range of physician and related health care personnel services provided in a variety of delivery methods (laboratory, clinic, outpatient hospitals, emergency room). As with all insurance, there is a cost for coverage (deducted from Social Security checks), there are deductibles that must be met, and there are payment limits.

## Workers' Compensation

Workers' compensation is required under state laws. Employers must purchase workers' compensation insurance either through private vendors or through a state administered fund. In addition, some states permit employers to insure themselves. As noted in Chapter 5, the premium rates are directly a function of claim experience. As a result, organizations are often motivated to keep claims to a minimum by stressing employee safety.

Each state can establish its own eligibility requirements, level of payment, and premium rate, but each state's workers' compensation program is expected to provide rehabilitation, medical, death, impairment, and disability benefits to employees and to employees' survivors and dependents.[18] The rehabilitation benefits normally cover cost of therapy, allowance during treatment, and indirect costs such as travel, meals, and lodging. The medical provision covers medical expenses due to an occupational injury and are not limited to coverage limitations associated with nonoccupational medical coverage (for example, deductibles). When the incident results in a death, the program must pay for burial of the employee and continuing income for survivors (spouse and dependents). Impairment occurs when an employee loses use of a part of his or her body (such as a finger). A schedule establishes the value that must be paid to the employee based on the kind and degree of the impairment and the worker's wages prior to the incident. The disability provision guarantees the injured employee a weekly income after a short waiting period. Payment to the injured worker from workers' compensation and Social Security cannot exceed 80 percent of the employee's wages prior to the injury.

## Unemployment Compensation

The federal government establishes the basic ground rules for unemployment compensation programs, but each state administers its own program and determines the benefits it will provide. For a state program to be federally qualified, it must establish a minimum earned income or minimum days worked requirement for benefit eligibility. Eligibility requires registration of the unemployed individual with the state unemployment office and a willingness on the part of the individual to accept comparable employment. In addition, the state must establish an appeal procedure for those denied benefits.

Just as with workers' compensation, organizations are required to pay state unemployment tax premiums on the basis of actuarial experience. To some extent employers have a motive to maintain stable employment and save on payments.

# Pension Benefits

## Issues in Designing Pension Plans

Pensions are clearly a significant cost component in the employee benefits package. Pension plans vary so much in operational detail that a specialist should be consulted by any organization considering introducing such a plan. In this text, only the basic features of pension plans are discussed.

ERISA is the main piece of legislation that regulates pension plans. ERISA resulted because pension plans were often unable to provide employees with the benefits promised. Society, concerned about the financial stability of employers' pension plans, passed protective legislation that deals with the issues, which are discussed in this section and summarized in Exhibit 13.3.

**Pension Plan Objectives**   Before implementing a pension plan, the compensation decision maker must ask, What are the objectives of the plan? For example, is the plan to provide for all the retirement needs of an employee and the dependent spouse, or is it intended only to supplement other income? Most pension plans today are not designed to stand alone as the sole income of a person in retirement; more than 60 percent are integrated formally with Social Security.[19] One typical approach to determining benefit levels under a pension plan is to make postretirement income from Social Security and the pension plan equal to a percentage of preretirement pay.[20] Retirement income should be at least 50 percent of preretirement income.[21]

**Who Qualifies?**   One important question in developing a pension plan is to determine eligibility to participate in the pension plan. Most employers have revised their pension plans during the past years to ensure that they meet IRS

---

**EXHIBIT 13.3**   **ERISA-RELATED ISSUES IN ESTABLISHING A PENSION PLAN**

| Issue | Consideration |
|---|---|
| Benefit level | How large will the pension benefit be? |
| Retirement age | What is the earliest age at which employees can retire under the plan? |
| Vesting | When does the employee have a right to the employer's contribution to the plan? |
| Funding | When must money be set aside to cover the pension liability? |
| Fiduciary standards | Is the fund managed in the interest of the participants? |
| Pension Benefit Guaranty Corporation | How does the Pension Benefit Guaranty Corporation become involved in private pension plans? |
| Pension plan objectives | What are the goals for income replacement, partial replacement, etc.? |
| Who qualifies? | Who is eligible to participate in the plan? |

regulations to be considered qualified plans and thus have tax-exempt status under existing IRS codes. It is estimated that corporate deductions for pension plans cost the U.S. Treasury about $52 billion in lost taxes in 1991.[22] Some employers have decided to forego tax-exempt status to maintain flexibility, to increase coverage to select employees, or to be selective in who can participate.

Under ERISA, if a pension plan is offered, an employee who is 21 years old and has one year of service must be eligible. This requirement applies only to employees who work more than half-time (defined as more than 1,000 hours in a calendar year). An employer wishing to avoid pension liability should be careful that its part-time employees do not exceed the ERISA standard. Employers of small business are permitted to establish simplified employee pension (SEP) plans in which contributions are made by employer and employee to a tax-exempt individual retirement account (IRA).[23]

**Benefit Level**   Although pension plan goals determine benefit levels, other factors influence benefit levels as well. The percentage of the preretirement income (sometimes referred to as the replacement ratio) is used to calculate the pension level.[24] Also of concern is whether the plan is based on a single employee or if it takes into account an employee and a dependent spouse. Today, experts suggest the use of the single-employee criterion, which results in higher benefit levels and higher costs.[25] Costs are higher under a single-employee criterion because the employee is not assumed to realize the economies of scale of two-person household or the spouse's Social Security benefit. ERISA has a series of supporting and disclosure provisions that require that all plan participants are provided with a summary of their benefits and that the plan supply the Secretary of Labor and the IRS with information pertaining to the plan benefits, financial stability, and its operations. Also, the 1986 Tax Reform Act limits the pension benefits available to employees if the organization wishes the plan to maintain its qualified status. Organizations, to provide better and more secure pensions for highly paid executives, are designing nonqualified plans for this group of executives; to protect them during a corporate merger or acquisition, the organizations are using trusts.[26] Monies to fund specified benefits are set aside in trusts that are independent of the corporate legal entity. This strategy enables key executives to protect their benefits regardless of the outcome of the attempted merger or acquisition.

**Retirement Age**   Every pension plan must specify a retirement age. Traditionally, 65 years has been used as the standard retirement age for private pension plans. Unions, for example, have pushed for 62, 60, and even 55 years of age in some cases, and in other cases, they have also pushed for a 30 years and out (mandatory retirement after 30 years of service) rule. At the same time that unions have been pushing to reduce the retirement age, amendments to the Age Discrimination in Employment Act have removed the minimum mandatory retirement age. Thus, although an employer may still specify age 65 (or younger) as its standard retirement age, the employer cannot force employees to retire at age 65 years. The 1986 Omnibus Budget Reconciliation Act (OBRA) enables an employee to continue to participate and accrue additional benefits after the established retirement age.

Although plans must set a standard retirement age, many pension plans also make provisions for early retirement. There is considerable variability in practice, but a common approach is to allow employees to retire at age 60 or 62 years at reduced benefit levels. The reduced benefit levels are based on the fact that younger employees will have paid into the plan for a shorter period of time and also are expected to draw against the plan longer. Some public and private sector organizations are encouraging employees to retire early as a cost saving strategy. For example, the State of Wisconsin, around 1990, established an early retirement window for employees. An *early retirement window* is a short period during which an employee who meets certain qualifications can retire early without penalty. The state had calculated that it would save money if employees with long tenure retired and were replaced with less experienced and cheaper employees. Some school districts had many experienced teachers take advantage of the early retirement program. This strategy did save payroll dollars but created a shortage of experienced personnel in some key areas.

**Vesting**    Vesting refers to the rights that an employee has to benefits that have accrued in a pension fund. Vesting is overseen by the IRS. In the case of contributory plans (plans in which employees contribute part of their salaries), the employee is always entitled to the individual share. However, when does the employee have a right to the company-contributed share in noncontributory or contributory plans? Under ERISA, the employer has 2 minimum options for vesting employees: (1) the employer can provide 100 percent vesting after 5 years of service; or (2) the employer can provide 20 percent vesting after 3 years of service, then 100 percent after 7 years. Employers who are part of a multiemployer plan must provide vesting within 10 years.[27]

**Funding**    Under ERISA, pension plans must also be funded and are overseen by the IRS. Liabilities incurred in a given year by a pension plan must be funded in that same year and are monitored and adjusted every third year to ensure financial stability. Expert accounting and actuarial advice are essential to arrive at realistic estimates of the employer's future expected liability under a pension plan. If the plan meets ERISA standards, then the employer can treat these liabilities as a business expense for tax purposes. Sometimes a number of employers will group together, pooling their employees in a single pension plan. These multiemployer plans are often created through an employers' association in an industry that is characterized by a large number of small employers as participants. A 1980 amendment to ERISA requires employers who withdraw from multiemployer plans to continue their liability.[28]

**Fiduciary Standards**    Compensation decision makers must be concerned that the fiduciary standards of ERISA are met. The funds placed in the pension plan must be managed by an individual or institution for the best interests of the participants in the plan. Normally, an organization will choose a bank, insurance company, or other financial institution to act as the fiduciary of the fund. This area of pension management is reviewed for compliance by the Department of Labor.

**Pension Benefit Guaranty Corporation**   The Pension Benefit Guaranty Corporation (PBGC), a nonprofit insurance corporation managed by the Department of Labor, administers insurance programs for defined benefit private pension plans that conform to ERISA standards. In the event that a private pension plan ceases to exist, the PBGC guarantees that an employee will be able to collect accrued benefits under the plan. Congress sets the premium rate for employers to ensure adequate funding to cover pension plans that cease to exist.

The PBGC also allows an employee to transfer funds from an employer's pension fund if the employer agrees. An employee may be able to transfer funds from one employer to another without incurring tax liability on the funds. Any transfer is contingent on the former employer being willing to release the funds and the new employer being willing to accept the funds. The individual can also leave the monies with PBGC and draw against those benefits at retirement age.

## Types of Pension Plans

It is misrepresentation to consider all pension plans as being the same. There is almost an unlimited array of options in setting up pension plans for employees. This section discusses several categories of the more common types of pension plans.

**Defined Benefits Plans**   The distinguishing feature of a defined benefits pension plan is that a participant in the plan will be entitled to a defined benefit level at retirement regardless of the cost to the employer. The amount is usually either a flat amount (for example, $800 per month), percentage of yearly income, or a combination of yearly income and years of service.[29] From the organization's standpoint, this plan is probably the most costly. The burden of ensuring that the funds are in the plan resides with the employer. As yield rates on the investments in the retirement fund change or as the demographics of the work force change, the employer must be sure that the funds are available to meet the obligations of the defined benefit level. Because of the financial obligations and the Tax Reform Act of 1986, 16,000 defined plans were terminated in 1990 and the number of new such plans has dropped by one-third.[30]

**Defined Contribution Plans**   In defined contribution plans, the employer contributes a fixed amount (so much per hour or a percentage of pay) into an employee's retirement account; however, there is no guarantee of a fixed benefit level when the employee retires. The amount the employee receives is based on how well the fund performs based on its investment strategy. This method is less risky and costly to the employer because the main commitment is to the initial level of funds. The employer carries no responsibility for the yield rate on the investments. The employee, however, incurs greater uncertainty because it is harder to plan for retirement and the risk is shifted to the employee. Benefits under such a plan may be highly variable.

**Salary Reduction Plans**   Salary reduction plans are special types of defined contribution plans. In this case, the employee contributes some portion of current earnings to the pension plan. Two types of salary reduction plans are extremely popular today: thrift plans, and 401K plans (the latter take their name from the legislation enacting them).

Salary reduction plans are of relative low cost to the organization because the funds are typically from employee salaries. Further, there is no liability for yield rates on investments, nor is there a defined benefit.

*Thrift Plans*   Thrift plans allow employees to contribute from current income into a pension plan that is invested on their behalf, and vesting rules apply. The advantage to the employee is that the interest earned is not taxed until they are paid back out of the plan. Typically, thrift plans involve an employer contribution as well. For example, the employer may contribute on a one-for-one basis with the employee—the employer matches each dollar the employee puts into the plan up to a prescribed limit (such as 6 percent of total pay).

*401K Plans*   401K plans allow an employee to defer current income into the future and to shelter the money from taxes until it is withdrawn. A typical 401K might work in conjunction with a profit-sharing plan. Once a year, an employee may be entitled to a share of the company profits. The employee may decide to invest this money in a pension fund, which means that the employee can defer the taxes on this money.[31] A similar plan in the nonprofit business sector is 403(b) or 501(c)(3) plans. The right of the employee to withdraw from this fund is restricted by the 1986 Tax Reform Act. The fund may not be drawn on before the employee's 59½ birthday unless the employee can prove hardship, employment termination, or disability. Any early withdrawals are taxed as income, and a penalty is imposed.

**Simplified Pension Plans**   A simplified pension plan might resemble an IRA. The employer might agree to put aside a fund of money into an IRA for each employee. This type of arrangement provides the least long-term financial commitment of the four types of plans discussed here. The employer's only involvement is the cash outlay. The employee is free to leave the money in the account or to withdraw it (and pay the tax).

**Stock Purchase Plans**   Employee stock ownership plans (ESOPs), tax reduction act stock ownership plans (TRASOPs), and payroll stock ownership plans (PAYSOPs) are all stock purchase plans that are used to fund pension programs. More formally, they are considered profit-sharing plans. The common theme that they share is enabling an employer to take advantage of tax law in granting stock to employees. The law also gives favorable tax treatment to employees when they redeem the stock at retirement.

## Pension Plan Costs

Pensions are the largest single component in the cost of employee benefits, if the costs of Social Security are counted as part of the pension package. In 1992, organizations paid 7.65 percent (6.2 percent Social Security tax and 1.45 percent Medicare tax) of each employee's gross pay (up to a maximum gross pay of $55,500) into the Social Security program. If an employer had a private pension plan to which it contributed 8 percent of an employee's gross pay, then the employer paid a total of 15.65 percent of gross pay into pensions. In addition to that 15.65 percent, the employee was required to pay 7.65 percent to Social Security and, in some cases, could contribute to the private pension plan as well, making the total contribution to the pension plan equal to at least 23.30 percent of gross pay.

## Pay for Time Not Worked Benefits

The second largest category of benefits is pay for time not worked. The most common type of pay for time not worked is vacation and holiday pay.[32] Also, there is a long list of other pay for time not worked that some organizations provide. Exhibit 13.4 summarizes the percentage of full-time employees receiving selected benefits.

### Vacation Pay

Most organizations have a policy governing vacation benefits. Some employers allow all employees the same number of weeks off with pay after a specified period of service. In other organizations, the employers vary the vacation time off with pay based on seniority. For example, an employer might have a policy of 2 weeks off with pay for employees with 1 to 5 years of service, 3 weeks off with pay for employees with 6 to 10 years of service, 4 weeks off with pay for employees with 11 to 15 years of service, 5 weeks off with pay for employees with 16 to 20 years of service, and 6 six weeks off with pay for employees with more than 21 years of service. Obviously, the more liberal the vacation policy, the more costly it will be to the organization. An example of two vacation policies appears in Exhibit 13.5. A key issue with the administration of this benefit is the development of a policy regarding employee requests for specific vacation weeks. A policy must consider the rights of senior employees, the efficient operation of the unit, and the morale of the junior employees. For this reason, many organizations permit the selection of weeks to be based on seniority but limit the number of weeks selected in the first round of choices (for example, 2 weeks) and grant the request only if it does not compromise the operation of the unit.

### Holiday Pay

Holidays are another major benefit that results in pay for time not worked.[33] The most common holidays are Christmas, New Year's Day, Memorial Day, July 4th, Labor Day, and Thanksgiving. Some organizations require the employee to work the day before and/or the day after the holiday to be paid. This is done to avoid excessive absences on those days as employees attempt to extend the holiday break.

| EXHIBIT 13.4 | PERCENTAGE OF FULL-TIME EMPLOYEES PARTICIPATING IN SELECTED EMPLOYEE BENEFIT PROGRAMS (1989 AND 1990)[a] |
|---|---|

| Employee Benefit Program | State and Local Governments (1990) | Small private Establishments (1990) | Medium and Large Private Establishments (1989) |
|---|---|---|---|
| **Paid time off** | | | |
| Holidays | 74 | 84 | 97 |
| Vacations | 67 | 88 | 97 |
| Personal leave | 39 | 11 | 22 |
| Lunch period | 11 | 8 | 10 |
| Rest period | 56 | 48 | 71 |
| Funeral leave | 63 | 47 | 84 |
| Jury duty leave | 94 | 54 | 90 |
| Military leave | 81 | 21 | 53 |
| Sick leave | 95 | 47 | 68 |
| Maternity leave | 1 | 2 | 3 |
| Paternity leave | 1 | b | 1 |
| **Unpaid time off** | | | |
| Maternity leave | 51 | 17 | 37 |
| Paternity leave | 33 | 8 | 18 |
| **Insurance** | | | |
| Sickness and accident insurance | 21 | 26 | 43 |
| Long-term disability insurance | 27 | 19 | 45 |
| Medical care | 93 | 69 | 92 |
| Dental care | 62 | 30 | 66 |
| Life insurance | 88 | 64 | 94 |
| **Retirement** | | | |
| All retirement[c] | 96 | 42 | 81 |
| Defined benefit pension | 90 | 20 | 63 |
| Defined contribution[d] | 9 | 31 | 48 |

[a] Except for maternity and paternity leave, benefits paid for entirely by the employee were excluded from the tabulations.

[b] Less than 0.5 percent.

[c] Includes defined benefit pension plans and defined contribution retirement plans. Some employees participated in both types of plans.

[d] Includes money purchase pension plans (plans providing retirement income based on fixed contribution rates plus earnings credited to the employee's account), savings and thrift plans, and Simplified Employee Pension plans in governments, and these plans plus deferred profit-sharing plans, employee stock ownership plans, and stock bonus plans in private industry. In all these plans, employer contributions must remain in the participant's account until retirement age, death, disability, separation from service, age 59 1/2 years, or hardship.

SOURCE: D. Hedger, "Benefits in State and Local Governments," *Monthly Labor Review* 115 (March 1992), 32–37.

---

**EXHIBIT 13.5**    **TWO VACATION POLICIES**

---

### Company A

**Nonofficer employees**

| | |
|---|---|
| Through the fifth year of continuous service | 10 days |
| January 1 following the year in which they complete 5 years of continuous service | 15 days |
| January 1 following the year in which they complete 10 years of continuous service | 20 days |

**Officers: vice-president and below**

| | |
|---|---|
| Through the eighth year of continuous service | 15 days |
| January 1 following the year in which they complete 8 years of service | 20 days |

**Officers: senior vice-president and above**

| | |
|---|---|
| January 1 following the date of employment | 20 days |

---

### Company B

Employees with 6 months or more service are eligible for paid vacation based on this schedule:

| Service | Vacation |
|---|---|
| 6 months | 1 week |
| 1 year | 2 weeks |
| 5 years | 2 weeks plus 3 days |
| 10 years | 3 weeks |
| 15 years | 3 weeks plus 3 days |
| 20 years | 4 weeks |

---

## Other Paid Time

Many other days can be considered legitimate occasions for time off with pay. Examples of these are:

1. Jury duty

2. Serving as an election official

3. Serving as a witness in court

4. Civic duty

5. Military duty (such as the National Guard)

6. Funeral leave

7. Maternity or paternity leave

8. Sick leave

9. Time off to vote

10. Personal leaves

11. Sabbatical leave

12. Time off for exercise

Specific time off with pay varies partly as a function of organizational philosophy. Two examples should make the point. In one case, an insurance company gives employees up to 90 minutes per day off with pay to use the company-operated physical fitness facility. This policy is consistent with a belief that employees who are in better physical condition perform better and are better actuarial risks. In the second case, a pharmaceutical company, believing that managers should be good citizens in the larger society, gives employees a sabbatical for 1 year at half-pay to serve in local political offices. The philosophy seems to be to encourage participation in local political affairs without penalizing the employee economically.

Anytime there is pay for days not worked, the organization must develop policies that apply to the use of the benefit. For example, are sick days not used during the year lost, carried over for future use, or cashed in for dollar value? If the policy is use it or lose it, it may encourage a rash of illness in the last quarter as employees use the benefits they believe they have earned. The point to be made is, as the organization considers adding these kinds of benefits, it must examine the administrative problems that may develop and plan a continuous education program to remind employees of the real purpose of the benefit.

### Indirect Costs of Pay for Time Not Worked

The direct costs associated with pay for time not worked are normally the hourly wage costs that are incurred plus the cost of other benefits (pension contributions, Social Security). However, many potential indirect costs are less obvious. For example, the work of an employee who is granted vacation time needs to be performed by someone else. Unless careful planning goes into scheduling vacations, the employer may have to pay other workers overtime, increase staffing levels, or run at reduced production levels.

Because these indirect costs can be substantial, careful administration of time off is necessary, including planning vacation and holiday schedules. This is especially true as cost becomes more critical and more customers adapt just-in-time inventory programs.

## Health and Welfare Benefits

Organizations usually provide an array of insurance benefits for employees on either a contributory or noncontributory basis. These include health insurance, life insurance, dental insurance, and all other forms of insurance. The more important of these are discussed in this section. Legislation prevents discrimination against certain groups of eligible employees in regard to benefit offerings. For example, because of the Age Discrimination in Employment Act as amended, benefits provided employees must not vary by age unless the difference can be justified based on costs.[34] In addition, the Pregnancy Discrimination Act prohibits employers from discriminating based on sex in the administration of all health care insurance plans. All health care problems and any disabilities resulting from pregnancy must be covered in the same way as all other health problems.[35]

## *Health Insurance*

Almost three-fourths of the employees in the private sector and about 80 percent of public sector employees are covered by some type of group health insurance program.[36] U.S. health care costs had reached $675 billion or 12 percent of gross national product in 1990.[37] Health care costs had risen from 4.4 percent of total compensation in 1980 to 6.4 percent in 1990.[38] Health insurance programs usually consist of two parts. One part is a plan to provide for basic medical services. Usually, this component has a deductible level ($50 to $500 per year) that the employee must pay, and the plan covers all other reasonable expenses (or a percentage of the expenses) up to some maximum. The second part of a typical plan is a main medical component. This component is designed to provide for catastrophic medical expenses, so that when the benefits under the first part of the plan are exhausted, the employee has continued coverage up to some maximum (for example, $250,000). Normally, major medical costs are shared on an 80 percent/20 percent split between the insurer and the employee, respectively. An example of one employer's health insurance plan is depicted in Exhibit 13.6.

When health insurance plans were introduced, they were generally *contributory plans*—employees usually paid all or part of the premium. Increasingly, these plans became *noncontributory:* the employer paid the entire cost of the plan. Currently, however, there is an increasing trend for employers to ask employees to help pay for the ever-increasing expense of these plans. Many plans today are designed so that all of the employee's individual premiums are paid by the employer, but the employees contribute to the premium charges for family and dependent coverage.

As stated earlier, the cost of health insurance coverage has grown substantially over the years as the cost of health care has grown (see Exhibit 13.7 on page 444).

This growth is attributable to at least three factors. First, health coverage costs have grown because of the increasingly comprehensive nature of coverage. As noted above, early plans often provided base care with few extas, whereas today's plans often cover many extras for which hospitals charge. For example, many early plans did not cover surgical procedures performed in the doctor's office (such as removal of warts). For the insurance to cover the procedure, the procedure would have to be performed in the hospital. Today, many plans do cover surgical procedures performed in the doctor's office.

Second, health care coverage costs have grown partly because of doctors' fears over malpractice charges. Because doctors are sued much more frequently today, they tend to order diagnostic tests that in the past they may not have ordered. This extensive diagnostic testing is billed back to the insurance carrier.

**EXHIBIT 13.6** **A HEALTH INSURANCE PLAN**

### Diagram of Your $100,000 Comprehensive Medical Insurance

| Type A (Hospital) | Type B (Surgical) | Type C (All Other) |
|---|---|---|
| Hospital room and board: standard semiprivate room rate | Surgery: in or out of hospital | Doctors calls—hospital, home, or office |
| | | Nurse's fees—O.P.N. or R.N. |
| | | Dental charges—due to accident |
| Hospital extras | Anesthetist | X-rays |
| | | Radiologic and laboratory |
| Ambulance (up to $30.00 round trip) | | Oxygen, blood, plasma |
| | | Artificial eyes and limbs |
| | | Casts, splints, trusses, braces |
| Emergency room within 72 hours after injury | | Crutches and surgical dressings |
| | | Rental of wheel chair, hospital bed, and iron lung |
| | | Rental of equipment for treatment of respiratory paralysis |
| | | Prescription drugs and medicines |
| 80 percent reimbursed up to $2,000, then 100 percent for balance of calendar year | 80 percent reimburses up to $2,000, then 100 percent for balance of calendar year | 80 percent reimbursed up to $2,000, then 100 percent for balance of calendar year |
| | | $100 calendar year deductible for all causes each year per person |
| No deductible | No deductible | (maximum of three deductibles per family), 12-month accumulation |

*Note:* Maternity benefits are payable as any other illness.

Third, health coverage costs have grown because both labor and capital costs have increased in hospitals. The cost of equipment has increased dramatically because of its greater sophistication and is passed on to the consumer. Similarly, health care is labor-intensive, and it is necessary to pass these costs on to the consumer. The consumer in this case is the health insurance carrier, which then increases the premiums.

Fourth, legislation now requires organizations to extend coverage to individuals who have not previously been covered, thus increasing costs. For example, the Consolidated Omnibus Budget Reconciliation Act (COBRA, 1985) extends coverage to departing employees; COBRA requires employers with 20 or more employees to offer continuation of health insurance for a limited time to divorced spouses of active employees and to terminated employees.[39] In general, 18 months coverage is required when termination is voluntary or mandatory, except in cases of gross misconduct. Thirty-six months is required in the event of the employee's death, employee's entitlement to Medicare, divorce, separation, or dependent coverage. The burden of proof is on the employer to be sure that employees know their rights and that these rights are clearly communicated in a timely manner. Under COBRA, the individual whose coverage is

**EXHIBIT 13.7  GROWTH RATES OF GROSS NATIONAL PRODUCT AND HEALTH EXPENDITURES**

| Year | Gross National Product (GNP) | | National Health Expenditures (NHE) | | NHE/GNP (%) |
|---|---|---|---|---|---|
| | Amount in Billions | Annual Growth Rate (%) | Amount in Billions | Annual Growth Rate (%) | |
| 1965 | $ 705.0 | 6.4 | $ 41.6 | 9.2 | 5.9 |
| 1975 | 1,598.0 | 8.5 | 132.9 | 12.3 | 8.3 |
| 1980 | 2,732.0 | 11.3 | 249.1 | 13.4 | 9.1 |
| 1985 | 4,015.0 | 8.0 | 420.1 | 11.0 | 10.5 |
| 1990 | 5,463.0 | 5.0 | 670.9 | 11.1 | 12.3 |
| 1995* | 7,284.0* | 6.4* | 1,072.7* | 9.9 | 14.7 |
| 2000* | 9,865.0* | 6.3* | 1,615.9* | 8.5 | 16.4 |

*Estimates.

SOURCE:  Health Care Financing Administration, Office of the Actuary; Data from The Office of National Health Statistics. In S. T. Sommerfield, D. R. Waldo, and J. A. Lemieux, "Projections of National Health Expenditures Through the Year 2000," *Health Care Financing Review* 13 (Fall 1991), 16.

continued is responsible for 102 percent of the insurance premium. The additional 2 percent above the cost of the plan is to cover administrative costs. At first glance, it would seem this legislation costs the employer nothing. But the concept of the employer's responsibility to educate and inform the employee adds a time and dollar cost in the benefits management area. A study by the National Association of Manufacturers and Towers, Perrin, Forster, and Crosby indicated that only 20 percent of eligible employees elected continuation.[40]

Another piece of legislation that has recently complicated the picture is the Family and Medical Leave Act of 1993 (FMLA). Under this act, health benefits must continue while an employee is on unpaid leave for any of the causes outlined in the act. FMLA applies to employers of 50 or more employees and allows 12 weeks of unpaid leave for the birth, adoption, or foster care of a child or for the care of a spouse, parent, or child (or self) in the case of serious illness. If the employee terminates employment for reasons other than the leave, the employer may recover health care premium costs from the former employee. The exact relationship of FMLA to such existing legislation as COBRA and its impact on benefits management will be determined over the next few years by agency rulings and court cases.

At present there is no legislation or guaranteed extension of health coverage to retirees, and this has been an area of friction between organizations and their retirees.[41] While Medicare provides basic coverage, additional coverage is almost essential. If organizations decide or are required to include retirees in their plans, costs for organizations will inevitably increase.

Despite increased coverage costs, insurance companies still declare that premiums are not keeping pace with payouts. The National Association of Manufacturers and Towers, Perrin, Forster, and Crosby found that insurers of large employers paid out $1.90 for every $1.00 premium collected in 1990 and $1.67 and $1.83 in 1989 and 1988. For insurers of employers with fewer than 2,000 employees, the payout was $1.55 in 1990 and $1.56 and $1.75 for 1989 and 1988.[42]

Health care is one of the most important and most debated issues facing the nation. One goal is the containment of health care costs, and a related goal is the establishment of reasonable (both in cost and availability) health care coverage. One of the main issues of national debate is the containment of health care costs. Some suggested approaches include pressuring doctors to keep fees down, increasing the deductible to discourage overuse of health care, introducing more competition (for example, allowing doctors to advertise their fees), and establishing national health insurance. Any one of these approaches is likely to be only partially successful because the causes of the growth of health care costs are many. The cost of health care has become such a concern that many private sector and public groups are in the process of developing proposals that would address the national health care problem. The groups studying the issue range from the National Leadership Coalition for Health Care Reform to the Democratic Party.[43]

The 1992 presidential campaign increased the focus on health care reform. President Clinton has made health care reform a priority issue. He has gathered a large group of experts to study the existing U.S. health care system and foreign health care systems, and to develop a comprehensive reform program. The question is not whether health care reform will take place, but what the specifics will be, how the program will be financed, and what impact it will have on existing health care.

### Dental Insurance

Early health insurance programs provided for rather limited coverage, and the trend is to broaden the coverage. One way in which coverage is expanding is by considering dental coverage as part of the basic health plan. One study found that availability of dental coverage increased from 8 percent of the firms surveyed in 1974 to 41 percent of the firms surveyed in 1981. In the survey, dental plans were noncontributory about two-thirds of the time.[44]

### Long-Term Care

The availability of long-term care in the form of nursing homes or in other forms has been of increasing interest. Nursing home costs require extensive cash reserves. Firms that offer this as an insurance option find only 5 percent to 15 percent of employees selecting it as part of their plan. The primary reason for the low enrollment is belief that the premiums are too expensive. Even with the ability to purchase the coverage though a group plan, the yearly premiums cost about $1,200 per year. This area will become an increasingly important benefit as the work force continues to age.[45]

### Other Related Health Benefits

The spectrum of benefits in the health care area has expanded significantly and now covers other related services such as psychiatric care, alcohol and drug treatment, counseling, vision care, chiropractic care, and prescription and other health-related services. These services may be part of a comprehensive insurance program or may be a series of independent insurance coverages.

Employee assistance programs (EAPs) are being offered by an increasing number of employers. EAPs are programs designed to help individuals deal with emotional, physical, financial, and personal problems that are influencing their job performance. The original purpose was to deal wlth alcohol and substance abuse, but EAPs have expanded to cover a broader array of individual problems, such as marital, child-related, and financial. In some organizations these are stand alone programs, while in others they are integrated within the organizations' comprehensive health programs depending on the specific coverage being provided through the EAP.

Many organizations prefer to have the EAP handled through a third party due to the sensitivity of the personal problems being treated. For example, many employees are reluctant to go to an in-house service that provides substance abuse counseling for fear that identification may harm their employment. To protect the individual using the service, the organization contracts with a third party to provide the service and pays a monthly per employee fee. The most confidential method is to permit employees to use the service without first obtaining permission from someone within the firm. Often the organization is provided a summary of the kinds of services being used by its employees, frequency of contact, and other pertinent data that may prove useful to the organization but does not compromise the employee's confidentiality.

## Life and Accident Insurance

Many employers provide life insurance, and the size of the policy is often determined based on the employee's salary. Under a typical plan, the employee's life in insured up to double the annual wage or salary. Life insurance plans can be contributory or noncontributory, but all have the advantage of lower group rates. Normally, companies put a limit on the size of the policy, and an employee will incur tax liability for coverage in excess of $50,000. That is, the premium for life insurance in excess of $50,000 is taxed as normal income.

A second type of plan provides accidental death and dismemberment insurance. These plans typically have a fixed scale of benefits so that an employee or a beneficiary receives a fixed amount in the event of accidental death or dismemberment. Such plans can also be contributory or noncontributory, and premium structures take advantage of group rates.

## Long-Term Disability Insurance

Employers typically cover short-term disability through their sick leave policy, discussed as pay for time not worked. There is also concern over long-range disability coverage when an employee is sick or injured and out of work for long periods of time. This situation is often covered through some form of long-term disability insurance. For example, an employee off the job for more than 6 months could draw against the disability insurance plan. These plans provide for coverage of up to 100 percent of a person's net pay. Any long-term disability program must be integrated with existing mandatory benefits, such as Social Security and workers' compensation. Proper integration should enable the organization to protect its employees at a reasonable cost.

Employers often make an effort to integrate the short-term and long-term disability plan. An example of one employer's plan is depicted in Exhibit 13.8.

# Methods of Providing Health Benefits

The methods for administration of health care benefits are varied. This section briefly discusses four methods: the traditional indemnity plan, health maintenance organizations, preferred provider organizations, and the self-funded approach.

## Traditional Indemnity Plan

The traditional method to handle health care coverage in the United States has been through an indemnity plan. An indemnity plan requires the employer to pay a monthly premium to an outside insurer for each employee covered

---

**EXHIBIT 13.8**    DISABILITY INSURANCE PLAN

---

If you become disabled, the Company will continue your salary based on your length of service.

At full salary:   3 months
At one-half salary:   3 months

Should total disability extend beyond 6 months, you will receive a monthly income from the long-term disability (LTD) plan.

Your monthly income would be $X,XXX.XX.

The benefits from the LTD plan are adjusted according to received benefits from governmental and other company-sponsored disability plans such as Social Security and workers' compensation.

**Additional Disability Benefits if Totally Disabled**

Your basic group life insurance will continue (after 123 months of total disability) to age 65 years, or to age 70 years if disability occurs after age 65, at no cost to you.

If you enrolled, Permaplan premiums will be waived up to age 65 years.

The long-term disability plan makes your contributions to the retirement system for as long as you are disabled up to age 65 years.

After 1 year of disability, you may elect to withdraw all or part of your profit sharing or all your retirement system accounts or both. The total value of your accounts was:

Profit sharing as of 10/1/XX:   $XX,XXX.XX
Retirement systems as of 9/30/XX:   $ X,XXX.XX

---

(family coverage is at times provided for at a higher rate). That payment enables those covered to select the physician, hospital, clinic, or laboratory of their choosing. This kind of delivery system provides the greatest freedom to the employees in regard to choice, but it is very common for this kind of plan to provide less benefits for the same cost or to carry higher premiums and higher deductibles than some of the newer approaches.

## *Health Maintenance Organizations*

The Health Maintenance Act of 1973 established the regulations under which health care coverage can be provided to employees. Due to the dual choice provision included as part of the legislation, HMOs have experienced significant growth since 1973. Participation in an HMO differs from traditional indemnity insurance in that participants must use only the doctors, clinics, and hospitals designated by the plan. Dual choice mandates that if an HMO is available in an employer's area (at least 25 employees live within the HMO service area), and if the HMO requests inclusion as an option to employees, and if the employer already provides health insurance, then the employer must provide the HMO option. The employer is obligated to provide coverage equal to the cost of the conventional health insurance provided but the specific coverage does not have to be equal. The dual choice provision has been repealed by the HMO amendment, which takes effect October 24, 1995.

Often the coverage under the HMO can be substantially larger for the same dollar cost than coverage under the more traditional health insurance programs. While it is hard to attribute this fact to a precise cause, it may be due to at least three factors. First, HMOs have fixed labor costs—doctors agree to work for a salary. Second, HMOs stress preventive features (it is presumably cheaper to cure someone at an early stage of illness). Third, some HMOs use paramedical personnel (doctors may delegate some duties to narrowly trained specialists).

While there is often more thorough coverage under an HMO, some employees resist these plans because of the loss of freedom. They are limited only to the physicians in the HMO. They are permitted to see other physicians only after receiving a referral from an HMO physician. This process can complicate an employee's desire to seek a specialist or to receive a second opinion. If an employee visits an outside physician without a referral, unless it is an emergency situation, the employee assumes full responsibility for the costs.

## Preferred Provider Organizations

The preferred provider organizations (PPOs) were designed as a compromise for employees who do not like the restriction in physician selection in HMOs, and for employers who are unwilling to continue the traditional health care provider system. In a PPO, the employer negotiates a discounted fee with a select number of physicians, hospitals, clinics, and laboratories to provide health care coverage to its employees. The incentive to health care providers for agreeing to the discounted fee is the increased volume of business and expedited claim processing. The employer can negotiate with the PPO to obtain information about the effectiveness and efficiency of services being provided by different physicians, clinics, hospitals, or laboratories that are associated with the PPO. In a PPO, an employee is not required to use the participating physicians; but when the employee does use these physicians, there is usually no charge for the services. If the employee uses the services of a physician outside the PPO, only 80 percent of the cost will likely be covered and the employee will be responsible for the difference.

## Self-Funded Plans

A number of organizations are involved in some degree of self-funding for their health care benefits. A survey by Foster, Higgins and Company (1990) found that 67 percent of employers with more than 1,000 employees were involved in self-funding. A common method of self-funding is a form of stop-loss insurance plan in which the employer assumes most of the cost of health care claims but does buy insurance to cover cost beyond some established level. For example, the employer covers all of an individual's cost up to $1,500 per year and all plan expenses up to $1,500,000. A company may stay with an insurance carrier to process its claims and to cover large risk claims. In this arrangement the company pays the carrier a small percent of what the normal annual premiums would be to cover processing of claims and to carry reinsurance for large claims. Normal claims' costs are the responsibility of the employer and are paid out of a pre–established fund.[46]

# Selected Benefits

Employers provide a wide range of other benefits. Most of these benefits not only provide advantages to the employees but also, in some way, serve to the advantage of the organization. Examples of some of these benefits are discussed below.

## *Other Insurance*

Just as health-related insurances have become more comprehensive over time, so have the types of group insurance offered in general. Today, some employers offer such benefits as auto insurance, legal insurance, liability insurance, home insurance, and bond insurance.

## *Discounts on Goods and Services*

Many employers allow their employees to purchase company products or services at reduced rates. A gas station owner may sell gas to employees at cost, or auto manufacturers may allow employees to purchase cars at a fixed discount. These programs stimulate demand for the organization's products or services, as well as allow the employee to obtain cheaper goods and services. A related benefit is when an employer arranges with other producers of goods and services to provide their output at reduced rates. For example, an employer may arrange with a local amusement park to give its employees a 50 percent discount on admission.

## *Subsidized Meals*

Many organizations provide for full or partially funded cafeterias. One reason may be a conviction on the part of the organization that employees who are well fed will work better. Another reason may simply be that there are inadequate meal facilities off premises. Still another reason may be that the company does not want employees to stray off for three-beer or martini lunches. Regardless of the motivations, these programs can be extremely costly.

## *Moving Expenses*

Employers with multiple operating sites often provide employees with relocation expense coverage. This benefit may be necessary to encourage employees to relocate without penalty. Even with relocation expenses covered, however, employers may find it difficult to get employees to relocate.

## Severance Pay

Very often an employer will provide an employee with the equivalent of 2 weeks of pay on termination (whether voluntary or not). Most companies provide severance pay to employees only if they are involuntarily terminated. This benefit is designed to aid the employee in the transition from one job to another.

An example of a severance pay policy schedule is depicted in Exhibit 13.9.

## Dependent Care

As more and more families have both husband and wife working (64 percent of families with children have working mothers) full-time, organizations[47] are under increasing pressure to provide dependent care. The primary dependent care is for children. In a survey, more than 70 percent of the respondents favored child care programs (34 percent on site, 38 percent allowance, 8 percent referral service) in which the employees could redesign their benefit coverage to pick up child care.[48] Many large companies are providing some form of on plant or subsidized day care.[49] Even prior to the FMLA, maternity leave is being provided to about 33 percent and paternity leave to about 20 percent of employees of medium- and large-size employers.[50] Some large organizations are providing employees with assistance with the care of elderly or ill relatives because of the cost of absenteeism and to attract and keep the best employees.[51] One survey found that 43 percent of the 1,000 firms surveyed offered time off to workers to care for ill family members. Also, 54 percent allowed employees to use their personal sick leave so they would not lose income.[52]

A study by the International Foundation of Employee Benefit Plans found that by the year 2000, the following services will be provided: 45 percent child care referral, 40 percent subsidization of child care, 28 percent on- or near-site child care; 53 percent elder service referral, 20 percent subsidization of elder care, and 18 percent respite care.[53]

---

**EXHIBIT 13.9    A SEVERANCE PAY POLICY**

| Time with Employer | Severance Pay[a] |
|---|---|
| Probationary period | None |
| Postprobationary period to 2 years | 2 weeks base pay |
| 2 to 5 years | 3 weeks base pay |
| 5 to 10 years | 5 weeks base pay |
| 10 to 15 years | 6 weeks base pay |
| 15 to 20 years | 7 weeks base pay |
| More than 20 years | 8 weeks base pay |

---

[a]Severance pay is paid only when the termination is company-initiated.

As the need for family assistance grows, companies are struggling to contain benefit costs. In a survey, it was shown that in 1987 there were hardly any paternity leaves or work-at-home policies. But a resurvey in 1991 showed that nearly half the firms had developed paternity leave, and 14 percent offered telecommuting policies for workers who needed to spend time at home.[54] Also, today's traditional family is changing. It is no longer seen as mother, father, and children. An increasing number of nontraditional families, such as homosexual couples and unmarried couples with children, have made employees change their definitions of employee benefits.

## Employee Stock Ownership Plans

ESOPs were designed for executive levels but have evolved to include most employees who wish to participate as a result of 1974 ERISA. Organizations set aside money in an employee trust that purchases the organization stock on the behalf of the employees. Each of the employees who participates has their own individual account to which the shares are allocated based on the established formula (based on percentage of salary and/or seniority). The original purpose of ESOPs was to provide employees a sense of ownership in the organization and was primarily used as part of an employee retirement program. The degree of real employee involvement in the decision making of the organization is very limited and usually covers little more than it did before the establishment of most ESOPs. The reasons for the low level of involvement is that the stake of the employees is relatively small, ownership of the shares do not transfer to the employees until they vest or leave (death, retirement, termination, resignation) the organization, and the plans cannot discriminate in favor of highly paid employees if the plan wants to maintain its qualified status.[55]

The tax changes and the wave of mergers and acquisitions during the mid-1980s changed the reasons that employers establish ESOPs. The primary reasons that most employers establish ESOPs is to reduce the threat of hostile takeovers and as a means of inexpensive financing. The tax laws permit organizations to finance a leveraged buyout (LBO) by the ESOP route. Often management terminates the employee pension plan, using money from the pension plan to buy an annuity to cover pension obligations and using the surplus to buy the company's stock. The cash available is often inadequate to purchase the full amount of stock, so the organization borrows the rest and pays off the loan from pre-tax earnings.[56] Thus the organization can deduct the interest and the dividends the organization pays on the stock in the ESOP.[57]

The Deficit Reduction Act of 1984 permitted those lending to ESOPs to defer tax on sales of ESOP stocks if the dollars gained through the sale are reinvested in a U.S. corporation within 12 months after the sale. The tax is permanently deferred if the replacement securities are held to death.[58] Also, investors can exclude 50 percent of the interest earned on loans to ESOPs with some limitations.[59] Because of the complications associated with ESOPs, it is necessary to employ the appropriate legal and accounting expertise before establishing an ESOP. This enables the management to fend off a hostile takeover and use pre-tax dollars to pay off the loan. ESOPs have enjoyed steady growth since 1975 and cover approximately 10 million employees at 10,000 companies in 1990.[60]

The financial success of LBO–ESOPs has been spotty. Some of the buy-outs have been successful (for example, Avis), whereas others have left workers with nothing or very shaky shares, while bankers and top management do very well.[61] Because of the varied success of these plans, the Department of Labor and Congress is increasing its scrutiny of LBO–ESOPs. A study by the National Center for Employee Ownership found that LBO–ESOPs were less likely to go bankrupt, and other studies have found that companies with ESOPs are more profitable than non-ESOP companies.[62]

### Other Benefits

Some employers are providing other services, such as preretirement planning, adoption assistance, financial planning, vacation spots, legal services (for example, wills, separation, divorce), long distance use of Watts lines during nonwork hours, and comprehensive wellness programs that cover education in smoking, drinking, eating habits, stress control, and access to physical exercise equipment and programs.

Executives have been identified by organizations as deserving a set of special service benefits because of the nature of their jobs. These benefits include health club memberships, country club memberships, high-level expense accounts, special parking privileges, cars, drivers, spouses' costs paid for on business trips, special personal and financial counseling, and special physical examinations. These benefits have been reduced in recent years because they often discriminate in favor of highly paid employees—thus tax benefits are lost—and because of the poor public image some of these benefits portray.

## Benefits Decision Making

Of central concern to compensation decision makers is the question of which benefits to offer. It is useful to think along two separate dimensions in answering this question. The first dimension is the benefit level (analogous to a wage level). Second is the dimension of the benefit structure (analogous to a wage structure). Benefit level is constrained by product market considerations, just as the wage level is constrained. The benefit structure is constrained by labor market considerations and employee preferences. Software is available to assist managers in making a wide array of benefit decisions.[63]

### Benefit Level and Product Market Benefit Surveys

The chapter on wage and benefit surveys suggests that organizations ought to survey their product market for benefits. The purpose of this survey is less to determine the actual components of the benefits package than to estimate the actual costs of such benefits. Just as ability to pay constrains wage levels, benefits levels are also constrained by ability to pay. The concern in product market surveys of benefits is the cost of those benefits, regardless of the composition of benefits.

## Benefit Structure and Labor Market Benefit Surveys

However, a survey of benefits in the labor market is particularly concerned with the structure of benefit packages. This concern stems from an assumption that benefit packages are compared when individuals make employment decisions. Under this assumption, it would be important for an organization to provide benefit packages of similar composition to its labor market competitors. However, if benefits are not used by employees in making decisions to join the organization, then such surveys are less critical.

Because of the fragmented nature of benefits, it is probably more important to offer roughly similar benefits than identical ones. For example, if the preponderance of firms in a labor market area offer dental coverage, then a low-wage firm might want to offer this, too, although it may make the plan contributory on the part of employees. Whether the organization can afford the plan at all, however, is a function of ability to pay constraints.

## Benefit Structure and Survey of Current Employees

A second way to assess which benefits the organization might offer is to survey present employees. Such a survey is particularly useful if the employer is considering increasing the benefits package. The rationale behind surveying present employees is that not all benefits are valued equally by all employees. The organization should spend the money on increased benefits in areas that will get the most recognition from employees.

## Benefit Structure and Goals

It should go without saying that the structure of the benefits package should reflect the goals of the organization (as constrained by the firm's ability to pay). The organization should question its values and goals and decide what it wants its benefits program to achieve. For example, some organizations may want to stress retirement programs; this would be logical for organizations whose labor forces become more valuable as they gain experience. Other organizations may want to stress both short-run and long-run disability programs; this would be logical for organizations with work environments that, by necessity, are somewhat hazardous.

## Contributory versus Noncontributory Benefits

An important decision-making issue centers on whether the benefit programs will be contributory or noncontributory. What percentage of the premium will the employee pay, or will the employer pay the entire cost? This decision has an impact on both the level of benefits and the benefit structure, because a higher level and a wider variety of benefits may be possible if employees share in the costs.

Another important consideration in deciding between contributory and noncontributory programs is guaranteeing that employees recognize the value of their benefits. One employer requires employees to pay 10 percent of the costs of all benefit plans where contributions are feasible. This employer's rationale is that employees have a greater appreciation of the true cost of benefits (and, therefore, realize their true value) when 10 percent of the cost is deducted from their paycheck each month.

## Trends in Employee Benefits

Trends in employee benefits are less than clear-cut. On the one hand, societal values seem to suggest that there will be a continued growth in benefit levels caused by continuing efforts to make benefit programs more comprehensive. For example, the recent trend to provide dental benefits can be viewed as one step in making health care coverage more comprehensive.

Also, organizations may make more systematic and sensible packages out of their short-term disability plans and their long-range disability plans. Today, many firms' sick-pay plans cover an employee only for two to four weeks. These firms' long-term disability plans do not begin until the employee has been off the job for six months. This gap in benefits is a natural one to fill, and benefit levels may continue to grow.

However, the serious structural changes in industry experienced during the early 1980s, along with the world recession, have made organizations more fiscally conservative, and as a consequence, they may be less likely to continue to increase benefit levels. Further, if benefits programs are taxed as direct income in the future, they may be less desirable to both employers and employees. Which of these forces will dominate in the future is not clear.

Organizations increasingly are looking to self-fund many of insurance-based benefits. The large employers are finding it cost-effective to self-insure in the areas of fire, health care, disability, dental, liability, and other areas of health and welfare plans. For example, in 1989 health insurance cost an average of $2,748 per worker.[64] Some organizations will pick up insurance coverage to cover huge cost items but may have very large deductibles before coverage kicks in. Self-insurance is usually done by large employers because small employers do not have the economic resources to assume the risk.

Because of the cost associated with benefits, many organizations have established programs to communicate to the employees the kinds of benefits they have, the cost of these benefits to the employer, and the impact the employee behavior can have on the cost of benefits (for example, health care) to the employer. There is an array of sophisticated methods to communicate the above to employees (for example, computer screens, pamphlets), but the key seems to be personal contact in which counselors can review each aspect and the potential impact of the employee on the costs of providing each benefit.

### *Cafeteria Benefit Plans*

One trend in benefits packages has been a flexible approach to benefits. Under this approach, an employee is provided with a core set of benefits and then may choose among other benefits.[65] The core benefits are those the organization believes are essential that all employees have and usually include health, life, disability insurance, and minimum vacation. Employees may only be able to opt out of these if they can prove coverage by some other means (for example, spouse coverage). For example, the employee with a very sick dependent might prefer more health care coverage, whereas an employee with many dependents may elect to carry more life insurance. There is a maximum total dollar amount to the benefits an employee may choose, and the employee can select a benefits package that fits his or her needs at a point in time. In some cases, the dollars not spent on benefits may be cashed in, at which time they are taxable. Also, if the employee exceeds the tax break limits, such as purchasing life insurance over the $50,000 limit, that will be taxable. Some organizations, instead of providing total freedom of choice after the core items, design a limited number of packages from which employees must pick. One package may be designed for young singles, one for young families, one for those families with no children at home, and so on.[66] A study found in 1990 that about two-thirds of the *Fortune* 500 top manufacturing and service firms that offer flexible plans permit full flexibility.[67] Flexible benefit plans have been found to be related positively to both employee satisfaction and understanding of their benefits.[68]

Flexible benefits plans have not enjoyed widespread use for at least two reasons. First, the IRS considers the cash/noncash options feature of flexible plans as placing the dollar value of those benefits in the wage/salary component of pay. (Some plans allow an employee the option of choosing between cash or benefits.) The dollar value of those benefits may not be tax-sheltered, and the employer and employee may lose the tax-sheltered advantage of traditional benefit packages. The tax status of certain benefits remains unclear, and it is unlikely that all questionable areas will be clarified in the near future.[69]

A second and perhaps more important reason why flexible plans are not offered more often is that they require both a solid core of benefits and optional benefits. A firm that can afford to provide a flexible plan must have a relatively high ability to pay in the first place. Many employers cannot afford such affluent benefit levels.

Other concerns about the feasibility of flexible plans are the administrative costs of constantly changing benefits levels for individual employees and the impact of self-selection of benefits on actuarially based costs. To deal with the first problem, organizations typically allow employees to change their benefit plan structure only once each year. The second problem is not well defined as of this date, but it makes intuitive sense, for example, that unhealthy workers would prefer higher health benefit levels. If enough unhealthy employees acted this way, the cost of the group plan would increase to provide the benefits. However, no good data are available on this point. It is unlikely that cafeteria plans will grow substantially.[70] Also, employers who provide counseling to employees on the selection of benefits may be held liable for poor counseling if employees later discover the benefit selection made does not provide adequate coverage.[71]

## Retirement Plans

Another area in which change may be on the horizon is private retirement plans. As the concept of Social Security has changed during the years from providing partial retirement income to providing a larger share of retirement income and as its costs have soared correspondingly, it would not be surprising if employers with private plans freeze their benefit levels and if employers without pension plans increasingly decide not to implement private plans. Organizations are taking a more active role in helping employees personally prepare better for their retirement years by providing retirement planning programs to offer suggestions and explain options (such as IRAs) far in advance of actual retirement.[77]

## Taxation of Benefits

In the 1990s one of the main issues is likely to be the taxation of employee benefits. To combat mounting federal deficits, Congress and the executive branch of government are looking for new ways to raise revenues. One approach is to take away the tax-sheltered status of employee benefits. Given that benefits have grown substantially because of this preferred status, it would not be surprising to see a cessation in benefit growth and perhaps even a decline if they lose this status.

# Summary

This chapter focuses on employee benefits. Links between theory and practice are discussed. Benefits in all likelihood do not influence performance, and they probably have little influence on joining behavior; their main impact is probably motivating retention. Reasons for the growth in employee benefits are societal and employer and employee attitudes toward income maintenance and preferential tax treatment of benefits.

Various forms of employee benefits, both legally required and voluntary, are discussed. The main benefits, in terms of costs, are pensions, pay for time not worked, and insurances. Health care is one of the big issues of the '90s. The type of coverage, cost of coverage, and methods of providing coverage are included in this chapter.

Recent trends in benefits are discussed. Health care benefits may change as a result of the President's commission. Cafeteria benefit plans will probably not become commonplace. There may actually be a decrease in the number of firms providing private pension plans if Social Security evolves into a comprehensive retirement plan. Many types of benefits may change if the government makes changes in their tax-sheltered status.

# Discussion Questions

1. Compare and contrast a defined benefit and a defined contribution pension plan.

2. Benefits do not motivate employees—discuss this proposition.

3. Why have benefits grown so much as a percentage of base pay?

4. List the main types of employee benefits. Which type has the greatest growth potential? Why?

5. Discuss an employer's concern with employee benefits from both a labor market and product market perspective. What strategies might be available to an employer whose benefits package is noncompetitive with other labor market firms but competitive with product market firms?

## EXERCISE

1. As a class project, each student is to identify five people who work full time. Develop a list of all the benefits discussed in this chapter. Ask each full-time worker which four of these benefits he or she prefers and why. In class, discuss and make some generalizations about your findings.

*References*

[1] "Benefit Boosts: Most Firms Expand Health Coverage to Keep Pace with Inflation," *The Wall Street Journal* (February 23, 1982), 1; "Big Changes in Employee Benefits Seen," *National Underwriter* 86 (August 27, 1982), 32.

[2] F. S. Hills and R. E. Hughes, *Salaries and Fringe Benefits in the Academic Labor Market: Internal/External Labor Markets and Geographic Differentials.* Paper presented at the National Academy of Management meetings, Orlando, FL, August 1977.

[3] T. J. Bergmann and M. A. Bergmann, "Empirical Analysis of the Role of Fringe Benefits in a Company's Compensation System," *Personnel* 64 (1987), 59–64.

[4] *Ibid.*

[5] *U.S. Chamber of Commerce Employee Benefits 1990* (Washington, DC: U.S. Chamber of Commerce, 1991).

[6] "Labor Letter," *The Wall Street Journal* LXXII (June 11, 1991), 1.

[7] C. Paternak, "Reasonable Mandate," *HRMagazine* 36 (December 1991), 27.

[8] J. McCroskey, "Work and Families: What Is the Employer's Responsibility?" *Personnel Journal* 61 (January 1982), 30–38.

[9] J. Solomon, "Companies Try to Measure Cost Savings from New Types of Corporate Benefits," *The Wall Street Journal* (December 29, 1988), B1.

[10] "Stock-Options Are Offered to More Employees, Due to Favorable 1981 Tax-Law Change," *The Wall Street Journal* (May 25, 1982), 1.

[11] L. Thornburg, "The Pension Headache," *HRMagazine* 37 (January 1992), 39–43.

[12] S. R. Leimberg and J. J. McFadden, "Non-Qualified Deferred Compensation: A Critical Look," *Journal of American Society at CLU & CHFC* 44 (May 1990), 32–45.

[13] B. R. Braden, "Increases in Employer Costs for Employee Benefits Dampen Dramatically," *Monthly Labor Review* 111 (1988), 3–7.

[14] "Families Paying the Price of Social Security: An Editorial Page Article Highlighting the Necessity for Social Security," *The Wall Street Journal* (April 2, 1982), 22.

[15] "Offbeat Benefits Multiply as a Way to Keep Workers Happy Inexpensively," *The Wall Street Journal* (July 7, 1982), 1.

[16] J. L. Martin, "A Payroll Tax Alternative Using FICA 2," *Compensation Review* (third quarter, 1979), 30–38.

17 _____, *Social Security and Medicare Fact Sheet* (Washington, DC: The Bureau of National Affairs, Incorporated, 1992), 1–4.

18 R. M. McCaffery, *Employee Benefit Programs: A Total Compensation Perspective* (Boston: PWS-Kent Publishing, 1992).

19 J. J. Maher and J. E. Kotz, "Defined-Benefit Versus Defined Contribution Pension Plans: How to Compare," *Compensation and Benefits Review* 23 (May/June 1991), 49–57.

20 R. D. Paul and J. M. Elkin, "Principles of Plan Design," in *Employee Benefits Handbook*, ed. Fred K. Foulkes (New York: Warren, Gorham, and Lamount, 1982), 2–8.

21 R. I. Mehr and S. G. Gustavson, *Life Insurance: Theory and Practice*, 3d ed. (Plano, TX: Business Publications, 1984).

22 L. Thornburg, "The Pension Headache," *HRMagazine* 37 (January 1992), 39–43.

23 S. A. Rubenfeld and M. Byerly, "Simplified Employee Pensions: A Retirement Alternative for Small Organizations," *Compensation Review* 13 (1981), 25–31.

24 B. Densmore, "More Firms Self-Funding Benefit Plans," *Business Insurance* 16 (April 26, 1982), 14–15; K. F. Maldonado, "Special Qualification Requirements for Defined Benefit Plans Covering Self-Employed Individuals or Shareholder Employees," *Taxes* 59 (November 1981), 784–796.

25 *Ibid.*, 786.

26 J. M. Benson and B. Walk Suzaki, "After Tax Reform, Part 3: Planning Executive Benefits," *Compensation and Benefits Review* 20 (1988), 45–56.

27 _____, "A Special Report to Clients" (Lincolnshire, IL: Hewitt Associates, October 22, 1986), 2.

28 D. S. Bowling III, "The Multiemployer Pension Plan Amendments Act of 1980," *Personnel Journal* 61 (1982), 18, 20.

29 J. Ledvinka and V. Scarpello, *Federal Regulation of Personnel and Human Resource Management*, 2d ed. (Boston: PWS-Kent Publishing, 1991).

30 R. T. Benna, "Forecast for Defined Benefit Pension Plans: Cloudy on the Horizon," *Personnel* 68 (June 1991), 5.

31 "Profit Sharing Arrangements in Cafeteria Plans," *CPA Journal* 52 (August 1982), 58-59.

32 M. Meyer, *Profile of Employee Benefits* (New York: Conference Board, 1981).

33 *Ibid.*

34 Mehr and Gustavson, *Life Insurance.*

35 *Ibid.*

36 *Daily Labor Report* (Washington, DC: Bureau of National Affairs, September 11, 1981), 1.

37 J. Dimeo, "National Health Care Reform Heats Up In Congress," *Pension World* 27 (October 1991), 38–39.

38 _____, "Health Care Reform: Tradeoffs and Implications," *EBRI Issue Brief* 125 (Washington, DC: Employee Benefit Research Institute, 1992), 1–64.

39 L. N. Vreeland, "Insurance Woes? Super-Cobra Comes to the Rescue," *Money* 20 (February 1991), 34–35; J. W. Lowry, "Explaining COBRA's Health Insurance Provisions," *Life Association News* 82 (1987), 53–56.

40 M. J. Fischer, "COBRA Cost Far Exceed Premiums, Study Says," *National Underwriters* 95 (July 8, 1991), 8.

41 R. J. Albert and N. S. Schelberg, "AIDS Has Damaging Effects on Employee Health Plans," *Pension World* 28 (March 1992), 52–53.

42 Fischer, "COBRA Cost Far Exceed Premiums, Study Says."

43 R. Kuttner, "Health Care: Why Corporate America Is Paralyzed," *Business Week* (April 8, 1991), 14; H. Schlossberg, "National Health Care Seen as Costly, Unwieldy," *Marketing News* 25 (May 13, 1991), 14–15; S. Brostoff, "Democrats Unveil Health Proposal," *Life & Health/Financial Services* 95 (June 10, 1991), 3;

K. Karlin, "Health Care Reform Proposed," *Legislative Scene* 2 (Scottsdale, AZ: American Compensation Association, August 1991), 1–2.

[44] Meyer, *Profile of Employee Benefits*, 13.

[45] C. D. Keen, "Few Employees Enroll in Long-Term Care Plans," *Issues in HR* (Society for Human Resource Management, October 1991), 4.

[46] _____, *Health Care Benefits Survey, 1989* (Princeton, NJ: Foster Higgins Survey and Research Services, 1990, Report 2), 15.

[47] J. Zampetti, "Building ABC's for an On-Site Child Care Center," *Management Review* 80 (March 1991), 54–55+.

[48] T. J. Slattery, "Dependent Care Benefits In Tug of War," *National Underwriters* 95 (May 6, 1991), 3+.

[49] C. Woolsey, "Flex Plans Meet Most Needs: Experts," *Business Insurance* 23 (October 2, 1989), 39.

[50] C. A. Cooley, "1989 Employee Benefits Address Family Concerns," *Monthly Labor Review* 113, 60-63; D. Klein and G. L. Stelluto, "Compensation Trends into the 21st Century," *Monthly Labor Review* 42 (1990), 76–78.

[51] K. Glynn, "Providing for Our Aging Society," *Personnel Administration* 33 (1988), 56–60; E. G. Gilbert, "J. P. Morgan, N.Y. Team Up on Elder Care," *National Underwriters* 95 (March 18, 1991), 18+.

[52] J. Dimeo, "Family Leave: A Campaign Issue Heating Up," *Pension World* 28 (March 1992), 6.

[53] B. K. Googins, "Corporate Work-Family Responses: Challenges and Opportunities for Compensation and Benefits," *Perspectives In Total Compensation* (Scottsdale, AZ: American Compensation Association 2, July 1991), 1–41.

[54] C. Trost, "To Cut Costs and Keep the Best People, More Concerns Offer Flexible Work Plans," *The Wall Street Journal* (February 18, 1992), B1.

[55] R. Russell, *The ESOP as a Form of Employee Participation in Decision Making and in Profits.* Paper presented at the Conference on Participative and Gainsharing Systems sponsored by J. L. Kellogg Graduate School of Management, Northwestern University, Profit Sharing Research Foundation and the Johnson Foundation, Wingspread International Conference Center, Racine, WS, October 8–10, 1986.

[56] A. B. Fisher, "Employees Left Holding the Bag," *Fortune* 123 (May 20, 1991), 83–93.

[57] R. J. Dema and D. Hardwood, "Tapping the Financial Benefits of an ESOP," *Journal of Accountancy* 171 (April 1991), 27–37.

[58] *Ibid.*

[59] *Ibid.*

[60] W. Smith, H. Lazrus, and H. M. Kalkstein, "Employee Stock Ownership Plans: Motivation and Morale Issues," *Compensation and Benefits Review* 22 (1990), 37–46.

[61] Fisher, "Employees Left Holding the Bag."

[62] Fisher, "Employees Left Holding the Bag"; Dema and Hardwood, "Tapping the Financial Benefits of an ESOP."

[63] "ACA Publishers Benefits—Software Directory," *American Compensation Association News* (October 1991), 1, 5.

[64] M. Bradford, "Benefit Administration," *Business Insurance* 24 (1990), 27–34.

[65] J. Geisel, "Bill Would Limit Types of Benefits Offered In Cafeteria Plans," *Business Insurance* 17 (August 1, 1983), 1.

[66] A. Cole, Jr., "Flexible Benefits are a Key to Better Employee Relations," *Personnel Journal* 62 (1983), 49–53.

[67] W. E. Lissy, "Currents in Compensating," *Compensation and Benefits Review* 23 (May/June 1991), 5–13.

[68] A. E. Barber, R. B. Dunham, and R. A. Formisano, "The Impact of Flexible Benefits on Employee Satisfaction: A Field Study," *Personnel Psychology* 45 (Spring 1992), 55–75.

[69] R. M. McCaffery, Employee Benefits Program: *A Total Compensation Perspective.*

[70] M. Zippo, "Flexible Benefits: Just the Beginning," *Personnel* 59 (July/August 1982), 56–58; R. B. Cockrum, "Has the Time Come for Employee Cafeteria Plans?" *Personnel Administrator* 27 (July 1982), 66-72; "Profit-Sharing Arrangements in Cafeteria Plans," *CPA Journal* 52 (August 1982), 58–59.

[71] Cockrum, "Has the Time Come for Employee Cafeteria Plans?"

[72] Thornburg, "The Pension Headache."

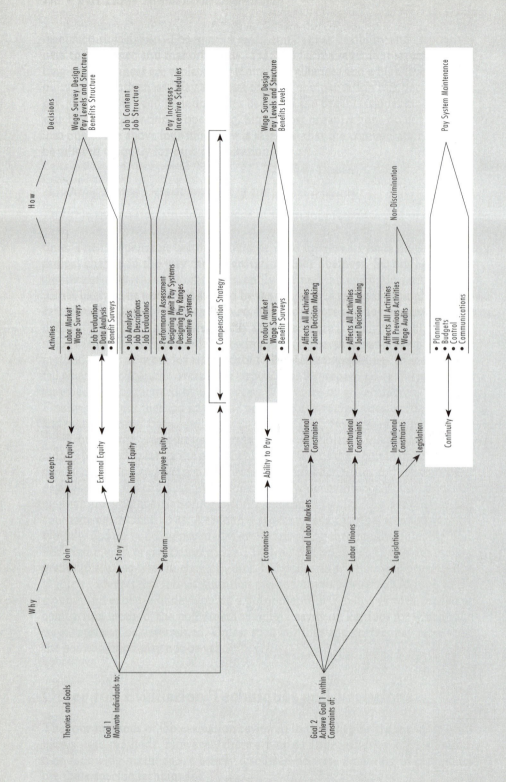

# VI

## Completing the Compensation Package

# 14

# Compensation Control and Administration

# Learning Objectives

**To learn the steps in the compensation budgeting process.**

**To learn the controls for evaluating the workings of the pay plan.**

**To learn how to assess and monitor employee acceptance of the pay plan.**

# Introduction

This chapter addresses pay-related controls and other administrative issues related to the pay plan. *Control* refers to the process of ensuring that the pay program is carried out as intended. Control takes many forms, including (1) budgets, (2) pay plan design processes and procedures, and (3) monitoring employee acceptance of the pay plan.

# Budget Controls

Organizations vary in the amount of money they can spend on compensation. On average, compensation costs between 30 percent and 50 percent of revenues. In labor-intensive firms, compensation costs may exceed 60 percent of revenue, whereas in capital-intensive firms costs may be as low as 12 percent of revenue. In all cases, however, the money available for compensation is limited.

Because compensation plays a central role in achieving organizational productivity and profit, one of the most important activities for the organization is the allocation of financial resources to compensation costs. That allocation happens through the budgeting process.

The compensation budget defines the money that will be available for compensation expenses for the coming planning period. The budget consists of all costs directly associated with employment. It is a gross figure that represents the money necessary to pay the total number of people who will work for the organization (as employees or contractors). Furthermore, the overall budget is a function not only of these people but of how the organization chooses to use them. Exhibit 14.1 lists the most common compensation costs and how they may relate to personnel.

Once the overall budget is determined, another budget, often called a "merit budget," "salary increase budget," or "pay adjustment budget," is determined from the overall budget. This latter budget, which normally represents the largest share of the overall budget increase, is the focal point of this chapter.

## Forecasting Need

The first step in the budgeting process is to forecast the money that the organization needs to meet its compensation costs for the following budget period. Organizations approach the forecasting process in two ways: "top down" and "bottom up."

| EXHIBIT 14.1 | COMMON COMPENSATION COSTS AND PERSONNEL USE |

## Wages and Salaries

Costs depend partly on:

- number employed
- whether full or part time
- whether paid to employees or subcontractors
- whether determined by management or negotiated with union

## Hours of Work Demanded

Costs depend partly on:

- number employed
- whether overtime is frequently or seldom required
- whether hours of work include premium pay for shift differentials and other undesirable work schedules

## Overtime Pay

Costs depend partly on:

- number employed
- whether mandated by law, custom, union, or subcontractor agreement
- amount of overtime paid (straight time, time and a half or higher)

## Pay for Time Not Worked

Costs depend partly on:

- number employed
- number of days off per year provided to employees or negotiated with a union

## Mandated Benefits

Costs depend partly on:

- number employed
- wages and salaries paid
- proportion of full-time and part-time employees

## Not Mandated Benefits

Costs depend partly on:

- number employed, but this relationship is curvilinear due to economies of scale achieved by large enrollments in group health and other programs
- employee experience with benefits

## Unemployment Compensation

Costs depend largely on layoff and turnover experience

## Workers Compensation

Costs depend largely on experience with accidents arising in the course of employment

*Top-down forecasting*[1] is normally done by the comptroller's office or the finance department. After review of expected activities for the coming year, projections of revenues and costs are generated and financial revenues allocated to various budgets. Sometimes the human resource department may also become involved in forecasting employment budgets and, by extension, compensation budgets, a process termed "top down compensation budgeting."

Firms using the *top-down* process assume that accurate forecasts can be made by a careful analysis of the past. Many companies use past sales dollars as the basis for all forecasts and budgets. Sales dollars are also used as the basis for forecasting employment needs and compensation budgets. This is done by first establishing a correlation between employment of a particular job family and company sales for the year. Next, the average amount of sales per each employee in the job family is determined. Once the relationship between employment and sales dollars is established, the organization can forecast employment for as many years into the future as available sales forecasts. Finally, the sales forecast for each year is divided by the average sales per employee within the employee group, and the result is the total number of employees needed for each year of the forecast years. By multiplying the number of employees each year by the turnover ratios for the year, and then adding the number of additional employees needed for the following year, the total number of employees needed for the next year can be calculated for each job family.

By this process, the company finds a relationship between sales dollars and average amount of sales per employee in each job family or organizational unit. The trend in sales per employee gives management an excellent picture of the needed size of the workforce. If the amount of sales per employee gets too high, for example, additional employees may need to be hired; if too low, other options such as hiring freezes or layoffs may be warranted. Once the relationship between number of employees needed to produce the expected sales dollars is determined, the change in total compensation outlay (pay and benefits) for the next year can be calculated from the expected percent change in sales dollars for the upcoming year. An example of employment forecasting for the sales job family is shown in Exhibit 14.2.

Note that the top-down budgeting approach does not take into account external changes such as job redesign or introduction of technologies that may significantly alter the relationship between average sales per employee and forecast sales dollars. The top-down approach also does not factor in the needs of specific organizational units and the diversity of skills normally present within any organization. Consequently, this approach results in establishing a "gross" budget, one incapable of allocating the pay portion of compensation in effective ways. To do the latter requires collecting data from within the organization, data provided by the "bottom up" budgeting approach.

*Bottom-up forecasting* uses supervisory pay adjustment recommendations to obtain expected changes in wages and salaries for the next budget period. Before supervisors can make such recommendations, however, the compensation department must supply pay adjustment policies and guidelines. Thus, before bottom-up forecasting can take place, top management must approve a change in the pay structure and a change in the guidelines for adjusting the pay of individual employees. These approvals must be obtained for each pay plan administered within the organization.

EXHIBIT 14.2 **EXAMPLE OF EMPLOYMENT FORECASTING FOR SALES JOB FAMILY**

| Year | No. of Sales Personnel End of Year | Average No. of Sales Personnel During the Year | Sales Dollars Per Sales Person in Thousands | Percent Turnover of Sales Personnel | 2000 Sales Forecast "Plus" or "Minus" in Thousands | No. of Employees Lost Through Turnover | "Plus" or "Minus" Employment Forecast |
|---|---|---|---|---|---|---|---|
| 1995 | 72 | 70 | $211 | 7 | | | |
| 1996 | 77 | 74.5 | $220 | 5 | | | |
| 1997 | 87 | 82 | $219 | 11 | $1,387 | | |
| 1998 | 93 | 90 | $234 | 8 | | | |
| 1999 | 92 | 92.5 | $210 | 6 | | 7 | None |
| Average | | | | 7 | | | |
| Average | | | | | $212 | | |

Adapted from W. W. Burton, "Forecasting Manpower Needs—A Tested Formula," in D. W. Ewing, ed., *Long-Range Planning for Management* (New York: Harper & Row Publishers Inc., 1958), 228–236.

Pay structure changes allow the organization to revisit its pay level policy, its pay system, and the ability of the pay system to support the organization's business goals and strategies. To change the pay structure, the organization must first determine the percentage by which average pay changed in the past year. The *level rise* is the move in average salary over a given period. A commonly used formula for determining the current year's percentage rise in the pay structure is

$$\text{percent level rise} = 100 \times \frac{\begin{array}{ccc} \text{average pay} & & \text{average pay} \\ \text{year end} & \text{minus} & \text{year beginning} \end{array}}{\text{average pay at beginning of year}}$$

The above level rise formula is normally computed for large groups. This is done by measuring the actual rise for the three quarters already experienced and projecting the percent answer for one more quarter to cover the forecast portion of the year. In small groups, the forecast can be used to project an actual payroll and population to the end of the forecast quarter; level rise is measured from the beginning-of-the-period average salary to that projected average salary.

Once the percent level rise is calculated, management can assess this figure against the desired pay level. For example, if the percent level rise is 6, management may choose to maintain current policy by adjusting the midpoint, minimum, and maximum of each pay grade within the pay structure by 6 percent. Or it can choose a pay level policy that is higher or lower than the current policy and adjust the pay structure accordingly. Establishing the percent level rise for the next budget year changes the pay structure and also helps establish the budget for the pay adjustments. Although pay adjustment budgets can be determined from the pool of money allocated for the percent level rise, these budgets are normally based on further analysis of results of the current year's spending and best estimates for next year's spending.

In the *bottom-up* approach to compensation forecasting, supervisory pay adjustment recommendations act as forecasts of labor cost changes for the next budget period and are therefore typically termed "salary forecasts." Exhibit 14.3 illustrates the type of information that may be incorporated within a salary forecast of companies with merit pay plans. The summation of all supervisor recommendations is the proposed pay adjustment budget derived from setting the spending goals for the next year. It is based on percent level rise decisions, analysis of the current pay plan's results, and determination of the dollar amount necessary for the coming year.

### Analysis of Current Pay Plan's Results

Analysis of the pay plan's results focuses on examining the way money was used in the past year, in order to project the amount that will be needed for the next year. Normally, the results of the current year's spending is measured by the following indices.

1. **Typical (Average) Increase Dollar Amount** This is the actual amount of dollars spent in 3 quarters plus the forecast amount for the

EXHIBIT 14.3　EXAMPLE OF SALARY FORECAST SHEET WITH MERIT PAY INCORPORATED

## SALARY FORECAST FOR PERIOD: JAN. 1 – DEC. 31, 1994

| | | Job family: ENGINEERING | Department: INFORMATION SYSTEMS | Section in department: NONE | Job grade: 3 | Recommending supervisor: FOARD JONES | | | | | APPROVALS 1st. 2nd. | | | | | |
|---|---|---|---|---|---|---|---|---|---|---|---|---|---|---|---|---|

| | | | Last Pay Decision | | | | Salary-Performance Position* | | | | | | | Proposed Salary Recommendation | Final | |
| Employee name and social security number | Job grade | Effective Date Mo Da Yr | Amount per month | % inc. | Frequency of inc. in months | Present Salary (month) | Last Period Pay Code | Last Period Perf. Code | Current Period Pay Code | Current Period Perf. Code | Amt per mo. | % | Freq n mo. | Eff. Date Mo Da Yr | New Salary | New Grade |
|---|---|---|---|---|---|---|---|---|---|---|---|---|---|---|---|---|
| J. B. RAY 300-34-2213 | 3 | 05 15 93 | | | | 2290 | B | A | B | A | 250 | 11.0 | 10 | 03 16 94 | 2540 | 4 |
| R. B. GRANT 460-76-3934 | 3 | 02 01 93 | | | | 2250 | B | A | C | A | 200 | 8.9 | 11 | 01 01 94 | 2450 | --- |
| P. M. WHITTLE 842-93-5265 | 3 | 11 01 93 | | | | 2225 | B | A | C | B | 180 | 8.0 | 12 | 03 01 94 | 2405 | --- |
| | | | | | | | | | | | | | | | | |
| | | | | | | | | | | | | | | | | |
| | | | | | | | | | | | | | | | | |
| | | | | | | | | | | | | | | | | |

Note:　Salary Performance Position is taken from the merit grid supervisors are instructed to use under merit pay programs. In this example, the pay code reflects the dollar amounts that should be given to A=exceptional performers; B=commendable performers; C=competent performers; D=developing employees. The performance code reflects the employee's actual performance.

fourth quarter divided by the actual and forecast number of increases given and to be given. Under merit pay systems, the formula is

TI $ = total merit dollars spent
(3 quarters actual, 1 forecast)
_____
total number of increases given during
the actual and forecast period

2. **Typical (Average Increase Percent)** This is the total amount of merit increase as defined above, expressed as a percentage of base salaries before the increase of employees receiving the merit increase. The formula is:

TI % = total merit dollars spent (as above) × 100%
_____
total base salary before increases of those receiving
increases during the actual and forecast period

3. **Participation Rate** This refers to the total number of increases given as defined above, expressed as a percentage of the total average population in a given time period. The formula is:

Actual
Participation % = total number increases given × 100%
_____
cumulative average population of total
group for the period covered

Averaging the population is designed to yield a more stable base on which to compute the pay raise participation percentage. This helps reduce the effect of seasonal or business fluctuations, changes in the economy, and other variances on the budget. To compute cumulative average population, one should use the population for the months covered in the program. Select four of the most recent quarterly populations and divide the total by four to obtain an average. For example, for a program to be effective April 1, take employee populations for the following periods:

| Employee Population | Time Period |
|:---:|:---:|
| 505 | March 31 |
| 471 | June 30 |
| 461 | Sept. 30 |
| 457 | Dec. 31 |

Average cumulative
population = 474 employees
(total employee population divided by 4)

**4. Merit Index** This is the total increase in dollars spent as defined by the typical (average) increase in dollars (first formula), expressed as a percentage of the average total monthly payroll for a group. All types of increases—merit, equity adjustments, promotional adjustments—are combined in this index to reflect dollars spent. The formula is:

MI $=$ $\dfrac{\text{total increase dollars spent}}{\text{cumulative average monthly payroll (computed in the same way as cumulative average population)}}$

## *Arriving at the Operations Budget*

After examining the results of the current year's program, cost of the proposed program can be estimated by setting goals for the coming year with respect to the desired merit index. For example, if the agreed on level rise is 6 percent, then the typical merit percentage increase is 6. To obtain the typical merit dollar increase, one can multiply the typical merit increase percentage by the actual present average salary of the group affected. Next year's pay adjustment budget can then be calculated by the formula

$$\begin{matrix}\text{Total Increase}\\ \text{Dollar Budget}\end{matrix} = \begin{matrix}\text{typical merit}\\ \text{increase percent}\end{matrix} \times \begin{matrix}\text{planned participation}\\ \text{percentage}\end{matrix}$$

The subsequent year's payroll cost can be calculated by the formula

$$\begin{matrix}\text{Payroll}\\ \text{Cost}\end{matrix} = \text{annual payroll dollars} \times \text{planned merit index percent}$$

A typical costing format is shown in Exhibit 14.4. The exhibit also shows the indices used in costing a pay increase program and how they are calculated.

# Pay Plan Design Processes and Procedures

The operational budget is normally not set without considering the current pay program's results in light of intended pay level policy and analysis of the movement of people within and across the organization's pay structures.

## *Analysis of Pay Level Policy-Practice Congruence*

Pay level policy reflects the organization's desired average pay position with respect to external competitors. In a pay rate structure, commonly used for hourly paid jobs, the line connecting all pay rates is the pay policy line. In a pay range structure, the line connecting the range midpoints normally reflects the pay policy line, as the midpoints represent average pay of jobs and positions within the pay grades. In broadly banded range structures, the pay policy line is not obvious. Because jobs of varying complexity are included in the broad band,

| EXHIBIT 14.4 | EXAMPLE OF COSTING FORMAT, INDICING USED IN COSTING A PAY PROGRAM, AND INDEX CALCULATION GUIDELINES |

**Typical Costing Format**

| Grade Level | Employees # | Average Salary | Proposed Merit $ | Typical Increase % | % Planned Participation | % Merit Index |
|---|---|---|---|---|---|---|
| 1 | 50 | $300 | $15 | 5.0 | 99 | 6.0 |
| 3 | | | | | | |
| 4 | | | | | | |
| 5 | | | | | | |
| etc. | | | | | | |
| Overall | | | | | | 6.0 |

**Indices Used in Costing a Pay Program**

(1) Merit Index

(2) Planned Participation

(3) Typical Merit Increase

(4) Population

(5) Average Salary

**Index Calculation Guidelines**

| Number | Index | Computation Guide |
|---|---|---|
| 1 | Typical Merit Increase $ | (Numbers 2 × 5) |
| 2 | Typical Merit Increase % | (Number 1 ÷ 5 or 3 ÷ 4) |
| 3 | Merit Index | (Numbers 4 × 2) |
| 4 | Planned Participation Rate | |
| 5 | Current Average Salary | |

the pay policy line is not the midpoint of the broad band range; rather, it can be determined by connecting the "target" points within the broad band ranges, as these reflect the "old" midpoints of traditional grades within the traditional pay range structure.

To examine whether managers comply with the organization's pay level policy, as well as to determine how the present pay ranges are being used, an index called the *compa-ratio* is calculated. The compa-ratio reflects the percentage relationship of average salary to the range midpoint or, in the case of broad band systems, to the target points within the broad band range. Compa-ratios may be calculated for individual employees, for each pay grade, for each pay structure, organizational unit, or organization. The standard compa-ratio formula is

$$\text{compa-ratio} = \frac{\text{average rates actually paid}}{\text{midpoint of the range}}$$

To compute an overall compa-ratio for a structure, weight each grade level average salary (or target range average salary) and range midpoint (or target point) by the employee population within the grade (or target range) to get the overall average figures, and then use the compa-ratio formula. The average salaries and populations used for this comparison are the latest actual available figures (usually from the end of the third quarter) and are not cumulative. To project the current compa-ratios to the end of the program year, add the fourth-quarter forecast increases to the latest payroll dollars for the group to obtain a projected payroll, and divide that payroll by the latest group population figures to get a projected actual average salary. Then use the formula to determine compa-ratios for these projected salaries.

To determine how the present pay ranges are being used, the position of pay rates within each pay range can be assessed. A compa-ratio range spread (CRRS) statistic can be calculated for this purpose

$$\text{CRRS} = 1 \ +/- \ \frac{\text{Range}}{2 + \text{Range}}$$

For example, if the range spread for the pay grade is 40 percent, then

$$\text{CRRS} = 1 \ +/- \ \frac{.4}{2 + .4} = 1.167 \text{ and } .833$$

With a 40 percent range spread for a grade or range of grades, a compa-ratio index of 1.167 indicates that all pay rates are at the maximum of the range. A compa-ratio of 1.0 indicates that the average pay rate equals the midpoint, and a compa-ratio of .833 indicates that all pay rates are at the minimum of the pay range. If an organization's midpoint reflects a pay policy of where the organization wishes to pay its fully qualified and fully satisfactory employees, a compa-ratio of 1.0 means that the average pay within the pay structure or pay grade is at the intended policy line. A compa-ratio of less than 1.0 means that the average pay is below the policy line. A compa-ratio of greater than 1.0 means that the average pay is above the pay line.

Organizations that use the range midpoints as the operationalization of pay level policy try to keep compa-ratios between .97 and 1.03. If promotions are rapid and the employee population is relatively new with low job tenure, the compa-ratio will be below 1.0. Conversely, if most employees have high seniority, promotion rates are low, and employees' performances have been satisfactory, the compa-ratio will be greater than 1.0. Thus, compa-ratios outside the desired range suggest managerial identification of the causes for the deviance and resolution of the observed policy-practice discrepancy.

Besides helping to control labor costs and to assess range utilization, compa-ratio analysis also can help assess managers' compliance with the Equal Pay Act and other employment legislation. For example, compa-ratio analysis by demographic groups can provide an indicator of the fairness of pay treatment within those demographic subsamples. In addition, comparisons of compa-ratios across departments can help determine managerial variability in compensation allocation practices.

## Analysis of People Movement within and across Pay Structures

Pay structure refers to the array of pay rates within the organization or job family. As noted, the pay structure may be designed solely from analysis of market pay for key jobs, or it may be designed through a process that integrates external market considerations with internal, relative job worth considerations. Most compensation experts agree that the integrated approach to development of pay structure is superior to the market approach, as the former considers both external competitiveness and internal job fairness. When using the integrated approach to pay plan design, a number of controls are imbedded into the pay techniques. These include:

1. Performance of task-oriented job analysis to determine who does what, when, why, how, and under what working conditions

2. Managerial approvals for implementing new jobs and their job descriptions

3. Use of the same compensable factors and weights when evaluating jobs that will be paid under the same pay structure

4. Use of multiple pay surveys to help identify the going rate of pay, hours of work, and other pay treatments for employees on benchmark jobs

5. Use of appropriately overlapping pay ranges

6. Use of the same rules, criteria, or standards for allocating pay raises and pay awards to individuals on given jobs

Nevertheless, the interaction between the pay plan and the way it is used produces a need to monitor employee positions within ranges and pay differentials between jobs linked by career progression ladders

**Employee Positions within Ranges**   In a job-based system, the job constrains the maximum pay the individual can receive. Still, supervisors sometimes succumb to pressure to pay over the range when senior employees are blocked from promotion to higher-level jobs because there are no vacancies. Normally, inexperienced people are hired at the minimum job rates. Sometimes, however, trainee pay rates may be above or below the minimum. The goal is to pay people properly for the jobs they perform. A useful index for assessing the pay position of employees within a pay grade is the range index

$$\text{Range Index} = \frac{\text{Actual Rate of Pay} - \text{Minimum Rate of Pay in Range}}{\text{Maximum Rate of Pay} - \text{Minimum Rate of Pay in Range}}$$

Range indices can be calculated for various employee groups to assess the movement of those groups within the pay structure. Besides the obvious concerns for fair treatment of demographically diverse employee groups, conducting a range index analysis of senior versus junior employees may help identify a wage compression problem. Recall that wage compression results when the ratio of pay within and/or between job grades decreases over time due to compensation policies and practices. Within grade, wage compression can occur from external and internal causes. One example of externally caused wage compression is having to pay new hires more than that paid current employees. One example of internally caused wage compression is pay adjustment guidelines that fail to differentiate the pay increase amounts to be allocated to employees at different performance levels. This normally occurs when pay adjustments are based on absolute dollar amount rather than percentage increase criteria. The percentage criterion is preferred since it allocates the same amounts of pay for the same levels of performance.[2]

Range index analysis can also help identify employees whose pay is not consistent with policy, that is, overpaid and underpaid employees. If workers are paid above the range maximum, their supervisors are generally instructed to freeze their pay (called "red circle") until the ranges shift upward as the pay structure adjusts to changes in market rates. If the pay rates are extremely out of line, supervisors may also be instructed to reduce the pay of the affected employees to bring it back into the range. Similarly, if employees are paid below the minimum of the range, their supervisors are often instructed on how long these employees may remain below the range minimum before being either terminated or brought up to minimum. Below minimum pay rates are normally called "green circle" rates.

**Employee Movement across Pay Structures**   Between job wage compression can occur when jobs are linked in a career progression ladder but are paid under different pay structures. Consider, for example, the jobs of quality control technician and sales representative in a manufacturing plant. The quality control technician job falls within the technical pay structure and the sales representative job is within the marketing pay structure. If the normal promotion path is from quality control technician to sales representative for the products produced by the plant, the jobs are hierarchically linked, even though they may be in different job families and therefore different pay structures. Because these jobs are linked by a common career ladder, it is important to ensure that the promotion from one to the other is accompanied by a meaningful pay increase. Even if the movement from quality control technician to sales representative is not a promotion but a lateral transfer, the organization must ensure that the transfer is indeed lateral, as reflected by maintaining the previous pay rate. These points may sound obvious, but employees have been known to refuse "promotions" from a quality control technician's job to sales representative because such movement would be accompanied by an $8,000 per year pay decrease.

Recognizing that wage compression between jobs linked by a career progression ladder reduces willingness to move into jobs of higher responsibility, organizations have traditionally provided pay differentials between supervisor and subordinate. Although the differentials vary across employment settings, the general rule is to pay the supervisor 10 percent to 15 percent more than that paid the highest paid subordinate. Few organizations, however, monitor the pay differentials for other jobs linked by a career progression ladder. Such monitoring is an important control mechanism and can easily be done by examining pay rates of jobs linked by a promotion ladder across affected pay structures.

# Monitoring Employee Acceptance

Pay systems are designed to affect the behaviors of individuals. Indeed, the ability of compensation to influence job performance and turnover behaviors, and subsequently, productivity and effectiveness, is the rationale for organizations ensuring that compensation is managed fairly.

There is no easy way of relating employee behaviors to acceptance of compensation. For one, self-interests and career progression goals may motivate employees to maintain high performance, even under inequitable conditions, when alternative job options are not available in the short run. Feelings of inequity may also motivate poor organizational citizenship, such as excessive absenteeism, theft, or sabotage. While accepting the difficulties in relating pay to employee behaviors, it is nevertheless useful to periodically assess the relationships between pay and (1) turnover, (2) performance, and (3) citizenship. It is also useful to assess employee opinions about the pay plan.

## *Monitoring the Pay System-Employee Behavior Relationship*

**Monitoring the Pay-Turnover Relationship**    Turnover may be monitored directly through exit interviews and indirectly through use of various indices presumed to relate to turnover.

*Exit Interviews*    These meetings attempt to determine the employee's reasons for leaving the organization. Although useful in assessing trends, the responses cannot be assumed to be valid. Some people may decide not to disclose the real reason for leaving: It may be uncomfortable to disclose negative feelings. Alternatively, some individuals may see no reason to disclose such feelings once the decision to leave has been finalized.

Sometimes a written questionnaire, asking the employee to check the main reasons he is leaving, provides more accurate information than a formal exit interview. Some companies also send such questionnaires to former employees, believing that people will be more willing to disclose their thoughts after they have left.

***Turnover Indices*** A variety of indices may be constructed to assess the relationship between the pay system and turnover. One commonly used compensation index is the *turnover effect*. The turnover effect is caused by such things as additions and deletions of employees to the group, promotions, and changes in salaries within the group. It can be either plus or minus but is usually the latter. The turnover effect calculation is:

TE = Level Rise % for Period A - Merit Index % for Period A
          (move in average salary) - (percent of pay adjustment money spent)

If there is no turnover effect, the level rise and merit index are, for all practical purposes, equal. To estimate the future effect of turnover, historical data are kept regarding the turnover effect by grade within salary programs. Other turnover indices may be devised, depending on interest in studying a variety of relationships between pay and turnover, such as (1) the relationship between pay level and turnover, (2) the relationship between compa-ratio trends and turnover for a given period, (3) the relationship between performance evaluations and turnover trends for employees at varying performance levels, (4) the relationship between pay and job and organization tenure of leavers versus stayers, and (5) the pay structure effects on career progression for stayers and leavers.

**Monitoring the Pay-Performance Relationship** Research on equity theory suggests that performance responses to underpayment may take two forms: decrease in quantity of output and decrease in quality of output.[3] Monitoring the relationship between pay and performance requires concern with two interrelated aspects of performance management: performance evaluation system and the link between the performance evaluation system and pay raise allocation.

Ensuring that employees perceive equitable treatment requires that the organization include quantity and quality standards in its pay adjustment policy. For example, if pay adjustments are based on work-group incentive plans, the plans should explicitly communicate the quantity and quality of output standards for receipt of different levels of incentive pay. If the pay adjustments are based on supervisory performance evaluations, these standards should flow directly from the employees' job descriptions and be contained on the performance evaluation form. Embedding the quality and quantity standards for pay adjustments in evaluations communicates the organization's performance expectations. If implemented as intended, such communication helps obtain desired levels of performance.

In most organizations, the supervisor is responsible for implementing performance evaluations and for recommending pay raises for subordinates. In most organizations, supervisors receive new pay range guidelines with information outlining the pay program, changes made to the program, the effective date for pay program implementation, and instructions for communication to employees. In merit pay systems, for example, supervisors are given guidelines on how to relate the individual's performance to recommendations for a particular pay raise.

Although the matching of pay raise recommendation with performance level seems straightforward, often it is not. Sometimes supervisors are reluctant to appraise the employee's performance as poor but eager to recommend a low pay raise. Other times, the supervisor recommends higher pay raises than warranted by performance. To deal with this problem, many organizations require employees to sign a statement that they have seen their performance evaluation, even though they may not agree with it. This process helps ensure that the employee is not surprised by the performance evaluation. It does not ensure that the organization's pay adjustment policy is implemented as intended. To assess the latter, some companies periodically audit the relationship between supervisory pay raise recommendations and the performance evaluation rating given by the supervisor. If a discrepancy is found, the compensation department asks the supervisor to reconcile it by either changing the performance appraisal to fit the pay raise recommendation or changing the pay raise recommendation to fit the performance appraisal. If the supervisor refuses to reconcile the discrepancy, he or she may be asked to communicate why to management. Ultimately, the responsibility for resolving the discrepancy rests with top management.

**Monitoring the Pay-Organizational Citizenship Relationship**    Equity theory suggests that employees may attempt to balance perceived pay inequity by engaging in various behaviors reflective of poor organizational citizenship, including (1) reducing the number of hours they are willing to work, (2) increasing absenteeism, (3) sabotage and theft of the employer's property and materials, and (4) refusing to accept promotional opportunities because they are viewed as either an increase in responsibility without appropriate increase in pay or a reflection of lack of commitment to continue employment within the organization.

Because these and other poor citizenship behaviors may reflect attempts at balancing pay inequity perceptions, organizations often examine the relationship between such negative behaviors and the pay system. Finding a relationship sometimes motivates changes in the system.

In combination, these indices enable the organization to obtain a fairly accurate picture of the relationship between the pay system and the behaviors it is intended to influence. Managerial perceptions of this relationship are considerations in setting the pay adjustment budget, the goals of the proposed pay plan, and the processes to be used for distributing the budget in the coming budget period.

## *Monitoring the Pay System-Employee Opinion Relationship*

Traditionally, pay system acceptance is inferred from surveys asking employees how satisfied they are with their pay. Surveying pay satisfaction reflects a belief in the equity theory assumption that pay satisfaction is an outcome of a perception that the ratio of one's inputs to outputs is in balance relative to the ratio of inputs to outputs of comparison others. Indeed, use of pay satisfaction as a criterion for assessing opinions about the fairness of pay received assumes that people will only be satisfied when they perceive the pay to be equitable with respect to comparison others. As equity theory views all input/output inequity as dissatisfying, being overpaid or underpaid is viewed as equally dissatisfying.

However, the situation is more complex than suggested by equity theory. First, a number of research studies have shown that the more pay individuals receive, the more satisfied they are with their pay.[4] Second, two studies have shown that employees on salaries and wages tend to equate perceptions of pay fairness with pay satisfaction.[5] Although numerous reasons can be found for these seemingly diverse findings, research has not yet provided a scientific explanation. Indeed, one worthy area of research is to determine the extent to which pay plan characteristics motivate perceptions of equivalence between pay satisfaction and pay fairness. It may be that people on fixed salaries or wages view pay satisfaction to be the same as pay fairness because they have no individual means of increasing their pay beyond an organizationally prescribed range. In contrast, people on variable pay plans, such as part salary and part incentive, may view pay satisfaction as being relatively independent of the fairness of pay. Because reactions to the two criteria—pay satisfaction and pay fairness—may be motivated by unique pay system and personal characteristics, organizations may find it useful to determine which of the criteria relate more strongly to organizationally relevant behaviors such as turnover, performance, and good citizenship and then use that criteria to assess pay plan acceptance.

Besides monitoring opinions about the fairness of pay received or satisfaction with the pay, research suggests the potential utility of monitoring perceptions about the fairness of major classes of procedures used to design and administer the pay plan. Although compensation researchers have implicitly recognized the potential of procedural justice perceptions to affect evaluative decisions, it was research in legal and political contexts that first identified and differentiated the impact of two distinct dimensions of justice (distributive and procedural) on attitudinal responses to decision outcomes.[6] One conclusion is that perceptions about the fairness of procedures used to arrive at a particular outcome (procedural justice perceptions) contribute to the attitude one holds about the outcome received and are also more important than perceptions of the fairness of the outcome received to evaluations of authorities and institutions responsible for the outcome.

Three studies have confirmed the proposed relationships between justice perceptions and attitudes about pay, supervision, and the employing organizations.[7] Specifically, these studies found that perceptions about the fairness of pay outcomes were the most important predictors of pay satisfaction, and perceptions about the fairness of pay procedures were the most important predictors of evaluations about supervisors and of organizational commitment.

One study also related the different classes of procedures to attitudes about pay, supervision, and the employing organization. Using the pay fairness model discussed in this book, Jones and Scarpello[8] proposed that the pay model of fairness results in concerns with three sources of fairness expectations: (1) external job—expectations that the pay for the job in one company is fair relative to the pay for the same job in another company; (2) internal job—expectations that the job the individual is performing is paid fairly relative to the pay of higher- and lower-level jobs in the same organization; and (3) internal employee—expectations of individuals on a given job about the fairness of their pay and pay raises as compared to the pay and pay raises of coworkers on the same job. Furthermore, the three sources of fairness expectations can be uniquely related to four classes of pay procedures. These include procedures for (1) determining the pay of jobs and the criteria to be used for pay adjustment purposes, (2) determining the process for making pay adjustments, (3) communicating information about the pay plan to affected employees, and (4) resolving disagreements about pay and the procedures used to set pay. Given that each class of pay procedures used to design and administer pay plans relates specifically to a particular fairness concern, Jones and Scarpello argued that it follows that the differing classes of pay procedures should have differential impact on work related attitudes. Using a stratified random sample of 612 employees from 86 departments and 4 broad job families within a large county government, Jones and Scarpello found:

1.  Perceptions about the fairness of pay determination procedures were the most important predictors of pay satisfaction and also contributed uniquely to the prediction of organizational commitment

2.  Perceptions about the fairness of the performance appraisal procedures were the most important predictors of satisfaction with the supervisor and also contributed uniquely to the prediction of organizational commitment

3.  Perceptions about the fairness of the pay communication procedures contributed uniquely to the prediction of organizational commitment

4.  Perceptions about the fairness of the appeals procedure did not contribute uniquely to the prediction of the three study criteria: pay satisfaction, supervisor satisfaction, and organizational commitment

Taken together, Jones and Scarpello confirmed previous research findings that distributive and procedural justice perceptions about pay should be recognized as distinct fairness concerns having significant but differential effects on relevant employee attitudes. The study also demonstrated that the fairness model of pay, discussed in this book, is a useful conceptual model for assessing employee reactions to pay treatment. Classes of procedures used in design and administration of fair pay plans clearly motivate differential evaluations of pay outcomes and agents and institutions responsible for those outcomes. Jones and Scarpello are currently working on relating pay procedures to turnover and job performance behaviors. At this writing, the studies have not been completed.

## Summary

This chapter discusses pay related controls and other administrative issues related to the pay plan. The chapter outlines the steps in the compensation budgeting process and provides formulas necessary for analyzing the performance of the current pay plan and for arriving at the operations budget. The chapter notes that the operations budget is normally set after considering the current pay plan's results in light of intended pay level policy and analysis of the movement of people within and across the organization's pay structures.

Analysis of the behavior of the pay plan, as designed, helps control labor costs and determine how the present plan's pay ranges are being used. It also helps assess compliance with the Equal Pay Act and other equal employment legislation.

The last section of the chapter focuses on ways of monitoring employee acceptance of pay. Although there is no easy way of relating employee behaviors to acceptance of compensation, ways of assessing relationships between pay and three classes of behaviors—turnover, performance, and organizational citizenship are discussed.

Also discussed are suggestions for assessing the relationship between justice perceptions and evaluations of pay outcomes and the agents and institutions responsible for them.

## Discussion Questions

1. Why should the organization be interested in assessing results of the current year's pay plan? What if the results are unexpected? Discuss two results that may not be expected and how the organization may deal with them.

2. What are the major ways of assessing congruence between pay level policy and pay plan administration processes?

3. What controls are embedded within the pay techniques? If contained within the pay techniques, should these controls be periodically assessed? Why or why not?

4. Develop an argument for why the organization may wish to assess employee pay satisfaction as opposed to perceptions of pay fairness, then take the opposite position and develop an argument for that position. After examining the issue from both perspectives, state and justify your position.

5. What are the main ways that you would monitor employee acceptance of the pay plan? Explain why the monitoring is useful.

6. Explain why perceptions about the fairness of pay procedures are important for organizations to monitor.

*References*

[1] W. W. Burton, "Forecasting Manpower Needs—A Tested Formula," in *Long Range Planning for Management*, ed. D. W. Ewing (1958), 228–236.
[2] H. Theeke, *Is Merit Pay Fair Pay?* Central Michigan University working paper (1993).
[3] J. S. Adams, "Injustice in Social Exchange," in *Advances in Experimental Social Psychology*, ed. L. Berkowitz (New York: Academic Press, 1965), 267–299.
[4] L. A. Messe and B. L. Watts, "Complex Nature of the Sense of Fairness: Internal Standards and Social Comparison as Bases for Reward Evaluations," *Personality and*

*Social Psychology* 45 (1983), 84–93; W. Austin, N. C. McGinn, and C. Susmilch, "Internal Standards Revisited: Effects of Social Comparisons and Expectancies on Judgments of Fairness and Satisfaction," *Journal of Experimental Social Psychology* 16 (1980), 426–441.

[5] V. Scarpello, *Pay Satisfaction and Pay Fairness: Are They the Same?* Paper presented at the Society for Industrial and Organizational Psychology meetings, Dallas (1988); L. A. Messe and B. L. Watts, "Complex Nature of the Sense of Fairness."

[6] E. A. Lind and T. R. Tyler, *The Social Psychology of Procedural Justice* (New York: Plenum Press, 1988); J. Thibaut and L. Walker, *Procedural Justice* (Hillsdale, NJ: Erlbaum, 1975).

[7] R. Folger and M. Konovsky, "Effects of Procedural and Distributive Justice on Reactions to Pay Raise Decisions," *Academy of Management Journal* 32 (1989), 115–130; D. B. McFarlin and P. D. Sweeney, "Distributive and Procedural Justice as Predictors of Satisfaction with Personal Organizational Outcomes," *Academy of Management Journal* 35 (1992), 626–637; F. F. Jones and V. Scarpello, *The Perceived Fairness of Pay Outcomes and Procedures as Predictors of Employee Attitudes.* Working paper (1993).

[8] F. F. Jones and V. Scarpello, *The Perceived Fairness of Pay Outcomes and Procedures.*

# 15

# Special Compensation Situations

## Learning Objectives

To understand the concern over executive compensation and the theoretic bases of compensating executives.

To know the different types of long-term incentives that can be used to attract, retain, and motivate executives.

To understand that executive incentive plans must be designed with the strategic goal of the organization in mind.

To be aware of unusual problems associated with the design of an executive incentive plan.

To understand the compensation components that make up the compensation package of employees in operations abroad.

To learn what comprises compensation for boards of directors.

To understand the kinds of two-tier pay plans available and the advantages and disadvantages associated with them.

To know the advantages and disadvantages of knowledge-based compensation plans.

To learn why incentive plans are used in compensating sales employees.

To have an understanding of the different sales compensation plans available.

## Introduction

Chapter 12 focused primarily on individual piece rate, standard hour, gainsharing, and profit-sharing plans. It included a discussion of the theoretic bases of incentive compensation as well as the conditions under which incentive plans are effective and the potential problems with incentive plans. This chapter focuses on special compensation situations. Even though executive and sales compensation could have been included in the chapter on incentives, the nature of the jobs and the conditions under which they are performed suggest that they be handled separately. The theoretic bases of executive compensation are discussed along with the kinds of incentive plans available and the problems associated with designing an executive compensation plan. A brief discussion of issues that pertain to international compensation, board of directors compensation, and two-tier compensation is included in the chapter. Also, this chapter explains knowledge-based pay, identifies its advantages and disadvantages, examines the effectiveness of such plans, and provides an example of one organization that has successfully implemented knowledge-based pay. This chapter concludes with a discussion of the main kinds of sales incentive plans and the problems associated with designing such plans.

# Executive Compensation

## Historical Perspective

Incentive pay for executives is not new. During the Roman Empire, Julius Caesar developed an incentive plan for his centurions. But longevity of an idea does not mean lack of controversy surrounding it. Controversy has raged, probably since Caesar's day, over two issues of executive compensation: The first involves the appropriate level of executive compensation; the second questions the appropriate composition of the executive compensation package.

It has long been common for executives of American businesses to receive large rewards for their leadership as their companies grow and prosper. The top executive at Bethlehem Steel in 1928 received a tax-free bonus of $1.9 million.[1] It has also long been common for Americans to voice their concern over executive pay. In a 1939 *Fortune* article, a poll found that more than half of the respondents believed executive pay was too high.[2] Currently, many Americans believe executive pay should be limited (for example, $1 million) or the criteria on which it is based should be significantly revised.[3] A review of the popular literature on executive pay during the past 50 years reveals the following main concerns: (1) executives are overpaid, (2) executive pay policies do not place adequate emphasis on increasing shareholders wealth, (3) golden parachutes (contracts that protect the economic wealth of key executives in case of change in control of the organization) and other perquisites (benefits tied to key management positions) overprotect the executive, and (4) there is not a relationship between executive compensation and corporate performance.[4]

In the past two decades, concern over executive pay has exploded. In recent years, the popular business press has been filled with articles questioning the size of the payouts to such business leaders as Iacocca (Chrysler), Wolf (United Airlines), and Eisner (Walt Disney). Articles in *The Wall Street Journal* and *Business Week* have indicated that many believe executive compensation is out of line with the compensation of others within the organization.[5] Why has the past 20 years resulted in this increased concern over executive compensation? Why has an issue that has been around for so long suddenly generated a wealth of articles concerned with the immediacy of the issue and analyzing its causes and potential solutions?

The economic position of the United States is a main reason for the increased scrutiny of executive pay. The decline of the basic United States industries (steel, auto) has drawn attention to the practices of firms within these industries. Analysts frequently suggest that a major cause of American decline is executives' emphasis on short-term perspective versus long-term goals. Executive compensation stands accused of reinforcing this short-term perspective.[6] Studies indicate that past executive compensation practices have not effectively aligned executive goals and objectives with corporate strategies.[7] Recently, organizations have begun to develop programs that examine the financial interests of their executives and stockholders.[8]

The environment in which most organizations developed their executive compensation programs was one of stability and prosperity, with little global competition.[9] That environment has changed. In the increasingly dynamic and potentially unfriendly global market place, executive compensation must take into consideration the perspective of all the relevant partners of the employment exchange, that is, shareholders, customers, suppliers, employees, and executives. Executive compensation plans must meet the specific needs of the organization and its partners; standard off-the-shelf plans cannot successfully shape corporate strategy that is beneficial to all. From the experiences and analyses of the last two decades, four beliefs have come to the forefront and serve as guiding principles in the examination and redesign of executive compensation. Thus, they are more important in the development of the field than any single plan that has been designed.[10] First is the belief that an incentive plan must influence behaviors that increase the firm's value for the stockholder. This puts special emphasis on cash flow (the actual flow of dollars into and out of the organization within a specified time period) and cash-flow-based returns, not just increases in stock price and dividends. Second is the belief that emphasis should be focused on the business unit results as well as on corporate results. This leads to more plans, including reference to cash-flow generation, market share growth, product innovation, and other strategic goals.[11] Third is the belief that the compensation plan may influence corporate culture, values, and use core skills.[12] Fourth, as implied earlier, is a belief that the increased skepticism is legitimate. Organizations are recognizing that past methods have not always lead to behavior that was best for the organization and that they need a new approach that will lead to behaviors that prepare for a competitive future. This will require plans that are more flexible, use different performance criteria (for example, cash flow), and offer a payout schedule that is tied to specific performance targets and not based solely on time.

This section on executive pay provides the foundation for the design of a pay plan that addresses the needs of all parties to the employment exchange. The active involvement of all relevant parties in designing the pay plan is essential.[13]

### Theoretic Bases

In theory, executive incentives are designed for attracting, retaining, and motivating executives, with special emphasis on motivating to ensure that the organization remains competitive today and tomorrow in its relevant markets. Earlier chapters dealt with the role of behavioral theories in influencing human behavior; these behavioral theories are relevant here, especially expectancy, equity, and reinforcement theories. This chapter briefly introduces agency theory as it relates specifically to executive compensation.

Agency theory attempts to explain the relationship between the agent (manager) and the principal (owner). It addresses the likelihood that the parties may have conflicting goals and the difficulty of measuring exactly what the agent is doing.[14] In general, agency theory acknowledges that humans may engage in behaviors that are self-serving and that mechanisms should be in place to channel the agents' activities to accomplish both their own and the principals' goals. Empirical evidence supports the role of agency theory in explaining executive behaviors.[15] Agency theory can be applied to executive compensation in that the incentive plan (governance mechanism) is designed to induce the executive to behave so that both the principal's and the agent's goals can be accomplished. Because the behaviors of executives are hard to measure and it is difficult to specify exactly what behaviors should be occurring, the emphasis shifts to outcomes. The organization permits its managers to engage in the behaviors they believe necessary (within the limits of ethical and legal considerations), and it measures them on the outcomes of those behaviors. One application is an incentive plan that links the reward of the executive, through stock bonus and options (rights to purchase a fixed amount of company stock at a fixed price over a stated period), to the performance of the organization (for example, return on investment, cash flow). A large percentage of the executive compensation package in this case must be contingency-based and not salary-based.[16]

## Executive Bonuses

The compensation plans for top executive officers are designed theoretically to motivate the behavior of those executives. Decisions regarding these bonuses are usually made by the compensation committee of the company's board of directors and rarely fall under the discretion of the company's compensation manager. Because 63 percent of all members of boards of directors are also CEOs, a great deal of the problem rests at the CEO level.[17]

Measuring the real contribution a management team makes to the performance of the organization can be difficult. The general economic conditions and the specific competitive market can strongly influence the normal measures of performance. The management team may have performed very well even though profits, earnings per share (a company's earnings divided by number of shares), and return on investments are down. Should the evaluation of performance be based on net improvement over previous years or should it be based on a comparative analysis with the competitor's change in performance over the same evaluation period? For example, performance based on last year may be down 5 percent to 10 percent, but the industry may be down 20 percent to 25 percent and thus on a relative basis, the firm performed well. The design of the executive compensation plan must determine whether, under these conditions, the team should be rewarded or get nothing in the form of bonuses. It is relatively clear, then, that judgment is required in compensating the top executives of any organization.

During the past few years, organizations have moved away from viewing pay as a fixed cost (for example, base pay and base benefits) and more to viewing it as a variable cost. The pay breakdown for top executive officers in 1985 was 52 percent base, 22 percent annual incentive, 8 percent long-term incentive, 2 percent perks, and 16 percent fringe benefits; whereas, in 1991, it was 35 percent base, 22 percent annual incentive, 31 percent long-term incentive, 1 percent perks, and 11 percent fringe benefits.[18] The use of "mega-grants" of stock options (size of grant larger than total annual compensation—up to 3 times for stock options) has increased from 28 chief executives in 1987 to 45 in 1990.[19] As one company president stated, "Once my salary reached $100,000, I was interested in tax sheltering as much of my income over that amount as I could. At my company we try to defer tax liability for senior executives as best we can."

In addition to cash bonuses, stock options, and base salaries, executives are eligible for an array of popular perks. In a 1990 survey by Hewitt Associates, the following perks were offered by more than 50 percent of the responding firms: company car, company plane, country club membership, estate planning, financial counseling, first-class air travel, income tax preparation, luncheon club membership, personal liability insurance, and physical examination.[20]

Many types of incentives are used to influence executive behaviors. Exhibit 15.1 shows the percentage of companies using different types of incentives according to a survey of 2,400 employers by William Mercer, Inc. The most common incentive granted executives during 1988 or 1989 was annual bonus (68 percent), and the least was phantom stock (3 percent).[21] *Phantom stock* does not involve the issuance of actual stock; rather, the executive receives units that can be cashed in for financial gain. In the same survey, it was found that 89 percent of the publicly held companies and 63 percent of the private companies used incentives. Size was related to the use of incentive plans; 89 percent of the companies with more than $100 million in revenues use incentives, while 64 percent with revenues less than $100 million use them. The Mercer survey also found organizations were granting incentives to positions lower in the organization than in past years. For example, annual bonuses were being extended to executives with annual median salaries of $40,000.

## Long-Term Incentives

In recent years, organizations have become increasingly concerned that executive decisions may not always be the firm's best interests. Many organizations view long-term incentives as a way to deal with that concern. The purpose of long-term incentives is to link executive and shareholder interest; encourage long-term thinking; attract, retain, and motivate; reward the executive for financial successes of the firm; and take advantage of tax regulations that benefit both the firm and the executive.[22] Most long-term incentive plans reward executives

---

| EXHIBIT 15.1 | TYPES OF INCENTIVES GRANTED |
|---|---|

| Incentive | Percent Granting |
|---|---|
| Annual bonus | 68 |
| Stock option | 32 |
| Nonqualified stock option | 23 |
| Incentive stock option | 15 |
| Restricted stock | 10 |
| Performance awards | 9 |
| Stock appreciation | 6 |
| Phantom stock | 3 |

SOURCE: *Employee Benefit Plan Review* Magazine, Vol. 45, October 1990, 42–44. Charles D. Spencer & Associates, Inc., Chicago, IL.

through a form of stock incentive. Some forms of stock incentives are described below; however, the tax implications for the individual or the organization are only briefly addressed because they are beyond the scope of this book. The popularity of each of the stock incentives is strongly affected by the current tax regulations; therefore, the organization must consult a tax professional at the time of design.

*Stock option* is a right granted an executive to purchase stock at a fixed price over a fixed period of time (up to 10 years). The employee has the right to purchase the stock at the option price and will exercise that option if the current market price is significantly above the option price. The difference between the option price and the market price is the financial gain to the executive. Recent practice has resulted in some executives receiving a much smaller base-salary increase or even a salary reduction, but they have realized significant stock options such that even a small increase in price of the stock can yield large returns for them.[23]

*Nonqualified stock options* do not have the restrictions that the qualified option plans discussed above have, such as minimum holding time or price requirements. Nonqualified stock options do not receive the favorable tax treatment that qualified stock options do. Instead, they can be taxed when the options are granted, when exercised, when sold, or when restriction of disposition of the option ends. The gain when recognized under one of these conditions is taxed as ordinary income. This type of option does not impact earnings, and the company can take a tax deduction if the option is granted at fair market value. *Incentive stock options* are granted at fair market value and are similar to nonqualified stock options, but the company is normally not allowed to take a tax deduction. The gain from the option is taxed as ordinary income if the employee does not hold the stock for a minimum of two years after it is granted or one year after it is exercised.[24] *Stock purchase plans* allow a short time to exercise purchase rights at a set price in comparison with the long period available in a straight option plan. Often organizations assist the executive in the financing so the stock purchase can be executed. The overwhelming desire to link employee goals to stockholder goals has resulted in organizations such as DuPont, Pepsico, Pfizer, and Wendy's expanding stock option and stock purchase plans to growing numbers of their employees.[25]

*Restricted stock* is the outright grant of stock to an executive at no or very low cost but subject to restrictions. The shares are registered to the employee along with voting and dividend rights, but the certificates are not actually transferred to the employee until the employee has fulfilled his or her employment conditions (usually continuation of employment for a specified number of years). On completion of the employment conditions, the stock is delivered to the employee to sell or hold as desired. There may be other restrictions in addition to employment length. A second version of restricted stock is called *phantom stock* (or restricted stock units). Here there is no actual stock held and thus no voting rights, but dividends are often paid. Once the employment conditions have been fulfilled, the award can be paid in cash, stock, or a combination. The award may be equal to the value of the phantom shares or to the appreciation in value over a set amount. A special case of a phantom stock involves *stock appreciation rights* (SAR). The right may be linked to a stock option or may be independent. The plan may specify the percentage of the appreciation that will be distributed to the executive in the form of stock or cash. This plan does not require the executive to exercise the option to receive the stock appreciation, and the amount received is taxed as ordinary income.[26] One difficulty is determining a market value for the phantom stock that is understandable to all parties. One valuation method is *book value*,[27] which is stockholders' equity divided by number of outstanding shares. When using book value, adjustments may be necessary to add value for nontangibles such as goodwill and customers lists. The granting of restricted stock is more popular among large companies. Forty-two percent of the *Fortune* 200 largest industrial companies make heavy use of this incentive, based on 1989 analysis of proxy statements.[28] Recently, some organizations have initiated *performance-acceler-ated restricted stock*, in which the shares can be earned earlier than scheduled if certain performance targets are met. This form of incentive is very effective in retaining key executives but is often perceived as a give away with no downward risk for the executive.

Performance-based plans are either goal attainment grants or formula-value grants.[29] *Performance-based goal attainment plans* essentially provide the executive a number of units or shares of stock if predetermined long-term performance goals are met within a specified time period. Usually the performance goals are corporate but may be based on a division or a strategic business unit. The goals may be compared with absolute standards or with company performance in comparison with its competitors.[30] The period varies from organization to organization. One survey found that 59 percent used a 3-year cycle, 32 percent used a 4-year cycle, and 9 percent used a 5- or 6-year cycle.[31] Payout can occur each year in the multiyear plan (after the initial cycle) or once at the end of the cycle. Executives can receive performance units for reaching set performance goals. The financial value of the units is a flat dollar amount ($50,000 or 1,000 units at $50 per unit) or a percentage of salary (30 percent of salary over the performance cycle). Executives receive performance shares in the form of actual shares or phantom shares. The financial value depends on the value of the stock at the time, and the number of shares awarded depends on goals attained during the performance cycle. A survey of *Fortune* top 200 industrial firms found 53 percent used either performance units or shares (sometimes both) during 1989, but only 37 percent of the top 200 service firms used either or both.[32]

With *formula value grants*, the value of the unit is usually based on a formula using such valuation indicators as earnings, cash flow, or book values. With *formula-value appreciation grants* (similar to stock appreciation rights), the financial gains to the executive are based on the value of the unit at the end of the performance period compared with the value of the units when they were granted.[33] *Full-value grants*, as the name implies, relate to full value, not just appreciation; they are paid out to executives based on continuity of employment and are calculated based on a predetermined formula. *Dividend units grants* entitle the executive to the dividends that would have been paid if the executive owned the shares. A survey of the *Fortune* 200 largest industrial firms revealed 2 percent use appreciation grants, 1 percent use full-value grants, and 16 percent use dividend units. The usage in 200 *Fortune* service firms was identical except that only 13 percent used dividend grants.[34]

## Executive Incentives and Strategic Management

The design of an executive incentive plan must consider the organization's goals and the environment within which the organization operates.[35] One incentive plan may serve for all executives in the organization; but if the organization has many distinct product lines or autonomous divisions, it will likely require several separate plans.[36] Organizations should link the level and form of executive compensation to the product life cycle and the level of competition in the product market.[37] If the firm has multiple divisions, it is quite common for the products of those different divisions to be at different stages in their life cycle and to face varying levels of competition (domestic and global). Because the managers of the different business units face different challenges, they must engage in different behaviors and strive for different goals. This would seem to call for different incentive packages.[38]

A business unit that is in the embryonic stage (new products with expanding markets; emerging from bankruptcy) will find that it is cash-poor and must reinvest in the organization every dollar generated if it is to position itself for the future.[39] Even though competition is often weak, the demand to expand its markets and to further develop its product consumes large amounts of cash, thus cash is not available to compensate executives at the appropriate labor market level. Such business units must pay moderate base pay and cash incentives but can supplement the executive's total compensation with lucrative stock incentives. One study found the fastest growing companies in an industry reserved twice the amount of shares for incentives as the industry in general did.[40]

In the growth cycle, a business unit is increasing market share and stabilizing operational costs. During this period, more cash is available to increase base salary and annual cash incentives; movement is away from heavy stock incentives.[41] Competition during this time, however, usually increases, which may reduce profit margins and lead to additional examination of the ability to fund the incentives.

Business units positioned in mature markets are concentrating on operational efficiency and the generation of improved cash flow. Managers' strategies should be directed toward these types of goals. The incentive mix shifts toward short-term performance-based plans and away from long-term incentives.[42] During this time, foreign competition may become severe and profit margins may change significantly. If the potential for renewed growth is slim, incentive plans must emphasize cost cutting and containment.

Managers operating units that are in the decline stage might attempt to maximize cash flow and operational efficiency. In this situation, base salary becomes a critical part of the executive total compensation with performance-based plans that emphasize short-term improvements in valuation of the unit (for example, cash flow).[43] During this phase, competition primarily involves product price, and executive strategy focuses on maximizing operational efficiency.

## Problems in Executive Compensation Design

Many of the problems discussed in the earlier chapter on incentive systems also apply to executive incentives, and they are not repeated. Some problems, however, are unique or have special importance to executive incentive programs.

The first such problem is the seemingly overwhelming need to maintain external market equity. Organizations sometimes incorporate an incentive because some of their labor market competitors have that incentive for their executives. The market for executives has been called a contrived market, and that may be a valid criticism. Because there are relatively few large firms and their executives form fairly closed ranks, they use each others' new incentives to argue for equal treatment. This results in a continuous increase in the variety of incentives offered but may not provide the organizations with any noticeable positive impact. The most important criteria to use in judging the value of any new incentive is whether it will increase the organization's ability to carry out its strategy effectively and efficiently.

A second problem results from an inappropriate mix of short- and long-term incentives. As mentioned earlier, organizations or their units go through different life cycles on their products, and the incentive program must take into consideration where in that life cycle the organization or unit is currently positioned and adjust the mix accordingly. In essence, the mix between base pay and short-term and long-term incentives must fit the strategic action plan of the unit.

A third problem occurs when there is overemphasis on a limited set of financial indicators such as earnings per share or return on investment. Some writers suggest that the financial indicators used to measure executive performance be expanded to include such performance standards as cash flow, market share, product innovation, and book value. This is not to say that the organization should disregard earnings per share or return on investment but rather that it should broaden performance standards to include a wider range of financial indicators and the strategic behaviors (for example, market expansion, new product innovation, product diversification, structural reorganization) of the management team.[44] Other writers, however, noting that company success usually depends on one or two factors, disagree with expanding the list of performance indicators. Measuring strategic behaviors is difficult. An organization increases its chances for acceptable measurement by using a team approach and by hiring consultants to facilitate the meetings and to review the objectivity of the plan.[45]

Fourth, using stocks as the primary financial incentive can be problematic. There are many reasons for the heavy emphasis on stocks, such as increasing employee involvement through ownership, but it can result in the dilution of ownership and earnings per share,[46] and it can take the focus away from long-term strategies and goals. Difficulties inherent in stock plans include the timing of the executives' exercise of their stock rights or options and the corresponding limitation of sale of these shares. Most programs require that the executives be current employees of the firm to receive the incentive; also, the executives must execute the purchase or option within a preestablished window. This provision accomplishes one of the objectives of the compensation program—retention. But it may be beneficial to both the organization and the individual to liberalize this requirement. Permitting executives who have moved on to other organizations or who have retired to exercise their options or rights might encourage them to develop goals and strategies that are truly long term because their continued employment is not a condition for reaping the financial rewards for which they are responsible.[47]

Occasionally, an organization changes its incentive plan solely to ensure that its executives receive a reward. An organization has a stock option incentive plan, but the stock market drops; this leaves the option price above the market price and makes the incentive worthless. Organizations have been known to cancel the existing incentive plan and initiate a new stock option plan with an option price below the current market price. This communicates to all that executives in the top levels of an organization will be taken care of and all downside risk will be eliminated. This kind of risk removal constitutes a fifth problem with executive incentives.

The sixth problem results when executives earn huge financial rewards by exercising stock options even though the organization itself has not performed well. The value indicators of the firm (for example, return on investment, cash flow, earnings per share) may not have increased dramatically but the price of the stock may have risen significantly because of a major overall advancement of the market. To avoid this situation—which both the public and all nonincluded employees view negatively—the organization could tie the number of stock options or rights to some specific measures of organizational valuation.

A seventh problem involves letting tax and accounting considerations dictate the composition of the executive incentive plan.[48] The tax implications must be an important consideration in the design of the incentive plan, but a more critical consideration is the role of the incentive in motivating managers to position the organization for long-term global competitiveness. That is, the organization must link the executive incentive plan to the strategic management of the organization. This requires the incentive compensation plan to be part of strategic planning, linked to both long- and short-term goals of the organization or unit; the plan must encourage teamwork, vary the compensation mix (base, short- and long-term) as necessary, and possibly reward executives after they have left the organization.[49]

# International Compensation

The global nature of today's marketplace requires increased exposure to foreign markets. The compensation of employees of U.S. operations in foreign countries is a significant managerial issue as firms attempt to be competitive in the new global marketplace. Companies operating abroad employ three kinds of employees—expatriates, third-country nationals (TCNs), and local-country nationals (LCNs). *Expatriates* are citizens of the country in which the parent company is located, who are working abroad usually for 5 years or less. *TCNs* are not citizens of the parent company's home country nor are they citizens of the country in which the foreign subsidiary is operating. These employees are citizens of a third country and usually move from country to country throughout their careers.[50] *LCNs* are citizens of the country in which the foreign operation is located.

The compensation of employees of U.S. firms operating abroad is made up of base salary, benefits, equalization benefits, and incentives. The goal of the total compensation package is to enhance the organization's ability to attract, retain, and motivate the best employees. Research has shown that cultural variations significantly affect the ratio of the compensation components to total compensation.

Product market constraints are the primary determinants of the level of total compensation, whereas local culture strongly influences the mix of direct pay, benefits, and incentives.[51]

### Base Salary

There may be serious equity problems among the three kinds of employees if different bases are used, resulting in the salary of one or more of them being significantly higher than the other. This is especially true if the work they are performing is relatively similar.[52] Thus the base salary of all employees will normally be established in accordance with the compensation policies and practices either of the country of the parent organization or of the country in which the foreign subsidiary is operating.[53] In some unusual situations (for example, trying to attract and retain employees with special skills in a tight labor market), salary may be based on the base-salary structure of the country of the TCNs. Home-based salary is calculated using the salary structure and policies of the parent organization. This policy is especially effective when assignments abroad are for short durations (3 to 5 years), few employees from other countries are employed at the same location, employees are high level (executives) or possess special skills, or the employees plan to return to the parent organization's country on completion of the assignment. This makes movement back to the employee home base simpler because major salary changes do not have to be made after the temporary assignment is completed.

Host-based salary is based on the policies and practices of the country in which the subsidiary is located. This is used when the staff is composed of employees from many countries, the employees are assigned at the location for an extended period of time (more than 5 years), cost of living in the foreign location is high (thus to keep the person whole, salary must be based on local costs of living), and maintenance of internal equity is critical.[54] This pay practice is also the norm for compensation when the plant employees are primarily LCNs because their relevant labor market is local and equity must be maintained with local customs and practices.

### Employee Benefits

The fringe benefit plans for expatriates and for most TCNs will be covered by the parent company benefit package. For some key TCNs, it may be necessary for tax reasons to develop a separate floating benefit plan, especially in the pension areas established in tax-haven countries.[55] In designing the benefit package for LCNs, the organization must review carefully local practices, customs, and laws. It must remember that it is a guest within the foreign country and act accordingly. Based on local customs, there may be different packages depending on the location of the operation (that is, rural or urban).[56] Design of the benefit package must also indicate an awareness of local economic conditions. For example, a defined benefit offered to employees in Brazil with its history of high inflation could burden the organization with significant long-term cost obligations, whereas that same benefit in a country with stable prices has more predictable cost projections. Consequently, experts recommend that benefit plans in all foreign operations should be defined contribution plans whenever possible. The organization must consider any legally required benefits; many European countries have retirement, disability, and termination requirements that are significantly broader and more costly than those U.S. organizations experience domestically.[57]

## Equalization Benefits

These benefits pertain primarily to expatriates and to some extent to TCNs. The purpose of equalization benefits is to keep expatriates whole (to prevent financial harm as a result of the move abroad) and to reduce the negative aspects of living abroad. For example, U.S. expatriates living abroad often receive one or two round-trip air fares each year to visit friends and relatives. To make day-to-day living more suitable, they are often provided private schooling for their children and subsidies for cost of housing, food, and other living expenses. In some locations, the organization supplies houses or apartments. Most organizations provide a tax equalization benefit (adjustment) so that an employee's income tax obligations do not negatively affect real earnings.[58] The adjustment ensures that the employee does not pay more taxes than if he or she were working in the United States. Some organizations pay a premium for accepting assignment in locations that impose significant hardships on the employee. The percentage premium is a function of the level of hardship that corresponds to the specific assignment. In many assignments, there is no hardship pay because the conditions are similar to those experienced in the employee's home country.

## Incentives

U.S. domestic organizations have shifted a larger proportion of executive and managerial pay from base pay to short- and long-term incentives, and that trend is starting to be more common in the design of pay plans for U.S. employees abroad.[59] In the past, the amount of stock available to executives of foreign subsidiaries in the form of options or grants has been small, which has reduced the incentive value to the executive. Most incentive plans have been tied closely to overall performance, with the reward to the executive in the form of stock options or rights. For executives operating foreign subsidiaries, contribution to overall corporate performance is as much a function of exchange rates and other noncontrollable factors as it is a function of effective and efficient management.[60] To provide a more meaningful incentive, more companies are designing incentive programs that are performance-based, but performance is measured at the strategic business unit (foreign subsidiary). How far down the organization the incentive plan extends depends on the philosophy of the organization and the customs of the country in which the operation is located. The basic principles discussed earlier as they apply to incentive plans also apply in this situation. Special considerations must be made for tax implications, especially for expatriates and TCNs, because of the possibilities of multiple taxing rules and regulations.[61] Employers under a tax equalization policy may incur significant foreign tax liability when U.S. expatriates are included in a stock option plan.[62] Assistance from a professional specializing in international taxation is essential.

# Board of Directors Compensation

The ultimate power within a U.S. corporation rests with the board of directors. A position on a board of directors is unique in that potential members do not apply but are often sought out by the company because of industry experience, specialized knowledge, or contacts they possess. Also, any new board member must be elected by the stockholders (through proxies) of the corporation. Designing a compensation package for this position is further complicated because most board members do not take board positions for financial rewards but for the challenge and prestige. Nevertheless, if the compensation package is not appropriate the potential board member may view the offer as an insult; a potentially good person may be lost and the organization's image may be damaged.

The compensation of board of directors may be composed of annual retainer, board meeting fees, committee meeting fee (for example, Executive Compensation Committee), stock options, stock grants, restricted stock options, restricted stock grants, and an array of other benefits (for example, pensions, life insurance, medical insurance).[63] The reader may wish to refer to the section on executive compensation for an explanation of the different stock incentives. The past decade has shown a significant increase in organizations using stock and pensions as part of the compensation of directors.

The pay of outside directors (directors not employed by the company in another capacity, such as vice-president) increased 27 percent from 1985 to 1990 according to a survey conducted by Korn/Ferry International. The average compensation for 1990 was $24,729, which included annual retainer and per meeting fee.[64] When the largest corporations are examined, the pay for board members is significantly higher with such major corporations as Pepsico paying $78,000, Philip Morris $54,675, Union Pacific $50,000, and Georgia-Pacific at $43,000 (these amounts for 1990 include annual retainer, meeting fees, and stock grants).[65] Many board members collect additional compensation for serving on special committees and are able to take advantage of lucrative stock option plans. The stock options or grants may replace the annual retainer or committee fee or may be paid in addition to the normal compensation. The expenses incurred by board members to attend meetings are reimbursed, and liability insurance is provided. Because of the increased litigation, the cost of liability insurance has increased dramatically and has become a significant factor.

Stock compensation has increased dramatically with more than 50 percent of 350 large companies surveyed by Towers Perrin providing this form of compensation to their directors in 1990. The companies surveyed provided stock grants valued at slightly less than $8,000.[66] This enables the organization to sweeten the compensation package without significantly increasing its direct cost. The most common form of stock option is either a restricted or unrestricted stock grant.[67] Stock compensation is an attempt to tie the interest of the directors more closely with the interest of the stockholders. The limited research available found that stock options are positively related to returns to shareholders, but grants of restricted stocks are negatively related. The negative relationship may be misleading. While it may be a negative relationship, it may not be a causal relationship. Some firms that offer restricted stock grants may already be in financial trouble, and it is not the grant that caused the poor organizational performance.[68] Some business analysts believe that all directors fees should be paid in stock and that all directors should be more than token stockholders.[69]

During the past years, the creation of pension plans for directors has increased significantly among the largest organizations with more than 50 percent offering them in 1990.[70] Those offering pensions usually set them at 93 percent of the director's annual retainer and require the director to serve on an average of 7 years.[71]

## Two-Tier Compensation Plans

Two-tier compensation plans pay new employees wages and/or benefits (for example, health insurance, holidays, sick days) that are less than those of employees who were hired before an established cut-off date. This form of differential pay is not new and dates back to the 1930s when it was first instituted by small organizations experiencing financial problems.[72] Two-tier pay plans became popular in the 1970s and 1980s when such industrial giants as Boeing, Lockheed, Safeway Stores, American Airlines, Great Atlantic and Pacific Tea Company, and Dow Chemical instituted plans to control costs.[73] The use of two-tier plans reached 11 percent of contract negotiated in 1985 but will likely decline in the future.[74]

### Types of Two-Tier Compensation Plans

The compensation plan may be a permanent pay differential or it may be temporary. With a permanent two-tier pay plan, the pay differential between employees hired after the cut-off date and those hired before remains constant. If the plan is temporary, new employees start at a rate less than existing employees doing the same work but move to the higher rate based on a predetermined time schedule. According to the Bureau of National Affairs, 90 days is the most common time delay before the new employees reach the regular pay rate for the job.[75] Some organizations have several steps before reaching full regular pay. For example, the new employees may start at 85 percent of normal pay and after 6 months move to 90 percent, with 95 percent after 1 year and 100 percent after 18 months. Most organizations that have two-tier pay plans have opted for a temporary wage differential rather than a permanent differential so that a group of workers do not think they are second-class members of the organization.

### Advantages and Disadvantages

There are several proposed benefits to a two-tier compensation plan.[76] First, the organization is able to reduce labor cost temporarily or permanently, depending on the type of plan installed. The objectives of the cost savings may be to achieve competitiveness after deregulation or to regain competitiveness after the introduction of new low-cost domestic or foreign competitors, or to seize a competitive advantage over existing competitors.[77] Second, it can aid retention of highly experienced employees because their pay is probably at or above market. Third, if the organization is experiencing high turnover and believes little can be done to reduce this problem, the two-tier plan shifts some of the training and selection cost to the new hires. This is an advantage only if the cost of any additional turnover is less than the money saved on wages and benefits. Fourth, one study found that, contrary to common belief, employees hired at less pay in a two-tier plan have a higher level of satisfaction with pay, work, and supervision. The explanation offered was that these employees may have lower initial expectations and may be using different referent groups to evaluate their work situation.[78]

There is a potential down side to initiating a two-tier plan. First, it may add significantly to turnover, which will increase the recruiting, selection, and training cost associated with replacing the departing employees and getting the new employees' performance up to standard.[79] This is true especially in a permanent two-tier system, but it may also be true in a temporary system when new hires are unwilling to wait out salary adjustments. Second, the quality of employee performance may be substantially below what the customer is accustomed to, and it may hurt future sales.[80] This was a problem several airlines faced when they instituted a two-tier wage rate for pilots and other airline personnel.[81] Third, the time between starting wage and standard may be too short to realize any significant cost savings and may actually cost the firm more than it saves because of costs associated with higher turnover, lower morale, and increased administrative work. Fourth, in permanent two-tier pay plans the firm must deal with questions such as the pay rate for employees who are promoted. Do they get paid at the percentage they would receive in their old job, or does the two-tier wage treatment only apply to the entry jobs? Also, are employees who are promoted from other jobs not included in the plan treated as if they were hired before the cut-off time? The latter would provide additional incentive for new employees to excel within the organization, but it also may significantly increase labor costs. Fifth, the organization may be charged with wage discrimination if the two-tier wage plan is proven to have an adverse impact on the economic status of protected groups and if the organization cannot prove that the plan existed for economic and business reasons. For example, an organization implements an affirmative action plan to hire a significant number of minorities but at the same time institutes a two-tier wage plan. Because the pay plan will have a significant impact on the wage level of new employees who are predominantly minorities, the organization may be requested to demonstrate that the plan was not designed to be discriminatory.[82]

One study that examined the effect of two-tier wage systems on firms' market value found half of the firms had a positive abnormal return and half a negative abnormal return, but the positive returns exceeded the negative returns in absolute value.[83] A second study found similar results, which led the authors to conclude that the lack of overall strong positive results may have led to the decrease in the use of two-tier wage systems.[84]

## Knowledge-Based Compensation

Traditionally, the pay assigned to a position is determined through formal job analysis and job evaluation. Recall that job evaluation is a process whereby the organization determines the relative value of a job. This traditional approach is generally called job-based pay. With knowledge-based pay, an individual's pay is based on the knowledge or the number and kind of skills the employee is capable of applying within the organization rather than on the job the employee is hired to do. This approach can also be called *person-based pay* or *skill-based pay*. The objectives of knowledge-based pay are to motivate the employee to learn multiple skills and perform multiple jobs, to provide the opportunity for the employee to invest in him- or herself, to improve the employee's self-image, to provide the employer increased flexibility in human resource allocation, and to decrease the employer's cost of doing business. An extensive survey conducted by the American Compensation Association found that knowledge-based pay had a positive influence on employee productivity and growth.[85] Nevertheless, these pay plans normally do not replace job-based pay plans. Rather, these plans are incorporated into job-based plans.

## Advantages

Knowledge-based pay has recently grown in popularity in both the manufacturing and the service industry, with adoption by organizational units of such firms as Anheuser-Busch, Atlantic Richfield, Borg-Warner, General Mills, Butler Manufacturing, Chrysler, Westinghouse, TRW, Aid Association for Lutherans (an insurance company), and Shenandoah Life.[86] Of 1,600 large organizations surveyed by the American Productivity Center and the American Compensation Association, two-thirds of the respondents using knowledge-based pay had implemented it in the last 5 years and 75 percent projected an increased use in the future.[87] The advantages that correspond to a knowledge-based pay plan are as follows.

First, the firm increases its flexibility in assigning workers to different jobs.[88] Employees who have skills to perform several jobs provide the employer with the flexibility to handle change in product or service demands and to deal more effectively with employee turnover and absenteeism.[89]

Second, the firm requires fewer job classifications because pay is not determined by the classification to which the job is assigned. Instead, the firm is concerned with broad categories of jobs and the skills required to do each, along with how to motivate each employee to learn these skills. The administrative problem of maintaining equity between many job classifications is reduced, as is the continuous pressure to move a job from one classification to a higher classification.

Third, lower staffing levels suffice because human resources are interchangeable and can handle increases and changes in product mix and service demands. Because the employees are able to staff a variety of positions at a high level of efficiency, the organization does not have to hire additional individuals to handle the fluctuating demands the operational units may experience. The employees feel a greater sense of team work and are often able to work with less supervision. Many of the routine tasks that supervisors often must perform are now carried out by the employee, freeing supervisors' time for activities they often must ignore or do inadequately.[90]

Fourth, the organization often experiences reduced turnover and absenteeism and improved recruitment. Employees with knowledge-based pay employers are able to grow and develop within the work unit, enabling them to satisfy some higher order needs (Maslow's Esteem and Self-Actualization; see Chapter 3), and thus reducing the need to change employers in order to use their abilities.[91] Also, potential employees are attracted by an organizational environment that enables them to develop their skills and talents.[92]

### Disadvantages

Implementing knowledge-based pay does have some potential problems. First, the direct wage cost for the organization may increase. The organization will be paying for skills that the employees apparently are not using on their current assignments. Unless the organization limits the premium available for learning additional skills, the number of skills some employees will learn and receive premiums for could increase dramatically.[93] This could result in the employer's payroll skyrocketing without a corresponding increase in productivity.[94]

Second, the amount of time and training resources required to execute the training program effectively may be more than the organization is willing to commit.[95] The real commitment comes in the form of time required to train multiple employees effectively in a basic set of skills. Not only must top management be committed but also each managerial level in the organization must accept this as the best way to manage the work force.[96]

Third, the firm must deal with the presence of employees who, because of limited ability or lack of self-confidence, will not participate in the learning of additional skills. If this number is large, it may severely limit the value of the knowledge-based pay, or if there are only a few, a feeling of isolation may develop among those who choose not to participate, resulting in a potentially negative situation.

Fourth, as employees move into different jobs, productivity is lost. The frequency of employee movement from one job to another must be monitored so it does not significantly hurt the ability of the firm to deliver goods and services in a timely manner.

Fifth, employees may top out by learning all the skills within their area and thus run the risk of lower morale. For those situations in which an employee has topped out, it may be advantageous to provide the employee with the opportunity to learn skills associated with jobs in a different work group—that is, if the employee has not already reached any premium cap and if the firm sees any potential use for the additional skills.[97]

Sixth, employees learn the skills associated with a new job with the expectation that the skills they have learned will be used. Employees unable to use the learned skills will often become disillusioned and may lose proficiency in the application of the new knowledge. Significant morale problems can result. Once an employee has been trained, if the organization cannot or does not use the skill, competitors may hire the trained employee.

Seventh, research points to an upper limit for the number of new skills an employee can be expected to learn with any level of proficiency. Between eight and ten skills is the limit.[98] Beyond that, the success of the plan diminishes and the administration becomes unmanageable.[99]

### Knowledge-Based Pay Plans Effectiveness

A survey was sent to compensation managers of the *Business Week* 1,000 firms to determine if knowledge-based pay was successful. The 30 responding compensation managers who had adopted knowledge-based pay stated that it increased employee understanding of organizational goals and motivated employees to learn a variety of new skills. However, the administration of the program was perceived as difficult, and the expected cost savings did not materialize.[100]

An in-depth study of 20 plants that had instituted knowledge-based pay tested certain commonly held beliefs regarding it.[101] First, knowledge-based pay was believed to be relevant only for production employees. In contrast, the study showed that firms apply knowledge-based pay to clerical, professional, and technical employees, not just to production employees. Second, the belief that first-line supervisors are a main obstacle to knowledge-based pay was not supported. Third, the idea that knowledge-based pay will only work in a new situation was partially supported. Three-fourths of the plants were start-up, but the remainder had switched from the traditional approach. Obviously, it is easier in a new operation because the excess baggage of the traditional system is not present, but firms have been successful in implementing knowledge-based pay in existing plants. Fourth, although most plants had a maximum of 15 skills and a minimum of 3 as their parameters, in practice employees had learned on average about 4 skills, which took about 49 months to learn. Fifth, the study revealed no relationship between the personal characteristics of the employee and the successful implementation of knowledge-based pay. Overall, the compensation managers believe there has been a strong relationship between anticipated and actual benefits (for example, lower labor costs and improved employee commitment) from instituting knowledge-based pay. They express satisfaction with the decision to use knowledge-based pay and believe it would be a mistake to discontinue its use.

## *Example*

Aid Associations for Lutherans (AAL), a leading insurance firm in providing fraternal benefits and financial security to Lutherans, has adopted knowledge-based pay in some areas of the organization to support the concept of self-managed work teams.[102] The employee's base pay is a function of experience, performance, and the service units that make up the job. Service units are composed of two types called "primary" and "additional." Primary service is determined by the Hay job evaluation process, which determines the wage range for a particular job (entry to maximum). An employee moves within the range based on years of experience and merit performance rating. The employee can add additional service units to increase the base pay. The value of the additional service units is a function of the level of know-how and the number of other service units added in the past. The first additional service unit added is valued more than the second, and so on, up to the tenth. A highly trained committee of AAL employees determined the value of know-how. This generates a matrix with different values of know-how on the horizontal axis, service units on the vertical axis, and corresponding dollar values within each cell of the matrix. The work team has an employee add responsibilities only if the team believes that doing so will accomplish team objectives more effectively. Total pay for an employee in a position is a summation of primary and additional service units. For example, an employee's job may have a range of $325 to $410 per week. The employee, based on experience and performance ratings, may personally have a primary wage of $380 with another $65 for 7 additional service units, bringing the total wage to $445. AAL is very pleased with the program and has shared the concept through its symposiums on self-managed teams.

# Sales Incentive Plans

## *Reasons for Sales Incentives*

Sales incentive plans are established in a manner very similar to incentive plans for production employees and are supported by the same theoretic background. However, the employee who is successful as a sales person is different from the production employee, the standards for determining the incentive are different, and the reasons for implementing an incentive plan are different.

One of the main reasons for the use of incentives for sales people is the difficulty of supervising these employees. Unlike production employees who are at work stations, most sales persons spend extended periods of time away from their company, making it difficult for management to observe and directly manage their behavior.

A second reason for incentive pay is that many sales persons see themselves as independent employees or entrepreneurs. Individuals with this orientation are highly motivated to perform, and money and awards are important reinforcers. At the extreme, some sales persons are in fact independent agents (for example, independent insurance agents and manufacturer's representatives); the only way the organization can entice them to sell its products is with an incentive system.

As with production employees, compensating sales people with incentive pay directly ties pay to performance. This becomes a third compelling reason for incentive pay. From a behavioral perspective, a commission incentive plan provides one of the clearest pay for performance relationships available. If an employee produces, he or she is rewarded; if not, there is no payment.

Fourth, the sales task is often composed of several independent tasks (such as negotiating price, qualifying accounts, and servicing accounts). This requires incentive plan developers to consider the relative weight of each activity based on how each fits into the organization's strategic action plan. To be effective, the plan must be flexible so that its elements and weights can change as the product life cycle changes or the degree of product competition changes.[103] Overall, the organization must integrate the incentive plan with corporate goals and strategies.[104] There has been an increased concern for integrating customer service and satisfaction in sales incentive plans. The most difficult aspect of this is the development of performance measures for those outcomes. In customer service, the focus could be on such measures as on-time delivery, returns, and credits, whereas for customer satisfaction it may be on information obtained through focus groups and surveys.[105]

Sales incentive plans usually use product price as the basis for setting commissions. A sales person receives a certain percentage of the premium value of an insurance policy or of the selling price of the product. This approach is similar to the piece rate plans for some production workers. It differs, however, from many plans where the standard is the labor savings realized by the employee during production.

There are many types of sales incentives plans. Some plans operate only during a special promotion, others operate for a specific period of time, and some are used to influence the behaviors of the sales person continuously.

Sales people are typically paid on some variation of four basic plans: straight salary, salary plus commission, draw plus commission, or straight commission.

## Straight Salary

Straight salary is not an incentive plan. It is primarily used when a team of specialists is needed to make a presentation to a client, when product servicing is critical, when seasonal variation is present, during the sales training phase, or when the sales person is primarily an order taker.

## Salary Plus Commission

A salary plus commission compensation plan amounts to a guaranteed minimum wage level (the guaranteed salary) plus the commission rate. This plan provides financial security to the employee, along with the opportunity for extra financial rewards. The most difficult aspect of this plan design is determining the proper mix between salary and commission. An organization should consider the following factors in determining the appropriate mix: importance of sales person skills, reputation of company, money spent on advertising and promotions, price and quality aspects of the product, amount of customer service required, importance of team selling, and the marketing objectives of the organization.[106] When salary and commission are used, the largest percentage, frequently 60 percent to 80 percent, goes to salary.[107] If, however, the task requires the sales person to possess special skills, the company lacks name recognition, little customer service is required, and teamwork is not relevant, then a larger portion of total compensation will usually be in the form of commission.

## Draw Plus Commission

Organizations that pay on a commission basis allow their sales people, under certain circumstances, to draw against future commissions. The basic philosophy behind a draw is that there may be considerable variation in sales over time and the organization wishes to smooth out income for the sales people over the selling period. This variation in sales may be because of seasonal variation in demand or because the employees are in the learning process. There are two kinds of draws. Recoverable draws are income advanced to the sales people when sales performance is less than the draw provided. This deficit must be repaid to the organization when the commission earned is greater than the draw for the selling period. The organization should put a cap on the deficit because if the employee leaves, the amount of the deficit is probably nonrecoverable. Nonrecoverable draws are not expected to be repaid and actually become a guarantee.[108] This kind of draw is usually used during the learning period and is actually a method the company uses to compensate a new sales person during the training period. Under this condition, the organization should systematically reduce the size of the draw over time so that at the end of the normal training period the draw is zero.

## Straight Sales Commission

Some organizations used a commission-only basis for paying trained sales people. An example of a sales commission schedule for insurance sales people is provided in Exhibit 15.2. In designing a commission-only plan, an organization must address several issues. First, what basis will be used to determine the commission? The two most common methods are overall sales volume or profit margin for each product or product line sold.[109] To encourage sales people to sell a complete product mix, the organization may provide a more lucrative commission schedule designed to accomplish this goal.[110] Second, should the commission schedule be a constant percentage, a increasing or decreasing percentage, or some combination? In selecting the schedule, the philosophy and objectives of the organization help determine which is best for the organization. For example, some organizations do not permit the salaries of sales people to exceed the compensation of select managerial positions, and thus an increasing schedule could compromise that policy. However, if the firm has excessive plant capacity it may have an increasing schedule up to the point at which a constant percentage becomes effective. Third, when will the sales person receive the commission: when the sale is made, when it is shipped, or when the invoice is paid in full? Obviously it is best for the cash flow of the organization to defer payment until the invoice is paid in full. This policy makes economic sense but violates the behavioral principle of having the reinforcer (money) closely linked to behavior (closing the sale). Caution must be taken not to delay the reward and thus reduce the cause-and-effect value of the financial incentive. Fourth, is the commission to be shared with others or does all of it go to the sales person? In some organizations, the sales manager or support staff share the commission. If the satisfaction of the customer requires cooperation of other members of the organization, a splitting of commission may be a reasonable policy. The organization must be able to identify who makes up the team and the appropriate contribution each makes to the long-term satisfaction of the customer.

## Special Sales Incentive Plans

Periodically organizations may stress some particular product or service more than others. The organization may put on a sales promotion specifically for that product or service. Reasons for a special promotion may include clearing out inventories of one product line, increasing market penetration for a particular product, balancing the sales mix, and introducing new products. Sales incentive programs usually run for a specified time period. An example of special sales promotion for insurance sales staff appears in Exhibit 15.3. Another example would be a company's offer of a 15 percent bonus on top of normal compensation for any sales person who can increase qualified (acceptable based on credit worthiness) new accounts by a set number or percentage within a specified time span. These bonus plans are normally used for accomplishing short-term

| EXHIBIT 15.2 | SALES COMMISSION SCHEDULE FOR INSURANCE |
|---|---|

### Schedule of First-Year Commissions

Contract Update (Agent)

This Update will be effective as of _____, 19 ____.

| Kind of Policy | Rate of Commission |
|---|---|
| Health Policies & Riders | 40 |
| Adjustable Life/Term Plans (illustrated below) | 50 |
| Convertible Annual Renewable Term | 25 |
| Adj. Life (nonrepeating premium) | 4 |

| Premium Paying Period | Kind of Policy and Rate of Commission Over Life of the Policy— Adjustable Life— Term Plans | Premium Paying Period | Kind of Policy and Rate of Commission Over Life of the Policy— Adjustable Life— Term Plans |
|---|---|---|---|
| 20 years or more | 50 | 12 | 37 |
| 19 | 48 | 11 | 36 |
| 18 | 46 | 10 | 35 |
| 17 | 44 | 9 | 32 |
| 16 | 42 | 8 | 29 |
| 15 | 40 | 7 | 26 |
| 14 | 39 | 6 | 23 |
| 13 | 38 | 5 | 20 |

Modified first-year commission on large premium policies:

We will modify first-year commissions on all policies with annual premiums of $100,000 or more. The modifications will apply to any excess over $100,000 as set forth in our rules.

We will credit you with all renewal commissions that would regularly be payable under the contract.

First-year commissions on large premium policies: Below explains how commissions are paid on policies that pay more than $100,000 in premiums. On these types of policies, your commission will be spread out over 3 years.

You will be paid 30 percent the first year, 15 percent the following year, and 10 percent in the third year, for a total of 55 percent. Production points, however, will be credited to you in the first year. The following table show how commissions on a large adjustable policy would be paid.

| Premium | Commissions | First Year 30 % | Second Year 15 % | Third Year 10 % |
|---|---|---|---|---|
| $100,000 | $50,000 | $100,000 × 0.30 = $30,000 | $100,000 × 0.15 = $15,000 | $100,000 × 0.10 = $10,000 |

Total commissions = $55,000

SOURCE: Adapted from various insurance companies' commission schedules.

| EXHIBIT 15.3 | EXAMPLE OF A SPECIAL SALES INCENTIVE SCHEDULE IN INSURANCE |
|---|---|

The purpose of this contest is to stir up interest in our fall business. It has been our history that almost every year for the past 33 years, we have done as much business from September 1 to December 31 as we do the other 8 months. We do not want this year to be an exception to that.

### Rules for the Contest

1. Prize for this contest is a suit of clothes purchased at XYZ clothing store.

2. Requirements: applications secured on September 1 to December 31, 1992. If you have 16 paid and delivered new applications during this time, you will be entitled to a suit of your choice not to exceed $400 at the above-named store.

3. If you do not have 16 cases written and delivered in this period but have 20 applications applied for with money on the applications, you will be entitled to this suit.

4. If you have $900,000 of paid volume, you will be entitled to this suit provided this amount is paid between September 1 and December 31, 1992.

5. If you have 16 paid applications and $900,000 of volume that has been paid between September 1 and December 31, you will be entitled to two suits or a suit and a dress coat.

---

goals and should be clearly identified as special bonuses since they will not continue after the specific goals are accomplished.

Specific sales promotion incentives operate very much like regular incentive programs. When they are added to already established incentive programs, the organization should make sure these promotions actually add to total sales over the long-term and do not detract from other sales areas. The special incentive rewards should be large enough to have value to the sales staff, but not so large that sales people ignore other lines of business or other aspects of their job. No research was discovered that addresses the size of incentive that satisfies these two constraints, but the problem is a potentially serious one.

Recognition plans are relatively popular among organizations attempting to motivate their sales force. These plans are also used with other employee groups. Surveys indicate that sales recognition programs are being viewed as important elements in any sales incentive program. A survey by Sales and Marketing Management found that a formal recognition program is highly related to sales force success.[111] Recognition awards may be monetary or product awards. When product awards are used, some writers noted that the most successful recognition programs include five elements.[112] First, the organization must have or develop a recognition symbol (for example, company logo or trademark) that will be enduring and easily recognized. Second, it must provide a gift as a vehicle for mobility of the recognition (for example, mugs, letter openers). Third, it must find a meaningful way to present the award to individuals. This may take the form of an awards banquet, an article in the company newsletter, or another means of public acknowledgment. Fourth, it must provide a presenter for the award whose stature increases the level of acceptance by employees. Fifth, it must periodically re-examine the award program to ensure that it is still directing behavior to the current organizational goals and that the awards are still valued by the employees. A recent study found the recognition programs of firms that acknowledged 31 percent to 50 percent of their sales force were more effective than those that acknowledged above or below this range.[113]

Support staff are critical for ultimate customer satisfaction. Some firms, for example, are finding that they must provide excellent follow-up service after the sale is made to be able to retain customers. Organizations are increasingly looking for ways to motivate their support staff. Xerox has established service goals for administrative and senior operating employees relating to their corporate goal of total customer satisfaction. The administrator of the billing department, for instance, can earn points based on handling bills in a proper and timely manner.[114] A survey of approximately 200 firms indicated that sales support incentives have grown significantly in the past decade.[115] One of the most common incentives is the travel award; small as well as large firms are using this incentive and applying it to technical, clerical, and telemarketing jobs.[116]

### Problems with Sales Incentive Plans

The same problems that plague piece rate and standard hour incentive plans exist with sales incentive plans. These problems are discussed in Chapter 12. A problem unique to sales incentives concerns setting standards and balancing territory opportunity. Just as production standards may vary across different units in a factory, performance standards may vary across sales territory. Sales territories may vary considerably in their potential for customers, and the same standard can be too high in one territory and too low in another. One territory may be so lucrative that by acting only as an order taker, the sales person can easily reach 150 percent of quota. However, in a different territory the sales person may have to work 60 hours a week to reach 80 percent of quota. This inequity can be incredibly demoralizing to the sales person. Probably the best solution is to set different standards based on the territory rather than reassigning or redesigning territories.

## Summary

This chapter on special compensation situations addresses six special situations: executives, international operations, board of directors, two-tier plans, knowledge-based plans, and incentive plans for sales staff.

First, the chapter presents background pertaining to executive compensation and discusses public concern with the level of such compensation. It explains the different kinds of short-term and long-term executive incentive plans. It stresses the importance of integrating executive incentive plans with corporate strategy and discusses the problems associated with designing an executive incentive plan.

Next, the chapter recognizes the importance of international compensation issues in the new global marketplace. It examines how an organization handles expatriates, local-country nationals, and third-country nationals. The chapter covers compensation for members of a board of directors, pointing out that these people serve primarily for reasons of challenge and prestige.

Two-tier compensation and knowledge-based pay are included as variations on traditional single-tier and job-based pay programs.

Finally, the chapter discusses the reasons incentives are used to compensate sales staff. It explains the compensation methods and presents the problems associated with sales incentive plans.

## Discussion Questions

1. What are the four fundamental beliefs that serve as guiding principles for the area of executive compensation?

2. Describe the special problems an organization faces in designing an executive compensation plan.

3. Discuss the four types of sales compensation plans and situations in which you would use them.

4. Describe a knowledge-based pay plan and discuss the advantages and disadvantages of such a plan.

5. Compare the home-based and host-based compensation plans for international organizations and discuss situations in which each would be used.

6. What is the two-tier compensation plan? What are the advantages of such a plan? Disadvantages?

7. What special problems are faced by organizations in determining pay for their board of directors?

*References*

[1] D. J. McLaughlin, "The Rise of a Strategic Approach to Executive Compensation," in *Executive Compensation: A Strategic Guide for the 1990s*, ed. F. K. Foulkes (Boston: Harvard Business School Press, 1991), 5–26.

[2] G. T. Milkovich and B. R. Rabin, "Executive Compensation and Firm Performance: Research Questions and Answers," in *Executive Compensation: A Strategic Guide for the 1990s*, ed. F. K. Foulkes (Boston: Harvard Business School Press, 1991), 81–97.

[3] J. A. Byrne, "Executive Pay," *Business Week* 3258 (March 30, 1992), 52–58; G. Colvin, "How to Pay the CEO Right," *Fortune* 125 (April 16, 1992), 60–70.

[4] Milkovich and Rabin, "Executive Compensation and Firm Performance."

[5] Byrne, "Executive Pay."

[6] I. I. Mitroff, *Business Not as Usual, Rethinking Our Industrial Corporate and Industrial Strategies for Global Competition* (San Francisco: Jossey Bass Publishers, 1987); C. J. Grayson and C. O. O'Dell, *American Business: A Two Minute Warning* (New York: Free Press, 1988).

[7] Deloitte, Haskins and Sells, *Review* 17 (August 18, 1986), 1.

[8] B. B. Overton and M. T. Steele, *Designing Management Incentive Plans: An Approach to Developing a Short-Term Incentive Plan for Managers* (Scottsdale, AZ: American Compensation Association, 1992).

[9] B. R. Baliga and T. J. Bergmann, "Design of an Executive Compensation System for Effective Management of Strategy," *Journal of Managerial Issues* 2 (Spring 1990), 60–74.

[10] McLaughlin, "The Rise of a Strategic Approach to Executive Compensation."

[11] Baliga and Bergmann, "Design of an Executive Compensation System for Effective Management of Strategy."

[12] G. B. Paulin and F. W. Cook, "What Should Be Done About Executive Compensation," *ACA Journal* 1 (Autumn 1992), 20–35.

[13] *Ibid.*

[14] K. M. Eisenhardt, "Agency Theory: An Assessment and Review," *Academy of Management Review* 14 (1989), 57–74.

[15] *Ibid.*

[16] Colvin, "How to Pay the CEO Right."

[17] *Ibid.*

[18] *Ibid.*

[19] A. Bennett, "Hard Times Trim CEO Pay Raises," *The Wall Street Journal* 75 (April 17, 1991), R1, 5.

[20] ———, "Popular Perks," *The Wall Street Journal* 76 (April 18, 1990), R25.

[21] ———, "Incentives Reach Deeper into Work Force," *Employee Benefit Plan Review* 45 (October 1990), 42–44.

[22] J. Bloedorn, "The Compensation Model: A Contemporary Design," in *Compensation Briefs* (Chicago: KPMG Peat Marwick, August 1992), 1–12.

[23] Bennett, "Hard Times Trim CEO Pay Raises."

[24] C. Breetwor, "Stock Plans Attract People, Nurture Loyalty," *Employee Benefit Plan Review* 45 (October 1990), 30–32.

[25] J. Weber, "Offering Employees Stock Options They Can't Refuse," *Business Week* 3234 (October 7, 1991), 34.

[26] A. Bennett, "Pay for Performance," *The Wall Street Journal* 76 (April 18, 1990), R7–8.

[27] J. D. England, "Don't Be Afraid of Phantom Stock," *Compensation and Benefits Review* 24 (September/October 1992), 39–46.

[28] B. W. Aisenbrey, "Long-Term Incentives for Management, Part 3: Restricted Stock," *Compensation and Benefits Review* 22 (November/December 1990), 34–46.

[29] J. M. Kanter and M. P. Ward, "Long-Term Incentives for Management, Part 4: Performance Plans," *Compensation and Benefits Review* 22 (January-February 1990), 36–49.

[30] J. S. Hyman, "Long-Term Incentives," in *The Compensation Handbook*, eds. M. L. Rock and L. A. Berger (New York: McGraw-Hill, 1991).

[31] Kanter and Ward, "Long-Term Incentives for Management."

[32] *Ibid.*

[33] *Ibid*; Hyman, "Long-Term Incentives."

[34] Kanter and Ward, "Long-Term Incentives for Management."

[35] Paulin and Cook, "What Should Be Done About Executive Compensation"; W. L. White, "Managing the Board Review of Executive Pay," *Compensation and Benefits Review* 24 (November/December 1992), 35–41.

[36] L. C. Brickford and J. E. Sorkin, "Long-Term Incentives for Management, Part 5: Selecting the Right Program," *Compensation and Benefits Review* 22 (March/April 1990), 38–46; B. M. Longnecker and C. L. Wood, "Compensation Under Seige: How to Win the Battle," *Compensation and Benefits Review* 24 (November/December 1992), 30–34.

[37] B. R. Ellig, Executive Compensation: A Total Pay Perspective (New York: McGraw-Hill, 1982).

[38] Baliga and Bergmann, "Design of an Executive Compensation System for Effective Management of Strategy."

[39] Overton and Steele, *Designing Management Incentive Plans.*

[40] J. D. McMillian and C. Young, "Sweetening the Compensation Package," *HRMagazine* 35 (October 1990), 36–39.

[41] Ellig, "Executive Compensation"

[42] *Ibid.*

[43] *Ibid*; Baliga and Bergmann, "Design of an Executive Compensation System for Effective Management of Strategy."

[44] G. J. Meng, "Returning the 'Incentive' to Incentive Pay," *Journal of Compensation and Benefits* 6 (September/October 1990), 38–42.

[45] W. J. Liccione and S. M. Podlogar, "How to Develop Compensation Plans with Incentive Value," *Journal of Compensation and Benefits* 6 (January/February 1991), 37–40.

[46] P. Chingos, "Executive Compensation in the 1990's: The Challenges Ahead," *Compensation and Benefits Review* 22 (November/December 1990), 20–30.

[47] Baliga and Bergmann, "Design of an Executive Compensation System for Effective Management of Strategy."

[48] G. S. Crystal, "Common Mistakes in Current Practice," in *Executive Compensation: A Strategic Guide for the 1990s*, ed. F. K. Foulkes (Boston: Harvard Business School Press, 1991).

[49] Baliga and Bergmann, "Design of an Executive Compensation System for Effective Management of Strategy."

[50] R. E. Heitzman, Jr. and K. Lipton, "Internation Employees: Are They Losing Out On Retirement," *Financial Executive* 6 (September/October 1990), 44–50.

[51] A. M. Townsend, K. D. Scott, and S. E. Markham, "An Examination of Country and Culture-Based Differences in Compensation Practices," *Journal of International Business Studies* 21 (1990), 667–678; R. M. Hodgetts and F. Luthans, "U.S. Multinationals' Compensation Strategies for Local Management: Cross-Cultural Implications," *Compensation and Benefits Review* 25 (March/April 1993), 42–48.

[52] L. P. Crandall and M. I. Phelps, "Pay For a Global Work Force," *Personnel Journal* 70 (February 1991), 28–33.

[53] *Ibid.*

[54] J. B. Anderson, "Compensating Your Overseas Executives, Part 2: Europe in 1992," *Compensation and Benefits Review* 22 (September/October 1990), 25–35.

[55] W. T. Cleary, "Guidelines for Establishing Overseas Employee Benefits Plans," *Pension World* 23 (July 1987), 48–49.

[56] *Ibid.*

[57] *Ibid.*

[58] R. B. Klein, "Exporting U.S. Stock Option Plans to Expatriates Overseas: Policy and Tax Planning Issues," *Perspectives in Total Compensation* 3 (Scottsdale, AZ: American Compensation Association, February 1992), 1–6; D. Sjoberg and B. Ernt, "European Harmonization: Effects of International Compensation Plans," *ACA Journal* 2 (Spring/Summer 1993), 62–73.

[59] B. J. Brooks, "Trends in Internation Executive Compensation," *Personnel* 64 (May 1987), 67–70.

[60] B. J. Brooks, "Long-Term Incentives: International Executives," *Personnel* 65 (August 1988), 40–42.

[61] M. J. Bishko, "Compensating Your Overseas Executives, Part 1: Strategies for the 1990s," *Compensation and Benefits Review* 22 (July/August 1990), 33–43.

[62] Klein, "Exporting U.S. Stock Option Plans to Expatriates Overseas."

[63] N. R. Fritz and A. Ritter, "Benefits for Outside Directors," *Personnel* 66 (September 1989), 38.

[64] B. Overton, "Remuneration of Outside Directors" in *Executive Compensation: A Strategic Guide for the 1990s*, ed. F. K. Foulkes (Boston: Harvard Business School Press, 1991), 383–398.

[65] J. H. Dobrzynski, "Directors' Pay is Becoming an Issue Too," *Business Week* 3212 (May 6, 1991), 94.

[66] ———, "Outside Directors," *ACA Resources* 2 (June 1991), 2.

67 ———, "Top Companies Offer Outside Directors Stock," *Personnel* 68 (February 1991), 9.

68 G. S. Crystal, "Do Directors Earn Their Keep?" *Fortune* 123 (May 6, 1991), 78–80.

69 Dobrzynski, "Directors' Pay is Becoming an Issue Too."

70 ———, "Outside Directors."

71 Crystal, "Do Directors Earn Their Keep?"

72 M. Grandel, "Two-Tier Pay Scales—Innovative or Destructive?" *Employment Relations Today* 12 (Summer 1985), 164–173.

73 M. J. Levine, "The Evolution of Two-Tier Wage Agreement: Bane or Panacea in Labor-Intensive Industries," *Labor Law Journal* 40 (January 1989), 12–20.

74 K. Jennings and E. Traynham, "The Wages of Two-Tier Pay Plans," *Personnel Journal* 67 (March 1988), 56–63.

75 Ibid.

76 Ibid.

77 S. L. Thomas and M. M. Kleiner, "The Effect of Two-Tier Collective Bargaining Agreements on Shareholder Equity," *Industrial and Labor Relations Review* 45 (January 1992), 339–351.

78 P. Cappelli and P. D. Sherer, "Assessing Worker Attitudes Under a Two-Tier Wage Plan," *Industrial and Labor Relations Review* 43 (January 1990), 225–244.

79 Jennings and Traynham, "The Wages of Two-Tier Pay Plans."

80 Thomas and Kleiner, "The Effect of Two-Tier Collective Bargaining Agreements on Shareholder Equity."

81 T. Harris, "Playing the Two-Tier Salary Scale," *Management Today* (September 1987), 23.

82 Grandel, "Two-Tier Pay Scales—Innovative or Destructive?"

83 Thomas and Kleiner, "The Effect of Two-Tier Collective Bargaining Agreements on Shareholder Equity."

84 K. J. Murphy, "Effect of Two-Tier Collective Bargaining Agreements on Shareholder Equity," *Industrial and Labor Relations Review* 45 (January 1992), 339–351.

85 N. Gupta, G. E. Ledford, C. D. Jenkins, and H. Doty, "Survey-Based Perceptions for Skill-Based Pay," *ACA Journal* 1 (Autumn 1992), 48–59.

86 E. Ingram II, "The Advantages of Knowledge-Based Pay," *Personnel Journal* 69 (April 1990), 138–140; M. Hequet, "Paying For Knowledge in 'Paper Factories,'" *Training* 27 (September 1990), 69–77.

87 G. E. Ledford, "Three Case Studies on Skill-Based Pay: An Overview," *Compensation and Benefits Review* 23 (March/April 1991), 11–23.

88 Gupta et al., "Survey-Based Perceptions for Skill-Based Pay"; E. E. Lawler and G. E. Ledford, Jr., "Who Uses Skill-Based Pay and Why," *Compensation and Benefits Review* 25 (March/April 1993), 22–26.

89 Ingram, "The Advantages of Knowledge-Based Pay."

90 R. L. Bunning, "Skill-Based Pay," *Personnel Administrator* 34 (June 1989), 65–70.

91 H. Tosi and L. Tosi, "What Managers Need to Know About Knowledge-Based Pay," *Organizational Dynamics* 14 (1989), 52–64.

92 Ingram, "The Advantages of Knowledge-Based Pay."

93 Gupta et al., "Survey-Based Perceptions for Skill-Based Pay."

94 M. Hequet, "Paying For Knowledge in 'Paper Factories,'" *Training* 27 (September 1990), 69–77.

95 Gupta et al., "Survey-Based Perceptions for Skill-Based Pay."

96 Ingram, "The Advantages of Knowledge-Based Pay."

97 Tosi and Tosi, "What Managers Need to Know About Knowledge-Based Pay."

98 Gupta et al., "Survey-Based Perceptions for Skill-Based Pay."

99 F. Luthans and M. L. Fox, "Update on Skill-Based Pay," *Personnel* 66 (March 1989), 27.

100 Ingram, "The Advantages of Knowledge-Based Pay."

101 N. Gupta, "Pay-for-knowledge Compensation Plans," *Monthly Labor Review* 110 (October 1987), 40–58.

[102]———, *The AAL Total Compensation Program* (Appleton, WS: Aid Association for Lutherans, 1991), 1–14.

[103]F. V. Cespedes, "A Preface to Payment: Designing a Sales Compensation Plan," *Sloan Management Review* 32 (Fall 1990), 59–69.

[104]R. Abratt and M. R. Smythe, "A Survey of Sales Incentive Programs," *Industrial Marketing Management* 18 (August 1989), 209–214.

[105]J. A. Colletti and L. J. Mahoney, "Should You Pay Your Sales Force for Customer Satisfaction?" in *Perspectives in Total Compensation* 2 (Scottsdale, AZ: American Compensation Association, November 1991), 1–4.

[106]A. Bau, R. Lal, V. Srinivasan, and R. Staelin, "Sales Compensation Plans: An Agency Theoretic Perspective," *Marketing Science* 4 (1985), 267–291.

[107]G. Cebryznski, "Sales Compensation Survey Shows Some 'Dramatic' Findings," *Marketing News* 20 (Nov. 7, 1986), 32.

[108]J. Dahm, "Using Draws Wisely in Your Sales Compensation Plan," *Sales & Marketing Management* 142 (August 1990), 92–93.

[109]Cespedes, "A Preface to Payment."

[110]S. A. Washbum, "Follow the Money," *Business Marketing* 75 (September 1990), 68–70.

[111]T. R. Wotruba, J. S. Macfie, and J. A. Colletti, "Effective Sales Force Recognition Programs," *Industrial Marketing Management* 20 (1991), 9–15.

[112]*Ibid.*

[113]*Ibid.*

[114]T. Harris, "Sales Support: No Longer Those Left Behind," *Sales and Marketing Management* 142 (April 1990), 102–114.

[115]*Ibid.*

[116]*Ibid.*

## Name Index

## Subject Index